Power Politics and Social Change in National Socialist Germany

# New Babylon

*Studies in the Social Sciences*

11

MOUTON · THE HAGUE · PARIS

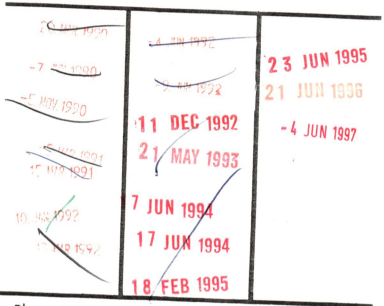

# Power Politics and
# Social Change in
# National Socialist Germany

*A Process of Escalation into Mass Destruction*

JOHN M. STEINER

MOUTON · THE HAGUE · PARIS

Photograph on page VI: Reproduced from *Das Ehrenbuch der SA* (photograph no. 121, January 30, 1933), officially suppressed in 1934.

ISBN: 90 279 7651 1

Printed in The Netherlands

*To the Victims of Totalitarianism*

*The smallest SA-man salutes Obergruppenführer Viktor Lutze*

# Foreword

*The mind is its own place, and in itself*
*Can make a heaven of hell, a hell of heaven.*
Milton: *Paradise Lost* (1667)

Evil is a curious thing. The infinite forms which evil may assume are constrained only by the limits of human imagination, but the recognition of evil in one's own actions is negated by man's capacity for self-justification, and in others' actions suffers from the transcience of memory.

It is just about four score years ago that the architects of the Third Reich erected a monument to evil unparalleled in modern history. They spread war, enslavement, and pestilence throughout neighboring countries of Europe, while at home they tortured and systematically destroyed millions of innocent men, women, and children of Jewish heritage along with Gypsies and other 'enemies of the state'.

Although individual members of the Nazi Party and SS officers were convicted at Nuremberg and Jerusalem of these crimes against the human status, the evil was an inherent part of the total social-political system. It was nurtured by petty opportunists, eager functionaries, anxious bureaucrats, tailors turned into traitors and convicts acting as Kapos. It was sustained through the exchange of individual responsibility, social conscience, and personal freedom for national pride, vicarious power of the State, and the illusion of security. But as Eli Wiesel suggests, the evil of inaction, of indifference to the plight of one's countrymen by the average German citizen is as significant as the evils of Nazi action.

Who, then, is responsible for these evils? Can we readily attribute the origin of such evil to Hitler, Himmler, Eichmann, and to other ap-

parently 'pathological personality types'? What is the message of Auschwitz, the lesson to be learned from Buchenwald and the Warsaw ghetto?

In John Steiner's brilliant analysis of the origins, operation and
impact of National Socialism, we are made to see the myriad ways in
which a social structure may come to shape and ultimately to control
individual patterns of thought and behavior. Once created, the Nazi
political system with its religious justification, economic and social
reward structure, and psychologically compelling network of interdependencies and identities could define reality, morality and justice
for *all* those living within its sphere of penetration. The ultimate evil
that he helps us to comprehend is the evil of the system itself – an
institutionalized system of power and control which transcends not
only its originators, but also transcends the boundaries of time, space,
and personalities.

Indeed, it would be comforting to be able to maintain that Naziism
was but a manifestation of Hitler's madness, or a political reaction
unique to the particular constellation of circumstances facing Germany
after World War I, comforting because of the distance which such
simplistic causal explanations allow us to put between 'us' and 'them',
between 'now' and 'then', between 'here' and 'there'. Once we establish
that evil is the product of an evil doer, it becomes easy to postulate
how different we are from such a person. Identification, empathy, and
guilt on our part then become rather improbable reactions, nor are we
implicated in any way for helping to create or perpetuate the environmental conditions which may have contributed to the evil. Finally, we
are comforted by the easy solutions which an 'evil seed' theory of
behavior provides – isolate, punish, or exterminate the sinner. We do
not have to generate complex, costly solutions tailored to remedy the
complex political, social, economic situation in which the crime or evil
is imbedded.

Although each individual must bear the responsibility for his/her
acts of cruelty or inhumanity, it is only by attempting to understand evil
as part of a matrix of prevailing situational forces acting upon individuals that we can cope with the insidious nature of such evil and
prevent its reappearance.

In the pages that follow, the reader will be guided through a unique
historical journey along the many paths which led to the hell of Nazi
Germany. The uniqueness of this venture lies both in what is to be

discovered as well as in the qualifications of the guide. John Steiner blends the formalism of sociological analysis – with its emphasis on structure, systems, and institutional functions – and a dynamic psychological approach to understanding individual behavior of the people involved in the system. His scholarship alone is a *tour de force*, as we are shown unpublished letters, documents, and biograms of the participants who constructed the social reality of the Third Reich. Skillful interpretations of history and astute political analyses are carefully documented with a truly remarkable diversity of original and secondary source materials.

But what makes this journey different from all the others into the same territory is that the academic, intellectual pursuit of knowledge is infused with the energy and is refined by the sensitivities of a man who was himself an actor in this drama – as victim.

John Steiner's years of struggle for survival through Auschwitz, the slave camps, the death marches, and destruction camps provide him with the vantage point of the participant-observer which he shares with us. But to be part of such a cataclysm was to be a subject in a diabolical experiment in which basic laws of human nature and humanity were shattered as fundamental conceptions of justice, causality, and rationality were suspended. This book is a personal account of the creation of a political-social system of power which imprisoned the author and is his attempt to understand how and why it happened.

To gain objectivity in his quest to unravel the mechanisms and mysteries of the events of these times, Steiner returned to Germany year after year (from his university position in the United States) to personally conduct several hundred interviews with his former captors, to gather retrospective autobiographical accounts from those men who had been in positions of power to decide the life and death of millions. But, to be sure, this is not a subjective account of the author's concentration camp experiences; those experiences are the barely perceptible loom on which is woven the fabric of a most scholarly reconstruction of an epoch, of a time unlike any other in the mind of man.

There is an urgency in the author's ultimate purpose for sharing his orientation, experience, and research labors with us in this book. It is his hope that the full understanding of the example he sets before us may indeed save lives in the future by preventing the reccurrence of such a totalitarian system. The urgency comes from a realization that many of the same forces which fueled the rise of the power elite in Nazi Germany are again gaining strength at this very time.

1984 is but a decade away, and the closer it comes the more we see Orwell's fantasy as a prophetic statement of what our lives are actually becoming. Recent research by psychologists has demonstrated that the majority of people can be easily led to yield up responsibility to authority and blindly obey orders to inflict extreme pain on a stranger (S. Milgram); that normal, healthy, adjusted college males can be transformed overnight into cruel, sadistic guards once they are made into an unquestioning cog in a simulated prison system (P. Zimbardo); that large numbers of Americans are already psychologically detached from the horror of the My Lai massacre in Vietnam (N. Opton); and finally, that the vast majority of those questioned (in a University of Hawaii study) believed the 'final solution' is a just means of handling the problem of the emotionally and mentally unfit (H. Mansson).

In these times of rapid change to which we can barely accommodate let alone control, history and its lessons are becoming expendable. John Steiner makes a very powerful and eloquent case for why *you* cannot allow that to be. If the distance between heaven and hell on earth is calculated by the human equation which John Milton proposes, then persons of good will must make every effort to guarantee that we do not surrender our Paradise once again.

PHILIP G. ZIMBARDO, PH.D.
*Professor of Social Psychology*
*Stanford University, Stanford, California, U.S.A.*

# Acknowledgements

Above all, the author wishes to express his deep gratitude to Professor Eduard Baumgarten, University of Freiburg, for his astute counsel and friendship and to Professor W. H. Nagel, University of Leiden, for his consistent interest and moral support. Both have been a source of inspiration.

For their help in making this book possible, the writer offers his thanks to the Alexander von Humboldt Stiftung, Bad Godesberg, especially to Professor Werner Heisenberg and to Dr. Heinrich Pfeiffer for their generous support of this study during the years 1964 to 1967.

The author gratefully acknowledges his indebtedness for the valuable advice and assistance given by Dr. Philip G. Zimbardo, Stanford University, Dr. Erich Fromm, and the Drs. Anton Hoch and Martin Broszat of the Institut für Zeitgeschichte, Munich. To Miss Susan Forney for her critical and skillful review of the manuscript and to the students in his seminars in Sociology of Power and in Personality and Social Structure, whose commentary have provided a continuous stream of stimulation, the author offers sincere thanks. In this regard, Dr. Stuart Hadden deserves particular mention.

The most personal debt is owed to his spouse, Ulrike Steiner. Her untiring and selfless assistance with every phase of the book made it possible for the manuscript to appear in print.

Sausalito, California                                                    J. M. S.
Spring, 1974

# Contents

Foreword by Philip G. Zimbardo                                            VII

Acknowledgements                                                          XI

Introduction                                                             XV

Part I.  Power, Ideology, and Political Crime                             1
1. *Towards a new conceptualization of power*                             3
2. *The historical setting of the National Socialist rise to power
   and its sociological implications*                                    8

Part II.  Sociological Factors in the Development of the NS
Party Bureaucracy                                                        13

Part III. The SS – An Example of a Totalitarian Bureaucratic
Institution                                                              45
 1. *Origin and early history of the SS*                                 47
 2. *Himmler's rise to power*                                            53
 3. *The emergence of the SS as an independent system of power
    and the role of its sub-systems*                                     60
 4. *Promulgation and application of racial doctrines in the SS*         71
 5. *Racial criteria for selection of personnel into the SS*             74
 6. *Ideological criteria for selection, indoctrination, and training*   77
 7. *'Lebensborn' – Example of an NS social institution*                 79
 8. *Jewish and non-German descent in the SS*                            81
 9. *The conception of morality and honor in the 'Schutzstaffel'*        86
10. *Consequences of Hitler's influence on NS ideology and
    the SS*                                                              93
11. *The perception of God in the SS*                                   104
12. *Discussion and conclusion*                                         120

Part IV.  Totalitarian Institutions and German Bureaucracy: A
Process of Escalation into Destruction                          129
1. *Discussion*                                                 155
2. *Conclusion*                                                 163

Part V. Sociological Implications of Deviance and Accountability in NS Political and Bureaucratic Institutions          167
1. *The sociological vision of Walther Rathenau's concept of
   social change*                                              169
2. *National Socialist aggression and psychoanalytic theory*   185

Notes and References                                           201

Appendices                                                     359

Bibliography                                                   425

Index                                                          445

# Introduction

What constitutes the substance of sociology as a calling – or, as Max Weber would say, a 'Beruf'? It appears to this writer that anyone who hopes to become a good sociologist should start with some hurt, some feeling of resentment against prevalent social trends which provokes him to find out what is wrong with his society. Wishing to relieve his own dissatisfaction, he will want to find out not only why human beings have to suffer, but also what can be done to alleviate their suffering. Thus, understanding – in contrast to mere dissecting, categorizing, and classifying – is seen as a major goal of the social sciences.

Although Weber, in his essay on 'Wertfreiheit,' held out for the sociologist the ideal of ethical neutrality, he was aware that this ideal, while worth striving for, could never be reached. Sociologists, being human, are limited by the content of their own life-histories – their own egos – by the prevalent cultural patterns of the nation and the social segment into which they were born. They can never be totally objective. Consequently, as John Madge writes in *The Tools of Social Science* (London, 1953): 'Instead of aiming to become the objective value-free theorist, the social scientist may without shame take on the job of social engineer, in which he may use his experience and special skills in the service of his chosen community.'

In our view, the sociologist can best serve in the role of the knowledgeable interpreter and critic who, when necessary, has the courage to become a socially constructive deviant in order to examine and comprehend social conventions. To obtain a broader perspective on his own society he must seek comparisons with other societies. Such a transvaluation of existing social forms can immensely increase productivity and foster international cooperation in the social sciences. Indeed, collective action should assist in the early detection, prediction, prevention, and control of brutality on a national as well as international level.

The purpose of this study is to trace and unravel but a few mechanisms which led to such a cataclysmic event; namely, the rise of a
political system and its numerous sub-systems which caused the death
of millions of innocent human beings. Early recognition and concerted
action might have prevented forfeiture of these lives; understanding
their example may save the lives of others in the future. In this spirit
and to this end, this investigation has been undertaken.

*Accountability, self-knowledge, and the relations between deviance and
identity*

We have implied that social scientists tend to be overly preoccupied
with methodology and neglectful of 'understanding' (in the Weberian
sense of 'verstehen'). After all, what does it avail us to describe social
processes and busy ourselves with functional or content analysis, social
structure, social institutions, social rules, or stratification if we are
unable to live up to our findings or if we simply escape into theory
because we cannot cope with everyday realities?

Isolated theoretical constructs are incomplete unless they can be
directly related to personal lives. Yet sociologists frequently overempha-
size the nomothetic approach, while the ideographic, essential to understanding human behavior, is consistently underestimated (Daniel L.
Haytin, *The Methodological Validity of the Case Study in the Social
Sciences,* Berkeley, 1969). We believe that a synthesis between these
two approaches must be effected (Bronislaw Malinowski, *A Scientific
Theory of Culture,* New York, 1966). In the Rorschach method, for
example, objective quantifiable variables are combined with subjective
and projective responses of individuals to interpret behavioral patterns.
Similarly, a sociologist may use his unconscious self and perhaps his
own socially destructive tendencies as instruments of insight into the
behavioral patterns of others. By developing an understanding of his
own anti-social drives, a constructive person can help the socially
destructive to harness theirs. Thus, in our subsequent study of National
Socialism, the approaches of Weber and Freud, of Simmel and Fromm,
will be conjoined, and the deviant behavior of the NS subculture interpreted as the collective behavior of German society at large of which
it was a part. In order to accomplish this goal, it has been necessary to

base this investigation on published and unpublished NS documents, interviews, case studies, and biograms. Case studies and personal documents have been of great assistance, especially when anomic, non-normative behavior is being interpreted.

## Sources of social deviance

Any given society has its distinctive way of viewing the universe – its 'Weltanschauung' – which determines its response to life situations and the selection of means to enhance survival. Among these responses and means will be characteristic acts of violence corresponding to the prevailing world view upon which man is constrained to function and to survive as an individual. These forms of violence will be reflected in behavioral norms, social contracts, socially sanctioned interaction between individuals, and indeed the entire structure of the society itself. For we maintain that in every society concepts of humaneness, kindness, and the like are not necessarily synonymous with 'good.' In some societies under certain circumstances cruelty and brutality may be considered 'good' and kindness a sign of weakness.

Teachers of human ethics have insisted over the ages that a cruel act is an 'evil,' but they are speaking of acts involving moral choice. A distinction must be made between mindless and malevolent cruelty, for only in the case of the latter is moral choice involved. A tiger's 'cruelty' when he chews a man is as impersonal as lightning or an earthquake; the mere satisfaction of animal hunger involves no malevolence. A butcher slaughtering a calf is similarly impersonal. Perhaps the major portion of human cruelty is non-malevolent – predominantly a result of oppressive dependency relations, insecurity, fear, deprivation, injustice, rejection, inertia, or merely poor judgment and misinterpretation of current realities.

In practice, if not in theory, man's attitude toward violence is ambiguous, reflecting the power structure of his society; that is, cruel acts are more likely to be termed evil when attributed to members of the outgroups in a given socio-political setting. They are less likely to be termed evil – that is, undesirable – when perpetrated by a power élite which has successfully propagated its norms through ingroups and promoted their acceptance by society at large.

Totalitarian sanction of cruelty or violence may be reinforced in societies where technological advancement has caused depersonalization of the individual and mechanization of the will. One of the most typical traits of contemporary civilization is a contradiction between the concrete and the abstract. A pilot who, by pressing a button, can kill thousands of people without a single tremor may weep at the loss of his pet dog. The thousands of people are an abstract idea while his dog is a concrete being.

The 'new' morality of modern technological warfare is an extension of a dangerously materialistic world view in which man sees himself as a machine, identifying himself with this means of conquering the universe. When the machine or technological device is viewed as the ultimate orientation of human value, the world surrounding man becomes 'mechanized' – inanimate and emotionally indifferent, if not hostile. In a society with this predominant world view, man is treated like a component of a machine with specific superior or inferior biological and physiological attributes which produces so much, must rest so much, and must be overhauled from time to time. Since a machine, or component thereof, can be manipulated at will, the millions of human 'wheels and cogs' which comprise the mechanized society may be set, steered, and removed at will: especially in a totalitarian system, it is even more so the will of the power élite.

Conversely, of course, man does not wish to be a cog. His sense of freedom revolts against it (Pavlov's escape reaction), as does his need for emotional response. Man, unlike a machine component, cannot remain emotionally untouched. He loves and hates and needs to be accepted or rejected. When he sees himself as part of a mechanized world, he feels abandoned, isolated, and imperiled. In this state he is likely to trade moral freedom for ego-survival by identifying with the will, with the norms and values of the power élite. Acts of cruelty perpetrated by this élite may thus be temporarily accepted as non-malevolent means to some transcendent unifying end such as socio-political order, national progress, national identity, etc. One must say 'temporarily' because history reveals that man will eventually reject a Caligula, Nero, Ghengis-Khan, Stalin, or Hitler and sicken at his memory. But this rejection may well come too late to save him from cooperating in his own destruction.

## *National Socialism: The price of social identity*

Despite the hope of many, Auschwitz and other brutalities committed during and after World War II have lost little of their horror with passing time. Moreover, the burden of responsibility that rests not only on the principal transgressors but, in a sense, on the whole of civilized society has not become lighter. Such questions as 'how?' and 'why?' are being asked with an increasing insistence and urgency by a multitude of people who are waiting for a satisfactory answer, so that future disasters of this magnitude can be avoided. How could these transgressions be perpetrated? How was it and is it still possible that the innocent could be treated with such cruelty, and how could the victim bear these atrocities?

Perhaps, as we will endeavor to show, the innocent were frequently not so innocent after all since they largely failed to recognize the early symptoms of the movement that brought about their doom. In a totalitarian state the sphere of influence of the dominant group or class is very much subject to change contingent upon the élite's ability to assert itself in a continuous power struggle. The élite, or any public authority, has no power in itself; power must be transferred to it by the people. As it appears, the German society was willing to make this transference. As early as 1788, Comte de Guibert recognized this trait. In his *Lobschrift auf Friedrich den Zweiten* (Berlin, 1788) he states:

> ... aber man muß auch die Preußischen Staaten, die durch *Friedrichs* Vorfahren an eine weit despotischere Regierung gewohnt waren, nicht mit den zarten Begriffen von Freiheit und Menschenrechten ansehn, welche etwa ein Engländer oder Amerikaner haben könnte.
> _____
> ... but one may not apply to the Prussian states – which through *Frederick's* ancestors had become accustomed to a far more despotic government – the delicate concept of freedom and human rights that an Englishman or an American might have.

The NS movement filled a specific socio-political vacuum created in German society by the lost war. The masses had been deprived of traditional authoritarian leaders whose decisions they were accustomed to abide by and upon whose judgments they relied and depended. Historically conditioned to this dependency, they had no opportunity to learn how to participate in a democratic process of decision-making with its contingent condition of public, more specifically, individual responsibility. They were used to delegating this responsibility to a privileged élite. Indeed, they resented having had a political system forced upon them which was not one of their own choosing, that is to say, one for which they were sociologically and psychologically unprepared.

It is not surprising, then, that after World War I the Germans persisted in supporting a charismatic leader, even when the latter went so far as to make injustice and cruelty norms of social behavior. It was not that they had lost their traditional revulsion against injustice and cruelty, but that they were willing to pay this price to preserve their 'follower' status even after the concentration camps had been established and the 'Röhm Putsch' staged. Many sanctioned and submitted to cruelty if it led to what was perceived as a reinstatement of 'law and order' and re-establishment of national self-respect and identity.

Throughout this study it will become more obvious that what a person, a group of persons, or a society does much depends upon the response elicited through interaction with others, especially others with whom a close dependency relationship has been formed. Thus, we cannot simply speak of responsibility as distinct from irresponsibility; the two are obviously interdependent. Those who dominate will only be successful if they find subjects who will submit to them.

It is in this light that National Socialist institutions – their function and their effect – will be examined with the hope that, through a better understanding of some of the sociological factors involved, a minute share can be contributed towards the prevention of similar social catastrophes.

Finally, as B. H. Liddle Hart has so aptly pointed out in his book *Strategy* (New York, 1954): 'The experience of history brings ample evidence that the downfall of civilized states tends to come not from the direct assaults of foes but from internal decay, combined with the consequences of exhaustion in war.'

*Part I*

Power,
Ideology,
and
Political Crime

'The man who will not act except in total righteousness achieves nothing. He does not enter the path of progress and he is not true because he is not real. . . . The man who seeks to be true must run the risk of being mistaken, of putting himself in the wrong.'

Karl Jaspers

'Nothing is permanent – except change.'

Heraclitus

# 1. *Towards a new conceptualization of power*

Prudent students of history will find that sincerity expressed in violence, in the guise of a civil but nonetheless ideologically entrenched wish to bring about radical socio-political change, has invariably been costly in human lives. Advocates of such change only rarely adhere to the blueprint of behavior purportedly designed to bring about the realization of the proposed change. The Crusaders, the Jacobins, the Bolsheviks, the Fascists, the Nazis, and the Maoists were by and large misguided by their 'sincere belief' in their respective causes. They all claimed to obey 'superior principles' (with their corresponding concept of law and order) to the utter disregard of existing 'mundane' morality and with complete disrespect for human life which they allegedly set out to improve. In point of fact, time after time ideology has been used as an excuse, license, and vehicle for the application of unconstrained power politics. Furthermore, it is a common occurrence that ideological (myth) systems are planned and developed to suit the creator's personal needs. Equally frequently they are subsequently adjusted better to serve the interests of the actors who, then, will apply them. Here, the vulgar interpretation of Marxist theory by Soviet imperialists appears to be a good case in point. More recently ideological reasons were used to justify the war in Vietnam, the occupation of Czechoslovakia by Soviet Russia and its satellite armed forces, and genocide committed in East Pakistan. As Ortega y Gasset observed in the late 1920s, . . . 'it is foolishness for the party of "law and order" to imagine that these "forces of public authority" erected to preserve order are always going to be content to preserve the order that that party desires. Inevitably they will end by themselves defining and deciding on the order they are going to impose which, naturally, will be that which suits them best.'[1] Indeed, the method by which an initial cause is advanced is invariably the most important factor in setting the stage for future action and in the subsequent adoption of policies once the system becomes established. One of the lessons which could have been learned by now is that the number of violent prophets a society can *absorb* with impunity is limited. Observations of this kind were made by Machiavelli in his treatise *The Prince*.[2] The methods by which 'causes' were advanced and institutionalized are, of course, primarily dependent upon the leadership's astuteness and ability to mobilize power in terms of 'popular' support for such causes. But the concept of power itself remains unclear without the recognition that *power is a product of social interaction only and not a mere attribute of the actor*. In this context, domination of others can be understood as an attempt to free oneself from oppressive interdependency relations by simply reversing them. The will to power, then, the wish to dominate others, can be viewed as a striving for greater independence and autonomy from others by forming interdependency patterns which the originator and his associates deem or experience as being more favorable (to them). In short, power becomes reality if a power-dependence relationship is established,[3] that is to say, if a potential power holder is in a position to secure and fill a vacant power role (in time and space) which enables him to structure the scope and radius of action of those who will submit to him. Thus a dependency relationship will become an essential basis for the perpetuation of a power position. This, in turn, will enhance the image, and the degree of freedom, of the actor holding power if he is successful in safeguarding his status by harnessing a hierarchical chain of command by bureaucratic and institutional means. In other words, his power position will enable him better to control and structure his environment and thereby improve the chances to satisfy his individual needs, as reflected in his *goal aspirations*.[4] So, for example, by virtue of his acquired power role, the actor will receive recognition in the form of material and non-material rewards which will be reflected in the realization of an aspired life-style. The power role will also place him in the limelight, which for many a power holder can become a source of satisfaction per se.[5]

This novel experience can stimulate in the actor *ecstatic joy* (or *elation*, a synonym used by Hannah Arendt) in response to a drift in emphasis to different areas of the actor's personality structure.[6] As a consequence of the newly acquired and more acceptable or satisfying identity as a power holder, the actor's self-image and social perspective will subsequently alter.[7] When the actor has been adequately prepared to play a specific power role (as, for example, in the case of the late President John F. Kennedy), elation will be kept to a minimum since he will not impute to the role more authority and influence than is in the interest of the people or warranted in a stable social order. Yet it should be understood that such a preparation itself does not ensure astute decision-making and does not produce a statesman out of an otherwise unqualified actor. However, if the legitimate social order is not stable, but is undergoing radical change, the possession of a power role may be a novel experience for the actor, and consequently he may lack the essential qualifications for the assumption of power and its corresponding responsibilities. In this instance, if it is a top leadership role (which is a relative concept in time and space), both the actor and his alters will mutually impute more authority and influence to the role than is traditionally ascribed to it. Hence, the actor may feel obliged to use his power to re-structure reality and, by doing so, serve as a *significant model* for others to follow.[8] So, for example, Hitler's expectations were treated as most important by the German people as long as the people were an actively involved, integral part of operative Nazi institutions. A more recent case in point is the My Lai 4 'incident,' a consequence and integral part of the war in Vietnam. This case has been aptly elaborated by the Afro-American G.I. Herbert Carter of Houston, Texas, former member of the Charlie Company under Captain Ernest L. Medina's command, serving in Lieutenant William L. Calley Jr.'s platoon, who observed: . . . 'what happened at My Lai 4 was not a massacre, but a logical result of the war in Vietnam. The people didn't know what they were dying for and *the guys didn't know why they were shooting them.*'[9] The confusion expressed here reflects the discrepancy of interests between the ruling élite which has become embroiled in a violent and seemingly unrealistic conflict with an 'enemy' (their enemy) and the soldier-citizen who has been enlisted to act upon *their behalf.* He is unable to perceive the validity of his involvement in the conflict as an existential necessity. Consequently, he may begin to doubt the wisdom of the leading actors and eventually reject those models which heretofore have served him as viable and therefore significant. This feeling of estrangement and gradual aliena-tion between the ruled and the ruling élite does not necessarily have to be a product of purely ideological differences or other, less immediate, social determinants, but is more based on the fact that the ruling élite has been unsuccessful in the realization of its aims. So for example, had the war in Vietnam been successful, questions about the underlying reasons for the conflict and the justification of its reality would have most likely not become a public issue. By way of illustration, this fact becomes even clearer when the motivation for Daniel Ellsberg's passing of most of the forty-seven-volume secret Pentagon study of U.S. involvement in the Vietnam war to the *New York Times* is more closely examined. From the results of such scrutiny, the researcher might come to the conclusion that Ellsberg's response to the death toll and ill success of U.S. Armed Forces in Vietnam was based less on humanistic than utilitarian considerations.

Unable to perceive the differences and ramifications between 'realistic and nonrealistic' social conflict,[10] top leaders will attempt to solve both types according to *their* social perspective and definition of the situation. If a non-violent solution either is not sought or cannot be found, an attempt will be made to resolve conflict by violent means or by re-structuring present realities. To accomplish this, policies and strategies will be promulgated and appropriate institutional channels found or, if not presently available, created along with corresponding sets of social roles necessary for the realization of such institutions or organizations. Low ranking officials at the end of the hierarchical chain of command will most likely be the ones to enact the orders passed down by the power élite. If, however, the initiated measures fail to resolve the conflict, and/or are rejected by the public at large as unacceptable, the low ranking officials who administered or implemented such measures in 'good faith,' upon explicit or implicit orders, and under considerable pressure, will usually be held responsible for the lack of success. After the Nuremberg Trial of the Nazi War Criminals (1945-46), conducted by the *victorious Allies*, the few high ranking, but lower echelon, policy making Nazi officials tried in *German* courts were sentenced to considerably lesser prison terms than many of their underlings. So, for example, we find that the lower ranking former SS staff members of concentration and destruction camps are chiefly held responsible for the massacres and are sentenced to long prison terms; this is done instead of bringing the roles of their superiors, the administrative initiators and high ranking desk-chair perpetrators, into proper context.[11] In the United States junior officers and lower ranks are called to account for the My Lai 4 massacre, instead of top leaders of the involved parties responsible for initiating and perpetuating violence in the Vietnam conflict. Almost all men of Charlie Company, despite warnings by military officials and civilian lawyers, were willing to talk about the My Lai massacre in interviews. There was a persistent feeling of shame. 'Don't mention my name,' one G.I. asked after an interview. 'I don't want people around here pointing to me when I walk down the street, saying, "There goes that storm trooper." '[12]

Social institutions and organizations can indeed become pliable instruments in the hands of power holders who have developed *expertise* in the technique of harnessing power as a tool for the realization of their designs. Thus, the absence of institutionalized (constitutional) checks and balances not only makes possible the rise of despotism but can also produce dependency relationships which are experienced by the submitting actors as excessive. Max Weber described this state as an 'iron cage' of modern, bureaucratic society from which there is no breaking out.[13]

Only by a contextual understanding of a given social setting in which interaction takes place (which includes competition for the playing of power roles) can we better accept the recognition that

> Majors and Minors differ but in name
> Patriots and Ministers are much the same
> the only difference, after all their rout,
> is, that the one is in, the other out!

With these verses C. J. Weber, in 1836, wanted to point out to his compatriots the circular nature of the élitist social system.[14]

How can this be interpreted sociologically? It means that within a given socio-political structure social institutions will be created which in turn will produce specific types of leadership roles. These roles will be filled by individuals whose personality characteristics may be more suited for such positions and who will derive more satisfaction from playing them than others with different personality profiles. It would be unreasonable to assume that most of these individuals decide to play such roles merely because of a 'situational accident.' It is more likely that they are available and ready to play these power roles because of their very specific psychogenic needs. They are prevented from playing them because heretofore in the socio-cultural blueprint there had been no socially approved or institutionalized outlets for such roles on the *sociogenic* level.[15] Conversely, for example, members of the SS lost their power roles after the defeat of National Socialism because institutions such as the SS had become obsolete and therefore no longer provided a source for total leadership roles. Indeed, in the new democratic social setting, power roles with a coercive, intimidating, or mass-destructive function had become dysfunctional. There was no longer any need to enforce social control by violent means or to restrict social interaction through rigid legal and social sanctions and tightly knit, hierarchically structured channels of communication. However, this is not to say that the personality structure of former members of the SS had undergone appreciable change in the democratic post-war German social setting. In fact, empirical evidence seems to indicate that this had not been the case. [16]

## 2.    *The historical setting of the National Socialist rise to power and its sociological implications*

When we view history from a sociological perspective, we are primarily interested in those events that have set the stage for structurally normative, relatively constant social patterns. One of the foremost and decisive factors is the concept of power which permits the ruling élite to impose social and ideological controls and new legal norms by which the means and degree of social contract and social sanction will be determined. In the case of National Socialism these social controls were not necessarily based on the basic needs of the people. Although Hitler's policies were at first actively supported by the public at large that had eagerly assumed a new identity as posited by Hitler's ideological rhetoric, [17] the scope of social interaction was solely determined by the 'Führer' and by the Nazi élite after their power became more firmly entrenched. [18]

By virtue of its strategic social position the ruling élite is best equipped to harness, safeguard, and perpetuate power. In practice, then, it can be observed that the interpretation and structuring of social reality tends to be largely determined by the current power élite. It is in their power to enact laws (the legal order being an integral part of the social order) which will reflect and represent their view of the world, their interests, their values and social norms. Yet, the values expressed in such norms should by no means be viewed as simply the ones of an elect few, but rather as those held in common and shared with the group of people, subculture, or class they represent, since, after all, the ruling élite is a product of the culture in which it has originated and in which a process of specific interaction has taken place. The power élite, however, defines and decides what does and what does not constitute deviant social behavior. Essentially, law is made by the power élite with an eye to protecting its own interests and that of the class with which it is affiliated and from which it derives identity and support. Consequently, as Vilfredo Pareto already recognized, exploitation of fellow men by corrupt politicians and desk-chair perpetrators (white collar criminals) as a rule does not take place by breaking the law but by using it. This can be done because these laws primarily serve the interests of the privileged to the disadvantage and at the expense of the less- or underprivileged. In point of fact, they provide the nucleus for acts which can escalate into economic and political crime. Both types are integral components of what has become a historical reality known as the ultimate crime, i.e., crime against the human status – genocide. Those who possess less can only be kept in place and exploited by those who possess more. By virtue of this fact, the latter are in a 'superior' position to generate power potential which then is used to create social differentiation and inequality. Hence, in a society with a relatively rigid social stratification in which the power élite has little direct interaction with other segments of society, there will be no sharing of a common life-style. Consequently, there will be also an experience of mutual social distance, eventual alienation, conflict, and an imbalanced dependence relationship between the lower and the upper social classes.[19] When power discontinues to be socially related, it ceases to be transmittable and thus becomes subject to challenge and seizure by a counter-élite. Subsequently, a power-circle will be closed again by the phase described by Pareto as the 'circulation of élites.' A case in point was provided by Hitler's National Socialism which brought about an escalation into destruction. A defunct post-World War I political élite was superseded by a new one, the Nazis. This counter-élite was able to muster the support of the drifting masses searching for a more effective and meaningful leadership. This counter-movement offered the people a popular political ideology (myth system) and, last but not least, social identity, deviant as it may have appeared to a non-involved, neutral observer.

Not only had joblessness and inflation threatened the existential security of the groping masses of Germans in search of an acceptable identity, but the socio-political climate after the military defeat of 1918 was neither conducive nor geared adequately to preparing the citizen to participate in a democratic process of decision-making. The post-war socio-political structure of the Weimar Republic was not the product of a free choice made by the people but had arisen out of the dictates imposed upon the defeated German nation by the victorious Allies. Moreover, in the primary sphere, the traditional German family structure was designed to leave decision-making solely to the head of the family who, in turn, expected the leaders and administrators of the state to make social and political decisions for him. Hence, this primary social structure rendered the man in the street unequipped to assume co-responsibility, via reflective participation, in the formulation of those policies and the steering of those activities which had a decisive effect on society at large.

More specifically, on a *sociogenic* level (or, as Ferdinand Toennies defined it, *Gesellschafts*-relationships),[20] this lack of active involvement resulted in an uneven power distribution and in dependency relationships which became increasingly 'authority' centered and coercive according to the formula: 'All for the State; nothing outside the State; nothing against the State.'[21] On the *primary* and *psychogenic* level (corresponding to Toennies's *Gemeinschafts*-relationships),[22] the imbalanced dependency relationships tended to impair the chances of the individual to develop an autonomous, well-rounded, integrated personality structure that would facilitate harmonious social interaction and stimulate the *capacity for concern* for the well-being of fellow men.[23]

Thus we can say: When we view personality, from a social-psychological perspective, as a process and not as a mere system of inner traits, the analysis of politically deviant behavior patterns takes on new dimensions. It is one thing to observe that a given individual is a political deviant or a Nazi, and another to state that he behaves deviantly under specific conditions. What constitutes politically deviant behavior is not so much determined by the 'Weltanschauung' held by an individual observer or by an outsider but is based on the consensus of those who have participated by way of interaction in the promulgation of social values and norms and on those segments of a populace which have a vested interest in the perpetuation of such norms. Cameron has suggested the search for the precipitating conditions. If, for example, fears, suspicions, threats, and aggressive actions of 'paranoia-prone individuals' heighten the anxiety of those around them, they 'inevitably arouse defensive and retaliatory hostility in others.'[24] Such a response tends to confirm their interpretation of the situation and promotes mutually aggressive tendencies. If, however, hostility-promoting responses are lacking and if, unlike Hitler, Mussolini, or Stalin, an objective statesman serves as a bridge to reality, the politically deviant-prone citizen 'can begin to entertain doubts and consider alternative interpretations'[25] suggested by responsible cultural, social, and political leaders. Only the most favorable social conditions can prevent hostile behavior. There is good evidence that social structure, 'class subcultures and variation in patterns of interaction are among the causes of this differential.'[26]

In summary, we find that power-relationships are products of social interaction, structured by the reality of a given socio-political system. A power-relationship, therefore, is an integral part of a given socio-cultural blueprint and needs to be interpreted in the context of a time and space perspective, that is to say, all social phenomena created and interpreted by man are relative, tenuous, and thus subject to change. Empirically, the functional importance of power can be best determined by the nature and number of significant dependence relationships a person or group of persons were able to establish in their interaction with others whereby the power status in terms of *exclusiveness* is advanced.[27]

In a final assessment of the foregoing thoughts, it can be found that if the socio-political structure is so constraining that the man in the street who becomes engulfed in it sees virtually no alternative but to assume the role assigned to him in order to survive existentially, he will serve those in power to enact the current administration's policies – even if they involve acts of injustice and violence. Such persons can be turned into SS- and party-men, Calleys, and similar leading and supportive perpetrators who will be in no position to extricate themselves from the system without incurring severely felt social sanctions and penalties.[28] In other words, not only will these actors be rarely capable of deviating from social norms and dictates imposed on them, but they will be pressured into conformistic behavior patterns, thus forming an integral link between policy makers and those who enact and perpetuate policies of deception, intimidation, coercion and violence.

*Part 2*

Sociological
Factors
in the
Development
of the NS Party
Bureaucracy

*To be is to be related.*

**C. J. K.**

During the nineteenth and twentieth centuries the majority of Germans saw themselves confronted with two increasingly dominant institutions which began to play a major role in molding their socio-political milieu: the bureaucrats on the one hand, and the political parties on the other. Both stood in particular contrast to the descending powers, primarily the feudal class.[1] Although the bureaucracy of the nineteenth century tended to be predominantly authoritarian and rigid, it was nevertheless frequently represented by true authorities and was by and large remarkably independent of public consensus and opinion. The average bureaucrat carried out orders of the administrators and rulers without necessarily considering the needs or wishes of the masses. The democratic liberals of the nineteenth century attempted to liberate the individual from the oppression of the bureaucrats by delimiting their powers, whereas the tendency of rising political parties of the late nineteenth and the twentieth century, especially the National Socialist movement, was to usurp, infiltrate, politicize, coordinate (or at least neutralize), and subdue the bureaucracy and thus render it instrumental for the realization of their political goals.[2] However, the individual citizen did not in general benefit from this change unless he learned to influence the political program of the party of his choice through an active participation and an intelligent, independent political reflection. This in turn was only possible when the political and social structure permitted, in Max Weber's terms, a 'Nivellierung der Beherrschten,' in which he saw a process of 'passive democratization.'[3] More specifically:

> ... die Minimisierung der Herrschaftsgewalt der 'Berufsbeamten' zugunsten der möglichst direkten Herrschaft des 'Demos', das heißt aber praktisch: seiner jeweiligen Parteiführer ... Das Entscheidende ist vielmehr hier ausschließlich die Nivellierung der *Beherrschten* gegenüber der herrschenden bürokratisch gegliederten Gruppe, welche dabei ihrerseits sehr wohl faktisch, oft aber auch formal, eine ganz autokratische Stellung besitzen kann.[4]

> ... it is understood to mean the minimization of the civil servants' ruling power in favor of the greatest possible 'direct' rule of the *demos*, which in practice means the respective leaders of the *demos*. The most decisive thing here – indeed

it is rather exclusively so – is the *leveling of the governed* in opposition to the ruling and bureaucratically articulated group, which in its turn may occupy a quite autocratic position, both in fact and in form.[4]

This was indeed the case with the rigid, hierarchical structure of Nazi leadership. Hence the majority of Nazi supporters could be and frequently were misused by the party as 'Stimmvieh' (voting cattle),[5] since there was at best merely an apparent increase in the participation of the people in the actual ruling process. The major decisions were left to relatively few political leaders whose personality profile or character structure,[6] social background, and intellectual endowment – to name a few dependent variables – also permitted them to play a dominant role in directing party policies and to appoint others to subordinate public offices to co-decide and administer state policy. This type of leadership, as recent history has shown, neglected to modernize outdated socio-political structures and institutions and furthermore all too often kept qualified mature citizens from participating in state control. Finally, this system failed to prepare the man in the street to assume his share of political responsibility for the direction of state affairs, opening instead avenues to drifting, transient, unintegrated individuals (irresponsible, power-hungry, aggressive, etc.) and, frequently, to emotionally unstable elements to act as decision makers and bureaucratic dirigists. This explains the vested interest in maintaining absolute dependency of the people upon frequently incompetent leaders. Moreover, the absence of effective institutionalized checks and balances further permitted unscrupulous demagogues, and in some cases entire subcultures,[7] to curtail and abuse human rights, civil liberties, and individual freedom.

As a newly established state Germany was during the Wilhelminian and Weimar era not only politically and economically unconsolidated but above all ethnically unintegrated. These factors and others such as the lost war stimulated nationalism and chauvinism creating an emotional climate which proved to be fertile soil for Hitler's racist and political ideology. Hitler exploited these trends and gave them further impetus and structured direction. The ideological context and infrastructure of his movement, the already existing disparities in the political and socio-economic sphere, the psycho-emotional state of the people

– all these appeared to have acted upon each other by way of mutual reinforcement. The upshot of this rather complex political and socio-psychological process was a relatively unified Germany under Hitler's ideological leadership and the domination of the society by the National Socialist party. Moreover, the recent innovations, especially in the field of electronics, resulting in readily available mass media of communication, were effectively employed to disseminate National Socialist target-oriented propaganda. For this purpose under the leadership of Hitler was created a specialized branch of party bureaucracy. Its function was to keep the people in a state of 'perpetual mobilization' and maximize the ethnic and national identity by inciting collective hostility against minorities and by intimidating dissenters and deviants into compliance. The urge to build theories about collectivities in order to mobilize public enmity has become a common occurrence and a universally prevalent socio-political phenomenon. However, Hitler's ultimate goal was not merely the destruction of pluralism and the creation of a 'Großdeutsches Reich' but a united Europe and world domination under National Socialism – in short, aggressive expansionism. Indeed the climax of extremist activity appears to have been reached in National Socialist Germany. A majority of Germans seemed to have found in Hitler a charismatic leader with whom they could identify; Hitler in turn found in men such as Göring, Hess, Goebbels, Bormann, Himmler, Speer, Keitel, Heydrich, Kaltenbrunner, Eichmann, and Höss – to name some of the more representative leadership types – the individuals he needed to carry out his policies of intimidation, persuasion, coercion, and destruction within a totalitarian framework. These were frequently persons with certain mental and emotional insecurities, disturbances, and unintegrated personalities. Others followed who were strongly attracted to this type of system, which promulgated and put into practice an ideology that appeared to correspond to their most intimate wishes. In this system, among other 'basically desirable attributes,' the traditional ethos of obedience was shifted from 'virtue' to crime. [8]

Weber has already partially explained the human shortcomings and personality disturbances of many bureaucrats and administrators which also applied to NS party functionaries. Among the most striking of these character deficiencies is a lack of 'capacity for concern' [9] (which is by no means restricted to German nationals). Weber ascribes the

change of attitudes and goals prevailing among contemporary bureaucrats to the shift of balance from the ancient traditional 'Kulturmenschentum' of the 'Anglo Saxon gentleman' type to the 'Fachmenschen'-
Typus.[10] In this important passage Weber writes the following:

> . . . in der Demagogenherrschaft der hellenischen sogenannten
> Demokratie war Ziel der Erziehung und Grundlage der sozia-
> len Schätzung, bei aller noch so großen Verschiedenheit dieser
> Fälle untereinander, nicht der 'Fachmensch', sondern – schlag-
> wörtlich ausgedrückt – der 'kultivierte Mensch'.
>
> Der Ausdruck wird hier gänzlich wertfrei und nur in dem
> Sinne gebraucht: daß eine Qualität der Lebensführung, die als
> 'kultiviert' galt, Ziel der Erziehung war, nicht aber speziali-
> sierte Fachschulung. Die, je nachdem, ritterlich oder asketisch
> oder (wie in China) literarisch oder (wie in Hellas) gym-
> nastisch-musisch oder zum konventionellen angelsächsischen
> Gentleman *kultivierte* Persönlichkeit war das durch die Struk-
> tur der Herrschaft und die sozialen Bedingungen der Zugehö-
> rigkeit zur Herrenschicht geprägte Bildungsideal. . . .
>
> Hinter allen Erörterungen der Gegenwart um die Grund-
> lagen des Bildungswesens steckt an irgendeiner entscheiden-
> den Stelle der durch das unaufhaltsame Umsichgreifen der
> Bürokratisierung aller öffentlichen und privaten Herrschafts-
> beziehungen und durch die stets zunehmende Bedeutung des
> Fachwissens bedingte, in alle intimsten Kulturfragen ein-
> gehende Kampf des 'Fachmenschen'-Typus das alte 'Kultur-
> menschentum'.[11]

Expressed in slogan-like fashion, the 'cultivated man,' rather
than the 'specialist,' has been the end sought by education
and has formed the basis of social esteem in such various
systems as the feudal, theocratic, and patrimonial structures
of dominion: in the English notable administration, in the old
Chinese patrimonial bureaucracy, as well as under the rule
of demagogues in the so-called Hellenic democracy.

The term 'cultivated man' is used here in a completely
value-neutral sense; it is understood to mean solely that the
goal of education consists in the quality of a man's bearing in
life which was *considered* 'cultivated,' rather than in a special-

ized training for expertness. The 'cultivated' personality formed the educational ideal, which was stamped by the structure
of domination and by the social condition for membership in
the ruling stratum. Such education aimed at a chivalrous or
an ascetic type; or, at a literary type, as in China; a gymnastic-
humanist type, as in Hellas; or it aimed at a conventional type,
as in the case of the Anglo-Saxon gentleman. . . .

Behind all the present discussions of the foundations of the
educational system, the struggle of the 'specialist type of man'
against the older type of 'cultivated man' is hidden at some
decisive point. This fight is determined by the irresistably ex-
panding bureaucratization of all public and private relations
of authority and by the ever-increasing importance of expert
and specialized knowledge. [11]

Furthermore, the National Socialist administrators and bureaucrats
frequently succeeded in avoiding any impairment of their power, which
was broad in sphere of influence, and any abridgment of their privileges
appertaining to their elevated social status, by deliberately keeping the
masses in a state of political ignorance and depriving them of basic
human rights. Thus it was possible for the Nazi leadership to manipu-
late the masses into assenting to the use of violence against the so-called
internal and external enemies or, in other terms, into supporting resolution of conflict with violent means, implicitly or explicitly.

In this context attention should be drawn to recent findings within
the growing discipline of social psychiatry. These findings show that:

Most individuals are unlikely to act in response to their violent
impulses. But in disguised forms they are responsible for perpetuating injustices, inequities, ghettos, and other social vio-
lences that lead to the secondary elaboration of violent interpersonal consequences. Obviously such social pathology
should not be accepted as inevitable. [12]

The foregoing recognition, however, does not specifically apply if such
stimuli are provided as rigid, normative, sanctioned behavior and as
institutionalized outlets tolerating, permitting, and encouraging discrimination or instigating the use of force against outgroups and so-

called undesirable elements. Coercive measures were used by the National Socialists' regime to introduce and enforce discriminatory and racist legislature.[13] There appears to be little doubt that these measures contributed decisively to the escalation into destruction, not only from a sociological point of view, but also from the standpoint of individual psychological receptiveness to National Socialist ideological indoctrination. This in turn brought about a weakening of humanitarian concern and resistance on the part of the populace to National Socialist discriminatory and persecutory measures. Furthermore, it encouraged those individuals with emotional insecurities, character disorders, authoritarian personalities, etc., to become actively engaged in carrying out these policies or at least to render passive cooperation.[14]

According to Peterson, prior to 1933 only about 4 per cent of the rightist bureaucrats supported the National Socialists.[15] After 1933 the majority of the public servants preferred to stay in office and therefore arranged themselves with the regime 'in one way or another.'[16] The relationship of the party to the state was further strengthened and clarified by numerous decrees in the time between 1933 and 1937. This step-by-step process of fusing party power with state authorities essentially began with the 'Gesetz zur Wiederherstellung des Berufsbeamtentums' of April 7, 1933, which was supposed to free public servants from undue influence of party politics. The real intention, however, was to remove all those individuals from public office who were 'not qualified' according to the judgment of the party's leadership or who were classified from the standpoint of racial and ideological policies as outgroups.[17] These groups were mostly made up of non-Aryans, Communists, Socialists, and all those 'die nicht die Gewähr dafür bieten, daß sie jederzeit für den nationalen Staat eintreten.'[18] Most of these measures and policies introduced by the Nazis after their rise to power obviously could not have been realized without the assistance of the bureaucrats. Without the cooperation of these latter, neither could mass extermination have taken place, nor could Hitler's war machine have functioned.[19] This is in accord with Max Weber's postulate that the expert knowledge of the bureaucrat – regardless of its limitations and minuteness – makes him indispensable and therefore powerful.[20] His persuasive influence is derived from the fact that any complex society requires the service of the bureaucrat's expertise and rewards him for his skills with status and power, the degree of which is determined by his functional importance measured in terms of exclusiveness. Determined authority is not necessarily equivalent to authoritative expert competence, and the two must be carefully distinguished. Both are present in a developed bureaucratic system, and firmly establish the executive ministerial, administrative, and other rank and file bureaucracy as a social force and institution which according to Weber is a precision instrument 'welches sehr verschiedenen sowohl rein politischen wie rein ökonomischen, wie irgendwelchen anderen Herrschaftsinteressen sich zur Verfügung stellen kann.'[21]

The following factors appear to play a paramount role in co-determining the status of the bureaucrat and the functions of the bureaucratic system in society as persuasive authority: (1) the predominant goal orientation of the administrative and bureaucratic institutions (a) coercive, (b) utilitarian, (c) normative, or (d) a combination of any of these; (2) the stage of development of public and private administration, the degree to which they have been bureaucratized as compared to other societies and cultures, and in what manner and to what purpose. In other terms: the present state of development from the standpoint of bureaucratization; (3) the degree of flexibility and the type of hierarchic power structure of the bureaucratic system; (4) the degree of dependency of the bureaucracy upon the political executive or the dominant political party, more specifically, the loosely or closely knit interdependence of the bureaucracy with the political and social establishment on the one hand and the bureaucratic system on the other; (5) the traditional and presently prevalent attitude (in time and space) of the bureaucrat towards superiors, subordinates, and those falling under his administrative jurisdiction; (6) the sphere of influence and power of the bureaucrat in a given society; (7) professional and social status, expert knowledge, technical skill, and administrative qualifications of the bureaucrat (although expertise is an essential qualification for anyone holding a public office, it cannot be regarded as the only qualifying criterion. Emotional maturity and integrity of character must be present to some degree); (8) a suitable personality and character profile (does the position occupied exert an influence which determines a predominantly negative selection process?); (9) presence or absence of institutionalized checks and balances which (a) provide reasonable insurance against misuse of power and authority, (b) uphold individual freedom and guarantee civil rights and liberties to all citizens, (c) guarantee safety from any willful injury, manipulation, negligence, incompetence, or corruption by holders of public office.[22]

Weber pointed out the interrelationship between the bureaucratization of state administration and state control (Herrschaftsbeziehungen):

> Wo die Bürokratisierung der Verwaltung einmal restlos durchgeführt ist, da ist eine praktisch so gut wie unzerbrechliche Form der Herrschaftsbeziehungen geschaffen. Der einzelne Beamte kann sich dem Apparat, in den er eingespannt ist, nicht entwinden. Der Berufsbeamte ist, im Gegensatz zum ehren- und nebenamtlich verwaltenden 'Honoratioren' mit seiner ganzen materiellen und ideellen Existenz an seine Tätigkeit gekettet. Er ist – der weit überwiegenden Mehrzahl nach – nur ein einzelnes, mit spezialisierten Aufgaben betrautes, Glied in einem nur von der höchsten Spitze her, nicht aber (normalerweise) von seiner Seite, zur Bewegung oder zum Stillstand zu veranlassenden, rastlos weiterlaufenden Mechanismus, der ihm eine im wesentlichen gebundene Marschroute vorschreibt. Und er ist durch all dies vor allem festgeschmiedet an die Interessengemeinschaft aller in diesen Mechanismus eingegliederten Funktionäre daran, daß dieser weiterfunktioniere und die vergesellschaftet ausgeübte Herrschaft fortbestehe.[23]

---

And where the bureaucratization of administration has been completely carried through, a form of power relation is established that is practically unshatterable.

The individual bureaucrat cannot squirm out of the apparatus in which he is harnessed. In contrast to the honorific or avocational 'notable,' the professional bureaucrat is chained to his activity by his entire material and ideal existence. In the great majority of cases, he is only a single cog in an ever-moving mechanism which prescribes to him an essentially fixed route of march. The official is entrusted with specialized tasks and normally the mechanism cannot be put into motion or arrested by him, but only from the very top. The individual bureaucrat is thus forged to the community of all the functionaries who are integrated into the mechanism. They have a common interest in seeing that the mechanism continue its functions and that the societally exercised authority carry on. [23]

Going a step further it may also be assumed that there exists a significant correlation and functional interdependence between organizational compliance, organizational structure, organizational goals pursued in time and space, and their effectiveness. [24] It stands to reason that the function and value of any given entity changes in time and space. To remain meaningful it must be considered in its context: Its original intention must be interpreted as well as its present purpose and interrelationship to other entities defined. Political organizations whose goal is control over the legitimate means of violence are more likely than other political organizations to apply coercive persuasion in the control of their members.

> ... political organizations with a culture goal, such as indoctrination, tend to emphasize normative compliance and to minimize both the use of coercion and remunerative allocation for internal control purposes. [25]

Political organizations are predominantly concerned with gaining control of command of sources of legitimate means of coercion, such as the armed forces and the safety, security, and political police. This seems in particular to be the central goal of revolutionary organizations which aspire to advance in status to become counter-élites, regardless of the ideological orientation, specifically 'shortly before and during the revolutionary episode itself.' [26] Some social movements and radical parties focus on the dissemination of a new ideology. These are usually revolutionary parties which are relatively unsuccessful in recruiting a large following and gaining power, and which operate in societies where the existing political structure is well established. During this phase their success depends heavily not only on the support they receive from the administration and bureaucracy in power but also on the number and intensity of ideological conviction of their followers. Max Weber observes the following concerning the dependency relationship of the governed to the bureaucracy:

Die Beherrschten ihrerseits ferner können einen einmal bestehenden bürokratischen Herrschaftsapparat weder entbehren noch ersetzen, da er auf Fachschulung, arbeitsteiliger Fachspezialisierung und festem Eingestelltsein auf gewohnte und virtuos beherrschte Einzelfunktionen in planvoller Synthese beruht. Stellt er seine Arbeit ein oder wird sie gewaltsam gehemmt, so ist die Folge ein Chaos, zu dessen Bewältigung schwer ein Ersatz aus der Mitte der Beherrschten zu improvisieren ist. Dies gilt ganz ebenso auf dem Gebiet der öffentlichen wie der privatwirtschaftlichen Verwaltung. Die Gebundenheit des materiellen Schicksals der Masse an das stetige korrekte Funktionieren der zunehmend bürokratisch geordneten privatkapitalistischen Organisation nimmt stetig zu, und der Gedanke an die Möglichkeit ihrer Ausschaltung wird dadurch immer utopischer. . . .

Die objektive Unentbehrlichkeit des einmal bestehenden Apparats in Verbindung mit der ihm eigenen 'Unpersönlichkeit' bringt es andererseits mit sich, daß er – im Gegensatz zu den feudalen, auf persönlicher Pietät ruhenden Ordnungen – sich sehr leicht bereit findet, für jeden zu arbeiten, der sich der Herrschaft über ihn einmal zu bemächtigen gewußt hat. Ein rational geordnetes Beamtensystem funktioniert, wenn der Feind das Gebiet besetzt, in dessen Hand unter Wechsel lediglich der obersten Spitzen tadellos weiter, weil es im Lebensinteresse aller Beteiligten, einschließlich vor allem des Feindes selbst, liegt, daß dies geschehe.[27]

---

The ruled, for their part, cannot dispense with or replace the bureaucratic apparatus of authority once it exists. For this bureaucracy rests upon expert training, a functional specialization of work, and an attitude set for habitual and virtuoso-like mastery of single yet methodically integrated functions. If the official stops working, or if his work is forcefully interrupted, chaos results, and it is difficult to improvise replacements from among the governed who are fit to master such chaos. This holds for public administration as well as for private economic management. More and more the material fate of the masses depends upon the steady and correct functioning of the increasingly bureaucratic organizations of private capitalism. The idea of eliminating these organizations becomes more and more utopian. . . .

The objective indispensability of the once-existing apparatus, with its peculiar, 'impersonal' character, means that the mechanism – in contrast to feudal orders based upon personal piety – is easily made to work for anybody who knows how to gain control over it. A rationally ordered system of officials continues to function smoothly after the enemy has occupied the area; he merely needs to change the top officials. This body of officials continues to operate because it is to the vital interest of everyone concerned, including above all the enemy.[27]

The underlying conscious and unconscious motivation of the masses for a need of institutionalized, bureaucratically structured 'safety, law, and order,' or simply for security, often compels them to yield to injustice, discriminatory acts of aggression, violence, even mass extermination and genocide – all of which, as history has shown, tend to be committed by the newly established revolutionary totalitarian regime's leadership and administration, which in turn is primarily interested in retaining its power position at any cost. These political crimes are apparently tolerated or passively accepted by the masses not so much from a decision either to accept or reject 'new' revolutionary political ideologies, but in the hope to preserve or regain personal well-being (prosperity, comfort, health, etc.). In other words they seek merely to protect their self-interests which again reinforce complacency and lack of concern. The demos apparently feels most secure when he is faced with easily followed rules and regulations and if decisions beyond his comprehension are made for him by his leaders and administrators.

In contrast to the assertion made by Burin who finds that 'Weber's position rested essentially on his exaggerated estimate of the *political* importance of technical expertness,'[28] this writer finds that Hitler in fact frequently found himself – to speak in Weber's terms – '. . . in the position of the "dilettante" who stands opposite the superior knowledge of the expert.'[29] Hitler, in the same way as Stalin, Ulbricht, Novotny, Brezhnev with Podgorny and Shelest who were chiefly responsible for the ruthless occupation of Czechoslovakia of August 1968,* and numerous other totalitarian leaders, was dependent on the technical and administrative skills of the bureaucracy and the system per se which enabled him to carry out both his own policies and those of the Nazi party. However, he used the 'bureaucrats' whom he despised only with great reluctance and precaution and replaced them whenever possible with ideologically orientated party members. Or, he directly commissioned the party bureaucracy to carry out his special orders (Führerbefehle). As Otto Strasser, Hermann Rauschning, Felix Kersten and others pointed out, Hitler and Himmler attempted to defend themselves vigorously against any dominant influence of the 'rational-legal type' bureaucracy.[30] Weber illustrates this phase (apparently encountered by most charismatic ruling 'masters') as follows:

> Mit zunehmendem qualitativen Umsichgreifen der Verwaltungsaufgaben und damit der Unentbehrlichkeit des Fachwissens, tritt daher in sehr typischer Art die Erscheinung auf, daß der Herr mit der gelegentlichen Konsultation einzelner bewährter Vertrauensleute oder auch einer intermittierend in schwierigen Lagen zusammenberufenen Versammlung von solchen nicht mehr auskommt . . .
>
> Diese Art von kollegialen Behörden sind also die typische Form, in welcher der Herrscher, der zunehmend 'Dilettant' wird, zugleich Fachwissen verwertet und sich – was oft unbeachtet bleibt – der steigenden Übermacht des Fachwissens zu erwehren und ihm gegenüber in seiner Herrenstellung zu behaupten trachtet. Er hält einen Fachmann durch andere in Schach und sucht sich durch jenes umständliche Verfahren selbst ein umfassendes Bild und die Gewißheit zu verschaffen, daß ihm nicht willkürliche Entscheidungen souffliert werden.[31]

With the qualitative extension of administrative tasks and therewith the indispensability of expert knowledge, it typically happens that the lord no longer is satisfied by occasional consultation with individual and proved confidants or even with an

---

* For an eyewitness, documented account of the invasion of Czechoslovakia in 1968, see Robert Littel (ed.), *The Czech Black Book* (New York: Frederick A. Praeger, 1969).

assembly of such men called together intermittently and in difficult situations.

... This kind of collegiate body is the typical form in which the ruler, who increasingly turns into a 'dilettante,' at the same time exploits expert knowledge and – what frequently remains unnoticed – seeks to fend off the over-powering weight of expert knowledge and to maintain his dominant position in the face of experts. He keeps one expert in check by others and by such cumbersome procedures he seeks personally to gain a comprehensive picture as well as the certainty that nobody prompts him to arbitrary decisions. [31]

In National Socialist Germany and other totalitarian regimes such as Stalinist Russia, Maoist China, etc., the position of 'collegiate' authorities (kollegiale Behörden) was and is in many cases predominantly occupied by the 'party bureaucracy' (Parteibürokratie). [32] This group or possibly subculture only rarely distinguishes itself – apart from qualifications involving mere routine performance – by professional or expert knowledge, but rather merely forms a closely knit group of party members with a certain measure of loyalty and opportunism. It must be remembered that the party bureaucracy is also frequently made up of insecure elements with characteristics typical of social, occupational, political, and ideological drifters who often are ready to seize any opportunity – especially during times of socio-political upheavals, instabilities, and changes – to improve their psycho-emotional, material, and social position. [33] They are eagerly trying to regain their lost self-confidence and emotional security, to better their self-image by climbing up the social ladder, to gain existential security and recognition and be accepted at almost any price. Many members of this subculture are emotionally unbalanced and immature individuals, ruthless in the choice of methods which they employ to gain or retain status, power, and influence. [34] They are often the ones who introduce, or at least cooperate in support of, persecutory measures directed against outgroups labeled as deviants and reactionaries, and who spread terror, brutality, violence, and the suppression of individual freedom and civil rights in general. The 'dominant, surgent and affectothyme psychopaths whose histrionics have crowded out better leaders' [35] and their corresponding deputies and supporters can be grouped roughly into three categories:

(1) individuals and political leaders who disguise their aggressive efforts in the form of persuasive ideologies supporting political, social, and party programs; (2) those who accept their political party program, their formulation of ideologies and policies, and are able to identify emotionally with the underlying values and norms, and, finally, are intellectually, professionally, and technically in a position to administer and execute them in a relatively organized manner; some of these have become infamously known as so-called 'Schreibtischmörder' (desk-chair perpetrators); (3) men from the lower or lowest class stratum who rarely possess special skills or schooling and are intellectually less endowed or less developed and tend to be insensitive towards the anguish and suffering of others. In order to reduce socioeconomic and emotional deprivation imposed upon them by society or brought about by their own inadequate ability to decrease their social distance, these individuals are eager to obtain a feeling of belonging, to be existentially upgraded – in short to feel more secure. To achieve this goal these persons are willing to join the ranks of extremist movements and serve them on low or even the lowest hierarchic levels, i.e., in subordinate positions as 'Handlanger' (underling, hireling, myrmidon, henchman, stooge, lackey, etc.) in a relatively low prestige 'body-contact relation' with the opponents and victims of the regime. Without their assistance, coercion, execution of persecutory measures, violence, and mass killings could not have been accomplished.[36] These three subgroups formed a symbiotic team which had set itself the task to realize NS ideologies and destroy what they considered to be the internal and external enemies of the Regime. It should be noted that the conceptualization, administration, detailed bureaucratic and actual application of these concerted acts of aggression and destruction could not have been carried out by merely one of these subgroups, probably because of psycho-emotional barriers on the one hand and their absence, accompanied by a lack of intellectual and professional achievement, on the other. This recognition seems also to verify 'Max Weber's statement about the relationship between revolution and the stability of personnel of governmental bureaucracies in modern society. Weber thought that the officials at the very top would be replaced, the bureaucratic machine with its necessity for special training and knowledge remaining intact and serving the new political master as it had the old.'[37]

Although some officials holding subordinate ranks were also replaced, the majority of key positions were soon delegated to party officials of old standing after the Nazi rise to power. Many bureaucrats
and administrators of all levels joined the party either for opportunistic
or ideological reasons in order to retain their positions.[38] Coercive pressure and control exerted by the party bureaucracy not only determined
the social and material security of the civil servant in general but also
the entire sphere of his social interaction. The social structure of the
German society itself was divided into the inner circles and the numerous variously stratified peripheral and outgroups of which the status of
the Jews and Gypsies was de facto the most irreversible by definition
and the most irreparable by fate. The bond of totalitarian bureaucratization, brought about by charismatic leadership coupled with ideologic,
economic, and military strategy, was successful 'until the National Socialist movement discredited itself by losing the war' (der Nationalsozialismus hat sich selbst widerlegt indem er gescheitert ist), as one
representative spokesman of the ultra-right wing NPD (Nationaldemokratische Partei Deutschlands) put it during the 1968 Baden-Württem-
berg election campaign in Freiburg/Breisgau. That is to say, the system
no longer functioned, i.e., it had become dysfunctional and was therefore no longer justifiable.

It should be remembered that the National Socialist party bureaucracy was essentially made up of men who not only were in a position
to do what was asked of them but who also had to identify themselves
with the cause and strategies of National Socialism. Hitler exemplified
the demands he made upon these people and characterized the 'types'
he needed in a conversation with Rauschning in 1934:

> Immerhin werden wir ohne einen Personenkreis, der mit Lust
> und Liebe an die Sache herangeht, nichts erreichen. Den Büro-
> kraten ist diese Aufgabe lästig; sie ist ihnen zu unsauber. In
> Wirklichkeit sind sie zu feige und zu dumm dazu. Aber den-
> ken wir an Frauen, an abenteuerlustige Damen der Gesell-
> schaft, überdrüssig ihres unnützen Daseins, denen Liebschaf-
> ten nicht mehr als Sensationen genügen. Ich werde mich nicht
> scheuen, anormale Männer zu verwenden, Abenteurer aus
> Lust am Metier. Es gibt unzählige solcher Menschen, die im
> bürgerlichen Leben zu nichts zu gebrauchen, hier aber einen

hervorragenden Platz ausfüllen können. . . .

Ich ziehe mir einen eigenen Apparat groß. Das kostet zwar viel Geld, aber ich komme schneller vorwärts. Ich habe einen Fragebogen zusammengestellt, nach dem mir über die mich interessierenden Persönlichkeiten zu berichten ist. Ich lasse eine umfassende Kartothek aller einflußreichen Persönlichkeiten in allen Ländern herstellen. Diese Kartenblätter werden alles Wichtige enthalten. Nimmt er Geld? Ist er anders zu kaufen? Ist er eitel? Ist er stark erotisch veranlagt? Welcher Typ? Ist er homosexuell? Das letztere ist besonders zu bevorzugen, weil es enge, nie mehr zu lösende Verbindungen gibt. Hat er in der Vergangenheit etwas zu verbergen? Kann man ihn erpressen? Welche Geschäfte treibt er? Besondere Liebhabereien, Sport, Marotten und Spleen. Reist er gern? Und so weiter.

Nach diesen Berichten such ich mir meine Leute aus. Damit mache ich wirkliche Politik. Nämlich ich gewinne mir Menschen, die für mich arbeiten. Ich schaffe mir eine Macht in jedem einzelnen Lande. . . .

Die Früchte meiner Tätigkeit werden wir erst im kommenden Kriege sehen. . . .

Ich aber treibe Machtpolitik, das heißt, ich bediene mich jedes Mittels, das mir dienlich erscheint, ohne die geringste Rücksichtnahme auf einen Komment oder Ehrenkodex. Und wer mir wie dieser Hugenberg mit seiner Sippe entgegenzetert, daß ich mein Wort breche, daß ich Verträge nicht halte, daß ich List, Betrug und Verstellung übe, dem antworte ich: bitte! tue desgleichen. . . . Gewiß bin ich heute im Vorteil vor diesen Bürgern und Demokraten, weil mich keine pedantischen und sentimentalen Rücksichten hindern. Soll ich edelmütig diesen Vorteil meiner Position verschmähen, nur weil meine Gegner noch nicht so weit sind? Wer sich betrügen läßt, braucht sich nicht wundern, daß man ihn betrügt. . . .

Ich gebe der Gewalt ihre angestammte Würde wieder, die Quelle alles Großen und die Mutter der Ordnung zu sein. . . .

Ich erkenne kein Moralgesetz in der Politik an. Politik ist ein Spiel, in dem jeder Trick erlaubt ist, und in dem die Spielregeln sich je nach Geschicklichkeit der Spieler ständig ändern. . . .

Man wirft mir vor, daß ich mich mit ehrgeizigen und strebe-
rischen Elementen umgebe. Welche Albernheiten! Soll ich mit
Betschwestern mein Reich bauen? Männer, die nicht ehrgeizig
sind, sollen mir vom Leibe bleiben. Nur wer sein eigenes Fortkommen mit der allgemeinen Sache so verknüpft, daß keins
mehr vom anderen zu trennen ist, nur auf den kann ich mich
verlassen. Leute, die von Patriotismus nicht bloß reden, sondern ihn zum einzigen Motiv ihres Handelns machen, sind
suspekt. Übrigens ist es nicht meine Aufgabe, die Menschheit
zu bessern, sondern mich ihrer Schwächen zu bedienen. Ich
will Menschen um mich haben, die gleich mir in der Gewalt
den Motor der Geschichte sehen und daraus die Konsequen-
zen ziehen. Aber ich habe durchaus nicht den Ehrgeiz, als besonderer Verächter der Moral zu erscheinen. Wozu es den
Leuten leicht machen. Es wird mir nicht schwer fallen, meiner
Politik einen moralichen Anstrich zu geben, und die Motive
meiner Gegner als Heuchelei zu entlarven. Für die Masse sind
moralische Gemeinplätze unentbehrlich und nichts ist verkehr-
ter, als wenn ein Politiker auch nach außen hin als der amora-
lische Übermensch erscheinen will. . . .

Ohne den Willen zur Grausamkeit geht es nicht. Übrigens
fehlt er unseren Gegnern nur, weil sie zu schwächlich sind,
nicht etwa, weil sie human sind. Herrschaft wird nie durch
Humanität begründet, sondern, vom bürgerlichen Winkel aus
betrachtet, durch Verbrechen. Der Terror ist absolut unentbehrlich bei jeder Begründung einer neuen Macht. Die Bolschewisten haben das noch auf alte Weise gemacht. Sie haben
die ganze frühere Herrschaftsklasse getötet. Das ist das alte,
klassische Mittel . . . Ich bediene mich der alten herrschenden
Klasse selbst. Ich halte sie in Furcht und Abhängigkeit. Ich
bin überzeugt, ich werde keine willigeren Helfer haben. Und
werden sie aufsässig, dann steht mir das alte, klassische Mittel
immer noch zu Gebote.

Zuviel Grausamkeit ist von Übel. Das stumpft ab. Wichtiger
noch als der Terror ist die systematische Umwandlung der
Begriffswelt und der Empfindungsschemata der Masse. Man
muß sich auch noch die Gedanken und Gefühle der Menschen

unterwerfen. Das wird uns heute in der Zeit des Radios unvergleichlich nachhaltiger glücken, als das in früheren Zeiten
möglich war. . . .

Unser Weg ist nicht sauber, . . . Ich kenne niemanden, der
sich nicht die Füße beschmutzt hat auf dem Weg zu Größe. [39]

---

Anyhow, we shall get nothing achieved without a staff who
have their hearts in the work. The officials don't like this
task; it's too dirty for them. So they say, but in reality it is
they who are too cowardly and too stupid. But consider the
women, the society ladies thirsting for adventure, sick of their
empty lives, no longer getting a 'kick' out of love affairs. And
I shall not shrink from using abnormal men, adventurers from
love of the trade. There are countless men of this sort, useless
in respectable life, but invaluable for this work.

. . . I am building up a great organization of my own. It
costs a lot of money, but it gets things moving for me. I have
drawn up a *questionnaire* covering details of the persons I am
interested in. I am having a comprehensive card index compiled of every influential person in the world. The cards con-
tain every detail of importance. Will he take money? Can he
be bought in any other way? Is he vain? Is he sexual? In what
way? Is he homosexual? That is of the utmost value, because
it provides close associations that can never be escaped from.
Has he anything in his past to conceal? Can he be subjected to
pressure? What is his business? His hobby, his favorite sport,
his likes and dislikes? Does he like travel? And so on. It is on
the strength of these reports that I choose my men. That really
is politics. I get hold of men who will work for me. I create
a force of my own in every country. . . .

We shall only see the fruits of my activity in the coming
war. . . .

. . . But I am concerned with power politics – that is to say,
I make use of all means that seem to me to be of service, without the slightest concern for the proprieties or for codes of
honor. And if people come blubbering to me, like that man
Hugenberg and his tribe, complaining that I am breaking my
word, that I am paying no regard to treaties, that I am

making a practice of trickery and deception and misrepresentation, I reply: 'Well, what of it? You are free to do the same. Nobody is preventing you.' ...

... I certainly have an advantage over these *bourgeois* democrats in my freedom from pedantic and sentimental inhibitions. Am I to be so generous as to throw away this advantage, simply because my opponents have not progressed so far? If anyone is prepared to be deceived, he must not be surprised that he is. ...

... I am restoring to force its original dignity, that of the source of all greatness and the creatrix of order. ...

... I recognize no moral law in politics. Politics is a game, in which every sort of trick is permissible, and in which the rules are constantly being changed by the players to suit themselves. ...

... I am charged with surrounding myself with ambitious and pushing elements. What rubbish! Am I to build my Reich with saintly sisters? If a man is not ambitious, I don't want him. Only on those whose own personal advancement is so bound up with the general movement that there is no longer any separating the two things – only on those men can I depend. Men who not only spout patriotism but make it the sole motive of their actions are suspect. In any case, my task is not to make men better, but to make use of their weaknesses.

The men I want round me are those who, like myself, see in force the motive element in history and who act accordingly. Not that I have any desire to appear as more contemptuous of the moral code than the generality of men. Why make it easy for people to attack me? I myself can quite easily give my policy a coloring of morality and show up my opponents' motives as hypocritical. Moral commonplaces are indispensable for the masses. Nothing is more mistaken than for a politician to pose as an amoral superman. ...

... Unless you are prepared to be pitiless, you will get nowhere. Our opponents are not prepared for it, not because they are humane or anything of that sort, but because they are too weak. Dominion is never founded on humanity but, regarded from the narrow civilian angle, on crime. Terrorism is absolutely indispensable in every case of the founding of a new power. The Bolsheviks applied it in the old style: they killed off the whole of the former ruling class. That is the ancient, classic method.* ... I make use of members of the old ruling class itself. I keep them in fear and dependence. I am confident that I shall have no more willing helpers. And if they become refractory, I can always return to the ancient, classic method.

Too much frightfulness does harm. It produces apathy. Even more important than terrorism is the systematic modification of the ideas and feelings of the masses. We have to control those. It is incomparably easier nowadays with the radio. ...

... Our path is not unsullied. I know of no case in which a man has trodden the path to power without wading through mud.[39]

It was not overly difficult for Hitler and later Himmler to find the types they needed for running a party bureaucracy which would assist them in realizing the ideological and emotional goals and needs. Hitler's ultimate goal was to create a tribal community (Volksgemeinschaft) out of the masses, this is to say a rigidly organized, self-confident nation: 'our party' (unsere Partei).[40] But the meaning of the word 'party' he deemed inadequate and therefore preferred the concept 'order' (Orden).[41] The party's inner circle, with its administrators and bureaucrats, was to assist him to create it. The rigidly stratified social structure of this system, of which the party with its ideological bureaucracy was to be a major part within the new German social order, had already been briefly outlined by Hitler in the summer of 1932:

> Wir stehen heute vor der ehernen Notwendigkeit, eine *neue soziale Ordnung* zu schaffen. Denn nur wenn uns das gelingt, werden wir die große geschichtliche Aufgabe lösen, die uns als Volk gestellt ist.

* 'To the best of my memory, it is recommended by Machiavelli; or, at least, he recommends extending goodwill only to the second stratum, those who were immediately below the ruling class.'

Die klassenlose Gesellschaft der Marxisten ist ein Wahnsinn. Ordnung heißt immer Rangordnung. Aber ebenso wahnwitzig sind die demokratischen Ideen einer Rangordnung auf Grund des Geldsackes. Echtes Herrentum entsteht nicht aus den zufälligen Spekulationsgewinnen von smarten Geschäftsleuten. Es ist das Geheimnis unseres Erfolges, das Lebensgesetz echten Herrentums wieder in den Mittelpunkt des politischen Kampfes gestellt zu haben. Echtes Herrentum entsteht nur da, wo auch echte Unterwerfung besteht. Es kommt nicht darauf an, die Ungleichheit der Menschen zu beseitigen, sondern im Gegenteil, sie zu vertiefen und, wie in alten großen Kulturen, sie durch übersteigbare Schranken zum Gesetz zu machen. Es gibt kein gleiches Recht für alle. Wir werden den Mut haben, dies nicht bloß zur Maxime unseres Handelns zu machen, sondern uns auch dazu bekennen. Nie werde ich daher anderen Völkern das gleiche Recht wie dem deutschen zuerkennen. Unsere Aufgabe ist es, die anderen Völker uns zu unterwerfen. Das deutsche Volk ist berufen, die neue Herrenschicht der Welt zu geben.

Die Rolle des Bürgertums ist ausgespielt. . . . Aber auch diese 'geschichtsbefugten Oberschichten', dieser Kalender-Adel, diese degenerierten Abkömmlinge alter Adelsgeschlechter haben nur noch die eine Aufgabe, in 'Schönheit zu sterben'. . . . Ich werde gewiß kein Herrentum zerstören, wo es heute noch echt ist. Aber wo gibt es solches? Und wenn es solches gibt, dann bekennt es sich zu mir. Nein, meine Parteigenossen, man diskutiert nicht über die Entstehung einer neuen 'Oberschicht'. Man schafft sie und es gibt nur *ein* Mittel, sie zu erzeugen: den Kampf. Die Auslese der neuen Führerschicht ist *mein* Kampf um die Macht. Wer sich zu *mir* bekennt, ist berufen eben durch dieses Bekenntnis und die Art, *wie* er sich bekennt. Das ist die große umwälzende Bedeutung unseres langen, zähen Kampfes um die Macht, daß in ihm eine neue Herrenschicht geboren wird, berufen, nicht bloß die Geschicke des deutschen Volkes, sondern der Welt zu lenken. . . .

Wie die künftige Sozialordnung ausschauen wird, meine Parteigenossen, das will ich Ihnen sagen: eine Herrenschicht wird es geben, eine historisch gewordene, aus den verschiedensten Elementen durch Kampf erlesene. Es wird die Menge der hierarchisch geordneten Parteimitglieder geben. Sie werden den neuen Mittelstand abgeben. Und es wird die große Masse der Anonymen geben, das Kollektiv der Dienenden, der ewig Unmündigen, gleichgültig, ob sie ehemals Vertreter des alten Bürgertums waren oder Großagrarier, Arbeiter oder Handwerker. Die wirtschaftliche Position und die bisherige gesellschaftliche Rolle wird da auch nicht die geringste Bedeutung haben. Diese lächerlichen Unterschiede werden in einem einzigen revolutionären Prozess eingeschmolzen werden. Darunter wird es aber noch die Schicht der unterworfenen Fremdstämmigen geben, nennen wir sie ruhig die moderne Sklavenschicht. Und über allem wird es den neuen Hochadel geben, die besonders verdienten und besonders verantwortlichen Führerpersönlichkeiten. Auf solche Weise, im Ringen um die Macht und Herrschaft innerhalb eines Volkes und außerhalb desselben entstehen neue Stände; niemals aber, wie sie sich diese Professoren und Stubenhocker es vorstellen, wie dieser Professor Spann, durch eine zusammengeleimte Verfassung, durch ein regierungsseitiges Dekret.

Was unser Parteigenosse Darré gesagt hat, billige ich. Hier im Osten ist unser großer Experimentierfeld. Hier wird die neue europäische Sozialordnung entstehen. ... ich denke in diesem einen Punkt ganz wie Darré und Himmler. Das Rassisch-biologische ist immer nur die *eine* Seite des ganzen Prozesses. Wir werden überhaupt sehr bald über die Grenzen des heutigen engen Nationalismus hinausgelangen. Meine Parteigenossen, Weltimperien entstehen zwar auf einer nationalen Basis, aber sie lassen diese sehr bald weit unter sich.[42]*

* Concluding this discourse, Hitler expressed the following notions concerning education and upbringing in his envisioned social order: 'Universal education is the most corroding and disintegrating poison that liberalism has ever invented for his own destruction. There must be only one possible education for each class, for each subdivision of each class. Complete freedom of choice in education is the privilege of the *élite* and of those whom they have specially admitted. The whole of science must be subject to continued control and selection. Knowledge is an aid to life, not its central aim. We must therefore be consistent, and allow the great mass of the lowest order the blessings

... Today we are faced with the iron necessity of creating a *new social order*. Only if we succeed in this we shall solve the great historical task which has been set our people.

The classless society of the Marxists was madness. Order always meant class order. But the democratic notion of a class order based on the moneybag was equally mad.

A genuine aristocracy was not born out of the accidentally successful speculations of bright businessmen. The secret of our success lay in the fact that we had once more placed the vital law of genuine aristocracy at the heart of the political struggle. True aristocracy existed only where there was also true subjection. We did not intend to abolish the inequality of man; on the contrary, we would deepen it and, as in ancient great civilizations, create insurmountable barriers which would turn it into law. There was no equal right for all. We would have the courage to make this denial the basis of all our actions, and to acknowledge it openly. Never would he concede to other nations equal rights with the German. It was our task to place other nations in subjection. The German people was called to give the world the new aristocracy. ...

The part played by the *bourgeoisie* is finished – permanently, my party comrades, ... But even these 'upper classes justified by history,' this paper aristocracy, these degenerate shoots of ancient noble families, have still one thing left, 'to die in beauty.'. . . I shall certainly destroy no aristocracy which today is still genuine. But where is there any such? If there is any, it will give its support to me. No, my party comrades, we shall not discuss the growth of a new upper class. We shall create it, and there is only one way of creating it: battle. The selection of the new Führer class is *my* struggle for power. Whoever proclaims his allegiance to *me* is, by this very proclamation and by the *manner* in which it is made, one of the chosen. This is the great revolutionary significance of our long, dogged struggle for power, that in it will be born a new *Herren*-class, chosen to guide the fortunes not only of the

---

of illiteracy. We ourselves, on the other hand, shake off all humane and scientific prejudices.'

German people, but of the world. . . .

As to the appearance of this future social order, my party comrades, I can say to you that there will be a *Herren*-class, an historical class tempered by battle, and welded from the most varied elements. There will be a great hierarchy of party members. They will be the new middle class. And there will be the great mass of the anonymous, the serving collective, the eternally disfranchised, no matter whether they were once members of the old *bourgeoisie,* the big land-owning class, the working-class or the artisans. Nor will their financial or previous social position be of the slightest importance. These preposterous differences will have been liquidated in a single revolutionary process. But beneath them there will still be the class of subject alien races; we need not hesitate to call them the modern slave class. And over all of these will stand the new high aristocracy, the most deserving and the most responsible *Führer*-personalities. In this way, in the struggle for power and mastery both within a nation and outside it, new classes emerge; never, as the professors and bookworms would have us believe, through a makeshift constitution, a government decree.

I fully approve of what our party comrade Darré has said. Our great experimental field is in the east. There the new European social order will arise, and this is the great significance of our eastern policy. . . .

Certainly we shall admit to our new ruling class members of other nations who have been worthy in our cause. On this point I entirely agree with Darré and Himmler. The racial and biological aspect is only one side of the total process. In fact, we shall very soon have overstepped the bounds of the narrow nationalism of today. My party comrades, it is true that world empires arise on a national basis, but very quickly they leave it far behind. [42]

The decree of December 1, 1933, was to guarantee the 'lawful' unity of the National Socialist party and the state. It stipulated that the NSDAP was 'die Trägerin des deutschen Staatsgedankens und mit dem Staat unlöslich verbunden.' [43] The bureaucrat was now forced either to cooperate and 'more or less' carry out the orders of the NSDAP or risk dismissal and suffer deprivation and hardship. The situation as described by Weber is also applicable to the rise to power of the National Socialists in 1933:

> Denn jeder Fortschritt der einfachen mit Ziffern rechnenden Wahltechnik, wie etwa (wenigstens unter Großstadtverhältnissen) das Proportionalwahlsystem, bedeutet straffe, interlokale bürokratische Organisation der Partei und damit zunehmende Herrschaft der Parteibürokratie und der Disziplin unter Ausschaltung der lokalen Honoratiorenkreise. [44]

---

> Every advance of the simple election techniques, for instance the system of proportional elections, which calculates with figures, means a strict and inter-local bureaucratic organization of the parties and therewith an increasing domination of party bureaucracy and discipline, as well as the elimination of the local circles of notables – at least this holds for great states. [44]

The national government was swiftly transformed into a personal agency of the Führer. Moreover, Hitler de facto took direct control of all governmental departments, the civil service, the armed forces, and the police. He held the power to decide between life and death for all his subordinates within the National Socialist party, and through the party for all Germans. Burin lists ten major measures introduced by the National Socialist party to gain control over the bureaucracy:

(1) Transfer of state functions from the 'formal' bureaucracy to the 'living organization,' i.e., the party; (2) personal union of governmental agencies and offices through appointments of party officeholders to state positions; (3) parallelism, i.e., creation of an analogous form of bureaucratic party offices to exert pressure on, and perhaps eventually to merge with, government departments; (4) Nazification at the top; (5) permeation; (6) conversion to National Socialism; (7) dismissal of undesirable personnel; (8) transfer of unreliable personnel; (9) enforced compliance; (10) replacement of law by discretion. [45] The almost ubiquitous Gestapo (the Nazi secret police) and other formations of the SS (élite Nazi guards) used terror to an unprecedented extent to control the bu-

reaucracy and the population in the interests of the party and the state. The Nazi authorities (and especially its terror organizations) were most adept at revealing just enough of their cruelties in prisons, concentration camps, and elsewhere to serve as a threat without disclosing enough to arouse a conscientious reaction on the part of a largely docile and easily intimidated populace. Until the enormity of Hitler's (and Himmler's) crimes against humanity became particularly obvious during the latter stages of the war, he seems to have enjoyed the more or less enthusiastic support of most Germans. By 1935 the entire mechanism of government had been predominantly 'coordinated' (gleichgeschaltet). Furthermore, Nazi control organizations moved practically into all cultural, professional, and economic areas to assure totalitarian rule in strict accordance with Hitler's wishes. By largely exempting acts of the Gestapo (and the Reichssicherheitshauptamt) – and in effect nearly all executive and administrative acts – from appeal to the courts, the Nazis also abrogated the principle of judicial review. At best the citizen could appeal to the same authority that had rendered the decision or seek intervention from high party circles. The rule of law, which had begun to take root under the Weimar Republic, was expurgated by basing the criminal code on the 'sound feeling of the people' as expressed through Nazi dogma. Judges were compelled to take an oath of personal allegiance to Hitler. A special court, the 'Volksgericht' (People's Court), was established to deal with acts against the state. Frequently its judges were not required to have any legal training and in reality meted out party justice. The land governments were placed under the direct control of national governors who in turn were responsible to the Führer, and the Ministry of the Interior was authorized to interfere directly in local affairs. In 1934 the land diets were abolished and their powers transferred to the Reich government. Consequently, as subsequent territory was integrated into the Reich, it became part of the unitary structure. The old ruling class – including bureaucrats, the military, and industrialists – for all practical purposes acceded to the dictatorship, the swift abrogation of the rule of law, and the suspension of politics.

During World War II the already advanced process of amalgamation between the party, the administration, and the bureaucracy was speeded up and reached a high degree of homogeneity, limited in its further development only by the additional external and internal emergencies and pressures. Simultaneously with this process of amalgamation there occurred a swift move toward decentralization of administrative and decision-making bodies. This move largely favored party functionaries, with three possible (and formidable) exceptions: Hitler's total assumption of leadership over the war machine, Himmler and his SS's total assumption of leadership in the Reichssicherheitshauptamt over internal security, and Party Secretary Bormann's parallel takeover of the party apparatus which was for all practical purposes assuming an absolute dominance over state affairs in general.[46] The technical difficulties experienced during the step-by-step adaptation and fusion of the bureaucratic and administrative machinery to party dictates and control brought with it some conflicts of sociological and psychological nature which were, however, of relatively little consequence in their influence upon the efficacious realization of National Socialist policies.[47] Indeed the particular stage of bureaucratic amalgamation achieved by the Nazi leadership was most appropriately described by Weber: 'Wo die Bürokratisierung der Verwaltung einmal restlos durchgeführt ist, da ist eine praktisch so gut wie unzerbrechliche Form der Herrschaftsbeziehungen geschaffen.'[48] Moreover, not only was the bureaucratic apparatus a most essential vehicle for the institutionalization and administration of NS ideological and political dogmas, but it also gave many an irrational concept an appearance of rational and legal validity with which the masses could be swayed. As Weber suggested:

> Eine einmal voll durchgeführte Bürokratie ist *das* spezifische Mittel, 'Gemeinschaftshandeln' in rational geordnetes 'Gesellschaftshandeln' zu überführen. Als Instrument der 'Vergesellschaftung' der Herrschaftsbeziehungen war und ist sie daher ein Machtmittel allerersten Ranges für den, der über den bürokratischen Apparat verfügt.[49]

> ⸻

> Once it is fully established, bureaucracy is among those social structures which are the hardest to destroy. Bureaucracy is *the* means of carrying 'community action' over into rationally ordered 'social action'. Therefore, as an instrument for 'societalizing' relations of power, bureaucracy has been and is a power instrument of the first order – for the one who controls the bureaucratic apparatus.[49]

The ambiguous wording of the first discriminatory decrees, and of others which followed, permitted the Nazi leadership to strengthen the esprit de corps of the ingroup at the expense of continuously arising and consistently purged outgroups. Coser insists that according to Simmel:

> Conflict with other groups contributes to the establishment and reaffirmation of the identity of the group and maintains its boundaries against the surrounding social world ... enmities and reciprocal antagonisms also maintain the total system by establishing a balance between its component parts.
>
> This takes place, according to Simmel, because members of the same stratum or caste are drawn together in a solidarity resulting from their common enmity to and rejection of members of other strata or castes. In this way a hierarchy of positions is maintained by the aversion that the various members of the subgroups within the total society have for each other.[50]

Furthermore, Else Frenkel-Brunswik pointed out that the ethnocentric personalities' 'hate is mobile and can be directed from one object to another.'[51] This became quite evident when Nazi leadership failed to recognize its final strategic, political, and economic objectives. The supreme leadership began to blame for their own ill success members of the ingroup, accusing them of flagrant negligence, insubordination, incompetence, lack of ideological identification or zealousness, etc. Shortly before his death on April 30, 1945, Hitler even turned against his SS and his closest collaborators Göring and Himmler.[52] Indeed the Nazis' choice of antagonists frequently did not depend on the choice of determinants directly related to a contentious issue but was largely – as in the case of the Jews, Gypsies, or Slavs – guided by the attainment of results which had hardly anything to do with objective improvement of the economic or socio-political state of affairs in Germany.[53]

However, from a pragmatic point of view, by excluding all those whom they thought capable of opposing or dissenting from their program, or of endangering it in any way, the spreading and practice of stereotype prejudice and scapegoating clearly assisted the Nazi leadership corps to realize their objectives, nebulous as they may have been, within the shortest possible time. Himmler expressed to his confidant

Kersten the following opinion concerning the characteristic features of a bureaucrat:

> Der Beamte ist der ewige Kriecher, ein Radfahrertyp, der alles, was er von oben einstecken muß und demütig einsteckt, nach unten weitergibt und jede Gelegenheit benutzt, um seinem Vorgesetzten, von dem er abhängig ist, zu zeigen, wie treu, ehrlich und anständig, wie fleißig und dienstbeflissen er ist. Das alles tut er aber nicht der Sache halber, sondern nur, um Karriere zu machen. [54]

> ... The civil servant is always servile; he humbly accepts everything that is passed down to him from above – why not? – he simply passes it on to the fellow below. Meanwhile he'll do everything in his power to show the boss on whose goodwill he depends how loyal, honourable, and decent he is, how industrious and conscientious. He behaves in this fashion not because he approves of it but for the sake of his career. [54]

and the following basic attitude, apparently prevalent among the leading National Socialists:

> Während der Kampfzeit, als uns die Bürokratie bedrückte, wo sie nur konnte, habe ich mir geschworen, mit dem Beamtenapparat Schluß zu machen, sobald wir an die Macht gekommen seien. Heute denke ich, nachdem ich die Geschichte des preußischen Staates kenne, darüber ganz anders. Man braucht die Beamten. Man muß sie jedoch in ihrer Mentalität genau kennen und sich dies nutzbar machen. [55]

> ... During our struggle for power, when the civil servants oppressed us as only they knew how, I used to swear to make an end of the whole system the moment we came to power. Now, knowing the history of the Prussian state, I think quite differently. The civil servants are a necessity. But you need to understand their mentality exactly before you can make use of it. [55]

To sum up: Only after the discriminatory and persecutory practice against the 'internal enemy' had been initiated by the Nazi movement and sanctioned by and incorporated into the legal and bureaucratic system had the initial phase of the perilous process of escalation into mass destruction begun. So, for example, the systematic step-by-step stripping process of human rights and dignity – depriving those defined as Jews of their German citizenship and forbidding them to enter into marriage with Aryans – started in principle with the passage of the Nuremberg racial laws in 1935 (Law for the Protection of German Blood and Honor, September 15, 1935, RGBl I, 1146).

Other more severe measures followed in quick succession: loss of employment, confiscation of property, concerted efforts by party bureaucrats to organize and execute the pogroms of the 'Reichskristallnacht' under Goebbels's leadership in 1938 (to be succeeded by the compulsion to wear the Yellow Star of David in 1941, Decree of September 1, 1941, RGBl I, 547), and the deportation of Jews to ghettos, forced labor camps, concentration camps, or killing centers.

Unlike the euthanasia program, which had not become an overt public issue and did not receive the support of the masses, the 'Jewish question' was 'solved' publicly, even though the specific methods of mass destruction and the deportees' 'final' fate in general were not known to most members of the German society. However, there was a failure on the part of the populace to take appropriate steps (similar to those which had brought an end to the euthanasia program) to prevent persecution and deportation of the Jewish and Gypsy minorities. Without the passive consent of the people and the cooperation of the bureaucracy, which had become an integral part of the NS power structure primarily through regional incorporation and infiltration of party members, acts of mass destruction could not have been carried out. Finally, it should be noted that there was virtually no resistance on the part of persecuted individuals, no attempt to defend their civil rights and freedom. And there was a striking lack of esprit de corps among the victims of NS aggression, especially in extreme stress situations. Exceptions to the rule were the Jewish uprising in the Warsaw ghetto (April-May, 1943) and incidental group and individual resistance at Auschwitz, Blechhammer (Ehrenforst), and other concentration camps. In short, there was little appreciable resistance by potential victims among the German populace against bureaucratized Nazi oppression and persecution.

*Part III*

# The SS - An Example of a Totalitarian Bureaucratic Institution

*Nevertheless, the consuming hunger of the uncritical mind for what it imagines to be certainty or finality impels it to feast upon shadows.*

E. T. B.

## 1. Origin and early history of the SS

The forerunner of the 'Stabswache' was the strong-arm squad known as the 'Ordnertruppe,' created by Hitler during the second part of the year 1920. As its leader Hitler appointed Emil Maurice, a watchmaker by trade and an ex-convict.[1] The 'Schutzstaffel' organization was formally founded in March 1923. Under the name of 'Stabswache' it was created on the order of Hitler, who appointed the naval officer Lieutenant Johann Ulrich Klintzsch to be its first commander.[2] In contrast to the SA (Sturmabteilung; that is, Stormtroopers),[3] whose task continued to be primarily the intimidation of opponents of Hitler and his National Socialist ideology, the major purpose of the 'Stabswache' was to protect Hitler and surround him by a kind of Praetorian Guard. However, it is quite probable that by creating the 'Stoßtrupp' in 1923, Hitler did not intend to limit its function to the protection of his person. He also wanted to create an instrument of power with which to hold his rivals, censors, and opponents within the party in check.[4] Originally this small unit was made up of eight men, who, because of their ruthlessness and their known devotion to Hitler, had been specially selected from the SA.[5] The members of the 'Stabswache' did not outwardly distinguish themselves from the SA except for a small silver-colored death's-head badge on their brown caps.[6] In May 1923, Lieutenant Klintzsch withdrew from the 'Stabswache.' Hitler, instead of appointing a successor, founded a new unit under the command of Joseph Berchtold. Berchtold, a newspaperman, seems to have preferred desk work at the newsroom of the *Völkische Beobachter* to strong-arm activity. All former members of the 'Stabswache' were transferred to this new unit 'Stoßtrupp Hitler',[7] but continued to be a subgroup of the SA until 1934. To their former main duty was added the protection of other high-ranking members of the party. While the 'Stabswache' had comprised eight men, the 'Stoßtrupp Hitler' already consisted of approximately fifty men by the fall of 1923. The new formation considered itself superior to the SA. This feeling was further emphasized – as was already pointed out – by the gradual differentiation of appearance. Members of the Shock Troop were now dressed in field-grey army blouses with black ties and black ski caps; they wore on their left sleeve armlets bearing a swastika with a black stripe at the top and at the bottom. All these paraphernalia and trimmings of power were simultaneously to symbolize each member's willingness to sacrifice his life for Hitler and his cause and to reflect the distinction of those selected for special duties – in fact constituting a certain type of élite. The 'Stoßtrupp Hitler' participated in the 1923 march to the Feldherrnhalle under the leadership of Berchtold.[8] Five men among those who lost their lives belonged to this unit, that is, the 'Stoßtrupp Hitler.' After the failure of the Hitler-Putsch, the 'Stoßtrupp Hitler' suffered the same fate as the NSDAP and SA, namely that of dissolution.[9] In April 1924, Herman Göring,[10] who had been commander of the SA since March 1923, appointed Ernst Röhm as deputy commander of the clandestine SA and SS-Shock Troop formations. Since the Bavarian authorities did not show any readiness to lift the ban against the SA in the immediate future, Röhm decided to convert the SA in a manner which would avoid his group's falling into political oblivion. He thus created a paramilitary unit called 'Frontbann.' Röhm acted as commander of the 'Frontbann,' which was placed under the protectorship of General Ludendorff. The shift from political to military matters and the association with Ludendorff motivated a number of veterans of World War I to join this organization.[11] Internal and local power struggles ensued during Hitler's incarceration.[12] After his hastened release from prison, Hitler, on February 26, 1925, not only reestablished the NSDAP but also demanded that the SA be reinstalled as political sub-formation of the party. Röhm, however, who had successfully led the 'Frontbann' during Hitler's absence, demanded that in the future the SA exist as a paramilitary force relatively independent of the party. The controversy between Hitler and Röhm arising out of these differences in policy reached a climax in May 1925. The result was Röhm's resignation as 'Frontbann' commander.[13] Röhm's intention had been to create a militia in which

> ... Parteipolitik nicht geduldet, politische Führer kein Weisungsrecht besitzen und die Organisation selbst verpflichtet sein sollte, den Anforderungen des Staates und der Reichswehr zu entsprechen, wenn es der Schutz des Vaterlandes verlangen sollte.[14]

> ———

> ... party politics are not to be tolerated, political leaders have no right to direct, and the organization itself would be

obligated to meet the demands of the state and of the Reichswehr when the protection of the Fatherland should require it.[14]

At the time of Röhm's resignation the number of men in the 'Frontbann' had reached approximately 30,000.[15] The SA units established
during the following period consequently became troops of loyal party
organizations. However, they lacked guidance and control from the
party center which at that time was located in Munich. It can be assumed that, because of increasing conflicts and dissenting views among
the SA leaders and their men, Hitler surrounded himself with and began to rely even more heavily on the 'Stoßtrupp' for his personal protection and power instrument. In this connection a significant correlation appears to be reflected in the festive act (the first 'Parteitag' in
Weimar, in July 1925) in which Hitler handed over the only swastika
flag – the 'Blutfahne,' rescued during the abortive march to the Feldherrnhalle – to the newly created 'Schutzstaffel.'[16] Already in April
1925, Hitler had ordered the establishment of this unit out of the 'Stoßtrupp Hitler.'[17] The new unit made its first public appearance during a
festivity at the Bismarck tower near Starnberg/Bavaria on April 5,
1925.[18] Hitler commissioned his driver Julius Schreck with the leadership of the 'Schutzstaffel' (SS).[19]

The SS was organized in Munich in spring, 1925, and at first consisted of a handful of men, including Schreck, Erhard Heiden, and
Emil Maurice, who had been members of the former 'Stabswache.'[20]
Within a year their number – according to Koch – increased to
seventy-five 'Staffeln.'[21] Of this group about seventy-five per cent were
veterans whose courage and readiness to fight had been tested during
World War I in combat at all fronts.[22] Generally, the ranks of the SS
in 1925 were filled by an appeal to SA men of old standing, and by
recruiting new members during propaganda rallies organized by the SS,
as well as by a public appeal in the *Völkischer Beobachter* which read:

> Nur wer in dem großen Kampf, den unsere Bewegung durch-
> fechten muß, in vorderster Linie sein will, trete in die Schutz-
> staffel ein.[23]

> Only he who wishes to serve in the front lines of the struggle
> which our movement must fight, join the SS.[23]

The manner in which the appeal to potential candidates for SS membership was formulated is of utmost significance. It reflected a specific attitude not only of those who recruited but also of those who responded to these requirements and ideals. Indeed, it predetermined the future form and goal orientation of the SS as an organizational entity and institution of the Third Reich. Hitler not only desired his SS to be bodyguards of fanatical conviction and dedication but demanded of them – if necessary – even to '... march against their own brothers.'[24] In addition to serving Hitler as his personal bodyguard, the new unit was given the task of protecting the party, its leading members as well as the party meetings.

Schreck, in his 'Rundschreiben' No. 1 of September 21, 1925, stressed that the 'Schutzstaffeln' were to be a formation distinct and separate from the SA.[25] By December 1925, the number of the SS had risen to approximately one hundred men[26] whose uniforms by this time were clearly distinguishable from those of the SA. Basically, the uniform of the 'Stoßtrupp Hitler' had been retained; only brown shirts were added. On April 14, 1926, Joseph Berchtold, after his return from Austria, replaced Schreck as commander of the 'Schutzstaffel.'

By *that* time Hitler realized that he could not win his political power struggle without relying on a mass formation. In spring, 1926, local SA units had already been re-established. With the support of a later member of the SS, Kurt Daluege, the first local formation of the SA had been re-established in Berlin-North in March, as were other SA units in the months to follow. On November 1, 1926, the highest SA leadership was established in Munich, and the existing local SA units were put under the command of Gauleiter and SA leader of the Ruhr, Franz von Pfeffer. In the same month the SS and the Hitler Youth were subordinated to SA leadership.[27] In spite of the fact that Berchtold was promoted to 'Reichsführer,' he still remained subordinate to von Pfeffer. The commander of the SA had also retained the right to decide when and where 'Schutzstaffeln' might be established. Since it was feared that in towns with small SA units the leaders might join the SS and thereby retard the growth of strong SA formations, 'Schutzstaffeln' generally were permitted only in those places where numerically strong SA units already existed. During the following years more effort was made to support the growth of a mass movement rather than to insist on attitudinal requirements as specified for the members in the SS. This helped to keep the SS in a marginal position. The lower hierarchical status of the SS was reflected in the chain of command. Whenever SA and SS formations joined in a common task, an SA leader outranked an even higher ranking member of the SS.[28] Perhaps this also explains why the members of the SS of that period played relatively subordinate roles as orderlies, distributors of printed propaganda material, news-vendors of party newspapers, and informers on opponents of the party. They were also given the task of finding new sources of financial support for the SS. Already in September 1926, Berchtold gave permission to members of the SS to tap the financial resources of potential sympathizers and opportunists. From that time on, anyone (with the exception of non-Aryans) could become a 'förderndes Mitglied' (contributing member) of the SS by making regular donations.[29]

In March 1927, Berchtold was released from his duties as commander and succeeded by his former deputy, Erhard Heiden. Heiden remained in this post until Heinrich Himmler, who in turn was his former deputy, was appointed 'Reichsführer-SS' on January 6, 1929. In this connection it should be stressed that although Heinrich Himmler is most frequently credited with having infused the SS with specific qualities which gave the organization its notorious reputation, many of these traits can already be detected in the 'Stabswache,' the 'Stoßtrupp Hitler,' and the 'Schutzstaffel' prior to his appointment. Although these characteristics can be traced to the similar background, value-norms, motivation, and attitude of those who joined the organization between 1923 and 1929, they should be primarily ascribed to Hitler's dominant influence.[30] Most members of the SS had been uprooted and traumatized by the events and outcome of World War I and had frequently joined the Armed Forces before having completed their secondary or basic education; or they had been prevented from finishing a training for a skill or trade.[31] The war had taught them that brute force often removes obstacles that seem otherwise impossible to eliminate. After the return from the front they were neither able to adjust to bourgeois life nor at ease in a society in which democratic political institutions and principles forced upon them by the Allies replaced those based on a belief system to which they had been exposed and had grown accustomed during their early formative age. This change of institutions did not occur because of an altered attitude or a new outlook, but rather as a result of a lost war. Consequently, they rejected the Weimar Republic and hoped to create in its place a socio-political order founded on a belief system which would more adequately satisfy their needs. Only through a radical change could they hope to advance swiftly into a higher socio-economic status. Social and political disorientation was not the only result of the war; the religio-ethical system previously adhered to had also been severely damaged. Instead of reconstructing a new personal ethical and social system they embraced an order almost religiously,[32] a 'Weltanschauung' which suited their concepts and value-norms and in addition promised material reward and security for the future. Unable to gain meaningful insight into causal factors and interrelations to objectify their problems and to resolve their conflicts, they instead adopted simple, popularized phrases and slogans which they could grasp and which had been coined especially by the National Socialist intellectual subculture for their consumption.

In an order issued on September 13, 1927, by the 'Oberleitung' of the 'Schutzstaffel,' SS men were forbidden to participate in political discussions. This order further stated that '. . . the SS man and SS leader keeps silent and never meddles in matters . . . which are none of his concern.'[33] Members of the SS who might have been inclined to act against this order were threatened with expulsion.[34] This order, generally obeyed throughout the history of the SS, conveyed to them the impression that they possessed something resembling a simple, absolute truth. Isolated from the interchange of ideas, incapable of carrying on dialogues, they developed in their need to compensate for their insecurity a 'Herrenbewußtsein' as individuals and an 'Elitebewußtsein' as a group.[35] There appears to be little doubt that Hitler himself was such a product. Since he was more eloquent and, apart from his non-normative drives (or because of them), possessed unchallenged leadership qualities as well as extraordinary charismatic appeal, he was accepted as their prophet.[36] Hitler realized that his SS men were not mere followers, but unconditional believers as well.[37] The creed of the SS demanded complete surrender of person and personality. They were ready to dedicate their lives to their charismatic 'Führer' and his gospel. They also accepted that an 'if' and a 'but' do not exist, but only a party discipline.[38] Hitler was also convinced that they would, if necessary, march against their own brothers, and the SS on various occasions confirmed his belief. Already on March 31, 1926, the SS had stood their men in Munich's Hackerkeller[39] against German Communists and Social Democrats. On January 28, 1928, they ruthlessly beat down opposition within the NSDAP in Nuremberg. Again, during the night from March 31 to April 1, 1931, under the command of Kurt Daluege, they suppressed the Stennes-Putsch in Berlin.[40] Afterwards, as reward for their faithful service, Hitler bestowed on the SS the motto: 'SS man, your honor is your loyalty.'[41] 'My honor is my loyalty' (Meine Ehre heißt Treue) was later engraved on the belt buckle and dagger worn by the SS men as part of their uniform. However, the greatest opportunity for the SS to prove unconditional obedience was the Röhm-Putsch. On January 6, 1929, through Hitler's order, the twenty-nine-year-old Heinrich Himmler was appointed 'Reichsführer'[42] of the 'Schutzstaffel' which at that time consisted of 280 men.[43] The appointment of this somewhat inconspicuous figure among the leaders of the National Socialist party came as a surprise. Why had Hitler appointed this medium-sized, rather unappealing Bavarian as the commander of the SS? It is conceivable that Hitler was aware of Himmler's loyalty to him as head of the party and knew him as a devoted and obedient disciple.[44] Especially in regard to racial theories and policies their views seem to have agreed.[45] Charles Wighton, a biographer of Reinhard Heydrich, expressed the view that Hitler had appointed Himmler as 'Reichsführer-SS' in order to keep better control over the rather rebellious leadership of the SA.[46] However, it is safer to assume that there were a number of relevant reasons for the appointment of Himmler.

## 2. *Himmler's rise to power*

It was a favorite practice of Hitler to create and strengthen rival offices and organizations so that they might neutralize one another and keep each other in check.[47] Thus, after Hitler had appointed Himmler as 'Reichsführer-SS,' he installed Kurt Daluege, formerly an engineer with the city of Berlin, as leader of the 'Schutzstaffel' in the capital of Germany. By the time Himmler moved his headquarters from Munich to Berlin (some time after January 30, 1933), Daluege had built up for himself a power position which virtually made him independent of

Himmler. Furthermore, in spite of Himmler's and later Heydrich's continued intrigues, he succeeded in retaining and even improving his position. He became chief of the 'Hauptamt' of the 'Ordnungspolizei.' As 'Reichsprotektor' of Böhmen and Mähren he became the successor of his assassinated colleague Heydrich, and as 'Generaloberst' of the 'Ordnungspolizei,' one of the four 'Oberst-Gruppenführer' of the SS. [48]

Himmler was born on October 10, 1900, in Munich, a son of the secondary school teacher (Gymnasialprofessor) Gebhard Himmler, Heinrich was the second oldest of three brothers. Ernst Himmler was born on December 23, 1905, and Gebhard, Heinrich's elder brother, was born on July 29, 1898. There is no indication that Heinrich Himmler's primary environment was not a harmonious, well-regulated, and socio-economically secure one. In 1917 he became a soldier in the eleventh Bavarian Infantry Regiment, [49] and by the end of the war he had attained the rank of officer-cadet (Fahnenjunker). The breakdown of discipline and the discrediting of military virtues after the dissolution of the imperial army appears to have impressed him most unfavorably. [50]

Having passed the 'Abitur' in 1910, Himmler studied agriculture and specialized in poultry science, which he chose as his future career. In the course of his studies at the Technical Agricultural College in Munich, he was especially interested in and fascinated by the results obtained from breeding various plants and animals. [51] While attending the college Himmler also joined a student fraternity (schlagende Verbindung) and during this time came increasingly into conflict with the teachings of the Catholic Church. After his graduation as agriculturist (Diplomlandwirt) in 1922, he accepted a position as a fertilizer salesman with the Stickstoff GmbH in Schleißheim. This activity was of short duration because of the economic crisis in Germany. Like many other veterans he joined those political organizations which not only absolved the former soldiers of the guilt of military defeat but also clamored for Germany's rise from defeat to a new and more grandiose future. Himmler joined the 'Reichskriegsflagge,' a veterans' organization which participated in the 'Bierhallen-Putsch' of November 8 and 9, 1923, in Munich. [52] Himmler's role in the Putsch was that of a standard-bearer of the 'Reichskriegsflagge.' After the Putsch Himmler seems to have been unemployed and restless. He moved with his family to Munich but could not find a position there either.

His alleged membership in various mystical organizations also falls into this particular period.[53] This is important because his inclinations introduced an entirely new emotional romanticism which was to have a decisive influence on the future organization and orientation of the SS. From 1921 to 1924 Himmler acted as Gregor Strasser's unpaid aid in Landshut. Despite the divergence of their personalities, Gregor Strasser confided without reservation in Himmler who in 1925 became deputy 'Gauleiter' of the Lower Bavarian NSDAP.[54] In August 1925, after Hitler had re-established the party when he was released from Landsberg prison, Himmler joined the NSDAP and received the party No. 14303. A year later Himmler became deputy 'Reichspropaganda' leader under Strasser and as of 1928 directly under Hitler. Also in 1926 Himmler became leader of a group of SS-men in Lower Bavaria; already in the following year he was appointed deputy to the 'Reichsführer-SS' Erhard Heiden.

It can be assumed that Himmler was aware of his personal limitations that would keep him from becoming the decisive leader or director of the party.[55] He possessed neither the persuasiveness and personality of a Hitler nor the intellect of a Goebbels. Himmler knew that in many respects he was mediocre, and, except perhaps for the final period of World War II, he never aspired to the highest office in Germany. He acknowledged Hitler as head of the party and, later, of the state. Yet in spite of his personal limitations, Himmler did aspire to an important post and hoped to attain it by creating an organization which would serve him as a basis for power. Perceiving Himmler's scheme, which eventually made the 'Reichsführer-SS' one of the most powerful men in the state, Hitler said that '... with intelligence and obstinacy, against wind and tide, he forged his instrument.'[56] To this goal of developing the SS into the most powerful organization within the party and state Himmler devoted his energies, his entire life. Immediately after his appointment on January 6, 1929, as 'Reichsführer-SS,' Himmler attempted to increase the size of the SS, at that time a group of only 280 men, while at the same time enforcing what he considered to be standards of quality and excellence. On April 12, 1929, Himmler, with the approval of Hitler and von Pfeffer, issued specific regulations concerning qualifications for membership in the SS. Had they been rigorously applied, many a faithful member would have been ousted. In order to retain them it was ruled that those who had fought in

World War I be exempted from these qualifications.[57] The same order stipulated that the SS should draw its new members from the SA. Those who had become increasingly dissatisfied with the development of the SA into a mass formation requested transfer to the SS. Others left the SA because the atmosphere within it was no longer revolutionary but had increasingly become bourgeois. From the spring of 1929 on, the SS developed more and more into a rival organization of the SA and by the end of this year had increased to approximately 1 000 men.[58]

During 1929 Himmler began his efforts to break all administrative links between SS and SA, and on December 1, 1930, a circular letter announced that a separation of the two organizations at the lower levels had been completed.[59] As for financial matters, the SS strove to remain as independent and self-sustaining as possible. Hitler had never revoked the privilege of the SS to secure funds from sustaining members, and Himmler never tired of tapping this and other sources[60] for the support and development of the SS.

On August 29, 1930, Franz von Pfeffer, simultaneously the commander of the SA and the commander in chief of the SS, resigned. Subsequently, Hitler took personal charge of the command over SA and SS and, from this date on, the rivalry between SA and SS appears to have increased noticeably. Both organizations raided one another for recruits, and each organization assumed that it was superior to the other. Command rivalries between the leaders of the two organizations tended to aggravate the conflicts. To avert serious difficulties or even open hostilities, Hitler, in early December 1930, issued appropriate orders. In these he stated that '. . . no SA leader has the right to give orders to the SS' and that 'no SS leader has the right to give orders to the SA.'[61] He prohibited all attempts to lure recruits from the rival organization but did permit transfer based on individual preference and decision. The fact that the SS received the right to act as the police force within the party was regarded by Himmler as a major step forward in moving the SS into a high strategic position. However, Hitler did not exercise supreme command over the SA and the SS very long. Already on September 2, 1931, Röhm resumed his duties with the SA, bearing the title of 'Chef des Stabes.'[62] Having sworn loyal obedience to Hitler, Himmler a few days later accepted Hitler's decision which also placed the SS under the command of Röhm. Once again the SS was reduced to an appendage of the SA. This, however, did not prevent

Himmler and Röhm from living in a state of open warfare with each other.[63] Himmler, viewing Röhm as the born revolutionary,[64] continued to build up his SS in order to gain more recognition and power. By June 14, 1932, the SS numbered approximately 41,000 and prior to Hitler's seizure of power had already reached about 52,000 men.[65]

In conclusion perhaps the following can be deduced about the young Himmler from original sources obtained from the 'Diaries of Heinrich Himmler's Early Years' (Angress and Smith):

Heinrich Himmler seems to have been on good terms with his parents and relatives and appears to have been quite attached to them. He appreciated his home atmosphere and his interrelations seem to have been cordial.[66] His interests, social activities, and preoccupations were largely determined by his middle-class background. He enjoyed fancy-dress parties and noted in detail his culinary delights. So, for example, on January 10, 1920: 'Drank coffee and ate marvelous cake.' On January 25, 1920: 'Ate sandwiches and goodies (Gutterle)'.[67] 'Took the streetcar to Thilde and her husband. I always like to be with dear folks. Throughout my visit I had to eat: dumpling soup, filet of veal, potato salad and noodles with beer, and then apple pie; then coffee and cake. . . . Thilde, that dear woman, accompanied me to the Harras. She gave me more cake, goodies, and an apple' (November 1, 1921).[68] In his teens and twenties Himmler was far more involved in mundane social activities than in political activities. Rather than creating the impression of a *homo politicus* Himmler was an inconspicuous, naive moralizer, a collector of trivia, and disseminator of platitudes. His views were dogmatic and conventional, his imagination barren, and his lack of humor striking.[69] Moreover, he was principled, abstinent, prudish, pedantic, and rather self-righteous.[70] 'The student Heinrich Himmler commented on men and events without extremism or passion. His observations, whether they refer to people, sex, religion, or politics, are usually naive, dogmatic, and commonplace, but devoid of fanatical overtones; nor are there traces of his later mysticism. . . . Style, grammar, and spelling are poor, and particularly conspicuous are Himmler's pedantry and his inability to distinguish between the important and the unimportant. Endless trivialities are carefully recorded, but only rarely is an idea clearly developed or a significant event treated with more than an oblique reference.'[71] In his interactions young Himmler reflected a distinct class consciousness and admiration for individuals in elevated social positions, specifically the aristocracy (Hochadel) and, last but not least, his superiors. He felt flattered when he was permitted to associate with them (Himmler's godfather was Prince Heinrich of Wittelsbach). [72] Himmler seems to have impressed his associates by his mildness of manner, his compassion and readiness to extend a helping hand, his kindness, faithfulness, and consideration for others. [73] During his childhood and as a student the to-be 'Reichsführer SS' appears to have been a devout Catholic. On December 15, 1919, Himmler records the following: 'I believe that I have come into conflict with my religion. Come what may, I shall always love God, shall pray to Him, and shall remain faithful to the Catholic Church and shall defend it even if I should be expelled from it.' [74] His doubts and conflicts concerning his faith seem to have reached a climax in 1924 and apparently prompted him to stop attending church altogether. [75]

Himmler seems to have identified with the spirit prevalent in German student fraternities (Schlagende Verbindungen) and on November 19, 1919, joined the 'Burschenschaft Apollo' in Munich. [76] Early in November 1921, Himmler became actively involved in ASTA (Allgemeiner Studentenausschuß) when he volunteered to accept minor duties in the local representative student association. However, his fraternity continued to hold his principal attention. [77] On January 17, 1920, Himmler appears to have played an active role, both as a nationalistic student and a military reservist, 'in a plot to liberate Count Arco-Valley, the assassin of Kurt Eisner,' by means of an abortive military coup. [78] Another of his few more specific political comments was occasioned by the assassination of Germany's first and only Jewish Foreign Minister, Walther Rathenau, on June 24, 1922. 'Rathenau has been shot. I am glad. . . . We would have never gotten rid of him by any other means. I am convinced that whatever he did, he did not do (it) for Germany.' [79]

There is virtually no indication that Himmler was at this time a violent anti-Semite. If he was, he seems to have kept his prejudice relatively well in check and appears to have been quite capable of drawing distinctions in individual cases. [80] So, for example, he limited himself to label a Jewish fellow-student of opposed political persuasion a 'Jewboy' and 'Jewish lout' (Judenlauser) (July 3, 1922). [81] On another occasion, but in the same entry, young Himmler concluded that a Jewish dancer whom he had met in one of the night clubs was 'a girl who deserves respect, the conceited bourgeois opinion notwithstanding.'[82]

Himmler frequently expressed the desire to prove himself in manly pursuits and engaged in military daydreaming, possibly to compensate for his feelings of inadequacy and to overcome his existential anxieties. Already during this period he must have been aware of his weak constitution and the discomforts due to his nervous stomach condition, that is to say, his nervous system in general. On November 4, 1919, he notes:

> I believe that we are facing grave times. . . .
>
> Perhaps I shall take part in fighting and war within a few years, and am looking forward to this war of liberation; I shall take part if I can still move a limb. . . .
>
> If I only could face danger now, could risk my life, could fight, it would be a relief to me. . . .
>
> If there is another campaign in the East I'll go along. The East is most important for us. The West will die easily. In the East we must fight and colonize. . . .
>
> Perhaps I'll join up in one way or another. For basically I am a soldier. But first I am going to take my exams.[83]

As time went by, Himmler's longing for military glory apparently did not leave him, and he continued to express his ambition to participate in Germany's future military pursuits.[84]

Himmler's self-concept and low self-esteem is perhaps best expressed by the following: 'I am too warmhearted and always talk too much' (November 4, 1921). . . . 'I still lack the gentlemanly sureness of manners. . . . When shall I stop talking too much?' (November 18, 1921). . . . 'I am a phrasemonger and chatterbox (Sprüchemacher und Schwätzer), and without energy; . . . they think me as a gay fellow who is amusing and takes care of everything, "Heini will see to it" (der Heini macht es schon).'[85] Nevertheless, he considered himself to be 'thick-blooded' and 'stern.'[86]

To alleviate the burden of his low self-esteem Himmler apparently enjoyed engaging in the spreading of rumors and gossip, especially by providing unsolicited character evaluations of individuals with whom he had come into proximate or only superficial contact.[87]

On January 26, 1922, Himmler mentions that he attended a meeting with Hauptmann (Captain) Röhm and Major Angerer at the Auerberger Keller, a Munich tavern, but he did not join the NSDAP until August 1923.[88] At that time Himmler thought rather highly of Röhm, which did not prevent him from organizing Röhm's liquidation and that of his close collaborators during the blood purge of June 30, 1934.

None of the entries in his diaries seem to convey that the 'diarist was inherently cruel or inhumane.'[89] Himmler created the impression of a gullible Bavarian 'Kleinbürger' and 'elementary believer' who was hardly the man to question seriously any popular leader.[90] Himmler did not strike his contemporaries as a leader, but rather impressed them as a 'Gefolgsmann' (follower).

3. *The emergence of the SS as an independent system of power and the role of its sub-systems*

Early in 1933 SS members began their duty with the SA as political police ('Hilfspolizei') in the political prison Columbia Haus in Berlin and in the first concentration camps, especially KL Dachau. So-called 'Sonderkommandos' (special detachments) were also formed, which constituted the nucleus from which the later armed SS force ('Verfügungs-Truppe,' VT) developed. On June 17, 1933, Hitler re-established his third 'Stabswache' of 120 men under the command of Josef (Sepp) Dietrich. During the occasion of the 'Parteitag' of the NSDAP this unit received the designation 'Leibstandarte Adolf Hitler,' and members pledged their allegiance to Hitler personally on November 9, 1933.[91] It can be assumed that Himmler welcomed the opportunity to free the SS of Röhm's dominant position during the blood purge in 1934. In his speech to Gestapo ('Geheime Staatspolizei') officials on October 11, 1934, Himmler attempted to justify the bloody extermination of the SA leaders. He claimed that the executed officials had conspired against Hitler and had wanted to start a new revolution which would have permitted a foreign power to march into Germany.[92] Thus Himmler's statement that June 30 (1934, 'the Röhm purge') ought not to be viewed as a day of victory or triumph sounds unconvincing.[93] For Himmler and the SS the purge had singular consequences. Upon Hitler's order of July 20, 1934, the SS was declared an independent organization within the structure of the NSDAP. On that occasion Hitler appointed Himmler and the newly promoted SA Stabschef Victor Lutze to 'Reichsleiter of the NSDAP.'[94] Hitler also awarded those active participants of the SS who had played an important role during the Röhm purge by promoting them to higher ranks; for example, the commander of the 'Leibstandarte' Sepp Dietrich was promoted from 'SS-Gruppenführer' to 'SS-Obergruppenführer' and the city aldermen of Munich, Christian Weber and Emil Maurice, were promoted to 'SS-Oberführer' and 'SS-Standartenführer.'[95]

Soon after Himmler had been appointed 'Reichsführer SS,' he began to transform the 'Schutzstaffel' into an 'élite.' Since under the given circumstances the SS could hardly have been developed along educational or social standards of excellence, the apparently most readily available basis for selection, which simultaneously could serve as a uniting bond, was to establish a physical selection process, founded on the spurious doctrine of racial purity. As well as making the 'Schutzstaffel' attractive to ambitious, 'racially qualified' individuals, this selection criterion also promised continued membership in the new élite to the upper bourgeoisie, and especially to the nobility. In other words, the new élite became attractive to all those whose status, prestige, and esteem had become insecure through socio-political changes and upheavals. This is reflected in the statistical figures compiled by SS statisticians in 1938 that give an occupational breakdown of those who had joined the 'Schutzstaffel' up to that time. The occupational background of those individuals flooding into all parts of the 'Schutzstaffel,' predominantly into the 'Allgemeine SS,' represents a widespread distribution of occupations but clearly does not constitute a balanced proportion of occupations prevalent in the German society of that time. The two largest groups represented in the 'Schutzstaffel,' together comprising 37 per cent of it, are denoted as 'Sonstige' (others) and 'Handel' (trade and business). The former, which constitutes 19 per cent of the SS and 17 per cent of the total populace of the Reich, is not made up of either academic or business professionals, or of skilled workers, but rather of individuals without any specific training. The latter, which constitutes 18 per cent of the SS and 9 per cent of the Reich, is made up of those in trade or business. Next are metal workers (Metall), representing 12 per cent of the SS and 11 per cent of the Reich. The fourth group, comprising clerical and public employees (Beamte u. Behördenangestellte), represents 10 per cent of the SS and 5 per cent of the Reich. The group of agricultural workers (Landwirtschaft) has a share of 10 per cent of the SS but 22 per cent of the Reich total. Next are skilled and unskilled laborers (ungelernte u. angelernte Arbeiter) with 8 per cent of the SS and a Reich total of 3 per cent; construction workers (Bau) comprise 5 per cent of the SS and 6 per cent of the Reich; those in food and consumers business (Nahrung u. Genuß), 4 per cent and 3 per cent respectively; traffic employees (Verkehr) 3 per cent and 4 per cent; woodworkers (Holz), also 3 per cent and 4 per cent; health and hygiene (Gesundheitspflege u. Hygiene), 3 per cent and 2 per cent; textile and clothing (Textil u. Bekleidung), 2 per cent and 4 per cent; free professions (Freie Berufe), 1 per cent and 6 per cent; paper and printing industry (Papier u. Druck), 1 per cent each; mining, stone, and soil workers (Bergbau-Stein u. Erde), 1 per cent and 3 per cent.[96] The preceding figures show that the socio-economically insecure groups, especially those who were apt to be unemployed due to the economic depression, were the ones to be primarily attracted by the 'Schutzstaffel.' Those least attracted were the free professions (intelligentsia) and such groups as the mining, stone, and soil workers, and to some extent the wood workers who were apparently able to secure employment because of their relative independence from political and economic changes. The members of these latter groups apparently did not suffer from existential and status anxiety to quite the same extent that members of the other groups did.

Immediately after the National Socialists' seizure of power many desired to join their ranks. Apart from the 'Allgemeine SS,' which formed the nucleus of the 'Schutzstaffel,' there developed the 'SS-Verfügungstruppen' (March 16, 1935), the later 'Waffen-SS' (Combat SS), and the 'SS-Totenkopfverbände' (Death's Head Units).[97] Besides the essential full-time staff for running such an organization, the 'Allgemeine SS' personnel were exclusively people who in addition to the service in the SS followed their own occupational activities.[98]

The 'SS-Verfügungstruppe' (SS-VT) was defined as an active division of the 'Schutzstaffel'; it was housed in barracks and equipped with light and heavy infantry weapons. The SS men, selected according to rigid criteria, committed themselves to a service time of at least four years. In addition to the SS ideological instruction, they also received full military training. Service in the 'SS-VT' was recognized as fulfillment of compulsory military duty. After the expiration of the committment time the members of the 'SS-VT' were transferred to the 'Allgemeine SS,' from which they had come – directly or indirectly.[99]

From the standpoint of structure, equipment, and training, the 'SS-Totenkopfverbände' essentially resembled the 'SS-Verfügungstruppe.' They, too, were housed in barracks and equipped with light and heavy infantry weapons. However, the foremost task assigned to them was the guarding of concentration camps. During the war they also served as combat and destruction units. In contrast to the 'SS-Verfügungstruppe,' the time served in the 'SS-Totenkopfverbände' was not always recognized as fulfillment of compulsory military duty, and it was expected that its members would commit themselves to a service time of twelve years. In regard to transfer to the 'Allgemeine SS' after the expiration of service time, the same rule applied as for the members of the 'SS-Verfügungstruppe.'[100]

As Himmler frequently stressed in his speeches, the interdependence of the three major units of the SS was intended and enforced. However, there was a marked difference in the target-orientation, especially between the 'Allgemeine SS' and the SS-VT on the one hand and the SS-TV on the other. In the SS-VT, the later 'Waffen-SS,' the tendency prevailed to suppress non-military considerations – i.e., to refrain from purely politically determined activities such as mass extermination of so-called inferior minorities – or, if they received any attention, it was because Himmler had given explicit orders to that effect. In the other two units political and ideological orientation played a foremost role.[101] The SS-VT and subsequent 'Waffen-SS' was headed by professional military men, usually adherents of the Prussian military tradition, as, for example, the later Generaloberst and Oberst-Gruppenführer of the 'Waffen-SS' Paul Hausser; the Obergruppenführer and Generals of the 'Waffen-SS' Felix Steiner, Wilhelm Bitterich, Herbert Gille, and Georg Keppler; the officers Lettow, Baron von Montigny, Freiherr von Scheele, Dörffler-Schuband, Dr. Voss, von Bülow, and others, who were not necessarily predestined to think only in terms of destructive, political, or ideological categories but placed greater emphasis on traditional military 'discipline, order, subordination, loyalty, and moral principles' per se.[102] However, most of these senior officers who joined the VT, or the later 'Waffen-SS,' in one way or another had come into conflict with the leadership or policies of the German Armed Forces. Many of them had lost their positions after World War I and because of political or other reasons decided to join the new élite units in the hope of furthering their careers.

After the completion of the so-called National Socialist revolution, in which the SS played an important role, Hitler assigned new tasks to the SS. On April 2, 1933, the 'Reichsführer SS' was installed as new political police commander of Bavaria.[103] In the following months he was appointed as head of all other corresponding offices of the German 'Länder.' On April 20, 1934, Himmler became deputy chief of the Prussian Ministerpräsident Hermann Göring, who also held the office of the 'Chef der Geheimen Staatspolizei' (Gestapo).[104] This institution was created and declared legal on April 26, 1933, by the Prussian Staatsministerium, ratified by the ministers Göring and Popitz, and became known as the 'Gesetz über die Errichtung eines Geheimen Staatspolizeiamts.'[105] The Gestapo not only provided the 'legal' framework for persecutory measures against real and spurious opponents of the Nazi regime but in fact also constituted the basis for the establishment of concentration camps (which during World War II escalated into destruction camps), since additional space had to be provided for all those against whom actions were being taken. This new development is described by Best in the following terms:

> Zum Aufbau einer selbständigen und schlagkräftigen politischen Polizei, die es bis dahin in Deutschland nicht gegeben hatte, wurden einerseits Fachbeamte der bisherigen Polizei und andererseits Angehörige der SS herangezogen. Die neuen Einrichtungen nahmen mit dem kompromißlosen Kampfgeist der SS die Bekämpfung der Volks- und Staatsfeinde zur Sicherung der nationalsozialistischen Führung und Ordnung auf. Die Angehörigen der 'Politischen Polizei' – zunächst noch: der 'Politischen Polizeien', der einzelnen deutschen Länder – wurden in zunehmendem Maße in die SS aufgenommen, so daß in ihnen sich zum ersten Male die gegenseitige Durchdringung von SS und Polizei vollzog. Etwa zur gleichen Zeit wurde die 'Waffen-SS' auf Befehl des Führers geschaffen, zunächst die 'SS-Leibstandarte Adolf Hitler'.[106]

In constructing an independent and swiftly striking political police, which Germany heretofore had not had, specialists from the existing police and members of the SS were called upon. With the uncompromising combative spirit of the SS, the new institutions took up the struggle against the enemies of the people and the state in the interests of the security of the National Socialist leadership and order. The members of the 'Political Police' — initially still the 'Political Police Forces' of the individual German states — were to an increasing extent incorporated in the SS, so that they offered the first perfect example of the mutual penetration of SS and police. At about the same time the 'Waffen-SS' — initially the 'SS-Leibstandarte Adolf Hitler' — was created at the command of the Führer. [106]

As the SS main offices, offices, and units (SS-Hauptämter, Ämter und Einheiten) began to emerge out of the 'Allgemeine SS,' the significance of this basic SS organization and executive body began to decline proportionally. The SS and Police were directed centrally by the main offices, whose chiefs were directly responsible to Himmler, and regionally through Higher SS and Police Leaders (Höhere SS und Polizeiführer), who were also directly responsible to Himmler. The central organization gradually developed into thirteen main offices. [107]

Since the tasks and objectives of the various and frequently heterogeneous groups incorporated in the SS were at times overlapping, power conflicts ensued even during the early stages of their existence. Himmler attempted to resolve these conflicts by rendering moral support to those departments and units which were targets of attacks and whose status and prestige were at the given time at a low point. The departments and units most frequently receiving Himmler's laudatory recognition were not those earning their laurels in combat in the front lines on the battlefields of World War II, but rather those guarding concentration camps, or members of the SD (Sicherheitsdienst, that is to say, the security service) or of the destruction units. Himmler, therefore, never tired of forging links between those groups and subgroups which lived in covert or overt conflict with each other; he saw his foremost task as shaping the SS into a monolithic organization. This he expressed clearly in his address to the officers corps of the 'Leibstandarte' on September 7, 1940:

Die Totenkopfdivision sagte: 'Ja, wir sind natürlich in der Beziehung besser, aber diese Regimenter da zu Hause, – ach Gott wie furchtbar – was haben die für alte Leute u.s.w..' ... daß nun einer den anderen über die Achsel ansah. Und nun war mir etwas klar: Wir mußten dazu kommen, diesen Gesamtkörper zusammenzuschweißen. Da habe ich dann eines Tages den Ausdruck 'Waffen-SS' genommen und habe ihn eingeführt....

Es ist bedeutend leichter in vielen Fällen, mit einer Kompanie ins Gefecht zu gehen, wie mit einer Kompanie in irgend einem Gebiet eine widersätzliche Bevölkerung kulturell tiefstehender Art niederzuhalten, Exekutionen zu machen, Leute herauszutransportieren, heulende und weinende Frauen wegzubringen ... Wir müssen beginnen, auch in der Gesamt-Waffen-SS, daß wir die übrige große Tätigkeit der Gesamt-SS und -Polizei erblicken und sehen, daß sie die Tätigkeit, die der Mann im grünen Rock tut, genau so als wertvoll ansehen, wie die Tätigkeit, die Sie tun. Daß Sie die Tätigkeit, die der Mann des SD oder der Sicherheitspolizei tut, genauso als lebensnotwendiges Stück unserer Gesamttätigkeit ansehen wie das, daß Sie mit der Waffe marschieren können. Sie sind die Beneidenswerten, denn wenn Sie etwas tun, wenn eine Truppe sich einen Ruhm erwirbt, dann kann von Ruhm gesprochen werden und dann kann sie ausgezeichnet werden dafür. Viel schwerer ist an vielen Stellen, – und ich will damit Ihre Taten wirklich nicht herunter tun, ..., aber viel schwerer ist, das glauben Sie mir, an vielen Stellen dieses stille Tun-müssen, die stille Tätigkeit, dieses Postenstehen vor der Weltanschauung, dieses Konsequent-sein-müssen, Kompromißlos-sein-müssen, das ist an manchen Stellen viel, viel schwerer. ... leben wird diese Waffen-SS nur dann, wenn die Gesamt-SS lebt. Wenn das gesamte Korps wirklich ein Orden ist, ... und sich darüber klar ist, daß ein Teil ohne den anderen nicht denkbar ist.[108]

---

The Totenkopf Division (Death's Head Division) said: 'Yes, we are, of course, better in this respect, but these regiments at home – God, how terrible – all the old men they have around – etc.' ... the result of which is that the one would look scornfully at the other. One thing became clear to me; we had to weld everybody together into one body. Then one day I decided to use the term 'Waffen-SS' and introduced it.

In many cases it is considerably easier to go into combat with a squadron than to serve in some area, holding down a recalcitrant, culturally inferior population, carrying out executions, selecting people for deportation, and taking away screaming and hysterical women . . . We have to begin in the whole 'Waffen-SS' to appreciate the range and scope of important tasks of the entire SS and police, and to realize that the activity performed by the man in the 'green uniform' is just as valuable as the one in which you are engaged. You must consider the activity of the SD man or the Security Police to be as vital for our over-all activity as your marching with weapons. You are the ones to be envied, for when you are in action, when a unit distinguishes itself, then one can speak of glory and the unit receives the recognition for it. In many other situations it is far more difficult — but believe me, often it is far more difficult in many places to do one's duty quietly and act quietly, to protect our Weltanschauung, and at the same time be unbending and uncompromising. Many times this is much harder than fighting a battle. The 'Waffen-SS' will live only when the entire SS lives, only when the entire corps is an order, and only when all parts realize that existence without the other parts is inconceivable. [108]

By December 31, 1933, the membership of the SS had increased to 209,014. [109] To check the flood of opportunists, Himmler, on July 10, 1933, issued an order to throttle the influx into the SS. This order remained in effect until September 1934. [110] Following the seizure of power, Himmler could select from a large number of candidates, since up to July 20, 1934, there were 400,000 available men of which 220,000 were registered. [111] Thus he could afford to dismiss those he now held unsuitable for membership. The majority of those who were dismissed between 1933 and 1936 (after July 20 the number of members was reduced to approximately 189,000 [112]) had proven to be rather disinclined to participate in the various activities of the 'Schutzstaffel.' [113] It is interesting to note that the criterion for dismissal was not so much 'racial deficiency' as lack of devotion and motivation. Others were ousted because they were considered undesirable elements, commonly referred to as 'old bruisers' (alte Schläger). Prior to 1933 they had primarily used their fists in behalf of the party, intimidating and beating down political opponents. Still others who qualified superbly according to the racial charts developed by the commission had to be dismissed because they were found incapable of controlling their consumption of alcohol.[114] Himmler also became aware of the fact that the physical appearance of those possessing leadership qualities was not necessarily identical with the image of an ideal Nordic type. To bring these useful, but racially frequently unattractive individuals into his organization, he established the rank of 'Ehrenführer,' that is to say, honorary leader. Besides being accepted into the SS as honorary leaders, men who fell into this category also had titles of rank bestowed on them. So, for example, was the later 'Reichspressechef' Otto Dietrich, on December 24, 1932, accepted as honorary leader and given the rank of 'Oberführer' and promoted to 'Gruppenführer' on January 27, 1934. Hermann Rauschning was given the rank of 'Standartenführer'; others in similar situations were Party Treasurer Franz Xaver Schwarz, the Gauleiter of Danzig Albert Forster, Gauleiter Wilhelm Kube, Wilhelm Grimm, Karl Kaufmann, Friedrich Hildebrandt, Wilhelm Loeper, Wilhelm Murr, Karl Wahl, Fritz Sauckel, etc.[115] In general many of the numerically few intellectually endowed career seekers had found positions in the 'Sicherheitsdienst' (SD) or other SS or party offices, while those remaining in the local SS groups were men of brawn, not of brain.

Of immediate concern to Himmler was the numerical strength of the SS. He was most anxious to achieve a speedy expansion of his instrument of power. Yet SS membership during the years 1935-1937 had not increased significantly. On December 31, 1935, the total membership (including 'Verfügungstruppe' and Death's Head Units) was 199,915 men. A year later it had risen to 200,129, and on December 31, 1937, it reached 208,364 men.[116] Following the 'Anschluß' of Austria and the annexation of Sudetenland, the strength of the SS increased to 238,159.[117] In 1939 the annexation of the Memel territory brought a small influx of eligible men which raised the number of SS personnel to a total of 258,456, including the 'Waffen-SS' and police units.[118] In addition, Himmler and SS-Brigadeführer Gottlob Berger, at that time

Chef Ergänzungsamt der Waffen-SS, viewed the occupation of Denmark, Norway, Holland, and Belgium as the opening up of a useful source from which to draw additional racially acceptable manpower. During an inspection of SS units in the Eindhoven-Tilburg area Himmler wrote:

> . . . the population is friendly and of good race and it is a joy to see the men, women, and children. They are a great gain for Germany. [119]

By means of this policy, not only would the Reich gain millions of new citizens but the 'Schutzstaffel' would also increase in numbers, power, and influence. Thus through the involvement of the SS in the expansion of the German Reich, Himmler's organization would become the dominating instrument in these newly occupied territories.

Himmler therefore accepted Gottlob Berger's (later chief of the SS Main Office – SS-Hauptamt – and 'Obergruppenführer') suggestion of the spring of 1940 to create European volunteer formations and incorporate them into the 'Waffen-SS.' [120] The justification frequently given for the establishment of these formations was that the multi-national volunteers with awareness of being responsible Europeans compelled them to unite with the Germans in the effort to save Europe from Communism. What has been frequently overlooked, however, is the fact that when Hitler agreed to the establishment of the first SS formations of predominantly non-German nationals, he thought that the enemy was Great Britain and not the Soviet Union. In fact, at that time, an open conflict between Germany and Russia was not even envisaged. Upon Hitler's order of April 20, 1940, the first SS formation recruited in the Scandinavian countries was formed; it received the name 'SS-Verfügungstruppe Standarte Nordland.' [121] Shortly afterwards Hitler agreed to Himmler's proposal, dated May 27, 1940, to establish an additional formation of foreign volunteers, named 'SS Standarte Westland,' which was to consist predominantly of Dutch and Flemish volunteers. [122] This policy of drawing 'Germanic blood' into the ranks of the SS and thereby furthering its sphere of influence was followed throughout the entire war. It is chiefly for this reason that members of foreign nations were frequently to be found not only in SS units with purely military functions but also in SS police and destruction units and as guards in German concentration camps.

An administrative and numerically leading position in the organization and execution of anti-Jewish policies – including the deportation and extermination of Jews – was occupied by Austrian members of the 'Reichssicherheitshauptamt' (RSHA), Gestapo, SS, police units, and 'Einsatzkommandos.' This fact has been pointed out by Simon Wiesenthal, head of the 'Dokumentationszentrum des Bundes jüdischer Verfolgter des Naziregimes' in Vienna, in a memorandum to the Austrian Bundeskanzler Dr. Josef Klaus, on October 12, 1966. Wiesenthal states that the participation of Austrian nationals in anti-Jewish measures was distinctly higher than their 8.5 per cent share of the total population of the Greater German Reich. [123]

The contrary formulation and the political ideological implications of the Führer decree of August 17, 1938, give the face-value impression that the 'SS-Verfügungstruppe' and the 'SS-Totenkopfverbände' were legitimate organizations in the service of the state. The decree clarified some differences between the 'SS-Totenkopfverbände' and the 'SS-Verfügungstruppe.' In essence the 'Death's Head Units' were more closely tied to the police than to the Armed Forces, but the decree stipulated that, unlike the 'SS-Verfügungstruppe,' the later 'Waffen-SS', although their political police duties were to be assigned by the Führer, they were not at his unconditional disposal. [124] At first their foremost task was limited to the guarding of concentration camps.

In contrast to the 'SS-Totenkopfverbände,' the 'SS-Verfügungstruppe' was a special formation unconditionally at Hitler's disposal and, as such, separated the later armed SS ('Waffen-SS') from the 'Wehrmacht' and from the police; but it was fashioned after the corresponding units of the army. [125] During peacetime it was to be commanded by the Reichsführer SS and chief of the German police, and regardless of its employment it was to remain 'a unit of the NSDAP.' The members were 'to be selected by the Reichsführer SS according to the ideological and political standards which I [Hitler] have ordered for the NSDAP and for the Schutzstaffel.' [126] The Führer decree of August 17, 1938, established a connection between the 'SS-Verfügungstruppe' and the 'SS-Totenkopfverbände' in the event of mobilization. In case of war certain parts of the 'SS-Totenkopfverbände' were to 'be transferred to the SS-Verfügungstruppe' to secure 'a reserve which would meet the ideological and political spirit' of that formation. [127] Eventually, after October 1939, all members of the 'SS-Totenkopfverbände' became officially a part of the 'Waffen-SS', and four 'Totenkopf-Standarten' (regiments), Oberbayern, Thüringen, Brandenburg, and Ostmark, formed one 'SS-Death's-head' division under the command of Theodor Eicke. [128] During the war former members of the 'SS-Totenkopfverbände' were to be found in the ranks of many field units of the 'Waffen-SS.' The 'SS-Totenkopfverbände' thus employed were frequently replaced, especially towards the end of the war, either by members of the 'Allgemeine SS' who were over forty-five years of age and had military training, or were physically less fit members of the 'Waffen-SS,' or by other formations of the Armed Forces. [129]

By the end of 1940 all members of the 'SS-Totenkopfverbände' were part of the 'Waffen-SS.' Three entire regiments of 'Totenkopf' troopers – about 6,500 men – became the nucleus of a new field division. Long before the end of the war former members of the 'SS-Totenkopfverbände' were to be found in the ranks of many field units of the 'Waffen-SS.' [130]

## 4. *Promulgation and application of racial doctrines in the SS*

Himmler's preoccupation with racial theories first became apparent in his fascination for eugenic breeding when he was studying poultry science. Between the years 1923-1926 he had been attracted to the ideas of the Artaman League and served as its leader in Bavaria. [131] This league had been founded and was led by Willibald Hentschel from Westernwanna (Elbe) and Bruno Tanzmann from Hellerau. [132] The name 'Artamanen' is derived from the middle-high German words 'art,' which means farming, and 'manen,' which means men. The members of the league believed that the industrialization of Germany lured some of the 'best blood' from the rural areas to the cities. Once in the cities, those of the 'good race' had chosen to limit the number of their descendants, or else their 'pure blood' had become contaminated through the intermarriage with the 'racially inferior.' Due to the migration to the city and the consequent labor shortage, which placed more and harder work on those who remained in rural areas, a decrease in the birthrate in the country had taken place. Himmler, as an 'Artaman,' advocated both the return of the racially uncontaminated to peasant life and their procreation in large numbers. The basic doctrine of the 'Artaman League' was the mystical belief in the relationship between blood and soil. Only those who made their livelihood by tilling the soil could bring forth 'racially desirable' offspring. [133]

As noted before, racial doctrines began to play an increasingly important role in socio-political movements in Central Europe in the last part of the nineteenth and the beginning of the twentieth century. [134] A diluted and crude Darwinism had filtered down to the lower strata of society and had become a conventional opinion. This notion, along with rising nationalism on the one hand and decreasing influence of Christian religious tenets – which up to this time had permeated internal policies and political movements – on the other, began to transform the religious basis of anti-Semitism into a racist anti-Judaism.

Hitler as well as Himmler had absorbed these racial notions, added some phrases of Nietzsche and other philosophers relative to race, and frequently quoted them out of context. Although there never seemed to have existed a close relationship between Hitler and Himmler, in regard to the subject of race they appear to have been in complete agreement. Hitler had laid the foundation of the future state in *Mein Kampf*, asserting that the folkish state '. . . must set the race in the centre of all life. It must take care to keep it pure.' [135] He believed the German people to be a mixture of predominantly Germanic blood. He held the 'Nordic race' to be the best of all, and therefore the best qualified to lead the nation and the world. Any mixing of Germanic blood with other 'races' – Slavs, Jews, Gypsies, Mongolians, Negroes, and others – he condemned; he rejected such mixing on the basis of the assumption that it brings in its wake the lowering of the level of the 'higher race' and 'physical and intellectual regression.' [136] It is therefore not surprising that in his conclusion to *Mein Kampf* Hitler writes:

> . . . a state [which] in this age of racial poisoning dedicates it-self to the care of its best racial elements must some day become master of the earth. [137]

The two foremost racial theorists of the Nazi movement, who believed that they had discovered in detail the prime role of the 'Nordic race' in history, were Alfred Rosenberg and Walter Darré. [138] Rosenberg held that the states of the Occident and their achievements had been the work of the 'Nordic race.' Through the ages the Nordic people had swept southward in various waves and had established the ancient culture of Greece and Rome. When ancient Rome began to break down, new waves arrived and Germanic states were established on Roman soil. Rosenberg believed that the 'Germanic races' had remained unmixed for some time because the Germanic tribes had adopted the Aryan type of Christianity. Following the conversion of the Germans to Roman Catholicism, the bastardization began, and continued through the centuries. He interpreted the Renaissance as an intoxicating remanifestation of 'Germanic blood.'[139] Following the Renaissance, the bastardization of Germanic elements increased. Liberalism, with its slogans of liberty, equality, and fraternity, undermined the racial instincts of many Nordic peoples in various countries of Europe, especially France. Rosenberg and fellow racists held that at the contemporary age the 'Untermensch,' under the banners of Marxism, prepared a new onslaught upon the 'racially pure' or 'Herrenmenschen.' In almost all revolts of the inferior against the superior, Hitler, Goebbels, Rosenberg, Himmler, and others suspected the Jew of being the prime instigator, who, through disguises such as Christianity, liberalism (French Revolution), democracy, and most recently Marxism, attempted to destroy the creator of culture, order, state, and morality, that is to say, the 'Nordic man.'

Significantly, the National Socialists managed for the first time in history to convert their doctrines of *racial* anti-Semitism (in contrast to the traditional, *religious* anti-Semitism) into a political-action program. Their theories were to a large extent taken over from the anti-Jewish racist ideology. This ideology had its beginnings in the second half of the seventeenth century when, for the first time, stereotype images appeared in the form of cartoons.[140] In these caricatures an attempt was made to discover 'typical' race characteristics in the Jewish minority group. In more recent times they can be found in a more artistic form in the drawings and verses of Wilhelm Busch, hailed by Rudolf Hess as 'Philosoph im heiteren Gewande,' and in a vulgar fashion in Streicher's 'Stürmer.'[141] The theory of the racists of the nineteenth century asserted that cultural features, positive or negative, were the product of physical characteristics. It was reasoned that since physical attributes did not change, social behavior patterns (including religion) were also immutable. The anti-Semites, therefore, began to regard the Jews as a 'race,' and the traditional discrimination based on religious motives played but a psychologically and legally supportive – and merely subordinate – role. However, it would be incorrect to assume that this radical racist anti-Semitism as propagated by the National Socialists was overly popular or that they received wide public support because of it. More accurately, they were supported in spite of it.[142] Acting under the orders of Hitler, Himmler formed the SS and indoctrinated it to become the major executive organ of the NS racist aggression policy. This policy had already been outlined in part in Dietrich Eckart's *Der Bolschewismus von Moses bis Lenin: Zwiegespräch zwischen Adolf Hitler und mir*, in Hitler's *Mein Kampf*, and Alfred Rosenberg's *Wesen, Grundsätze und Ziele der NSDAP*, and in other Nazi publications and speeches. However, prudently enough, the so-called 'Aryan-paragraph' was not so much based on racial characteristics as on descent. An objective evaluation of racial characteristics would have quickly uncovered the missing basis for scientific evidence. Indeed there was a sufficient number of Jews whose appearance, habitus, and mannerisms were far more 'Germanic' than those of their 'Aryan' persecutors, if one would be willing to use the ideational imagery and norms of NS racists.

## 5. *Racial criteria for the selection of personnel into the SS*

Himmler readily adopted the racial ideas of Hitler, Darré, Günther, and their forerunners. He believed that Germany was predominantly inhabited by six European 'races': The Nordic, the Phalic, the Dinaric, the Alpine, the East-Baltic, and the Mediterranean. The average German he believed to be a mixture of these races. However, the strongest element in the majority of Germans, and also the element uniting them, he held to be the 'Nordic race,' ranking between 50 and 60 per cent.[143] He believed that no other people in Europe were as 'Nordic' as the Germans and as well qualified for leadership.[144] Hitler and Himmler favored an 'Aufnordung' of the German people and the regeneration of the people of those regions where degeneration had appeared.[145] Both were convinced that the effectiveness of a military unit depended directly upon its 'Nordic' elements.[146] Consequently they sought to recruit as many so-called Nordic Germans into the SS as possible. They planned to eliminate gradually all 'non-Nordic' races from the SS, either through expulsion or through selective breeding.

Through a process of refinement, the SS was to achieve 'racial purity' and Himmler visualized the SS as a new representative German tribe.[147] After January 8, 1929, those men who appeared to be of 'Nordic' stock, at least 1.70 m tall, blond, and blue-eyed, were especially welcome in the SS.[148] However, prior to January 30, 1933, these criteria were not applied as absolute standards. An individual who proved himself as a 'tough bruiser' (Schläger) in the skirmishes with political opponents was accepted even if he possessed what were considered 'Slavic' or 'Mediterranean' features. Those who had served in the front lines during World War I were also considered fully qualified for the SS, having proven their membership in the 'Nordic' race by bravery in attack and trench warfare.[149] After the National Socialist seizure of power, Himmler issued a number of orders to exclude those individuals from membership whom he considered racially unfit for the SS. To be accepted, most of the candidates had to appear before a commission of SS physicians who examined prospective members for 'Nordic' characteristics.[150] The commission followed certain directives which had been worked out by the 'SS-Hauptsturmführer' Dr. B. K. Schultz. In regard to physical appearance a scale from nine to one was applied.[151] Those who obtained ratings from nine to six were accepted into the SS. Those who received ratings five and four were accepted only after having proven the 'Nordic' qualities in their behavior. Ratings three to one were regarded as unacceptable. Himmler also required that those selected possess a 'well-balanced' physique:

> Uns kommt es . . . nicht nur auf die Länge und auf die Augenfarbe an, sondern wir lehnen auch viele Leute ab, die vielleicht 1,80 oder 1,85 m lang sind, wenn sie körperlich falsch gewachsen sind. . . . Wenn also die Unterschenkel in einem völlig falschen Verhältnis zu den Oberschenkeln stehen, wo die Unterschenkel in einem völlig falschen Verhältnis zum Oberkörper stehen, so daß der Körper bei jedem Schritt eine unerhörte Hubleistung aufwenden muß, um diese Marschleistung zu vollbringen, . . . [152]

We take into consideration not only height and eye color, but indeed reject many people even if they are 1.80 m or 1.85 m tall but whose physical build is otherwise faulty. If, for example, the shanks are in a wholly improper relationship to the thighs and the trunk has a completely wrong relationship to the shanks so that at every step the body must make a tremendous heaving effort when marching, . . .[152]

In regard to racial appearance the following classification was applied:[153]

a) purely Nordic;
b) predominantly Nordic or Phalic;
c) harmonious bastard with slight Alpine, Dinaric, or Mediterranean characteristics;
d) bastard of predominantly East-Baltic or Alpine origin;
e) bastard with extra-European blood.

Ratings of a, b, or c qualified for membership in the SS. To eliminate from the SS anyone who might have 'undesirable' blood, Himmler ordered that every SS man establish his genealogical record. An officer had to establish the proof that since 1750 no Jewish individual of an extra-European race was among his ancestors.[154] Enlisted men had to establish genealogical records back to 1800. However, in developing the future élite, Himmler envisaged a certain type of individual who not only possessed specific characteristics but also identified himself through his behavior. It was expected that a member of the SS behave as a 'Herrenmensch.' Anyone who possessed a weak will or moved about in a rather relaxed fashion was disqualified.[155] What should be stressed here is the fact that to begin with, no specific moral or intellectual aptitude was required for qualification as a 'Herrenmensch.' However, 'racial purity,' bravery, unconditional obedience, and ideological conviction were the desirable criteria for the new élite. To achieve some uniformity of behavior and conduct, future members were then screened and classified as follows:[156]

A I    – very much qualified for the SS
A II   – qualified for the SS
A III  – scarcely suitable for the SS
B I    – by and large undesirable for the SS

B II   – unsuitable for the SS
C       – unsuitable for becoming a soldier of the 'Wehrmacht'

That these criteria for selection did not provide any guarantee of the suitability of those newly admitted can be concluded from the evidence given by Himmler himself. In January 1937, he stated that from the end of 1933 to the end of 1935, 60,000 newly admitted recruits had to be discharged (herausgesetzt) because 'they were of no use.' [157]

## 6. *Ideological criteria for selection, indoctrination, and training*

The selection according to biological criteria alone was no assurance of obtaining those most desirable for membership; proper indoctrination and training were considered of utmost importance. Although Himmler emphasized the need for physical fitness through exercise and sport, he placed equal emphasis on ideological indoctrination. This took place once a week during the so-called 'Schulungsabend.' Subject matters were historical and political themes, and several pages of *Mein Kampf* had to be discussed. [158] The ideological training was carried out by political officers, [159] later on better known under the name of 'Nationalsozialistische Führungsoffiziere' (NSFO). Their functions were patterned after those of the Soviet political commissars.

While still a member of the 'Streifendienst' (a branch of the 'Hitler Youth'), a boy was closely observed by the local leaders of the SS. After release from this organization at the age of eighteen, the young man became a candidate for the SS for approximately one year, during which time he had to acquire the 'Reichssportabzeichen' and the 'SA-Sportabzeichen,' considered by Himmler to be the foremost criterion of physical and racial excellence.

On March 16, 1935, Hitler issued an order to establish a fully militarized formation of the 'SS-Verfügungstruppen' to serve as a nucleus for an SS division. Prior to World War II, SS officers were trained at two academies, the 'SS Junkerschule Bad Tölz' and the 'SS Junkerschule Braunschweig.' The officer academy at Tölz was established in 1934 and that at Braunschweig in 1935. [160] Forty per cent of the officer candidates accepted before 1938 had only rudimentary school education. [161]

For the 'SS-Verfügungsdivision' and the 'Leibstandarte SS Adolf Hitler,' applicants had to be between seventeen and twenty-two, and for the 'SS-Totenkopfdivision' the maximum age was twenty-six. The minimum height for these field divisions was 1.70 m, except for the élite 'Leibstandarte' which required the minimum to be no less than 1.84 m. Circulars giving detailed requirements for admission into the 'Waffen-SS' concluded with the remark that 'service in the Waffen-SS counts as military service.'[162]

After having served as a candidate of the SS for one year the young man was expected to fulfill his 'Reichsarbeitsdienst' and Wehrmacht obligation in the following two or three years. Upon his release from both organizations he was still considered a candidate until he was properly instructed in the marriage order and honor law of the SS.[163] November 9 was chosen as the day for taking the oath of loyalty and obedience to Hitler, and as a symbol of acceptance to full membership the candidate received the dagger. On the same day the new member of the SS had to take an additional oath swearing that he and his future family would be obedient to the marriage order of the SS.[164] From this time on he received the right and had the duty to defend his honor with the weapon – according to the honor laws of the SS.[165] From eighteen to twenty-five an SS man belonged to the active SS No. 1, from twenty-five to thirty-five to the active SS No. 2, from thirty-five to forty-five to the SS reserve, and after forty-five to the 'Stammabteilung.'[166] Due to the brief period between the seizure of power and the beginning of World War II, the establishment of these subdivisions actually remained in the planning stage.

To assure a racially pure posterity for the SS, Himmler issued the order No. A-65 of December 31, 1931, commonly referred to as 'Heiratsbefehl' (marriage order),[167] which became effective on January 8, 1932. It stated that the future of the German nation depended on '. . . the selection and preservation of the racially and hereditarily healthy good blood . . . .'[168] The chief aim, stated in article three, was the subsequent establishment of the '. . . hereditarily valuable clan of Germanic-Nordic kind.'[169] Article five stipulated that every member of the SS intending to marry had to apply for marriage approval. The office responsible for processing the documents necessary for marriage approval, under the leadership of Standartenführer R. Walter Darré[170], was named 'Race Office.' Questionnaires were devised by the 'Race

Office' (later renamed 'Race and Settlement Main Office'), and the prospective marriage partners had to appear before a physician of the SS for an examination of hereditary diseases. The SS physician had to determine whether or not both applicants were desirable from the point of view of racial propagation and membership in the clan. Photographs showing the applicants in trunks had to be attached to the application. They also had to submit a statement concerning their financial status, especially in regard to debts.[171]

When the approved marriage had taken place the names of the couple and their subsequent offspring were recorded in the clan book of the SS. The degree of enforcement of the marriage order varied in the course of time. During the first years after its proclamation, the marriage order was not observed rigorously, but after August 1, 1935, members of the SS (except officers) who dared to marry without consent of the 'Race and Settlement Main Office' were to be reported to the SS court in Munich. By trial it was established whether the offender was to be excluded or expelled from the 'Schutzstaffel.' However, if he could prove to the court that he had married without having had cognizance of the marriage order, he was severely reprimanded, but not expelled. If the offender was an officer of higher rank, the decision rested with Himmler personally and was withdrawn from the jurisdiction of the SS court.[172] For obvious reasons there was a relaxation of the enforcement with the beginning of the war; but as of January 1, 1940, members of the 'Allgemeine SS,' the 'Waffen-SS,' or SS men who served in the German Armed Forces again had to submit to a more rigorous examination prior to receiving permission for marriage.[173]

## 7. 'Lebensborn' – Example of an NS social institution

The ideal image of an SS family as portrayed in the SS 'Leithefte' consisted of a young couple surrounded by a large number of children of 'Nordic' appearance. The youthfulness of both parents, the obvious virility of the father, and the femininity of the mother conveyed to the on-looker the impression that no greater contribution to the 'Aufnordung' of the SS and German nation could be expected. However, this image was false and statistics for 1937, for example, belie this picture.[174] They show that the leaders of the SS, who most frequently had adequate incomes, by and large remained captives of 'bourgeois customs.' They enjoyed the conveniences their positions afforded them but were reluctant to assume the inconvenience and burden of a large family.

To remedy this situation Himmler, on December 12, 1935, founded the 'Lebensborn e.V.' which, prior to March 1, 1938, functioned in Berlin and later moved its office to Munich. The purpose of this institution was to encourage the propagation of the 'Nordic race' and to secure as much 'Nordic blood' for the SS as possible. Consequently, the tasks of the 'Lebensborn' were, first, to offer support and aid to racially and hereditarily healthy families and, secondly, to care for women pregnant by racially and hereditarily acceptable men. These women were 'expected to give birth to equally valuable children.'[175] Unwed mothers and women who expected children out of wedlock with SS men could give birth in the homes of the 'Lebensborn.'[176] Racially valuable women were also admitted even though the father of the expected child was not a member of the SS. A number of women who expected children by high NS-functionaries delivered these children in the homes of the 'Lebensborn.' In addition, Himmler desired the 'Lebensborn' to perform yet another task. In a conversation with Felix Kersten on May 9, 1943, Himmler said that privately he let it be known that '. . . any unmarried woman who was alone in the world but longed for a child might turn to the Lebensborn with perfect confidence.'[177] Himmler assured the rather astounded Kersten that '. . . we only recommend valuable and racially pure men as "procreation-assistants".'[178] The future of the child thus conceived would be assured since 'the "Reichsführung SS" would sponsor the child and provide for its education.'[179] Himmler had to admit to Kersten that at first the women had not availed themselves readily of the procreation-assistants but that in time the situation had slightly improved. Through the use of propaganda, Hitler planned to change middle-class prejudices and make this kind of motherhood acceptable and even honorable.

The 'Lebensborn' was financed predominantly by the SS officers. Every month a certain amount of their salaries, usually ranging between 1 and 5 per cent, was withheld. The largest part of the money used for the support of the society came from high SS officers who were either single, married with no children, or married with one child or one minor to support. Furthermore, for the duration of the war, the

'Schutzstaffel,' through the 'Lebensborn,' would care for all legitimate and illegitimate children of SS men, and assume responsibility for the children's and the mothers' physical well-being. This order, dated October 28, 1939, gave rise to objections, especially by those members of the SS who still adhered to 'bourgeois moral ideals' and by those who feared that their wives, daughters, brides, and sweethearts might become targets for libidinous fellow comrades.[180] Himmler calmed their uneasy feelings by assuring them he was thinking of those un-married women who out of '. . . deepest, ethical seriousness wanted to have children by their sweethearts who soon could leave for the front-lines . . . .'[181]

Yet another order which was decreed from Himmler's 'Feldkomman-dostelle,' dated August 15, 1942, entitled 'SS Orders to the Last Sons', [182] permitted, upon the order of the Führer, the withdrawal of certain members of the SS from front line duties so that their families might not die out. Article II announced the withdrawal from front line duty for one year: 'It is your duty to see to it that as quickly as possible, through the begetting and birth of children of good blood, you will no longer remain the last sons.'[183] The language of these orders is devoid of human compassion and empathy; it does not make any allowance for individual difference. The orders bluntly indicate that two creatures are to meet once more in order to produce an offspring for state and nation.

## 8. *Jewish and non-German descent in the SS*

Whenever the Jewish ancestry of an SS man was discovered, he was requested by his superior to petition for release. Failure to comply with the request would cause the SS court in Munich to announce his ex-pulsion.[184] Exceptions were made in some cases involving high-ranking members; the most well-known case is said to be that of Reinhard Heydrich, at first head of the Security Police (Sipo), of the Secret State Police (Geheime Staatspolizei or Gestapo), the Criminal Police (Kripo), and in 1939 chief of the Reich Security Main Office (RSHA).[185]

In 1931 two men had been accepted into the SS who during sub-sequent years had rendered faithful service. When their genealogical records had been assembled it was found out that they were of partially

Gypsy origin. Himmler ruled – in these and similar cases – that since these two men were good enough to fight for the party before 1933, they now should not be excluded from the SS. However, a notice was inserted in their dossiers stating that their children could not be accepted into the SS.[186]

Most of those judged unsuitable for membership in the SS either had Jewish ancestors or had married women of Jewish descent. A deciding factor was the rank of the SS members in question, since the rules were not quite so rigorously applied to those who were officers.[187]

Somewhat different was the ruling concerning those who were partially 'un-Nordic' in appearance and racial origin. It was expected that after a few generations of intermarriage with 'Nordic' people, traces of 'Mediterranean,' 'Alpine,' and perhaps 'East-Baltic' blood could be eliminated (ausgemendelt).

Generally, in the literature about the SS insufficient emphasis has been given to the fact that the Slavs were considered by the racial ideologists – especially Hitler and Himmler[188] – as not much less 'art-fremd' than the Jews. Ever since Himmler had become 'Reichsführer SS' his major endeavor was to create an Order of 'good blood' which was to serve Germany. He wanted to create an Order

> ..., der diesen Gedanken des nordischen Blutes so verbreitet, daß wir alles nordische Blut in der Welt an uns heranziehen, unseren Gegnern das Blut wegnehmen, es uns einfügen, damit niemals mehr, jetzt in der ganzen Politik gesehen, in großen Mengen und in nennenswertem Umfange, nordisches Blut, germanisches Blut, gegen uns kämpft.[189]

> ──────

> ... which would so spread the notion of Nordic blood, that we would attract all Nordic blood in the world to us, deprive our opponents of it and incorporate it to the extent that, viewed from a political vantage point, Nordic blood, Germanic blood, would never again fight against us in large masses and on a noteworthy scale.[189]

In Himmler's opinion: 'The Slav is never able to construct anything of his own.'[190] He stated that, with the exception of a few personalities which Asia produces every couple of centuries, as for example, Attila,

Ghengis-Khan, Tamerlane, Lenin, and Stalin, the masses of the Slavs
are a race-mixture, in short: '. . . aufgebaut auf einer Unterrasse mit
eingesprengten Blutstropfen unseren Blutes, einer führenden Rasse,
nicht fähig, sich selbst zu beherrschen und Ordnung zu halten.'[191] Consequently Himmler was not eager to include in the SS individuals of
Slavic origin. So, for example, von dem Bach-Zelewski related before
the court at Nuremberg that Himmler had accepted him into the SS in
spite of his 'Slavic blood.' However, in order to decrease the 'Slavic
blood' in the family, Himmler had reserved the right to approve the
brides of the general's three sons.[192] To remedy such 'racial impurities,'
Himmler intended to permit marriages of his SS-men to blonde, blue-
eyed women only.[193] According to his interpretation of the Mendelian
laws Himmler calculated that within 120 years the SS, and thereby the
German nation, would become 'pureblooded' again, provided that such
a 'breeding policy' was carried out systematically.[194] Himmler explained
his stand on racial hygiene to Kersten in the following terms:

Wer wird einmal nach 300 oder 500 Jahren fragen, ob ein
Fräulein Müller oder Schulze unglücklich war? Das ist im
Großen gesehen ganz gleichgültig, nicht gleichgültig aber ist
es, ob in diesem Raume, in dem wir leben, ein rassisch und
körperlich hochstehender Menschenschlag lebt, der in der
Lage ist, das ihm überlassene Erbe zu verwalten und stets von
Neuem zu sichern. Gewiß, man soll, wo man es kann, auf
Gefühle und Empfindungen Rücksicht nehmen, aber da, wo
es um das Glück von Generationen und den Bestand des Rei-
ches geht, muß man steinhart sein und nicht mit Weichheit
und zarten Gefühlen die Existenz künftiger Generationen aufs
Spiel setzen. Nehmen Sie sich als Beispiel einmal den Wald.
Da herrscht zunächst eine üppige Vegetation der verschiedensten Pflanzen und Sträucher, solange die Bäume, die den künftigen Wald tragen, noch klein sind. Schauen Sie sich denselben
Wald zwanzig Jahre später an! Die gesamte üppige Vegetation
ist verschwunden, die zum Licht strebenden Bäume haben das
Lebensgesetz des Waldes erfüllt, um leben zu können wurde
diese Vegetation vernichtet. Wieviele pflanzliche Einzelschick-
sale sind dabei betroffen worden! Wir finden das ganz in der
Ordnung und stellen es als das Gesetz des Waldes hin. Im

Leben der Völker und des Reiches ist dies nicht anders, man
muß es nur erkennen und sich selbst bewußt machen, um sich
vor Gefühlsduselei, die gar nicht am Platz ist, zu hüten.[195]

---

... After 300 or 500 years who will ask if Miss Mueller or
Miss Schulze was unhappy? On the whole that is quite unimportant; the important thing, however, is whether in the space
we inhabit a racially and physically superior type of man lives,
who will be capable of administering his bequeathed heritage
and continually safeguard it. Certainly, wherever it is possible,
one should take into consideration the feelings and emotions
of our people. But when the happiness of generations and the
existence of the Reich are at stake, one has to be as hard as
stone and not endanger the existence of future generations with
softness and tender feelings. Let us take the example of the
forest. At first there is an abundance of luxurious vegetation
of plants and bushes of all kinds while the trees, which carry
the germ of the future forest, are still small. Look at the same
forest after twenty years have gone by! All the luxurious vegetation is gone. The trees, pressing upwards towards the sun-
light, have fulfilled the forest's law of life. And so, for the
trees to live, the vegetation was destroyed. How many individual fates of plants were affected by this. We find this quite
proper and accept it as the law of the forest. The same applies
to the life of the people and the state. We only need to recognize this fact and be aware of it in order to guard against petty
sentimentality which is quite out of place.[195]

Himmler severely reprimanded and often punished those SS-men who
either entertained intimate relations with or were married to women
of non-German, particularly Jewish, descent, even if such relationships
had already existed prior to the 'Machtergreifung' of 1933.[196] So, for
example, Himmler complained to Kersten that in spite of all propaganda in favor of 'Germanic,' blonde, blue-eyed women, his SS-men
persisted in marrying brunettes.[197] Despite the introduction of punitive
measures Himmler's breeding policies were condemned to failure.

In addition to experiencing considerable difficulty in carrying out
his eugenic program, Himmler appears to have been even more troubled

with the non-Aryan background of some of his SS-men and that of their spouses.[198] One of the most prominent cases was the appearance of the apparently quite virile Mosaic Abraham Reinau (1663), who was christened in 1685, on the genealogical scene of the SS (1938).[199] In this connection Himmler wrote to the 'Reichsbauernführer' and 'SS-Obergruppenführer' Richard Walther Darré on March 29, 1938:

> Lieber Richard!
> Anliegend übersende ich Dir den Abstammungsnachweis des SS-Standartenführers Friedrich Engler-Füßlin (E.-F. was 'Landesbauernführer' of Baden) Dieser Jude Reinau muß verheerend in der dortigen Gegend gewirkt haben. Heute habe ich schon einen SS-Führer entlassen müssen, da er und seine Frau 1 mal und ein Teil sogar 2 mal von diesem Reinau abstammen.
>
> Bei Engler-Füßlin sehe ich einen Ausweg, wenn er sich verpflichtet, von dieser Frau keine Kinder mehr haben zu wollen, und wenn weiter stillschweigend darüber Klarheit herrschte, daß die Kinder aus dieser Ehe nicht in die SS aufgenommen werden können.
>
> Heil Hitler!<br>Dein HH[200]

---

> Dear Richard:
> Enclosed you will find the evidence of SS-Standartenführer Friedrich Engler-Füßlin's ancestral origin. (E.-F. was 'Landesbauernführer' of Baden.) This Jew Reinau must have been devastatingly active in that area. Today I was forced to dismiss still another SS leader because he and his wife are in one line of descent – and one of them even in two lines – from this Reinau.
>
> With Engler-Füßlin I can think of one way out. He must promise not to have any more children out of his present marriage, and furthermore, it will be tacitly understood that his present children be forbidden to join the SS.
>
> Heil Hitler!<br>Your HH[200]

Because of this rather active ancestor Reinau, SS-Untersturmführer

Küchlin (born on May 2, 1910, in Freiburg i. Brsg. SS-Nr. 104 845) was first discharged from the SS by Himmler (April 3, 1940) who then reversed his decision and ordered Küchlin to be retained under the provision that further investigation and clarification would be forth-coming.[201] In the case of the SS-Rottenführer Katzenstein and the SS-Obersturmführer Julius and Rolf Sütterlin, also descendents of Reinau, Himmler once more decided to defer his final decision (December 17, 1943) regarding their retention in the SS.[202] Nevertheless he ruled that the offspring of these three kinsmen would not be accepted into the SS or, if this was not applicable, would not be permitted to marry an SS-man.[203] It stands to reason that Himmler became somewhat more lenient as the German strategic situation deteriorated and the manpower shortage during the war became more critical. Neither would it be realistic to overrate Himmler's influence as a decisive policy maker nor does it correspond with facts.[204] In reality, the SS as an organiza-tional entity was permeated with and built up along Hitler's terms and ideologies. This left a margin for exceptions due to Hitler's utilitarian inconsistency and Machiavellian outlook. Reinhard Heydrich's em-ployment and retention in the SS may be considered as a reflection of this attitude. In spite of recent controversies on that subject a careful evaluation of available sources still indicates that the zealous chief of the 'Reichssicherheitshauptamt' (RSHA), deputy 'Reichsprotektor von Böhmen und Mähren' and SS-Obergruppenführer Reinhard Heydrich – in Nazi racist terminology – appears to have been a Jewish 'Misch-ling.'[205]

## 9.  *The conception of morality and honor in the 'Schutzstaffel'*

Perhaps it can be stated that by and large those who were attracted to the SS were marginal individuals in search of an identity. Their self-concept and level of achievement were low, their need for dependency relations and reassertion high. They apparently felt secure in a close-knit, rigid, hierarchical social system in which responsibility and deci-sion-making were delegated to a superior authority. It seems that the SS-men felt relieved when they were permitted to function in a relative-ly sheltered collective in which they 'merely' had to carry out clear-cut orders. The SS was essentially an anti-intellectual organization.[206]

Individualism and independence were experienced as burdensome and undesirable. Values, norms, and rules were accepted – indeed, all that which was gradually emerging as the moral code of honor. The SS-men abided by it without necessarily coming into conflict with their conscience or, in Freudian terms, with their superego. That is to say, they let themselves be guided by a very oppressive set of rules and regulations which were recognized as valid and which contributed to 'law and order' as it was perceived by the SS. There appears to be little doubt that the propagation and enforcement of these concepts filled the needs of many an SS-man.[207] However, the attitude and sentiment, which also made up the esprit de corps of the SS, quickly changed as it became obvious that the war could not be won. During this time splinter groups emerged and the already existent gap between the SS combat groups and other SS units widened considerably.[208] In fact, some fundamental SS policies began to be challenged and moral issues were raised by an increasing number of SS leaders.[209]

After the consolidation of power Hitler delegated to Himmler the unrewarding task of uniting under one name a multi-purpose organization with highly diverse tasks. He ordered this unit inoculated with racist doctrines, and introduced a code of behavior. The former was to be applied to Germans and the latter to non-Germans. This was clearly expressed by Himmler in his speech to the Gruppenführer in Posen on October 4, 1943;

> In unseren Reihen leben wir nach unseren germanischen Gesetzen, von denen ein wunderschönes heißt: Ehre ist Zwang genug. – Den fremden Völkern gegenüber wollen wir asiatische Gesetze zur Anwendung bringen. .... Haben wir einen unseres Blutes, einen gutrassigen Norweger oder Niederländer vor uns, dann können wir sein Herz nur nach unseren, das heißt seinen und unseren gesamtgermanischen Gesetzen gewinnen. Haben wir einen Russen oder einen Slawen – blutlich gesehen – vor uns, dann wollen wir ihm gegenüber niemals unsere heiligen Gesetze anwenden, sondern die erprobten russischen Kommissarsgesetze. ....
>
> Ein Grundsatz muß für den SS-Mann absolut gelten: ehrlich, anständig, treu und kameradschaftlich haben wir zu Angehörigen unseres eigenen Blutes zu sein und zu sonst nieman-

dem. Wie es den Russen geht, wie es den Tschechen geht, ist mir total gleichgültig. Das, was in den Völkern an gutem Blut unserer Art vorhanden ist, werden wir uns holen, indem wir ihnen, wenn notwendig, die Kinder rauben und sie bei uns großziehen. Ob die anderen Völker in Wohlstand leben oder ob sie verrecken vor Hunger, das interessiert mich nur soweit als wir sie als Skaven für unsere Kultur brauchen, anders interessiert mich das nicht. Ob bei dem Bau eines Panzergrabens 10 000 russische Weiber an Entkräftung umfallen oder nicht, interessiert mich nur soweit, als der Panzergraben für Deutschland fertig wird. Wir werden niemals roh und herzlos sein, wo es nicht sein muß; das ist klar. Wir Deutsche, die wir als einzige auf der Welt eine anständige Einstellung zum Tier haben, werden ja auch zu diesen Menschentieren eine anständige Einstellung einnehmen, aber es ist ein Verbrechen gegen unser eigenes Blut, uns um sie Sorge zu machen und ihnen Ideale zu bringen, damit unsere Söhne und Enkel es noch schwerer haben mit ihnen.[210]

———

Among ourselves we live according to our Germanic laws of which one very beautiful is expressed in: Honor is obliging enough. – To alien peoples we want to apply Asiatic laws. . . . When we are faced with one of our blood, a racially pure Norwegian or Dutchman, we can win his heart only by appealing to our laws, that is, his and ours, derived from commonly held Germanic laws. If, however, we are dealing with a Russian or a Slav – as far as blood is concerned – we never want to apply our sacred laws to him, but rather the proven Russian commissar's rules. . . .

One basic principle must be the absolute rule for the SS man: We must be honest, decent, loyal, and comradely to members of our own blood and to nobody else. What happens to a Russian, to a Czech, does not interest me in the slightest. What the nations can offer in the way of good blood of our type, we will take, if necessary by kidnapping their children and raising them here with us. Whether nations live in prosperity or starve to death interests me only in so far as we need them as slaves for our culture; otherwise it is of no interest to me. Whether 10,000 Russian females fall down from exhaustion while digging an anti-tank ditch interests me only in so far as the anti-tank ditch for Germany is finished. We shall never be rough and heartless when it is not necessary, that is clear. We Germans, who are the only people in the world who have a decent attitude towards animals, will also assume a decent attitude towards these human animals. But it is a crime against our own blood to worry about them and give them ideals, thus causing our sons and grandsons to have a more difficult time with them. [210]

All those who were not willing to accept this moral code de facto did not belong in the ranks of the SS because of their 'pessimism and lack of faith.' [211] The basis of the underlying moral concepts by which the SS was guided had its origins predominantly in petty bourgeois prejudices, unexamined traditions, and opportunistic considerations to which these attracted individuals could readily adjust. Himmler and his followers served Hitler as willing instruments to carry out his ambition of introducing a 'new world order.' The methods employed to realize this goal in fact constituted the NS moral revolution.

Himmler justified his changing the world in the following arguments:

Das Wichtigste aber ist die tiefste weltanschauliche Durchdringung unseres ganzen Volkes, die tiefste Erkenntnis, daß unser Volk, eine Minderheit von 70 Millionen im Herzen Europas, nur bestehen konnte, weil wir qualitativ wertvoller waren als die anderen ... Wir sind wertvoller, weil unser Blut dazu befähigt, mehr zu erfinden als die andern, weil es uns befähigt zu besseren Soldaten, zu besseren Staatsmännern, zu höherer Kultur, zu besseren Charakteren. Wir haben die bessere Qualität, wenn ich jetzt auf Ihr Gebiet übergehe, weil eben der deutsche Soldat pflichttreuer, anständiger und intelligenter ist als der Soldat der anderen. Diese Qualität erhalten wir so lange, als dieses Volk die alten Gesetze erkennt und befolgt, die Gesetze der Erhaltung eines Volkes, die der Nationalsozialismus dank Adolf Hitler ihm wieder gebracht hat. [212]

---

... But the most important thing is the thorough ideological penetration of all our people with the profound realization that our people, a minority of 70 million people in the heart of Europe, could stand only because we are qualitatively more valuable than the others.

. . . We are more valuable because our blood enables us to invent more than others, to lead our people better than the others; because it enables us to have better soldiers, better statesmen, higher culture, better characters. We also have better quality, speaking of your profession, because the German soldier is more devoted to duty, more decent, and more intelligent than the soldiers of other countries. And we shall maintain this quality as long as we keep our blood and people healthy, so long as this people recognizes and obeys the ancient laws for preservation of a people which National Socialism, thanks to Adolf Hitler, restored to it.[212]

Having accepted these basic premises and having acknowledged Hitler's role as initiator and supreme leader of the NS program, members of the 'Schutzstaffel' considered loyalty and obedience their prime virtue. After the seizure of power every member of the SS subjected his will and personality without mental reservations to the Führer. The promise of unquestioning obedience was expressed in the following oath:

I swear to you, Adolf Hitler, as Führer and Chancellor of the Reich, loyalty and bravery. I promise to you and the superiors appointed by you, obedience unto death. So help me God.[213]

As already stated, to most of the members of the SS, unquestioning obedience to orders seems to have come easily.[214] Yet, in 1938, more than half of the individuals excluded from the SS were discharged for lack of discipline.[215] The next largest number ousted from the SS was made up of those who had violated the marriage order.[216]

More specifically, the SS introduced its own code of honor on November 9, 1934.[217] Until then the SS had been subject to the same code of conduct as the SA. The new code gave the 'Schutzstaffel' an unusual position within the NSDAP. The code of honor granted the right to challenge the offender. The duel was permissible not only among members of the SS but also between SS-men and members of SA and NSDAP student organizations. Rehabilitation through duelling was possible until an order of Hitler, promulgated in spring 1940, forbade duelling.[218] The war afforded ample opportunity to find an outlet for aggression; the shedding of blood by duelling seemed rather inappropriate. From that time on differences had to be referred to the SS court of honor.

Rehabilitation through suicide was also considered permissible as a means of atonement for misconduct. Himmler held suicide justifiable in cases in which a man by committing a crime had defiled his own honor or had harmed the interests of the SS and his nation. In 1937 eighty-five SS-men,[219] and in 1938 ninety-four SS-men,[220] had committed suicide, and six had attempted it. According to Himmler only 15 per cent of the attempted or successful suicides were justifiable.[221] Most of the 85 per cent had been precipitated by fear of punishment, reprimand of superior, quarrel with parents, dissolution of engagement, jealousy, and unhappy love. Suicides committed for these reasons were acknowledged not as an act of heroism but as '. . . flight, as an effort to escape from the struggle and life itself. . . .'[222]

Homosexuality, according to the ethics of Himmler, was a transgression which demanded the life of the offender. In 1937 Himmler proposed to punish and execute the offender in the following manner: Homosexuals '. . . in every case will be publicly demoted, expelled, and handed over to the court. After having served the sentence handed down by the court, upon my order they will be transferred to a concentration camp and shot to death while escaping.'[223] A year later Himmler already '. . . could imagine that in a few years hence a homosexual in the SS would be punished with death.'[224] In August 1941, Hitler spoke about the evil of homosexuality. He stated that 'in one organization, namely the SS, every case of homosexuality must be punished with death; when it aspires to be the élite of the nation there cannot be any other punishment for offences committed within this order.'[225] Appropriate legislation affecting the SS and the police appeared in November 1941. In this Hitler ruled that 'a member of the SS and police who commits immoral acts with another male or who permits himself to be used for immoral acts will be punished by death.'[226] In addition other offences, considered serious, but not punishable by death, were misuse of alcohol, social relationships with Jews,[227] and theft from a comrade. Crimes punishable under the criminal code, such as homicide, fraud, and treason, committed by SS-men were also tried by SS judges in SS courts which were under the jurisdiction of the 'Hauptamt-SS Gericht.'[228] The ethics of the SS did not allow social or human relationships with those who were – according to the Nazi laws – considered subhuman (Untermenschen). Immediately after the seizure of power the prohibition against association with the Jewish 'race' even forbade purchases in Jewish stores. In 1934 Himmler reprimanded two high-ranking SS officers (Standartenführer) for having shopped in a Jewish store;[229] in the same document he threatened those SS-men with expulsion who either shopped in a Jewish store, sought treatment from a Jewish physician, or consulted Jewish lawyers and physicians.[230] In 1938 fifty SS-men were excluded for having had some sort of association with Jewish people.[231] An intimate relationship with a Jewish person was, of course, most reprehensible in Himmler's view, and punishment for the crime of 'Rassenschande' was very harsh.[232] The 'racially' inferior was an outcast of society, doomed to annihilation, and any meddling or interference with this policy was severely punished. Himmler decreed that 'the solution of the Jewish question . . . is a worry for the "Führer" and not a worry for the individual. Contravention, even in the slightest form, will be punished by expulsion from the SS.'[233]

According to Obergruppenführer and General of the 'Waffen-SS' Felix Steiner[234], in contrast to Himmler's 'Ordensgedanke' and his Germanic mysticism, the indoctrination of the SS with ideas of racial materialism was difficult to realize, specifically for SS leaders with dissenting opinions. Although Himmler's own appearance provided the most effective depreciation of his racial theories, for disciplinary reasons it could not be used as a counter argument.[235] Therefore 'sound reason and humor' were used to combat these 'absurd theories,' thus preventing them from becoming dangerous.[236] Unfortunately, in reality this was difficult to accomplish, and Steiner's efforts to change the prevalent sentiment among his men fell somewhat short when we examine a selection of personal letters by men of the 'Division Wiking' of which he was the Commanding General from 1940 to 1942.[237] Out of a selection of letters written by forty-nine voluntary 'Germanic' members of the 'Waffen-SS,' twenty overtly identified themselves with NS racial doctrines and twenty-nine did not refer to them directly.[238] However, as would be expected, all letters reflect a highly positive identification with National Socialist ideology and justification of the war.

10. *Consequences of Hitler's influence on NS ideology and the SS*

Hitler envisaged the future SS in the following terms:

> Mein Ziel ist, daß ein beruflich auserlesenes und besonders geschultes Spezialkorps, die künftige Stoßarmee, die aus lang dienenden Parteigenossen besteht, auch gesinnungsgemäß den nationalsozialistischen Kern in der allgemeinen Wehrmacht verkörpert.[239]

'My aim is to get a specially trained and technically first-rate corps, shock troops consisting of long-serving party comrades, which will at the same time represent the National Socialist spirit in the national defence.'[239]

He further carefully planned the establishment of a terror system with which he wanted to intimidate foes and friends alike:

> Sie halten mich für ungebildet, für einen Barbaren. Ja, wir sind Barbaren. Wir *wollen* es sein. Es ist ein Ehrentitel. *Wir* sind es, die die Welt verjüngen werden. Diese Welt ist am Ende! Es ist unsere Aufgabe, Unruhe zu stiften ... Die Leute haben erwartet, daß ich sie mit Glacéhandschuhen anfassen werde, oder daß ich mich mit Reden begnügen werde. Wir sind nicht in der Lage, auf humane Gefühle Rücksicht zu nehmen. Ich kann auch nicht erst langatmige Untersuchungen anstellen, wer guten Willens ist und ob einer unschuldig ist. Wir müssen uns von allen sentimentalen Gefühlen frei machen und hart werden. Wenn ich eines Tages den Krieg befehlen werde, kann ich mir nicht Gedanken machen über die zehn Millionen jungen Männer, die ich in den Tod schicke. Es ist lächerlich, ... von mir zu verlangen, daß ich nur die wirklichen Verbrecher unter den Kommunisten festsetze. Es ist diese feige bürgerliche Inkonsequenz, sich mit einem Rechtsverfahren die Gewissen zu beruhigen. Es gibt nur *ein* Recht, das Lebensrecht der Nation ... Ich muß Dinge tun, die nicht mit dem Maßstab bürgerlicher Zimperlichkeit zu beurteilen sind. Dieser Reichstagbrand gibt mir den Anlaß einzugreifen. Und ich werde eingreifen. ... Die Welt wird nur mit Furcht regiert.[240]

They regard me as an uneducated barbarian. Yes, we are barbarians! We want to be barbarians! It is an honorable title. *We* shall rejuvenate the world! This world is near its end. It is our mission to cause unrest. . . .

These people thought I would handle them with kid gloves, that I would be satisfied with speeches. We are not in a position to dally with humane feelings, nor can I undertake tedious investigations into anyone's good-will or innocence. We must shake off all sentimentality and be hard. Some day, when I order war, I shall not be in a position to hesitate because of the ten million young men I shall be sending to their death. It is preposterous to expect me to look only for the real criminals among the Communists. It is just like the cowardly, inconsistent *bourgeoisie* to pacify their consciences with legal proceedings. There is only *one* legal right, the nation's right to live.

. . . I must do things that cannot be measured with the yardstick of *bourgeois* squeamishness. This Reichstag fire gives me the opportunity to intervene. And I shall intervene. . . .

The world can only be ruled by fear.[240]

Hitler's response to threatening stimuli was especially reflected in the realm of his racial aggression policy and his unscrupulous, compulsive drive of destruction. His sentiments were frequently projected in his definition of the NS Weltanschauung – as, for example, in his speech at the Reichsparteitag in Nuremberg, in September 1933, entitled 'Nationalsozialismus als Weltanschauung':

Der Nationalsozialismus ist eine Weltanschauung. Indem er die ihrer innersten Veranlagung nach zu dieser Weltanschauung gehörenden Menschen erfaßt und in eine organische Gemeinschaft bringt, wird er zur Partei derjenigen, die eigentlich ihrem Wesen nach einer bestimmten Rasse zuzusprechen sind.[241]

----

National Socialism is a Weltanschauung. While it seizes those persons whose inner-most make-up causes them to share this Weltanschauung and brings them into a natural community, National Socialism becomes a party of those who, in accordance with their disposition, are to be considered of a certain race.[241]

Hitler apparently 'felt' that the source of those ego-threatening feelings
and ideas to which he reacted with aggressions, preoccupations, obsessions, etc., could be alleviated by the destruction of individuals or
groups whom he believed to be their chief carriers. According to
Treher:

> ... Hitler lived in a world of his own – with his own laws,
> norms and values which had little or almost no connection
> with mundane reality situations. Hitler's anti-ego is the Jew,
> to him this is reality just as his mission to which he was select-
> ed by the 'Vorsehung', namely to become the leader of the
> German 'Volk'. It appears that Hitler's obsessions mobilized
> his defense-mechanism which in turn produced a pattern of
> systematized schizophrenic murder (in defense). With his
> leadership principle, i.e., by means of a hierarchic chain of
> responsibility, he wanted to lead the nation to immortal heights
> using measures such as mass murder and world conquest. Im-
> mortality he sought to achieve by mass destruction. This points
> into the direction of a true schizophrenic coincidentia opposito-
> rum. *[242]

Himmler, the 'Gefolgsmann' and a man of limited creativity, and his
SS, bore in a most striking fashion the stamp of Hitler's ideology. The
SS was conceived to a large extent by Hitler and his disciple Himmler
as a natural and biological élite, a new ruling class of the Nazi aristocracy, essential in providing the leadership necessary to establish and
maintain the 'new order' in a German dominated anti-Bolshevistic,
'united' Europe.[243] To the SS was assigned the responsibility for the
'elimination of all racially and biologically inferior elements and the
radical removal of all incorrigible political opposition that refuses on
principle to acknowledge the ideological basis of the National Socialist
state and its essential institutions.'[244] Ever since Hitler's leadership of
the NS party, the main enemy was conceived to be, as Himmler put it,
'the Jewish-Bolshevistic revolution of subhumans.'[245] Himmler consider-

---

* According to Prof. Dr. Hans Karl von Hassenbach, Hitler's personal assistant
surgeon, Hitler did not suffer from schizophrenia at any time. He had been
ill in 1936 and from August to September 1944 suffered from Icterus. Later he
showed symptoms of Parkinson's disease in an early stage. This information
was given by von Hasselbach to Prof. Dr. Eduard Baumgarten in two written
statements of February 4 and 9, 1975.

ed the foremost task of the 'Schutzstaffel' to be essentially an anti-Bolshevistic combat organization:

> Wir werden dafür sorgen, daß niemals in Deutschland, dem Herzen Europas, von innen oder durch Emissäre von außen her die jüdisch-bolschewistische Revolution des Untermenschen entfacht werden kann. Unbarmherzig werden wir für alle diese Kräfte, deren Existenz und Treiben wir kennen, am Tage auch nur des geringsten Versuches, sei er heute, sei er in Jahrzehnten oder in Jahrhunderten, ein gnadeloses Richtschwert sein.[246]

> We shall take care that never again in Germany, the heart of Europe, will the Jewish-Bolshevistic revolution of subhumans be able to be kindled either from within or through emissaries from without. Without pity we shall be a merciless sword of justice for all those forces whose existence and activity we know, on the day of the slightest attempt, may it be today, may it be in decades or may it be in centuries.[246]

Thus it can be understood why it was exceedingly difficult for all members of the SS to separate themselves from these convictions. After the beginning of the war against Russia this enemy was also to be eradicated from all of Europe. It was a struggle between 'Nordic-Germanic Europe' and the 'Jewish-Bolshevik imperialism of subhumans.'[247] After the war the SS apologists, especially strongly represented in the ranks of the 'Waffen-SS' veterans association (HIAG),[248] stressed that they saw it as their foremost task – and that it was their privilege to be the first – to save Europe and Western civilization from being overrun by 'Asiatic Communist hordes.'[249] It is conceivable that the ideological indoctrination of the SS was reflected in the manner in which its 'Ämter' and 'Hauptämter' operated and, last but not least, in the distinctive unrelenting fighting style of the 'Waffen-SS.'[250] In the military leadership of the 'Waffen-SS,' the ideological emphasis was placed more on German nationalism, political influence and power, specifically the realization of the idea of an anti-Communist united Europe dominated by Germany, rather than on Hitler's and Himmler's racist lines.[251] There appears to be a consensus among the interviewed

'Waffen-SS' officers and men, who claim (ex post facto) that Himmler's 'unrealistic ideological rantings' were generally not taken seriously and that his romantic whims were accepted as a necessary evil and merely laughed off. Even if this was the case among the men of the 'Waffen-SS,' this view does not seem to have been that of officers and men of other SS formations, and also not of those who had volunteered for membership during the early stage of the organization.[252] The actions of those members of the SS, running concentration camps, ghettos, slave labor or destruction camps, behind the desk or in the camp proper, presupposed at least a certain measure of identification with the racist ideology – with NS ideology in general.[253] Without this attitude such close cooperation or collaboration with initiators, administrators, and executives of the destruction programs such as the 'Final Solution' would not have been possible.[254] However, in one of his weaker moments the commandant of Auschwitz, SS-Obersturmbannführer Höss, admitted:

> Wohl stand für uns alle der Führer-Befehl unverrückbar fest, auch daß die SS ihn durchführen mußte. Doch in allen nagten geheime Zweifel. Und ich selbst durfte auf keinen Fall meine gleichen Zweifel bekennen. Ich mußte mich, um die Beteiligten zum psychischen Durchhalten zu zwingen, felsenfest von der Notwendigkeit der Durchführung dieses grausam-harten Befehls überzeugt zeigen.[255]

> There was no doubt in the mind of any of us that Hitler's order had to be obeyed regardless, and that it was the duty of the SS to carry it out. Nevertheless we were all tormented by secret doubts.
> I myself dared not admit to such doubts. In order to make my subordinates carry on with their tasks, it was psychologically essential that I myself appear convinced of the necessity for this gruesomely harsh order.[255]

This somewhat ambivalent attitude towards the tasks concerned with persecution, concentration, or destruction appears to have its origin in the marked dichotomy of value-norms. The value-norms introduced by leading Nazi ideologists, especially during the thirties, stood in vivid contrast to traditional ones. It was these latter, however, that had, at least partially, molded the perpetrators' attitudes during their formative age. Even in high SS circles this dichotomy was manifest. In this connection it also seems apparent that a close relationship existed between the ambivalent attitude of the initiators (as well as perpetrators) and the introduction of euphemisms, code communications, and general language, i.e., 'Sprachregelung,' used by them in connection with killing and mass extermination orders. The effect of the NS indoctrination, in which the 'Sprachregelung' played an important role and contributed to this ambivalence, was expressed by von dem Bach-Zelewski during his cross-examination before the IMT on January 7, 1946:

> Wenn man jahrelang predigt, jahrzehntelang predigt, daß die slawische Rasse eine Unterrasse ist, daß die Juden überhaupt keine Menschen sind, dann muß es zu einer solchen Explosion kommen.[256]

> ⸻

> If for years, indeed for decades, you hear that the Slavs are inferior, that the Jews are not even human, then it must be expected that such an explosion is bound to occur.[256]

Yet – in spite of it – a sizable number of higher SS leaders and party functionaries had apparently assisted in the protection of Jews, especially Jewish 'Mischlinge,' from persecution or deportation to concentration camps. Himmler admitted this in his speech to the Gruppenführer during the Gruppenführertagung in Posen on October 4, 1943:

> ... – 'Das jüdische Volk wird ausgerottet', sagt ein jeder Parteigenosse, 'ganz klar, steht in unserem Programm, Ausschaltung der Juden, Ausrottung, machen wir.' Und dann kommen sie alle an, die braven 80 Millionen Deutschen, und jeder hat seinen anständigen Juden. Es ist ja klar, die anderen sind Schweine, aber dieser ist ein prima Jude.[257]

> ⸻

> ... – 'The Jewish people is to be destroyed,' says every party comrade. 'That is quite clear, it is in our program: elimination of the Jews, their destruction. We'll do that.' And they all come, our 80 million good Germans, and each one has his

decent Jew. It is clear, the others are swine (Schweine), but this one is a first-class Jew.[257]

This shows that the integration of NS values, especially the racist one, was not as complete as Himmler or other National Socialist extremists within or outside the SS might have wished. In other words, in spite of Himmler's dictum: 'Ich bin überzeugt von der Weltanschauung, daß letzten Endes in der Welt nur das gute Blut, auf die Dauer gesehen, die beste Leistung hervorbringt,'[258] many members of the 'Black Order' were not at all convinced of the validity of this Weltanschauung, let alone had integrated it into their ideas.[259] Yet these men actively took part in other endeavors leading to aggression and destruction, and indirectly supported, tolerated, or merely disregarded those ego-threatening situations which they felt were of no direct concern to them.[260] Obviously they must have been drawn into the SS by other, to them more attractive, elements which made up the SS Weltanschauung.

This eclecticism within the SS appears to have been far stronger than many otherwise objective students of the SS are willing to admit. As far as this writer was able to ascertain in his research (interviews and 234 questionnaires), to a large extent this eclecticism was reflected in the respective position and capacity in which SS officers and men had served. The research results also indicate that it was quite frequently within the SS-men's discretion to choose their field of activity in the organization or to find ways and means to avoid disagreeable assignments as, for example, service in concentration camps or action groups (Einsatzgruppen). This choice of an alternative was dependent not so much upon rules and regulations or upon unconditional obedience, based on a hierarchical chain of command, but more upon the individual's measure of courage, sound logic, and ability to interpret perceived events impartially. Yet it should be obvious that in spite of these attributes, deviation from organizational constraints prevalent in Nazi institutions, especially the SS, was not a simple act but indeed a perilous one. An incident experienced by this writer in Ehrenforst, where the slave labor camp of Blechhammer was located, in the spring of 1944, corroborates this view: After a cabaret performance in which camp life was parodied and which was staged by a group of inmates some of whom were professional actors, one of the SS NCOs and SD members present spontaneously stood up and declared to the

SS and inmate audience: 'Man sagt uns immer, was für ein Abschaum der Menschheit, was für Ungeziefer Ihr seid; wer aber unter diesen Umständen so eine glänzende Vorstellung geben kann und sich so verhält wie Ihr, verdient größte Hochachtung und Bewunderung' ['We have always been told that you are vermin and the scum of humanity; yet, who, under these circumstances, can give such a brilliant performance and conducts himself as you have deserves highest respect and admiration']. Shortly afterwards, this SD-man and SS-Scharführer disappeared from the camp and it was said that he had been transferred.

We are confronted with a somewhat more complex situation when we examine the personality-profile and attitude of members of the execution squads of the 'Einsatzgruppen,' and of those who were directly concerned with the killing of prisoners. Many of these men were either deliberately misinformed by the SS leadership about the extent of the crime and objective guilt of those who were to be executed, or so thoroughly indoctrinated that they were able to identify themselves with their role. Others may have come into the units emotionally unprepared, naive, and without a realistic expectation of the duties which were awaiting them, or they may have been simply coerced.[261] Himmler did his best to indoctrinate all those to be assigned to these or similar tasks and presented the following viewpoint to stimulate those who were to be sent to the Eastern Front to aggression and violence:

> On the other side stands a population of 180 millions, a mixture of races, whose very names are unpronounceable, and whose physique is such that one can shoot them down without pity and compassion. These animals that torture and ill-treat every prisoner from our side, every wounded man that they come across and do not treat them the way decent soldiers would, you will see for yourself. These people have been welded by the Jews into one religion, one ideology, that is called Bolshevism, with the task: now we have Russia, half of Asia, a part of Europe, now we will overwhelm Germany and the whole world.[262]

It stands to reason that this kind of indoctrination was not limited to members of the 'Waffen-SS' or 'Totenkopfverbände' but was applied in an equal measure to all SS formations and parts of the German populace which could be reached by NS propagandists. The SS indoctrination was reinforced by 'Das Schwarze Korps' and the NS press in general. As far as it could be established by this writer in interviews with former members of the SS, the most frequently read papers were *Der Völkische Beobachter, Das Reich, Das Schwarze Korps,* and, by those holding non-commissioned or lower ranks, especially among the 'Totenkopfverbände' and police units, Streicher's *Der Stürmer.* [263] For the most sophisticated, propagandistic material was disseminated by organizations such as the *Nationalsozialistische Monatshefte (Wissenschaftliche Zeitschrift der NSDAP),* published by Adolf Hitler and edited by Alfred Rosenberg. Some of the more representative and well-known titles of this monthly periodical were:

| | |
|---|---|
| No. 14, May 1931: | 'Der nationale und soziale Verrat der SPD'. |
| No. 17, August 1931: | 'Neuer Adel. Bauer in Not!' |
| No. 24, March 1932: | 'Rassenhygiene'. |
| No. 25, April 1932: | 'Hitler gegen das "System" '. |
| No. 26, May 1932: | 'Kampf um den Osten'. |
| No. 34, January 1933: | 'Ein abschließendes Wort zur Judenfrage'. |
| No. 37, April 1933: | 'Novemberverbrecher'. [264] |

| | |
|---|---|
| No. 34, January 1933: | 'The National and Social Treason of the SPD' (German Social Democratic Party); |
| No. 14, May 1931: | 'New Nobility. Farmer in Need'; |
| No. 17, August 1931: | 'Racial Hygiene'; |
| No. 24, March 1932: | 'Hitler against the "System" '; |
| No. 25, April 1932: | 'Struggle for the East'; |
| No. 26, May 1932: | 'A Final Word on the Jewish Question'; |
| No. 37, April 1933: | 'November Criminals'. |

On a somewhat lower level of sophistication were the *Schulungsbriefe des Reichsschulungsamtes der NSDAP und der Deutschen Arbeitsfront* to which a broader indoctrinating function was ascribed. The following titles can be cited as examples:

| | |
|---|---|
| No. 3, August 1933: | 'Die Schutzfärbung; unsere Führer!'. |

No. 4, September 1933:   'Parteidisziplin; der zweite **Punkt im**
                          Parteiprogramm der NSDAP.'.
No. 8, August 1937:      'Friedrich Nietzsche, der unerbitt-
                          liche Werter des neunzehnten Jahr-
                          hunderts'. [265]

---

No. 3, August 1933:      'Friedrich Nietzsche, der unerbitt-
No. 4, September 1933:   'Party Discipline; the Second Point
                          in the Party Program of the NSDAP';
No. 8, August 1937:      'Friedrich Nietzsche, the Relentless
                          Assessor of the 19th Century'.

The systematic dissemination of prejudicial ideas and discriminative measures justifying acts of terror and persecution was often accepted by the masses. So, in fact, were those playing a major role in these practices. Thus no decisive opposition arose. In addition, psychological defense-mechanisms, such as displacement, repression, regression, and rationalization, began to play an increasingly important role. Although the intensity of reaction to and effect of indoctrination and propaganda differed widely, it was to a large extent possible to alleviate the capacity for concern. So, for example, Speer responded in the following words in an interview with staff-members of the news magazine *Der Spiegel* when confronted with the statement:

> 'Manche Zeithistoriker, die sich mit Ihrer Rolle im Dritten Reich beschäftigt haben, bescheinigen Ihnen persönliche Integrität aber zugleich die Amoral eines in seiner Sachwelt befangenen Technokraten – also die Verhaltensweise eines Mannes, der Charakter wahrt, aber sich gegenüber dem Terror, etwa in den Konzentrationslagern, verschließt, als fände dieser gar nicht statt, . . .'
>
> (Speer) 'Ja, es war das fundamental Falsche in dieser Zeit, daß man sich von den Ereignissen separierte, die einem unangenehm waren. Man fühlte sich nur verantwortlich für einen Sektor.' [266]

---

Many a contemporary historian who has concerned himself with your role in the Third Reich testifies to your personal integrity, but also to the amorality of a technocrat who is trapped in his sphere of activity – that is, the behavioral pattern of a man who maintains strength of character, but closes his eyes to terror, as in the concentration camps, as if such did not exist, . . .

(Speer) 'Yes, there was something fundamentally wrong about this time that caused one to separate oneself from the events that were unpleasant. One felt responsible only for one's own sector.' [266]

In conclusion, it should be stressed that there were indeed ways and means to resist or at least neutralize indoctrination leading to acts of violence and crimes against humanity, or as the French prosecutor François de Menthon called it, 'crimes against the human status.' [267] As mentioned earlier, an ability to resist was largely dependent upon such factors as individual difference, primary milieu, IQ, personality profile, educational and professional background, etc. So, for example, interviews with officers and men who had been trained or had served under the command of the unorthodox SS-Obergruppenführer and General of the 'Waffen-SS' Felix Steiner have revealed that, as far as could be established, almost no one had served, before or at a later date, in any capacity in concentration camps, Eicke's Death's Head formation or division, 'Einsatzgruppen,' or 'Sonderkommandos.' Furthermore, there appears to be an understanding – if not a consensus – among 224 interviewed SS officers and men of all ranks that ways and means could be found to avoid assignments to the above-mentioned formations and commands, including duty in concentration camps. Or one could at least obtain a transfer to regular SS combat units. [268] This realistic alternative has been frequently denied, especially by those individuals who served in some capacity in these non-military commands or formations. The most common justifications given for reluctance to apply for a transfer or seek to avoid such commands were: too severe institutional constraints, strict obedience to orders, ignorance of rules and regulations or means to effect such a transfer, belief in the necessity for and identification with measures applied in concentration camps or destruction commands, unrealistic expectations (or aspirations) as to the duty and conditions prevailing in camps or extermination squads, intimidation by superiors, lack of courage, and finally, the appeal of serving in a secure post rather than in regular combat units.

Thus the so-called 'Befehlsnotstand' – so frequently appealed to before German courts – was applicable only in a minority of cases. It appears that the readiness of SS personnel to serve in concentration camps or special commands must have been due not only to the institutionalization of mass murder but also to Himmler's successful strategy of socializing the SS to the NS ideology, the legitimized myth system. Himmler's strategies of indoctrination had enhanced the swift uncritical execution of orders, especially in situations of stress. Moreover it had increased the totalitarian potential of the NS leadership and, permitting a more successful manipulative activity, lowered the capacity for concern, not only for basic human rights in general, but particularly for those of the outgroups, by delimiting the actors' opportunity to choose *alternative* social roles.

## 11.  *The perception of God in the SS*

The 'Schutzstaffel' was not only a political and military organization. It was also one of the militant, quasi-religious orders of the twentieth century, with its own image of the absolute and a creed called 'gottgläubig,' which did not develop beyond its initial stage. In this connection Himmler stated:

> Alles ist noch im Fluß. Wir ringen selbst noch um die letzte Form. Von erwachsenen Menschen kann man verlangen, daß sie an dem Ringen teilnehmen, auch auf die Gefahr hin, daß sie einige Zeit sozusagen formlos dahinleben müssen. [269]

> ... Everything is still in a state of flux. We're struggling towards a final form of belief. You can expect mature men to take part in this struggle and to share the dangers of having no fixed creed. [269]

The creed stated that the members believed in God (whom they called 'der Uralte' or 'Altvater'), [270] in Germany, '... and in the Führer Adolf Hitler whom He has sent to us.' [271] Himmler asserted to Kersten:

> Er (Hitler) ist dazu von dem Karma des Germanentums der

Welt vorbestimmt, den Kampf gegen den Osten zu führen und
das Germanentum der Welt zu retten, eine der ganz großen
Lichtgestalten hat in ihm ihre Inkarnation gefunden. ... zu
dem nach Jahrhunderten die Menschen ebenso gläubig auf-
schauen würden, wie sie es zu Christus getan hätten.[272]

... – It has been ordained by the Karma of the Germanic
world that he [Hitler] should wage war against the East and
save the Germanic peoples – a figure of the greatest brilliance
has become incarnate in his person. ... whom men would
regard in centuries to come with the same reverence that they
had accorded to Christ. [272]

The 'Schutzstaffel,' under Himmler's leadership, regarded itself as the
'elect' (auserwählt) who were called upon to assist the 'Führer' in his
great task.

... unsere innere und äußere Situation drängte einfach auf die
Zusammenlegung zwischen Reichsführer-SS und Chef der
Polizei, das war eben auch ein Karma, mit dem ich (Himmler)
mich abfinden und daß ich selbst zu meinen Gunsten wenden
muß.[273]

... But the present state of things both at home and abroad
demands the fusion of Reichsführer SS and Chief of Police –
that, too, is a Karma, which I [Himmler] must come to terms
with and turn to my own use.[273]

Himmler believed himself to be the reincarnation of Heinrich der
Löwe* and felt elated when his SS men referred to him as 'König Heinrich' or 'Der schwarze Herzog.'[274] Himmler read and held in high
esteem the Bhagavad-Gita, the Eddas, the Veda, the Rig-Veda, the
speeches of Buddha, the Visudi-Magga, the Book of Purity, and various
astrological writings.[275] In contrast to his previous persuasion, Himmler now adhered to the Indo-German belief and became an advocate of
reincarnation.

* Henry the Lion, Duke of Saxony and Bavaria (1129-1195).

Die Indogermanen glauben an die Wiedergeburt. Mit *einem* Leben ist das Leben nicht zu Ende. Was der Mensch an guten, aber auch an schlechten Taten auf dieser Erde vollbracht hat, wirkt sich im nächsten Leben als sein Karma aus, das für ihn wiederum nicht ein unerbittliches Schicksal ist, sondern mit dem er fertig werden und es wenden kann. Es entspricht germanischem Denken, nicht der Gnade ausgeliefert zu sein, sondern zu wissen, was Du hier getan hast, wird für Dich oder gegen Dich zeugen, Du entrinnst nicht. Du hast aber die Möglichkeit, durch Deine eigene Kraft in einem neuen Leben das Schicksal zu wenden. [276]

---

The Indo-Germanic peoples believe in rebirth. Life doesn't come to an end with *one* experience of it. The good and evil deeds which man does on this earth affect his next life in the form of his Karma, which is not an inexorable fate, but one which he can control and alter. The Germanic belief entails no surrender to divine grace, but the knowledge that what you have done on this earth will witness for you or against you, inescapably. But you have a chance to alter your fate by your own efforts in a new life. [276]

However, this doctrine did not deter him from persecuting theosophists and anthroposophists whose conviction in some respects was not all too different from the one he now professed. [277] At this point Himmler strictly rejected the teachings of the Catholic Church and characterized it as

... eine Aktiengesellschaft, in der die Hauptaktionäre seit ihrem Bestehen – also immerhin fast zweitausend Jahre – hundert- und tausendprozentige Gewinne ziehen und nichts dafür geben. Dieser Riesenbetrugs-AG gegenüber sind die Versicherungsgesellschaften, die immer dann, wenn man etwas von ihnen will, darauf hinweisen, daß dies nicht im Kontrakt stehe, kleine harmlose Anfänger im Betrügen. ...

Überall finden Sie in den entscheidenden Momenten den Eingriff von zwei großen Weltmächten, der katholischen Kirche und der Juden. Beide streben die Weltherrschaft an, sind sich im Grunde spinnefeind, aber im Kampf gegen das Germanentum sind sie sich einig. Die eine dieser Mächte haben wir wenigstens für Deutschland beseitigt, mit der anderen werden wir nach dem großen Kriege abrechnen. Heute sind uns leider die Hände gebunden, aus diplomatischer Klugheit müssen wir mit unseren wahren Gefühlen zurückhalten, aber diese Zeiten werden sich ändern. Dann werden wir den Pfaffen die Kutten ausziehen, da hilft ihnen kein Gott und auch keine Jungfrau Maria. Am liebsten möchte ich einmal selbst hier in Rom unter dem Pfaffenvolk aufräumen und mit dem Heiligen Vater abrechnen. . . .

Ich bewundere die Weisheit der indischen Religionsstifter, die von ihren Königen und höchsten Würdenträgern verlangten, daß sie sich jedes Jahr für zwei bis drei Monate zur Meditation in ein Kloster zurückzogen. Solche Einrichtungen werden wir später auch schaffen.[278]

―――

. . . a corporation from which the chief shareholders – since its foundation and for nearly two thousand years – draw a hundred or a thousand per cent profit and give nothing in return. Insurance companies which always say that it's not in the contract whenever you make a claim are mere novices in the art of deception compared with this gigantic swindle.

. . . In every crisis you'll trace the influence of two great world powers, the Catholic Church and the Jews. They're both striving for world leadership, basically hostile to each other, only united in their struggle against the Germanic peoples. We've already removed one of these powers, at least from Germany; the time will come to settle accounts with the other after the war. At the moment, unfortunately, our hands are tied; diplomatic caution demands that we should mask our real feelings, but this will change. Then we'll unfrock these priests – neither their God nor their Virgin Mary will be able to do a thing for them then. What I'd like best would be to liquidate the clergy here in Rome and settle accounts with the Holy Father. . . .

. . . I admire the wisdom of those Indian religions that insisted that their kings and high state officials should withdraw and meditate in a monastery for two or three months every year. One day we'll institute something on those lines.[278]

Many high leaders of the SS, however, perceived their task as primarily military and political. The religious notions preached to them by Himmler were often viewed as a mystical romanticism which had to be tolerated as one of his idiosyncrasies.[279] But to Hitler, undoubtedly, National Socialism was, to be sure, something more than a political movement and even more than a religion. Already in 1934 Hitler declared to Rauschning:

> Wer den Nationalsozialismus nur als politische Bewegung versteht, weiß fast nichts von ihm. Er ist mehr noch als Religion: er ist der Wille zur neuen Menschenschöpfung.[280]
>
> ———
>
> . . . Those who see in National Socialism nothing more than a political movement know scarcely anything of it. It is more even than a religion: it is the will to create mankind anew.[280]

Hitler perceived himself not only as a statesman, lawmaker, artist, and city architect but also as a prophet and founder of a new religion.[281] His new 'Menschheitsreligion' was to create a new 'Menschheit.' The prototype of the new man, to be fashioned by his order, was to have the characteristics of

> wehrhafte Ritter, kluge Verwaltungsmänner, zugleich aber geistliche Leute, die ihre 'Heimlichkeit' haben, ein der profanen Welt verborgenes Wissen, eine hierarchische Ordnung . . .[282]
>
> ———
>
> . . . armed knights, who had to be capable administrators but also formed a priesthood with its mysteries (Heimlichkeit), a hierarchical organization with a knowledge hidden from the profane world.[282]

functioning under a specific type of leadership. In essence Hitler envisioned the future man as fearless and cruel.[283] The SA had proved unsuitable for this purpose. Among its members there were hardly any individuals fit to become members of a secret priesthood, capable in times of danger to preserve and safeguard the seeds of an ideology which would serve the German nation until the time when its members would have become more receptive to new modes of perception.[284]

The first attempts to develop such types were made in the various newly established 'Junkerschulen,' led by Reichsleiter Ley and later by Himmler and his deputies in the training centers of the 'SS-Verfügungstruppen.' On an even higher level, the so-called 'Ordensburgen' were established under Himmler's immediate supervision.[285]

Hitler was not interested in offering the young future leaders an intellectual education, for he held that knowledge despoils the youth.[286] Hitler preferred the learning process to be based on their 'natural play-drive activity.'[287] The future heroic youth was to learn self-discipline and the overcoming of the fear of death:

> In meinen Ordensburgen wird eine Jugend heranwachsen, vor der sich die Welt erschrecken wird. Eine gewalttätige, herrische, unerschrockene, grausame Jugend will ich ... Es darf nichts Schwaches und Zärtliches an ihr sein ...
> In meinen Ordensburgen wird der schöne, sich selbst gebietende Gottmensch als kultisches Bild stehen und die Jugend auf die kommende Stufe der männlichen Reife vorbereiten.[288]
>
> ---
>
> '... In my Ordensburgen a young generation will grow up before which the world will shrink back. A violently active, dominating, intrepid, brutal youth – that is what I am after. ... There must be no weakness or tenderness in it. ...
> ... In my academies the figure of the magnificent, self-ordaining godman will stand as an idol; it will prepare the young men for their coming period of ripe manhood.'[288]

To complete his religious mission, the new Aryan 'super-religion' was to be rendered more veritable by substituting Nordic paganism for the Judeo-Christian traditional elements prevalent in contemporary German culture. Hitler, who never ceased to pay his church tax, wanted to sacrifice his life for the nation in its hour of greatest danger: '... ich muß mich dem Volk in der Stunde der höchsten Gefahr zum Opfer geben.'[289] By this act Hitler apparently intended to become the Third Reich's Aryan, Germanic prophet-savior. Himmler, whom Hitler regarded somewhat as a modern Ignatius von Loyola,[290] not only created and forged this new militant order, pledging unswerving obedience to Hitler, but was also ready to build SS cloisters. Of special note is the Wewelsburg near Paderborn in Westfalia, which was to be used in his honor.[291] In this renovated castle of the Middle Ages, annual, secret consistories were held by members of the inner cricle. Here they were to meditate and hold occult exercises. In the large council hall every member of this consistory occupied his own chair, to which a silver plate with his name and insignia was fastened.[292]

Hitler had made it clear to his confidants that he wanted to see Christianity exterminated in Germany.[293] To him the Christian faith was Jewish and therefore weak. The Christian morality of compassion was to be supplanted by a heroic creed, the belief in the God of nature, the God of one's own nation, destiny, and blood.[294] Jesus could not be very well converted into an Aryan, so for the cross was to be substituted the swastika and for the holy blood of the Savior, the 'pure blood' of the Germanic tribe.[295] Nevertheless, the Catholic Church as an institution, having survived, after all, for two thousand years, was to serve as a model for the new Nazi religion.[296] Wodan, the age-old hunter, and Thor, the god of thunder, once again were to return from oblivion and with them heathen customs and traditions; the eternal flame was to burn again on the hearth (Herd).[297]

Hitler's aim was to free men from the compulsion of an

> . . . Selbstzweck gewordenen Geistes; von den schmutzigen und erniedrigenden Selbstpeinigungen einer Gewissen und Moral genannten Chimäre und von den Ansprüchen einer Freiheit und persönlichen Selbständigkeit, denen immer nur ganz wenige gewachsen sein können.
>
> Der christlichen Lehre von der unendlichen Bedeutung der menschlichen Einzelseele und der persönlichen Verantwortung setze ich mit eiskalter Klarheit die erlösende Lehre von der Nichtigkeit und Unbedeutendheit des einzelnen Menschen und seines Fortlebens in der sichtbaren Unsterblichkeit der Nation gegenüber. An die Stelle des Dogmas von dem stellvertretenden Leiden und Sterben eines göttlichen Erlösers tritt das stellvertretende Leben und Handeln des neuen Führergesetzgebers, das die Masse der Gläubigen von der Last der freien Entscheidung entbindet.[298]

———

... intelligence that has taken charge; from the dirty and degrading self-mortifications of a chimera called conscience and morality, and from the demands of a freedom and personal independence which only a very few can bear.

To the Christian doctrine of personal responsibility and infinite significance of the individual human soul, I oppose uncompromisingly the saving doctrine of the nothingness and insignificance of the individual human being and his continued existence in the visible immortality of the nation. The dogma of vicarious suffering and death through a divine savior gives place to that of the representative living and acting of the new leader-legislator, which liberates the mass of the faithful from the burden of the free.[298]

Hitler's notion of a new German cult is developed even more clearly in another comment made to Rauschning: 'Has it not occurred to you that the Jews are the counterpart of the German in everything and all and yet they are so much alike as only two brothers can be?' Shortly afterwards he answered his own question by saying: 'There cannot exist two chosen peoples. We are the people of God ... two worlds are confronted with each other! The man of God (Gottesmensch) and the man of Satan! (Satansmensch). The Jew is man's antagonist, the anti-man. The Jew is the creature of another God. The Aryan and the Jew have their stand opposite each other and if I call the one man, I have to give the other a different name. They are so far apart from each other as the animal from man. Not that I would call the Jew an animal. He stands much farther apart from the animal than the Aryans do. He is a being alien to nature and apart from nature (naturfernes Wesen).'[299]

Hitler denied the existence of a Jewish religion. As he had written in *Mein Kampf* there exists only a Jewish race disguised as religious community:

Das Judentum war immer ein Volk mit bestimmten rassischen Eigenarten und niemals eine Religion, nur sein Fortkommen ließ es schon frühzeitig nach einem Mittel suchen, das die unangenehme Aufmerksamkeit in Bezug auf seine Angehörigen zu zerstreuen vermochte. Welches Mittel aber wäre zweckmäßiger und zugleich harmloser gewesen als die Einschiebung des geborgten Begriffs der Religionsgemeinschaft? Denn auch hier ist alles entlehnt, besser gestohlen – aus dem ursprünglichen eigenen Wesen kann der Jude eine religiöse Einrichtung schon deshalb nicht besitzen, da ihm der Idealismus in jeder Form fehlt und damit auch der Glaube an ein Jenseits vollkommen fremd ist. Man kann sich aber eine Religion nach arischer Auffassung nicht vorstellen, der die Überzeugung des Fortlebens nach dem Tode in irgendeiner Form mangelt. Tatsächlich ist auch der Talmud kein Buch der Vorbereitung für das Jenseits, sondern nur für ein praktisches und erträgliches Leben im Diesseits. Die jüdische Religionslehre ist in erster Linie eine Anweisung zur Reinerhaltung des Blutes des Judentums sowie zur Regelung des Verkehrs der Juden untereinander, mehr aber noch mit der übrigen Welt, mit den Nichtjuden also. [300]

---

The Jews were always a people with definite racial qualities and never a religion, only their success made them look very early for a means which could divert disagreeable attention from their identity. What would have been more useful and at the same time more harmless than pretending to be a religious community? For here, too, everything is purloined, or, rather, stolen because by his own original nature, the Jew cannot possess a religious institution for the very reason that he lacks all idealism in any form and he also does not recognize any belief in the hereafter. In the Aryan conception, one cannot conceive of a religion which lacks the conviction that life will continue after death in some form. Indeed, the Talmud is not a book of preparation for the life to come but rather for a practical and bearable life in this world.

The Jewish religious doctrine is primarily directions for preserving the purity of Jewish blood. It regulates Jews' intercourse with one another, with the rest of the world, that is, and especially with non-Jews. [300]

This passage not only indicates with great clarity Hitler's attitude towards the Jewish minority but also delineates the policy which was to guide the subsequent anti-Judaic measures after his rise to power. In essence we find embodied in it what later became known as the Nuremberg racial laws. Therewith, anyone defined by Hitler – and after 1933 by the Régime's administrators – as Jewish was deprived of the right to become affiliated with a denomination of his choice which would also have met with official approval and recognition. Furthermore, according to Hitler's notion, religious affiliation was predestined by racial characteristics rather than determined by religious contemplation and identification with a specific creed. In short, this implied that only Aryans (ari-stos) could find salvation.

Thus it can be understood why Himmler, in establishing the SS as an order, not only provided it with certain racial rules and regulations based on the religious philosophies of NS leaders – as, for example, Hitler, Darré, Rosenberg, and others – but also posited a new metaphysics as a substitute for the Judeo-Christian heritage from which he derived religious and ethical principles. Had he merely claimed that this new faith was custom-tailored to bind together the members of the new order, perhaps a certain degree of tolerance and forbearance towards the other groups and individuals would have been the result. The harshness, intolerance, and brutality of the SS towards others had their origin precisely in the claim and conviction that such actions were in accordance with what members of the SS understood to be the eternal and immutable laws of the universe and nature which had their origin in God or Providence. Himmler, Bormann and other high-ranking party members frequently stated that they believed in the existence of God or that they were affiliated with a religious denomination designated as 'gottgläubig.'[301] According to Kersten, Himmler's opinion was:

Schon die bloße Vernunft muß einem sagen, daß hinter all dem Werden der Natur, hinter dieser wunderbaren Anordnung, wie wir sie im Menschen-, Tier- und Pflanzenreich finden, ein planendes höheres Wesen stehen muß, mögen wir das nun Gott oder die Vorsehung oder sonst irgendwie nennen.[302]

——

... Surely common sense must tell you that some higher being – whether you call it God or Providence or anything else you like – is behind nature and the marvellous order which exists in the world of men and animals and plants.[302]

So, as an example, in April 1945, Himmler wrote to a friend about his unusual conversion:

> Ich weiß, ... daß ich allgemein als ein unbesonnener Heide betrachtet werde, aber im Grunde meines Herzens bin ich ein Gläubiger: ich glaube an Gott und die Vorsehung. Im Laufe des letzten Jahres habe ich wieder an Wunder zu glauben gelernt. Die Rettung des Führers am 20. Juli war ein Wunder, und ein weiteres habe ich in meinem eigenen Leben just in diesem Frühling erfahren ...[303]

> I know ... that I am generally regarded as a heedless pagan, but in the depth of my heart I am a believer; I believe in God and Providence. In the course of the last year I have learned to believe in miracles again. The Führer's escape on the 20th of July was a miracle; and I have experienced another in my life, this very spring ...[303]

SS ideology (being identical with NS ideology) and active Christian faith were considered incompatible. During World War II, this rule was largely ignored. For instance, it was possible to fight in the ranks of the 'Waffen-SS' and to receive the sacraments of one's church.[304] In fact, Himmler stressed that atheists were not tolerated in the SS:

> Wenn ich von meinen SS-Männern verlange, daß sie gottgläubig sein müssen, ist das nicht, wie mir dies oft ausgelegt wird, eine Tarnung oder eine Konzession, sondern es ist mir damit sehr ernst. Menschen, die kein höheres Wesen oder eine Vorsehung oder wie sie das sonst nennen wollen, anerkennen, möchte ich nicht in meiner Umgebung haben.[305]

> It's no pretense, nor concession, as is often alleged against me, but a very serious matter, when I insist that members of the SS must believe in God. I'm not going to have men around me who refuse to recognize any higher being or Providence or whatever you like to call it.[305]

The official attitude of the 'Schutzstaffel' toward those who did not believe in God has been defined in instructional material. It was phrased '. . . the Schutzstaffel thinks them to be conceited, to be megalomaniacs and stupid . . .' [306], unfit for membership. God, as perceived by the leaders of the National Socialist movement, was different from God as understood by the various Christian traditions. He was not perceived as the God of love and kindness. He did not even permit the sun to shine upon and the rain to refresh both the strong and the weak. The God of the National Socialists was partial, harsh, and cruel. He was believed to interfere occasionally in the events of history (Vorsehung), but more often he was presumed to remain withdrawn. In the distant past, God was believed to have established certain laws and principles which assured the proper course of history. The struggle for survival was held to be the most basic of all eternal laws. 'Everything in life is struggle. Everything is selection. That which survives in the final analysis through the centuries is always the better and the stronger.' [307] The German nation, and within it the 'Nordic' element, had passed through the test tubes of history and had come out refined, purified, and superior. It was for this reason that Hitler and other Nazi ideologists perceived in the British somewhat of a model. [308] Other nations and peoples in the past had not withstood these rigorous tests, or were in the process of being cast aside, particularly the Jews, the major target of National Socialist aggression. The 'Chosen People' Hitler feared most; they, like the Germans, had survived for thousands of years, thus evidently constituting an existential, ideological, and psychological threat to the universe. [309] The belief of racial superiority preached to the members of the SS kindled in them the certainty that they were the élite, instilling not only arrogance but also the wish to determine the fitness of others to survive. Himmler related that he and his associates had '. . . already during the "Kampfzeit" made it their task, "den Untermenschen niederzuhalten".' [310] This attitude necessitated, as he openly acknowledged, the committing of illegal acts. The sanctions for the unlawful acts committed were derived from '. . . the laws of reason and natural perception. . . .' [311]

As in the majority of religious orders, there existed a hierarchy in the 'Schutzstaffel.' The most fundamental distinction was to be found between officers and enlisted men. In addition, Himmler introduced three honorific symbols, the death's-head ring, the sword, and the dagger. The bestowal of these symbols did not always take place according to fixed norms and criteria. The ring was given primarily to those who had shown great devotion to the 'Schutzstaffel,' both as an organization and as a 'Weltanschauung.' The honorary dagger was bestowed rather arbitrarily, mostly upon higher-ranking leaders of the SS, including 'Ehrenführer' and individuals who, for instance, had participated in the actions of June 30, 1934,[312] or had distinguished themselves in a similar capacity. When an SS candidate received the dagger as a status symbol of his mission, he was accepted into the order and bound to serve faithfully the one who had been sent by 'Him' to lead the 'Ecclesia militans,' that is to say, the SS, and with their assistance the German nation, and eventually all the Aryan peoples of the greater Germanic Reich. The honorary sword reflected the highest mark of distinction, denoting membership in the innermost circle of the 'Schutzstaffel.'[313] Himmler envisaged the entire 'Schutzstaffel' functioning as a kind of hierarchical monastic order, and special distinction was to be placed on obedience, loyalty, and devotion rather than on charismatic gifts. After the war this order was to give the German people a new '. . . upper class (Oberschicht) which would bind this Germanic people and Europe together. . . .'[314] In reality, the mysticism of the 'Schutzstaffel' reinforced the original purpose of this institution, namely to proliferate the National Socialist system in which human interaction had been reduced to virtually nothing but fear, mutual intimidation, coercion and violence.

The 'Schutzstaffel,' like every religious movement, had its special festivals, celebrations, and holy days. Some of them were to be observed and celebrated in a small circle, that is, by the family or primary groups; others were to be observed by the local or regional unit. Two of the most important celebrations in the family were the wedding and the birth of a child. In general, SS ideology objected to church weddings, and SS members were advised not to have their marriage before a priest or a minister. After the exchange of the marriage vows before a civil authority, an appropriate celebration was to take place, attended by the family and invited fellow SS members, which usually included a superior SS officer. The purpose of this celebration was to offer the bride a substitute for the church ceremony, to introduce her to the SS community, and to impress upon her her membership in and subordination to the rules of the order. Frequently the commander of the local SS unit was to speak and rings were to be exchanged. Himmler also endorsed the offering of bread and salt to the bride and groom, and both received from the 'Schutzstaffel' a silver cup.[315] The birth of a child was to be celebrated amidst the family and the circle of friends, excluding church officials. Himmler proposed that as a gift the child should receive a silver cup, a silver spoon, and a blue ribbon of silk.[316] Attendance of a clergyman at a funeral was likewise discouraged, but if the family insisted on a religious burial, the church service was to take place on the day preceding the SS funeral ceremony. Himmler was opposed to a service attended by both SS and clergy. In such a case '... we are delivered to the priest, and when he makes some tactless attacks ... we cannot remove him from the graveside, but out of respect for the dead we must suffer it.'[317] Only the commander of the SS unit was to deliver the funeral sermon. The mourners were expected to draw comfort from the knowledge that the deceased had been a link in the great chain of which they all were a part.[318] At the close of the ceremony, the members were to form a circle around the tomb and join together in singing the SS 'Treuelied.'[319]

Since Christmas was not to be observed by SS members, the 'Jul-Fest' was to take its place. Himmler, however, desired the 'Jul-Fest' to be observed on the last day of the year. In this connection it should be noted that the 'Jul-Fest' has survived National Socialism and is being celebrated by many former SS members to the present day.[320] At no time was the significance of a symbol considered as important as during this season. Himmler annually mailed to his SS families as a token of his esteem all the 'Jul-Leuchter' (candle holders made of ceramic) the SS could afford to mail.[321] These symbols were also meant to serve as consolation especially to those women who, by having married into the SS order, had renounced the spiritual shelter and service of their church.[322]

Some holidays were observed both by the church and the SS, whereas others were exclusively celebrated by the SS: for instance, summer and winter solstice (Mittsommernacht und Sonnenwendfeier). Summer solstice was observed as the victory of light over darkness; winter solstice was celebrated because the sun, after having reached its lowest point on the horizon, was on the rise again. Both festivals were interpreted as symbols of dying and resurrecting (Stirb und Werde!). Winter solstice was basically viewed as a substitute for Christmas, or, as it was claimed, as a pre-Christian Germanic holiday which was to facilitate the breaking away from Christianity.

The holidays observed jointly were the twentieth of April (1889), the birthday of the 'Führer,' and the ninth of November (1923), the commemoration of the first National Socialist 'martyrs.' The thirtieth of January (1933) was to be a reminder of the new millennium.

Thus, having established its own peculiar creed, the SS frequently clashed with Christian religious traditions. Consequently, the SS considered it its duty to fight against '. . . priesthood and priestly fraud, against mystification, superstition, and mediatorialism which forces itself between Nordic men and the divine governments of providence.'[323] So, for example, Himmler declared in Posen on October 4, 1943:

> Wir haben automatisch jeden gegen uns, der überzeugter Kommunist ist, wir haben jeden Freimaurer gegen uns, jeden Demokraten, jeden überzeugten Christen. Das sind die weltanschaulichen Gegner, . . .[324]

> We have against us automatically every person who is a convinced Communist; we have every Freemason against us, every Democrat, every convinced Christian. These are the ideological opponents. . . .[324]

The Reichsführer-SS was aware that a great number of SS men wanted to maintain at least a nominal membership in existing churches. Therefore, pressure was put upon the individual members of the SS to realize their separation from the church. Frequently Himmler succeeded in his policy of effecting an estrangement of SS corps members from their original church and substituted for it the NS creed.[325] Yet, especially during the war, a nominal church membership was tolerated.[326] However, the promotion to the rank of officer frequently depended upon whether or not the candidate had left his church. Figures show that by the end of 1938, 21.9 per cent of the 'Allgemeine SS' had become 'gottgläubig.' The percentage of those who declared themselves to be 'gottgläubig' was highest in the 'Totenkopfverbände' with 69.0 per cent and in the 'Verfügungstruppe' with 53.6 per cent.[327]

The SS ideology and mysticism, as advocated and practiced by those SS leaders and men who had left their respective churches to become affiliated with the creed of the 'gottgläubig,' was in essence a synthesis of Germanic paganism, misinterpretations of the Old Testament, and other occult and ritual elements.[328] The basis for the creed was deeply rooted in rigid retributory categories as, for example, laid down in the lex talionis (an eye for an eye, a tooth for a tooth). However, the underlying structure of the SS creed was also molded out of racial materialism. Hans F. K. Günther, the 'Wegbereiter der deutschen Rassenforschung,' expressed this in the following terms:

> Eine Rasse stellt sich dar in einer Menschengruppe, die sich durch die ihr eignende Vereinigung körperlicher Merkmale und seelischer Eigenschaften von jeder anderen (in solcher Weise zusammengefaßten) Menschengruppe unterscheidet und immer wieder nur ihresgleichen zeugt.[329]

> ———

> A race embodies a group of human beings which, by means of its appropriate union of physical characteristics and spiritual attributes, distinguishes itself from every other group of humans (composed in such fashion) and reproduces only its own kind.[329]

To conclude: In agreement with Elizabeth Nottingham's statements on the functional position of the sociology of religion,[330] we find that the creed of the 'gottgläubig' has in essence fulfilled the same functions as the more traditional religious denominations. Firstly, this creed provided values that served to channel the attitudes of members of the SS and that defined for them the content of their social obligations to the SS as an institution and NS model organizations of the German society. In other words, in this role the creed of the 'gottgläubig' also helped to create systems of social values which were integrated and coherent. Secondly, it may be assumed that this creed also played a vital role in supplying the constraining power that underwrites and reinforces custom, custom which was to strengthen the NS Regime and the SS as an order. Furthermore, the creed was to make an important contribution towards social change aspired to by the NS leadership corps.

It can be readily perceived why the institutionalized NS-SS religion of the 'gottgläubig' became a significant social force which placed its members in direct conflict with the traditional German secular and ecclesiastic institutions. The NS and SS ecclesiarchs, therefore, had to develop their own 'logic,' their own 'world,' backed up by their institutions to alleviate socio-psychological tension and to render their ideology veritable.[331] This in turn brought about a period of transition in which traditional social, political, and religious institutions were co-ordinated with new ones, that is to say, adjusted to current realities, in order to secure a maximum degree of functionality and rationale.

## 12.  *Discussion and conclusion*

The SS was a complex heterogeneous organization headed and developed by Heinrich Himmler, who attempted to unify an array of Main Offices (Hauptämter), Offices (Ämter), departments, units, and sub-organizations with highly diverse functions under one ideological denominator. Overtly this was reflected in the wearing of a distinct uniform and in a ranking system with specific designations, insignia, and paraphernalia (trimmings of power such as the death's-head emblem) which differed from those worn by traditional German military organizations and which dated from the time-period when the 'Schutzstaffel' was still a subordinated unit of the SA. To provide potential candidates for membership with additional incentive, rewards were offered in the form of social status (to counter the feeling of status anxiety), power positions, titles, promotion opportunities, material security, and a feeling of belonging (Ordensgemeinschaft), which included a pronounced esprit de corps. Himmler indoctrinated and motivated members of the 'Schutzstaffel' with the National Socialist 'Weltanschauung' which provided them with a frame of reference and target orientation which facilitated the process of rationalization and reinforced their motivation for aggression.

Basically, the majority of personnel in various formations of the SS – with the possible exception of those with a higher intellectual level in the 'SD-Ausland' under the leadership of SS-Brigadeführer Schellenberg, and to some extent those in the 'SD-Inland' run by SS-Brigadeführer Ohlendorf who had access to foreign sources of information and thus were exposed to cross-cultural influences – were socially isolated young men frequently coming from a socio-economically deprived milieu whose level of existential achievement and sophistication was delimited.[332] The potential SS candidates joined the 'Schutzstaffel' between 1923 and 1933. Their predominant motivations were ideological convictions or opportunistic considerations. They were trained to accept the SS discipline and the principle of unconditional obedience to authority. This obedience was to authority, rather than to the individual representing such authority. Hitler's charismatic appeal may provide an exception here, but even that was probably limited to the period of success (1926-1943). Those who were not ready to accept these conditions were either discharged, expelled, or transferred; only in exceptional cases were they exposed to more severe punishment.[333]

Careful distinction must be made among the political police, members of 'Einsatzgruppen,' concentration camp personnel, and combat formations, although they were all unified in one organization under the leadership of Himmler and appointed by Hitler to act as 'Schutzstaffel der NSDAP.' Under civilian conditions and exposed to democratic social institutions with their inherent control systems, the majority of the personnel would most likely not have come to the attention of any civil or international tribunal, not more so than any other average citizen of that nation, age group, and socio-economic background. It is interesting to note that the great majority of former members of the SS – including those who served in some capacity in concentration camps – did not come into conflict with the laws of a constitutional state after the conclusion of World War II. In contrast to other SS formations, where brutalities and atrocities had become more or less an established rule, mass destruction and acts of cruelty committed by the 'Waffen-SS' appear, at least from available evidence, to have been exceptions to the rule. Towards the end of the war – especially when their depleted ranks were refilled with draftees – to become a member of the 'Waffen-SS' was no less a situational accident than it was to be drafted into other formations of the German Armed Forces.

Although the escalation from detention in concentration camps to extermination and genocide primarily involved those defined by Nazi racial laws as Jews, Gypsies, and to some extent Slavs, this process had already begun with the Röhm purge in 1934. This was followed by Hitler's Nuremberg anti-Jewish laws, by the Reichskristallnacht, by the relatively short-lived euthanasia program, i.e., the gassing of so-called incurably ill German 'Aryans' at Schloß Grafeneck (Württemberg), in Brandenburg, in Bernburg (Anhalt), at Schloß Hartheim, at Burg Sonnenstein near Pirna, at Hadamar near Limburg,[334] and finally by the execution of a group of men who stood in opposition to Hitler known as the Twentieth of July (1944) Movement. This incident and what followed illustrate the dynamics of an escalation of violence. Now a trend began to engulf more and more members of ingroups, no longer limiting persecution only to 'marginal' Germans or strictly to members of outgroups. In increasing numbers, this persecution wave subsequently also involved other low and high ranking German 'non-conformists' to National Socialist law and order.

The victims of Hitler's policies were members of ethnic groups, real and spurious opponents of Hitler and the Nazi Régime, and ideological and social deviants of all nationalities including Germans. Notable examples were those executed at the discretion of ardent Nazis acting as one-man 'Standgericht' (emergency court) or by so-called people's courts. The most common official accusations were treason and 'cowardice in the face of the enemy.' At this stage even some high-ranking officers of the 'Waffen-SS,' interviewed by this writer, claimed that they expected to be executed if the Nazis had been victorious.[335] Finally millions of Germans and non-Germans would have been resettled, including members of the SS. Towards the end of the war the NS moral and racist revolution began to devour its own children.

Apart from political and psychological considerations, perhaps one of the major reasons why the German democratic authorities were at first not overly motivated to bring the perpetrators of 'crimes against the human status' (Hannah Arendt) to justice is the fact that these individuals did not commit mass murder of their own free will.[336] They were incited, persuaded, and coerced by the Nazi leadership, and thus acted within the confine of the law of that time. Atrocities, judged posthumously from a democratic point of view as crimes, were in those days 'mere' acts of the state on which official recognition was bestowed.[337] These acts fall under a classification which can be called 'crimes in retrospect.' The question should be asked whether or not the individuals who committed these acts had a feeling of guilt or have at any time come into conflict with their consciences. In most of these cases this question would have to be answered affirmatively, since it was most certainly their guilt feeling and fear of punishment which made them change their names or go into hiding before a prosecution of Nazi criminals had even begun. A more significant example appears to be the 'Sonderkommando 1005' of Standartenführer Paul Blobel who had been given the task to 'erase the traces of Einsatzgruppen executions in the East.'[338] There was, of course, a variety of responses set off by the defense mechanisms which deal with guilt feelings. Perhaps one of the more interesting rationalizations was that of Ernst Kaltenbrunner who stated in his heretofore unpublished autobiographical notes of October 1945, that his entire endeavor was devoted to bringing about 'a democracy in an independent Austria.'[339]

Were it not for the Eichmann trial in Jerusalem, world public opinion, and the initiative of certain legal authorities such as the late Attorney General of Hessen, Fritz Bauer, trials against individuals who committed 'crimes against the human status' would hardly have assumed present proportions. However, only too frequently do we find that 'the SS' has been used by many other German contemporaries as the scapegoat with which to extricate themselves from their involvement in National Socialism, a movement which, after all, was not exactly an unpopular one. Indeed, it was not 'the SS' or any individual or organization that was solely responsible for the National Socialist excesses; moreover, the National Socialist movement ought to be viewed as a complex process of interlocking socio-cultural interdependencies. Adenauer's and Lübke's assertions 'that only a relatively small percentage of Germans had been Nazis'[340] does not correspond with reality, just as it is not correct to claim that Nazism was 'merely' a racist, anti-Jewish movement.

Finally, from a standpoint of group-dynamics – if we accept the theorem that social structure influences behavior – it seems probable that a closed society with rigid bureaucratic and hierarchic institutions will foster human relations which are anonymous and abstract and will very likely produce individuals with an authoritarian personality structure (Else Frenkel-Brunswick) and an affinity to acts of cruelty. Societies in which interaction and social institutions are built upon *dialogue*,[341] and where positions of authority are filled by competent individuals with an integrated, autonomous personality, will tend to be more resilient against totalitarian or dictatorial misuse. Furthermore, this attitude will promote alternative, relatively more liberal institutional and bureaucratic response and practices.[342]

The intense feeling of resentment prevalent in the German society at large against Jews, Slavic nations, and Western democracies was further developed through effective NS propaganda into a 'frustration-aggression pattern' (Dollard, Fromm) which increasingly isolated the people and impaired meaningful cross-cultural as well as inter-societal communication. It was in this context that, through decisive alterations of the social structure and value system, it became possible for many 'banal individuals'[343] to become 'perpetrators of evil' through a mere obedient and uncritical following of orders of the Régime's leadership.

The fact that the guards of concentration camps were nominal members of the 'Waffen-SS' has been passed off by apologists of the 'Waffen-SS' as a betrayal of the combat troops. Karl O. Paetel correctly summarizes that 'the soldiers of the Waffen-SS were brave fighters, suffered big losses, and, as far as they served in the front line, did not run extermination camps.'[344] A detailed discussion from a legal viewpoint of the criminal acts committed by the SS has been attempted by Herbert Jäger in 'Verbrechen unter totalitärer Herrschaft.'[345]

We arrive at a different position from a sociological or social-psychological point of view when we examine more closely the functions, norms, and values of the members of 'Death's Head Units' and police units who were linked with concentration camps, special commands, mass destruction activities, or with so-called special 'police tasks' in German occupied territories.[346] They were also responsible for deportations in connection with the racial policy, but eventually turned over these latter tasks to other SS and police formations after they had been transferred to Eicke's 'Death's Head' regiments. They were directly responsible to Himmler, and frequently, under the disguise of fighting partisans behind the front, they were employed in mass exterminations of civilians and Russian prisoners of war. Towards the end of the war an increasing number of these men were serving in front-line formations of the 'Waffen-SS.' In August 1940, Himmler established the Main Leadership Office of the SS (SS-Führungshauptamt), installed Hans Jüttner as its chief, and subordinated to him all formations of the 'Waffen-SS.'[347] The inspectorate of concentration camps, formerly under the Main Office of the SS (SS-Hauptamt) and Eicke's leadership, now became 'Amt VI' under SS-Brigadeführer (Major-General) Richard Glücks.[348] On March 3, 1942, SS-Obergruppenführer and General of the 'Waffen-SS' Oswald Pohl, chief of the SS Main Economic and Administrative Office (WVHA), took over the entire concentration camp system from the Operational Main Office (SS-Führungshauptamt) as 'Amtsgruppe D.'[349] What further added to the difficulty in distinguishing between the 'Waffen-SS' and other SS formations was the fact that all general officers – from Brigadeführer to Oberstgruppenführer – regardless of their functions, automatically received nominal 'Waffen-SS' ranks, that is, the military rank of a general even without ever having served in SS combat formations.[350]

The interchange of enlisted personnel and officers between the combat troops of the 'Waffen-SS' and those on duty in concentration camps – serving there in increasing numbers especially towards the end of the war – will add to the confusion of anyone who attempts to view the SS as an organization composed of distinct, homogeneous formations with exclusive functions.[351] The extent of this practice can only be estimated until the records of SS personnel are more thoroughly examined. In the final period of the war the recruited guard personnel was frequently composed of older men, coming from various branches of the German Armed Forces or party formations, who were incorporated into the 'Waffen-SS.'[352] Furthermore, Stein's assertion that 'competent combat officers were rarely transferred to concentration camps unless wounded or otherwise rendered unfit for front-line duty' can be corroborated fom this writer's own extensive experience, but especially from the results of his interviews with former members of the 'Waffen-SS' and 'Death's Head Units.'[353] It was ascertained that many members of the 'Waffen-SS' apparently were quite successful in avoiding assignments to concentration camps or Eicke's 'Death's Head' troops. It can be concluded that for administrative reasons and from the standpoint of internal unification of the SS, Himmler put the 'Death's Head' formations and the 'SS-Verfügungstruppen' under a common denominator which frequently led to ideological and practical incompatibilities as well as conflicts.[354] By combining these two SS formations Himmler hoped to elevate the status and prestige of the 'Death's Head Units' and police units during the war. However, these formations essentially remained separate organizations in spite of a frequent transfer of personnel. Material published by the SS statisticians shows that 1) the socio-economic backgrounds of these two formations do not seem to reflect a significant difference and that 2) the thorough ideological and racist indoctrination played a dominant role in both cases with regard to the shaping of social values, norms and attitudes towards those defined as enemies of the German nation by the NS, and acted upon by the SS leadership.

As of March 3, 1942, the guard batallions and concentration camp administrations became a part of the 'Amtsgruppe D' of the WVHA which – from the standpoint of survival – had an immediate effect on the camp inmates. There was an increasing tendency to exploit the physically qualified inmates as slave laborers until their collapse rather than put them to death upon their arrival in destruction camps.

The replacement of younger, more ideologically indoctrinated camp personnel by older men of different background and combat experience – wherever it occurred – could reduce the plight of the inmates to some extent because of a less rigid interpretation of camp policies.[355]

There appears to have been relatively little uniformity among the various components of the SS at any time. Especially during the war, the concentration camp system, the police system, and the 'Waffen-SS' followed a course distinct from that of any of the others. Finally, it should be noted that after the war the already existing chasm between SS combat and non-combat formations widened considerably. This fact found its explicit reflection in an editorial of *Der Freiwillige*, the official organ of the HIAG, in July 1967, entitled 'Allan Dulles und der Nazi-General.' In this article 'der Höchste SS- und Polizeiführer' for the entire occupied Italy, SS-Obergruppenführer und General der Waffen-SS (and, as he claimed to this writer, on April 20, 1945, promoted to Oberstgruppenführer) and only surviving senior general officer of the 'political sector' of the SS, Karl Wolff, was publicly deposed from his pedestal by his 'comrades.' The anonymous spokesman of *Der Freiwillige* writes:

> Wir beneiden keinen, der um des Ganzen willen den Vorwurf des Verrats oder doch den der Zweideutigkeit seiner Haltung auf sich nehmen zu müssen sich gezwungen sah. Festzuhalten ist, daß die drei Männer, die einen fragwürdigen Weg einschlugen, unsere Uniform trugen, ja geradezu, von damals aus gesehen, die Verkörperung dessen waren, was der Begriff der SS umfaßte. Für uns heute sind andere Männer die Verkörperung der SS: unsere eben von uns gegangenen Kommandeure Sepp Dietrich, Felix Steiner, Keppler, Herbert Gille, unsere Panzermayer-Soldaten! Die Drei, die im Zwielicht stehen, waren von anderer Art: einer der Stellvertreter des Staatsoberhaupts, der andere Träger der stärksten Gewalt nach innen, der dritte war als Höchster SS- und Polizeiführer der 'Himm-

ler Italiens'. Sie gehören hinüber in den politischen Bereich. Nehmen wir den abenteuerlichen SD-Amtschef Schellenberg hinzu, der für Himmler über Bernadotte in Verbindung mit den Westmächten zu kommen versuchte, dann haben wir die Extreme der Gesamt-SS. Zwischen ihnen liegt viel.[356]

———

We don't envy anyone who, in the interest of the nation, saw himself compelled to chance charges of treason – or, at least, of an ambiguous stance. Certainly the three men who followed a questionable path wore our uniform, indeed, from the viewpoint of that time, were the personification of the SS. For us today, other men are the personification of the SS: our commanders who just left us – Sepp Dietrich, Felix Steiner, Keppler, Herbert Gille, our Panzermayer soldiers! The three who stand in the twilight were of another kind: one the deputy head of state; the second, holder of the greatest power in domestic affairs, and the third, the highest SS and Police Commander, the 'Himmler of Italy'.* They belong to the other sector, the political sphere. Add in the adventurous Chief of the SD, Schellenberg, who attempted through Bernadotte, to establish contact with the Western powers on behalf of Himmler, and we get the extremes of the entire SS. There is a wide gap between them.[356]

Thus, expressis verbis, the frequently held opinion that 'the SS' was and to some extent still is a monolithic institution with an unparalleled esprit de corps does not hold true any longer, if this – and there is sufficient evidence to disprove such an assertion – was ever the case.[357]

---

* The writer of the editorial is referring to Rudolf Hess, Heimrich Himmler, and Karl Wolff.

*Part IV*

Totalitarian Institutions
and German Bureaucracy:
A Process of Escalation
into Destruction

*Das erschütterndste Umsturzwort, das je aus königlichem Munde kam, sprach Friedrich der Große, indem er den Herrscher als Staatsdiener definierte. Nicht in der Offenbarung preußischer Sachlichkeit und Pflichtbewußtheit lag das Entscheidende dieses Wortes, sondern vielmehr darin, daß das Königtum vom Mysterium, der Staat vom mystischen Königtum losgebunden wurde, und daß nunmehr der Staat nach Auffassung des königlichen Freigeistes zwar als höchste Einrichtung, immerhin aber nur als Einrichtung der Nützlichkeit und Wohlfahrt und als Menschenwerk dastand.*

Walther Rathenau: *Zur Kritik der Zeit*

*The most stirring revolutionary words uttered by a king were those by Frederick the Great when he defined the ruler as the servant of the state. The decisive impact of these words lay, not in the revelation of Prussian realism and its awareness of duty, but rather in the fact that royalty had become detached from mystery (Mysterium) and the state from mystic royalty. From now on the state, in the view of the royal freethinker, was the supreme institution, to be sure, but an institution to be valued only from the standpoint of utility and welfare and as man's creation.*

Walther Rathenau: *Zur Kritik der Zeit*

In the following brief passages an attempt is made to shed some light on the process of escalation into mass destruction. This is done by (1) examining the interrelations among (a) the charismatic leadership, (b) NS party-initiated acts of violence, (c) the role played by former administrative and bureaucratic institutions, and (d) the participation of the victims themselves; (2) by drawing attention to the rise of organizations such as the Gestapo, the development of concentration and destruction camps, and the fusion of party organizations with the bureaucratic apparatus in the implementation of the destruction policies; and (3) by showing through what stages the elimination process of undesirable German and non-German individuals and groups passed before their destruction. In short, a chain of events was triggered by what at first appeared to many to be a relatively harmless ideological prejudice and merely a party program to attract support of the masses.

The policy against those defined as enemies of the Nazi movement was already outlined in a relatively uniform fashion in numerous speeches and publications during the period between 1920 and 1934 by leading members of the National Socialist party.[1] The policy paving the way for the future course of the movement was laid down in *Mein Kampf*, reiterated in variations on the theme, and reinforced by other Nazi leaders after the abortive march to the Feldherrnhalle in Munich on November 9, 1923. At this time the Nazi functionaries realized that the overt revolutionary methods which were to bring them into power were rejected by German society, due largely to the widely prevalent 'Obrigkeitshörigkeit,' including that of the German political leaders. What seems to be a fairly representative example of a then-prevalent attitude was expressed by Hitler's opponent, Commissar-General of the State (Generalstaatskommissar) of the Bavarian state government Dr. von Kahr, during the Hitler-trial (Hitler-Prozess) in Munich (February 26 through March 27, 1924): 'Master of this land may only be the state, state power and no one else.'[2] State attorney Dr. Stenglein in his plaidoyer against Hitler stated:

> Das schroffe einseitige und enge Parteiprogramm, das jeden als Schädling verurteilt, der nur um eine Linie abweicht, wenn er noch so sehr auf vaterländischem Boden steht.
> ... eine Ungeduld, die da meint, sie könne mit einem Ge-

waltstreich das alte Deutsche Reich in seiner strahlenden Herrlichkeit wiederaufrichten.

... Abgesehen von diesen beiden schädlichen Erscheinungen liegt die tiefe Wurzel der Geschehnisse in der Zerrüttung der Staatsautorität und der sittlichen Achtung vor dem Gesetz. Ein Staat, in dem die Heiligkeit der Gesetze nicht mehr feststeht, wird stets schweren Erschütterungen ausgesetzt sein.

Die Erkenntnis, daß die Staatsautorität die Lebensnotwendigkeit eines Staates ist, muß wieder hergestellt werden.

Ein hohes, vielleicht auch an sich gerechtfertigtes Ziel rechtfertigt nicht die Anwendung verbrecherischer Mittel. ... Die Weimarer Verfassung bildet die Grundlage des Reiches. Die Gegnerschaft dieser Verfassung, mag sie auch aus nationalen Gründen berechtigt erscheinen, darf niemals dazu führen, daß die Verfassung mit Gewalt zu ändern oder zu beseitigen versucht wird.[3]

---

The harsh, one-sided, and narrow party program which condemns as a parasite everyone who dissents in the slightest from the party line, however firm his patriotic stance;

... an impatience which holds that by means of a coup d'état it can restore the old German Reich in all its splendor.

... Apart from these two pernicious phenomena, the deep root of these events lies in the dissipation of the authority of the state and of moral respect for the law. A state in which the sanctity of the law is no longer an established fact will be subject to ever more serious upheavals.

The recognition must be restored that the authority of the state is vital to its survival.

A noble goal, which may be justifiable in itself, does not justify the use of criminal means ... The Weimar Constitution is the foundation of the Reich. Opposition to this constitution, however warranted it may appear from the point of view of national interest, must never be allowed to lead to attempts to alter or abolish the constitution by violent means.[3]

Another revealing view concerning Hitler's public image and that of his party at the time of the trial was given by the commander of the

Bavarian 'Reichswehr' Lieutenant-General Otto von Lossow, who stated:

> Die hinreißende und suggestive Beredsamkeit Hitlers hat auch auf mich anfangs großen Eindruck gemacht. Es ist ohne weiteres klar, daß Hitler in vielem recht hatte. Je öfter ich aber Hitler hörte, desto mehr schwächte sich der erste Eindruck ab. Ich merkte, daß die langen Reden doch fast immer das gleiche enthielten, daß ein Teil der Ausführungen für jeden national eingestellten Deutschen selbstverständlich ist und daß ein anderer Teil davon Zeugnis ablegte, daß Hitler der Wirklichkeitssinn und der Maßstab für das, was möglich und erreichbar ist, abgeht.
>
> ... Seit dem Deutschen Tag in Nürnberg schien mir der Maßstab für das wirkliche Kräfteverhältnis auf seiten des Kampfbundes mehr und mehr geschwunden zu sein. Man glaubte, man könne jetzt alles tun. Hitler war denn auch nicht mehr so selbstlos. Er hielt sich für den deutschen Mussolini, für den deutschen Gambetta, und seine Gefolgschaft, die das Erbe des Byzantinismus der Monarchie angetreten hatte, bezeichnete ihn als den deutschen Messias. Er war der 'Berufene', und die damalige Misere verstärkte natürlich diesen Glauben. ... Ich habe damals wie Oberst v. Seißer die Besuche Hitlers nicht abgelehnt, wir haben vielmehr immer den Versuch gemacht, Hitler auf den Boden der Wirklichkeit und der Tatsachen zurückzuführen, weil wir den gesunden Kern der Hitlerbewegung erkannt hatten, den wir darin sahen, daß die Bewegung die werbende Kraft für die nationale Einstellung der Arbeiterschaft besaß. ... Als mitverantwortlicher Träger der Staatsautorität war es meine Pflicht, ohne Rücksicht auf meine Person und moralische Hemmungen, alles einzusetzen, um unabsehbare Folgen für das Reich und für Bayern hintanzuhalten, die eingetreten wären, wenn die Diktatur Hitler auch nur einige Tage gedauert hätte.[4]

---

Hitler's captivating and suggestive rhetoric at first made a great impression on me, too: It is quite clear that Hitler was right in many respects. However, the more often I listened to him, the weaker that initial impression became. I noticed that his long speeches were almost always the same, that one portion of the exposition is self-evident to every German concerned about the national interest, and that another portion bore witness to the fact that Hitler lacks a sense of reality and perception of what is possible and attainable.

. . . Since the German Day (Deutscher Tag) in Nuremberg, the judgment of the Kampfbund – as to the actual power relationships – seemed to have become increasingly unrealistic. They thought they could do anything now. Hitler was no longer so selfless either. He considered himself the German Mussolini, the German Gambetta, and his followers, who had entered upon the inheritance of the Byzantine monarchy, called him the German Messiah. He was the 'Chosen One' and the misery of the times naturally strengthened this belief. . . . Like Colonel von Seisser, I did not refuse Hitler's visits. Rather, we always attempted to bring Hitler back to face reality and facts, because we had recognized the healthy core of Hitler's political movement. Essentially, we saw that the movement possessed the power to enlist the working class in the national interest. . . . As co-responsible holder of the state authority, it was my duty – without consideration for my person or any moral qualms – to do everything in my power to prevent the incalculable consequences for the Reich and for Bavaria that would have ensued even if Hitler's dictatorship had lasted only a few days.[4]

Finally the commander of the Bavarian police (Landespolizei), Colonel von Seißer, evaluated Hitler and his movement in the following terms:

Der Deutsche Tag in Nürnberg hat der Bewegung neuen Auftrieb und den Führern einen ins Maßlose gesteigerten Größenwahn gegeben. Die glänzende Rednergabe Hitlers, sein suggestiver Einfluß, eine mit außerordentlichen Geldmitteln arbeitende Propaganda haben einen Beifall erzeugt, dem Herr Hitler erlegen ist, und aus dem Trommler einer großen Sache wurde der Mann, der allein die Geschicke des Reiches leiten wollte. Was nicht zum Kampfbund gehörte, war Nachtwächter, war separatistisch, donaumonarchistisch, päpstlich oder französisch gesinnt. . . .

Dann kamen die bekannten Vorgänge im Bürgerbräukeller. Die Tat war geschehen. Ein Zurück gab es nicht mehr, wie Hitler uns selbst gesagt hat. Eine Hitler-Regierung aber hätte über das Land und über das Reich ein Unheil gebracht, das so schnell nicht wieder gutzumachen gewesen wäre. Proben davon haben wir ja in der Nacht und am Morgen erlebt.[5]

The German Day (Deutscher Tag) in Nuremberg gave the (NS) movement a new impetus and produced in its leaders a boundless megalomania. Hitler's brilliant rhetorical gift, his suggestiveness, and a propaganda which was supported by an extraordinary amount of money, met with such approval that Herr Hitler succumbed to it. The drummer of a great cause became the man who strove to control the destiny of the Reich by himself. Whoever did not belong to the Kampfbund was considered backward, separatist, Danube-monarchical, papal, or pro-French. . . .

Then came the well-known events in the Bürgerbräukeller. The die was cast. There was no turning back, as Hitler himself told us. But a Hitler administration would have brought such disaster to the state of Bavaria and the Reich that it could not have been easily remedied. We received proof of this during the night and the following morning.[5]

Hitler, in his speech of November 8, 1933, at the Bürgerbräukeller in Munich, gave the following explanation for his actions leading to the events of November 8 and 9, 1923:

We have opened the eyes of the entire German nation and have put into the cradle of the movement heroism which it needed later on, and above all: that evening and that day they have made it possible for us later to fight ten years long legally, and do not deceive yourselves: if we had not acted at that time I could have never created, formed and retained a revolutionary movement and at the same time still remained legal.[6]

The basis for Hitler's actions was the rejection of the binding nature of the traditional moral and social order. To realize one of his foremost goals, namely the establishment of a racist world, it was declared that one racial or ethnic group is condemned by nature to hereditary inferiority and another group is destined to hereditary superiority. For this purpose the Nazi leaders first had to destroy the social system of which they had been a part and from which they had never quite succeeded in emancipating themselves. This undercurrent ambivalence permeated almost every institution established by the NS leadership and contributed a great deal to the confusion of those persecuted, and especially of the inmates of concentration camps, in seeking an appropriate modus vivendi from the standpoint of adjustment to prison and camp environment. Basically – from 1923 on – the following policy prevailed, and Goebbels openly declared in 1934:

> Wir haben offen erklärt, daß wir uns demokratischer Mittel nur bedienen, um die Macht zu gewinnen, und daß wir nach der Machteroberung unseren Gegnern rücksichtslos alle die Mittel versagen würden, die man uns in Zeiten der Opposition zugebilligt hatte.[7]

> ----

> We have publicly declared that we would only make use of democratic means in order to seize power, and that, once we possessed it, we would relentlessly deny our opponents all those means that had been granted to us during the time that we were in opposition.[7]

Furthermore, the measures to be taken against internal enemies after the gain of power were also explicitly expressed in Goebbels's essays and articles written during the 'time of struggle.' The basic notion was that of intolerance to any type of dissent or deviation from what constituted NS values and norms (chiefly based on racial materialism):

> Es gibt keinen Frieden, bis der Gegner in die Knie gezwungen ist. Es ist gar nicht von Belang, ob er das Gute will, wenn er das Böse tut. Auch Dummheit wird in der Politik bestraft. Wir verspüren nicht im mindesten Lust, uns an einen lebenden Leichnam binden zu lassen, damit er auch uns allmählich mit dem Tode anstecke. Erkennt Eure wahren Feinde rechts und links![8]

There can be no peace until the adversary is brought to his knees. It is of no importance whatsoever whether he intends to do good when, in fact, he does harm. Stupidity is also punished in politics. We do not have the slightest desire to let ourselves be tied to a living corpse that could then gradually also infect us with death. Recognize your true enemies both on the right and on the left![8]

Consequently radical measures were advocated for combating those who were stepping out of line according to the party authorities. What appears to be a representative reflection on this policy can already be found in a written statement made by Goebbels in 1929:

Wir verlangen viel mehr noch als der bürgerliche Staat abzubauen beabsichtigt. Todesstrafe für Mörder, das ist für uns eine Selbstverständlichkeit. Darüber hinaus aber haben wir die Absicht, auch mit Schiebern, Wucherern, Vaterlandsverrätern und Verbrechern an der Ehre und an der Existenz des Volkes ebenso kurzen Prozess zu machen. Zu dieser Absicht bestimmen uns nicht irgendwelche Bedürfnisse nach Rache oder Vergeltung, wir wollen nur das Volk beschützen und sein Leben sicherstellen. Das Volk steht uns höher als die verbrecherischen Komplexe irgendeines asozialen Individuums. Wer dagegen anschreit, der ist dringend verdächtig, daß er ihn verdient.[9]

---

What we demand is much more than the bourgeois state is prepared to surrender.With us the death penalty for murderers is a matter of course. But we intend to go much further: racketeers, profiteers, traitors against the fatherland and those who commit crimes against the honor and existence of the people will also be made short work of. In this we are not motivated by any notions of revenge or retribution, we only wish to protect the nation and guarantee its existence. In our view the nation takes precedence over the criminal obsessions of some anti-social individual. Anyone who raises his voice against this renders himself extremely suspect of deserving the same fate.[9]

With this kind of reasoning[10] Goebbels clearly delineated the National
Socialist policy of aggression which reserved for its functionaries the
arbitrary right to decide who was 'friend' and who was 'foe.' Justice,
equality before the law, and humanistic considerations were viewed by
the Nazis as reactionary and 'bürgerlich' and therefore in direct conflict
with their interests.[11] However, traditional attitudes and social values
and norms affecting all segments of German society could only be
changed after the seizure of power. With the 'Machtergreifung' intolerance and terror were introduced as official means of enforcing
governmental policies and were programmed into the antecedent social
institutions.[12] For this purpose not only the institutions but also the
bureaucratic machinery underwent changes to the extent that individuals constituting the links in the chain of command became still more
authoritarian, the channels of communication more rigid, and – most
important of all – the target orientation of the administrative apparatus
was shifted to accommodate the new belief system. The Nazis aimed at
eradicating the patterns of conduct which may be subsumed under the
term 'substantive rationality.' This notion is explained by Burin as
follows:

> To the Nazis, politics and propaganda were one and the same:
> each meant indoctrination practised in a climate of controlled
> rather than competitive thought. The indoctrination of the
> people with Nazi irrationalism was a form of 'violence to the
> mind' requiring, as a condition of success, the elimination of
> all non-conformist, i.e., non-directed ideas. The Party's ap-
> paratus of surveillance and control was geared to that mis-
> sion.[13]

These modifications were especially reflected in the suppression of
meaningful dialogue and the rise to power of new bureaucratic organizations whose ethos and social composition expressed the essence of the Nazi
system.[14] This system made it also possible to successfully prevent the
ascension of a counter-élite. However, unlike the Bolshevik revolution
of 1917, National Socialism did not cause a violent break with all
existing economic and socio-political institutions.[15] Yet, as mentioned
earlier, the German judicial and law-enforcing institutions of the nineteenth and twentieth century Wilhelminian and Weimar era in partic-

ular were not prepared to deal with such persecutory measures as were introduced by the Nazi leadership corps. To cope with new NS objectives, Göring, who especially during the initial stage of the Régime was instrumental in introducing such 'innovations,' gave the following explanation for his action:

> Wochenlang arbeitete ich persönlich an der Umgestaltung der IA-Abteilung (section of the political police) und schließlich schuf ich allein aus eigener Entschließung und eigener Überlegung das 'geheime Staatspolizeiamt'. Jenes von den Staatsfeinden so sehr gefürchtete Instrument, das in erster Linie mit dazu beigetragen hat, daß heute von einer kommunistischen und marxistischen Gefahr in Deutschland und in Preußen keine Rede mehr sein kann ... So entstanden die Konzentrationslager, in die wir zunächst Tausende von Funktionären der kommunistischen und sozialdemokratischen Partei einliefern mußten. Selbstverständlich sind im Anfang Übergriffe vorgekommen. Selbstverständlich wurden da und dort auch Unschuldige betroffen. Selbstverständlich wurde auch da und dort geschlagen und es sind Rohheitsakte verübt worden. Aber gemessen an allem Gewesenen, an der Größe des Vorgangs, ist doch diese deutsche Freiheitsrevolution die unblutigste und disziplinierteste aller Revolutionen in der Geschichte gewesen.[16]

For weeks on end I personally worked on the reorganization of the IA-Section [IA-Abteilung = section of the political police], and in the end I, alone, acting on my own decision and at my own discretion, created the 'Secret State Police Bureau' – the instrument, so greatly dreaded by the enemies of the state, which above all has made it possible today that, by and large, there is no longer any necessity to speak of a Communist or Marxist threat in Germany or in Prussia. . . . This is how concentration camps were started. We used them at first for the detention of thousands of functionaries of the Communist and Social-Democratic parties. Naturally, innocent individuals were also affected now and then. Naturally, also, blows were struck occasionally, and some persons were treated roughly. But taking into account everything that happened, and the extent of the action, the German freedom revolution was the least bloody yet and the most disciplined of all revolutions in history.[16]

The relatively clearly defined groups and individuals most frequently and deeply affected by these measures were Jews, Communists, Gypsies, Social Democrats, Liberals, opponents and dissenters, or merely those who were discontented outside as well as inside the NSDAP. In order to enable the party leadership to keep the multitudes of these real and spurious enemies in check, the SS and the political police system were built up and developed under Göring who was assisted by Diels, Hinkler, and especially Himmler, who in turn had Heydrich, Kaltenbrunner, and Müller as his deputies. Covered by the cloak of legality and under Himmler's leadership, some formations of the SS, but primarily the RSHA (Reichssicherheitshauptamt) and WVHA (SS Wirtschafts-foremost instruments of terror, were not only misleading the German und Verwaltungshauptamt), which ultimately had become the Régime's populace, whose interests they pretended to serve in an official capacity (by upholding the nation's 'safety, law, and order'), but also to a great extent those they had drawn into their own ranks. Potential SS 'human material' was largely attracted by propaganda, deceptive information, spurious facts, false evidence. and non sequitur argumentation and conclusions.[17]

The traditional German civil service and ministerial bureaucracy were substantially rational institutions; primarily because of this, they commanded implicit confidence of the people.[18] The Nazi Régime utilized this confidence and the attitude of the people to further its own aims.[19] Immediately after the seizure of power, totalitarianism was injected into the inherited bureaucratic system primarily through its ideological party and terror-bureaucracy. This was accomplished by the fusion of both the new and the old systems, which the party leadership succeeded in integrating to a large extent, thus ensuring a reasonably smooth functioning of the bureaucratic apparatus. In the party and its formations, especially in the SS and the political police system, this was achieved with great expediency if one considers specifically the odious efficiency of the destruction machinery during the war years.[20] This could only be accomplished by a 'symmetrical, hierarchic structure and characteristically "bureaucratic" procedures combined with ideological fanaticism and the charismatic legitimation of authority.'[21] The product of a change from a basically rational, subsequently traditional, state machinery to an apparatus governed predominantly by an extremist party ideology may be appropriately named 'ideological bureaucracy.'[22] In somewhat less complex terms, this social-psychological process was named and popularized by the NS leadership corps 'leadership of the personality' (Führung der Persönlichkeit).[23]

Hitler envisaged the executive and administrative division of labor, i.e., the function of the party and that of the bureaucracy, in the following terms:

> The task of the leadership and, in effect, that of legislation is in the hands of the party. The state is administration and its function is that of execution.[24]

In practice this had the following three major consequences: (1) The bureaucracy ceased to be a leading political order in the state and thereby no longer constituted a political class in the traditional sense. It was deprived of its 'substantive rational' control function in terms of checks and balances, and its activity was reduced to carrying out orders of the party, particularly of its authoritarian leadership, as was, for example, the case with the numerous 'Führer decrees.'[25] (2) The civil servants, judges, and administrators were thereby transformed into a corps of obedient, efficient, uncritical 'political soldiers' and thus became a part of Hitler's National Socialist totalitarian system.[26] (3) With the infiltration of NS rank and file party members into all echelons of the administration and bureaucracy, an inflation of positions of authority was enhanced. These posts were frequently filled by people who may have been authoritarian, but were no authorities in any field (Menschen mit Autorität, ohne Autoritäten zu sein). The effect of their activity brought about a profound change not only in their own attitude towards others but also in the attitude of those who were subject to their jurisdiction. The stimulated response among the populace to its totalitarian administration ranged from identification, collaboration, accommodation, opportunism, passive submission, disorientation, unconcern, and apathy to dissent and passive or active resistance, including other forms of opposition and assent.[27]

The collaboration of 'non-political experts,' at times lacking even ideological conviction – regardless of nominal party membership – with 'Nazi activists in every government bureau assured both technically effective administration and subservience to the political leadership.'[28]

At the party congress in 1935 Hitler revealed what also in essence constituted the basis of the NS revolution:

> I would like to state that the battle against the internal enemies of the nation will never fail because of a deficient formal bureaucracy. Instead where the normal bureaucracy of the state should prove to be unfit to solve a problem, the German nation will charge its more vital organization with the assertion of its existential necessities.[29]

Although the German bureaucratic machinery was modified and adjusted to the deviant aims[30] of the NS leadership, it was still not in an adequate position directly to concern itself with activities of terror and destruction. This function was assigned predominantly to special organizations and formations which the party leadership, specifically Hitler, had created for this purpose. In particular Göring and later Himmler, acting upon his immediate orders and, responsible only to Hitler, created the SA, the 'Allgemeine SS,' the 'SS-Totenkopfverbände,' the 'Gestapo,' the 'SD,' the 'SS-Verfügungstruppe' (later 'Waffen-SS'), the 'Reichssicherheitshauptamt' (RSHA), etc., and influenced other agencies administering the political justice of the National Socialist state, as for example the people's courts.[31]

Furthermore, by the fusion of high positions in the party with high positions in the state, which were filled by appointees of the party such as 'Gauleiter' (province party leader), 'Kreisleiter' (district party leader), district presidents, etc., the party or SS leadership gained a dominant influence over the bureaucratic apparatus.[32] The transfer or dismissal of undesirable personnel (coercion) fostered compliance, and the promotion of active party members created opportunism and conformism. At an even higher level, decisive pressure was exerted on the bureaucratic machinery by the appointment of party leaders to ministerial, quasi-ministerial, state-secretarial, 'Reichsleiter' (Reichs-leader), 'Reichsstatthalter' (Reichs-governor), 'Reichskommissar' (Reichs-commissioner), 'Generalgouverneur' (governor-general), and other elevated administrative and political posts. Well-known cases in point were Wilhelm Frick, Minister of the Interior, who was succeeded in 1943 by Reichsführer-SS Heinrich Himmler; Joseph Goebbels, Minister of Propaganda, Gauleiter of Berlin, and during the last stage of the Régime 'Reichsbevollmächtigter für den totalen Kriegseinsatz'; and Alfred Rosenberg 'Reichsleiter und Beauftragter für weltanschauliche Schulung der NSDAP' and later Minister for the East, etc. Due to this combination of subjective ideological party leadership with the administrative system of the state, arbitrary discretion prevailed and 'the legal state was submerged in a chaos of irrationality and violence'[33] while yet retaining the facade of traditional law and order. By these acts, the inherited traditional bureaucracy was reduced to an adjunct of the new ruling class and became merely an administrative instrument.[34] It is, therefore, no situational accident that Himmler and his organization eventually became the most powerful and influential force of the Reich after Hitler and possibly Bormann who had succeeded Rudolf Hess as head of the party chancellery.[35]

As a consequence, the change from a legal state to a police state inevitably brought with it a drastic decline of the traditional judiciary. Concessions and adjustments to Nazi ideological requirements had to be made and took the form of the practice of discrimination, intimidation, terror, and violence.[36] Law was increasingly replaced by the application of political and ideological directives, while still retaining a quasi-judicial form.[37] Individuals, such as the dedicated Nazis Gürtner, Schlegelberger, Thierack, and Freisler, were appointed to the highest judiciary posts. The first three became Ministers of Justice and the fourth President of the People's Court. They were frequently referred to as models of legal excellence by many an eminent contemporary German jurist.[38] In an official note of October 13, 1942, Thierack expressed the National Socialist concept of the role of criminal justice to 'Reichsleiter' and deputy leader of the party, Bormann, in the following terms:

> With a view to freeing the German people of the Poles, the Russians, the Jews, and the Gypsies, and with a view to making the eastern territories which have been incorporated into the Reich available for settlement by German nationals, I intend to transfer criminal jurisdiction over Poles, Russians, Jews,

and Gypsies to the Reichsführer-SS. I do so on the principle that the administration of justice can only make a small contribution to the extermination of these peoples. The judicial administration undoubtedly pronounces very severe sentences on such persons, but that is not enough in order to constitute any material contribution towards the realization of the above-mentioned aim. [39]

This attitude constituted a complete break with the system of values of traditional German jurisprudence. It reflects the inroads of National Socialist ideology into German bureaucratic institutions in general, thus paving the way for the process of escalation into destruction. Finally, at least during the war, there was hardly a single organization or public institution that had not become involved in one way or another in criminal transactions and atrocities. [40] This state of legal lawlessness enabled Himmler and his SS formations to increase their power, build up their social and military status, and extend their dominant influence over almost all party, governmental, and industrial organizations and institutions. Nevertheless, despite his continuous efforts, Himmler never quite succeeded in appreciably raising the quickly declining esteem of his organizations. [41] Possible exceptions were certain combat formations and a few individual leaders of the 'Waffen-SS.' This demonstrates the fact that, in one way or another, every ruling class is dependent upon the general public to whom eventually it has to turn for support to retain its power status. This type of dependence ensures that a so-called total control can in reality never be complete. Thus, as Theodore Abel observed, 'correcting factors' are 'present in any organization by virtue of the fact that what is organized are human beings and not robots.' [42]

Soon after the NS seizure of power in 1933, the SS quickly developed into a complex bureaucratic organization. The adherence to non-normative rules in the early stage of its function as 'Stabswache' – originally conceived as transitional and as means only – became transformed into an end in itself; it is thus an excellent example of the familiar process of displacement of goals whereby something of 'instrumental value becomes a terminal value.' [43] The SS leadership readily provided the ideological rationalization to justify its role, its methods, and its course of action. It avoided public discussions about its techniques and, as a matter of policy, strengthened its 'structural sources of over-conformity.'[44]

Apart from serving the NSDAP as 'Schutzstaffel,' the SS also performed public functions, the foremost of which was to safeguard the internal security of German nationals. Thus many of its members served in the government and were 'servants of the people,' but in fact they were very much more than government officials, due to their position of power and the arbitrariness inherent in the NS notion of justice. Because of this discrepancy between ideology, public claims, assumed function, and reality (incompatibility of roles), a growing tension developed not only among the SS. The public at large lived in constant fear of being persecuted by the Gestapo (while denying the reality of destruction camps) and the military perceived the 'Waffen-SS' as a rival. But also among the various SS formations, Main Offices and Offices, and individual leaders themselves tension arose, quite apart from the presence of internal rivalries, intrigues, and power struggles.[45] The structural profile of the SS was further complicated due to Himmler's relative independence from other bureaucratic organizations. His organization was not an integral part of any hierarchy, but he had his men in almost every hierarchy. Thus, the position of the SS and its machinery of destruction was placed between the ministerial and the party. As Hilberg correctly observes, 'Himmler received most of his funds from the Finance Ministry and recruited most of his men from the party. Both fiscally and in its personnel structure, the SS and police were consequently a civil service-party amalgamation.'[46]

From 1941 the Reichssicherheitshauptamt and, in 1942, the Wirtschafts- und Verwaltungshauptamt had gained control over the entire concentration camp system and were chiefly responsible for carrying out the policy of mass destruction. Their function included the seizure, that is to say, the rounding-up and transportation, of deportees into camps or similar total institutions. Here the persecuted either could be exploited as slave-laborers or, if the object was to achieve the exclusion of inconvenient witnesses and the killing of 'inferiors,' they could be exterminated by a variety of 'ingenious' means. The RSHA, a subsystem of the SS and essentially a unique combination of party men and civil servants, was to a degree also characteristic of the German administrative and bureaucratic apparatus in general. It was established largely due to the efforts of Reinhard Heydrich.[47] In his initial step,

Heydrich succeeded in amalgamating the offices which were already in his charge, namely the 'Geheime Staatspolizei' (Secret State Police, or Gestapo) and the 'Landeskriminalpolizeiamt' (Criminal Police, or Kripo), into the 'Hauptamt-Sicherheitspolizei' (Main Office Security Police, or Sipo). Furthermore, the Security Police, as an agency of the state, was accompanied by a parallel formation of the party intelligence, the 'Sicherheitsdienst' (Security Service, or SD).[48] Thus, Heydrich was now in charge of two Main Offices, the 'Hauptamt-Sicherheitspolizei' (Sipo), a state organization, and the 'Sicherheitshauptamt,' a party organization. On September 27, 1939, Himmler ordered in a decree that the two Main Offices were to be amalgamated into the 'Reichssicherheitshauptamt' (Reich Security Main Office, or RSHA).[49] Now Heydrich had become 'Chef der Sicherheitspolizei (SP) und des Sicherheitsdienstes (SD).'

Heydrich's power position and the official status of the RSHA permitted, for example, the following negotiation: In a proposed Army-RSHA agreement drafted on March 26, 1941, which the General Quartermaster of the Army, Major-General Wagner, sent to Heydrich, the crucial sentence read: '. . . within the framework of the instructions and upon their own responsibility, the Sonderkommandos are entitled to carry out executive measures against the civilian population.' (Die Sonderkommandos sind berechtigt, im Rahmen ihres Auftrages in eigener Verantwortung gegenüber der Zivilbevölkerung Exekutivmaßnahmen zu treffen).[50] The final version of the agreement between the OKH (Oberkommando des Heeres, i.e., High Command of the Army) differed from the preceding draft in so far as 'the "Einsatzgruppen" were to be permitted to operate not only in army group rear areas, but also in the corps areas right on the front line.'[51] Although not explicitly stated in the agreement, it was generally understood that Jews, Russian commissars, mentally disturbed individuals, and others belonging to undesirable categories were to be killed on the spot.[52] Similar orders followed to improve the efficacy of mass destruction by the use of mobile and stationary gassing facilities.[53] More specifically, in a draft letter written by the 'Referent des Ostministeriums,' Amtsgerichtsrat Dr. Wetzel announced on October 25, 1941 (to the 'Reichskommissar für das Ostland,' Lohse), that gassing machinery (Vergasungsapparate) was to be introduced. In addition he points out who was to be primarily affected by this killing procedure:

Ich darf darauf hinweisen, daß Sturmbannführer Eichmann, der Sachbearbeiter für Judenfragen im Reichssicherheitshauptamt mit diesem Verfahren einverstanden ist. Nach Mitteilung von Sturmbannführer Eichmann sollen in Riga und in Minsk Lager für Juden geschaffen werden, in die evtl. auch Juden aus dem Altreichgebiet kommen. Es werden zur Zeit aus dem Altreich Juden evakuiert, die nach Litzmannstadt, aber auch nach anderen Lagern kommen sollen, um dann später im Osten, soweit arbeitsfähig, in Arbeitseinsatz zu kommen.

Nach Sachlage bestehen keine Bedenken, wenn diejenigen Juden, die nicht arbeitsfähig sind, mit den Brackschen Hilfsmitteln beseitigt werden. Auf diese Weise dürften dann auch Vorgänge, wie sie sich bei den Erschießungen von Juden in Wilna nach einem mir vorliegenden Bericht ergaben, und die auch im Hinblick darauf, daß die Erschießungen öffentlich vorgenommen wurden, kaum gebilligt werden können, nicht mehr möglich sein. Die Arbeitsfähigen dagegen werden zum Arbeitseinsatz nach Osten abtransportiert. Daß bei den arbeitsfähigen Juden Männer und Frauen getrennt zu halten sind, dürfte selbstverständlich sein . . .[54]

---

In this connection I have to inform you that Sturmbannführer Eichmann, who is in charge of the Jewish question at the Reichssicherheitshauptamt, is in agreement with this procedure. He tells me that camps for Jews are to be established in Riga and in Minsk, to which Jews from the Altreich will eventually be sent. For the present Jews from the Altreich will be evacuated to Litzmannstadt and other camps, and those who are 'fit for work' subsequently transferred further east for use as labor.

In our present situation we cannot afford to have scruples about taking advantage of Brack's facilities for the elimination of Jews who are not fit for work, as these will provide a way of avoiding any possible recurrence of the events which occurred, according to a report which I have in front of me, at the shooting of the Jews in Vilna. Incidentally, I see from the report that the shootings took place in public, which can hardly have been approved.

> Jews fit for work, on the other hand, are to be transferred
> further east for use as labor. It goes without saying that the
> men are to be separated from the women.[54]

This is but one example to show how many of the various organizations
were involved and to what extent they were cooperating with the RSHA
in the destruction process.

Furthermore, it should be noted that in the party's penetration into
and domination over every stratum of German society, and later on of
the occupied territories, it not only transformed public organizations,
systems, and sub-systems into more or less pliable instruments but also
deeply affected the fate of previously relatively independent political,
religious and social groups.

Since there is no evidence to the contrary, it may be assumed that
the majority of German, Austrian, Czech, Hungarian, and similarly
situated Western European Jews who were born at the turn of the century or later had been brought up in a cultural milieu not appreciably
different from that of the gentile majority group apart from dissimilari-
ties in their religious belief. In fact a good many 'Jews' either were only
nominal members of this minority group or were agnostics, atheists, or
had become Christian in their religious orientation and affiliation.
They had assimilated the cultural values and norms of the society in
which they were born and brought up.[55] Thus, for example, they had
supported and identified themselves with the Wilhelminean or Weimar
era, or were just as 'good' or 'bad' patriotic Austro-Hungarian monar-
chists or Czechoslovak democrats as their fellow countrymen had been.
That is to say, they had thought, acted, and responded to pleasing,
frustrating, or threatening stimuli in a similar fashion and under
practically the same conditions as the members of the majority group.
It is true that anti-Judaism existed, but it was hardly disturbing enough
to cause serious psychological trauma or distort the views and the cur-
ricula vitae of those who may have been subjected to it – until the
time of Hitler's influence, when racism became a dominant social
factor. It is in this light that we have to understand Hitler's remark to
Rauschning:

> Übrigens sind die Juden bereit gewesen, mir in meinem poli-
> tischen Kampf zu helfen. In den Anfängen unserer Bewegung

haben mich sogar einige Juden finanziell unterstützt. Ich
brauchte nur den kleinen Finger auszustrecken und sie hätten
sich alle um mich gedrängt. Sie wußten schon, wo etwas Neues
und Lebendiges war. Der Jude ist es doch gewesen, der diese
Wirtschaft der dauernden Bewegung und Steigerung erfunden
hat, die man Kapitalismus nennt. Diese geniale Schöpfung mit
einem raffinierten und doch simplen selbsttätigen Mechanismus. Machen wir uns nichts vor, es ist genial, es ist teuflisch
genial.

Die moderne Wirtschaft ist eine Schöpfung der Juden. Sie
wird von ihnen ausschließlich beherrscht. Das ist ihr Über-
reich, das sie über alle Reiche der Welt und ihre Herrlichkeit
ausgespannt haben. Aber nun sind wir es, die mit der Weltanschauung der ewigen Revolution ihnen Konkurrenz machen.
Ist Ihnen nicht aufgefallen, wie der Jude in allem und jedem
das genaue Gegenteil des Deutschen ist und ihm doch wieder
so verwandt ist, wie es nur zwei Brüder sein können? [56]

---

Jews have been ready to help me in my political struggle.
At the outset of our movement some Jews actually gave me
financial assistance. If I had but held out my little finger, I
should have had the whole lot of them crowding round me.
They knew well enough where there was a new thing on, with
life in it. It was the Jews, of course, who invented the economic
system of constant fluctuation and expansion that we call
Capitalism — that invention of genius, with its subtle and yet
simple self-acting mechanism. Let us make no mistake about
it — it is an invention of genius, of the Devil's own ingenuity.

The economic system of our day is the creation of the Jews.
It is under their exclusive control. It is their superstate, planted
by them above all the states of the world in all their glory.
But now we have challenged them, with the system of unend-
ing revolution. Has it not struck you how the Jew is the exact
opposite of the German in every single respect, and yet is as
closely akin to him as a blood brother? [56]

The Enabling Act (Ermächtigungsgesetz) of March 24, 1938, which
gave **Hitler** power of legislation through decree (Führer decree), abol-

ished all rights and privileges of citizenship for the Jews. In April of
that year all non-Aryans were removed from public offices including
those of 'auctioneers' and 'meat inspectors.' Thus, after January 1939,
no professional positions were open to Jews any more. So-called 'mixed' marriages or intimate relationships between Jews and Aryans had
already been declared criminal by the Nuremberg Laws (Reichsbürgergesetz, Gesetz zum Schutze des deutschen Blutes und der deutschen
Ehre) of September 15, 1935. Jewish businessmen were forced out of
their commercial enterprises. On November 7, 1938, the third secretary of the German Embassy in Paris, Legationsrat Ernst vom Rath, was
assassinated by the seventeen-year-old Jewish refugee of German-Po-
lish background, Herschel Grynspan. This act precipitated the pogroms
in Germany and Austria of November 9 and 10, infamously known as
the 'Reichskristallnacht' (night of the broken crystal glass), which
were primarily staged by Dr. Joseph Goebbels with the approval of
Hitler.[57] Violent anti-Jewish persecutory measures introduced during
this time mark the beginning of a phase which found its climax in the
'Final Solution' (Endlösung der Judenfrage).[58]

By placing most of the blame for Germany's internal and international conflicts on the Jews, a certain psychological escape mechanism and prop to German defeatism and disunity was erected. It was
not the Germans that had triggered their national crisis but 'enemies'
from within. The outcome of the intensive campaign of aggression and
violence against the Jews and other similarly situated groups and individuals in Germany by public authorities was not only that antagonism towards Jews spread and deepened among the populace and
even in concentration camps but also that the capacity for concern
was considerably impaired.[59]

The Jewish minority was neither conditioned nor ready to deal with
such a sudden, massive onslaught of aggression and violence. They
were caught by surprise as were all the others who had not anticipated
and, therefore, were not prepared to deal with the measures with which
Hitler had threatened and which were realized after he had come into
power. The Jews, like many others, were almost immediately affected
by Hitler's persecutory measures from the very start of the Régime's
existence right up to the realization of the 'Final Solution.' Yet they
frequently did not take Hitler's threats and open declarations to this
effect seriously until it was too late appreciably to influence or effec-

tively to change the course of events by opposition or resistance.

One of the most dramatic cases in this respect was the 'Reichsver-tretung der Juden in Deutschland' (Reich representation of the Jews in Germany). Early in 1933, the Jewish communities in Germany, as well as in the territories later occupied by Germany, were still decentralized. Each city which had a large Jewish community had its own Jewish administration which took charge of the social, educational, and religious activities of its members. At the end of 1933, the recently established national organization 'Reichsvertretung' was activated largely by the efforts of Director Heinrich Stahl, the chairman of the 'Vorstand' of the Berlin Jewish Community. One of the chief purposes of this new organization, which was headed by Rabbi Dr. Leo Baeck and his deputy Stahl, was to enter into open discussions (offene Aussprache) with the Nazis on the subject of anti-Semitism and the Jewish future in Germany.[60] According to the decree of July 4, 1939, drafted by Ministerialrat Bernard Lösener and a co-worker named Schiedmair of the Ministry of the Interior, and signed by the Minister of the Interior, Frick, the Deputy of the Führer, Hess, the Minister of Education, Rust, and the Minister of Church Affairs, Kerrl, the name of this organization was changed from 'Reichsvertretung' to 'Reichsvereinigung' (Reich Association). The decree empowered the Ministry of the Interior, but de facto Heydrich's State Security Police, to assign additional tasks to this Reich Association.[61] By this provision the Jewish administrative apparatus with its network of communal organizations gradually became an integral, collaborative part of the bureaucratic machinery of destruction without any significant change of personnel.[62] The members of this association, namely all persons classified by the Nuremberg Laws as 'Jewish,' were directly affected by this decree. To begin with, the territorial jurisdiction of the 'Reichsvereinigung' was limited to the Old Reich and to the Sudeten area. Eventually it was extended by the RSHA[63], more specifically Eichmann's office IV B 4, to all the territories of Greater Germany (with the exception of Denmark) in which Jewish 'Kultusgemeinden' (Jewish communal organization) centers were being transformed on similar lines to assume a self-destructive function.[64] This activity reached its climax in ghettos and in destruction- and slave labor camps, in which so-called 'Ältestenräte' or 'Judenräte' were directly responsible to the SS camp leadership and, upon its orders, assisted in the realization of the destruction policy.[65]

The Jewish communal organizations not only provided the Security Police with complete lists of their members but also had to select the Jewish persons who were to be deported according to a quota system dictated to them from above. They also had to arrange for the notification of the victims through their own Jewish 'Ordnungsdienst' (Jewish auxiliary police). [66] Thus Eichmann's office forced the Jewish leaders to comply with and to participate in the NS destruction program which involved their own charges. By means of a well-calculated policy of intimidation and deception, the Reich Security Main Office induced the Jewish national and communal leaders and especially later the Jewish Councils of Elders which operated in ghettos (Warsaw, Lodz, Theresienstadt, etc.) gradually to transform the basically religious organizations into a self-destructive administrative machinery. Many non-Jewish inmates who were detained in concentration and death camps for their political or criminal activities also operated as office holders on similar lines. Thus many individuals and groups became essential components of the National Socialist bureaucratic deportation- and destruction-apparatus without necessarily identifying themselves with the Régime's aims. [67] This transformation, however, could only be realized because of (1) the NS arbitrary definition of an enemy of the Régime, i.e., the Reich (this included anyone who for one reason or another did not suit the NS leadership corps); (2) the social, cultural, and political isolation of those who were thus defined; (3) tacit consent or open dissent de facto led to the identical effect: discrimination and arbitrary acts of persecution or violence (SA, SS); and (4) the introduction of discriminatory legislation effecting the deprivation of civil rights and legal protection for individuals and groups which were excluded from the social body (deportation, concentration, or ghettoization) and subjected to persecution, exploitation, or annihilation. [68]

Furthermore, a review of the way in which the escalation of violence tends to develop through legitimation into extreme forms reveals that a sequential three-stage process appears to be involved: (1) initial covert or overt support by the public for coercive, mild violence committed by a special interest group (usually social, political, or deviant); (2) support for the special group in the planning and perpetration of extreme forms of violence; and (3) the actual practice of extreme forms of violence by a relatively small number of people who appear to find some fulfillment or satisfaction in their acts (for example, some members of the SA, the SS Death's Head Guard battalion [Totenkopfwach-sturmbanne], the RSHA, the WVHA, the Special Command [Sonder-kommando], the Police battalions, the Action Group [Einsatzgruppe], etc.). Such a paradigm of development of violence can frequently be applied to milling crowds, to police squads facing an unruly crowd, and especially to total systems and institutions such as concentration camps.[69] The process of destruction finally found its acme in situations of extreme stress, especially in ghettos, concentration-, slave labor-, and AEL (Arbeitserziehungslager) camps, killing centers, during death marches, and during the transportation of deportees in closed or open cattle wagons. Hitler's policies, Weltanschauung, and program, which frequently had not been taken too seriously by the public at large, gradually became a reality.[70] Hitler instituted the killing of Germans and non-Germans who were considered to be useless or disloyal. With the assistance of his paladins, the party, the bureaucracy, other supporters, and the general populace including people in countries which were later occupied by Germany (with the exception of Denmark and Finland), he was able to put the 'Final Solution' into effect.[71] From the time when they were conceived these acts appeared to have constituted real solutions to problems and conflicts as Hitler perceived them.[72] The following passages from *Mein Kampf*, unique in Nazi literature, provide the blueprint for future action, namely gassing:

> Hätte man zu Kriegsbeginn und während des Krieges einmal zwölf- oder fünfzehntausend dieser hebräischen Volksverder-ber so unter Giftgas gehalten, wie Hunderttausende unserer allerbesten deutschen Arbeiter aus allen Schichten und Be-rufen es im Felde erdulden mußten, dann wäre das Millionen-opfer der Front nicht vergeblich gewesen. Im Gegenteil: Zwölf-tausend Schurken zur rechten Zeit beseitigt, hätte vielleicht einer Million ordentlicher, für die Zukunft wertvoller Deut-schen gerettet . . .
>
> Solch eine Abrechnung von wirklicher, weltgeschichtlicher Größe findet allerdings nicht statt nach dem Schema irgend-eines Geheimrats oder einer alten, ausgetrockneten Minister-seele, sondern nach den ewigen Gesetzen des Lebens auf dieser Erde, die Kampf um dieses Leben sind und Kampf bleiben. Man mußte sich vergegenwärtigen, daß aus den blutigsten

Bürgerkriegen häufig ein stahlharter, gesunder Volkskörper
erwuchs, während aus künstlich gehegten Friedenszuständen
öfter als einmal die Fäulnis zum Himmel emporstank. Völker-
schicksale wendet man nicht mit Glacéhandschuhen.[73]

--------

... If, at the beginning of the War and during the War, twelve
or fifteen thousand of these Hebraic corrupters of the nation
had been subjugated to poison gas such as had to be endured
in the field by hundreds of thousands of our very best German
workers of all classes and professions, then the sacrifice of
millions at the front would not have been in vain. On the contrary: if twelve thousand scoundrels had been opportunely
eliminated, perhaps a million orderly, worthwhile Germans
might have been saved for the future. ...

Such an historic, genuinely momentous settling of accounts,
of course, does not occur as the result of a scheme of this or
that privy counsellor or dried-up bureaucrat, but in line with
mundane laws of life, which are and remain the struggle for
existence. It should have been realized that a steely, healthy
body national has often grown out of the most bloody civil
wars, while the rottenness of artificially nurtured conditions of
peace has more than once stunk to high Heaven. National
destinies are not altered with kid gloves.[73]

Indeed, Hitler and his followers succeeded in changing the course of
the German nation and, for that matter, also of world history by the
revolutionary act of stripping off the 'gloves of civility' and exposing
the social body to an escalation into unrelenting brutality.

It should be understood that in both democratic and non-democratic
political systems leaders will conform to group norms only if their
leadership as well as their policies are dependent on their being accepted by their followers. It has been suggested that popular mass leaders
embody the wishes and expectations of their supporters. Erich Fromm's
social psychological analysis of the reasons for Hitler's success supports
this point of view:

I have tried to show in Hitler's writings the two trends that we
have already described as fundamental for the authoritarian

character: the craving for power over men and the longing for submission to an overwhelmingly strong outside power. Hitler's ideas are more or less identical with the ideology of the Nazi Party. ... This ideology results from his personality which, with its inferiority feeling, hatred against life, asceticism, and envy of those who enjoy life, is the soil of sadomasochist strivings; it was addressed to people who 'on account of their similar character structure', felt attracted and excited by these teachings and became ardent followers of the man who expressed what they felt.[74]

Thus, it is quite conceivable that the charismatic leader, whose singular gift of appeal and influence sets him apart from others in comparable positions of power, most likely also reflects the strivings and desires of those who have submitted to his leadership. Paul Halmos, in his study on leadership, has followed Weber's suggestion that charisma is derived from the internal suffering of the leader, simultaneously corroborating Fromm's views by claiming that '. . . the charismatic leader is no other than the one whose private misery is the ideal type of misery prevalent in his culture.'[75] So, for example, the leader can appeal to a defeated, resentful people, or to a people of frustrated ambitions, or again to those experiencing an acute need for an identity who are in search of a unifying belief system which would satisfy unfulfilled needs. In these cases, and in others like them, he will then promise to make amends for the grievance of his people.

## 1. *Discussion*

Especially in times of stress we tend to be preoccupied with the meaning and purpose of our existence and with the fulfillment of our life's task, our social roles.[76] One convenient and relatively easily available solution to satisfy the acute needs of the masses in times of general disorganization and disorientation (anomie), when obvious and mundane solutions have failed, can be found in the escape into a supernatural ideology.[77] In so doing an attempt is being made to find meaning in what is thought to be a chaotic life. In his despair man feels that he is dependent on a force outside of and superior to himself (in Hitler's case the 'Vorsehung'). Moreover, he hopes to partake in this power by allying himself with it. Ideally, then, a mortal can be transformed into a superman as long as he follows the biddings of this super force and abides by its laws. Man preoccupied with trouble frequently does not know how to resolve his 'problem of living'[78] and simply defers or transfers it to the supernatural sphere, not so much to obtain additional insight (to seek to know-why, for example, by viewing human existence in terms of sub specie aeternitatis) but to obtain additional power (techniques, know-how, etc.) to make his life more bearable and manageable. In a state of desperation man becomes not only a pragmatist but also an opportunist. 'Out of what is only one thought among many he will make his only thought, his obsession.'[79] He becomes an extremist, a dreamer, a fanatic. In a condition of elation he sees himself in a more favorable, superior light which he feels gives him extraordinary powers over others, over hostile nature, and which encourages him to deal with issues that he otherwise would feel incapable of acting upon. By withdrawing from reality, from the pressures of this hour and the 'spirit' (or mood) of the times[80], he is also deferring the solution of his conflicts. As these pressures alter in time and space, many other factors change simultaneously: the order of man's urgencies (priorities), his perspective on issues, on life relative to his physical, emotional, and spiritual survival.[81] Yet his perspective remains in accordance with the factors of environmental dependency. The irreversible alone remains constant, never the manner in which man deals with it. In situations in which normlessness prevails, or in extreme dependency situations when man feels compelled to concentrate his attention and efforts in a specific direction pertaining to his immediate needs, he will tend to lose a balanced overall perspective (individual difference notwithstanding).[82] Means, purpose, the interdependencies involved in the perception and attainment of long-range goals (including a consistent goal orientation) may gradually become more and more obscured. The result of such a frame of mind may be a dissociation of intellect and emotion, that is to say, a state of moral and mental confusion.

> Man who is lost in complications aspires to save himself in simplicity – a universal return to nudity, a general call to rid oneself of, to retire from, to deny, all richness, complexity, and abundance. . . .

The man, then, who retreats to that single question of social justice exaggerates it, becomes exacerbated and exasperated by it, removes it from its proper place, refuses with any genuineness to accept life as it is; and, by means of a personal and intimate fiction which his desperation inspires in him, he reduces life to an extreme in which he installs himself and gives himself over to extremism. And from that extreme he will fight all the rest of the enormous sector of human affairs, will deny science, morality, status, truth, and so on.[83]

During the decline of an epoch when traditional institutions have become dysfunctional and ferocious crises erupt, 'cultured men' frequently turn into 'barbarians.'[84]

If the sum and entirety of living lacks meaning, if one lives for nothing, then all the internal justifications which I find for my life in its acts are an error of perspective. This conclusion imposes a radical change, another perspective . . . Culture is only the interpretation which man gives to his life, the series of more or less satisfactory solutions which he invents in order to handle his problems and the needs of his life. These include the material order of things as well as the so-called spiritual. . . . He who creates an idea does not have the impression that it is any thought of his; but rather he seems to see reality itself in immediate contact with himself. . . .

Every culture or every great phase of culture ends in man's socialization, and vice versa; socialization pulls man out of his life of solitude, which is his real and authentic life. Note that man's socialization, his absorption by the social self, appears not only at the end of cultural evolution, but also before culture begins.[85]

Under these species of Syndicalism and Fascism there appears for the first time in Europe a type of man who does not want to give reasons or to be right, but simply shows himself resolved to impose his opinions. This is the new thing: the right not to be reasonable, the 'reason of unreason'. Here I see the most palpable manifestation of the new mentality of the

masses, due to their having decided to rule society without the
capacity for doing so. In their political conduct the structure
of the new mentality is revealed in the rawest, most convincing
manner: but the key to it lies in intellectual hermetism. . . .

Civilisation is nothing else than the attempt to reduce force
to being the *ultima ratio*. We are now beginning to realise this
with startling clearness, because 'direct action' consists in in-
verting the order and proclaiming violence as *prima ratio*, or
strictly as *unica ratio*. It is the norm which proposes the an-
nulment of all norms, which suppresses all intermediate process between our purpose and its execution. It is the Magna
Charta of barbarism.

It is well to recall that at every epoch when the mass, for
one purpose or another, has taken a part in public life, it has
been in the form of 'direct action'. This was, then, the natural
*modus operandi* of the masses. . . .

All our communal life is coming under this regime in which
appeal to 'indirect' authority is suppressed. In social relations
'good manners' no longer hold sway. Literature as 'direct action' appears in the form of insult. The restrictions of sexual
relations are reduced.

Restrictions, standards, courtesy, indirect methods, justice,
reason! Why were all these invented, why all these complica-
tions created? They are all summed up in the word civilisation,
which, through the underlying notion of *civis*, the citizen,
reveals its real origin. By means of all these there is an attempt
to make possible the city, the community, common life. . . .
All, in fact, presuppose the radical progressive desire on the
part of each individual to take others into consideration. Civilisation is before all, the will to live in common. A man is un-
civilised, barbarian in the degree in which he does not take
others into account. Barbarism is the tendency to disassocia-
tion. Accordingly, all barbarous epochs have been times of
human scattering, of the pullulation of tiny groups, separate
from and hostile to one another.[86]

Consequently, the ensuing retrogression into 'unreason' is the first step
towards 'barbarism' and constitutes a denial of civilizational accom-

plishments.[87] So, for example, social institutions and organizations are means designed to perpetuate impulses of reason and expediency in a civilized manner. We might therefore ask why people periodically seem to retrogress into savagery. It seems that those who do so, lacking historical and personal experience, are unable to avoid commonplace pitfalls and erroneous conclusions in regard to their endeavors. They are those who for a number of reasons, which should be further researched, have been by-passed by the civilizational process and instead have chosen to participate in a process of retrogression, involution, and decay. Ideally, therefore, an avoidance of such behavior patterns by introducing non-violent changes can be brought about only by men of genius who are better equipped to avoid 'false dawns.'[88]

> Consequently, without a spiritual power, *without someone to command*, and in proportion as this is lacking, chaos reigns over mankind. And similarly, all displacement of power, every change of authority, implies a change of opinions, and therefore nothing less than a change of historical gravitation.[89]

Since we 'are constantly seeking an internal justification for life,'[90] and are unable to find satisfactory answers ourselves, we will tend to turn to spiritual leadership. However, in times when traditional spiritual leadership has come to an end and man's judgment is impaired, the opportunity for new prophets is enhanced. Mao, Stalin, Mussolini, and Hitler not only were pacemakers of new socio-political trends but also revaluated the current ethical concepts and practices. Theirs was the power to perpetuate civilized practices or to retrogress into primitivism. Each of them became obsessed with an idée fixe of his own. Yet it would be a mistake to assume that their individual preoccupations were not similar to the ones prevalent among the larger segments of the populace which gave them their support. 'Hence there are periods in which it is enough only to give a shout, no matter how arbitrary its phrasing, for everyone to surrender themselves to it. These are periods of *chantage* in history.'[91] The socio-political system then most likely to be imposed will be regarded primarily as a means to safeguard the newly established leadership position. Once the masses become a part of the new system they are rendered helpless.[92] Those especially who are experiencing a change of mind, or who otherwise become disenchanted with the new leadership and system, now find themsleves in a cul-de-sac which can be even more oppressive than the one they were in before. 'Man,' however, '... adapts himself to everything, to the best and the worst. To one thing only does he not adapt himself: to being not clear in his own mind concerning what he believes about things.'[93] Hitler was well aware of this and saw to it that National Socialist ideology catered to this need. National Socialism as a mass movement attracted and was able to hold a following not because it was designed to satisfy a need for self-advancement but because it could satisfy a desire for self-renunciation.

Some light has been shed on the question of why people supported Hitler and his system – but who were they, in what ways did they cooperate? Walther Rathenau envisioned them as a 'vertical invasion of the barbarians' and Breysig has viewed them as ' "peoples of perpetual dawn" (those who have remained in a motionless, frozen twilight, which never progresses towards midday).'[94] More specifically, Hitler's supporters came predominantly from the lower middle class. This class appears to make fascism in general an essentially petit bourgeois movement.[95] The 'vertical invaders' now became the administrators, bureaucrats, and desk perpetrators, as well as the 'Handlanger' (helpers, handymen), all of whom perceived it as their duty to aggress upon or shed the blood of their fellow men. These men perpetuated the system either because they were unable to see alternative modes of behavior or, if they were aware of alternatives, because they were not ready to act upon their recognition and risk a loss of personal security or otherwise imperil their mundane existence. By acting as they did

> these men were trying to resolve their problem of living ... by reducing contact to a minimum. The withdrawal by man into a corner of the world is an accurate symbol of the first stage of desperation. It means that man, in effect, reduces life and the world to a corner, to a single fragment of what it was formerly.[96]

This withdrawal from threatening or unbearable social situations can be regarded as a specific type of moral and mental confusion (dementia) in which individual and collective responsibility is surrendered to a charismatic personage or superior force. In the case of National Socialism it was Adolf Hitler and his 'Vorsehung.' Simultaneously during this phase of demoralization a growing impatience with reason and reasoned action occurred among the masses which gave expression to what is known as anti-intellectualism.[97] Impulsive action was advocated to bring about immediate drastic changes regardless of sacrifices or consequences involved. Yet such movements are also occasionally led by intellectuals, professionals, and educated individuals whose frustration with the present situation of unrest and unresolved conflicts has reached its upper limit (e.g., Otto and Gregor Strasser, Hermann Rauschning, Hans Frank, etc.). They find relief in a highly structured system and in direct rather than contemplated action, for which they delegate responsibility to the supreme leader. However, if they fail to achieve the desired relief, they may soon find themselves not only relieved of their leadership role but also in greater anguish than before. The vacated positions are quickly filled with people who have little regard for the future of civilization and have virtually no experience in policy making, administrative work, and complex human interaction in general. In short, they are the 'perennially primitive'[98] who have therefore not participated in the civilizational process of mankind. As Ortega y Gasset astutely observed:

> The man who despairs of culture turns against it and declares its laws and its norms to be worn out and abolished. The mass man who in these days takes on the directing of life feels himself deeply flattered by this declaration, because culture which is, after all, an authentic imperative, weighs on him too heavily; and in their abolition of culture he sees a permit to kick up his heels, get out of himself, and give himself over to a life of licentiousness.[99]

Finally, there are several other factors which must be considered for a complete understanding of the organs of violence, be it at the juvenile, student- and racial-rioting, or revolutionary level, or in a process of escalation into cold or hot war. These factors are the leader's psychological makeup, his interaction with others, and his socio-economic background. These three must also be considered with respect to his leadership corps and his immediate followers. Without a clearer understanding, especially of the forces that shape the individual, we will fail to understand the direction that local or international violence will take.[100] Furthermore, it is being suggested that closer attention and more support should be given to a slowly developing branch of criminology, namely that of political crime.[101] More specifically, the term political crime, or crime against humanity, is used in connection with all those offenders who have been charged by the people with executive and administrative authority who have neglected or misused their political, professional, or social responsibility and have thus jeopardized individual freedom (freedom of expression and movement) and caused serious damage to the safety, health, or lives of individuals, groups, or society at large, by whom they are liable to be called to account. It appears that this type of offense is even more dependent upon societal norms and values which are still adhered to and considered to be valid than many other types of crime which are more readily detectable in their early stages because they are viewed as so 'clearly' deviant. The numerous trials of concentration camp officials and similar 'offenders against humanity',[102] especially initiators and perpetrators of mass persecution and extermination, have demonstrated that since 1945 most of these individuals have not come into overt conflict with the law. That is to say, they conformed to the laws of the land when society and its legislation were predominantly guided by humanitarian and democratic principles, just as they had obeyed the laws of the NS-Régime. Such findings indicate that the political safety of society could be reinforced even more effectively if the contributions of the social sciences were utilized more appropriately.

In essence, the starting position for the foregoing discussion on the process of escalation into destruction can be found in a notion expressed by the party ideologist, Alfred Rosenberg, in his prison cell in Nuremberg on December 15, 1945:

> Ich glaube, er (Hitler) wurde einfach mitgerissen. Wir dachten am Anfang nicht daran, irgend jemanden zu töten, das kann ich Ihnen versichern! Ich trat immer für eine friedliche Lösung ein. Ich hielt vor 10 000 Leuten eine Rede, die dann gedruckt und in großen Mengen verteilt wurde, in der ich für eine friedliche Lösung eintrat. Die Juden sollten lediglich aus ihren einflußreichen Positionen heraus, das war alles.[103]

――

... I don't know. I guess it just ran away with him [Hitler].

We didn't contemplate killing anybody in the beginning; I can assure you of that. I always advocated a peaceful solution. I held a speech before 10,000 people which was later printed and distributed widely, advocating a peaceful solution. Just taking the Jews out of their influential positions, that's all.'[103]

## 2. *Conclusion*

It was not merely Hitler's preoccupation with racist ideas and aggression, but rather the NS system, per se, created by him and his leaders, which precipitated an escalation into destruction. However, this could only be accomplished with the support of the masses who had permitted themselves to be engulfed by the system. The majority of the populace had accepted the rigid, hierarchical chain of command and more or less uncritically followed the biddings of those in authoritative positions. The influence of the NS subculture of violence, i.e., its underlying myth system, had a deeply demoralizing effect upon German society, bringing about a change of attitude towards traditional values and norms as reflected in human interaction. Passive acceptance of the 'inevitable' appeared to prevail, partly because in German society there was a striking lack of social imagination, capacity for concern, and ability to function without a rigidly structured socio-political system. A basic traditional obedience to, trust in, and respect and admiration for authority and its administrative apparatus, as well as a strong emphasis on social status differentiation, enhanced totalitarian leadership roles.[104] Attention has been drawn to the Prussian tradition in which the state is placed above the individual to whom the status and role of a servant is assigned.[105] Christian Fürchtegott Gellert (1715-69) reflects on this interdependency relationship in his fable 'Die Bienen' (1746):

. . . .

Der Weiser rief darauf den Rest der Unterthanen
Um sie zur Eintracht zu ermahnen.
Der Unterschied in eurer Pflicht
Erzeugt, sprach er, den Vorzug nicht.
Nur die dem Staat am treusten dienen,
Dieß sind allein die bessern Bienen.[106]

> Thereupon the sage called upon the rest of the subjects
> To warn them of the need of harmony.
> The difference in your duties, he said,
> Does not give rise to any system of preferences.
> Only those who serve the state most faithfully,
> Only those are the better bees. [106]

Y Gasset predicts: 'Society will have to live *for* the State, man *for* the governmental machine . . . Society begins to be enslaved, to be unable to live except *in the service of the State*. The whole life is bureaucratised . . . The bureaucratisation of life brings about its absolute decay in all orders. . . . Then the State, in order to attend its own needs, forces on still more the bureaucratisation of human existence. This bureaucratisation to the second power is the militarisation of society. The State's most urgent need is its apparatus of war, its army. Before all the State is the producer of security (that security, be it remembered, of which the mass-man is born).' [107] Eventually, '. . . the State gets the upper hand and society has to begin to live for the State.' [108] Stalin, Mussolini, Mao, and Hitler acted upon the formula: 'All for the State; nothing outside the State; nothing against the State.' [109] An indication of a rise of anti-democratic thinking and radicalism is frequently expressed in the out-cry for 'law and order.' [110] Simultaneously, it is a symptom of anti-intellectualism and lack of sophistication to imagine that these forces of public authority, or the dictates of a majority and in some cases the coercion of a minority, will bring about a less problematic and stratified interaction among various segments of people within a given society. Force and fear are unsuited to creating insight, acceptance, and respect for the beliefs, customs, and values of others, or a willingness to cooperate because of a better understanding. The forces that are willing to preserve and uphold the status quo of institutions which have clearly outlived their socio-political usefulness are also likely to impose that order which suits them best. This is frequently done by increasing coercive pressures and enforcing submission to their norms and rules of the game. Especially during this phase retrogression into direct action takes place. This action crushes independence and individualism and negates civilizational achievements. During this stage of demoralization man begins to seek a new meaning for his existence, a new purpose in life which would help him towards an acceptable identity. [111]

The choice of a new leader will then determine to what extent he will be able to find an equanimity. Whether the new ethos will also bring a new ideology (or vice versa) will much depend on the formerly adhered to beliefs and the degree of dissatisfaction with them. If there has been a high degree of dissatisfaction, the aspiration and revelation of seers will then introduce the Leitmotiv of a new 'Zeitgeist' which will be implemented by the leaders and handed down to the masses.

Imbalance of power and authority provides a fertile soil for the rise of despotism and totalitarianism in general. Man has been taught for ages to delegate responsibility for his socio-political welfare to the state, more specifically, to the public service élite. Neither has man learned to become authoritative in governing himself nor has he successfully learned the art of rational decision-making. Hitler and his hierarchically structured leadership corps – extending down to the ordinary party member – successfully exploited this traditional frame of mind by keeping its subjects in a state of unprecedented political dependency, ignorance, and powerlessness. After a brief initial period (1933-1934) of assertion, re-grouping, and consolidation (in terms of Pareto's circulation of the élite), power, status, and privileges were given to the newly installed Nazi administration and bureaucracy. Thus, once more, the people were induced and gradually coerced into subservience to the state – except this time a state dominated by one party.

However, these are but a few of the numerous factors which triggered the escalation into violence. To begin with, although the Jews as an ancient historical minority and traditional target of aggression served as foremost victims of the NS ingroup's racist policy, persecution spread quickly to other groups which the Régime declared to be its antagonists. Again it should be stressed that anti-Semitism was but one integral part, one consequence, of National Socialist ideology. None of the aforementioned factors alone suffices to explain *the* cause of the holocaust. Rather, they must be viewed as clusters of interdependent correlates which precipitated socio-political violence in German society. To identify, while they are still in a formative stage, the consequences of specific social patterns appearing in the aforementioned clusters and leading to an escalation of violence, should become one of the foremost predictive functions of contemporary social scientists.

*Part V*

Sociological Implications
of Deviance and
Accountability in
NS Political and
Bureaucratic Institutions

*Who, then, is sane? (Quisnam igitur sanus?)*

Horace: *Satires*, II

*Wer immer strebend sich bemüht, den können wir erlösen.*

Goethe: *Faust*, II

*Whoever strives with all his power,*
*We are allowed to save.*

Goethe: *Faust*, II

# 1. The sociological vision of Walther Rathenau's concept of social change

The fate of Jews in Nazi Germany led usually to one of two alternatives. They could either take advantage of their already limited freedom by hiding within German territory or escaping from it – a choice which avoided deportation into concentration or destruction camps but which subjected them to an unknown, insecure, and unsupportive social setting – or they could submit to the incompassionate whims of state authority, accepting, in a perhaps deterministic way, a structured, totalitarian institution. The overwhelming majority chose the latter alternative, whose almost inevitable result was the loss of life. Otto Rank (1885-1939) in his social philosophy[1] offers an interesting psychological explanation for this type of response. He perceives the interaction and role of the neurotic 'victim' and that of 'the lordly natures, the men of will,' or simply the superman, in the following terms:

> If one conceives of the neurotic as a type, with psychological significance in itself, and not as a person deviating from a social norm, then one can see that there exists a place for this type socially, yes, a real need, otherwise he would perhaps not have come into existence in our civilization at all. If the fundamental life fear of the individual leads, figuratively speaking, to the end that he has no other choice than to be slain or slay, the question is who are the sacrifices that must constantly fall in this way? I think it is the type which we today designate as neurotic which the New Testament characterizes as 'christian' and which Nietzsche in the ideology of earlier times has described as the slave type. . . . In offering themselves up as it were in a Christian sense, they make it not too hard for the others who slay, the lordly natures, the men of will. In view of the difficulties of the therapy one must ask whether it is not a vain therapeutic ambition to want to transform this sacrificial type into god-men. . . .[2]

The frequent assertion of psychoanalytically oriented writers that victims of aggression – the Jews persecuted by the Nazis, for example – tend to identify with their aggressors is ill-conceived. Instead of identifying with their aggressors, the persecuted Jews continued to adhere to their accustomed frame of reference and to find their identity as before within the predominantly just and generally acceptable norms and values of the society in which they lived, of which they were a part, and which they believed to be upheld by responsible representatives of state authority, namely the administrators and bureaucrats.

Indeed, for the injustices and atrocities committed by the Nazis, especially in camps and prisons, there was no historical precedent. Once a victim had entered the National Socialist machinery of destruction there was no way, at least physically, of defending his liberty or civil rights. Hence for most the experience was a road of no return – a one-way ticket. Those who first recognized and accepted Nazi authority frequently also viewed its representatives as authorities and not merely as authoritarian and unjust. They were not capable of living, or indeed of viewing their lives, without accepted rulings and decisions made by state authority. Thus most of them preferred to submit their fate to verdicts originating with NS state authority regardless of the outcome. We need, therefore, to raise one basic question: can society exist and function without what is perceived and accepted as authority? We need to examine our atomic age in this regard. Has authoritativeness become obsolete? If so, and if an alternative is necessary, should it perhaps be that, in the future, all those vested with authority become 'authorities' in the true sense of the word?

Walther Rathenau (1867-1922) drew up in 1912 a model of the function of authority and its division of labor. This model was especially representative of Central European society at that time, and may still be valid for ours. He states:

> ... der Obere herrscht, leitet, verantwortet und schützt, der Untere gehorcht, leistet, dient und strebt. Der Obere erzieht sich zur Gesinnung und Freiheit, der Untere zur Ausdauer und Fertigkeit. Daß solche Arbeitsteilung Großes hervorzubringen bestimmt ist, zeigt jede bewußte Organisation bis in die jüngste Zeit.[3]

> ------

> ... the executive rules, guides, protects, and assumes responsibility; the subordinate obeys, performs, serves, and strives. The executive seeks to attain conviction and freedom,

the subordinate seeks endurance and skill. That such a division of labor is capable of great accomplishment has been borne out by any thoughtfully designed organization up to most recent times.[3]

Rathenau was basically in agreement with Frederick the Great, who was first to define the role of the sovereign as servant of the state.[4] Frederick the Great perhaps fashioned this role after the traditional ecclesiastical role, namely that of the servus servorum dei. Frederick the Great believed that anyone in authority serving the people and the state was in fact to play the role of a servant, a servant of humanity. Rathenau felt that these concepts had undergone a transition and were in a state of flux due to novel and conflicting values and norms resulting from the mechanization of the world – in short, as a product of cultural and social change. One of the basic changes occurred in the function of labor itself. He writes:

Die Arbeit selbst aber ist nicht mehr eine Funktion des Lebens, nicht mehr eine Anpassung des Leibes und der Seele an die Naturkräfte, sondern weitaus eine fremde Funktion zum Zweck des Lebens, eine Anpassung des Leibes und der Seele an den Mechanismus. Denn mit Ausnahme der wenigen freien Berufe, deren Wesen ungeteilt und Selbstzweck ist, der künstlerischen, wissenschaftlichen und sonsthin schöpferisch gestaltenden Arbeit, ist der mechanisierte Beruf Teilwerk. Es sieht keinen Anfang und kein Ende, es steht keiner vollendeten Schöpfung gegenüber; denn er schafft Zwischenprodukte und durchläuft Zwischenstadien. Auch er kann angepaßten Naturen eine absolut erscheinende Befriedigung gewähren, insbesondere da, wo er mit Privilegien und Befugnissen operiert; im allgemeinen aber trägt er seine Belohnung nicht in sich, sondern hinter sich, er verlangt nicht sowohl Liebe als Interesse.

Mit der Abkehr des Berufes von der Natur zur Mechanisierung haben sich weitere Änderungen seines Wesens vollzogen.

Zum ersten: der alte Beruf war gegründet auf Erfahrung und Erlernung. Der Sohn vollbrachte im Kreislauf des Jahres, was der Vater im Kreislauf des Jahres vollbracht hatte. Der

Alte hatte die längere Übung, er hatte mehr Zwischenfälle erlebt: so war er geschulter und weiser. Zu ihm blickte man auf, er war Autorität. Was das junge Geschlecht zum Ererbten hinzufügte, war freiwilliger Tribut an die langsam sich ändernde Meinung der Zeit, nicht Not und Zwang.

Wollte heute einer sein Land bestellen, seine Schuhe fertigen, seine Schnittware verkaufen, wie es ihn seine Vorfahren gelehrt, er wäre bald mit seiner Weisheit am Ende; könnte er sie bei seinen wechselnden Zwischenfällen um Rat fragen, er erhielte falsche Auskunft. Er muß wie ein Fechter der launischen Mechanisierung ins Auge schaun, ihre Finten parieren, ihren Stößen zuvorkommen. Er muß planen, erfinden, nachahmen, ausprobieren, um sich zu erhalten. Den Begriff der Autorität versteht er nicht mehr, und Respekt hat er nur da, wo er Erfolg sieht.[5]

----

But labor itself is no longer a function of life, no longer an adaptation of body and soul to the powers of nature, but, rather, more an alien function for the purpose of life, an adaptation of body and soul to mechanization. For with the exception of the few free professions that are essentially an end in themselves – work which is artistic, scientific and otherwise creative – the mechanized occupation is fragmentary work. It knows no beginning and no end; it will not be faced with a creation, for it makes intermediate products and passes through intermediary stages. It appears to offer an absolute satisfaction to those who have been able to adjust, especially where such activity is rewarded with privileges and authority. But in general it does not bring reward itself, but rather promises it. The mechanized occupation requires neither dedication nor interest.

With the turning away of labor from nature towards mechanization, further changes in its character have taken place.

Firstly: the old vocation was based on experience and the learning process. The son accomplished in the course of the year what the father had accomplished in the course of his year. The older man had more practice, he had more experience; hence, he was more schooled and wiser. One looked up to him, he was an authority. What the younger generation added to its inheritance was a voluntary contribution to the slowly changing mood of the times; it was not based on need and coercion.

If someone today wanted to cultivate his land, manufacture his shoes, or sell his dry goods the way his ancestors had taught him, he would soon be at his wit's end. If, amidst these changing circumstances, he could ask his ancestors for advice, he would receive wrong information. Like a fencer, he must face ill-humored mechanization squarely in the eye, parry its feints, anticipate its blows. He must plan, invent, experiment to survive. He no longer understands the concept of authority, and he has respect only for that in which he sees success. [5]

The conceptual alteration of the traditional division of labor, and therefore also of authority and its implications, is, according to Rathenau, chiefly responsible for bringing about a radical change in certain basic social norms and values. This, in turn, brought about certain attitudes which have often had a deeply alienating and dehumanizing effect upon interpersonal relations in general. The basic forms of man's struggle for survival have likewise undergone alterations, especially in those parts of the world in which Western civilization prevails. In fact, nothing has remained static: our standards, values, goals, indeed our basic philosophies of life are all subject to constant change and re-evaluation. Rathenau asserts that these factors must be reflected also in our ideals, in the political sphere, in our leisure time activities, in our consumer habits, and in the introduction of innovations in general. In Germany the responsibility for some of the modern changes, which were in fact brought about by the technical age, was placed squarely upon the 'un-German' spirit, but even more specifically upon the Jews:

Daß ungermanischer Geist für die Gestaltung der Moderne verantwortlich ist, hat mancher unwilliger Denker dem Volksgewissen ins Ohr geraunt, doch stets in der Meinung, zu entarteten Germanen zu sprechen. So suchte man nach einem Ferment und entdeckte es im Judentum. Der Antisemitismus ist die falsche Schlußfolgerung aus einer höchst wahrhaften Prämisse: der europäischen Entgermanisierung; und somit kann

derjenige Teil der Bewegung, der Rückkehr zum Germanentum wünscht, sehr wohl respektiert und verstanden werden,
wenn er auch die praktische Unmöglichkeit einer Volksent-
mischung postuliert.

Die Lehre von der semitischen Gährung hat jüngst ein geist-
voller Nationalökonom in anziehender Weise mit einer Art
verdrießlicher Bewunderung des schuldigen Teils entwickelt,
indem er das Neuzeitwesen auf den Kapitalismus, den Kapitalismus auf das Judentum zurückführt. Er denkt also im Ernst
daran, dem kleinen Volksstamm, dem die Welt die Hälfte ihres
Gesamtbesitzes an religiöser Transzendenz schuldet, nun auch
die Summe der materiellen Lebensordnung zuzuschreiben. Der
Irrtum liegt in der Verkennung der Tatsache, daß Kapitalismus, so gut wie Technik, Wissenschaft, Verkehr, Kolonisa-
tion, Städteentwicklung oder Weltpolitik, nur Einzelerschei-
nungen der Grundfunktion bedeuten, die in der Verdichtung
und ihrer Selbstbehauptung, der Mechanisierung, liegt. . . . Am
schwersten aber wird der Gärungstheorie der Nachweis fallen,
daß durch große Einwirkung eines Fermentes aus taciteischen
und karolingischen Germanen preußische Kaufleute, Fabrik-
arbeiter, Gelehrte und Beamte werden konnten.[6]

---

Many an indignant theorist (Denker) was whispering to the
people's conscience that an un-Germanic spirit is responsible
for the fashioning of modernism, always, however, assuming
that he was speaking to degenerated Germans. Hence, a
fermenting agent was sought, and was discovered in Jewry.
Anti-Semitism is the false conclusion drawn from a perfectly
valid premise: the de-Germanization (Entgermanisierung) of
Europe. Part of the movement, which wishes a return to the
Teutonic state, can very well be respected and understood,
even if it postulates the practical impossibility of a segregation
of the peoples.

The doctrine of the Semitic fermentation has, in an alluring
way, been recently developed by an ingenious economist, with
a kind of vexed admiration for the guilty party, deriving
modernism from capitalism, and capitalism from Jewry. Thus,
he seriously believes that one can attribute to this small tribe,

to which the world is indebted for half of its total knowledge
of religious transcendentalism, the entire material way of life
(Lebensordnung) as well. The error lies in the lack of appreci-
ation of the fact that capitalism, as well as technology, science,
transportation, colonization, urban development, and world
politics, are but manifestations of the basic function which, in
its compressed and self-asserted form, is mechanization. . . .
The most difficult task in support of the fermentation theory,
however, will be to prove that the strong influence of a fermenting agent could have transformed the Teutons of Tacitus
and the Carolingian Teutons into Prussian merchants, factory
workers, scholars, and civil servants. [6]

According to Rathenau, the restraining influence of social antecedents
is reflected not only in the gradual processes of social change but also,
and especially, in the revolutionary mechanization of the world. The
following are some of the social factors reflecting such major inter-
vening influences which bring about a fusion of traditional, antecedent
values, norms, and behavioral paradigms with innovative social forces:

(1)   The contemporary consumer habits:
Wie die Eroberer des Pekinger Kaiserpalastes bis an die
Knie in seidenen Stoffen wateten, so stampft der erwerbende
Mensch durch Ströme von Waren, mit denen ihn keine einge-
wohnte Liebe zum Gerät verbindet, und läßt Ströme von Ab-
fällen hinter sich zurück. Wir lesen vom Reichtum einer
griechischen Stadt und bedenken nicht, daß im Hause des
Bürgers nichts anderes zu finden war, als ein paar Tische und
Betten, ein Dutzend Tongefäße, Decken und vielleicht ein
kupferner Kessel. Die jährlichen Abgänge einer unserer bürgerlichen Wohnungen sind umfangreicher als dieser ganze
klassische Besitz.
Ehrgeiz und Warenhunger arbeiten sich in die Hände. Der
eine zwingt den Menschen, sich immer fester in das Joch der
Mechanisierung einzupressen; er steigert seine Erfindungs-
kraft, seinen produktiven Willen. Der andere erhöht sein Kon-
sumbedürfnis und läßt ihn doch gleichzeitig empfinden, daß
nur ein emsig schaffendes Organ die Lust des Kaufens dauernd
genießen darf. [7]

(1)  The contemporary consumer habits:
As the conquerors of the Emperor's Palace in Peking waded in silken fabrics up to their knees, so the acquisitive man stomps through streams of goods to which he is not bound by any accustomed love of his tools, and leaves streams of refuse behind. We read about the wealth of a Greek city and do not realize that in a citizen's house there was nothing to be found but a couple of tables and beds, a dozen earthen vessels, blankets, and perhaps a copper kettle. What is discarded annually in one of our bourgeois households is more extensive than this entire classical possession.

Ambition and appetite for consumer goods reinforce each other. The one forces man to settle ever more firmly in the yoke of mechanization; he increases his inventiveness and his productive will. The other augments his need to consume, yet at the same time makes him aware that only an assiduously industrious being may continue to enjoy the pleasure of buying.[7]

(2)  The human and ethic ideals:
Der Aufrührer, der Revolutionär, der kirchliche Empörer, der Konquistador werden gepriesen, verehrt und zuweilen staatlich anerkannt, wenn sie Erfolg haben. . . .

Amerikanische Menschen des Erfolges beginnen den Massen zu imponieren; mutige Erfinder und Entdecker werden höher gefeiert als vordem Kriegshelden; zum Lesebuch des Volkes ist nach Ritter- und Indianergeschichten der Detektivroman geworden. Ja es beginnt hier bereits eine gewisse Verwirrung des bürgerlichen Empfindens: in einer Zeit, die den Erfolg an die Stelle des Sieges gesetzt hat, kann man nicht umhin sich einzugestehen, daß den Helden von ehedem die Eigenschaften fehlen, welche die Mechanisierung verlangt. Man strebt, den Erfolgreichen nachzuahmen, und kann somit nicht unterlassen, sie zu bewundern, wo nicht gar zu lieben. Roosevelt kämpft mit Blücher und gedenkt zu siegen. Das germanische Ideal, das dem Ansturm des Christentums durch ein Jahrtausend standhielt, ist durch die Mechanisierung erschüttert. . . . So begnügte sich die ältere Zeit hinsichtlich aller

Wohlfahrtsbestrebungen damit, Siechenhäuser, Irrenkerker und Klostersuppen zu stiften, und alles übrige der privaten Barmherzigkeit anheimzustellen. Die mechanistische Epoche dagegen übernahm von ihren Schöpfern, unterdrückten und furchthaften Stämmen das Mitleid, das nichts anderes als eine altruistische Furchtempfindung ist. In der Verherrlichung dieses Pathemas zum ethischen Ideal lag zweifellos eine gewisse Diesseitigkeit der Anschauung, ja ein ethischer Materialismus; doch ist durch die gesetzgeberische und organisatorische Ausgestaltung des Wohlfahrtswesens, vor allem aber durch die Überzeugung des öffentlichen Gewissens, daß alles menschliche Elend als Blutschuld der Gesellschaft zu erachten sei, ein Wert von so gewaltiger Positivität entstanden, daß jede künftige Einschätzung der Mechanisierung ihn in Rechnung zu stellen haben wird.[8]

---

(2)   The human and ethic ideals:
The agitator, the revolutionary, the religious insurgent, the conquistador are praised, honored, and occasionally receive recognition by the state if they succeed . . .

American men of success are beginning to impress the masses. Courageous inventors and discoverors are more celebrated than military heroes in former times; stories of knights and Red Indians, formerly the popular literature of the masses, have now been succeeded by the detective novel. Indeed, we can see the beginning of a certain confusion in the bourgeois perception: in a time which has replaced victory by success, one cannot avoid the admission that the heroes of former days lack the attributes which mechanization demands. One strives to imitate the successful, and thus one cannot help but admire or even love them. Roosevelt fights with Blücher and intends to win. The Germanic ideal, which resisted the assault of Christianity for a thousand years, is shaken by mechanization. . . . Thus, with respect to attempts to improve welfare, men of former times were content to found infirmaries, lunatic asylums, and soup kitchens in cloisters, and leave everything else to private charity. The mechanistic epoch, on the other hand, adopted from its creators, the repressed and fearful tribes, compassion which is nothing but an altruistic feeling of fear. In the glorification of this 'pathema' to an ethic ideal lay, no doubt, a certain worldliness, indeed, an ethic materialism. Nevertheless, the legislative and organizational development of the welfare system and, above all, the conviction of the public conscience that all human misery is to be regarded as a capital crime of society, have engendered a value that is so strongly positive that every future assessment of mechanization will have to take it into account.[8]

(3) The religious ideals:
So mächtig die Kirche das Leben der früheren Jahrhunderte durchdrang, so gering war die Wirkung der in ihr verkörperten reinen christlichen Ideen auf das Germanentum. Widerwillig aufgenommen, durch Höllenzwang gefestigt, konnte die Kirche den Abgrund, der zwischen dem Worte Christi und ihren hierarchisch-politischen Aufgaben lag, nicht überbrücken. Mit dem Mutideal des Germanen, das ihren Lehren der Demut widersprach, mußte sie sich abfinden; die wenig evangelischen Sitten abendländischer Lebensweise, Politik, Kriegsführung mußte sie dulden, ja ihren irdischen Zielen dienstbar machen. Den letzten transzendenten Inhalt dieser Verkündigung durfte sie den Massen nicht übermitteln, um nicht die weltliche Ordnung zu stören oder aufzuheben. Die Lehre von der Liebe, der Weltflucht, der Demut, der Kindlichkeit, der Zweckfreiheit, dem Gottesreich blieb esoterisch, ein Besitz der Heiligen. Ins Volk drang der Mariendienst, die Geschichte der Geburt und der Leiden Jesu, der Olymp der Heiligen, der Begriff der Sünde und der Gnade, Himmel und Hölle. . . .
  Die Anschauung dieser Welt geht eben dahin, alles Geschehene sei unerstaunlich, von ausschließlicher Realität, nicht ethischen, sondern mechanischen Gesetzen unterworfen, ohne absolute Werte, durch Vernunft erschöpfbar. Diese Anschauung ist aber nichts anderes als die Gefühlslokalisierung der Tatsache, daß der noch junge mechanistische Prozeß die Seelenkräfte zugunsten der Geisteskräfte unterdrückt.[9]

---

(3) The religious ideals:

The penetration of Germanic life by the Church in earlier centuries was as powerful as the influence of the pure Christian ideas it incorporated was weak. Involuntarily received and established on the fear of Hell, the Church was unable to bridge the gap that lay between the word of Christ and its hierarchic-political tasks. It had to come to terms with the Germanic ideal of courage, which contradicted its doctrine of humility. The Church had to put up with the mores of occidental life style, politics, warfare – unevangelical as they were – indeed, put them in the service of its worldly goals. In order not to distrub or abolish the wordly order, the Church could not transmit the ultimate transcendental content of its preaching to the masses. The doctrine of love, withdrawal from life, humility, childlike innocence, freedom from self-interest (Zweckfreiheit), the Kingdom of God, remained esoteric – a possession of the Saints. What penetrated to the people was the service of Mary, the story of the birth and sufferings of Jesus, the Olympus of the Saints, the concept of sin and grace, Heaven and Hell. . . .

The view in this world tends to be that all events are explainable, of exclusive reality, not subject to ethical but to mechanistic laws without absolute value, and can be grasped by reason. This view, however, is nothing but the emotional realization of the fact that the still recent mechanistic process already represses the spiritual powers in favor of the mental powers.[9]

(4) The political ideals:
Es braucht wohl nicht ausgesprochen zu werden, daß der Name des Nationalismus hier nicht als Synonym des Wortes Patriotismus genannt wird, daß vielmehr unter jenem Begriff die Tendenz verstanden ist, die Nationen in ihren Lebensfunktionen abzusondern, ihre Vergesellschaftung zu hindern. Auch in dieser Bedeutung bleibt der Nationalismus in seiner Urform berechtigt: es darf einer Nation nicht zugemutet werden, fremder Sprache, fremdem Glauben, fremder Kultur und fremder Obrigkeit sich zu fügen; das Weltcäsarentum hat seine Berechtigung verloren, und ein absoluter Kosmopolitismus wird

als politisches Ideal schwerlich wiederkehren. Indessen ist es durchaus denkbar, daß die staatlichen Organisationen über den Rahmen des Staates hinaus einen unvergleichlich weiteren Ausbau erfahren, als bisher durch völkerrechtliche, schiedsrichterliche und postalische Vereinbarungen geschehen.[10]

------

(4)  The political ideals:
It is surely not necessary to emphasize that 'nationalism' is not used here as a synonym of 'patriotism'. Rather, the term 'nationalism' denotes the tendency to separate nations in their vital functions, to prevent the process of socialization (Vergesellschaftung). Also in this sense nationalism remains justified in its original form (Urform): a nation cannot be expected to yield to a foreign language, a foreign belief, a foreign culture, or a foreign authority; imperialism (Weltcäsarentum) has lost its justification and an absolute cosmopolitanism as a political ideal will probably not return. However, it is perfectly conceivable that state organizations will undergo an incomparably greater development, beyond the framework of the state than heretofore, with respect to agreements on international law, arbitration, and the postal system.[10]

In the final assessment of his social analysis and observations Rathenau reflects on what he defines as the 'yearning of the time' (von der Sehnsucht der Zeit), in which he most aptly captures the prevailing tendencies and moods of the era. These perspectives, relevant not only to the present atomic age, can also serve as a key to a better understanding of the antecedents which played a dominant role in the development and character of National Socialism and its consequences. Rathenau asserts:

Trotzdem aber die Mechanisierung noch lange nicht ihren Zenith erreicht hat, trotzdem sie ihre Aufgabe, den Weltkreis zu europäisieren, erst nach Generationen erfüllen und vielleicht auch dann auch noch nicht kulminieren wird, trägt sie schon heute den Tod im Herzen. Denn im Urgrund ihres Bewußtseins graut dieser Welt vor ihr selbst; ihre innersten Regungen klagen sie an und ringen nach Befreiung aus den Ketten unablässiger Zweckgedanken.

Die Welt sagt, sie weiß, was sie will. Sie weiß es nicht, denn sie will Glück und sorgt um Materie. Sie fühlt, daß die Materie sie nicht beglückt, und sie ist verurteilt, sie immer von neuem zu begehren. Sie gleicht Midas, der im Goldstrom verschmachtet.

Die Hoffnungen, die aus der Tiefe aufsteigen und im Geiste Einzelner Bewußtsein erlangen, sind widerspruchsvoll und daher dem Gemeingeist unklar. . . .

Es ist, als sei die Welt flüssig geworden und zerrinne in den Händen. Alles ist möglich, alles ist erlaubt, alles ist begehrenswert, alles ist gut. Zuletzt tut der Abgrund der Zeiten sich auf, und es zeigt sich wie in Macbeths Spiegel jedes der Gesichte zu schwankenden Generationsreihen erweitert; jeder Mosaikstein des flimmernden Bildes wird zum endlosen Bande, und in jedem Querschnitt des Bündels erscheint ein neues Symbol unsäglicher Relativitäten.

Der Mensch aber begehrt Glauben und Werte. . . .

Die Welt erhielt ihr Gepräge von den Rebellen; an die Stelle der Kaste trat die Organisation, an die Stelle des Frohns die Maschine. . . .

Vor Jahren habe ich entwickelt, daß Furcht und Zweckhaftigkeit auf der einen, Mut und Zweckfreiheit auf der anderen Seite die Grundstimmungen des Menschengeistes ausdrükken. . . .

Ein Drittel, vielleicht die Hälfte der Weltarbeit geht auf, um der Menschheit Reizungs- und Betäubungsmittel, Schmuck, Spiel, Tand, Waffen, Vergnügungen und Zerstreuungen zu schaffen, deren sie zur Erhaltung des leiblichen, zur Beglükkung des seelischen Lebens nicht bedarf, die vielmehr dazu dienen, den Menschen dem Menschen und der Natur zu entfremden. . . .

Auch die Mechanik des Denkens ist höher gesteigert als zu irgend einer früheren Zeit. Denn das materielle Wissen ist gewaltig, die Menge der erkannten Zusammenhänge, der beobachteten Tatsachen, der verfügbaren Analogien unermeßlich. Vor allem aber sind wirksame, der Mechanisierung angepaßte Methoden und Formen des Denkens verfügbar, die früheren Zeiten unbekannt, heute von jedermann mühelos gehandhabt werden, vom Politiker, Dichter, Reporter und Landwirt. Beherrschend für unser Denkwesen ist die Form geworden, die man als Fluxionsmethode bezeichnen könnte. Sie besteht darin, daß die Erscheinung nicht mehr als ein fest Gegebenes angesehen wird, sondern als kontinuierliche Funktion variabler Faktoren. Auf ihr beruht die mathematische Analysis, die Entwicklungslehre, die historische Betrachtungsweise, das naturwissenschaftliche Messen, die Statistik. In Verbindung mit ihr haben mathematisch-physikalische, philosophisch-kritische, vergleichend naturwissenschaftliche, mechanisch konstruktive, praktisch organisatorische Methoden sich der Geister bemächtigt, und neue Begriffe, Verständigungsmittel, Lehren und Sprachformen geschaffen. . . .

Sie (die Sehnsucht unserer Zeit) schafft sich Gemeinden, Tempel und Altäre, und empfindet verzweifelnd, daß sie das Einzelne nicht glauben kann, weil sie alles glaubt, daß sie alles glauben muß, weil sie nichts glauben kann. Die Zeit sucht nicht ihren Sinn und ihren Gott, sie sucht ihre Seele, die im Gemenge des Blutes, im Gewühl des mechanistischen Denkens und Begehrens sich verdüstert hat. . . .

. . . diese Not entspringt nicht physikalischen und klimatischen Umwälzungen; sie ist von der Menschheit selbst geschaffen, die nunmehr, hinreichend entwickelt, ihrem eigenen Inneren überlassen, mit den gleichen Mitteln sich Qualen bereitet und Erlösung sucht.[11]

---

But despite the fact that mechanization is still far from its zenith, despite the fact that it will fulfill its task of Europeanizing the world only after generations have passed – and perhaps even then will not have reached its culmination – it is clearly carrying death in its heart. For in the very depths of its consciousness, this world has a horror of itself; its innermost emotions accuse it and struggle to be freed from the shackles of unceasing goal-oriented thought (Zweckgedanke).

The world says that it knows what it wants. It does not know, for it wants happiness, yet concerns itself with material things. It feels that material things do not make it happy, yet it is condemned always to desire them anew. It resembles Midas who languished in a stream of gold.

The hopes which ascend from the depths and attain awareness in the minds of a few are contradictory and hence unclear to the unsophisticated mind (Gemeingeist).

It is as if the world had become fluid and were melting in one's hand. Everything is possible, everything is permitted, everything is desirable, everything is good. Finally, the abyss of the times opens and one sees, as in Macbeth's mirror, each of the faces expanded into swaying rows of generations; every mosaic stone of the flickering picture turns into an endless ribbon, and in every cross-cut of the tangled skein appears a new symbol of immense relativities.

But man desires faith and values . . .

The world was moulded by the rebels; the caste was replaced by the organization, the serf by the machine . . .

Years ago I developed the theory that fear and expediency, on the one hand, and courage and freedom of purpose, on the other, express the fundamental moods of the human spirit . . .

A third, perhaps one half, of the work of the world is aimed at the production of stimulants and narcotics, jewelry, games, trinkets, weapons, recreation – diversions for mankind – which are not needed for the maintenance of bodily life nor for the happiness of psychic life; rather, they serve to alienate man from man and from nature . . .

Also, thinking has become more mechnized than at any time in the past. For material knowledge is immense, and the mass of recognized relationships, observed facts, and available analogies is immeasurable. But above all, we have available methods and forms of thinking which are effective and adapted to mechanization, methods and forms unknown to earlier times but which can easily be manipulated by everyone today – the politician, the poet, the reporter, and the farmer. The form which one could characterize as 'the method of fluxions' (Fluxionsmethode) has come to govern our way of thinking. It consists in regarding a phenomenon, no longer as a given datum, but rather as a continuous function of variable factors. On this method are based mathematical analysis, the doctrine of evolution, the historical viewpoint, scientific measurement, statistics. In connection with it, our minds have been seized by mathematical-physical, philosophical-critical, comparative-scientific, mechanical-constructive, and practical-organizational methods; and new concepts, means of understanding, doctrines, and linguistic forms have been created . . .

The yearning of our time creates for itself congregations, temples, and altars, and feels despairingly that it cannot believe a particular thing because it believes everything, that it must believe everything because it cannot believe anything. The time does not seek its meaning and its God; it seeks its soul, which has become darkened in the mingling of blood, in the tumult of mechanistic thinking and desiring . . .

. . . this distress does not originate in physical and climatic upheavals; it is created by mankind itself, which now has reached a stage where, left on its own, it torments itself and seeks redemption with the same means.[11]

With considerable foresight and sociological perception, Rathenau depicts a society and world in transition. His main theme, and the one of special interest here, is that no social force in the history of mankind has had such a singular, all-embracing influence in re-shaping social institutions and organizations and changing social interaction as the process of mechanization in our technical epoch. Its inescapable powers dominate the sources and methods of production and influence means of survival. Indeed, they are life-determinants, and in the final analysis have become a power-source of life itself. Up to the present time this power has been predominantly based on, and governed by, reason, with such formidable exceptions as Nazi Germany, Hiroshima and Nagasaki, and other courses of action taken by present-day major world powers and totalitarian régimes. These deviations from reasoned and reflected action should serve as a warning, especially in extreme stress situations when traditional solutions to social conflicts are no longer readily available. Then, indeed, as a West-German politician has unwittingly but aptly pointed out, a situation arises when 'a radical fringe whether of the left or of the right' can become 'an inevitable part of a democracy.'[12] However, one should hasten to add that under given circumstances – as recent history has shown – it can also devour it.

Rathenau, Oswald Spengler (1880-1936), and others have reflected upon an intellectual climate (Zeitgeist) in which totalitarian movements such as communism, fascism, and National Socialism can develop and thrive.[13] The antecedents of an absolute state have already been explicated by Nicolò Machiavelli (1469-1525) in his treatise *Il Principe* (*The Prince*). In this study Machiavelli searched for an ethical justification for the so-called evil.[14] He found it in a philosophy which claims an ominipotent sovereignty of the state and its principle ruler to which society with all its individually differentiated members is totally subordinated. Thus the state can formulate and reject moral principles according to situational requirements in time and space. Consequently, the powerless individual becomes increasingly confused and manipulable.

## 2. *National Socialist aggression and psychoanalytic theory*

Many contemporary psychotherapists in Western civilization have assumed the role of socio-moral leaders. Frequently they possess the advantages of an elevated social status and an authoritative medical frame of reference. One of the best-formulated statements representative of the values and objectives of these professionals has been given by the psychoanalytic theorist Erich Fromm:

> In the field of psychotherapy . . . the fundamental concepts of aim and method depend on one's personal religious, philosophical, political and social opinions. Answers to the questions – what is a neurotic, what is the aim of therapeutic treatment, what is psychic health – all depend on what the therapist considers 'best' for man.[15]

The notion of what is 'best' for man will certainly reflect the advocate's social background, level of intellectual and emotional maturity (holy alliance between intellect and emotion), milieu, socio-economic class affiliation, education, group, sub-group, or subculture membership, etc., but it will hardly constitute a correlate of his medical artistry.

The cure for social 'ills' does not therefore lie so much in the sphere of medical science as in the ability to solve social conflicts in a manner which avoids physical suffering and mental anguish. But this attitude, at least from a sociological point of view, clearly constitutes a bias. This bias, so prevalent in Western society, owes its existence to positivistic-materialistic philosophy (which includes Social Darwinism) and the Judeo-Christian heritage as well as the Greco-Roman antecedents of Western society. These are the fibers from which the value system, social norms, and moral code are woven. Nonetheless the keynote of most social conflicts seems to be aggression originating from the need to free oneself from intolerable dependency relations. This aggression most often arises during specific phases of socio-cultural change in which traditional social institutions are rendered dysfunctional. In addition, the urge permeating many a political philosophy to mobilize the hostility of the masses is still a dominant factor. Totalitarian organizations and institutions have been designed to bring about a total social control of their charges, to engage and implicate the masses in all activities and strategies of their leaders, including those that are injurious, destructive, and eventually frequently self-destructive. Thus intolerable dependency relations are most often encountered in situations where restrictive, highly manipulative authority roles predominate. Those who become implicated, or are co-opted (and therefore also inculpated), have little or no opportunity to assert the individual human needs by which men enhance their chances of self-realization. This is not to suggest that whenever intolerable dependency relations develop, a liberation from oppressive restraints will not be attempted whenever there is a viable chance or stimulus to do so.

Dependency relations can be roughly grouped into the following categories: emotional, mental (including intellectual), physical-material, and a combination of all three. There are several stages of dependency, of which the most extreme usually occur under normal circumstances during early childhood and old age (geriatric stage). Under non-normative conditions extreme dependency relationships can be found in cases of severe illness, or of deprivation of freedom of movement (as, for example, in total systems [Goffman], deprivation of expression, action, or basic bodily and emotional needs. Frequently dependency relationships are freely interchangeable; that is, specific dependency relationships may end or be done away with only to be replaced by others. In specific situations, restraint from freedom may not appear restrictive to the extent that an escape into a dependency is actually sought in the belief that it will free one from another intolerable state (such as, for example, the unknown or uncertainty). A dependency relationship is of course not limited to humans, but may also be extended to material objects and ideational and ideological concepts. In general the experience of dependency is ubiquitous but differs in time, space, and degree of oppressiveness. And at times, satisfaction is derived from a dependency relationship, until it becomes burdensome or intolerable. Dependency relations are thus in a continual, dynamic state of flux. They follow a specific attraction-repulsion pattern, frequently resulting in feelings of ambivalence. This transformative interplay within individually determined but very specific narrow confines perpetually vacillates from a state of relative freedom to a state of extreme dependency. If a meaningful and functional balance between these two is to be maintained for any one individual, he must activate his will and mobilize his intellectual and emotional faculties. Responsibility and concern cannot come about without the experience of dependency and some conception of freedom from it.

Finally, it should be remembered that the type of dependency is also closely related to socio-economic background and class affiliation. Most of the students of Nazism are agreed that lower middle class tradesmen and shopkeepers and artisans together comprised a disproportionately large segment of the supporters of Nazism before the Nazis took power.[16] And they did so, these observers agree, because of their deep-seated fear of radical proletarianism (communism) on the one hand and of the rapid rationalization of production and distribution, that is to say, the large corporation and the department store, on the other. These fears involved their concern both with material and status security. To the small German proprietor Hitler promised to crush radical proletarianism and control big business.[17] To the industrialists and big business tycoons he promised non-interference.[18] Those belonging to a socio-economically deprived class or to an ethnic minority in similar conditions will be more likely to have a dependency relation to material values and social status than the more secure and affluent members of society. These latter will be more inclined towards a dependency on social and cultural values.

It becomes evident that our temporal existence is dominated by concern for the solution of 'problems in living'[19] and by a search for an identity. These, again, are determined by a perpetual attraction-repulsion pattern, a dynamic force which demands a 'coming to terms' with temporal and spatial environmental restrictions imposed on the human organism due to its dependency on material and non-material entities. The successful continuation of human life is largely based on the ability to hold the forces of freedom and dependency in balance. Examples of patterns in which these opposites sometimes manifest themselves can perhaps be expressed as follows: satisfaction-frustration, sustenance-deprivation, sympathy-antipathy, love-hate, life-death, success-failure, balance-imbalance, understanding-confusion, sensitivity-callousness, concern-complacency, organization-disorganization. The intent and function of authority is usually to dominate, to eliminate personal freedoms, and thus to increase dependency relations. If the intent and functions of authority (as opposed to authoritarianism) were also to educate (not merely to train) individuals towards self-realization, that is achievement of a maximum of possible freedoms, then ideally the task of those in authority would be a transient one of providing guidance until all individuals become themselves *independent* authorities in their specific sphere of endeavor. The National Socialist leadership was increasingly preoccupied with the assumption of authority roles, which, however, were only rarely filled by authorities who had earned their position based on expertise in a reputable field. To the Nazis authority was merely a vehicle to gain, retain, and further their power. This they did by binding the masses to them with bonds of extreme dependency, officially referred to as 'unconditional obedience' to the charismatic leader Adolf Hitler. The dependency links within their hierarchically structured institutions had essentially the same purpose, namely to bring about group homogeneity and to activate esprit de corps, not by furthering of individual insight and authoritativeness, but by coercion to keep the rank and file party members in line. In other terms, in exchange for total social control, the Nazi leadership offered to the people what appeared as a secure system of checks and balances. This is reflected in party slogans, such as the well-known 'Führer, befiehl, wir folgen Dir' (leader command, we shall follow you). The pivotal point of Hitler's 'Machtpolitik' was strongly influenced by Nicolò Machiavelli's pessimistic realism and utilitarianism. However, it is quite doubtful that Hitler's dissociation of Christian ethics from political philosophy, originating from Machiavelli's insistence that morality is not related to acts of the state, by the same token made him an expositor of 'Realpolitik.'

From Freud whose 'intellectual framework, his whole orientation, despite his preoccupation with the mind, is a mechanistic-materialistic one'[20], we learn that: 'The tendency to aggression, . . . is an innate, independent, instinctual disposition in man, and . . . constitutes the most powerful obstacle to culture.'[21] Freud posited that:

> the meaning of the evolution of culture is no longer a riddle to us. It must present to us the struggle between Eros and Death, between the instincts of life and the instincts of destruction, as it works itself out in the human species. This struggle is what all life essentially consists of and so the evolution of civilization may be simply described as the struggle of the human species for existence.[22]

Thus, according to the neo-Freudian theorist Karen Horney:

> As (Freud) saw it, man is doomed to dissatisfaction whichever way he turns. He cannot live out satisfactorily his instinctual drives without wrecking himself and civilization. He cannot be happy alone or with others. He has but the alternative of suffering himself or making others suffer.[23]

Another neo-Freudian stand, and one also acceptable from an interactionist's approach, has been presented by Read Bain, who states that:

> The fundamental Freudian assumption is that the human personality is a more or less abnormal or supervenient by-product of non-social, or even anti-social, instinctual tendencies. . . . This failure to recognize the organic relationship of culture and personality, . . . this assumption that there is something 'unnatural' if not abnormal about culture, runs like a red thread through the whole theory of psychoanalysis and leads inevitably to the mysticism which Freud so vehemently denies and condemns. It is the old Darwinian concept of evolution, red in tooth and claw, applied to intrapersonal and familial development.[24]

Frederic Wertham with some validity has pointed to the 'great loopholes for reactionary mysticism' provided by Freudian theory. Wertham notes that the death instinct philosophy also shows up in the writings of Martin Heidegger, the existentialist philosopher who for a brief period became a prominent Nazi apologist.[25] Wertham states: 'It is significant how often . . . Freud refers to race, heredity and the primitive phylogenetic element. . . . Here again Freud comes close to those existentialists who invoke "the call of our ancestors". . . . The whole concept of race as Freud uses it includes the idea of higher and lower races.'[26]

Although the Nazis did not have a specific reason for disagreeing with Freud's theories per se, they nevertheless did so because he happened to be – according to their definition, which reduced millions of human beings to an abstraction to which a social stigma was attached – a Jew.[27] From this and other examples it can be readily seen that hardcore determinism has been a dominant factor in the contemporary history of totalitarian socio-political thought, specifically in National Socialist ideology.[28] Therefore attention should once more be drawn to the dominant 'mood of the times,' especially that prevailing in Central Europe, where the political and emotional climate was charged with racist concepts. These were the concepts that superiority and inferiority were biologically determined, which in National Socialist ideology made the Aryan a superman and the Jew an underling. The foremost advocate of this extreme racism was Hitler. His political ideology was chiefly based on aggressive discriminative materialism.[29] Hitler's ultimate naive extremism found its climax in the 'Final Solution'[30] to conflicts which – it was claimed – were a result of immutable physical and personality traits.[31] Personality characteristics were attributed to hereditary determinants. 'Disease' of the mind, in fact anything classed by the Nazis as deviant, now not only belonged to the domain of the biological and medical sciences but also fell under the jurisdiction of party leadership. Hence all those who, according to NS definition, possessed 'negative' traits had to be removed in order to bring about 'Aryan harmony.' In Nazi terminology, what could not be 'ausgemendelt' ('Mendeled out')[32], was to be 'ausgemerzt' (effaced) or 'ausgerottet' (exterminated).[33] Himmler gave a very accurate account of this activity to his medical advisor and physiotherapist Felix Kersten:

Er (Himmler) habe die Juden hinausschaffen wollen, das

sei aber nicht gelungen, trotz anfänglicher Erfolge sei die Aktion durch die Ablehnung des Auslands schließlich steckengeblieben. Nun lege man ihm die Vernichtung der Juden nahe. ... Man geht von folgenden Erwägungen aus: Die Juden erschüttern die verschiedenen Staatssysteme immer wieder durch Kriege und Revolutionen. Nicht nur politische, sondern auch finanzielle und geistige Revolutionen sind es. Man denke nur an die Vernichtung der Ehrbarkeit des Kaufmannsstandes, die Zersetzung des Kunstbegriffes, der Währungen, kurzum alles dessen, was einem Staat Stabilität verleiht. Dies führt zur materiellen und geistigen Enterbung der Völker und zu einer allgemeinen Proletarisierung. Da aber Proletarier keinen Staat lenken können, kommt die Führung in die Hände der sich gegenseitig abstützenden und sich entproletarisierenden Juden. Die Juden verursachen die Fäulnis, von der sie dann gut leben. Sie beherrschen über die ganze Welt hin die Nachrichtenzentren, die Presse, die Filmproduktion, die Kunst und damit praktisch alles andere. Der Schaden, den die Juden seit vielen Jahrhunderten angerichtet haben und künftig in noch viel größerem Umfang anrichten werden, ist derart umfassend, daß dem nur noch durch ein völliges Ausscheiden der Juden begegnet werden kann. Alle Uneinigkeit in Europa ist von den Juden durch ihren zersetzenden Geist angerichtet worden, somit alle Kriege und alles Elend. Das ist eine Blutschuld der Juden, die unzählbare Millionen von Opfern verschlungen hat und noch verschlingen wird. Man kann dem Juden nur mit seiner eigenen Methode und seinen eigenen Worten begegnen: Auge um Auge und Zahn um Zahn. Die unendlichen Millionen von Toten, die das Judentum seit Jahrhunderten immer wieder verursacht hat, müssen mit ihnen abgerechnet werden. Schon früher haben diese Zusammenhänge zur teilweisen Ausrottung der Juden bei verschiedenen Völkern geführt. Erst wenn der letzte Jude von der Welt verschwunden ist, wird die Völkerzersetzung und der Krieg als Milliardengeschäft verschwinden und unübersehbare Millionen künftiger Geschlechter werden dadurch bewahrt, für das unsichtbare Reich der Juden wieder und wieder im gegenseitigen Kampf zu Grunde gehen zu müssen. ...

Es ist der Fluch des Großen, daß es über Leichen schreiten muß, um neues Leben zu schaffen. Wir müssen aber neues Leben schaffen, der Raum muß keimfrei sein, sonst kann es nicht gedeihen. Ich werde schwer daran zu tragen haben. Himmler zitierte dann das Wort 'Unerbittlich schreitet durch die Weltgeschichte die Vergeltung.'[34]

---

He [Himmler] claimed he had wanted to move the Jews out [of Germany: trans.] but did not succeed; in spite of initial success, the scheme finally broke down due to the refusal of other countries to accept the Jews. Now their destruction is suggested to him . . . 'These are the points to consider: time and again the Jews have stirred up the various systems of government by means of wars and revolutions, not only political but economic and intellectual revolutions. One need only consider the destruction of the good repute of the merchant class, the undermining of the concept of art, the erosion of currencies – in short, the destruction of everything that lends stability to a state. This leads to nations being robbed of their material and intellectual heritage, and to a general proletarization. But as the proletariat cannot lead a state, leadership comes into the hands of the Jews, who render support to each other and deproletarize themselves. The Jews cause the rottenness on which they thrive. Throughout the world they dominate the communications centers, the press, motion picture production, the arts, and thereby practically everything else. The damage which the Jews have caused for many centuries, and will cause in the future to an even greater extent, is so comprehensive that it can be countered only by eliminating them entirely. All disunity in Europe – and hence all wars and all misery – has been caused by the subversive spirit of the Jews. This is a blood debt which has swallowed up countless millions of victims and will consume more. One can fight the Jews only with their own method and their own words: an eye for an eye, and a tooth for a tooth. One must settle accounts with the Jews for the infinite millions of deaths that they have caused again and again for centuries. These interrelated facts have already led to the partial extermination of the Jews by various peoples in the past. Only when the last Jew will have disappeared from the world will there also be an end to the disintegration of nations and to war waged as a business enterprise worth millions; countless future generations will be saved from mutual slaughter on behalf of the invisible Jewish Empire. . . .

'It is the curse of greatness that it must step over dead bodies to create new life. Yet we must create new life, we must cleanse the soil from germs or it will never bear fruit. It will be a great burden for me to bear.'

Himmler then quoted the phrase: 'Retaliation strides remorselessly through the history of the world.'[34]

The basis for these views, value judgments, and actions of members of this subculture of violence, namely the NSDAP, and its subsidiary protective and reinforcing agency the SS (Schutzstaffel der NSDAP), are to be sought, as already suggested by Walther Rathenau, in the mechanistic-materialistic concept of the world (Weltanschauung). The socio-political antecedent of Nazism, the authoritarian and highly structured feudal society which in 1918 came to an abrupt end, did not render the masses a body of responsible, politically aware individuals. Instead, charismatic authoritarian leaders filled the leadership positions, specifically the Kaiser's, vacated by the defunct aristocracy. These leaders then continued to relieve the people of complex, cumbersome decision-making in societal and state affairs. For obvious reasons the socio-political process of democratization had not yet become an integral part of the Central European milieu.

Certain fallacious trends of thought, frequently outgrowths of traditional but obsolete social systems and institutions, have contributed significantly to social disorganization and disorientation. This was suggested in the past by the well-known Orwellian thesis: a society becomes totalitarian when its ruling class has lost its functions but succeeds in clinging to power by force and fraud. These factors can easily lead to cataclysmic events of which some only now are beginning to be recognized and identified as consequential. Hence there is a need for new perspectives concerning the function of social factors and their consequences. There is likewise a need to re-evaluate some of the prevalent philosophies about social ecology, etiology, and interaction. Such perspectives and re-evaluations may shed light on the function of social conflicts and thus ultimately serve the interests of mankind. In other words, the function of social theory should be to assist modern man in his search for a soul, for the meaning of his existence, by paying 'equal regard to the physiological and the spiritual factor,' and by transferring 'the objective, empirical methods of science to the study of the phenomenology of the spirit.'[35] An important (yet little recognized and frequently misunderstood) step in this direction has been taken by Rudolf Steiner in his *Philosophie der Freiheit* as well as in some of his other writings.[36]

A reasonable and hopefully logical conclusion of the foregoing considerations, which have been a continued preoccupation of mankind, can be found in an article by M. Brachyahu entitled 'A Contribution Towards the Psychology of the Parties.' He states:

> At the extreme of the parties stand the 'radicals'. What outlooks and strivings do we see in this radicalism? They are directed towards absolute changes in the existing state of affairs, to a complete revolution. We do not use the word 'radical' when we speak of acts or strivings of construction or reconstruction. The essence of the radical striving is the act of uprooting, not the act of ploughing or sowing. Thus there is no difference if a man is a radical of a left or of a right party. Both of them are alike in their essential aim – to bring the building down in ruins. If one pays careful regard to the mentality of radicals . . . you find in many of them that they are influenced more by hate than they are by love.[37]

Partly in response to expressions such as the ones cited above, dissatisfaction is growing with those psychologists and psychiatrists who designate as neurotic, psychopathic, deviant, etc., those who attempt to effect fundamental change in contemporary institutions. Helen Merrell Lynd writes: 'No one would deny that some radicals are neurotic. But that is a very different thing from saying that only neurotics develop radical social views, or that radical programs are necessarily evil or undesirable.'[38]

Yet from a sociological point of view we recognize, along with Dewey, Horney, Fromm, Erikson, Mead, Blumer, Szasz, Gerth, Mills, Shibutani, Goffman, Abel, Scheff, and others, that given a minimum biological substratum, human personality is essentially the product of interactions with other persons. Already Sullivan has posited that two goals condition human behavior: the pursuit of satisfaction (in which biological needs predominate), and the pursuit of security (in which socio-cultural activities play a dominant role). Thus, according to Sullivan, the process of becoming a human being is almost synonymous with the process of socialization. This does not necessarily imply, however, that man's biological nature condemns him to perpetual conflict with society. It suggests, in fact, that anxiety and conflict, being the product of man-made social institutions, are subject to alteration, that is, to social change. It has been seen above that this is also the case with dependency relations. Therefore it is reasonable, as Kluckhohn and Murray propose, to approach social processes in a manner which regards

> the conventional separation of the 'organism and his environment', the drama of 'the individual *versus* his society', the bipolarity between 'personality and culture' as false or at least misleading. . . . In actual experience, individuals and societies constitute a single field.[39]

It is suggested that the Third Reich, with its National Socialist institutions (indeed *all* totalitarian and non-totalitarian institutions that lead to a state of anomie and violent conflict) has to be understood and interpreted in this regard. As these institutions and social systems decay and rapidly become dysfunctional, our orientation and identity which are anchored in them will likewise become affected. This will be reflected in our insecurities, anxieties, and world image – and indeed in the manner in which socio-political conflicts will be resolved.[40]

If then the social and existential therapist of tomorrow is to meet the needs of his clients in the Nuclear Age, the remarks presented in Erik Erikson's book *Insight and Responsibility* seem most appropriate:

> Clinical evidence . . . will be decisively clarified, but not changed in nature, by a sharpened awareness (such as now emanates from sociological studies) of the psychotherapist's as well as the patient's position in society and history.
>
> The relativity implicit in clinical work may, to some, militate

against its scientific value. Yet, ... this very relativity, truly acknowledged, will make the clinicians better companions of today's and tomorrow's scientists than did the attempts to reduce the study of the human mind to a science identical with traditional natural science. [41]

Perhaps sometime in the future we shall be able to control – if not prevent – acts which escalate into violence and lead, as in Hitler's NSDAP, to the massacre of millions of human beings.

For the present let it suffice to say that one of the decisive mutual characteristics and dilemmas existent among potential and actual members of radical movements or subcultures of violence appears to be an inability to distinguish personal frustrations – more specifically, unresolved 'problems in living' – from public issues (that is to say, until society is forced to deal with them, at which time these problems indeed will have become a public issue).

All that we view, define, reject, and judge as 'good' or 'evil' is a part of us and we are also its product. How else could we distinguish between 'good' and 'evil' or define what we have not experienced – of which we are not a part ourselves? Essentially these elements make up our 'moral' fiber, the ethos of the time, which enables us to respond 'morally.' Consequently, the social scientist ought to be engaged in a continuous search or re-search for new alternative interpretations of social conflict and be actively involved in what C. W. Mills has so aptly described as *ventures of social imagination.* It is in this context that tolerance of ambiguity should be viewed as a means to achieving such a goal, not necessarily as an end in itself. Any experience is real to those who experience it even though others may not be in a position to share or accept it. [42] Yet we cannot simply divorce thought from experience, experience from behavior, behavior from the individual actor, and the individual actor from his biosocial system, just as we cannot separate on a macrocosmic level the influences which the universe has on the world we live in. All these elements will produce unique social patterns of human interaction in which individual experience becomes a paramount factor. Interdependencies and interaction, then, are the social fiber out of which man's reality is woven, a reality which man shapes and in which he strives to survive. Viewed from this perspective, the individual's differential experience of what constitutes *his* reality (and the consensus of those similarly situated) not only appears to be at the bottom of what produces social conflict but also will determine the means which will be chosen from the number of available alternatives to resolve it.

I perceive our last decade in America as a period of deception and conspiracy, of mediocrity and complacency. Ethical considerations in our national life have yielded to norms of expediency and promises of immediate gratification. 'Actors' replace leaders, playing public roles in the appearance of authority, without being authoritative. Without the necessary qualifications for leadership, without expertise, circumspection, and propriety, they manufacture images through the aid of agencies of public relations and mass media. This process of deception in our national political culture follows the course of deception analyzable in interpersonal relations. Glaser and Strauss, for example, note how the clients tend to defend the very con men or quack doctors who mislead them. The public is as client to the corporations, agencies, and governments that manage the world's resources. To preserve the continuity of his accustomed life style and his beliefs, the public as client listens receptively. He believes 'the agent's justifying explanations about why things are going wrong or are not getting better, and believes that matters will improve'[43] (e.g., that there will be no inflation or recession in America, that the government has improved the state of affairs and is generally in control, that the citizens have it better than ever before, or that when the Arab countries lift the oil embargo, the price of gasoline will be reduced).

The man in the street is confused by the onslaught of abruptly changing stimuli which he is fed by the mass media, fashionable ideological movements, fads and personality cults to which he readily conforms because he lacks autonomy. He is constantly bombarded by subliminal penetration in the form of advertising and propaganda based on motivational research. These symbolic value images tend to further distort his sense of identity, his self-image, human status, indeed, his very humanness, and embroil him in interactions ranging from fratricide to genocide, *egocide*[44] to ecocide. Unable to resist popular trends and traits, the insufficiently educated citizen, ignorant of history, is poorly equipped to face the realities of the day and to assume civic responsibility by a judicious participation in decision making processes. In failing to make reflected choices, and incapable of solving conflict situations, he renders himself dependent on those whom he elects to power positions, in the belief that they will respond to his needs. More frequently than not, the state of mind of the voter reflects the state of mind of the elected. Certainly on a societal level, both share at least the consequences of the collective experience. Hence it is ludicrous to assume that the individuals the citizen has elected into power positions will exceed the expectations he has of himself. It is in this respect that the citizen gets what he deserves. The final stage of this drama is a rude awakening which often comes too late, after the damage has already been done.

If authority is not to turn into tyranny, it has to close the gap between knowledge and ignorance. Only by matching authority with responsibility can competence in its true sense be attained. In this context let us consider the danger of our era of Imperial Presidency and Watergate. When the moral order of a society is deteriorating, or becomes anomic, the political order will reflect this state. During such times social conditions provide a fertile ground for the rise of demagogues. Such deterioration of political, social, and moral standards was, indeed, the case in Nazi Germany, as it is today exemplified by periodical assassinations of innovative political and public figures, Watergate, and similar 'plumber' ventures. Commonly these activities are attempts of powerful interest and pressure groups to institutionalize private, secret policing agencies which, if successful, create a hidden government, rendering the visible, traditional-legal one powerless – exactly as Hitler, Himmler, Bormann, and Goebbels produced a state within a state – the outcome when power is monopolized by a few. Such individuals use a public forum as a vehicle for the satisfaction of their personal needs. The consequences of such idiosyncratically tainted centralization of power – if not curbed in time by appropriate awareness and social response, specifically the application of checks and balances – can escalate into totalitarianism.

Vigilance, social imagination, and assumption of responsibility by the public at large can produce an alternative scenario to the one created by those actors whose state of mind compels them to follow blindly the example of their peers and the biddings of their superiors. Instead, we must develop in every citizen the ability to understand the issues at hand, so that he can act judiciously. To facilitate the understanding (Verstehen) of interrelationships and decision making processes, the citizen should be given the best possible educational exposure a society has to offer. Liberal learning is the pre-eminent source of the higher order of critical intelligence that is capable of judging both means and ends, and without it citizens will produce a society, in Max Weber's words, of 'sensualists without spirit, specialists without heart.'

Notes
and
References

I. POWER, IDEOLOGY, AND POLITICAL CRIME

1. José Ortega y Gasset, *The Revolt of the Masses* (New York: W. W. Norton, 1960), p. 123.
2. Cf. Niccolo Machiavelli, *The Prince*, trs. and ed. by Thomas G. Bergin (New York: Appleton-Century-Crofts, 1947), pp. 19-20, 23-26.
3. Cf. Richard H. Emerson, 'Power-Dependence Relations,' *American Sociological Review*, Vol. XXVII (February, 1962), pp. 31-37, 39-41, and John M. Steiner, *Social Institutions and Social Change under National Socialist Rule: An Analysis of a Process of Escalation into Mass Destruction*, Ph. D. Dissertation (University of Freiburg, 1968), pp. 178-180.
4. From careful study of biograms of power holders it becomes evident that compensation for low self-esteem is one of the important driving forces behind the search for power. This can be mitigated by a domination of others in which the individuality of those who submit is being effaced. Cf. F. S. Perls, *Ego Hunger and Aggression* (New York: Vintage Books, 1969), Chpt. XII, pp. 169-173. So, for example, Woodrow Wilson, in his Kansas address of May 1911, based in part on self-recognition, said the following: 'The man with power, but without conscience, could, with an eloquent tongue, if he cared for nothing but his own power, put this whole country into a flame, because this whole country believes that something is wrong, and is eager to follow those who profess to be able to lead it away from its difficulties.' Quoted in Franz Neumann, *Behemoth: The Structure and Practice of National Socialism* (Toronto: Oxford University Press, 1942), p. 33.
Cf. also Alexander L. and Juliette L. George, *Woodrow Wilson and Colonel House* (New York: Dover Publications, 1956), and Sigmund Freud and William C. Bullitt, *Thomas Woodrow Wilson: Twenty-Eighth President of the United States* (Boston: Houghton Mifflin, 1967).
Efforts to relate German family structures to political authoritarianism include Erik H. Erikson, *Childhood and Society* (New York: W. W. Norton, 1963), Chpt. IX: 'The Legend of Hitler's Childhood,' pp. 326-358; see Appendix XIV.
5. A stimulating portrayal of the process of a gradual change in the personality profile of power holders has been presented by Ladislav Mňačko in his book, *Taste of Power* (New York: Praeger, 1967), in which the author describes the rise and decline of a Communist statesman.
6. Cf. Hans Gerth and C. Wright Mills, *Character and Social Structure* (New York: Harcourt, Brace and World, 1964), pp. 96-97 and Hannah Arendt, *Eichmann in Jerusalem* (London: Faber and Faber, 1963), pp. 59, 42, 48, 50, 231. In referring to the function of personality structure, Mills observes the following: 'Although men sometimes shape institutions, institutions always select and form men. In any given period we must balance the weight of the character or will or intelligence of individual men with the objective institutional structure which allows them to exercise these traits.' C. Wright Mills, *The Power Elite* (London: Oxford University Press, 1969), p. 96. Cf. also *ibid.*, p. 357.

See also Irving Louis Horowitz, *The War Game* (New York: Ballantine Books, 1963), Chpt. I, 'Arms, Policies and Games,' pp. 11-28.

7. In this context Colonel Burton C. Andrus's (U.S. Army Retired) book *I was the Nuremberg Jailer* (New York: Tower Publications, 1970) should be mentioned. A discriminative reader of Andrus's account will find that the victorious Allies' concern for human status and dignity, while sitting in judgment over the defeated top Nazi leaders, was, relatively speaking, not significantly different from that of the condemned while they had been in power. One of the basic notions underlying this attitude prevalent in Western societies, cultural differences notwithstanding, can be found in the traditional legal ethos expressed in the *lex talionis.*

Attention should also be drawn to the utilization of biograms as helpful indicants of changes occurring in the power holder's self-image, identity, attitude and to other *shifts* taking place, not only in the actor's personality structure and social perspective after he has attained a high level of exclusiveness, but also in those of his followers who have formed a dependence relationship with him.

8. Cf. George H. Mead, *Mind, Self, and Society* (Chicago: University of Chicago Press, 1934), pp. 154-156. See also Bernard N. Meltzer, 'The Social Psychology of George Herbert Mead,' in Stephan P. Spitzer (ed.), *The Sociology of Personality* (New York: Van Nostrand Reinhold, 1969), pp. 60-61.

9. Seymour M. Hersh, *My Lai 4: A Report of the Massacre and Its Aftermath* (New York: Random House, 1970), p. 187. For a detailed portrayal and legal, political, and psychological account of the violent conflict in Vietnam involving political crime, i.e., crime against humanity, see Richard A. Falk, Gabriel Kolko, and Robert Jay Lifton (eds.), *Crimes of War* (New York: Vintage Books: A Division of Random House, 1971), *passim.*

10. Lewis A. Coser, *The Functions of Social Conflict* (New York: The Free Press, 1968), pp. 48-55.
    Cf. also Horowitz, *op. cit.*, Chpt. IV, 'Conflict, Consensus and Cooperation,' pp. 147-169.

11. See biograms and personal accounts (in this writer's personal archives) of former members of the SS currently serving life sentences in German penitentiaries. Cf. also John M. Steiner, 'Bureaucracy, Totalitarianism, and Political Crime,' in *Essays in Criminology. Zum zehnjährigen Bestehen der Deutschen Kriminologischen Gesellschaft und dem 50. Geburtstag ihres Präsidenten, Prof. Dr. Armand Mergen* (Hamburg: Kriminalistik Verlag, 1969), pp. 35-38.

12. Hersh, *op. cit.*, p. 183.

13. Cf. Arthur Mitzman, *The Iron Cage: An Historical Interpretation of Max Weber* (New York: Alfred Knopf, 1970), *passim.* See also Franz Kafka, *The Castle* and *The Trial*, any edition, *passim.*

14. Quoted by Carl Julius Weber in *Das Ritterwesen* (Stuttgart: Hallberger'sche Verlagshandlung, 1836), Vol. I, p. 42.

15. Durkheim asserts that a social fact must always be explained by a social fact. This concept of social facts corresponds to the organization of behavior at the sociogenic level and bears a stable relationship only to causes at that level.

Relationships to other levels, though important while they exist, are less permanent and subject to greater fluctuation. Cf. Emile Durkheim, *Les Règles de la méthode sociologique* (Paris: Librairie Félix Alcan, 1927), pp. 120-137.

16. Cf. John M. Steiner and Jochen Fahrenberg, 'Die Ausprägung autoritärer Einstellung bei ehemaligen Angehörigen der SS und der Wehrmacht,' *Kölner Zeitschrift für Soziologie und Sozial-Psychologie*, Vol. XXII (1970), No. 3, pp. 551-566.

17. Cf. Hugh Dalziel Duncan, *Communication and Social Order* (New York: Oxford University Press, 1962), Chpt. XII: 'Hitler's Theory of Rhetoric as a Means toward Social Identification,' pp. 225-236.

18. Cf. Albert Speer, *Erinnerungen* (Berlin: Propyläen Verlag, 1969), *passim*.

19. Cf. Steiner, Ph. D. thesis, *op. cit.*, pp. 179-180.

20. Cf. Ferdinand Toennies, *Community and Society*, trs. by Charles P. Loomis (New York: Harper and Row, 1957), p. 191. Toennies's description of the ideal type of *Gesellschafts*-relationship involves strangers whose only principle in this interaction is: 'What I do for you, I do only as a means to effect your simultaneous, previous, or later service for me. Actually and really I want and desire only this.' *Ibid.*, p. 252.

21. Ortega y Gasset, *op. cit.*, p. 122.

22. Cf. Toennies, *op. cit.*, p. 191.
Toennies's description of *Gemeinschafts*-relationships involves 'concord' or 'family spirit.' He states: 'All intimate, private, and exclusive living together, so we discover, is understood as life in *Gemeinschaft*.' *Ibid.*, p. 33.

23. Cf. D. W. Winnicott, 'The Development of the Capacity for Concern,' *Bulletin of the Menninger Clinic*, Vol. XXVII, No. 4 (Topeka, Kansas, 1963), pp. 167-176.

24. Norman Cameron, 'The Paranoial Pseudo-Community Revisited,' *American Journal of Sociology*, Vol. LXV (July, 1959), p. 58.
Existential *fear* can be viewed as the expression of an unsatisfied need for survival and security in which the momentum of the unknown dominates. Fear is also artificially induced and manipulated by power holders, specifically in totalitarian societies, as, for example, the Soviet Union and Communist China, to bring about submission to their authority. It is used for Pavlovian conditioning, indoctrination, conversion, or persuasion of recalcitrant non- or anti-communists. Such 'mind reform,' better known as brainwashing, produces a deliberately induced *paranoid* state which is maintained by a conditioned or controlled environment usually hermetically sealed by an 'iron-bamboo curtain.' See Edward Hunter, *Brainwashing* (New York: Pyramid Books Edition: second printing, 1961), pp. 224-243.

25. Cameron, *loc. cit.*, p. 58.

26. J. Milton Yinger, 'Research Implications of a Field View of Personality,' in Spitzer, *op. cit.*, Chpt. XII, p. 180.

27. Cp. Robert Dubin, 'Power, Function, and Organization,' *Pacific Sociological Review*, Vol. VI, Spring 1963, pp. 16-22.

28. Cf. Arthur Everett *et al.*, Calley (New York: Dell Publications, 1971), *passim*.

## II. SOCIOLOGICAL FACTORS IN THE DEVELOPMENT OF THE NS PARTY BUREAUCRACY

1. Cp. E. N. Peterson, 'Die Bürokratie und die NSDAP,' *Der Staat, Zeitschrift für öffentliches Recht und Verfassungsgeschichte*, Vol. VI, No. 2, 1967, p. 151.
2. Cp. Hans Gerth and C. Wright Mills, *Character and Social Structure* (London: Routledge and Kegan Paul, 1961), p. 364.
3. Max Weber, 'Bürokratie und die NSDAP' in C. Wright Mills, *Klassik der Soziologie: eine polemische Auslese* (Frankfurt/M.: S. Fischer Verlag, 1966), p. 174.
4. *Ibid.*
5. *Ibid.*, p. 151.
6. Cf. Gerth and Mills, *op. cit.*, pp. 19-34.
7. For a more detailed description on the study and definition of subcultures see John Madge, *The Origins of Scientific Sociology* (Glencoe/Ill.: Free Press, 1964), Chpt. VII, pp. 210-254.
8. Cf. E. Federn, 'Some Clinical Remarks on the Psychopathology of Genocide,' *Psychiatr. Quart.*, Vol. XXXIV, No. 3, 1960, pp. 538-549.
9. Cf. D. W. Winnicott, 'The Development of the Capacity for Concern,' *Bulletin of the Menninger Clinic*, Vol. XXVII, No. 4, 1963, pp. 167-176.
10. Max Weber, in Mills, *op. cit.*, p. 189.
11. *Ibid.*
12. Louis Jolyon West, 'The Psychobiology of Radical Violence,' *Mental Health Digest*, December 1966, p. 24.
13. Cf. Joseph Goebbels, 'Rassenfrage und Weltpropaganda,' in Julius Streicher (ed.), *Reichstagung in Nürnberg 1933* (Berlin: Vaterländischer Verlag C. A. Weller, 1933), pp. 135-142.
    See also Walter Groß, 'Politik und Rassenfrage,' in *ibid.*, pp. 154-158.
    Adolf Hitler, 'Die Nationalsozialistische Führer-Hierarchie und die Europäische Mission Deutschlands' (Schlußansprache auf dem Parteikongreß), in *ibid.*, pp. 215-244. See especially *ibid.*, p. 219: 'Die Spanne, die zwischen dem niedersten noch sogenannten Menschen und unseren höchsten Rassen liegt, ist größer als die zwischen dem tiefsten Menschen und dem höchsten Affen.'
    ['The span which exists between the lowest yet still so-called man and our most advanced races is greater than the one between the lowest man and the most developed ape.']
14. A good if somewhat extreme case in point as to the stimulation of incentives for the outlet of violent impulses through 'legalized' NS institutions, which were created for that purpose, we may find reflected in the writings of a former SS-Hauptscharführer and staff member of a notorious concentration camp. The following excerpts are taken from autobiographical reflections and notes addressed to this writer in 1968 (name withheld):
    'Ich bin Jahrgang 15, hatte eine ordentliche aber straffe Jugendzeit, ... mein Vater prügelte oft. Mal hatte ich ein altes Glasauge aus seinen Schreibtisch mit in die Schule genommen und es dem anderen gezeigt, es dann unter der Bank liegen lassen, der Lehrer schickte es meinem Vater und der hätte mich fast tot-

geschlagen, daß ich es genommen hatte, ohne ihn gefragt zu haben. Zum Spielen, bin ich als Kind auch so gut wie nicht gekommen. Mit 10 Jahren, mußte ich von Frühjahr bis Herbst schon morgens um 3 Uhr aufstehen und die Pferde auf das Kleefeld bringen. So sind mir zu Schularbeiten nur immer eine Stunde morgens vor der Schule geblieben und durch die harte Behandlung im Elternhause hat es mich auch zur SS getrieben und seit dieser Zeit, war mein Vater mit mir verfeindet, und dies hat bis 1957 angehalten!

'Mit 15 Jahren gab mich mein Vater in die Lehre zu einem ehem. Offizier, da ich ein Pferdeliebhaber war, nahm er mich mit in den Reitverein, dieser ging dann in der Reiter-SS auf und so war ich schon ohne mein Dazutun dabei. 1934 meldete ich mich zur Kavallerie bei der Reichswehr, hörte aber nichts auf mein Gesuch, so sagte ein Freund zu mir: in Dresden wird eine SS-Truppe aufgestellt, dorthin machte ich ein Gesuch und am 15.5.34 erhielt ich die Einberufung für das 3. SS-Sonderkommando auf vierwöchentliche Probezeit. . . . Damals, gab es noch keine Häftlingsprobleme, die Politischen wurden von der SA bewacht. Welcher Junge, hat nun nicht den Ehrgeiz, eine Probezeit zu bestehen, um nicht als lächerliche Figur zu seinen Schulkameraden zurück-zu-kehren. Hätte man natürlich 34 die Entwicklung voraussehen können, so wäre es schon besser gewesen, eine lächerliche Figur zu sein. 1935 kam die Wehrpflicht und da verpflichtete ich mich auf 12 Jahre. Es lagen also keine politischen, ideologischen, materielle-sicherheit oder Geborgenheit vor, sondern eine reine militärische Laufbahn! Im Juni 36 hatte ich einen Motorradunfall mit einer Knieverletzung, die mir die Versetzung am 30.7.37 zum Kdt. Stab des KL Bu. (Buchenwald) einbrachte. Und hier war Koch Kommandant.

'Wie stand es nun mit dem Mittleid. Dazu kann ich sagen, es waren meist junge SS-Männer, die überhaupt keinen Kontakt mit den Häftlingen hatten, sie taten Dienst, was ihnen befohlen wurde, über andere haben sie sich keine Gedanken gemacht, die nur beim Ausgang, Urlaub und Frauen waren. Es bestand bei keinen ein Philantrop – Menschenfreund – keine Ahnung von Phisiognomik, von Psychologie wird keiner etwas gehört haben. Durch das sture Befehlen und psychischen Suggestionen: Der Häftling ist unser Feind!

'. . . Leid zuzufügen! Ich sage, dies war in der damaligen Zeit zu 99 % unvermeidlich, ohne es willentlich begehen zu wollen! Wieviel Leid wird heute noch anderen zugefügt?

'. . . bei der SS, konnte man gar keine eigenen Gedanken sich machen, weil diese doch nicht verwandbar waren und die Führung, die Richtlinien der Gedanken bestimmte!! . . . Schauen wir uns die Umjubelung Hitlers bei Kundgebungen, Radioansprachen usw. die Hitlerjugend, BDM usw. an, diese machten doch zum großen Teil die öffentliche Meinung. Eltern hatten doch über ihre Kinder kein Recht mehr. Schon vom Blockleiter aufwärts wurde die Meinung gemacht, die Presse schrieb fast nur, was ihr vorgeschrieben wurde.

'. . . Mir wäre auch nie im Leben der Gedanke gekommen, aus eigenen Willen einen anderen zu töten! Ich habe auch keinen Rassenhaß gekannt, daß wohl unflegelhafte Worte gefallen sind, ist in der Sprache der Soldaten aller Nationen, in meinen Elternhaus verkehrten Juden und alle Kleidung, die ich bis 34 trug,

war vom Juden gekauft. Das Wort "Antisemitismus" ist mir erst 1950 klar geworden, was es bedeutet. Ich habe auch nie Hitlers "Mein Kampf" gelesen,
obwohl ich zwei Stück zu meiner ersten Eheschließung bekam!
'... Kontakt hatten die anderen Häftlinge mit dem Juden, sogut wie keinen, das
Wort "Dreckjude" war bei Häftlingen und SS die Umgangssprache! Ein besonderer Judenhasser, war der Österreicher und Gärtner Untersturmführer Dummbeck, der wollte die Juden nur zur Scheiße tragen haben. Wenn ich die Frage
beantworte, was mich am meisten beeindruckt hat, so muß ich sagen alles, oft
habe ich mir in Gedanken vorgestellt, einer könnte mein Vater sein!
'... Der Haß wurde von der Lagerleitung über die politischen Schulungsleiter
geschürt, wurde aus Filmen, vom Urlaub und aus der öffentlichen Meinung
mitgebracht. Da auch der Film "Jud-Süss" dem Häftlingen vorgeführt wurde,
entstand ein Haß der einzeln Kategorien, gegen die Juden und dieser bestand
von rot, über grün bis schwarz! ... Die gesteigerte Brutalität, brachte der ständige einpeitschende Druck und die Ständige weitere Verrohung des Krieges mit-
sich! Die Führung, sah in ihren Feinden ein Ventil was vernichtet werden mußte,
sie sah diese Menschen nicht mehr als Menschen an, sondern nur als unnötige
Belastung für die Volksernährung, darum war, jemehr zu Grunde gingen, es
ihnen willkommen! ... Wenn ich in 20 Fällen Beihilfe geleistet habe, dann nur
aus der militärischen Abhängigkeit zum eigenen Schutze meines Lebens ...
'Es ist wohl ein Unterschied, wenn einen ein Vorgesetzter und Gerichtsherr sagt,
es ist ein Sabotör, oder Wehrkraftzersetzer, dies kann man bei Kindern und
Frauen sofort erkennen, daß es Unrecht ist und kann sich dagegen wehren und
vielleicht damals in der Öffentlichkeit Verständnis gefunden, aber nicht bei
Sabotage usw. ...
'Wie stellen Sie sich nur eine Verweigerung vor? Der damalige Staat, bestimmte
doch über Leben und Tod. Die Gestapo, nahm doch sogar dem Richtern die
Menschen weg, die sie töten lassen wollten. Kennen Sie einen Richter, der damals Strafantrag gegen dem Staat wegen Mord gestellt hat!
'Ich will Ihnen es auch frei sagen, wenn wir auch in Innern die Rechtmäßigkeit
bezweifelt haben, aber so waren wir doch völlig Machtlos, dagegen etwas zu
unternehmen, sagen Sie mir bitte, bei wem wir dies Vorbringen sollten? Weiter
will ich Ihnen sagen, daß viele in Bu. für befohlende Tötungen mit dem Kriegsverdienstkreuz mit Schwertern ausgezeichnet wurden, aber ich habe es nicht
bekommen!! ...
'In welcher ständigen psychischen Bedrücktheit ich von Juli 37 bis Ende 42
gelebt habe, ist nicht zu schildern, immer das Gefühl es könnte etwas in dieser
oder der nächsten Stunde schief gehen, SS, Häftlinge hängten einen hin, weil
man dem oder dem etwas gegeben hatte, oder wie ich es mit dem Strafverfü-
gungen machte, viele als durchgeführt unterschrieben, wo dann die Betr. nicht
bestraft wurden. ... Wie ich zu dem Exekutionen gekommen bin, ... natürlich
wurden diese in Schriftstücken von Berlin angewiesen. Aber, konnte ich dem
Kommandanten sagen: erst will ich das Urteil einsehen? Ich muß immer wieder
wiederholen, ich habe nie den Willen gehabt, einen Menschen zu töten und daß
ich auf Befehl des Kommandanten, dem Ärzten dabei behilflich sein mußte,

diesem Befehl konnte ich mich nicht entziehen, durch Selbstmord ja, aber anders nicht! Wenn ich aus eigenen Entschluß einen Menschen getötet hätte, dann wäre ich ein Mörder. So hat aber der Staat und der, der unter Ausnützung des militärischen Gehorsams es angeordnet hat, es zu vertreten. Wer aus einen eigenen Entschluß handlungen vorgenommen hat, dessen eigene Person, muß auch zur Verantwortung gezogen werden! Ich glaube auch heute noch sagen zu können, wenn man von mir verlangt hätte, ich sollte bei Tötungen von Frauen und Kindern behilflich sein, daß ich dies verweigert hätte. So aber, hat mir der Kommandant erklärt, daß es sich um Sabotöre, Wehrkraftzersetzer, Wirtschaftsverbrecher usw. handelt und darauf, stand im Kriege die Todesstrafe. ...
'Nun will ich zu dem Exekutionen kommen und wie ich dazu kam. Mitte Sept. 39 kam Dr. Ding zu mir und sagte zu mir: "holen Sie mir mal dem – Namen weiß ich heute nicht mehr –, auf meine Frage, was er mit ihm wolle, sagt er, er müßte ihm eine Spritze geben. Als ich mit dem Häftling ins Dienstzimmer zurückkam, sagt Dr. Ding zu ihm, legen Sie sich auf das Bett, machte dem rechten Arm frei, legte einen Schlauch um dem Oberarm und sagt zu mir, halten Sie dem Schlauch, dann nahm er eine Spritze, stach in die Armbeugvene ein, zog Blut an und drückte die Flüssigkeit in die Vene, als diese leer war rührte sich der Häftling nicht mehr, auf meine Frage, der ist doch nicht etwa tot, sagt Ding, ja der ist tot, dies ging von Koch aus." Als Ding weg war, rief ich Koch an (Koch was commandant of the concentration camp Buchenwald) und erklärte ihm, das Dr. Ding soeben hier gewesen sei und einen Häftling eine Spritze gegeben habe, der nun tot sei, ja sagt Koch: "Ich weiß Bescheid, laßen Sie ihm zur Leichenhalle bringen."
'Und so, hatte mich Ding mit der 1. Tötung überfahren! Nun sagen Sie mir, wo, bei wem, sollte ich diese Tötung vorbringen? Nach einer längeren Zeit, ließ mich Koch kommen und erklärte mir, es werden hier nun Exekutionen vorgenommen werden, es handelt sich dabei um Sabotage, Wirtschaftsverbrechen, Wehrkraftzersetzung, Einbruch unter der Verdunkelung usw. Da wir noch keinen Schießstand haben, habe ich angeordnet, daß diese von dem Ärzten im Arrest vorgenommen werden und Sie haben dem Ärzten dabei zu helfen, die Durchführung haben Sie mir sofort zu melden. Koch schrieb mir die Personaligen von Fernschreiben und Schriftstücken ab. Auch hier muß ich Sie fragen, konnte ich den mächtigen Koch fragen: sind das rechtskräftige Urteile, oder ich will erst das Urteil lesen? ... Ich weiß, Sie werden sagen, ich hätte mich von der Rechtmäßigkeit überzeugen müssen und die Beihilfe verweigern müssen? Was wäre mir geschehen, wenn ich die Exekutionen als Mord hingestellt hätte und hätte das RSHA, (Reichssicherheitshauptamt, i.e., Reich's Security Main Office), Himmler, Koch, als Mörder beschuldigt? Bleiben wir doch bei den damaligen Verhältnissen, das RSHA, Hitler, Himmler, entschieden über Leben und Tod. Haben Sie je gehört, daß ein Staatsanwalt, Richter einen Strafantrag gegen Hitler, Himmler wegen Mord und Völkermord gestellt haben? ...
'Die Hauptverantwortlichen für die Vernichtung sind: Hitler, seine Kanzlei, Himmler mit seinem Stab, das Reichssicherheitsamt, Heydrich, Kaltenbrunner, Müller der alle Vernichtungen an die untergeordneten Stellen anordnete. Ohlen-

dorf mit seinen Einsatzkommandos. An der Judenvernichtung war auch das Reichsaußenministerium, Innen- u. Verkehrsministerium beteiligt. An Politkommissaren und Partisanen das Oberkommando der Wehrmacht, die Politkommissare lieferte sie an die KL's zum Erschießen, wie nach Bu. Exekutionskommando 99 (Pferdestall). Eichmann, hatte schon eine untergeordnete Stelle!

'... Wie man aber verhintern kann, daß dies nicht geschieht, dazu finde ich keine Antwort, weil es im Leben Situationen gibt, wo der, der Leid zufügt, es selbst nicht weiß, was er tut. Und warum nicht: weil er nicht in der Haut dessen steckt, dem das Leid zugefügt wird! Jeder, dem Menschen unterstellt werden, müßten selbst erst einmal Haft und Leidensjahre verbringen, um in die Seele der gequälten Menschen sehen zu können. Dann dürfte niemand vor dem 35. Lebensjahr über Gefangene gestellt werden, weil in jüngeren Jahren sich die Quäler noch keine Gedanken über das Seelenleben des anderen machen. (Jugend ohne Gedanken).

Mein Dienst in Bu. konnte mich niemals befriedigen, weil ich selbst nicht frei war u. man wie eine Maschine durch befehlen und kommandieren in Trab gehalten wurde – und dies wirkte sich bis zum Letzten aus, also an Häftlingen. Ich lebte immer in der Seelennot, wann geht etwas schief, oder halten Sie in der damaligen Zeit einen Selbstmord aus Widerstand, Verfehlungen für Opportun, gegenüber seiner Frau, Eltern, Geschwister? Und was für einen Sinn hätte es nützen sollen, ein anderer wäre an die Stelle getreten oder sollte ich meine Vorgesetzten wegen der Anschnauzerei erschießen?

'... Die Worte: Menschlichkeit, Humanität habe ich von meinen Vorgesetzten nie gehört, auch nicht von dem Schulungsleiter einen Studienrat, oder Prof. Schröder! Der Krieg hat sie noch Machthungriger gemacht, ihm wurde die Entscheidung über Leben und Tod der "Staatsfeinde" übertragen mit der inneren Furcht, vorher noch viel geleistet zu haben, lebten sie ihr Leben, von oben nach unten stossend, dies war mein Eindruck, ... Ich weiß auch Sie beschäftigt noch die Grundfrage: wie konnte er sich damals dem Machthabern willenlos ausliefern und dessen Unrecht ausführen. Dazu kann ich immer nur wieder sagen, der Wille zum eigenen Überleben.'

---

['I was born in 1915 and had a well-ordered but strict upbringing ... my father often beat me. Once I took an old glass eye from his desk to show it to the others at school. I left it under the desk. The teacher sent it to my father who almost beat me to death because I had taken it without asking. I virtually never got a chance to play either. At the age of ten, I had to get up as early as three a.m., from spring until fall, to lead the horses out to the clover field. That way I had only one hour left in the morning before school in which to do my homework. The harsh treatment in my parents' home drove me to join the SS. At that time I incurred my father's enmity, and that lasted until 1957!

'When I was fifteen, my father arranged for me to become an apprentice with a former officer. Since I liked horses, he took me along to the riding club. This club was taken over by the mounted SS (Reiter-SS) and I found myself a member without actually having done anything about it myself. In 1934 I volunteered for the cavalry of the Reichswehr (German Armed Forces), but received no reply. Then a friend told me that in Dresden an SS unit was being formed. I applied there, and on May 15, 1934, I was called up for a four-week-trial period in the Third SS Special Squad (Drittes SS-Sonderkommando). At that time there did not yet exist a problem with prisoners and the political prisoners were guarded by the SA. What boy does not have the ambition to prove himself during a trial period, so as not to be sent back to his schoolmates to cut a ridiculous figure? Of course, if, in 1934, one had been able to foresee future developments, it would have been better to cut a ridiculous figure. In 1935 conscription was introduced, and I enlisted for twelve years. This decision was not based on political or ideological grounds, or on a search for material security and a place of safety, but simply to start a military career! In June 1936, I had a motorcycle accident in which I injured my knee. Unhappily, this injury caused me to be transferred, on July 30, 1937, to the commandant's staff at the Buchenwald concentration camp, and Koch was the commandant there. [SS-Standartenführer Karl-Otto Koch was commandant of Buchenwald from August 1, 1937 to December 1941: trans.]

'As to the question of compassion: I can say that there were mostly young SS men who had no contact with the prisoners at all. They carried out their duties as ordered. They did not think about anyone else, but only of getting a pass, leave, and women. No one was a philanthropist – friend of mankind – no one had any concept of physiognomy and none of them would have heard about psychology either. We were conditioned by the bullheaded orders and the psychological indoctrination: the prisoner is our enemy!

'As to the question of harm: I can tell you that this was at that time 99 % unavoidable, even without the intention of doing so. How much harm is done to others today?

'In the SS you did not form your own opinion because your own ideas would not be applied anyway. The leadership determined the general line! ... Just look at the exultation surrounding Hitler during rallies, radio speeches, etc. The Hitler Youth, the BDM [Bund Deutscher Mädel, that is, Union of German Girls: trans.], etc. – they, for the most part, created public opinion. Parents had no right over their children any more. Opinion was created from the block-leader (Blockleiter) on up; the press wrote almost exclusively what was dictated to them.

'... Neither would the idea ever have entered my mind to kill someone of my own free will. I also experienced no race hatred. The use of vulgar language did not make the soldiers different from those of any other nation. Jews had been frequent visitors in my parents' home, and all the clothing that I wore until 1934 had been bought from Jews. The meaning of the word "anti-Semitism" did not become clear to me until 1950. I never read Hitler's *Mein Kampf* either, although I received two copies on the occasion of my first marriage!

'... The other prisoners had virtually no contact with the Jews and the word "dirty Jew" (Dreckjude) was in everyday use among the prisoners and the SS.

A particularly virulent Jew hater was the Austrian gardner, Untersturmführer Dummbeck, who only wanted the Jews for carrying shit. To answer the question as to what impressed me most, I have to say, everything. I often thought to myself, one of them could be my father.

'... Hate was stirred by the camp administration through the leaders of political indoctrination and was conveyed by films, by personnel returning from leave, as well as imposed by public opinion. Since the motion picture "Jud Süß" was also shown to the inmates, hatred of Jews developed among the various categories of prisoners, those classified as "reds" [Politische, that is, political prisoners: trans.], "greens" [Berufsverbrecher, that is, habitual criminals: trans.], and "blacks" [asoziale Elemente, that is, asocial elements: trans.].

'... The heightened brutality was brought about by the pressure which was constantly whipped up and the increasingly brutalizing effect of the war. The leadership perceived its enemies as parasites that had to be destroyed, using them as an outlet for their own aggression. The prisoners were no longer considered human beings, but an unnecessary burden on the people's food supply. Therefore, the more who perished, the more welcome it was to the leadership. If I aided and abetted in twenty cases, I did it only on grounds of military subordination, that is, to protect my own life. . . .

'It certainly makes a difference whether one's superior and law lord accuses a man of being a saboteur or defeatist, or whether women and children are accused. I can easily recognize that to bring such charges against them is unjustified, and, perhaps, one can resist such orders. One might even have met with some public support at that time, but not in cases of sabotages, etc. . . .

'How do you think a refusal was possible? The state, at that time, decided on life and death. If the Gestapo wanted to kill certain individuals, it took them away, even from the courts. Do you know of a single judge who charged the state with murder at that time?

'I am going to be quite frank with you: Even if we had secret doubts about the legality of what was happening, we were still completely powerless to oppose it. Please tell me to whom we could have complained? Furthermore, I would like to mention that many of the concentration camp SS personnel were decorated with the War Service Cross with Swords (Kriegsverdienstkreuz mit Schwertern) for having complied with orders to kill inmates. However, I did not receive it.

'It is impossible to describe the constant psychological distress in which I lived from July 1937 until the end of 1942. There was always that feeling that something might go wrong at any given moment. The SS or inmates might tell on you because you had given something extra to this or that prisoner. Or, in the case of the imposition of penalties, I signed many such orders as if they had been carried out, whereas the prisoners involved actually had not been punished.

'I will now go into the question of how I got involved in executions: They were, of course, authorized in written instructions from Berlin. However, could I say to the commandant: "First I want to check into the verdict?" I have to repeat, again and again, that I have never had the desire to kill a human being. I had to assist the physicians at the order of the commandant. Only by committing suicide – but in no other way – could I have gotten around that order. If I had killed a person of my own accord, then I would have been a murderer. Thus, it is the state, and the individual who ordered the killings – exploiting the concept of military obedience – that have to bear the responsibility. It is the individual who carried out acts (of violence) as a result of his own decision that has to be held responsible. I think I can say, even today, that, had I been ordered to assist in the killings of women and children, I would have refused to do so. As it was, however, the commander explained to me that the persons involved were saboteurs, defeatists, economic criminals, etc. During the war such crimes were punished by death.

'I will now discuss the execution and how I got involved in them. In the middle of September 1939, Dr. Ding [SS-Hauptsturmführer Dr. Erwin Ding-Schuler was the camp physician at Buchenwald: trans.] came to me and said "Go and get ..." (I do not remember the name). When I asked him why he wanted to see this inmate, he said he had to give him an injection. After I returned to Dr. Ding's office with the prisoner, Dr. Ding told him to lie down on the bed. The doctor then rolled up one sleeve, placed a tourniquet around the upper right arm and told me to hold the tourniquet. Then he took a syringe, inserted it into the elbow vein, drew blood, and injected the fluid into the vein. When the syringe was empty, the prisoner did not move any more. To my question, "He, surely, is not dead?", Dr. Ding answered, "Yes, he is dead. This was ordered by Koch."

'After Ding was gone, I called Koch and explained to him that Dr. Ding had just been there and had given an injection to a prisoner who was now dead. "Yes," said Koch, "I know about it. Have him taken to the morgue."

'So this is how Ding had taken me by surprise with my first killing. Now tell me, where, to whom, could I have reported this killing? Some time later, I was summoned to Koch who explained to me that from now on there would be executions in cases of sabotage, economic crimes, defeatism, break-ins during blackout, etc. Since there still was no firing range, "I ordered," Koch went on, "that these individuals be handed over to the physicians, to carry out the executions, and you have to assist the physicians." Koch copied the identifications (of the prisoners) from teletype and other records for me. Here, again, I have to ask you whether I could have asked the powerful Koch about the legality of these verdicts or said, "First I want to read the verdict."? I know that you will say that I should have ascertained the legality of the verdicts and refused to participate. What would have happened to me if I had exposed the executions as cases of murder, if I had charged the Reich Security Main Office (RSHA), Hitler, and Himmler with murder? Let us be realistic about what was possible at that time: The Reich Security Main Office, Hitler, and Himmler decided on life and death. Have you ever heard of a prosecutor or a judge who filed suit against Hitler and Himmler for murder and genocide?

'The primary responsibility for the exterminations rests with Hitler, his chancellery, Himmler and his staff, the Reich Security Main Office, Heydrich, Kaltenbrunner, and Müller, who ordered all exterminations to be carried out by the lower ranks, as well as Ohlendorf with his task force units [Einsatzkommandos, operational units of the Sipo, Sicherheitspolizei, that is, Security Police, and the SD, Sicherheitsdienst RFSS, that is, Security Service Reichsleader SS, for special missions, usually including liquidations in occupied territory. Six Einsatzkommandos formed an Einsatzgruppe, that is, operational groups or task force: trans.]. The Reich Foreign Ministry, the Ministry of the Interior, and the Ministry of Transport also participated in the destruction process. The High Command of the German Armed Forces was responsible for measures taken against political commissars and guerrillas. Political commissars were handed over to the concentration camps, such as the firing squad 99 (Exekutionskommando 99) "Horsebarn" ("Pferdestall") in Buchenwald. Eichmann held a subordinate position.

'I have searched in vain for an answer to the question how all this could have been prevented, for there are situations in life in which the individual who inflicts pain does not know himself what he is doing. Why is this? Because this individual cannot put himself into the shoes of the one to whom harm is done. Everyone who is put in charge of others, should first himself spend years of suffering and imprisonment, so that he might gain some insight into the souls of tormented human beings. Moreover, nobody under thirty-five years of age should be given authority over prisoners. In their younger years, tormentors do not yet reflect on another person's emotional state of mind (youth with a lack of concern and compassion).

'My service in Buchenwald never satisfied me, because I, myself, was not free. Like a machine, I was kept moving with orders and commands, which affected everyone in the chain of command, most seriously the prisoners. I lived in constant mental agony that something might go wrong. In your opinion, would committing suicide, for fear of the consequences of mistakes or the resisting of orders, have been opportune, considering that one had responsibility towards one's wife, parents, brothers and sisters? And what would have been the use? Someone else would have taken my place; or should I have shot my superiors for their high-handedness?

'Words like human kindness, compassion, I never heard from either my superiors or the political indoctrinator (Schulungsleiter), a high school teacher or professor, by the name of Schröder. The war had made these individuals more power hungry than they had been before. They had been given jurisdiction over life and death of the "enemies of the state." Obsessed with fear of running out of time, they lived their lives, exerting constant pressure on anyone under their influence, at least, that was my impression. ... I know you, too, are concerned with the basic question: How could one, at that time, surrender so weak-mindedly to those holding power and commit crimes for them? Again, I can only say that it was the desire for my own survival.']

A former Untersturmführer of the 'Geheime Staatspolizei' relates the following concerning measures against German Jews and the standpoint and frame of mind of some Gestapo officials who implemented them (name withheld):

'Die erste deutsche Stadt, die die Amerikaner besetzten, war am 21. Oktober 1944 (Samstag) Aachen. Einige Tage später . . . brachte die damalige "Rhein-Mainische-Volkszeitung" – Nachfolgerin des "Frankfurter Volksblattes" – eine kleine Zeitungsnotiz, in der gemeldet wurde, daß die Amerikaner in Aachen deutsche Männer als "Hilfspolizisten" ausbilden würden. Am gleichen Tage hatte ich nachmittags eine Rücksprache mit Grosse. Ich erstattete ihm Bericht über die Tätigkeit von Mack und mir im Heddernheimer-Kupferwerk. Wir zwei waren zu dieser Zeit Sachbearbeiter im Sabotagereferat und arbeiteten als "Studenten im Ferieneinsatz" seit 6.9.44 . . . abwechselnd in der Betriebsschlosserei dieser Fabrik, um Sabotagefälle zu verhindern oder aufzuklären. Im Laufe des Gesprächs erwähnte ich den genannten Zeitungsartikel und sagte zu Grosse: "Wenn die Amerikaner nach Frankfurt/Main kommen, können sie auch uns als Polizisten übernehmen, da wir keine Ausbildung mehr benötigen." "Die werden uns höchstens an die Wand stellen, wenn sie uns erwischen, aber nicht als Polizisten nehmen," sagte Grosse zu mir. Auf meinen Widerspruch, daß wir doch keine Verbrechen begangen hätten, die eine derartige Maßnahme rechtfertigte und wir doch *nur* eine polizeiliche Tätigkeit, wenn auch politisch, ausgeübt hätten, meinte Grosse: "Wir werden aber auch für die Anderen mitbüßen müssen!" Zu dieser Bemerkung sagte ich: "Man kann uns doch nicht bestrafen für das, was Andere gemacht haben." Hier wurde Grosse sehr unruhig und sagte zu mir, ohne mich anzusehen: "Wissen Sie denn nicht, daß man die Juden im Osten und in Auschwitz hat arbeiten und sterben lassen? Für den Tod dieser Juden wird man auch uns zur Rechenschaft ziehen!" Darauf konnte ich *keine* Antwort geben und verließ das Zimmer, zumal auch die eigentliche Rücksprache beendet war.

'Diese Mitteilung traf mich wie ein Blitz aus heiterm Himmel. Bisher hatte ich noch *nie* etwas davon gehört, daß man die Juden sterben ließ. Es war auch das *erste* Mal, daß Grosse mir gegenüber eine derartige Bemerkung machte mit dem Zusatz: "Mehr kann ich Ihnen zu dieser Sache nicht sagen!" Bis zu diesem Tage wußte ich *nur* von gelegentlichen Erschießungen und hatte geglaubt, es handelt sich um "Partisanen". Ein ähnlicher Fall war mir als Teilnehmer des Polenfeldzuges bekannt, in dem im September 1939 in Sanok 11 jüdische Partisanen erschossen worden sind . . ., so daß ich mir auch keine Gedanken darüber machte, wenn von gelegentlichen Erschießungen im Osten die Rede war. Von einer planmäßigen Vernichtung der Juden hatte ich *nie* etwas erfahren. Bei Dienstbesprechungen hatten Poche/Breder oder einer der Stellvertreter immer erklärt, daß die Juden im Lager ein sehr schweres Leben hätten.

'Nachdem ich Grosse verlassen hatte, ging ich erst einmal auf mein Dienstzimmer. Dort hielt ich es aber nicht lange aus und begab mich zur Schutzhaftabteilung – IID –, da ich über die jüdische Angelegenheit Klarheit haben wollte. Allerdings war *nur* die Angestellte Erna Hammeran anwesend. Wir zwei sprachen uns schon seit langer Zeit mit den Vornamen an. Als ich das Zimmer betrat, sagte Erna zu mir: "Heiner! Wie siehst Du denn aus? Du bist ja ganz blaß!" Ich brachte vorerst kein Wort heraus und setzte mich erst einmal. Nach einer kurzen Pause fragte ich: "Erna, ist es wahr, daß man die Juden, die nach

Auschwitz kamen, hat sterben lassen?" Erna lachte ganz laut und sagte: "Weißt Du das erst jetzt, wir wissen das schon lange, die Juden werden vergast! Darüber brauchst Du Dir doch keine Gedanken zu machen." Das war der zweite Blitz, der mich traf. Ohne ein Wort zu sagen, verließ ich Erna und ging direkt zu Nellen.

'Nellen empfing mich mit den Worten: "Na, Kamerad B., was gibt's?" "Herr Kommissar, stimmt es, daß man die Juden in Auschwitz mit Gas getötet hat?", meine Frage. Er sagte ganz offen: "Ja, aber wir haben damit nichts zu tun!" Auf meine weitere Frage wie das erfolgt sei, erklärte er mir: "Die Juden kommen in einen Raum, der mit Gas gefüllt wird." Ich fragte weiter und wollte wissen, ob dieser Raum mit dem Gasraum in der Gutleutkaserne zu vergleichen sei, in dem wir mit Gasmasken üben mußten. Nellen bejahte diese Frage und sagte mit seiner Kommandostimme: "Kamerad B., ich empfehle Ihnen, *nie* darüber zu sprechen!" Diese Empfehlung befolgte ich zu meinem eigenen Schaden bis zum heutigen Tag und habe geschwiegen.

'. . . Gegen 20 Uhr kam Erna . . . ich brachte das Gespräch auf die "Vergasungen" und bat sie, mir doch zu erzählen, was sie davon weiß. Sie lehnte ab und meinte: "Es gibt doch schönere Themen, über die wir uns unterhalten können." Daraufhin sagte ich zu ihr, daß ich sie nicht eher nach Hause lasse und wenn es die ganze Nacht dauert, bis sie mir Aufklärung gegeben habe. Nach einigem hin und her, erzählte Erna:

> "Im Sommer 1943 mußten Karl – gemeint ist Krim. Sekr. Klöppel – und ich zu Weymar in sein Zimmer. Dieser eröffnete uns, daß die Akten jüdischer Häftlinge des KZ-Auschwitz nicht mehr auf "Wiedervorlage" zum "Haftprüfungstermin" zu legen sind. In diesem Lager würden die Juden mittels Gas getötet, somit entfalle der Haftprüfungstermin. Ebenso machte uns Weymar auf die Schweigepflicht aufmerksam. Bei Verstoß gebe es nur eins, die Todesstrafe. Auf die Frage Klöppels, wie die Vergasungen durchgeführt werden, sagte Weymar, in einem Gasraum, mehr darf ich nicht sagen."

'. . . Köhler sagte: "Die Amerikaner werden uns ebenso vergasen, wie man in Auschwitz die Juden vergast hat!" Diesen Ausspruch nahm ich zum Anlaß, Blüth zu fragen: "O-Stuf., wußten Sie das von Auschwitz?" "Ich wäre ein schlechter Kommissar, wenn ich die Lagerverhältnisse und die Vergasungen nicht kennen würde", war seine Antwort. Im gleichen Atemzug und *nur mich* ansehend, sagte er weiter: "Übrigens kann mir in dieser Hinsicht nichts passieren!" "Mir vielleicht?" erwiderte ich. "Sie waren immerhin Judensachbearbeiter", war Büths Antwort.

'Jetzt entspann sich ein sehr lautes Streitgespräch, in dem ich Büth vorwarf, daß er den Juden Strauß, Kettenhofweg 72, nach Auschwitz habe bringen lassen, um dessen wertvolle Wohnungseinrichtung und Teppiche für ein Butterbrot (Schunk) zu erwerben.

'. . . Am Freitag, den 9.2.1945, besuchte mich Bierwirth auf der Dienststelle . . . er wollte wieder einmal von mir geholfen haben. Hierbei erfuhr ich, daß seine jüdische Frau am Mittwoch, den 14.2.1945, für einen Judentransport von Frankfurt/Main nach dem Osten vorgesehen war. Mit der Zusammenstellung des Transportes hatte Breder den Krim. Sekr. Thorn und den Verw. Insp. Hummel beauftragt. Diese beiden hatten im Erdgeschoß rechts das Eckzimmer für die Tage der Transportvorbereitungen belegt, sonst waren sie in Cronburg/Ts. Ich begab mich zu ihnen und bat um Rückstellung von Frau Bierwirth, da sie krank sei und den Transport mit großer Wahrscheinlichkeit *nicht* überleben würde. Hierbei ergab sich nun sinngemäß folgendes kurze Gespräch:

| | |
|---|---|
| *Thorn* (sehr scharf) | – Früher warst Du Judensachbearbeiter, heute bin ich es und lasse mir in meine Arbeit *nicht* reinreden! |
| *Hummel* (spöttisch) | – Die Staatspolizei kapituliert *nicht* vor den Juden! |
| *Ich* (leise) | – Wißt Ihr denn *nicht*, daß die Juden im Osten umgelegt werden? |
| *Beide* | – Dies interessiert *nicht*, was mit den Juden im Osten passiert. Aus Frankfurt/Main kommt diese Bagage auf alle Fälle heraus! |
| *Hummel* | – Übrigens, woher weißt Du eigentlich, daß das Judenmensch Bierwirth weg soll? |
| *Ich* | – Ihr Mann, der mit mir bei der Schupo war, Rudi – gemeint war Thorn – kennt ihn auch, war bei mir und steht vor der Tür. Er wartet auf Bescheid. |

'Darauf verließ Hummel das Zimmer und warf den "Rassenschänder", wie er Bierwirth bezeichnete, aus der Dienststelle. Die Jüdin kam weg. Nach dem Zusammenbruch holte Bierwirth seine todkranke Frau von Theresienstadt nach Frankfurt, wo sie nur noch einige Tage lebte."

———

['The first German city that the Americans occupied on October 21, 1944, (Saturday) was Aachen. A few days later the newspaper *Rhein-Mainische Volkszeitung* – successor of the *Frankfurter Volksblatt*, published a short article which stated that the Americans in Aachen were going to train German men as auxiliary police (Hilfspolizisten). That same afternoon I had a conference with Grosse. I reported to him the activities of Mack and myself in the Heddernheim copper works. At that time the two of us were working on cases of sabotage and since September 6, 1944, had been working alternately as "students on vacation duty" in the fitting shop of that factory to prevent or uncover sabotage activities. In the course of the conversation I mentioned the article in question and said to Grosse, "When the Americans reach Frankfurt, they can take us in as policemen, too, since we do not need any more training." "At best, they will stand us up against the wall if they catch us, but they will not take us as policemen," Grosse said. When I objected that we had committed no crime that would justify such measures, and that we had acted *only* as police, even though political police, Grosse remarked, "But we will also have to pay for the crimes of others." To this I replied, "But surely, they cannot punish us for what others have done." At this point Grosse became very nervous and said without looking at me, "Don't you know that in the East and in Auschwitz they made the Jews work and then die? We will also be called to account for the deaths of those Jews!" To this I did not have an answer and left the room, especially as the actual conference was over.

'This information hit me like lightning from a clear sky. Up to that time I had *never* heard anything about the Jews being killed. It was also the first time that Grosse had made such a remark to me with this addition: "I cannot tell you anymore concerning this matter!" Until that day I had known *only* of occasional executions and had assumed that they concerned "guerrillas" only. As a participant in the Polish campaign (Polenfeldzug), I got to know about such a case in September of 1939, when eleven Jewish guerrillas were shot in Sanok, ... I, therefore, did not think anything of it when there was talk of occasional executions in the East. I had never learned anything of a systematic extermination of the Jews. During conferences, Poche, Breder, or one of the deputies had always explained that life in the camps was very difficult for the Jews.

'After leaving Grosse, I first went to my office. However, I could not stand being there very long; so I went over to the Department for Protective Custody (Schutzhaftabteilung), the IID, because I wanted to find out for myself how the Jewish problem was being handled. The only person present, however, was Erna Hammeran. The two of us had been on a first-name basis for a long time. When I entered the room, Erna said to me, "Heiner, what's the matter? You look quite pale!" For a while I could not speak and sat down first. After a brief pause I asked, "Erna, is it true that the Jews who were sent to Auschwitz, were taken there to be killed?" Erna laughed aloud and said, "You only know that now? We have known that for a long time, the Jews are gassed! Well, you don't have to be concerned about that." That was the second lightning that hit me. Without a word I left Erna and went directly to Nellen.

'Nellen received me with the words, "Well, comrade B., what's up?" "Inspector, is it true that the Jews in Auschwitz have been killed with gas?" I asked. He was quite frank. "Yes, but we have nothing to do with that!" When I asked how it was done, he explained, "The Jews go into a room which then is filled with gas." I went on to ask if this room could be compared to the gas room in the Gutleut Barracks, in which we had to train with gas masks. Nellen answered in the affirmative and said in his commanding voice, "Comrade B., I advise you *never* to speak about that!" I followed this advice, to my own detriment, to this day, and remained silent.

'... Shortly before eight p.m. Erna came to my office and I brought the conversation around to the "gassings." I asked her what she knew about them. She declined to answer and said, "There are more pleasant subjects to talk about." Thereupon I told her that I would not let her go home until she had given me the information, even if it took all night. After some hemming and hawing, Erna told me the following:

"In the summer of 1943, Karl – meaning Krim. Sekr. [Kriminal Sekretär, junior rank in the German criminal police, Section V of the RSHA, headed by Gruppenführer Arthur Nebe: trans.] Kloppel and I, were summoned to Weymar's office. He disclosed to us that the records of Jewish prisoners in the Auschwitz concentration camp were no longer to be subject to reconsideration of the sentence. The Jews in this camp were killed with gas; therefore, reconsideration would no longer be necessary. Weymar also brought to our attention the obligation to remain silent. In case of violation, there would be but one thing, the death penalty. In answer to Kloppel's question as to how the gassings were implemented, Weymar replied, "In a gas chamber; I am not allowed to say more." "

'. . . Köhler said, "The Americans will gas us in the same way that the Jews were gassed in Auschwitz!" This statement was the reason for me to ask Büth, "Obersturmbannführer, did you know about Auschwitz?" "I would be a bad inspector if I did not know about the conditions in the camps and the gassings," was his answer. In the same breath, and looking *only* at me, he continued, "Incidentally, nothing can happen to me in this respect." "To me, perhaps?" I countered. "After all, you were the expert on Jewish affairs," was Büth's answer.

'There then ensued a very loud dispute in the course of which I accused Büth of having had the Jew Strauss, of Kettenhofweg 72 (in the city of Frankfurt), sent to Auschwitz in order to acquire his valuable furnishings and rugs for a song.

'. . . On Friday, February 9, 1945, Bierwirth visited me in my office. He wanted my help again. On this occasion I learned that his Jewish wife was marked down for a Jewish transport, leaving Frankfurt/Main for the East, on February 14, 1945. Breder assigned the organization of the transport to Krim. Sekr. Thorn and Administrative Inspector Hummel. These two had reserved the corner room to the right on the ground floor for the days on which deportations to camps were being prepared; usually Thorn and Hummel were in Cronburg/Taunus. I went to them and asked for the withdrawal of Mrs. Bierwirth's name from the list (of those who were scheduled to leave for the East: trans.), because she was ill and would most likely *not* survive the transport. In substance, the following short conversation occurred:

| | |
|---|---|
| *Thorn* (very harshly) | – You used to be the expert on Jewish affairs. Now I am the expert and will *not* be told by anyone how to do my job. |
| *Hummel* (mockingly) | – The State Police does not surrender to the Jews! |
| *Myself* (softly) | – Don't you know that the Jews are finished off in the East? |
| *Thorn and Hummel* | – It is of no interest what happens to the Jews in the East. In any case, this scum has to get out of Frankfurt/Main. |

| | |
|---|---|
| *Hummel* | – By the way, how do you actually know that that Jewess (Judenmensch) Bierwirth has to go? |
| *Myself* | – Her husband who was with me in the Police – Rudi (meaning Thorn) knows him, too, – came to me and is now outside the door, waiting for an answer. |

'At that point Hummel left the room and threw the "race defiler" (Rassenschänder), as he characterized Bierwirth, out of the building. The Jewess was deported. After the collapse (of Germany), Bierwirth brought his wife, who was dangerously ill, from Theresienstadt back to Frankfurt, where she lived only a few more days.']

Another account of effective NS-indoctrination was given by a former member of the Waffen-SS (name withheld):
'Am 20. Juli 1940, kurz nach Vollendung meines 16. Lebensjahres trat ich als Freiwilliger in die Waffen-SS ein.
'Nach der Ausbildung erfolgte meine Versetzung zur Ehrenkompanie Feldherrnhalle nach München, 3 Monate später nach Obersalzberg und so war ich längere Zeit immer in unmittelbarer Nähe Hitlers. Durch die dortige intensive NS-Politische Schulung und Erziehung wurde ich in politischer Hinsicht zu einem vollkommen einseitigen und restlos der Sache ergebenen Menschen. Eine Tatsache, an deren Folgen ich bis heute zu tragen habe. Man kann heute darüber urteilen und denken wie man mag, aber wer so wie ich damals, täglich die höchsten Offiziere und Würdenträger von Partei und Staat im Umgang mit dem Führer gesehen hat und deren Benehmen ihm gegenüber, für den jungen Menschen gab es nichts anderes mehr, als den Nationalsozialismus und dessen Ideen. Mit Beginn des Rußlandfeldzuges meldete ich mich sofort an die Front, kam zur Division Das Reich in den Mittelabschnitt. Nach einer am 19.11.41 vor Moskau erlittenen schweren Verwundung zurück zum Feldersatzbatl. nach Prag.
'Anläßlich der Heydrich-Aktion erlebte ich zum 1. Male den S.D. im Einsatz, möchte aber davon nicht berichten.
'Im Frühjahr 42 kam ich wieder zur Feldtruppe in den Kaukasus. Auf dem Wege dorthin mußte ich über Lublin, um von dort aus einen Nachschubtransport vom Hauptnachschublager zu übernehmen. In diesem Lager waren nur Juden beschäftigt. Was ich hier zu sehen bekam, überstieg jegliches menschliche Fassungsvermögen. Zum ersten Male sah ich, wie gewisse Leute zu Reichtum und ihrem späteren Vermögen gelangten.
'Nach dem Rückzug aus dem Kaukasus und einigen Monaten Einsatz im Südabschnitt kam ich nach einer weiteren Verwundung über Warschau nach Beneschau bei Prag.
'In Warschau war damals gerade die Ghettoaktion abgeschlossen und ich besichtigte mit einigen Kameraden den Schauplatz. Auffallend für uns war, daß die meisten dort eingesetzten Soldaten an die Front versetzt wurden, die Offiziere aber mit großem Gepäck Richtung Heimat fuhren.
'Zum 3. Male erlebte ich, daß für gewisse Leute das Problem Vermögenserwerb eigentlich gar kein Problem war.

'In Beneschau war ich dann Zugführer und Ausbilder beim SS Fallschirmjäger-batl. Während dieser Zeit wurde einer meiner besten Freunde aus der Rekruten-zeit damals Oberscharführer wegen angeblicher Fahnenflucht vom Höh. SS u. Pol. Gericht in Prag zum Tode verurteilt und vor unserem Batl. erschossen. In Wirklichkeit stand dahinter aber keine Fahnenflucht, sonder Intrigen, Hass und Neid, hervorgerufen durch einen S.D. Führer wegen einer Frau tschechi-scher Abstammung.

'Hier wurde mir endlich klar, daß es selbst in unseren Reihen kein Vertrauen und keine Kameradschaft mehr geben konnte. Ich ließ mich zurück versetzen nach Prag und ging von dort aus wieder zu meiner alten Einheit, dem Rgt. Deutschland – Div. Das Reich – in die Gegend von Toulouse.'

---

['On July 20, 1940, shortly after I had completed my sixteenth year, I joined the Waffen-SS as a volunteer. After my training, I was transferred to the Guard of Honor (Ehrenkompanie) "Feldherrnhalle" in Munich and three months later to Obersalzberg. Thus I spent considerable time in the immediate vicinity of Hitler. There the intensive National Socialist political schooling and training made me a completely one-sided person, thoroughly dedicated to the cause. To this day I have to bear the consequences of this fact. Today this may be judged and considered in whichever way; but for a person like myself, who saw the highest officers and dignitaries of party and state in daily association with the Führer and observed their behavior towards him – for such a young man there existed nothing else any more but National Socialism and its ideas. At the beginning of the Russian campaign (Rußlandfeldzug), I promptly volunteer-ed for the front and was assigned to the division "Das Reich," in the central section (of the front). I was wounded severely on November 19, 1941, outside of Moscow, and sent back to join the Field Reserve Battalion (Feldersatz-bataillon) in Prague.

'During the Heydrich affair, I had the experience of seeing the Security Service (SD) in action for the first time, but would rather not discuss that.

'In the spring of 1942, I was assigned to the front again, this time to the Caucasus. On my way I had to pass through Lublin to take command of a supply convoy from the main supply depot. The only people working in that camp were Jews. What I witnessed there exceeded any human imagination. For the first time I saw how certain people acquired their wealth and accumulated their subsequent fortunes.

'Following the retreat from the Caucasus and several months of duty in the southern section (of the front), where I was wounded again, I came by way of Warsaw to Beneschau near Prague.

'In Warsaw the ghetto operation had just come to an end, and I visited the scene of action with some comrades. To us it was quite obvious that most of the enlisted men who had participated in the operation there, were sent to the front, whereas the officers were headed home with a lot of luggage. For the third time, I learned that for certain people the problem of acquisition of wealth actually was no problem at all.

'In Beneschau I became platoon leader and instructor in the SS-Paratroop Battalion (SS-Fallschirmjägerbataillon). During that time one of my best friends from the time of my basic training, then an Oberscharführer, was sentenced to death by the Higher SS and Police Court (Höheres SS und Polizeigericht) in Prague for alleged desertion and was shot in the presence of the battalion. In reality, however, this had not been a case of desertion, but rather one of intrigues, hate, and envy, instigated by an SD leader over a woman of Czech origin.

'At this point I finally realized that even in our own ranks there could no longer be trust and comradeship. I applied for my transfer to Prague, and from there returned to my old unit, the "Regiment Deutschland" of the "Division Das Reich", in the Toulouse area.']

15. Cf. Peterson, *loc. cit.*, p. 153.
16. *Ibid.*
17. Cf. Law for the Re-establishment of the Professional Civil Service, April 7, 1933 (RGBl I, 175).
    For a detailed review and comparison between canonical and NS-introduced anti-Jewish measures and legislation, see Raul Hilberg, *The Destruction of the European Jews* (Chicago: Quadrangle Books, 1961), pp. 5-7.
18. *Ibid.* 'Nach dem Wortlaut des Deutschen Beamtengesetzes vom 26. Januar 1937 war das Berufsbeamtentum von der NS-Weltanschauung durchdrungen und es war der Vollstrecker des Willens der Partei.' *Loc. cit.*

['According to the wording of the German Civil Service Law (Deutsches Beamtengesetz) of January 26, 1937, the professional civil service was permeated by the NS-Weltanschauung and was the executor of the will of the party.']

19. Cf. Hilberg, *op cit.*, pp. 390, 434, 438, 439-442. See especially SS-Obergruppenführer Wolff's and Himmler's communications in the years 1942 and 1943 with Dr. Ing. Theodor Ganzenmüller, 'Staatssekretär' in the Transport Ministry and Deputy 'Generaldirektor' of the 'Deutsche Reichsbahn,' concerning the transportation of Jews to the death camp Treblinka and other killing centers. (Ganzenmüller to Wolff July 28, 1942, No-2207; Wolff to Ganzenmüller August 13, 1942, No-2207; Himmler to Ganzenmüller January 20, 1942, No-2405.) *Ibid.*, pp. 313-314. Cp. *ibid.*, pp. 34-35.
20. Cf. Max Weber, in Mills, *op. cit.*, pp. 179-183.
    E. N. Peterson in his article 'Die Bürokratie' asserts: 'Das nationalsozialistische Deutschland mit seiner ungeheuerlichen Steigerung in Auschwitz dürfte bewiesen haben, daß die Bürokratie – entgegen dem Postulat *Max Webers*, daß die Fachkenntnis des Bürokraten ihn unentbehrlich und damit mächtig macht – nicht Widerstand leisten kann oder will.' *op. cit.*, pp. 151-152.

['National Socialist Germany, with its monstrous climax in Auschwitz, appears to have proved that the bureaucracy – contrary to Max Weber's postulate that the expert knowledge of the bureaucrat makes him indispensable and therefore

powerful – cannot or will not offer resistance.']
Unfortunately Peterson's assertion falls somewhat short insofar as it neither proves nor disproves Max Weber's thesis and thus contributes but little to a better understanding of the bureaucrat's role in Nazi Germany.
21. Weber, in Mills, *op. cit.*, pp. 178-179.
22. So, for example, Lorenz von Stein points this out most aptly by characterizing the modern university as a 'school for bureaucrats' of which – according to H. H. Gerth – 'Germany is a neat case in point.' H. H. Gerth and Mills, *op. cit.*, p. 254.
23. Weber, in Mills, *op. cit.*, p. 176.
24. Cf. Amitai Etzioni, *A Comparative Analysis of Complex Organizations* (New York: The Free Press, 1965), p. 71.
25. *Ibid.*, p. 77.
26. *Ibid.*, p. 76.
27. Weber, in Mills, *op. cit.*, pp. 176-177.
28. Frederic S. Burin, 'Bureaucracy and National Socialism: A Reconsideration of Weberian Theory,' in Robert K. Merton (ed.), *Reader in Bureaucracy* (Glencoe/Ill.: The Free Press, 1952), p. 43.
29. Max Weber writes: 'Stets ist die Machtstellung der vollentwickelten Bürokratie eine sehr große, unter normalen Verhältnissen eine überragende . . . – stets befindet er (der Herr) sich den im Betrieb der Verwaltung stehenden geschulten Beamten gegenüber in der Lage des "Dilettanten" gegenüber dem "Fachmann". . . . Auch der absolute Monarch und in gewissem Sinne gerade er am meisten ist der überlegenen bürokratischen Fachkenntnis gegenüber machtlos.' Weber, in Mills, *op. cit.*, pp. 180, 181.
Cp. Burin, in Merton, *op. cit.*, p. 43.

['Under normal conditions, the power position of a fully developed bureaucracy is always overtowering. The "political master" finds himself in the position of the "dilettante" who stands opposite the "expert," facing the trained official who stands within the management of administration. . . . The absolute monarch is powerless opposite the superior knowledge of the bureaucratic expert – in a certain sense more powerless than any other political head.']

30. In a conversation with Hitler in 1934 Rauschning has the following to report: 'Er (Hitler) wurde ungeduldig, wenn man ihm mit Detailproblemen kam. Er hatte eine große Abneigung vor reinen "Fachmännern" und hielt auf ihr Urteil gar nichts. Er betrachtete Fachmänner nur als Handlanger, als Pinselwäscher und Farbenreiber, um in der Begriffswelt seines Malergewerbes zu bleiben. "Sie müssen sich von Akten freimachen", riet er mir bei dieser Gelegenheit. "Für den Bürokram haben Sie andere Leute. Man muß den Blick frei behalten. Man sieht sofort, Sie beschäftigen sich zuviel mit Details. Kommen Sie bloß nicht in die unglückliche Leidenschaft von dem früheren Reichskanzler Brüning, der jedes Gesetz eigenhändig veröffentlichungsreif machte. Das charakterisiert diesen Mann. Deshalb behielt er auch keine Kraft zu großen Entschlüssen.

Haben Sie nie den falschen Ehrgeiz, sich mit Einzelheiten zu befassen oder Gesetze selbst zu entwerfen." ' Hermann Rauschning, *Gespräche mit Hitler* (Wien: Europa-Verlag, 1940), p. 172.
See also *ibid.*, pp. 96-97, 99-100, 173, 204, 250-251.

---

In a conversation with Hitler in 1934 Rauschning has the following to report: ['He (Hitler) quickly became impatient if the details of a problem were brought to him. He was greatly averse to "experts" and had little regard for their opinions. He looked upon them as mere hacks, as brush-cleaners and color-grinders, to use the terms of his own trade.
' "You must keep free of red tape," he advised me on this same occasion. "You have other people to attend to such things. You must keep your vision clear. Very evidently you pay too much attention to details. You mustn't fall into the unhappy habit of the former Chancellor Brüning, who prepared every law for publication with his own hands. So typical for the man! That's why he had no strength left for great decisions. Don't lose yourself in the false ambition to deal with details. Don't formulate the laws yourself." ']

Concerning the bureaucrats Himmler expressed the following views to Kersten on July 17, 1941:
'Der oberste Parteirichter und der oberste SS-Richter sind keine Juristen und sollen niemals Juristen sein ... Die Juristen in den Stäben brauchen wir in der Übergangszeit, um uns gegen die Maßnahmen der Bürokratie, deren Stärke und scheinbare Unangreifbarkeit in ihrem Paragraphennetz beruht, wehren zu können. Wir schlagen die Juristen mit den Juristen. Hier handelt es sich um Not-maßnahmen. Unsere Juristen versuchen wir dadurch, daß wir sie in die SS stecken und mit unserem Geist durchdringen, umzuschulen.

'... Immer wieder ertappt man sie dabei, wie sie ausbrechen und in ihre alten Bahnen zurückfallen. ... Wenn ich da nicht aufgepaßt hätte, hätten die Juristen in meinen Stäben und nicht ich geherrscht. Ich hätte bei jeder meiner Maßnahmen erst einmal bei meinen Herren Juristen anfragen müssen, ob sie richtig seien und dem überkommenen Rechtsdenken entsprächen, demselben Rechtsdenken, das wir gerade auf das Bitterste bekämpfen und das uns mit allen seinen Möglichkeiten den Weg zur Macht verlegt hatte.
'... Überall stieß ich auf an und für sich nette, liebe, anständige Leute in SS-Uniform, die ihre Aufgabe darin sahen, mir zu allen meinen Befehlen eine Art Rechtsgutachten zu liefern und mir zu beweisen, in welchen Punkten meine Maßnahmen dem geltenden Recht widersprächen und daher nicht rechtsverbindlich seien. Sie taten aus bester Absicht, um mich, wie sie sich ausdrückten, vor Schaden und Regreßansprüchen zu bewahren und sahen gar nicht, daß sie selbst die Gefangenen eines Systems waren. ... Es war mir immer ein besonderer Spaß zu sehen, wie so ein im Grunde armes Würstchen aufatmete, wenn ihm ein Gesetz untergeschoben wurde, an das er sich klammern konnte, und wie er

nun mit geschwellter Brust mit den Gesetzesparagraphen jonglierend, unsere
Maßnahmen als juristisch einwandfrei hinstellte.' Felix Kersten, *Totenkopf und
Treue* (Hamburg: Robert Mölich Verlag, 1952), pp. 138-139.

['Supreme judges – whether in the Party or the SS – are no lawyers and never
will be. . . . In the past we needed lawyers on our staff to protect us against
bureaucratic measures, whose strength – which seemed invulnerable – rested on
a network of paragraphs. We fought lawyers with lawyers. This was a matter
of necessity.
'We try to train our lawyers by putting them in the SS and infusing them with
our own spirit. . . . You're always catching them at it, breaking out and falling
back into their old ways. . . . Before I got it right it was the lawyers, not I,
who controlled my staff. I had first to consult my legal gentry about all my
measures to find out whether they were correct and corresponded with accepted
legal ideas, the same ideas which we were bitterly fighting, which had put
every possible obstacle in our way to power.
'. . . Everywhere I was knocking up against people in SS uniform, in themselves
dear, nice, decent people, who saw their task as that of supplying all my orders
with a kind of legal respectability and pointing out to me at what points my
measures contradicted existing enactments and were therefore not binding in
law. They did that from the best motives, in order to save me, as they expressed it, from damages and recourse to claims, never seeing that they themselves were the prisoners of a system. . . .
'It always particularly amused me to see what a sigh of relief came from some
poor pudding-head when a law was substituted which he could grasp, and how
he would puff himself out and juggle with the legal paragraphs to make our
measures legally unobjectionable.']

In a conversation with Felix Kersten on September 24, 1943, the SS-Brigadeführer Otto Ohlendorf stated the following concerning Himmler's tactics and
manipulative practices within his own organization and in his interaction with
other institutions:
'Er beauftragt sehr oft mit neu anfallenden Aufgaben nicht die bestehenden In-
stitutionen, sondern Einzelpersonen, mit derselben Aufgabe manchmal mehrere
zugleich. Das nennt er dann Taktik. Praktisch geht ein Nebeneinander- und
Gegeneinander-Arbeiten auf der ganzen Linie vor sich, die Kräfte werden un-
nütz verbraucht und gebunden und der Sinn für jede Autorität zerstört. Hier
ahmt er im kleinen den Führer nach, der ja aus dem Mißtrauen gegen jede
staatliche Einrichtung aus der Kampfzeit solche Sonderbeauftragungen vor-
nimmt. . . . Tatsächlich organisiert er die staatliche Unordnung. Die Folge dieses
Organisationsprinzipes ist, daß hinter einer scheinbar höchsten autoritären dik-
tatorischen Gewalt eine Vielzahl von Gewalten entsteht, die alle behaupten, nur
ihrem Auftraggeber verantwortlich zu sein. Dieser hat gar nicht die Zeit, die
Möglichkeit und die Kenntnisse, sie in ihrem Aufgabenbereich zu überschauen
und zu kontrollieren. So entsteht eine Vielzahl unabhängig schaltender autori-

tärer Gewalten. Das Führungsinstrument des Staates wird dadurch völlig entwertet.' *Ibid.*, pp. 261-262. See also *ibid.*, pp. 63-64, 142-143, 165.

['He frequently entrusts new tasks as they arise to individuals, instead of giving them to institutions which already exist. Often several men will be given the same job. He calls that tactics. This leads to every sort of confusion and contradiction, abilities are wasted and respect for authority destroyed. In doing this, he's really copying the Führer, who inherits from his early struggles a preference for these personal appointments and distrusts government institutions. ... In fact, he's really organizing disorder. The logical result of this principle is that, while power seems to be concentrated in an authoritative dictatorship, in reality it is dispersed over a host of people, each of whom asserts that he's the only responsible authority. But he has neither the time, nor the ability, nor the knowledge required to supervise and control all the tasks assigned him. So numbers of independent and divided authorities come into being. The government's dictatorial powers quite lose their value.']

For an evaluation of Kersten's activity and reliability of his statements cf. H. R. Trevor-Roper, 'The Strange Case of Himmler's Doctor,' *Commentary*, April 1957, Vol. XXIII, No. 4, pp. 356-364; Walter Schellenberg, *Hitler's Secret Service* (New York: Pyramid Books, 1958), pp. 198-209.

31. Weber, in Mills, *op. cit.*, p. 183. Cf. also *ibid.*, p. 173.
32. *Ibid.*, p. 183.
33. H. H. Gerth elaborates this point by observing the following:
'Persons whose career expectations are frustrated or who suffer losses in status or income in the intensive vocational competition of modern capitalism should be especially likely to accept the belief in the charismatic leader. Those placed on the disadvantaged side of life always tend to be interested in some sort of salvation which breaks through the routines associated with their deprivation. Such "unsuccessful" persons were to be found in every stratum of German society. Princes without thrones, indebted and subsidized landlords, indebted farmers, virtually bankrupt industrialists, impoverished shop keepers and artisans, doctors without patients, lawyers without clients, writers without readers, unemployed teachers, and unemployed manual and white-collar workers joined the movement. National Socialism as a salvationary movement exercised an especially strong attraction on the "old" and "new" middle classes, especially in those strata where substantive rationality is least developed, and will be the most highly represented among those seeking salvation by quasi-miraculous means – or at least by methods which break through the routines which account for their deprivation.' Hans H. Gerth, 'The Nazi Party: Its Leadership and Composition,' in Robert K. Merton *et al.* (ed.), *op. cit.*, pp. 105-106. Cf. also *ibid.*, pp. 104-112.
Cp. also Morris Janowitz, 'Soziale Schichtung und Mobilität in Westdeutschland,' *Kölner Zeitschrift für Soziologie und Sozialpsychologie*, Vol. X (1958), pp. 32-33.

See also John M. Steiner and Jochen Fahrenberg, 'Die Ausprägung autoritärer Einstellung bei ehemaligen Angehörigen der SS und der Wehrmacht,' *ibid.*, Vol. XXII, No. 3 (1970), pp. 551-566.

34. See especially Raymond Cattell, *The Scientific Analysis of Personality* (Harmondsworth, England: Penguin Books, 1965), Chpt. II: 'Mental Measurement and Sociopolitical Life,' pp. 353-361.
35. *Ibid.*, p. 357.
36. See footnote 14. Cf. also Walter Poller, *Arztschreiber in Buchenwald* (Offenbach/M.: Verlag Das Segel, 1960), pp. 97-104, 114-115, 164, 189, 196-197, 213.
37. H. H. Gerth, 'The Nazi Party: Its Leadership and Function,' in Merton *et al.*, *op. cit.*, p. 111.
38. Gerth states: 'National Socialism, however, replaced officials of all ranks and stations from top to bottom.' This, he thought, invalidated Max Weber's claim as stated before. However, figures cited by Gerth in support of his point seem to disprove rather than prove this conclusion. *Ibid.*
39. Rauschning, *op. cit.*, pp. 250-253, 255-258.
40. *Ibid.*, p. 187.
41. *Loc. cit.*
42. *Ibid.*, pp. 44-46.
43. Peterson, *op. cit.*, p. 154.
44. Weber, in Mills, *op. cit.*, p. 173.
45. Cf. Burin, in Merton, *op. cit.*, pp. 42-43; see also Peterson, *loc. cit.*, p. 154. According to the *Deutsches Beamtengesetz* of January 26, 1937, 'war das Berufsbeamtentum von der NS-Weltanschauung durchdrungen und es war Vollstrecker des Willens der Partei.' *Ibid.*

['The professional civil service was permeated by the NS-Weltanschauung and was the executor of the will of the party.']

46. Cf. *ibid.*, pp. 160-161. See also Joseph Wulf, *Martin Bormann, Hitlers Schatten* (Gütersloh: Sigbert Mohn Verlag, 1962), *passim*.
47. For a more detailed description of quarrels and controversies between party and bureaucracy, ideology and competency, conflict in personalities and actual ability to cope with a task-oriented, effective solution of problems and power struggle in general, see Peterson, *loc. cit.*, pp. 159-171.
48. Weber, in Mills, *op. cit.*, p. 176.
49. *Ibid.*
50. Louis A. Coser, *The Function of Social Conflict* (Glencoe/Ill.: The Free Press, 1956), pp. 38, 35. For ingroup and outgroup hypothesis see *ibid.*, pp. 34-36, 53-54, 57, 69-70, 87-95, 104-110.
51. Els Frenkel-Brunswik, 'Interaction of Psychological and Sociological Factors in Political Behavior', *American Political Science Review*, Vol. XLVI, 1952, p. 63.
52. See Trevor-Roper, *Hitlers letzte Tage* (Frankfurt/M.: Ullstein, 1965), pp. 176-179, 187, 231-232.
53. Cf. Coser, *op. cit.*, pp. 49-50.

54. Kersten, *op. cit.*, p. 63.
55. *Ibid.*, p. 64.

## III.  THE SS – AN EXAMPLE OF A TOTALITARIAN BUREAUCRATIC INSTITUTION

1. Cf. William L. Shirer, *The Rise and Fall of the Third Reich* (Greenwich/Conn.: Fawcett Publications, 1962), p. 70.
Cp. Helmut Heiber (ed.), *Reichsführer!* ... *Briefe an und von Himmler* (Stuttgart: Deutsche Verlags-Anstalt, 1968), p. 12.
2. Cf. Ernst Bayer, *Geschichte, Arbeit, Zweck und Organisation der SA. Aus den Schriften der Hochschule für Politik* (Berlin: Junker und Dünnhaupt Verlag, 1938), in *Der Prozess gegen die Hauptkriegsverbrecher vor dem Internationalen Militärgerichtshof* (IMI), Nuremberg, 1948), Vol. XXIX, p. 283, PS-2168.
3. The SA '... wurde im Kampf geboren und erhielt vom Führer selbst den Namen "Sturmabteilung" nach jener denkwürdigen Saalschlacht im Hofbräuhaus zu München am 4. November 1921.' *Ibid.*, p. 281.
'... am 4. November 1921 geschah es, daß irgend jemand, ohne daß man heute feststellen kann wer es war, das Wort "Sturmabteilung" als Bezeichung für den Saalschutz der Ordnertruppe prägte, ...' Karl W. H. Koch, *Das Ehrenbuch der SA* (Düsseldorf: Friedrich Floeder Verlag, 1934), p. 17.

---

[The SA '... was born in battle and received from the Führer himself the name "Sturmabteilung" (Storm Detachment) in memory of that remarkable battle in the Hofbräuhaus in Munich on November 4, 1921.'
'... on November 4, 1921, it happened that somebody – and today it is impossible to determine who it was – coined the word "Sturmabteilung" as the designation for the Ordnertruppe maintaining meeting-hall security ...']

4. Cf. Oron James Hale, 'Gottfried Feder calls Hitler to Order: An Unpublished Letter on Nazi Party Affairs' (Document), *The Journal of Modern History*, December 1958, Vol. XXX, No. 4, pp. 358-362.
See also Otto Strasser, *Hitler und Ich* (Buenos Aires: Editorial Trenkelbach, 1940), pp. 75-78, 97-98, 143-151, 172-198; Hermann Rauschning, *Gespräche mit Hitler* (Wien: Europa-Verlag, 1940), pp. 80-82; Shirer, *op. cit.*, pp. 72-73.
5. Koch, *op. cit.*, p. 53. See also *Statistisches Jahrbuch der Schutzstaffel der NSDAP 1937* (Berlin: März, 1938), p. 3.
6. Cf. *SS-Leitheft*, Vol. VII, No. 1b, 1941, pp. 10-11. See also *Geschichte, Aufbau und Aufgaben der SS*, German Records Microfilmed at Alexandria/Virginia (GRMA), T-175, R. 180, Fr. 2 715 222.
7. Cf. 'Nationalpolitischer Lehrgang der Wehrmacht vom Januar 1937: Vortrag Himmlers über Wesen und Aufgabe der SS und der Polizei,' in IMT, Vol. XXIX,

*op. cit.*, p. 206, PS-1992 (A).
8. Cf. Koch, *op. cit.*, pp. 39-41.
9. 'Nationalpolitischer Lehrgang der Wehrmacht vom Januar 1937,' in IMT, *op. cit.*, p. 206.
10. 'Ich erhielt von ihm (Adolf Hitler) den Auftrag, die SA zu organisieren.' Unpublished handwritten autobiographical notes by Hermann Göring, Nuremberg, May, 1945, p. IV. See also Bayer, *op. cit.*, p. 283. See Appendix XIII.

['I received from him (Adolf Hitler) the assigment of organizing the SA.']

11. Cf. Felix Steiner, *Die Armee der Geächteten* (Göttingen: Plesse Verlag, 1963), p. 41.
See also Koch, *op. cit.*, pp. 44-46.
12. *Ibid.*, p. 47.
13. *Ibid.*, p. 48. Cp. also Steiner, *op. cit.*, pp. 40-41.
14. Ernst Röhm, *Geschichte eines Hochverräters* (München: Franz Eher Nachfolger GmbH, 1930), p. 314.
See also Steiner, *op. cit.*, pp. 42-44.
15. Cf. Koch, *op. cit.*, p. 48.
16. *Ibid.*, p. 55. Other authors (Hans Buchheim, 'Die SS – Das Herrschaftsinstrument, Befehl und Gehorsam,' in Hans Buchheim *et al.*, *Anatomie des SS-Staates* [Freiburg: Walter-Verlag, 1965], Vol. I, p. 33; Ermenhild Neusüss-Hunkel, *Die SS* [Hannover: Norddeutsche Verlagsanstalt, 1956], p. 7) give the date of July, 1926.
17. Cf. Werner Best, *Die Deutsche Polizei* (Darmstadt: Wittich Verlag, 1940), p. 85.
Cp. also *Geschichte, Aufbau und Aufgaben der SS*, GRMA, *op. cit.*, see also Koch, *op. cit.*, p. 48.
18. See *ibid.*
19. Cf. Buchheim, *op. cit.*, p. 31. Cp. Heiber, *op. cit.*, p. 12.
20. For a first-hand observation of the early SA, SS, and NS party leaders see Otto Strasser, *Hitler und ich* (Konstanz: Johannes Asmus Verlag, 1948), pp. 76, 97-100; Steiner, *op. cit.*, pp. 35-81; Hermann Rauschning, *Gespräche mit Hitler* (Wien: Europa-Verlag, 1940), pp. 18-20; Koch, *op. cit.*, see especially Chpts.: 'Der Gang zur SA,' pp. 57-91, 'Der Kampf um die Strasse,' pp. 92-109, 'Vom Leben der SA,' pp. 209-221.
21. A 'Staffel' consisted of ten men, not counting its commander. Cf. 'Nationalpolitischer Lehrgang der Wehrmacht vom Januar 1937,' in IMT, *op. cit.*, p. 206.
22. Cf. Koch, *op. cit.*, p. 53.
23. *Ibid.*
24. H. R. Trevor-Roper (ed.), *Hitler's Secret Conversations 1941-1944. With an Introductory Essay on the Mind of Adolf Hitler* (New York: Farrar, Strauss and Young, 1953), p. 138. Cp. also Strasser, *op. cit.*, p. 101.
25. See German Records Microfilmed at Berlin Document Center (BDC), T-580, R. 87, F. 425.

26. Cf. *Statistisches Jahrbuch der Schutzstaffel der NSDAP 1937, op. cit.*, p. 3.
27. Cf. Bayer, *op. cit.*, p. 286.
28. For von Pfeffer's order of November 4, 1926, see BDC, T-580, R. 85, F. 403.
29. Cf. Ausschnitt aus Lagebericht N/Nr. 51 w, September 22, 1926, *ibid.*, R. 87, F. 425.

Prior to January 30, 1933, the number of contributing members of the SS was approximately equal to the number of active members. To recognize the service of the early contributors, Himmler, in 1934, awarded an honorary silver pin. In April 1934, the *FM-Zeitschrift* (FM meaning 'Förderndes Mitglied') appeared for the first time. By 1939, the circulation of this periodical had reached approximately 365,000 copies. See newspaper clipping of July 12, 1939, *ibid.*, T-611, R. 10, F. 444.

'Fördernde Mitglieder der SS (FM)' were defined as follows: 'Der Dienst bei der Schutzstaffel, der vornehmlich bei den Führerversammlungen außerordentliche Anforderungen stellt, ist wirtschaftlich aus dem Grund ungleich schwerer, weil die einzelnen Verbände der Schutzstaffel räumlich weiter auseinandergezogen sind als die Verbände der SA. Dies bedingt ungleich höhere Transportkosten zur Ausübung des Dienstes.

'Der Führer hat deshalb der Schutzstaffel die Errichtung der FM-Organisation gestattet. Die Fördernden Mitglieder, die nicht Parteigenossen sein brauchen, zahlen monatlich bestimmte Beträge. Zum Inkasso dieser Beträge sind nur die Dienststellen der SS ermächtigt, die vom RFS (Verwaltungsamt SS) hierzu beauftragt sind. Die FM-Organisation ist für den Bestand der Schutzstaffel von größter Bedeutung und darf in ihrer Arbeit durch keine andere Dienststelle gestört werden. Während des Krieges werden die Beiträge nicht kassiert.'

*Die Organisation der NSDAP*, edited by Der Reichsorganisationsleiter der NSDAP (München: Zentralverlag der NSDAP, Franz Eher Nachf., 1943), 7. Auflage, p. 423-424.

---

[Contributing Members of the SS (FM, that is, Fördernde Mitglieder: trans.) were defined as follows: 'Service in the Schutzstaffel, which especially in the case of the Führer's rallies presents extraordinary demands, creates economic burdens which are considerably more difficult. The reason is that the individual units of the Schutzstaffel are more widely dispersed than the units of the SA. This fact entails disproportionately higher transportation costs for the performance of duty.

'Therefore, the Führer has authorized the Schutzstaffel to establish the FM-Organization. The Contributing Members, who need not be party members, make given contributions monthly. The only offices of the SS that may collect these contributions are those authorized by the administrative office of the SS (RFS, that is, Verwaltungsamt SS). The FM-Organization is of the greatest importance to the existence of the Schutzstaffel and must not be hindered in its work by any other organization. During war-time the contributions will not be collected.']

30. Hitler to Rauschning: 'Ich brauche Leute, die fest zupacken und sich nicht erst besinnen, wenn sie jemanden niederschlagen sollen. Es kümmert mich einen Dreck, ob sie ein paar Wertsachen für eigene Rechnung mitgehen lassen.' Rauschning, *op. cit.*, p. 95. See also *ibid.*, pp. 22, 81.

[Hitler to Rauschning: 'I need men who will not stop to think if they're ordered to knock someone down! I don't care a tinker's damn if they knock down a few valuables on their own account as well.']

31. Cp. *ibid.*, pp. 235-236. Note especially: 'Diese Generation mußte erst einmal verbraucht werden, ehe aus der Partei das neue fremdartige Gebilde eines weltlichen Priesterstaates herauswuchs.' *Ibid.*, p. 236.

['The present generation would first have to be used up before the party could grow into the new and unfamiliar shape of a secular priesthood in control of the state.']

32. See *ibid.*, pp. 208-215, 240.
33. For order No. 1 of the 'Schutzstaffel,' 'Oberleitung,' of September 13, 1927, see BDC, T-580, R. 87, F. 425.
34. *Ibid.*
35. Cf. Eugen Kogon, *Der SS-Staat. Das System der deutschen Konzentrationslager* (München: Karl Alber, 1946), p. 293.
36. *Ibid.*, pp. 18-23.

Rauschning makes the following sober comment about Hitler's appeal: 'Hitler hat nichts Anziehendes. ... damals fabelte man von seinen tiefen blauen Augen. Sie waren weder tief noch blau. Sie blickten starr oder erloschen. ... Die Färbung seiner dunklen, fremdartigen Stimme ist für den Norddeutschen abstoßend. Der Ton ist voll, aber gequetscht, als wenn die Nase verstopft wäre. ... Es ist mir aufgefallen, daß Hitler auf solche Persönlichkeiten den stärksten Eindruck machte, die entweder suggestionsfähig waren und einen femininen Einschlag hatten oder an Byzantinismus und Personenkult durch Erziehung und gesellschaftliche Stellung gewohnt waren. Das Äußere Hitlers trägt sicher nicht dazu bei, seinen persönlichen Eindruck zu erhöhen.' Rauschning, *op. cit.*, p. 19.

['Hitler is not physically attractive. ... But at that time stories were circulated in the party and among sympathizers about his deep blue eyes. They are neither deep nor blue. His look is staring or dead, ... The timbre of his harsh, strange voice is repellent to the North German. The tone is full, but forced, as though his nose were blocked. ... I have noticed that Hitler made the strongest impression on people who were either highly suggestible or somewhat effeminate or accustomed by their education and social background to formalism and hero worship. Hitler's physical appearance certainly does not improve the personal impression he creates.]

On page 188 Rauschning describes his own response to Hitler's speech as follows: 'Hitler redete weiter über die Größe der nationalsozialistischen Bewegung. ... Ich gestehe, von seiner begeisterten Rede beeindruckt worden zu sein. ... Hitler ist Prophet. Weit über die Bedeutung eines Politikers strebte er in die Gefilde eines übermenschlichen Daseins als der Prophet einer neuen Menschheit.' *Ibid.,* pp. 188, 231.

---

['Hitler talked on about the greatness of the National Socialist movement. ... I must confess to having been swayed by his impassioned speech ... Hitler is a prophet. Far from being a mere politician, he aimed for the realm of a superhuman existence as the prophet of a new mankind.']

In contrast to the above description compare Hitler's portrayal drawn by Goebbels, entitled 'Adolf Hitler,' in Dr. Goebbels (ed.), *Knorke, ein neues Buch Isidor für Zeitgenossen* (München: Verlag Franz Eher Nachf., 1929), pp. 36-37. See also Appendix XIV, Hitler's biogram of November 29, 1921.

37. Cf. Trevor-Roper, *op. cit.,* p. 138. There are valid indications that there existed a difference between those who joined the SA and those who joined the SS. Those who joined the SA anticipated the re-establishment of a petty bourgeois existence in case of a realization of a National Socialist state. Strasser writes: 'Die SA war diszipliniert wie eine gute Armee; sie hatte keine politische Überzeugung, – die Uniform und der Gehorsam, das war ihre Religion.' Strasser, *op. cit.,* p. 152. The SS, on the other hand, aspired to an élitist status and power.

---

['The SA was disciplined like a good army. It had no political convictictions. Uniform and obedience – those were its religion.']

38. For Berchtold's directives concerning the establishment of 'Schutzstaffeln' of the NSDAP, dated early 1927, see BDC, T-580, R. 87, F. 425. See also Rauschning, *op. cit.,* p. 66.
39. See Koch, *op. cit.,* p. 53.
40. See Otto Strasser's report on the origin and development of the Berlin SA formation revolt (headed by Captain Stennes) against Hitler's corruption. The revolt was set off by Gregor and Otto Strasser's disclosures in their paper 'Die Schwarze Front.' Cf. Strasser, *op. cit.,* pp. 159-160; cp. also Strasser's Buenos Aires edition of 1940, pp. 117-129.
41. See *Die Organisation der NSDAP, 1943, 7. Auflage, Hrsg. Der Reichsorganisationsleiter der NSDAP* (München: Zentralverlag der NSDAP, Franz Eher Nachf., 1943), p. 417. See also Best, *op. cit.,* p. 86.
   According to Kurt Lewin, in German culture 'loyalty is frequently identified with obedience.' Gertrud Weiß-Lewin (ed.), Kurt Lewin, *Resolving Social Conflict* (New York: Harper and Row, 1948), p. 51.
42. Cf. 'Nationalpolitischer Lehrgang der Wehrmacht vom Januar 1937,' im IMT, *op. cit.,* p. 207. See also *Dienstaltersliste der Schutzstaffel der NSDAP, Stand vom 1. Juli 1935, bearbeitet von der Personalkanzlei des Reichsführers-SS*

(Berlin, 1935), p. 2.

43. Cf. *Statistisches Jahrbuch der Schutzstaffel der NSDAP 1937, op. cit.,* p. 3. Cp. Heiber, *op. cit.,* p. 13.

44. See footnote 54.

45. Cf. Rauschning, *op. cit.,* p. 46.

46. Cf. C. Wighton, *Heydrich, Hitler's Most Evil Henchman* (Philadelphia: Chilton Company, 1962), p. 43.

47. Strasser writes: 'Wenn Pfeffer sich als unfähig erwiesen, wenn Stennes ihn (Hitler) verraten hatte, dann könnte sich eines Tages auch Röhm, mit dem schon so heftige Zusammenstöße vorgekommen waren, gegen ihn wenden. Um dieser Gefahr vorzubeugen, brauchte Hitler eine starke Stoßtruppe, die ihm bis in den Tod ergeben war. Die kleine SS Formation nahm von hier aus ihren schnellen Aufschwung, und Himmler machte eine schwindelerregende Karriere. Zwischen Röhm, dem Führer der SA, und Himmler, dem Führer der SS, herrschte offen Kriegszustand. Hitler sah die Rivalität gern.' Strasser, *op. cit.,* p. 162.

———

[Strasser writes: 'If Pfeffer had proven incompetent, if Stennes had betrayed him [Hitler], then it was possible that Röhm – with whom there had already been such strong clashes – might also turn against him some day. In order to preclude this danger, Hitler needed a strong body of shock troops who were dedicated to him unto death. From that initial point the small SS formation experienced its rapid growth, and Himmler launched his dizzying career. There was often a state of open war between Röhm, the leader of the SA, and Himmler, the leader of the SS. Hitler was pleased to see this rivalry.']

48. Cf. *Dienstaltersliste der Schutzstaffel der NSDAP. Stand vom 9. November 1944, hrsg. vom SS-Personalamt* (Berlin, 1944), p. 7. The three other 'Oberstgruppenführer' were Franz Xaver Schwarz, Josef Dietrich, and Paul Hausser; see *ibid.*

During the numerous interviews with this writer (1967/1968) the former 'Obergruppenführer' and General of the 'Waffen-SS,' Karl Wolff, claimed to have been promoted on April 20, 1945, to 'Oberstgruppenführer.'

49. Cf. *Geschichte und Daten der SS,* GRMA, T-175, R. 180, Fr. 2 715 223. For a detailed account of Himmler's early years, see especially Werner T. Angress and Bradley F. Smith, 'Diaries of Heinrich Himmler's Early Years,' *The Journal of Modern History,* September 1959, Vol. XXXI, No. 3, pp. 206-224.

50. Cf. *Rede des Reichsführers-SS auf der Ordensburg Sonthofen, May 5, 1944,* GRMA, T-175, R. 92, Fr. 2 613 469.

51. Cf. W. Frischauer, *Himmler: The Evil Genius of the Third Reich* (Boston: The Beacon Press, 1953), p. 20.

52. See *ibid.* Cf. also Angress and Smith, *op. cit.,* pp. 211-212; Steiner, *op. cit.,* p. 59; Ludwig Voggenreiter (ed.), *Der Hitler-Prozess* (Potsdam: Ludwig Voggenreiter, 1934), pp. 8-13.

The march to the Feldherrnhalle on November 9, 1923, was described by Koch as follows: 'Voran die beiden Fahnen, dann der Führer mit seinen Begleitern, hierauf Teile vom Stoßtrupp Hitler und im Anschluß daran Teile vom ersten und zweiten Batallion vom Regiment München in Marschkolonne neben Oberland, Publikum davor, auf beiden Seiten und dahinter, so bewegte sich der Zug durch Münchens Straßen. Schwache Absperrungsketten der Landespolizei verschwanden in der Höhe der Residenz in den wogenden, singenden Menschenmassen, die immer wieder in das Deutschlandlied der SA einfielen.' Koch, *op. cit.*, p. 40.

['In front the two flags, then the Führer with his escorts, then portions of the Hitler shock troops followed by parts of the 1st and 2nd Battalions of the München Regiment in marching order beside Oberland; the public in front, on both sides, and to the rear – in this fashion the procession moved through the streets of Munich. Around the Residenz, the weak restraining chains of the local police disappeared among the surging, singing masses, who again and again joined the SA in the national anthem (Deutschlandlied).']

53. See Steiner, *op. cit.*, pp. 59-62. Cp. also Dietrich Bronder, *Bevor Hitler kam* (Hannover: Pfeiffer Verlag, 1964), pp. 239-241. In his chapter 'Okkulte Wurzeln' the author describes the nature and objectives of the Thule-Order in which Heinrich Himmler supposedly played a prominent role. See *ibid.*, pp. 219-244.
54. See Strasser, *op. cit.*, p. 47, and G. Reitlinger, *The SS: Alibi of a Nation, 1922-1945* (New York: Viking Press, 1957), p. 23.
   In an interview with this writer in Freiburg/Breisgau on November 4, 1966, Otto Strasser stated that his brother Gregor was a rather poor judge of people. After Himmler had betrayed his confidence, Gregor Strasser could still not believe in Himmler's 'faithlessness' because of his 'clear blue eyes.' See also Otto Strasser's letter to the editor: 'Er (Himmler) war damals völlig "Strasser-Mann" und versuchte mir einmal zu erklären, daß die SS, die er aufbaute, "das Gewissen des NS" sein sollte, "notfalls auch gegen Hitler", wenn der dem Mussolini-Faschismus zu weit entgegenkommen würde. Daß er später (aber lange nach Goebbels) sich änderte, ist für den Kenner der menschlichen Natur nicht verwunderlich!' *Der Spiegel*, November 14, 1966, No. 47, pp. 14-15.
   Cf. also Heiber, *op. cit.*, pp. 10-11.

['He [Himmler] was, at that time, a convinced follower of Strasser, and he once attempted to explain to me that the SS, which he was building up, was to be "the conscience of National Socialism, even, if need be, against Hitler," if the latter were too accommodating to the Mussolini type of Fascism. The fact that he later changed his mind (but long after Goebbels) is not surprising for those with a knowledge of human nature!']

55. The former General and 'Obergruppenführer' of the 'Waffen-SS,' and commander of the 'Division Wiking,' Felix Steiner, related in numerous interviews

with this writer that he had always considered Himmler a 'schlampiger Romantiker.' Similar views were expressed by Himmler's former Chief of Personal Staff (Chef des Persönlichen Stabes Rf-SS), General and 'Obergruppenführer' Karl Wolff, as well as by 'Obersturmbannführer' Fritz Lechler, former Chief of Amt B-II and Amt W-VI (clothes of the SS and inmates of concentration camps, textiles and leather), who considered Himmler as a weak but strongheaded person. Cp. also Steiner, *op. cit.*, pp. 60, 61, 63, 65, 232, 240. Cp. Angress and Smith, *op. cit.*, p. 215.

56. Cf. Trevor-Roper, *op. cit.*, p. 138.
57. For this order entitled CRUSA VII, April 12, 1929, see BDC, T-580, R. 87, F. 425.
58. Cf. *Statistisches Jahrbuch der Schutzstaffel der NSDAP 1937*, *op. cit.*, p. 3.
59. For Himmler's SS-Befehl No. 20, December 1, 1930, see BDC, T-580, R. 87, F. 425.
60. In two letters, one from late 1929 and the other dated January 29, 1930, Himmler attempted to secure money from the German settlers in Oruro, Bolivia, through the services of Ernst Röhm. Himmler appealed to Röhm by stating that, in his opinion, the SS carried on the tradition of the 'Reichskriegsflagge.' See GRMA, T-175, R. 199, Frs. 2 739 868, 2 739 874-2 739 875.
61. Auszug aus Lagebericht München, December 4, 1930, see BDC, T-580, R. 85, F. 403.
62. Cf. Koch, *op. cit.*, p. 240.
63. It is interesting to note that Koch – in his Ehrenbuch der SA, published a few months before the Röhm-Putsch in June 1934, and in which he describes the history and development of the SA in detail – does not mention Himmler's name once, although those of his predecessors appear.
64. *Himmler to Röhm, June 26, 1930,* see GRMA, T-175, R. 194, Fr. 2 739 869.
65. Cf. *Statistisches Jahrbuch der Schutzstaffel der NSDAP 1937*, *op.. cit.*, p. 3.
66. Cf. Angress and Smith, *loc. cit.*, p. 214.
67. *Ibid.*, p. 209.
68. *Ibid.*
69. Cf. *ibid.*, pp. 213, 214, 215, 216. Cp. Heiber, *op. cit.*, p. 16.
70. Cf. Angress and Smith, *loc. cit.*, p. 218. See also Heiber, *op. cit.*, p. 16.
71. Cf. Angress and Smith, *loc. cit.*, p. 213.
72. Cf. *ibid.*, pp. 213, 219. Cp. Heiber, *op. cit.*, p. 15.
73. Cf. Angress and Smith, *loc. cit.*, pp. 214-215.
74. *Ibid.*, p. 217.
75. Cf. *ibid.*, p. 218.
76. Cf. *ibid.*, p. 210.
77. Cf. *ibid.*
78. *Loc. cit.*
79. *Ibid.*, p. 220.
80. Cf. *ibid.*
81. *Loc. cit.*
82. *Ibid.*, p. 221.

83. *Ibid.*, p. 216. See entries of November 14, 1919; of November 28, 1919; of November 22, 1921; of June 11, 1922.
84. Cf. *ibid.*
85. Cf. *ibid.*, pp. 215-216.
86. *Ibid.*, p. 218.
87. Cf. *ibid.*, pp. 215-216.
88. Cf. *ibid.*, p. 211.
89. *Ibid.*, p. 222.
90. Cf. *ibid.*, pp. 222-223. Cf. also Felix Kersten, *Totenkopf und Treue* (Hamburg: Robert Mölich Verlag, 1952), pp. 389-407.
91. Cf. Buchheim, 'Die SS – Das Herrschaftsinstrument, Befehl und Gehorsam,' in Buchheim, *op. cit.*, p. 191.
92. For Himmler's 'Ansprache vor den Beamten und Angestellten des Geheimen Staatspolizeiamtes,' on October 11, 1934, see GRMA, T-175, R. 89, Fr. 2 611 537.
93. *Ibid.*, Fr. 2 611 536.
94. 'Der Führer erhebt die SS zur selbständigen Organisation. München 25. Juli. Die Reichspressestelle der NSDAP gibt folgende Verfügung des Führers bekannt: Im Hinblick auf die großen Verdienste der SS, besonders im Zusammenhang mit den Ereignissen des 30. Juni 1934, erhebe ich dieselbe zu einer *selbständigen Organisation* im Rahmen der NSDAP. Der Reichsführer der SS untersteht daher, gleich dem Chef des Stabes, dem obersten SA-Führer direkt. Der Chef des Stabes und der Reichsführer der SS bekleiden beide den parteimäßigen Rang eines Reichsleiters.
München, den 20. Juli 1934. gez. Adolf Hitler.'
See *Völkischer Beobachter, Ausgabe A/Süddeutsche Ausgabe*, München, July 1, 1934, p. 1.

['The Führer makes the SS an independent organization. Munich, July 25. The Reich Press Office of the NSDAP announces the following instruction of the Führer: "In view of the great services of the SS, especially in connection with the events of June 30, 1934, I raise the SS to the level of an *independent organization* within the framework of the NSDAP. The Reichsführer of the SS (RFSS) is, therefore, directly subordinate to the supreme SA-Führer as is the Chief of Staff. The Chief of Staff and the Reichsführer of the SS both hold the party rank of Reichsleiter (Reich leader). Munich, July 20, 1934, signed Adolf Hitler." ']

95. Cf. *Dienstaltersliste der Schutzstaffel der NSDAP, Stand vom 1. Juli 1935, bearbeitet von der Personalkanzlei des Reichsführers-SS* (Berlin, 1935), p. 2. Cf. Appendix I.
96. *Statistisches Jahrbuch der Schutzstaffel der NSDAP 1938, op. cit.*, p. 107. See Appendix IV a-d. Cf. also Appendix IVe.
Cp. Hans H. Gerth, 'The Nazi Party: Its Leadership and Composition,' in Robert K. Merton *et al.* (ed.), *Reader in Bureaucracy* (Glencoe/Ill.: The Free

Press, 1960), pp. 104-107, and John M. Steiner and Jochen Fahrenberg, 'Die Ausprächung autoritäter Einstellung bei ehemaligen Angehörigen der SS und der Wehrmacht,' *Kölner Zeitschrift für Soziologie und Sozial-Psychologie,* Vol. XXII, No. 3 (1970), pp. 555-556.

97. Cf. *ibid.,* p. 9. See also 'Die Waffen-SS als Teil der ehemaligen Kriegs-Wehrmacht, Eine Antwort an das Institut für Zeitgeschichte,' *Wiking-Ruf* (Hameln: Wiking-Ruf-Verlag, June 1955), Vol. IV, No. 6, pp. 13-15, 18.

98. Cf. *Statistisches Jahrbuch der Schutzstaffel der NSDAP 1937, op. cit.,* p. 10.

99. Cf. *ibid.,* p. 12. See also Steiner, *op. cit.,* pp. 250-251; Best, *op. cit.,* p. 17; Robert Ley (ed.), 'Bericht über die SS seit dem Reichsparteitag 1938, in Nationalsozialistisches Jahrbuch 1940,' in IMT, *op. cit.,* pp. 275-277, PS-2164.

100. Cf. *Statistisches Jahrbuch der Schutzstaffel der NSDAP 1937, op. cit.,* p. 14; Best, *op. cit.,* p. 17; Ley, *op. cit.,* pp. 277-278. See also 'Nationalpolitischer Lehrgang der Wehrmacht vom Januar 1937,' *op. cit.,* pp. 221-222. Also cp. 'Rede Himmlers bei der SS-Gruppenführertagung in Posen am 4. Oktober 1943,' in IMT, *op. cit.,* pp. 145-146, PS-1919.

101. See testimony given by former members of the 'Waffen-SS' before the IMT in Nuremberg on August 5 and 6, 1946, IMT, Vol. XX, pp. 371-471. See also Steiner, *op. cit.,* pp. 79-81.

102. *Ibid.,* pp. 79-98. Cp. George H. Stein, *The Waffen-SS, Hitler's Elite Guard at War 1939-1945* (Ithaca, N.Y.: Cornell University Press, 1966), pp. XXX-XXXII, 291. See especially 'Fanatismus oder Verantwortung?,' *Wiking-Ruf, op cit.,* pp. 3-4, and 'Letztes Geleit' and 'Abschied von Georg Keppler,' in *Der Freiwillige, Kameradschaftsblatt der HIAG (Hilfsgemeinschaft auf Gegenseitigkeit)* (Osnabrück: Munin-Verlag GmbH, 1966), Vol. XII, No. 7, pp. 2-9, 19-20.

103. Cf. Best, *op. cit.,* p. 86.

104. Cf. *ibid.*

105. See 'Preußisches Gesetz vom 26. April 1933 über die Errichtung eines Geheimen Staatspolizeiamts,' in IMT, Vol. XXIX, *op. cit.,* pp. 250-251, PS-2104. Cf. also 'Preußisches Gesetz vom 30. November 1933. Betrifft den Aufgabenkreis der Geheimen Staatspolizei,' *ibid.,* pp. 251-252, PS-2105; 'Preußisches Gesetz vom 10. Februar 1936 zur Ausführung des Gesetzes über die Geheime Staatspolizei vom gleichen Tage,' *ibid.,* pp. 255-258, PS-2109; 'Verordnung Görings vom 8. März 1934 zur Durchführung des Gesetzes über die Geheime Staatspolizei vom 30. November 1933,' *ibid.,* pp. 258-260, PS-2113; 'Aus dem Völkischen Beobachter vom 22. Januar 1936: Auszug aus einem Artikel über die Bedeutung und Aufgaben der Geheimen Staatspolizei,' *ibid.,* pp. 178-180, PS-1956: 'Die Geheime Staatspolizei ist ein kriminalpolizeilicher Behördenapparat, dem die besondere Aufgabe der Verfolgung von Verbrechen und Vergehen gegen den Staat, vor allem die Verfolgung des Hoch- und Landesverrats, obliegt ... Während kurzfristige Schutzhaft in Polizei- und Gerichtsgefängnissen vollzogen wird, nehmen die der Geheimen Staatspolizei unterstehenden Konzentrationslager diejenigen Schutzhäftlinge auf, die für längere Zeit aus der Öffentlichkeit herausgenommen werden müssen.' *Ibid.,* pp. 178, 180.

['The Secret State Police (Gestapo) is a criminal investigation unit in charge of the special duty of prosecuting crimes and offenses against the state, above all treason and high treason . . . While periods of short-term preventive custody are served in police and court prisons, those prisoners who must be removed from the public for longer periods are sent to the concentration camps, which are under the control of the Secret State Police.']

106. Best, *op. cit.*, p. 86.
'Die Waffen-SS entstand aus dem Gedanken heraus, dem Führer eine auserlesene, länger dienende Truppe für die Erfüllung besonderer Aufgaben zu schaffen. Sie soll es den Angehörigen der Allgemeinen SS sowie Freiwilligen, die den besonderen Bedingungen der Schutzstaffel entsprechen, ermöglichen, auch mit der Waffe in der Hand im Kriege in eigenen Verbänden zum Teil im Rahmen des Heeres für die Verwirklichung der nationalsozialistischen Idee zu kämpfen. Der Führer befahl daher die Schaffung einer kasernierten Truppe, der heutigen Waffen-SS. Sie verbindet mit der soldatischen Haltung eine straffe geistige Ausrichtung und erzieht ihre Männer auch zu politischen Kämpfern.

'Die Waffen-SS kennt neben den gezogenen Reservisten zur Zeit auch Freiwillige auf Kriegsdauer. Den dauernden Mannschaftsbestand geben 4- bis 12-jährig dienende Männer ab.
'Die Führer, Unterführer und Männer sowohl der aktiven Teile wie auch die Freiwilligen und Reservisten sind hinsichtlich Besoldung und Versorgung den Angehörigen der Wehrmacht gleichgestellt. Der Dienst in der Waffen-SS ist Erfüllung der gesetzlichen Wehrpflicht.
'Die Anfänge der Waffen-SS gehen auf die am 17.3.1933 befohlene Aufstellung der "Stabswache" in Stärke von zunächst nur 120 Mann zurück. Aus dieser kleinen Gruppe entwickelte sich die spätere SS-Verfügungstruppe bzw. die Leibstandarte SS "Adolf Hitler". Im Laufe dieses Krieges wuchsen diese Verbände zu Divisionen:

     Leibstandarte-SS "Adolf Hitler"
     SS-Division "Reich"
     SS-Totenkopf-Division
     SS-Polizei-Division
     SS-Division "Wiking"
     SS-Gebirgs-Division-Nord
     SS-Kavallerie-Division

dazu während des Krieges die

     SS-Freiwilligen-Division "Prinz-Eugen" und die 1. und 2.
     SS-Infanterie-Brigade.

'Die SS-Division "Wiking" setzte sich zusammen aus Reichsdeutschen, germanischen Freiwilligen und dem Finnischen Freiwilligen-Bataillon.

In den SS-Brigaden befinden sich die germanischen Freiwilligen-Legionen "Nor-
wegen", "Niederlande", "Flandern" und das Freikorps "Danmark".'
*Die Organisation der NSDAP, op. cit.*, pp. 427a-b.

'Sie (Leibstandarte "Adolf Hitler") sind das älteste Regiment dieser Waffen-SS
und nach Ihnen kamen dann die Standarten "Deutschland" und "Germania"
und dann kam die Standarte "Der Führer" und dann wurde aus diesen einzelnen
Infanterieregimentern eine Division . . . im Polenfeldzug waren wir noch gar
keine eigene Division und jetzt im Westfeldzug hatten wir bereits die Leibstandarte als Détachement, wobei erst im 2. Teil die Artillerieabteilung dazu
kam, die Verfügungstruppendivision, die Totenkopfdivision, dann die Polizei-
division.' 'Ansprache Himmlers an das Offizierkorps der Leibstandarte-SS "*Adolf
Hitler*" am 7. September 1940,' in IMT, Vol. XXIX, *op. cit.*, p. 99, PS-1918.

――――

['The Waffen-SS originated in the idea of creating for the Führer a body of
selected troops, serving longer for the execution of special tasks. It shall make
it possible for members of the General SS (Allgemeine SS) as well as for
volunteers who meet the special requirements of the Schutzstaffel to also bear
arms in war-time in their own units, in part within the framework of the army,
and to fight for the realization of the National Socialist idea. Hence the Führer
ordered the creation of a barracks-based body of troops, the Waffen-SS of today. It combines soldierly behavior with rigid mental discipline and also trains
its men to become political combatants.
'The Waffen-SS also includes reservists who have been called up, as well as
volunteers serving for the duration of the war. Men serving from four to twelve
years constitute the permanent body of troops. With respect to pay and provision, the leaders, deputy leaders, and men in the active units as well as the
volunteers and reservists are on a par with the members of the Wehrmacht.
Service in the Waffen-SS fulfills the legal obligation of military service.
'The beginning of the Waffen-SS dates back to March 17, 1933, when the
creation of a "staff guard" (Stabswache) was ordered, with an initial strength
of only one hundred and twenty men. From this small group there developed
the later SS-Verfügungstruppe (special disposition troops; the militarized formations of the SS, renamed Waffen-SS in the winter of 1939/40: trans.) and the
"Adolf Hitler" Leibstandarte SS (the Adolf Hitler bodyguard: trans.). In the
course of this war the following units acquired divisional status:

> SS-Leibstandarte "Adolf Hitler"
> SS-Division "Reich"
> SS-Death's Head Division
> SS-Police Division
> SS-Division "Viking"
> SS-Mountain Division North
> SS-Cavalry Division

these were joined during the war by

SS-Volunteer Division "Prinz Eugen" and
First and Second SS-Infantry Brigades.

'The SS-Division "Viking" was composed of German nationals, volunteers of
German extraction, and the Finn Volunteer Battalion. The SS brigades include
the Germanic volunteer legions "Norway", "Netherlands", "Flanders", and the
volunteer corps "Denmark".' *Die Organisation der NSDAP, op. cit.*, pp. 427a-b.

'You (the Leibstandarte "Adolf Hitler") are the oldest regiment of this Waffen-
SS. After you came the Standarten (a formation approximately equivalent to a
regiment: trans.) "Deutschland" and "Germania", then the Standarte "Der
Führer". These individual infantry regiments subsequently developed into
divisions ... In the Polish campaign we were not yet a real division, and now
in the Western campaign we had the Leibstandarte as a detachment. It was
only in the second part of the campaign that the artillery section joined us,
followed by the division of Verfügungstruppen, the Death's Head Division, and
then the Police Division.']

107. By the end of 1943 there were twelve 'SS-Hauptämter' with the following functions:

'Gliederung und Aufgabenbereiche
Aus der Vielseitigkeit der Aufgaben der Schutzstaffel ergibt sich ihre Gliederung. Der Reichsführer SS übt die Kommandogewalt über die gesamte SS aus.
Zur Herausgabe und Durchführung seiner Befehle und Anordnungen für die
gesamte SS, die Polizei und ihm sonst übertragene umfangreiche Arbeitsgebiete
bedient er sich der ihm unmittelbar unterstellten Hauptämter der Reichsführung
SS sowie einiger anderer, ihm unmittelbar verantwortlicher Dienststellen. Letztere sind nach dem Stande vom September 1942 der Reichsarzt SS und Polizei
und der Chef des Fernmeldewesens.
Die Hauptämter der Reichsführung SS sind im Laufe der Zeit in nachstehender
Reihenfolge gebildet worden:

SS-Hauptamt,
Reichssicherheitshauptamt,
Rasse- und Siedlungshauptamt SS,
Hauptamt Ordnungspolizei,
SS-Wirtschafts-Verwaltungs-Hauptamt,
Persönlicher Stab Reichsführer SS,
SS-Personalhauptamt,
Hauptamt SS-Gericht,
SS-Führungshauptamt,
Dienststelle SS-Obergruppenführer Heißmeyer,
Stabshauptamt des Reichskommissars für die Festigung deutschen Volks-
tums,

Hauptamt Volksdeutsche Mittelstelle.

## Arbeitsgebiete der SS-Hauptämter

*Das SS-Hauptamt*
Aufgabe des SS-Hauptamtes ist die weltanschauliche und politische Führung, Schulung und Erziehung der SS, die Ergänzung der gesamten SS und Polizei und der Verbände, die der SS unterstellt sind, und die Erfassung der SS-Angehörigen und deren Sippen. Weitere Aufgaben sind die körperliche Erziehung und die kulturelle Betreuung der SS. Von besonderer Wichtigkeit ist der Aufbau und die Führung der SS in den germanischen Ländern.

*Das Reichssicherheitshauptamt*
Im Reichssicherheitshauptamt werden alle organisatorischen, personellen, wirtschaftlichen und technischen Angelegenheiten der Sicherheitspolizei und des SD bearbeitet. Daneben ist es die Zentrale der staatspolizeilichen und kriminalpolizeilichen Exekutive sowie die Zentralleitung des Nachrichtennetzes des SD.

*Das Rasse- und Siedlungshauptamt*
Das Rasse- und Siedlungshauptamt SS bearbeitet in seinen Ämtern die rassische Auslese des SS-Nachwuchses, lenkt die Gattenwahl der SS-Männer und fördert die Bildung erbbiologisch wertvoller kinderreicher Familien. Geeigneten und siedlungswilligen SS-Männern wird der Weg zum eigenen Hof ermöglicht.

*Das Hauptamt Ordnungspolizei*
Aufgabengebiete des Hauptamtes Ordnungspolizei sind Polizeiverwaltung sowie Betreuung und Führung der Schutzpolizei des Reiches, der Gendarmerie, der Schutzpolizei der Gemeinden, der Wasserschutzpolizei, der Luftschutzpolizei, der Feuerschutzpolizei, der Schutzmannschaften in den besetzten Gebieten, der Kolonialpolizei, der Freiwilligen Feuerwehr, der Pflicht- und Jugendfeuerwehren, der Technischen Nothilfe und der Technischen SS- und Polizei-Akademie.

*Das SS-Wirtschafts-Verwaltungs-Hauptamt*
Das SS-Wirtschafts-Verwaltungs-Hauptamt bearbeitet alle ihm vom Reichsführer SS und Chef der Deutschen Polizei, Heinrich Himmler, auf wirtschaftlichem und verwaltungsmäßigem Gebiet übertragenen Aufgaben.

*Der Persönliche Stab Reichsführer SS*
Der Persönliche Stab ist das zentrale Hauptamt. Entwickelt aus der Adjutantur des Reichsführers SS unterstehen ihm darüber hinaus alle Dienststellen, die mit der Verwirklichung der besonderen Pläne des Reichsführers SS betraut sind. Der Chef des Persönlichen Stabes ist ständiger Verbindungsführer des Reichsführers SS im Führerhauptquartier und bearbeitet dort alle Fragen der SS einschließlich der Waffen-SS und der Polizei.

*Das SS-Personalhauptamt*

Das SS-Personalhauptamt umfaßt folgende Arbeitsgebiete: Bearbeitung der Personalangelegenheiten von sämtlichen Führern der Schutzstaffel, sowohl Allgemeine SS wie Waffen-SS und SD in bezug auf Aufnahme, Beförderung und Entlassung. Weiter wird bearbeitet die SS-Dienstaltersliste, die Verleihung von Totenkopfringen und Ehrendegen sowie die Stellenbesetzung der Allgemeinen SS.

*Das Hauptamt SS-Gericht*

Das Hauptamt SS-Gericht bearbeitet Disziplinar- und Beschwerdesachen sowie Ehrenschutzangelegenheiten für den Reichsführer SS. Es ist darüber hinaus Zentralstelle und Ministerialinstanz für die Sonderstrafgerichtsbarkeit der SS und Polizei (ihm sind u.a. das Oberste SS- und Polizeigericht und 30 SS- und Polizeigerichte angeschlossen). Das Hauptamt SS-Gericht erledigt auch sonstige ihm vom Reichsführer SS zugewiesene Rechtsaufgaben.

*Das SS-Führungshauptamt*

Der Reichsführer SS bedient sich des SS-Führungshauptamtes als Kommandostelle zur Führung der Waffen-SS und zur vor- und nachmilitärischen Führung und Erziehung der Allgemeinen SS. Das SS-Führungshauptamt entstand im August 1940 aus der Notwendigkeit heraus, alle Funktionen, die mit dem Einsatz, der Führung, Organisation und Ausbildung der Einheiten zusammenhängen, an einer Stelle zu vereinen. Im SS-Führungshauptamt arbeiten folgende Ämter: Kommandoamt der Waffen-SS, Kommandoamt der Allgemeinen SS, SS-Verwaltungsamt, SS-Waffenamt, Amt für Führerausbildung, SS-Sanitätsamt, Amtsgruppe Inspektion.

*Dienststelle SS-Obergruppenführer Heißmeyer*

Die Dienststelle SS-Obergruppenführer Heißmeyer hat die Aufgabe, die Nationalpolitischen Erziehungsanstalten zu betreuen, für deren Neuentwicklung zu weiterem Ausbau Sorge zu tragen und weiter die Umwandlung der Internatsschulen im Reich in Deutsche Heimschulen durchzuführen, diese weiter auszubauen und neu auszurichten. In die Deutschen Heimschulen werden vorwiegend Kinder von gefallenen Soldaten, Beamten und aller der Volksgenossen aufgenommen, die auf Grund häufiger beruflicher Dienstsitzveränderungen sonst nicht die Gelegenheit haben, ihren Kindern eine ordnungsgemäße Ausbildung zukommen zu lassen.

*Das Stabshauptamt des Reichskommissars für die Festigung deutschen Volkstums*

Dem Stabshauptamt des Reichskommissars für die Festigung deutschen Volkstums liegt im Reich und in den unter der Oberhoheit des Reiches stehenden Gebieten die gesamte Siedlungs- und Aufbauplanung und deren Durchführung ob, einschließlich aller mit der Siedlung zusammenhängenden Verwaltungs- und Wirtschaftsfragen, insbesondere der Menscheneinsatz zum Zwecke der Siedlung.

*Das SS-Hauptamt Volksdeutsche Mittelstelle*
Das SS-Hauptamt Volksdeutsche Mittelstelle bearbeitet Volkstumsfragen, insbesondere Angelegenheiten des deutschen Volkstums. Es führt volkstumspoli-
tische Aufträge des Reichsführers SS durch, wobei im Vordergrund dieser Arbeit die Stärkung des Zusammengehörigkeitsgefühls aller Deutschen mit den
sich daraus ergebenden praktischen volkstumspolitischen Folgerungen steht.'

---

*Structure and range of duties*
From the diversity of the tasks of the Schutzstaffel followed its structure. The
Reich SS Leader exercises command over the entire SS. He makes use of the
Main Offices of the SS ((SS-Hauptämter) of the Reichsführung (the High Command of the SS, comprising Himmler's Personal Staff and the Hauptämter:
trans.) as well as other departments directly responsible to him, to issue and
execute his orders and instructions for the entire SS, the Police, and any
other executive duties assigned to him. As of September 1942 these departments are the SS-Reich and Police Physician and the Chief of Telecommuni-
cation.
The Main Offices of the Reichsführung-SS, in the course of time, have been
developed in the following sequence:

SS-Main Office (*SS-Hauptamt*)
Reich Security Main Office (*Reichssicherheitshauptamt*)
Race and Settlement Main Office SS (*Rasse-und Siedlungshauptamt*)
Police Main Office (*Hauptamt Ordnungspolizei*)
SS-Economic and Administrative Main Office (*SS-Wirtschafts-Verwal-
tungshauptamt*)
Personal Staff Reich SS Leader (*Persönlicher Stab Reichsführer SS*)
SS-Personnel Main Office (*SS-Personalhauptamt*)
Main Office SS-Tribunal (*Hauptamt SS-Gericht*)
SS-Operational Main Office (*SS-Führungshauptamt*)
Administrative Office SS-Obergruppenführer Heißmeyer (*Dienststelle
SS-Obergruppenführer Heißmeyer*)
Staff Main Office of the Reich Commissar for the Strengthening of
German Nationality (*Stabshauptamt des Reichskommissars für die
Festigung deutschen Volkstums*)
Main Office: Center for Nationals of Germanic Race (*Hauptamt Volks-
deutsche Mittelstelle*).

## SS-Main Offices and their scope of activity

*SS-Main Office*
Its task is the ideological and political leadership, indoctrination and education
of the SS; the recruitment of the entire SS, Police, and those formations that
are subordinated to the SS, as well as the keeping of records of the families of
the SS-men and their kin. Further tasks are the physical education and cultural

care of the SS. The development and leadership of the SS in Germanic countries are of special importance.

### Reich Security Main Office

The Reich Security Main Office handles all organizational, personal, economic, and technical matters of the Security Police and the Security Service. In addition, it is the center of the State Police and Criminal Police executive branch as well as the center of the intelligence network of the Security Service (SD).

### Race and Settlement Main Office SS

The Race and Settlement Main Office SS handles the racial selection of SS recruits, guides the SS-men's choice of mates, and promotes the development of genetically valuable prolific families. It will help suitable SS-men, who are willing to settle, to get their own farms.

### Police Main Office

The scope of activity of the Police Main Office is Police administration as well as care and guidance of the Protection Police, the Sheriff's Office (gendarmes), the Local Police, the Coast Guard, the Air-Raid Shelter Police, the Fire Protection Police, the Protection Units in the occupied territories, the Colonial Police, the Voluntary Fire Brigade, the Professional and Youth Fire Brigades, the Technical Emergency Corps, and the Technical SS and Police Academy.

### SS Economic and Administrative Main Office

The SS Economic and Administrative Main Office handles all tasks in the economic and administrative areas assigned to it by the Reich Leader SS and Chief of German Police, Heinrich Himmler.

### Personal Staff Reich Leader SS

The Personal Staff is the central Main Office. Developed from personnel surrounding the Reich Leader SS, it is also in charge of all administrative offices entrusted with the realization of special plans of the Reich Leader SS. The chief of the Personal Staff is the permanent liaison-officer of the Reich Leader SS in the Führer's Headquarters where he handles all questions concerning the SS, including the Waffen-SS and Police.

### SS Personnel Main Office

The SS Personnel Main Office includes the following fields of activity: Administration of personnel matters concerning all leaders of the Schutzstaffel, as well as the General SS, Waffen-SS, and Security Service (SD) regarding admission, promotion, and dismissal. Furthermore, the SS Personnel Main Office processes the SS seniority list (Dienstaltersliste), the granting of Death's Head Rings and Honorary Swords, as well as filling posts in the General SS.

## Main Office SS Tribunal

The Main Office SS Tribunal handles matters concerning discipline, complaints, and affairs of honor for the Reich Leader SS. Moreover, it is the central office and has jurisdiction over (Ministerialinstanz) special criminal justice of the SS and Police (attached to it are, among others, the Supreme SS and Police Court as well as thirty SS and Police Courts). In addition, the SS Tribunal takes care of other legal matters assigned to it by the Reich Leader SS.

## SS Operational Main Office

The Reich Leader uses the SS Operational Main Office as command post for the guidance of the Waffen-SS, as well as the pre- and post-military guidance and education of the General SS. The SS Operational Main Office emerged in August 1940 from the necessity to unite in one place all functions concerning the deployment (Einsatz), leadership, organization, and training of units. The following agencies work in the SS Operational Main Office: Commanding Office of the Waffen-SS, Commanding Office of the General SS, SS Adminstration Office, SS Weapons Office, Office of Leadership Training, SS Medical Service Office, Office for Inspections.

## Administrative Office SS-Obergruppenführer Heißmeyer

It is the task of the Administrative Office SS-Obergruppenführer Heißmeyer to tend to the National Socialist educational institutions, be concerned with their future development and expansion and continue to transform boarding schools in the Reich into German Home Schools (Heimschulen), to further their expansion as well as give them a new outlook. Primarily accepted into German Home Schools will be children of soldiers killed in action, of civil servants, and of all those fellow Germans (Volksgenossen), who, due to frequent occupational transfer, do not have the opportunity to furnish their children with an orderly education.

## Staff Main Office of the Reich Commissar for the Strengthening of Germanic Nationality

The Staff Main Office of the Reich Commissar for the Strengthening of Germanic Nationality is in charge of all plans for settlement and construction and their execution in the Reich and those territories that are under the sovereignty of the Reich, including all administrative and economic questions, in particular those concerning the development of manpower for the purpose of settlement.

## Main Office: Center for Nationals of Germanic Race

The Main Office: Center for Nationals of Germanic Race handles questions of nationality (Volkstum), especially matters of German nationality. It carries out orders of the Reich Leader SS concerning policies of German nationhood, emphasizing the strengthening of the feeling of solidarity among all Germans with all the resulting practical political consequences.]

*Die Organisation der NSDAP, op. cit.,* pp. 419-442. See Appendix II.
See also Best, *op. cit.,* pp. 88-95. Also cp. 'Rede Himmlers bei der SS-Gruppenführertagung in Posen am 4. Oktober 1943,' in IMT, *op. cit.,* pp. 138-139.
108. 'Ansprache Himmlers an das Offizierskorps der Leibstandarte-SS *Adolf Hitler*
am 7. September 1940,' in IMT, *op. cit.,* pp. 104, 105, 107.
Cp. also 'Rede Himmlers bei der SS-Gruppenführertagung in Posen am 4. Oktober 1943,' in IMT, *op. cit.,* pp. 166-167.
109. See Der Inspekteur der Statistik of the 'Schutzstaffel,' March 1, 1943, BDC,
T-580, R. 88, F. 436.
110. See newspaper clipping of an article by E. J. Cassel, entitled 'Des Führers
Schwarzes Korps' of April 5, 1938, BDC, T-580, R. 87, F. 425.
111. See *Statistisches Jahrbuch der Schutzstaffel der NSDAP 1937, op. cit.,* p. 4.
112. See *ibid.*
113. Himmler states in January, 1937: '. . . wir haben dann von Ende 1933 bis Ende
1935 von den Neuaufgenommenen wieder alles das herausgesetzt, was nichts
taugte. In diesen Jahren habe ich etwa 60 000 Männer herausgesetzt; die heutige
Stärke der Schutzstaffel beträgt rund 210 000 Mann.' 'Nationalpolitischer Lehrgang der Wehrmacht vom Januar 1937,' in IMT, *op. cit.,* p. 210.

['. . . then from the end of 1933 to the end of 1935 we expelled all of the new
recruits who were no good. During those years I expelled about sixty thousand
men. The present strength of the Schutzstaffel (SS) is about two hundred and
ten thousand men.']

See also Appendix V, loose attachment marked 'Geheim' (secret), giving reasons
for exclusion and dishonorable expulsion (discharge) from the SS. *Statistisches
Jahrbuch der Schutzstaffel der NSDAP 1938, op. cit.*
114. Rede des Reichsführers SS am Brocken, May 22, 1936, see GRMA, T-175,
R. 89, Fr. 2 611 585. Cp. also Rede Himmlers bei der SS-Gruppenführertagung
in Posen am 4. Oktober 1943, *op. cit.,* p. 165. See Appendices V, VI, *Statistisches Jahrbuch der Schutzstaffel der NSDAP, 1937, op. cit.,* pp. 55-56 (1937),
68-69 (1938).
115. See *Dienstaltersliste der Schutzstaffel der NSDAP, Stand vom 1. Juli 1935,*
*bearbeitet von der Personalkanzlei des Reichsführers SS, op. cit.,* p. 2.
116. See *Statistisches Jahrbuch der Schutzstaffel der NSDAP 1937, op. cit.,* p. 16.
See Appendix VII and *ibid.,* pp. 51, 47, 19. See Appendices VIII, IX, X.
117. By December 31, 1938, there were 14 234 in the VT, 9 172 in the TV, and
214 753 in the 'Allgemeine SS' (total of 238 159 men), See *Statistisches Jahrbuch der Schutzstaffel der NSDAP 1938, op. cit.,* p. 16. See Appendix XI,
*ibid.,* p. 79.
The average age of members of the SS was 26.8 years in 1934, 29.6 in 1936,
29.9 in 1939, and 28.7 in December 1938. In 1938 the most frequently represented age-groups of men drawn into the SS were those born in 1913
(17,188), 1914 (16,549), 1912 (16,484), 1911 (15,288), 1910 (13,837), 1915
(13,397), 1909 (12,408), 1908 (10,945). The least represented group was born

in 1883 (214). *Statistisches Jahrbuch der Schutzstaffel der NSDAP 1937 and 1938, op. cit.,* pp. 42, 19. In 1938 the most frequently represented age groups of men in the 'Totenkopfverbände' (Death's Head Units) were born in 1920 (1,695), 1919 (1,438), 1921 1,286). *Ibid.* (1938), p. 81.

118. See Der Inspekteur der Statistik of the 'Schutzstaffel,' March 1, 1943, see BDC, T-580, R. 88, F. 436.

119. For Himmler's observations in the Eindhoven-Tilburg area on May 18, 1940, see GRMA, T-175, R. 119, Fr. 2 644 360.

120. Cf. Kersten, *op. cit.,* p. 300.

121. Himmler to Brauchitsch, April, 1940, see BDC, T-580, R. 89, F. 440.

122. Report of Himmler to Hitler, Bad Nauheim (or Neuheim), May 27, 1940, see GRMA, T-175, R. 94, Fr. 2 615 217. See also Himmler to Brauchitsch, Sonderzug Heinrich, June 7, 1940, see BDC, T-580, R. 89, F. 440.

123. In his letter to the Austrian Bundeskanzler Klaus, Simon Wiesenthal writes: 'In dem beigeschlossenen Memorandum habe ich die mit zahlreichen Beweisen untermauerte These aufgestellt, daß Österreicher während der NS-Zeit am Tode von etwa drei Millionen Juden schuldig wurden ... Es ist erwiesen, daß Österreicher ihren Platz bei allen wichtigen Stellen der NSDAP, der SS, der Gestapo, des SD sowie anderer Körperschaften und Organisationen hatten, die sich mit der Vernichtung der Juden befaßten ... Unter ihnen befand sich eine erstaunlich hohe Anzahl von Österreichern.' Simon Wiesenthal, *Memorandum, I. Die Beteiligung von Österreichern an Nazi-Verbrechen und deren strafrechtliche Verfolgung.* Mimeographed memorandum (Vienna, October 12, 1966), pp. 1-2, 6.

['In the enclosed memorandum I have made the assertion, based on ample evidence, that during the National Socialist period Austrians became guilty of the deaths of three million Jews ... It has been proved that Austrians occupied positions in all important institutions of the NSDAP, SS, Secret State Police, Security Service as well as in other corporate bodies and organizations which were engaged in the destruction of the Jews ... In these NS corporate bodies there was an astonishingly high number of Austrians.']

The following individuals were mentioned as chiefly responsible: Dr. Ernst Kaltenbrunner, chief of RSHA and Gestapo; Adolf Eichmann, head of Amt IV B4; Odilo Globocnik, higher SS and police leader, district Lublin, responsible for the camps Belzec, Sobibor, and Treblinka, responsible for the 'Aktion Reinhard' and the first to use gas vans as a means of mass destruction; Eichmann's transportation chief, Franz Novak, Anton and Alois Brunner, responsible for the transportation of Jews from Austria, Greece, and Slovakia; Dr. Erich Rajakowitsch, in charge of deportations from Holland; Dr. Seidl and Dr. Burger, in charge of the ghetto Theresienstadt; Hermann Höfle, chief of staff of the 'Aktion Reinhard'; Franz Stangel, commandant of Treblinka; Dr. Gustav Otto Wächter, governor of the district Galizien; Dr. Johann Kunz, chief of the commando of the Sicherheitspolizei in White-Ruthenia; Franz Murer, in charge of the ghetto of Wilna; Eduard Roschmann, in charge of the ghetto Riga; Amon Goeth, Commandant of the concentration camp Plaszow; Dr. Hanns Rauter, Generalkommissar (director) in Holland; Dr. Hans Fischböck, Generalkommissar für Finanz und Wirtschaft (director of economic affairs); Dr. Artur Seyss-Inquart, Reichskommissar in Holland, and many others. *Ibid.*, pp. 4-13.

124. According to Hitler's secret decree of August 17, 1938, the 'SS- Totenkopfverbände' were: '... weder ein Teil der Wehrmacht noch der Polizei. Sie sind eine stehende bewaffnete Truppe der SS zur Lösung von Sonderaufgaben polizeilicher Natur, die zu stellen ich mir von Fall zu Fall vorbehalte. Als solche und als Gliederung der NSDAP sind sie weltanschaulich und politisch nach den von mir für die NSDAP und die Schutzstaffeln gegebenen Richtlinien auszuwählen, zu erziehen und durch Einstellung von SS-tauglichen Freiwilligen, die ihrer Wehrpflicht grundsätzlich in der Wehrmacht genügt haben, zu ergänzen.' Steiner, *op. cit.*, p. 344. See also *ibid.*, p. 345. Cp. Ley in IMT, *op. cit.*, p. 276, PS-2164.

['... neither a part of the Armed Forces nor the Police. They are a permanent, armed troop of the SS for carrying out special tasks of police nature, which I reserve the right to assign to them from case to case. As such and as a branch (Gliederung) of the NSDAP, they are to be selected and trained according to ideological and political guidelines given by me for the NSDAP and the Schutzstaffeln; they are to be educated and their ranks supplemented with ablebodied SS volunteers who have satisfied in principle the requirements of compulsary military service in the Armed Forces.']

125. Cf. *ibid.*: 'Die Gliederung der einzelnen Verbände der SS-Verfügungstruppe ist aus organisatorischen Gründen den entsprechenden Einheiten des Heeres angeglichen. Die Truppen rekrutieren sich aus Freiwilligen aus der Zahl der Wehrpflichtigen; diese sind jedoch neben den Tauglichkeitsbestimmungen der Wehrmacht den besonderen Auswahlgesetzen der Schutzstaffel unterworfen. 'Sie erfüllen in der SS-Verfügungstruppe, in der sie sich zu vier Jahren Dienst verpflichten müssen, in den ersten zwei Jahren ihre gesetzliche aktive Dienstpflicht.'

['For organizational reasons, the structure of the individual units of the SS-Verfügungstruppe is adjusted to that of the corresponding units of the army. The troops are recruited from volunteers among the conscripts, but they are subject to the special selection statutes of the Schutzstaffel as well as the fitness criteria of the Wehrmacht. 'The first two years of their service in the SS-Verfügungstruppe, which requires enlistment for four years, fulfill the legal active-duty requirement.']

126. Walter Hofer (ed.), *Der Nationalsozialismus, Dokumente 1933-1945* (Frankfurt: Fischer Bücherei, 1957), pp. 110-111. See also Steiner, *op. cit.*, p. 20.

127. *Ibid.*

128. Cf. Stein, *op. cit.*, p. 33. See also 'Gutachten des Bundestags-Abg. Oberst a.D. Alfred Burgemeister (CDU) an seine Fraktion auf Grund seiner Studien,' in Steiner, *op. cit.*, p. 345.

129. Cf. Stein, *op. cit.*, p. 23. Cp. Steiner, *op. cit.*, pp. 259-260.

130. Cf. Stein, *op. cit.*, pp. 23, 33.

131. Cf. Steiner, *op. cit.*, p. 59. See also Bronder, *op. cit.*, p. 197.

132. Cf. *ibid.*, pp. 196-197.

133. Cf. 'Heinrich Himmler, Die Schutzstaffel 1936: Äußerungen über Gehorsamspflicht und über Sicherheitsdienst und GESTAPO,' in IMT, Vol. XXIX, *op. cit.*, p. 14, PS-1851.

In his address to the Gruppenführer in Posen on October 4, 1943, Himmler said the following: 'Ich glaube auch, daß aus dem Unheil des Bombenkrieges eine Auflockerung der Großstädte kommt, so daß wir vom gütigen Herrgott etwas auf das Land hinausgetrieben werden. Dann wird mancher sagen: Na, auf dem Lande ist es doch gar nicht so schlecht, ich habe eine Ziege, der andere hat ein Schwein, wir haben ein paar Kartoffeln. Das sind sehr reelle Grundlagen. ... – Das Geld, um die Städte abzureißen, hätten wir nie aufwenden können. Jetzt hat das Schicksal sie abgerissen, . . .' in IMT, *op. cit.*, p. 164.

['I also believe that a decongestion of the large cities will result from the calamity of the bombing, so that we are forced by the good God somewhat out into the country. Then some will say: Well, it is really not so bad in the country; I have a goat, somebody else has a pig, we have a few potatoes. That is a very real basis ... – We would never have been able to find the money to tear down the cities. Now fate has torn them down ...']

134. See Peter G. J. Pulzer, *Die Entstehung des politischen Antisemitismus in Deutschland und Österreich 1867-1914* (Gütersloh: Sigbert Mohn Verlag, 1966), *passim.*

135. Adolf Hitler, *Mein Kampf*, Vol. II (München: Zentralverlag der NSDAP, 1940), p. 41.

136. *Ibid.*, Vol. I, p. 282. See also pp. 283-291 and 295-323.

137. *Ibid.*, Vol. II, p. 331. Hitler to Strasser: 'Die nordische Rasse hat das Recht, die Welt zu beherrschen, und dieses Recht der Rasse wird das leitende Prinzip unserer Außenpolitik werden.' In Strasser, *op. cit.*, p. 139. See also Rauschning, *op. cit.*, pp. 222-223, and Julius Streicher (ed.), *Reichstagung in Nürnberg 1933* (Berlin: Vaterländischer Verlag, 1933), pp. 54-56.

['The Nordic race has a right to rule the world, and this right will be the leading principle in our foreign policy.']

Prior to committing suicide on April 29, 1945, at sixteen hours, Hitler wrote in his political legacy: 'Vor allem verpflichte ich die Führung der Nation und die Gefolgschaft zur peinlichen Einhaltung der Rassengesetze und zum unbarmherzigen Widerstand gegen den Weltvergifter aller Völker, das internationale

Judentum.' Raul Hilberg, *The Destruction of the European Jews* (Chicago: Quadrangle Books, 1961), p. 635, PS-3569.

['Above all I pledge the nation's leadership as well as their followers to painstakingly adhere to the recial laws and merciless resistance to international Jewry, poisoner of all nations.']

138. Cf. Walter Darré, *Das Bauerntum als Lebensquell der Nordischen Rasse* (München: Lehmann, 1933), *passim*. See also Darré, 'Erhaltung des Bauerntums zur Erhaltung des Volkes,' in Streicher (ed.), *op. cit.*, pp. 185-190, and Alfred Rosenberg, 'Die rassische Bedingtheit der Außenpolitik,' in *ibid.*, pp. 103-128. See also Rosenberg, *Der Mythos des 20. Jahrhunderts* (München: Hoheneichen-Verlag, 1941), *passim*. See especially Rosenberg's letter to Major Kelley of December 26, 1945 (see Appendix XV). Cp. G. M. Gilbert, *Nürnberger Tagebuch* (Frankfurt: Fischer Bücherei, 1963), p. 101.

139. Cf. Rosenberg, *Der Mythos des 20. Jahrhunderts, op. cit.*, p. 81.

140. Cf. Eduard Fuchs, *Die Juden in der Karikatur. Ein Beitrag zur Kulturgeschichte* (München: A. Langen, 1921), pp. 160-166. See also Otto Strasser, *Der Faschismus: Geschichte und Gefahr* (München: Günter Olzog Verlag, 1965), p. 34.

141. Wilhelm Busch (1832-1908), one of the most popular and widely read German caricaturists and poets, depicted the Jews as repulsive and evil, simultaneously ascribing to them immutable racial characteristics. The following two excerpts are to serve as an illustration:

 1. 'Und der Jud mit krummer Ferse,
   Krummer Nas' und krummer Hos'
   Schlängelt sich zur hohen Börse
   Tiefverderbt und seelenlos.'

 2. 'Kurz die Hose, lang der Rock,
   Krumm die Nase und der Stock,
   Augen schwarz und Seele grau,
   Hut nach hinten, Miene schlau –
   So ist Schmulchen Schiefelbeiner.
   (Schöner ist doch unsereiner!)'

 ['1. And the Jew with crooked heel,
   Crooked nose and crooked pants
   Slithering towards the stock exchange
   Deeply corrupted and without soul.

  2. Short the pants, long the jacket,
   Crooked the nose as is the cane,
   Eyes black and grey the soul,

Hat to the rear, shrewd the mien –
Such is Sammy Crookedlegs.
(Our type is more appealing!)']

*Wilhelm Busch-Album. Humoristischer Hausschatz* (*Jubiläums-Ausgabe*), (München: Verlag Friedrich Bassermann, 1924);
1. from 'Die Fromme Helene,' (1872), Chpt. I, p. 3.
2. from 'Plisch und Plum,' (1882), Chpt. V, p. 56.
Cp. the caricatures in 'Auf gut Deutsch,' *Wochenschrift für Ordnung und Recht*, Dietrich Eckart (ed.), München, 1920, *passim*. Cf. also Albert Reich, *Dietrich Eckart* (München: Franz Eher Nachf., 1933), pp. 79-82. See especially the editorial 'Staat und evangelische Kirche im 19. Jahrhundert,' *Schulungsbriefe*, IV, 8, 1937, p. 317, and Eckart, *Der Bolschewismus, op. cit.,* p. 47.

142. See interrogation of Hjalmar Schacht of October 17, 1945, PS-3792, in which he pointed out that the anti-Jewish decrees were 'not important enough to risk a break' with Hitler; cit. in Hilberg, *op. cit.,* p. 22.

143. Cf. *Der Reichsführer SS/SS Hauptamt, Rassenpolitik* (Berlin, 1943), pp. 17-19.

144. Cf. Rede des Reichsführers SS vor den Leitern, Erziehern und Jungmannen der 8. Klasse der Nationalpolitischen Erziehungsanstalten im Zeltlager Ahrenshoop, July 3, 1938, see GRMA, T-175, R. 90, Frs. 2 612 349-2 612 350.

145. Cf. Trevor-Roper, *op. cit.,* p. 352. These services Hitler preferred to have performed by the SS. In this conversation Hitler delighted in the racial improvement of the native population living in the vicinity of Berchtesgaden. This improvement was credited to SS men stationed there.

146. Cf. Rede des Reichsführers SS vor den Leitern, Erziehern und Jungmannen der 8. Klasse der Nationalpolitischen Erziehungsanstalten im Zeltlager Ahrenshoop, July 3, 1938, see GRMA, T-175, R. 90, Fr. 2 612 351.

147. Cf. Rede des Reichsführers SS auf der Tagung für Befehlshaber der Kriegsmarine in Weimar, December 16, 1943, see *ibid.,* R. 91, Fr. 2 613 340. According to the *Statistisches Jahrbuch der Schutzstaffel der NSDAP 1938, op. cit.,* p. 66, the most frequently occurring heights of SS trainees in this year were: 1.70 m: 1,683 men; 1.76 m: 1,661 men; 1.74 m: 1,574 men; 1.62 m: 1,520 men; 1.68 m: 1,370 men.

148. Cf. 'Nationalpolitischer Lehrgang der Wehrmacht vom Januar 1937,' in IMT, *op. cit.,* pp. 207-208, 210-211.

149. *Ibid.,* p. 207.

150. Rede des Reichsführers SS am Brocken, May 22, 1936, see R. 89, Fr. 2 611 582. The following categories of SS affiliation were established according to *Statistisches Jahrbuch der Schutzstaffel der NSDAP 1938, op. cit.,* p. 8:

'*SS-Bewerber*
Es sind dies Männer, die sich um Aufnahme in die Schutzstaffel beworben haben und bei der SS-Annahme-Untersuchung sowohl SS-tauglich als auch SS-geeignet befunden wurden, über deren vorläufige Aufnahme jedoch noch nicht entschieden ist.

'*SS-Anwärter*
Dies sind diejenigen SS-Angehörigen, die unter Zuteilung einer SS-Nummer vorläufig in die SS aufgenommen sind d.h. sämtliche Staffel-Männer und Staffel-Dienstgrade.

'*SS-Männer*
SS-Männer sind alle SS-Angehörigen, die entweder am 30. Januar 1936 drei Jahre der SS angehörten oder nach Erfüllung der vorgeschriebenen Bedingungen als solche anerkannt und damit endgültig in die SS aufgenommen sind. Jeder SS-Führer ist in erster Linie SS-Mann.
SS-Angehörige, die ihrer Dienstpflicht beim Reichsarbeitsdienst oder der Wehrmacht genügen, scheiden für die Dauer dieser Zeit aus dem Befehlsverhältnis der SS aus. Sie werden in dieser Zeit als "SS-Zugehörige" geführt.
Unabhängig von vorgenannter Unterscheidung sind die SS-Angehörigen altersmäßig, gegebenenfalls auch nach der körperlichen Leistungsfähigkeit aufgeteilt in SS-I, umfaßt SS-Angehörige vom 18. bis 25. Lebensjahr, SS-II, umfaßt SS-Angehörige vom 25. bis 35. Lebensjahr, SS-Reserve, umfaßt SS-Angehörige vom 35. bis 45. Lebensjahr und SS-Stammabteilung, umfaßt SS-Angehörige über 45 Jahre. Die Altersgrenze von 45 Jahren bei der SS-Stammabteilung gilt jedoch nur als Anhalt. Alte, verdiente Männer, die aus beruflichen oder gesundheitlichen Gründen tatsächlich nicht in der Lage sind, Dienst zu verrichten, werden nicht ausgeschieden, sondern zur SS-Stammabteilung überwiesen, auch wenn sie das vorgeschriebene Alter noch nicht erreicht haben. Gerade durch die Errichtung der SS-Stammabteilung unterscheidet sich die SS als Orden von einer soldatischen Organisation.
Ausgenommen von der Aufteilung nach dem Alter sind die Angehörigen der Stäbe.'
. . .
'Dagegen gibt es bei der SS-Verfügungstruppe keine "SS-Zugehörigen", da der Wehrpflicht in ihr selbst genügt wird.
Auf Grund ihres Charakters als aktiver, kasernierter Truppe entfällt ebenfalls die altersmäßige Aufteilung in "SS-I, SS-II, SS-Reserve und SS-Stammabteilung".' *Ibid.*, p. 10.
*Ibid.*, p. 12: 'Die zur Ableistung ihrer Dienstpflicht beim Reichsarbeitsdienst oder bei der Wehrmacht befindlichen Angehörigen der SS-Totenkopfverbände werden in derselben Weise wie die entsprechenden Angehörigen der Allgemeinen SS als "SS-Zugehörige" geführt. Durch Erlaß des Führers vom August des Jahres 1938 ist jedoch bestimmt, daß künftig nur bereits in der Wehrmacht gediente Männer, sofern sie den Bedingungen entsprechen, eingestellt werden dürfen. Eine altersmäßige Aufteilung der SS-Totenkopfverbände ... besteht nicht.'

['*SS-Applicants*
These are men that have applied for admission into the Schutzstaffel and were found both fit for active service and suited for the SS – according to the ac-

ceptance examination – on whose provisional acceptance, however, a final decision has not yet been made.

*'SS-Candidates*
These are those members of the SS who have been assigned an SS-number and have been provisionally accepted, that is, all detachment-men and detachment-service ranks.

*'SS-Men*
SS-men are all those members of the SS who on January 30, 1936, either had belonged to the SS for three years or, after having fulfilled the prescribed conditions, have been recognized as such and thereby have been permanently accepted into the SS. Every SS leader is first and foremost an SS-man.
SS members who are serving conscription duty in the Reich Labor Service Reichsarbeitsdienst) or the Armed Forces are during this period not subject to orders from the SS (Befehlsverhältnis). During this time they are listed as "SS-affiliated" ("SS-Zugehörige").
Regardless of the above-mentioned distinctions, those classified as members of the SS are subdivided according to age and, if necessary, also on the basis of their physical stamina (Leistungsfähigkeit) in:
SS-I – comprises SS members from 18 to 25 years of age,
SS-II – comprises SS members from 25 to 35 years of age,
SS-Reservists – comprises SS members from 35 to 45 years of age, and
SS-core-branch – comprises SS members over 45 years of age.
However, the age limit of 45 years in regard to the SS-core-branch is meant as a frame of reference only. Men who have distinguised themselves, and who because of professional or health reasons are actually not in a position to serve, even though they have not yet reached the prescribed age limit, will not be excluded but transferred to the SS-core-branch. It is the SS-core-branch that distinguishes the SS as an order from a military organization.
Staff members are exempted from this grouping based on age.
In contrast to the Schutzstaffel, there are no "SS-affiliated" men in the SS-Verfügungstruppe since service in them satisfies the requirements of conscription duty.
On account of its being an active, barrack-stationed troop, the division into "SS-I, SS-II, SS-Reservists, and SS-core-branch, based on age, does not apply either." *Ibid.*, p. 10.
*Ibid.*, p. 12: "Those members of the SS-Death's Head Formations who in order to comply with their military conscription duty are serving in the Reich Labor Service or the Armed Forces are also classified as SS-affiliated, just as the corresponding members of the General SS. According to the Führer's decree of August 1938, however, it was ruled that in the future only those men may be enlisted that have already served in the Armed Forces, provided they meet the requirements. Grouping on the basis of age does not exist in the Death's Head Formations." ']

151. For 'Rassenkunde und rassische Richtlinien bei der SS Musterung,' see BDC, T-580, R. 88, F. 436.
152. 'Nationalpolitischer Lehrgang der Wehrmacht vom Januar 1937,' in IMT, *op. cit.*, p. 211.
153. For 'Rassenkunde und rassische Richtlinien bei der SS Musterung,' see BDC, T-580, R. 88, F. 436.
154. Cf. 'Nationalpolitischer Lehrgang der Wehrmacht vom Januar 1937,' in IMT, *op. cit.*, p. 210.
155. *Ibid.*, p. 211: 'Es kommt nun also darauf an, wie sich der junge Mann vor dieser Kommission benimmt. daß er also nicht bloß stramm die Hände an die Hosennaht legt, sondern daß er bei aller Diszipliniertheit doch nicht wie ein Knecht auftritt, daß er, wenn man sich mit ihm unterhält, wenn er gefragt wird, tatsächlich frei und ordentlich antworten kann, daß sein Gang, seine Hände, daß all das wirklich dem entspricht, was wir nach unserer nunmehr achtjährigen Erfahrung als Ideal wollen. Darnach wird geprüft, ob wir den Mann aufnehmen oder nicht.'

['So it depends now upon the manner in which the young man behaves before this commission. It is important that he not merely stiffly place his hands on the seams of his trousers; that while behaving in a disciplined manner, he does not have the air of a servant; that he speaks freely and well when one speaks with him or when he is questioned; that his walk, his hands, and all the rest are in accordance with the ideal we have developed after more than eight years of experience. These criteria determine whether we accept the man or not.']

See also Rede des Reichsführers SS am Brocken, May 22, 1936, GRMA, T-175, R. 89, Fr. 2 611 581.
156. For 'Rassenkunde und rassische Richtlinien bei der SS Musterung,' see BDC, T-580, R. 88, F. 436.
157. 'Nationalpolitischer Lehrgang der Wehrmacht vom Januar 1937,' in IMT, *op. cit.*, p. 210. See Appendices VI a-d.
158. *Ibid.*, p. 216.
159. Cf. Rede des Reichsführers SS auf der Tagung der RPA-Leiter am 28. Januar 1944, see GRMA, T-175, R. 94, Frs. 2 614 803-2 614 805.
160. Cf. Rede des Reichsführers SS am 23. November 1942, SS Junkerschule Tölz, see GRMA, T-175, R. 90, Fr. 2 612 778. For details concerning the origin and development of the 'Führerschulen,' see Steiner, *op. cit.*, pp. 342, 86-102, 129-132, 296. See also Buchheim, *loc. cit.*, pp. 193-194.
161. Cf. Himmler's speech of November 8, 1937, see GRMA, T-175, R. 90. Frs. 2 612 395-2 612 397.
    Cp. also Steiner, *op. cit.*, pp. 96-97.
162. 'Merkblatt für den freiwilligen Eintritt in die Waffen-SS 1940,' see GRMA, T-175, R. 104, Fr. 2 626 172.
163. Cf. 'Nationalpolitischer Lehrgang der Wehrmacht vom Januar 1937,' in IMT,

*op. cit.*, p. 213.
164. *Ibid.*, November 9 was chosen to commemorate the dissolution of the 'Stoß-trupp Hitler' in 1923. *Ibid.*, p. 206.
165. *Ibid.*, p. 213.
166. Cp. footnote 150.
167. Cf. Günter d'Alquen, *Die SS, Geschichte, Aufgabe und Organisation der Schutz-staffeln der NSDAP* (Berlin: Schriften der Hochschule für Politik II: *Der organisatorische Aufbau des Dritten Reiches*, No. 33), pp. 9-10, 18-19.
168. *Ibid.*, p. 10.
169. *Ibid.*
170. See *Dienstaltersliste der NSDAP vom 1. Juli 1935, op. cit.*, p. 2.
171. For Himmler's revised marriage order of January 26, 1940, see GRMA, T-175, R. 188, Fr. 2 726 256.
172. For Himmler's order of June 6, 1935, see BDC, T-611, R. 10, F. 446.
173. For Himmler's order of January 26, 1940, see GRMA, T-175, R. 188, Fr. 2 726 255-256

In the 'Verordnungsblatt der Waffen-SS' of December 1, 1940, we find that the marriage order had been altered again: 'Nur zur Kriegsdienstleistung einge-zogene Angehörige der Waffen-SS, die der Allgemeinen SS nicht angehören, brauchen die für die Waffen-SS übliche Heiratserlaubnis nicht einzuholen.' Rasse- und Siedlungshauptamt, Dok. SS-42, in IMT, Vol. XLII, *op. cit.*, p. 490.

['The only men who need not obtain the marriage permission otherwise custo-mary in the Waffen-SS are those members of the Waffen-SS who have been conscripted for military service and do not belong to the Allgemeine SS.']

174. Cf. Der Reichsführer SS, *Statistisches Jahrbuch der Schutzstaffel der NSDAP 1937*, see GRMA, T-175, R. 192, Fr. 2 730 929. See also *ibid.*, Fr. 2 730 918.
175. *Ibid.*, R. 188, Fr. 2 725 189.
176. In the course of this writer's interviews with former high SS officers it was disclosed that the offspring of extra-marital unions of SS officers were frequent-ly delivered in 'Lebensborn' homes. So, for example, SS General Karl Wolff, Himmler's former adjutant, disclosed during his trial in Munich on July 14, 1964, that Himmler had two illegitimate children stemming from an extra-marital relationship with his secretary. Cf. Himmler's letter of February 12, 1945, to SS-Ogruf. Schleßmann, Heiber, *op. cit.*, p. 305.
177. Kersten, *op. cit.*, p. 230. See also *ibid.*, p. 231. Cp. Heiber, *op. cit.*, p. 24.
178. Kersten, *op. cit.*, p. 230.

Himmler expressed the following opinion to Kersten on May 4, 1943: 'Ich per-sönlich bin der Ansicht, ... daß unsere Entwicklung dazu führt, mit der Einehe zu brechen. Die heutige Form der Ehe ist ein satanisches Werk der katholischen Kirche, die Ehegesetze selbst sind unmoralisch. ... Im Falle der Doppelehe wird die eine Frau für die andere der Ansporn sein, dem Idealbild in jeder Beziehung nahezukommen, die Haare auf den Zähnen und die Schlampigkeit werden ver-schwinden ... Da ein Mann im Normalfall unmöglich ein ganzes Leben lang mit einer Frau auskommen kann, zwingt man ihn zur Untreue und, um diese zu verdecken, zur Heuchelei. Die Folgen sind Zerwürfnisse innerhalb der Ehe. 'Die steigenden Verluste an der Ostfront bereiteten Hitler, ... große Sorgen. Der Führer habe sich deshalb entschlossen, unmittelbar nach dem Kriege eine tiefgreifende Änderung der jetzigen Ehegesetze vorzunehmen und die Doppelehe einzuführen. Dies werde jedoch zunächst nicht in der Form geschehen, daß allgemein die Einehe aufgehoben werde, vielmehr soll als hohe Auszeichnung den Helden dieses Krieges, den Trägern des deutschen Kreuzes in Gold sowie den Ritterkreuzträgern, das Recht verliehen werden, eine zweite Ehe einzugehen. Dieses Recht werde dann auf die Träger des eisernen Kreuzes 1. Klasse, sowie auf diejenigen, die die silberne und goldene Nahkampfspange trügen, ausgedehnt werden.' Kersten, *op. cit.*, pp. 224, 223.

------

['My personal opinion ... is that it would be a natural development for us to break with monogamy. Marriage in its existing form is the Catholic Church's Satanic achievement; marriage laws are in themselves immoral. ... But with bigamy, each wife would act as a stimulus to the other so that both would try to be their husband's dream-woman – no more untidy hair, no more slovenliness. ...

'The fact that a man has to spend his entire existence with one wife drives him first of all to deceive her and then makes him a hypocrite as he tries to cover it up. The result is dissension between the partners. ... Mounting losses on the Eastern front were causing Hitler great anxiety. ... Therefore the Führer had decided, the moment the war was over, to make comprehensive changes in the existing marriage laws and to introduce bigamy.

'In its first stage this would not mean the general abolition of monogamy, but the right to contract a second marriage would be granted to holders of the German Cross in Gold and holders of the Knight's Cross as a special tribute to heroism in battle. This right would next be extended to holders of the Iron Cross First Class and to those who held the Silver and Gold Clasps awarded for service in front-line fighting.']

179. *Ibid.*, p. 230. During his trial in Munich on July 14, 1964, the former SS-Obergruppenführer and General der Waffen-SS, Karl Wolff, asserted that Martin Bormann asked Himmler to deny requests of those SS members who asked his permission for a divorce. The reason for Bormann's request was to counter the divorce wave of high Nazi officials in the early forties. These officials were divorcing their older wives in order to marry younger ones. As a consequence – according to interviews with former SS officers – Himmler eventually opposed the continuously increasing requests of his men. A case in point was Himmler's close co-worker SS-Obergruppenführer and General der Waffen-SS, Karl Wolff, who fell somewhat out of favor with his chief after Wolff's insistence on divorcing his first wife in order to marry the Countess Ingrid von Bernstorff née von Christensen. Shortly afterwards Wolff was removed from his post as chief of the 'persönliche Stab Reichsführer SS' to become the only

'Höchster SS- und Polizeiführer und Bevollmächtigter General der Deutschen Wehrmacht' (Highest SS- and Police Leader and Plenipotentiary General of the German Armed Forces) in Italy, in September 1943. See also Kersten, *op. cit.*, p. 103.

180. For Himmler's clarification of the order of October 28, 1939, addressed 'An alle Männer der SS und Polizei,' January 30, 1940, see GRMA, T-175, Frs. 2 672 045-2 672 046.

181. *Ibid.*, Fr. 2 672 045.

182. Report by Himmler to Hitler, Winnitza (Ukraine), August 15, 1942, *ibid.*, Fr. 2 615 178, and for 'SS Befehle an die letzten Söhne,' Feldkommandostelle, August 15, 1942, see *ibid.*, R. 161, Fr. 2 693 305.

183. *Ibid.*

184. For Himmler's order of March 31, 1939, see BDC, T-611, R. 26, F. 158.

185. Many authors, as for example Hermann Rauschning, Otto Strasser, Raul Hilberg, Hannah Arendt, Dietrich Bronder, Walter Hagen (alias Höttl), and others, claim that many of the leading men of the Third Reich, including Hitler, were at least partially descendents of Jewish ancestry. The SS historian Sturmbannführer Dr. Höttl asserts that the first commander of the SS, Emil Maurice, was a 'Mischling' of the 'second degree.' Furthermore, it is claimed that Himmler had a Jewish relative and that the RSHA-chief Heydrich was motivated to persecute Jews because they formed at least 'a part of his ancestry.' Cf. Walter Hagen, *Die geheime Front* (Linz und Wien: Nibelungen-Verlag, 1950), pp. 19-39. Cp. also Hilberg, *op. cit.*, p. 677, and Bronder, *op. cit.*, p. 204.

Shlomo Aronson, in his doctoral dissertation 'Heydrich und die Anfänge der Gestapo und des SD,' Berlin, 1966, claims to have traced Heydrich's genealogy back to 1788 without having detected any Jewish ancestor. This is not in itself conclusive evidence, since it was in Reinhard Heydrich's power to alter relevant documents.

In Hugo Riemann's *Musik-Lexikon* (Leipzig: Max Hesse Verlag, 1916), p. 467, the following can be found concerning Reinhard Heydrich's father: 'Heydrich, Bruno (eigentlich Süß), geb. 23. Febr. 1865 in Leuben (Sachsen), Sohn eines Pianofortebauers . . .'

['Heydrich, Bruno (actually Süss), born on February 23, 1865, in Leuben (Saxony), the son of a pianoforte builder. . . .']

In this connection Kersten writes on August 20, 1942: ' "Es geht das Gerücht, daß Heydrich nicht rein arisch gewesen sei, das kann doch kaum stimmen", fragte ich.' (Kersten to Himmler) To this Himmler responded: ' "Doch, es stimmt." "Wußten Sie das schon früher oder haben Sie es jetzt erst bei seinem Tode erfahren? Weiß das auch Herr Hitler?" ... "Das wußte ich schon, als ich noch Chef der bayrischen politischen Polizei war. Ich habe damals dem Führer Vortrag gehalten, daraufhin ließ dieser sich Heydrich kommen, hat mit ihm lange gesprochen und einen sehr günstigen Eindruck von ihm bekommen.

Später erklärte mir der Führer, dieser Heydrich sei ein hochbegabter, aber auch sehr gefährlicher Mann, dessen Gaben man der Bewegung erhalten müsse. Solche Leute könnte man jedoch nur arbeiten lassen, wenn man sie fest in der Hand behielte und dazu eigne sich seine nichtarische Abstammung ausgezeichnet, er werde uns ewig dankbar sein, daß wir ihn behalten und nicht ausgestoßen hätten und werde blindlings gehorchen. Das war dann auch der Fall".'

On August 25, 1942, Kersten reports: 'Heydrich sei im Grunde ein armer Mensch gewesen, innerlich völlig gespalten, wie man das oft bei Mischlingen finde. Diese litten unter ständigen Minderwertigkeitskomplexen und versuchten, sie in irgendeiner Form abzureagieren. Dann käme es zu solchen Erscheinungen, wie man sie bei Heydrich in gesteigerter Form zu verzeichnen gehabt habe. "Sehen Sie, lieber Herr Kersten, Heydrich litt unendlich unter der Tatsache, daß er nicht reinrassig war. Durch erhöhte Leistungen, besonders auf dem Gebiet des Sports, der ja dem Juden an und für sich nicht liegt, wollte er den Beweis bringen, daß der germanische Anteil in seinem Blute überwiegend sein mußte. Er freute sich wie ein Kind, als er das Sportabzeichen in Silber und das Reiterabzeichen erworben hatte, wenn er Sieger im Fechtkampf war, gut schoß oder prachtvolle Trophäen von der Jagd nach Hause bringen konnte oder gar, als er das E.K.I bekam. Aber bei all dem verfolgte er einen Zweck, wahre innere Freude hat er nicht daran gehabt, auch wenn er sich das selbst vormachte. . . . Ich habe mich oft mit ihm unterhalten und versucht, ihm zu helfen, sogar gegen meine Überzeugung ihm gegenüber die Möglichkeit der Überwindung des jüdischen Blutanteils durch das bessere germanische Blut zugegeben und ihn selbst als ein Beispiel dafür bezeichnet. Wie freute er sich, als dieser Gedanke für Vierteljuden, jedoch nur aus rein staatspolitischen Gründen, um die Judenfrage endgültig einer Regelung zuzuführrern, in der Rassegesetzgebung zum Ausdruck kam. Im Augenblick war er mir für solche Hilfe zwar sehr dankbar und kam sich wie erlöst vor, aber genützt hat es auf die Dauer nichts." . . . Himmler sprach weiter: "Er hatte in sich den Juden rein intellektuell überwunden und war auf die andere Seite übergeschwenkt. Er war davon überzeugt, daß der jüdische Anteil an seinem Blut verdammenswert war, er haßte dieses Blut, das ihm so übel mitspielte. Der Führer konnte sich im Kampf gegen die Juden wirklich keinen besseren Mann aussuchen als gerade Heydrich. Dem Juden gegenüber kannte er kein Mitleid und keine Gnade".' Kersten, *op. cit.*, pp. 128-131.

See also Heiber, *op. cit.*, pp. 18-19.

———

['There's a rumor that Heydrich was not entirely Aryan. That can hardly be **true, can it? I** asked. (Kersten to Himmler) To this Himmler responded: "Yes, it's true enough." "Did you know that before, or have you only learned it since his death? Does Herr Hitler know it, too?" "I already knew it when I was still head of the Bavarian political police. I made a report to the Führer at the time; he summoned Heydrich, talked to him for a long time and received a very favorable impression. Later the Führer explained to me that this Heydrich was a highly gifted but also very dangerous man, whose gifts the movement had to retain. Such people could only be used as long as they were kept well in hand and for that purpose his non-Aryan origin was extremely useful; for he would be eternally grateful to us that we kept him and not expelled him and would obey blindly. That was in fact the case." '

On August 25, 1942, Kersten reports: 'Heydrich had basically been an unhappy man, completely divided within himself, as often happened with those of mixed race. Such people suffered from persistent inferiority complexes and tried to react in one way or another. Then such phenomena appeared as had become noticeable in Heydrich in increased form. "You know, my dear Kersten, Heydrich suffered immensely from the fact that he was not racially pure. He wanted to prove that the Germanic elements in his blood were dominant, by distinguishing himself, particularly in the field of sport, in which Jews do not play any part. He had a childish pleasure in winning the Silver Sport Badge and the Riding Badge, in being the victor in fencing bouts, in shooting well, or in bringing home fine hunting trophies, or, especially, in getting the Iron Cross First Class. But in all activities he was only pursuing a purpose; he found no real pleasure in it, even though he pretended to himself that he did so. ... Often I've talked to him and tried to help him, even against my own convictions, pointing out the possibilities of overcoming Jewish elements by the admixture of better Germanic blood, citing himself as a case in point. How pleased he was when this attitude to those who were a quarter Jewish found expression in the racial laws; though this sprang only from political reasons, in order finally to regulate the Jewish question. For the time being, it is true, he was grateful to me for such help and seemed as if liberated, but nothing was any use in the long run." ... Himmler went on: "He had overcome the Jew in himself by purely intellectual means and had swung over to the other side. He was convinced that the Jewish elements in his blood were damnable; he hated the blood which had played him so false. The Führer could really have picked no better man than Heydrich for the campaign against the Jews. For them he was without mercy or pity." ']

186. For Himmler's order of March 31, 1939, see BDC, T-611, R. 26, F. 158.
187. For Himmler's order concerning 'Nachfahren des Juden Lazarus Samuel' of April 19, 1939, see GRMA, T-175, R. 145, Fr. 2 672 047.
188. Hitler stated: 'Die Tschechen müssen heraus aus Mitteleuropa. Solange sie dort sind, werden sie immer ein Herd hussitisch-bolschewistischer Zersetzung sein.' Rauschning, *op. cit.*, p. 42.

['The Czechs must get out of Central Europe. As long as they remain, they will always be a source of Hussite-Bolshevik disintegration.']

189. 'Ansprache Himmlers an das Offizierskorps der Leibstandarte SS "Adolf Hitler" am 7. September 1940,' in IMT, Vol. XXIX, *op. cit.*, p. 109, PS-1918.
190. 'Rede Himmlers bei der SS-Gruppenführertagung in Posen am 4. Oktober 1943,' in IMT, *op. cit.*, p. 118, PS-1919.

191. *Ibid.*
192. Cf. Erich von dem Bach-Zelewski, 'Leben eines SS-Generals,' *Aufbau (Recon-struction)*, (New York, 1946), p. 40.
     Similar difficulties were experienced by SS-Hauptsturmführer Mauersberg, whom Himmler first refused to give permission for the short-lived marriage with the Czech film actress Lida Baarová, a favorite of Goebbels, who wanted to have her 'eingedeutscht.' Her marriage to the 'Leibstandarte' officer took place only after the intervention of leading Nazi personages, specifically Goebbels. This information was obtained by this writer during an interview with Mr. Mauersberg in September 1962, in the presence of SS-Obergruppenführer and General d. Waffen-SS a.D. Felix Steiner.
193. Cf. Kersten, *op. cit.*, p. 329.
194. Cf. *ibid.*, pp. 392-393.
195. *Ibid.*, pp. 233-234. Cp. *ibid.*, pp. 92-93, 99. See also Heiber, *op. cit.*, p. 213.
196. Cf. *ibid.*, pp. 152-154.
     In a note to the 'Rasse- und Siedlungshauptamt SS' (RuSHA) of April 19, 1939, Himmler wrote the following concerning 'Nachfahren des Juden Lazarus Samuel': 'SS-Unterscharführer Poppen muß wegen seiner jüdischen Abstammung und Staffel-Unterscharführer Hüls wegen der jüdischen Abstammung seiner Frau aus der SS entlassen werden.' Heiber, *op. cit.*, p. 64.
     In a letter of September 13, 1939 to SS-Gruppenführer Walter Schmitt, chief of the 'SS-Personalhauptamt' (SSPHA) Himmler wrote: 'SS-Obersturmführer Mayr/Miesbach ist mit Frau Sigrid, geb. Magnussen verheiratet. Sigrid Magnussen ist nach ihrer Abstammung zu einem Viertel jüdischen Blutes. SS-Obersturmführer Mayr hat sich verpflichtet, keine weiteren Kinder mit seiner Frau zu erzeugen und weiß, daß die 3 vorhandenen Kinder niemals die Genehmigung zur Verheiratung mit einem SS-Angehörigen bekommen werden.' Heiber, *op. cit.*, p. 66.
     On October 17, 1940, SS-Sturmbannführer Dr. Brandt (Himmler's personal secretary) wrote to the 'Hauptamt SS-Gericht' (HASS-Gericht): 'Der Reichsführer-SS ist nach eingehender Prüfung auf Grund der positiven Stellungnahme des Reichssicherheitshauptamtes der Ansicht, daß SS-Sturmbannführer Dr. Karl Feitenhansl wegen seiner Verfehlung (geschlechtlicher Verkehr mit einer Jüdin), die bereits in den Jahren 1926 und 1927 liegt, nicht aus der SS auszutreten braucht. Der Reichsführer-SS schlägt vor, F. vom Gau Sudetenland in einen anderen Gau zu versetzen und ihm dort die gleiche Stellung zu geben, die er bis jetzt innehat. Ihm soll nahegelegt werden, solange er noch im Sudetenland ist, die SS-Uniform nicht zu tragen.' Heiber, *op. cit.*, p. 82.
     On November 7, 1942, Himmler wrote to SS-Obergruppenführer of the SS-Panzerkorps, Paul Haußer, the following: '... Die Versetzung des SS-Obersturmbannführers Harmel sowie die 7 Tage Stubenarrest hebe ich damit auf. Trotzdem halte ich es für notwendig, den Sachverhalt nochmals vor Augen zu führen, denn die Tatsache, daß ein SS-Mann ein niederländisches Mädchen, das er niemals heiraten durfte, trotz der seit 11 Jahren bestehenden Heiratsgesetze der SS geheiratet hat und mit ihr Kinder unerwünschten Blutes in die Welt

setzt, ist nicht wegzudebattieren. ... Ich sehe diese Frage als so ernst an, daß ich lieber einen meiner Kommandeure, wenn er zwar nicht aus bösem Willen, aber aus Unachtsamkeit die Verletzung des Gesetzes ermöglicht hat, Unrecht tue und zu hart strafe, als daß ich eine solche Sache durchgehen lasse.

'... Wenn ich als erster Reichsführer-SS zulasse, daß unsere Grundgesetze gebrochen würden, dann würde ich gegen uns alle und gegen Deutschland handeln. Dies könnt Ihr alle von mir nicht erwarten, auch wenn mancher junge, von sich selbst überzogene Führer der Waffen-SS auch heute noch glaubt, ohne diese Dinge auskommen zu können, und ein anders uniformierter Offizier zu sein. ...

'Ich werde durch einen Befehl nunmehr einwandfrei klarstellen, daß die Truppe keine dienstliche Genehmigung zu erteilen hat. Genehmigt, freigegeben oder abgelehnt wird eine Heirat durch den Reichsführer-SS. Die Truppe hat zu befürworten oder nicht zu befürworten.'

---

[In a note to the 'Rasse- und Siedlungshauptamt SS' (RuSHA) of April 19, 1939, Himmler wrote the following concerning 'Nachfahren des Juden Lazarus Samuel': 'SS-Unterscharführer Poppen, because of his Jewish descent, and Staffel-Unterscharführer Hüls, because of the Jewish descent of his wife, must be dismissed from the SS.' Heiber, *op. cit.*, p. 64.

In a letter of September 13, 1939, to SS-Gruppenführer Walter Schmitt, chief of the 'SS-Personalhauptamt' (SSPHA) Himmler wrote: 'SS-Obersturmführer Mayr/Miesbach is married to a woman named Sigrid, née Magnussen. According to her descent, Sigrid Magnussen is one fourth Jewish.

'SS-Obersturmführer Mayr has obligated himself to conceive no more children with his wife and knows that the three existing children will never receive approval to marry a member of the SS.' Heiber, *op. cit.*, p. 66.

On October 17, 1940, SS-Sturmbannführer Dr. Brandt (Himmler's personal secretary) wrote to the 'Hauptamt SS-Gericht' (HASS-Gericht): 'After thorough examination, on the basis of the positive evaluation of the Reich Main Security Office, the Reich Leader SS is of the opinion that SS-Sturmbannführer Dr. Karl Feitenhansl need not resign from the SS because of his offence (sexual intercourse with a Jewess), which dates back as far as 1926 and 1927. The Reich Leader SS suggests transferring F. from the Sudetenland district to another district and giving him the same position there which he has occupied up to now. It should be made clear to him that as long as he remains in the Sudetenland, he is not to wear the SS uniform.' Heiber, *op. cit.*, p. 82.

On November 7, 1942, Himmler wrote to SS-Obergruppenführer of the SS-Panzerkorps, Paul Haußer, the following: '... Therewith I suspend the transfer of SS-Obersturmbannführer Harmel as well as the seven days of confinement to quarters. Nevertheless I consider it necessary to review the circumstances once more, for one cannot explain away the fact that despite the marriage laws of the SS, which have existed for eleven years, an SS man has married a Dutch girl, whom he should never have been allowed to marry, and is producing undesirable blood with her children. ... I consider this question to be so serious that, rather than let such a matter pass, I would do an injustice to one of my commanders and punish him too severely if he has made possible a violation of the law by his inattentiveness, even though not as a result of ill will.

'. . . If, as first SS Reich Leader, I allowed our basic laws to be broken, I would be acting against all of us and against Germany. None of you can expect this of me, even if many a young, self-centered leader of the Waffen-SS still believes, even today, that he can get by without these things and that he is an officer wearing a different uniform. . . .
'I will issue an order to make it perfectly clear from now on that the troop has no right to issue official approvals. A marriage is approved, allowed, or rejected by the Reich Leader SS. The only role of the troop is to recommend or not to recommend approval.']

This letter was not dispatched; instead Himmler noted down 'mündlich besprochen 7.XI.42 München.' Heiber, *op. cit.*, pp. 152-153, 154. See Appendix V.
197. Cf. Kersten, *op. cit.*, p. 99.
198. Cf. Heiber, *op. cit.*, pp. 52, 66.
On August 22, 1943, Himmler wrote the following note to SS-Gruppenführer Walter Krüger, 'Kdr. SS-Panzergrenadier-Division "Das Reich" ': 'Lieber Krüger! SS-Obergruppenführer Berger hat mir beiliegende Akte übersandt, die ich Ihnen zuleite. Nach bestem Wissen und Gewissen konnte ich aber zu keiner anderen als der beiliegenden Stellungnahme kommen.
'Ich rate Ihnen, lieber Krüger, daß Sie nun von sich aus mit der Begründung "Sie wollten wegen der Jugend Ihrer Tochter noch keine Verheiratung und gäben von sich aus Ihre väterliche Genehmigung dazu nicht", dem SS-Sturmbannführer Klingenberg Ihre Einwilligung zur Verheiratung mit Ihrer Tochter ablehnen. Auf diese Weise ginge die Ablehnung von Ihnen und Ihrer Familie aus und würde in keiner Weise von Seiten der SS ausgesprochen.
'Daß Ihre Stellung in der SS durch meine Stellungnahme sowie durch das ganze Unglück, das in der Ahnentafel Ihrer Frau beruht, in keiner Weise berührt wird, wissen Sie, und ich versichere es Ihnen als Reichsführer-SS mit diesen Zeilen erneut. Ich verweise Sie hier noch einmal mit allem Ernst auf den von mir im Jahre 1937 eingeführten Eid der Gruppenführer, den ich aus der Erwägung, daß derartige schwere Fälle an den Einzelnen sowohl wie an den Gesamtorden herantreten können, einführte. . . .
'Anlage: 22.8.43; Stellungnahme RF
Meine Stellungnahme zu dem Heiratsgesuch des SS-Sturmbannführers Klingenberg mit Fräulein Elisabeth Krüger, Tochter des SS-Gruppenführers Krüger und seiner Ehefrau Elli geb. Reichard.
1.) Die vorgelegte Ahnentafel von Fräulein Elisabeth Krüger weist in der mütterlichen Linie im Jahre 1711 einen volljüdischen Ahnen auf.
2.) Nach den Gesetzen der SS ist damit eine Verheiratung des SS-Sturmbannführers Klingenberg mit Fräulein Elisabeth Krüger unmöglich.
3.) **Auf Grund** einzelner Anhaltspunkte ist die Möglichkeit, daß die mütter-

liche Ahnenlinie durch eine außerhalb der geschlossenen und urkundlich nach-
gewiesenen Ehen erfolgte Zeugung nicht der durch die Urkunden dargelegten
Abstammung entspricht, nicht ausgeschlossen, jedoch durch den erfolgten Tod
aller in Frage kommenden Personen nicht beweisbar.'
['Dear Krüger, SS-Obergruppenführer Berger has sent me the attached document, which I am sending on to you. In all good conscience, however, I have
been unable to take a position different from that in the attached document.
'I advise you, my dear Krüger, to refuse to give your consent to the marriage
of SS-Sturmbannführer Klingenberg with your daughter, and that you justify
it on the grounds that "because of her youth you did not want your daughter
to be married yet, and, therefore, as far as you are concerned, you did not
give your paternal consent." This way the refusal would come from you and
your family, and not in any way from the SS.
'You know – and as Reich Leader SS I assure you of this once more with these
lines – that your position in the SS is not jeopardized in any way by my attitude
or by the whole unfortunate business, the origin of which lies in the family
tree of your wife. In all earnestness I refer you once more to the Gruppenführer oath, which I introduced in the year 1937 with the thought that such
difficult cases could occur to an individual as well as to the entire order
(the SS) . . .
'Enclosure: August 22, 1943; position of Reich Leader. My position on the
petition of SS-Sturmbannführer Klingenberg for marriage to Miss Elisabeth
Krüger, daughter of SS-Gruppenführer Krüger and his wife Elli, née Reichard.
1.) The family tree of Miss Elisabeth Krüger which has been submitted shows
a maternal ancestor of full Jewish blood, in the year 1711.
2.) Therefore, in accordance with the laws of the SS, a marriage between SS-
Sturmbannfürer Klingenberg and Miss Elisabeth Krüger is impossible.
3.) Individual indications make it impossible to exclude the chance that
the maternal line of descent does not correspond to that indicated by the
documents, due to the birth of a child outside the marriage that took place and
are proven by the documentation; the deaths of all concerned, however, make it
impossible to prove this chance.']

Heiber, *op. cit.*, pp. 230-231. See also Himmler's letter concerning Mrs. Krüger
and her offspring, *ibid.*, pp. 231-232.
199. Cf. Heiber, *op. cit.*, pp. 245-247.
200. *Ibid.*, p. 52.
201. Cf. *ibid.*, pp. 75-76.
On April 3, 1940, Himmler wrote to Gefreiter Walter Küchlin: '. . . In den
Fragen des Blutes habe ich für die Schutzstaffel festgesetzt, daß das Ende des
30-jährigen Krieges der Stichtag ist, bis zu dem jeder verpflichtet ist, nachzu-
forschen und von dem ab ich rechne. Ist nach diesem Stichtag ein jüdischer
Ahne in der Ahnenreihe, so muß der Mann aus der SS ausscheiden. Milder
rechne ich, wenn bei der Frau in der Ahnenreihe weit zurückliegend ein jüdischer Vorfahre ist.' Heiber, *op. cit.*, p. 75.

['... In questions of descent, I have decreed for the Schutzstaffel that the end of the Thirty-Year-War is the key date back to which everybody is obligated to research his ancestry, and from which I calculate. If there is a Jewish ancestor in the family tree after this date, the man must leave the SS. I take a more lenient position if, in the case of the wife, there is a Jewish ancestor far in the past.']

202. Cf. *ibid.*, pp. 245-246.
203. Cf. *ibid.*, p. 246. See also *ibid.*, p. 247.
204. Cf. Kersten, *op. cit.*, pp. 156-157, 215, 217, 258, 344, 383, 395-399, 406-407. See also Heiber, *op. cit.*, pp. 15-17.
205. The result of this writer's research in the years 1962-1968 and of interviews conducted with Reinhard and Heinz Heydrich's close relatives revealed that the two brothers and their father Bruno had been targets of anti-Semitic discrimination and aggression while residing in Halle.

In an unpublished letter of January 3, 1967, to the editor of *Der Spiegel* Heinz Höhne, Mrs. Ellie Bommersheim of Munich, formerly of Halle, wrote the following: '... Gerade weil Ihre SS-Serie den Personen und Handlungen jener Zeit so genau auf den Grund geht, ist mir unverständlich, wie Sie trotz Helmut Maurer, Robert Kempner und Reitlinger dem SD-Chef Reinhard Heydrich "keinen Tropfen jüdischen Blutes" bescheinigen. Sie "glauben", doch derjenige Teil der Bevölkerung Halles, der ihn (und das waren die meisten, da er äußerst markant war!!) hegten nicht den geringsten Zweifel über seine jüdische Abstammung. Sie (die Hallenser) wissen, daß die Himmler-Beauftragten nicht nur die standesamtlichen, sondern auch die kirchlichen Urkunden vernichteten. ... Aus Halle schreibt man soeben aus Musikerkreisen: "... Selbstverständlich sind uns alten Hallischen Musikern die Dinge um Heydr. und Familie bekannt. Wir wissen, können aber aus bekannten Gründen nichts belegen. Auch Rabbiner bestätigen uns die Abkunft und den Namen Isidor *Süss* ..." ... Ich finde es durchaus verständlich, daß diese benachteiligten Menschen sich taufen und ihren Namen ändern ließen. Br. H. tat dies schon in jungen Jahren, um als Hofopernsänger in Meiningen und Weimar zu bestehen.'

['... It is precisely because your SS series goes to the root of the characters and actions of that time that I find it incomprehensible that – despite Helmut Maurer, Robert Kempner, and Reitlinger – you do not acknowledge that SD Chief Reinhard Heydrich had "a drop of Jewish blood." You "believe" this, yet that segment of the population of Halle which knew Dir. Heydrich (and that included most of the inhabitants, as he was extremely prominent!!), had not the slightest doubt about his Jewish origin. The townspeople know that Himmler's emissaries destroyed not only the civil records, but also those of the church. ... The following has just come from musical circles in Halle: "Of course, the truth about Heydrich and his family is known to us old musicians of Halle. We know it, but, for well-known reasons, cannot prove it. Rabbis, too, corroborate for us the origin and the name Isidor *Süss* ..." ... I find it completely understandable that these disadvantaged people had themselves baptized and their name changed. Bruno Heydrich did this when he was still young, in order to succeed as a court opera singer in Meiningen and Weimar.']

As children the two brothers were frequently engaged in altercations in which the younger Heinz frequently had to defend his weaker brother Reinhard. Such factors may have been of decisive psychological significance. Exposure to anti-Semitic discrimination can have a strong influence upon the victim's attitude towards the Jews, particularly when there is no feeling of identity with this minority. This undoubtedly occurred in the case of Reinhard Heydrich who developed a massive negative transference towards the Jews.

When questioned by this writer as to Reinhard Heydrich's partially Jewish origin, the Heydrichs did not exclude this possibility.

See also Gilbert's dialogue with H. Frank in which Gilbert refers to Frank's Jewish background and a possible psychological reaction resulting from it. Gilbert, *op. cit.*, p. 128. Rauschning concedes that the roots of Hitler's anti-Semitism lay in the 'fact' that Hitler was, according to the Nuremberg racial laws, a 'Mischling.' Rauschning, *op. cit.*, p. 221.

Cp. also footnote 185.

206. See Appendix IVd. Cf. also Kersten, *op. cit.*, pp. 247-265. Cp. Appendix IVe (1937).

207. Cf. Rauschning, *op. cit.*, p. 80.

The former SS-Obergruppenführer and General of the 'Waffen-SS,' Felix Steiner, describes those SS leaders and men concerned with 'Spezialkommandos' (special tasks: concentration camp duties, police actions, etc.) as: '... Condottieri-Figuren, die in ihrem Character Unterwürfigkeit mit Brutalität und Feigheit verbanden und in keiner Diktatur fehlen können. ... Peinlich genau suchte er sich dafür die Helfershelfer aus und wies sie persönlich und ohne Zeugen in ihre verbrecherischen Aufgaben ein. Er fand sie in Ehrgeizlingen, Primitiven und Brutalen. Der Rest sind meist unglückselige Befehlsausführer.' Steiner, *op. cit.*, p. 233.

------

['... condottieri types, whose character combined servility with brutality and cowardice, and who are never missing in any dictatorship ... He (Himmler) painstakingly selected his accomplices and personally introduced them, without witnesses, to their criminal duties. He found them among the ambitious, the primitive, and the brutal. The rest were mostly unfortunates who obediently carried out orders.']

Steiner also considered the former inspector of concentration camps, SS-Obergruppenführer Theodor Eicke, as belonging to this group. Eicke died in 1943 as commanding general of the 'SS-Totenkopf-Division' at the Eastern Front. Cf. *ibid.*, pp. 34, 114-115.

Höss observes in the unpublished part of his autobiography: 'Unfähige' (concentration camp personnel) 'kamen dann zum Umziehen nach Auschwitz, das

allmählich der Personal-Schutt-Ablageplatz der K.L. war.'
['Incompetents (among concentration camp personnel) came for re-education to Auschwitz which gradually became the personnel refuse dump of the concentration camps.']
*The Höss-File,* p. 5, Institut für Zeitgeschichte, Munich. See also John M. Steiner and Jochen Fahrenberg, 'Die Ausprägung autoritärer Einstellung bei ehemaligen Angehörigen der SS und der Wehrmacht,' *Kölner Zeitschrift für Soziologie und Sozial-Psychologie,* Vol. XXII, No. 3 (1970), pp. 551-566.

208. Cf. Steiner, *op. cit., passim.*
209. Cf. *ibid.*
The attempts of the SS-Brigadeführer Otto Ohlendorf and Walter Schellenberg, the SS-Obergruppenführer and Generals of the 'Waffen-SS' Felix Steiner and Karl Wolff, and to some extent the SS-Standartenführer Rudolf Brandt, and others, may be considered as efforts to bring about changes in prevailing destruction policies. See especially Kersten, *op. cit.,* pp. 247-265, 339-381.
According to an affidavit by Dr. jur. Konrad Morgen, SS judge and 'Untersuchungsführer des Reichskriminalhauptamtes' (RKPA), of July 13, 1946, legal proceedings were to be initiated against persons who were chiefly responsible for mass killings in concentration and destruction camps. Morgen states:
'... Gegen die Ausführenden von Blutbefehlen waren von mir bereits Verfahren eingeleitet unter anderem an markanten Persönlichkeiten:
SS-Obersturmbannführer Eichmann, dem Leiter der Aktion Endlösung der Judenfrage im RSHA,
SS-Sturmbannführer Höss, Kommandant Auschwitz,
SS-Oberführer Loritz, Kommandant Dachau und Oranienburg,
SS-Untersturmführer Grabner, Leiter der politischen Abteilung Auschwitz. Gegen ihn hatte ich bereits Anklage wegen Mordes in mindestens 2 000 Fällen erhoben. Gegen SS-Obergruppenführer Pohl und Frank liefen bereits Voruntersuchungen. Beide waren schon erheblich bloßgestellt. Bei den Untersuchungen hat jegliche Unterstützung geleistet insbesondere an örtlichen Instanzen: Höhere SS und Polizeiführer Kassel, Erbprinz zu Waldeck und der Chef des SS und Polizeigerichtes Kassel, SS-Sturmbannführer Dr. Paulmann, Höhere SS und Polizeiführer Niederlande, SS-Gruppenführer Rauter und der Chef des SS und Polizeigerichtes Den Haag, SS-Obersturmbannführer Härtel.
An zentralen Dienststellen: SS Richter beim RFSS, SS-Oberführer Bender ...
'5. Die Hauptschuldigen an den KZ Greueln ... In erster Linie SS-Obergruppenführer Pohl ... SS-Gruppenführer Müller, der Chef der Gestapo ... Werkzeuge dieser beiden Männer ... SS-Obersturmbannführer Schmidt-Klevenow, Chef der Rechtsabteilung bei Pohl, Standartenführer Voigt, Chef des Prüfungsamtes des Verwaltungs- und Wirtschaftshauptamtes ... Reichsarzt SS, SS-Gruppenführer Dr. Grawitz.
An der Spitze des Unternehmens stand der SS-Obersturmbannführer Eichmann vom RSHA mit seinem Stab. Eichmann gab als Inhalt seiner Aufgabe Umsiedlung von Juden in die Ostgebiete bzw. ihre Überführung in den deutschen Arbeits- und Rüstungseinsatz. Dieselbe Terminologie galt auch intern. Eichmann

verhandelte zu Beginn seiner Tätigkeit mit den örtlichen politischen und Verwaltungsstellen über die Zahl der zu evakuierenden Juden, Gestellungstermine und Fragen über das Judenvermögen ... Der Widerstand ausländischer Stellen wurde meist schnell überwunden durch Überlassung des unbeweglichen Judenvermögens an das fremde, besetzte Land. Waren Kontingente und Termine ausgehandelt und Eichmann in diesem Rahmen freie Hand und Unterstützung durch die fremden Polizeiorgane zugesichert worden, so wandte sich dieser an die jüdischen Zentralorgane, Kultusgemeinden und Ältestenräte mit der Auflage, eine bestimmte Zahl von Juden für die Umsiedlung schriftlich namhaft zu machen. Dabei wurden diesen jüdischen Zentralorganen Befreiung von der Aussiedlung zugesichert und im Nichtbefolgungsfalle Zwangsmaßnahmen angedroht. Die namhaft gemachten Juden wurden dann von der örtlichen Polizei schlagartig verhaftet oder aber da, wo man sich absolut sicher fühlte, von der Judengemeinde selbst an die Bahn gebracht. Vorher fanden einflußreiche Juden noch immer den Weg zu Eichmann, um ihre Befreiung unter Hinweis auf Deutschfreundlichkeit und Unentbehrlichkeit für die Kriegswirtschaft zu erwirken. Die Bahn mußte die Judentransporte unter Fahrtnummern wie Kriegstransporte befördern, so daß Abgangs- und Durchgangsbahnhöfe nicht das Bestimmungsziel wissen konnten. Die Leitung der Züge lag bei den Wehrmachttransportkommandanturen.

Das Begleitpersonal bis zur Reichsgrenze stellte die fremde Polizei, innerhalb des Reichsgebietes dann deutsche Polizei oder Transportbegleitkommandos der Waffen SS, welche generell für Begleitung von Kriegstransporten aller Art abgestellt waren. Nur bei der Verlegung von einem Lager zum anderen fuhren Angehörige der Wachverbände des betreffenden KZ mit. Auf diese Weise kamen die Transporte im Vernichtungslager an, ohne daß bis zu diesem Augenblick einer der bisher Mitwirkenden den geheimen Zweck dieses Transportes hätte ahnen können.

Am Zielbahnhof angekommen, fand die Ausladung in einem abgesperrten Gebäude statt, das vorher vom Bahn- und Begleitpersonal verlassen werden musste ... Die Entladung erfolgte durch ein Kommando jüdischer Häftlinge. Hierauf erfolgte eine Aussonderung der Arbeitsfähigen durch SS Ärzte und die Arbeitsunfähigen wurden auf LKWs verladen und rollten alsbald mit sehr geringer Bedeckung weiter. In Auschwitz lag das Vernichtungslager Kilometer entfernt vom eigentlichen Konzentrationslager. Die Innensicherung dieses Vernichtungslagers lag ebenfalls in den Händen einer mit Knüppeln bewaffneten jüdischen Ordnertruppe. Die Außensicherung vor dem Draht erfolgte durch ukrainische-baltische SS Freiwillige. In dem Vernichtungslager waren die Krematorien äußerlich nicht als solche erkennbar. Man konnte sie durchaus für Großbadeeinrichtungen halten. Das wurde den Ankömmlingen auch gesagt. Sie kamen dann sofort in einen großen Auskleideraum in dem wiederum jüdische Häftlinge die Aufsicht führten. Für ihre Garderobe bekamen sie eine Marke. Dann gingen sie in den Duschraum, der geschlossen wurde. In diesem Augenblick trat ein SS Mann im Gasanzug über einen äußeren Luftschacht und goß eine Büchse mit Blausäure in den Raum. In dem vorgewärmten Raum ent wickelte sich das Gas sehr schnell und tötete in Minuten alle. Nach Entlüftung traten wiederum jüdische Arbeitskommandos in Tätigkeit. Sie forschten die äußeren Körperhöhlen nach versteckten Wertsachen ab und brachen etwaige Goldplomben aus dem Gebiß der Leichen.

Sodann wurden diese in einen Nebenraum mittels Aufzugs in den Oberstock vor die Krematorien gebracht und durch polnische Häftlinge verbrannt. Die Mitwirkung von SS Angehörigen beschränkte sich demnach auf Kommandant, Arzt, Kraftfahrer, Vergaser und Wachtruppe. Nur Kommandant, Arzt und Vergaser waren dabei durchwegs deutsch.

Zur weiteren Tarnung war es in Auschwitz zudem Brauch, von der Vernichtung jene Juden auszunehmen, welche über Ruf und Beziehungen im Ausland verfügten wie Rabbiner, Gelehrte, Literaten, Wirtschaftler. Diese waren gesondert untergebracht und besonders gut behandelt mit der einzigen Verpflichtung, überallhin nach dem Ausland zu schreiben, wie gut sie es in Auschwitz hätten . . .

'Aus persönlichem Vortrag habe ich später ersehen, daß von den geschilderten Vorgängen selbst Hauptamtschefs der SS keine Ahnung hatten. Wie der Chef des Hauptamtes SS Gericht, SS Obergruppenführer Breithaupt und mein letzter Gerichtsherr nach meiner Versetzung, der Chef des Rasse- und Siedlungshauptamtes, SS Obergruppenführer Hildebrandt. Erst recht konnte wegen der unheimlichen Technik andere SS Angehörige geringeren Dienstgrades, die örtlichen Stapostellen und erst gar nicht die Truppe und die Bevölkerung erfahren.'

['. . . I had already initiated legal proceedings against those who had carried out death orders; among others against the following persons:

'SS-Obersturmbannführer Eichmann, the leader of the Action Final Solution of the Jewish question within the RSHA (Reich Security Main Office);
SS-Sturmbannführer Höss, commandant of Auschwitz.
SS-Oberführer Loritz, commandant of Dachau and Oranienburg;
SS-Untersturmführer Grabner, leader of the political section of Auschwitz. I had already charged him with murder in at least two thousand cases. Preliminary investigations were already being made of SS-Obergruppenführer Pohl and Frank. Both were already considerably compromised. Among the local authorities which were particularly noteworthy in offering all possible support to the investigations were:
'The Higher SS and Police Leader of Kassel, Erbprinz zu Waldeck, and the Chief of the SS and Police Court of Kassel, SS-Sturmbannführer Dr. Paulmann; the Higher SS and Police Leader of the Netherlands, SS-Gruppenführer Rauter, and the Chief of the SS and Police Court of The Hague, SS-Obersturmbannführer Härtel.
'In central offices: The SS judge in the RFSS (Office of the SS Reich Leader), SS-Oberführer Bender . . .
'5. The principal guilty parties in the horrors of the concentration camps . . . In

the first place SS-Obergruppenführer Pohl ... Chief of the Gestapo, SS-Gruppenführer Müller ... Tools of these two men ... the Chief of the Legal Department in Pohl's organization, SS-Obersturmbannführer Schmidt-Klevenow; the Chief of the Controller's Office of the SS Main Economic and Administration Office, Sandartenführer Voigt;* ... the SS Reich Physician, SS-Gruppenführer Dr. Grawitz.

'The head of the operation was SS-Obersturmbannführer Eichmann of the RSHA, and his staff. Eichmann stated that his task was to resettle the Jews in the East or to transfer them to the German labor and armament installations there. The same terminology was also used internally. At the beginning of his activity, Eichmann negotiated with the local political and administrative offices as to the number of Jews to be evacuated, reporting dates, and questions concerning Jewish possessions ... Resistance from foreign quarters was for the most part quickly overcome by turning over Jewish real estate to the occupied foreign country. When the quota and the reporting dates were settled and Eichmann was assured of a free hand and support in this respect from the organs of the foreign police, he turned to the central Jewish agencies, religious communities, and councils of elders and gave them the assignment of indicating in writing the names of a specified number of Jews for resettlement. In this process the Jewish central agencies were assured that they would be exempted from resettlement, and that failure to comply would result in the use of force. The thus selected Jews were then quickly arrested by the local police or, in cases in which it was considered absolutely safe, were taken to the railroad cars by delegated members of the Jewish community itself. Before that time influential Jews always found their way to Eichmann in order to obtain their freedom by referring to their pro-German sentiments and their indispensability to the war economy. The railroad officials had to number and handle the box cars carrying Jews as if they were carrying war material, so that people at the departure or intermediate stations could not tell the destination. Control over the trains was in the hands of the transport commands of the Wehrmacht.

'The foreign police constituted the accompanying personnel up to the border of the Reich. Within the Reich territory German police or transport escort squads of the Waffen-SS were generally assigned to escorting military shipments of every sort. It was only in cases of transfer from one camp to another that members of the guard squad of the concentration camp in question rode along. In this way the transports arrived at the destruction camps without any of the personnel so far working on the shipment being able to guess the secret purpose of the transport.

'When the transport reached its destination, the unloading took place in a closed-off building which had to be vacated by all railroad and escort personnel prior to the unloading. ... A squad of Jewish prisoners carried out the unloading. Subsequently, SS physicians singled out those able to work, and those unable to work were loaded onto trucks and were moved on at once with a very small

* Correct: Vogt.

escort. At Auschwitz the destruction camp was kilometers away from the concentration camp proper. The internal security of this destruction camp was also in the hands of a Jewish order squad armed with clubs. Ukrainian-Baltic SS volunteers were responsible for external security around the fence. The crematoria of the destruction camp were not recognizable as such from the outside. One could easily take them to be large-scale washrooms, and this was also what the arrivals were told. They were then immediately taken to a large undressing room, again supervised by Jewish inmates. Upon checking their clothes they received a chit. Then they went into the shower room, which was locked. At that moment an SS man in a gas-proof suit stepped up to an external air-shaft and emptied a can of prussic acid into the room. The gas spread very quickly throughout the pre-warmed room and killed all present within minutes. After the room was aired out, Jewish work squads again went into action. They searched the external body cavities for concealed valuables and removed any gold fillings from the mouths of the corpses.

'The bodies then were transported by means of elevators to an adjoining room on the upper story, in front of the crematoria, where Polish inmates burned them. Thus the collaboration of SS members was limited to the commandant, doctor, truck drivers, gassers, and guard squad. Only the commandant, doctor, and gasser were invariably German.

'For further camouflage, it was the custom at Auschwitz to exempt from death those Jews who had a reputation and relationships abroad, such as rabbis, scholars, authors, and economists. They received separate lodgings and were treated especially well, the only obligation being to write to all those abroad about how good life was in Auschwitz . . .

'From personal experience I later realized that even heads of Main SS Offices had no idea of the events that I have described. Examples are the Chief of the Main Office SS-Tribunal, SS-Obergruppenführer Breithaupt, and the Chief of the Race and Settlement Main Office SS, and, after my transfer, my superior to whom I was answerable (Gerichtsherr), SS-Obergruppenführer Hildebrandt. The sinister procedures prevented even more the other SS members in the lower ranks, the local State Police offices, and certainly the troops and the people, from learning what was going on.']

'Eidesstattliche Erklärung des Dr. Konrad Morgen vom 13. Juli 1946,' in IMT, Vol. XLII, *op. cit.*, pp. 556-557, 559-561, 562, Affidavit SS-65. Cp. *ibid.*, Affidavit SS-67.

210. 'Rede Himmlers bei der SS-Gruppenführertagung in Posen am 4. Oktober 1943,' in IMT, *op. cit.*, pp. 152, 122-123, PS-1919.
211. *Ibid.*, p. 153.
212. IMT, *op. cit.*, p. 230, PS-1992 (A).
213. Der Reichsführer SS, *Dich ruft die SS* (Berlin, 1942), p. 18.
214. In his speech to the Gruppenführer in Posen on October 4, 1943, Himmler said: 'Gehorsam wird im soldatischen Leben morgens, mittags und abends gefordert und geleistet. Der kleine Mann gehorcht auch immer oder meistens.

Gehorcht er nicht, so wird er eingesperrt. ... Wer den Befehl ausführt, hat dies zu tun als getreuer Walter, als getreuer Vertreter der befehlsgebenden Gewalt. ... Wenn also einer glaubt, er könne die Befolgung eines Befehles nicht verantworten, dann hat er das ehrlich zu melden: ich kann es nicht verantworten, ich bitte, mich davon zu entbinden. Dann wird wohl in den meisten Fällen der Befehl kommen: Sie haben das doch durchzuführen. Oder man denkt: der ist mit den Nerven fertig, der ist schwach. Dann kann man sagen: Gut, gehen Sie in Pension. Befehle müssen aber heilig sein. Wenn die Generäle gehorchen, dann gehorchen die Armeen von selbst.' IMT, *op. cit.*, pp. 150-151, PS-1919.

['In the military life, obedience is demanded and given morning, noon, and night. The little man obeys, too, that is, usually. If he does not obey, he will be locked up ... He who executes an order must do it as a faithful manager, a faithful representative of the commanding power ... So if somebody thinks that he cannot accept the responsibility for complying with an order, he should report this honestly: I cannot accept this responsibility; please excuse me from executing this order. In most cases, no doubt, the order will then be: You have to execute it nevertheless. Or one may think: This fellow's nerves are shot; he is weak. Then one can say: Very well, go and retire, but orders must be sacred. If the generals obey, then the armies will obey by themselves.']

Similar thoughts were expressed by Rudolf Höss in his conversation with Gilbert: 'Wir waren alle auf bedingungslosen Gehorsam gedrillt, ganz gleich, welcher Art die Befehle waren. ... Wenn nun Hitler den Befehl gab, das Judenproblem auf diese Weise endgültig zu lösen, blieb nichts weiter übrig, als zu gehorchen. Jeder andere SS-Mann hätte das gleiche getan.' Gilbert, *op. cit.*, p. 327. Cp. *ibid.*, pp. 278, 318-319, 356-358.

['We were all drilled into unconditional obedience, no matter what kind of orders were given ... Now, when Hitler gave the order to solve the Jewish problem permanently in this fashion, there was no alternative but to obey. Any other SS man would have done the same.']

215. Cf. Der Reichsführer-SS, *Statistisches Jahrbuch der Schutzstaffel der NSDAP 1937, op. cit.*, pp. 55-56. Of a total number of 11,253 men discharged, 2,489 were excluded and 286 expelled. Both groups were dismissed for dishonorable reasons (dishonorable discharge); 7,960 were released, that is 22 % excluded, 3 % expelled, 70 % released; 5 % (518) sick had died. See Appendices VI a-b. Out of the 7,960 men released (100 %), 6,721 (84,4 %) left on their own request, 794 (10.0 %) left because they were unfit for service, 211 (2.6 %) left because they were unsuited because of ill health, 198 (2.5 %) left because their personality was unsuitable (charakterlich ungeeignet), and 36 (0.5 %) were unsuitable for ideological reasons. *Ibid.*, p. 56.

216. For having committed this offence, 307 SS members were excluded and one was expelled during 1938. See Appendix V.

217. See GRMA, T-175, R. 130, Fr. 2 656 672.

218. For the proclamation of Hitler's order issued by the Hauptamt SS Gericht, April 23, 1940, see *ibid.*, R. 199, Fr. 2 739 976.
219. Cf. Der Reichsführer-SS, *Statistisches Jahrbuch der Schutzstaffel der NSDAP 1937, op. cit.*, p. 91.
220. *Ibid.*, 1938, p. 123. The highest number of suicides was committed by SS-men between the ages of 26-30 (25) and between 31-35 (22). The most frequent motives were: unknown (22), depression and mental illness (11), embezzlement and fraud (10), marital discord (9), unhappy love (8), occupational reasons (8), not specified dishonorable offenses (8); total number of suicides in 1938: 94. From this total 79 (84%) were members of the 'Allgemeine SS,' 4 (4.3%) members of the 'Verfügungstruppe' (VT), and 11 (11.7%) members of the 'Totenkopfverbände.' *Ibid.*, p. 123.
     In 1937, a total number of 85 had committed suicide. Some of the motives given were: 14 unknown, 14 depression and mental illness, 9 unhappy love; the age-groups most frequently represented were: 26-30 (23) (among these there was one man who committed suicide because of his non-Aryan origin); 21-25 (18); 31-35 (17); 41-50 (7); up to 20 (7). The breakdown of their religious affiliations appeared as follows: Evangelic 50 (59%), Gottgläubig 22 (36%), and Catholic 13 (15%). Cf. *ibid.*, 1937, p. 91.
221. For Himmler's order of April 1, 1939, see GRMA, T-175, R. 190, Fr. 2 727 854.
222. *Ibid.*
223. Rede des Reichsführers-SS anläßlich der Gruppenführerbesprechung in Tölz, February 18, 1937, *ibid.*, R. 89, Fr. 2 611 881.
224. Ahnen- und Enkelrede des Reichsführers-SS auf der Tagung der Auslandsorganisation in Stuttgart, September 2, 1938, *ibid.*, R. 90, Fr. 2 612 587.
225. For Aktenvermerk, August 19, 1941, see BDC, T-611, R. 11, F. 447. In 1937 the same act (§ 175) was punished merely by exclusion (23) or expulsion (29). See *Statistisches Jahrbuch der Schutzstaffel der NSDAP 1938, op. cit.*, loosely attached enclosure 267 38 II E, marked 'Geheim.' See Appendix V.
226. For Erlaß des Führers zur Reinerhaltung von SS und Polizei, November 15, 1941, see GRMA, T-175, R. 161, Fr. 2 693 487.
227. In the unpublished part of his autobiographical notes the Commandant of Auschwitz, SS-Obersturmbannführer Rudolf Höss, relates that Obersturmbannführer Arthur Liebhenschel was removed from Auschwitz as commandant because it became known that his second wife had come into conflict with the SD due to her association with Jews after the enforcement of the Nuremberg laws: 'Diese Tatsache wurde in Auschwitz bekannt und Liebhenschel war da nicht mehr tragbar.' Unpublished manuscript, Institut für Zeitgeschichte, Munich, *Höss-folder*, p. 2.

___

['This fact became known in Auschwitz, and Liebhenschel was no longer acceptable there.']

228. A somewhat modified example was the sentence of a former SS judge and colonel of the 'Waffen-SS' (there was a total of about 70 judges in the SS), inter-

viewed by this writer (name withheld) who sentenced a non-commissioned SS officer (Unteroffizier) to death because he had shot a Jewish woman after he had raped her. In the trial against the former SS and Gestapo officer Walter Thormeyer, accused of murder near Mielec in 1942-1943, a witness, Wilhelm Glamann, also a Gestapo official, testified before the court on December 15, 1966, in Freiburg i. Brsg., that the accused shot his eighteen-year-old Jewish mistress and her young brother in the nearby woods. However, this act was apparently not revealed to his superior authorities.

According to Hannah Arendt, Eichmann, too, seems to have had a Jewish mistress in Vienna. Cf. Arendt, *Eichmann in Jerusalem, op. cit.*, p. 27.

Höss writes: 'Im Verlauf des Krieges, als selbst Himmler die Todesurteile zu viel wurden – er mußte ja jedes bestätigen – errichtete man die SS-Bewährungs-abteilungen an der Front, – "Himmelfahrtskommandos" genannt – die zum Minensuchen oder fast aussichtlosen Widerstandsunternehmen eingesetzt wurden. Nur wenige haben diese Bewährungseinsätze lebend oder unverwundet überstanden, danach waren sie allerdings rehabilitiert. Homosexuelle Vergehen, Fahnenflucht, Feigheit vor dem Feind oder Dienstverweigerung wurden grundsätzlich mit dem Tode bestraft, ebenso Rassenschande und später das sich aneignen von ehemaligem Judeneigentum. Streng geahndet wurden auch Verfehlungen gegen die Dienstaufsicht . . . Die Straflager der SS – Matzkau und Dachau –, die den Zuchthäusern bzw. Gefängnissen entsprachen, und in die die verurteilten SS und Polizeiangehörigen eingeliefert wurden, zur Verbüßung der erkannten Freiheitsstrafen, waren gefürchtet . . . Da diese Straflager bald überfüllt waren, schickte man den größeren Teil der Insassen ebenfalls zur Frontbewährung in die Bewährungsabteilungen. –' *Höss-Folder, op. cit.*, p. 9.

[Höss writes: 'In the course of the war, when the death verdicts became too numerous even for Himmler – after all he had to confirm each one – the SS Probationary Units (Bewährungsabteilungen), called "Ascension Commandos" ("Himmelfahrtkommandos"), were established at the front. They were assigned to mine-sweeping or to resist the enemy where the situation was almost hopeless. Only a few men ever came out of these Probationary Units alive and unwounded, but those who did were, to be sure, subsequently rehabilitated. Homosexual offenses, desertion, cowardice in the face of the enemy, or refusal to perform one's duty were punished by death as a matter of principle, as were race defilement and, later, appropriating formerly Jewish property for oneself. Disciplinary violations were also severely punished . . . The men feared the punishment camps of the SS – Matzkau and Dachau – which corresponded to penitentiaries or prisons, respectively, and to which the convicted members of the SS and the Police were delivered to serve their sentences . . . Since these punishment camps were soon overcrowded, the majority of the inmates were sent to join the Probationary Units at the front. –']

See also Fa 91/5 Bl. 1251, Institut für Zeitgeschichte, Munich, Appendix XIX. Cp. Heiber, *op. cit.*, pp. 86, 54-55.

As another example one can cite the former Obersturmführer of the 'Waffen-SS' Richard Schädig, presently inmate of the Landesstrafanstalt Ziegenhain, Hessen, who was sentenced by an SS court and expelled (ausgestoßen) from the SS because he had 'wrangled' (organisiert) army supply. This information was received by this writer during an interview at Ziegenhain.

229. For Himmler's order of November 5, 1934, see BDC, T-580, R. 90, F. 449.

230. Cf. *ibid.* According to a notice in the file of the NSDAP Hauptarchiv, of December 8, 1938, Hitler's correspondence with the Jewish family physician, Dr. Eduard Bloch in Linz, in which Hitler repeatedly expressed his gratitude for services rendered to his mother, was confiscated by the Gestapo on March 28, 1938, on his order. See also Eduard Bloch, 'My Patient Hitler' (*Collier's*, March, 1941), *passim*.

231. Cf. Der Reichsführer SS, *Statistisches Jahrbuch der Schutzstaffel der NSDAP 1938, op. cit.*, loosely attached enclosure 267 38 II E, marked 'Geheim' (secret). See Appendix V.

232. See footnote 228.

233. For Himmler's order of August 16, 1935, see BDC, T-580, R. 90, F. 449.
However, paradoxically enough, there existed, indeed, SS-men who were 'Mischlinge' of the first or second degree.
This fact was made known and documented in detail by Simon Wiesenthal in his Dokumentationszentrum des Bundes Jüdischer Verfolgter des Naziregimes (BJVN) in Vienna.

234. Steiner's strict adherence to the decrees of the Geneva Conventions was pointed out in a testimony before the International Military Tribunal. Cf. IMT, Vol. XX, *op. cit.*, pp. 451-452. See also Steiner, *op. cit.*, pp. 302-303.

235. Cf. *ibid.*, pp. 79-80, 94-95.
Similar remarks about Himmler's 'racial' appearance were made by the Gauleiter of Danzig, Albert Forster. This was asserted by Obergruppenführer and General of the 'Waffen-SS', Karl Wolff during his trial in Munich on July 13, 1965.
Kersten, too, observes that officers of the 'Waffen-SS' 'lachten über seine militärischen Anwandlungen, sein gänzlich unmilitärisches Äußere und seine unglückselige Figur.' ['laughed about his military airs, his utterly unmilitary appearance, and the unfortunate figure he cut at Hitler's parades.'] Kersten, *op. cit.*, p. 404. This fact was corroborated by the former SS-Obersturmbannführer Fritz Lechler and other high-ranking SS officers who, when interviewed by this writer, frequently referred to Himmler as 'Reichsheini.'

236. Steiner writes: 'Sie' (die Truppe) 'verbannte jede Möglichkeit überheblichen Rassenwahns in ihren eigenen Reihen einfach durch die kameradschaftliche Verspottung besonders hervorstechender, betont nordischer Erscheinungstypen, als "Doppelarier" oder "Reichsführer SS befohlene Ausgabe" und ähnlicher harmloser Ulkbezeichnungen, womit sie solchen absurden Theorien von vornherein ihre ursprüngliche Gefährlichkeit nahm.' Steiner, *op. cit.*, p. 80.

---

[Steiner writes: 'It (the troop) banished any possibility of exaggerated racism in its own ranks by simply making fun, in comradely fashion, of particularly outstanding, notably Nordic types. They called them "double Aryans" or "Reich Leader SS recommended edition", or applied similar harmless, silly designations by which they immediately stripped such absurd theories of their original dangerousness.']

Apparently attempts were also made by other leaders of the 'Waffen-SS' to discuss the racial ideologies in a more objective fashion. *Ibid.*, p. 131.

237. Cf. *ibid.*, p. 352.

238. Cf. Aufbruch, *Briefe von germanischen Freiwilligen der SS-Division Wiking* (Berlin: Nibelungen Verlag, 1943), *passim*.

239. Rauschning, *op. cit.*, p. 148. See also *ibid.*, pp. 80-82, and Hitler, *Mein Kampf*, Vol. II, *op.cit.*, pp. 9-22.

An example of the tasks assigned by Hitler to such 'special NS corps' was given by the former SD-chief Otto Ohlendorf, who related to the IMT in Nuremberg on January 3, 1946, how orders for mass-murder originated, how they were executed, and how he was ordered to take command over a 'Sondereinsatztruppe' which was given the assignment to kill 90,000 Jews. He further described in detail the mass shooting of men and the destruction of women by means of mobile gassing-vans. 'Es wurde alles direkt von Himmler auf Weisung des Führers befohlen, so mußte . . . (Ohlendorf) . . . gehorchen.' Gilbert, *op. cit.*, p. 104.

['Himmler's orders were based on direct instructions by the Führer, so he . . . (Ohlendorf) . . . had to obey.']

Cp. Heiber, *op. cit.*, pp. 83, 131, 133, 134, 151-152.

240. Rauschning, *op. cit.*, pp. 78, 79.

241. A. Hitler, 'Nationalsozialismus als Weltanschauung,' in Streicher (ed.) *op. cit.*, p. 81. See also *ibid.*, pp. 82-84.

242. W. Treher, *Hitler, Steiner, Schreber. Ein Beitrag zur Phänomenologie des kranken Geistes* (Emmendingen: im Selbstverlag, 1966), pp. 101-104. Treher's attempt to draw case analogies between Hitler, Rudolf Steiner, and Schreber appears persuasive enough but does not seem to be scientifically convincing.

On December 12, 1942, Himmler disclosed the following information to Kersten: ' "Können Sie einen Mann behandeln, der unter starken Kopfschmerzen, Schwindelgefühl und Schlaflosigkeit leidet? . . . Hier lesen Sie. Es ist die Geheimakte mit dem Bericht über die Krankheit des Führers." Der Bericht umfaßte 26 Seiten, wie ich beim ersten Durchblättern feststellte, ganz offensichtlich war jedoch das Krankenblatt Hitlers aus der Zeit, als er blind im Krankenhaus zu Pasewalk lag, benutzt. Von dieser Zeit ging der Bericht aus und stellte fest, daß Hitler als junger Soldat im Felde von einer Kampfgasvergiftung befallen worden wäre, die schlecht behandelt worden sei, so daß zeitweilige Erblindungsgefahr bestand. Dazu seien Anzeichen einer syphilitischen Erkrankung aufgetreten. Er wurde in Pasewalk auskuriert und als geheilt entlassen. Im Jahre 1937

traten Erscheinungen auf, aus denen man schließen konnte, daß die syphilitische
Erkrankung ihr unheimliches Zerstörungswerk fortsetzte, und der Beginn des
Jahres 1942 habe derartige Erscheinungen gezeigt, daß nicht daran zu zweifeln
sei, daß Hitler an progressiver Paralyse leide, die alle Symptome zeigte mit
Ausnahme der Starrheit der Pupillen und Sprachstörungen.' Kersten, *op. cit.*,
pp. 209-210. See also *ibid.*, pp. 211-218.

------

[' "Can you treat a man who suffers from severe headaches, dizziness, and in-
somnia? . . . Here, read this. It is the secret document containing the report on
the Führer's illness." The report contained twenty-six pages, as I saw upon
leafing through it for the first time. However, it was quite apparent that Hitler's
sickness report from the time when he lay blinded in the hospital at Pasewalk
had been used. The report dated from this time and in it it was declared that
Hitler had been subjected to a poison-gas attack while he was a young soldier
in the field, and that his condition had been badly treated, so that for a time
he was in danger of blindness. Moreover, indications of syphilis were said to
have been noted. He was cured in Pasewalk and was released as healed. In the
year of 1937 symptoms appeared from which one could conclude that the
syphilis was continuing its sinister ravages; and it was said that at the beginning
of 1942 such serious symptoms occurred that it could not be doubted that
Hitler was suffering from progressive paralysis, showing all symptoms with the
exception of fixity of the pupils and speech disorders.']

243. Cp. Stein, *op. cit.*, p. 244.
244. Kogon, *op. cit.*, p. 20.
245. 'H. Himmler, Die Schutzstaffel 1936,' in IMT, Vol. XXIX, *op. cit.*, p. 14,
PS-1851.
246. *Ibid.*, pp. 14-15.
247. Cf. Alfred Rosenberg, *Wesen, Grundsätze und Ziele der NSDAP* (München:
Deutscher Volksverlag, 1932), pp. 7-13. Cp. Rauschning, *op. cit.*, pp. 124,
126-127, 129, 139, 179, 210-211, 210-228.
248. The 'Mutual Aid Society' of the 'Waffen-SS,' 'HIAG' (Hilfsorganisation or Hilfsgemeinschaft auf Gegenseitigkeit), was established in Hamburg in June 1950,
as a local organization of former members of the 'Waffen-SS,' headed by the
former Brigadeführer and Generalmajor of the 'Waffen-SS' Otto Kumm. After
an amalgamation of numerous smaller interest organizations of former members of the 'Waffen-SS' in 1952, the 'HIAG' gradually developed into a nation-
wide organization, the 'Bundesverband der (Hilfsgemeinschaft) Soldaten der
ehem. Waffen-SS e.V.,' chiefly due to the efforts of the former senior general
officer of the 'Waffen-SS' and 'spiritus rector,' Oberst-Gruppenführer and Generaloberst of the 'Waffen-SS' Paul Hausser ('Papa Hausser'; for some of his
views see his open letter in *Wiking-Ruf*, No. 11, November 1955, p. 6), and the
former Obergruppenführer and Generals of the 'Waffen-SS' Herbert O. Gille
and Felix Steiner. (See declaration made during the 'Arbeitstagung der HIAG-
Referenten in Hannover,' in *Wiking-Ruf*, No. 10, August 1952, p. 2.)

The monthly *Wiking-Ruf* (Mitteilungsblatt der ehemaligen Soldaten der Waffen-SS für Vermißten-, Such- und Hilfsdienst) was first published and edited by the general of the 'Waffen-SS' Herbert O. Gille in Hameln/Weser, in November 1951, then at Stemmen, and later in Hameln again, published by the Wiking-Ruf-Verlag and edited by Kurt Kanis. Already during the first year of its appearance, the *Wiking-Ruf* became the official organ of the 'HIAG.' (See *Wiking-Ruf*, No. 4, February 1952, p. 7, and No. 14, December 1952, p. 16.) In 1958 this monthly periodical was renamed *Der Freiwillige (Für Einigkeit und Recht und Freiheit)*, edited by Cornelius van der Horst at Elmshorn in Holstein, and published by the Munin-Verlag, Osnabrück.

Especially during its early existence the 'HIAG' concentrated on 'help-find-lost-comrades' actions (Kameraden-Suchdienst 'Kamerad, wo bist Du?'), and lobbied to achieve rehabilitation and legitimacy of the 'Waffen-SS' on a basis of equal status with –and as– recognized formations of the Third Reich's German Armed Forces. In addition, it staged rallies (Kameradschaftstreffen) once per year. Although any political affiliation of the 'HIAG' has been strongly discouraged by its leaders, ideological tendencies advocated and political leanings expressed are to be kept, according to Gille, '. . . im Geiste . . . europäischer und vaterländischer Gesinnung' ['. . . in the spirit of European and patriotic sentiment'] (*Wiking-Ruf*, No. 1, Hameln, November 1951, p. 1) and were more specifically outlined by 'HIAG's' first chairman and spokesman (Bundes- resp. Landessprecher) Otto Kumm on June 6, 1952:

'Es hat eine infame und verlogene Propaganda schon während des Krieges, vor allem aber nach dem Kriege, verstanden, mit all den unerfreulichen Erscheinungen, die dem 3. Reich und auch der SS anhafteten, alles das herunterzumachen und in den Dreck zu ziehen, was uns heilig war und ist und was dazu geeignet ist, im deutschen Volk die wertvollsten Eigenschaften und besten Kräfte zu fördern, zum Wohle und Gedeihen eben dieses Volkes. Denn wir wollen uns doch darüber im klaren sein, daß der Kampf nicht allein dem autoritären Regime des 3. Reiches, sondern vor allem dem Wiedererstarken des deutschen Volkes galt. Das hat nackt und klar die Forderung der bedingungslosen Kapitulation schon während des Krieges bewiesen, . . .'

'Wir haben in der Waffen-SS zweifellos einem falschen Nationalismus gehuldigt und erst der Krieg mit seiner gewaltigen Ausweitung hat uns gelehrt, daß es mehr sein muß als Deutschland, dem wir unser Leben weihen. So entstand in uns zwangsläufig, erheblich gefördert durch die vielen tausend Kameraden aus allen europäischen Nationen, die Idee eines großen, das ganze Abendland umfassenden Europas.

Das Ziel unseres eigenen Lebens muß sein, daß das Höchste auf der Welt die Unantastbarkeit der menschlichen Persönlichkeit ist, die für das Recht des Schutzes durch die Gemeinschaft freiwillig die Pflicht auf sich nimmt, der Gemeinschaft zu dienen und sie zu verteidigen. Jeder Versuch aber, die Aufgabe der Persönlichkeit zu fordern, zur besseren Lenkung der Gemeinschaft, muß von uns schärfstens zurückgewiesen werden, denn alle menschliche Leistung erwächst überhaupt nur aus der in sich freien starken Persönlichkeit, wie auch nur Gemeinschaftsleistungen hervorgebracht werden können von starken freien Völkern.

Wir wollen keine neue Bewegung schaffen, schon gar keine neue Partei, obgleich wir der Meinung sind, daß es endlich Zeit ist, diese Gedanken auch einmal vor einem größeren Forum des Volkes, besonders der Jugend, auszusprechen.' (*Wiking-Ruf*, No. 10, Hannover, August 1952, pp. 5-6.)

['Even during the war, but especially after the war, infamous and lying propagandists have been able to make use of all the unfortunate events connected with the Third Reich and also with the SS to destroy and drag through the mud all of what was and is sacred to us and which is capable of furthering the most precious attributes and the best powers of the German people, in the interest of the welfare and prosperity of this very people. Let us be clear about it: the battle was directed not only against the authoritarian régime of the Third Reich, but, above all, against the resurgence of the strength of the German people. This fact was made perfectly clear by the demand for unconditional surrender during the war itself . . .

'In the Waffen-SS we no doubt paid hommage to a false nationalism, and it was only the war and its enormous expansion that taught us that there must be more to which we dedicate our lives than just Germany. Thus, out of necessity, the idea of a greater Europe, embracing the entire Occident, developed within us an idea notably furthered by many thousands of comrades from all European nations. It must be the goal of our lives to make the inviolability of the human personality the highest earthly value which, in exchange for the right of protection by the community, voluntarily assumes the obligation of serving and defending this community. However, we must vigorously reject any attempt to demand the denial of one's personality in the interests of a better direction of the community, for all human accomplishment is developed only in a strong personality that is free in itself, just as communal accomplishments can only be produced by strong, free peoples. We do not want to create a new movement, and certainly not a new party – although we are of the opinion that it is finally time to express these thoughts for once to a larger forum of the people, particularly the young.']

For an apologetic and nationalistic point of view, cp. Paul Krauss, 'Eine Mahnung zur Pflicht der ehemaligen Waffen-SS: Die Wurzeln tief im Volk,' *Der Freiwillige*, No. 7, July 1967, pp. 10, 11.

Furthermore, an anonymous 'HIAG' spokesman demands: 'Wir fordern die Einsicht, daß man das Recht auf politischen Irrtum keiner Person absprechen kann und darf und daß Erkenntnisse und Läuterungen zu achten sind.' (Unsigned editorial, 'Gleichberechtigung und Gerechtigkeit,' *Wiking-Ruf*, No. 2, February 1957, p. 13.)

['We demand understanding of the fact that one cannot and may not deny the right of political error to any person, and that realization, learning, and purification are to be respected.']

On April 23, 1962, the 'HIAG' created a mutual benefit association 'Sozialwerk Paul Hausser e. V.' (until recently Paul Hausser was the only surviving senior General of the 'Waffen-SS') for needy former members of the 'Waffen-SS,' disabled war veterans, and survivors of men killed in action.

'HIAG's' most popular and eloquent chief spokesman (Bundessprecher) so far was the former commander of the 12th SS-Panzerdivision 'Hitlerjugend,' the late former Brigadeführer and Generalmajor of the 'Waffen-SS' Kurt Meyer ('Panzer-Meyer'). (See Meyer's public declaration in protest against the identification of the 'Waffen-SS' with other non-military SS formations, prejudicial treatment, collective condemnation, and defamation of 'the SS' in Steiner, *op. cit.*, pp. 249-251, and the editorial signed 'S.,' entitled 'Die Waffen-SS als Teil der ehemaligen Kriegs-Wehrmacht. Eine Antwort an das Institut für Zeitgeschichte,' *Wiking-Ruf*, No. 6, June 1955, pp. 13-15, 18.)

For a detailed but somewhat erroneous account of the 'HIAG,' cp. Stein, *op. cit.*, pp. 254-257.

249. Cf. Felix Steiner, *Die Freiwilligen: Idee und Opfergang* (Göttingen: Plesse Verlag, 1958), p. 57.

250. Stein refers to this fighting style as a '... blend of determination and ruthlessness.' *Op. cit.*, p. 122.

251. In an interview on September 16, 1962, General Steiner told this writer that after Himmler's infamous speech at Posen on October 4, 1943 (at which Steiner was present), he went to see Himmler to protest against what Himmler had said. '... So etwas kann man doch nicht verantworten ...'; Himmler brushed Steiner off without a reply.

['... How can one assume responsibility for such things ...']

252. Cp. Stein, *op cit.*, pp. 125-126.

253. According to results of a research project entitled 'The Marks of the Authoritarian Attitude in Former Members of the SS and the Armed Forces,' conducted by this writer, presently available figures show that the Nazi ideological doctrines held by the SS supported aggression and war morale, while those oriented to different values –which appears to have been prevalently the case with members of other comparable German military formations– did not give such strong support. *Abstracts on Criminology and Penology*, Vol. X, No. 4 (July/August 1970), pp. 225-236. Cf. also Robert Ley (ed.), 'Aus dem nationalsozialistischen Jahrbuch 1941: Bericht über die SS im Kriegsjahr 1939/40: Beteiligung an Kriegshandlungen,' in IMT, Vol. XXIX, *op. cit.*, pp. 269-274, PS-2163.

254. Höss gave the following explanation concerning his attitude towards his post at the concentration camp Auschwitz and the destruction program in general:

'Ich war zu der Zeit rein zufällig Kommandant von Auschwitz und er' (Himmler) 'hatte beschlossen, Auschwitz zu dem Hauptausrottungslager zu machen. Es blieb mir nichts weiter übrig, als die Befehle auszuführen. Jeder andere SS-

Mann hätte das gleiche getan. Ebenso ging es Eichmann, der mit dem gesamten Ausrottungsprogramm beauftragt gewesen war, und auch den Führern der Einsatzgruppen, wie z.B. Ohlendorf. Uns wurde eingebläut, Befehlen zu gehorchen, und auch eingeimpft, die Juden seien unsere Feinde. Wir glaubten zu dieser Zeit nicht, daß es Propaganda war. Wir wurden mit Leib und Seele da hinein verwickelt. Wenn nun Hitler den Befehl gab, das Judenproblem auf diese Weise endgültig zu lösen, blieb nichts weiter übrig, als zu gehorchen. Jeder andere SS-Mann hätte das gleiche getan.' Gilbert, *op. cit.*, p. 327.

——

['By pure coincidence I was, at the time, commandant of Auschwitz, and he (Himmler) had decided to make Auschwitz the principal extermination camp. There was nothing I could do but execute the orders. Any other SS man would have done the same. It was the same with Eichmann, who had been charged with the entire program of extermination, and with the leaders of the task forces (Einsatzgruppen: trans.), such as Ohlendorf. We were imbued with the idea that we must obey orders, and inoculated with the notion that the Jews were our enemies. At that time we did not believe that this was propaganda. We were implicated in this body and soul. So when Hitler now gave the order for a definite solution of the Jewish problem in that way, there was nothing one could do but obey. Any other SS man would have done the same.']

255. Rudolf Höss, *Kommandant in Auschwitz, autobiographische Aufzeichnungen,* Martin Broszat (ed.), (München: Deutscher Taschenbuch Verlag, 1964), p. 132. See Appendices XIX, XX.
256. Gilbert, *op. cit.*, p. 116. Cp. also Höss, *op. cit.*, p. 111. See also Cornelia Berning, *Vom 'Abstammungsnachweis' zum 'Zuchtwart'. Vokabular des Nationalsozialismus* (Berlin: Walter de Gruyter, 1964), *passim.*
257. 'Rede Himmlers bei der SS-Gruppenführertagung in Posen am 4. Oktober 1943,' in IMT, Vol. XXIX, *op. cit.*, p. 145, PS-1919.
   The fact that some SS officers and men assisted in the survival of the persecuted was revealed during the interviews with former members of the SS, specifically with Karl Wolff, Felix Steiner, and others, and during this writer's experiences in various concentration camps. Also cf. Steiner, *Die Armee der Geächteten, op. cit.*, pp. 186, 181-182.
258. 'Nationalpolitischer Lehrgang der Wehrmacht vom Januar 1937', in IMT *op. cit.*, p. 207.
259. This was most clearly expressed by Steiner. See especially Steiner, *op. cit.*, pp. 80-83, 94, 98, 114-115, 131-132, 178, 190, 220, 227-229, 233, 240.
260. During an interview with this writer in Munich on July 23, 1960, Steiner responded to the question why he had not opposed atrocities committed by other formations of the SS: 'Ich hatte keine Zeit, mich um Angelegenheiten zu kümmern, mit denen ich nichts zu tun hatte, und die hinter der Front geschahen' [here Steiner refers to concentration camps and 'Einsatzgruppen': trans.], 'ich kämpfte an der Ostfront auf Leben und Tod.' Cp. Steiner, *op. cit.*, pp. 184-185.

——

['I had no time to concern myself with matters with which I had nothing to do, and which took place behind the front lines; I was in a life-and-death fight on the Eastern front.']

During the same interview Steiner related to this writer his position expressed by him in a conversation with Fritz Graf von der Schulenburg, in May 1943, during which Steiner rejected Schulenburg's suggestion to remove Hitler – by force, if necessary – as inopportune. Cp. Steiner, *op. cit.*, pp. 185-186.
Concerning the events of July 20, 1944, Steiner essentially took the same position and added that he disagreed not only with the manner of assassination, but also with the timing and circumstances. If it had been successful, the German nation – in its precarious strategic position – would have been subjected to an even greater bloodshed than had been the case already, mainly because of a disunited leadership. For a representative view expressed by a former 'Waffen-SS'-man concerning the July 20 uprising, see K. Kutzner, 'Sie waren Soldaten!,' *Wiking-Ruf*, No. 9, 1955, pp. 8-10.

261. See Appendix XX.
262. 'Der Reichsführer SS zu den Ersatzmannschaften für die Kampfgruppe "Nord" am Sonntag, dem 13. Juli 1941, in Stettin,' Geheim, RFSS, T-175, 109/2632 083 ff., in Stein, *op. cit.*, pp. 126-127.
263. Hitler and Himmler referred to Streicher's 'Stürmer' as model for anti-Jewish propaganda. Cf. Rauschning, *op. cit.*, 223, and Heiber, *op. cit.*, p. 212.
The 'Stürmer' seems to have had a stronger indoctrinating effect than it has been generally assumed, especially among the less endowed members of the SS. Höss writes in his memoirs: 'Die Juden in Dachau hatten es nicht leicht. Sie mußten die körperlich für sie sehr schwere Arbeit in der Kiesgrube machen. Die Bewachung war auf sie besonders scharf gemacht durch Eicke und den "Stürmer", der ja in den Kasernen und den Kantinen überall aushing. Sie wurden als die "Verderber des deutschen Volkes" genug gehetzt und getrieben, auch von ihren Mitgefangenen. Da auch im Schutzhaftlager ein 'Stürmer'-Aushängekasten angebracht war, war die Wirkung auch unter den sonst absolut nicht antisemitischen Häftlingen doch spürbar.' Höss, *op. cit.*, p. 111.
This fact can be corroborated by this writer's experience while an inmate at Dachau in 1945.
Höss to Gilbert on April 12, 1946: 'Verstehen Sie nicht, wir SS-Leute sollten nicht über diese Dinge nachdenken; es kam uns nie in den Sinn. Und außerdem war es gewissermaßen eine Selbstverständlichkeit geworden, daß die Juden an allem schuld hatten. ... wir haben nie etwas anderes gehört. Es stand nicht nur in Zeitungen wie dem Stürmer, sondern wir hörten es überall.' Gilbert, *op. cit.*, p. 252. Cp. *ibid.*, pp. 295-296.
Höss to Gilbert on April 16, 1946: 'Er sagte, er hätte seit Jahren jede Woche Goebbels Leitartikel im "Reich" gelesen, ebenso seine Bücher und seine verschiedenen Reden; ferner Rosenbergs Mythos des 20. Jahrhunderts und einige seiner Reden; und dann natürlich Hitlers Mein Kampf, und die meisten seiner Reden hätte er gelesen oder gehört. Außer den Werken dieser Verfasser gab

es noch ideologische Kampfschriften und anderes Unterrichtsmaterial der SS. Streichers Stürmer las er nur gelegentlich, weil er zu oberflächlich war. (Er erwähnte, daß diejenigen seiner Untergebenen, die regelmäßig den Stürmer lasen, Leute mit sehr begrenztem Horizont waren.) Goebbels, Rosenberg und Hitler regten ihn mehr zum Nachdenken an. In allen diesen Schriften und Reden wurde ununterbrochen gepredigt, daß das Judentum Deutschlands Feind sei.' Gilbert, *op. cit.*, pp. 259-260.

The following titles and excerpts from the '*Stürmer*' have been selected from editions published in the years 1940-1944.

*Vol. XVIII, 1940*:
'Der in Wien geborene, zuletzt in Znaim wohnhaft gewesene Jude Hugo Israel Weiss hatte das Parteiabzeichen getragen und sich als Parteimitglied ausgegeben. Er wurde zu 13 Monaten Zuchthaus verurteilt.'
'Der staatenlose Ostjude Alexander Israel Popper stand bereits einmal vor Gericht, weil er sich mit der Beschaffung gefälschter Taufscheine und sonstiger Ausweispapiere für jüdische Auswanderer befaßt hatte. Die damalige Amnestierung wurde aber vom Oberlandesgericht aufgehoben. Diesmal erhielt er 2 Monate Kerker.' *Der Stürmer*, No. 6. February, pp. 9, 10.
'Seit dem 1. Januar 1939 sind in Deutschland alle jüdischen Personen verpflichtet, Vornamen zu führen, aus denen ihre Rassenzugehörigkeit deutlich hervorgeht. Ein Jude, der bisher "Karl Franck" hieß, muß sich nun "Karl Israel Franck" nennen. Oder eine Jüdin, die den Namen "Elli Fürst" trug, heißt nun "Elli Sara Fürst".'
'Die Juden sind schuld am Kriege!'
'Masaryk, der Judensprößling. Eine tschechische Zeitung veröffentlichte Einzelheiten über die Person des Gründers des ehemaligen tschechoslowakischen Staates. Danach war der erste Präsident T. G. Masaryk ein Halbjude. Sein wirklicher Vater, sein Erzeuger, war der Jude Samuel Redlich, der mit der Mutter Masaryks, einer armen Dienstmagd, ein Verhältnis hatte. Als sich die Folgen einstellten, verheiratete der Jude sie an seinen Kutscher, dem er als Entgeld dafür eine Schafferstelle auf einem Gute gab. Masaryk wieder heiratete eine Volljüdin, die amerikanische Staatsbürgerin Charlotte Garrigue Wright.' *Der Stürmer*, No. 9, February, pp. 1-2, 7.
'Churchill Judenstämmling (Warum lügt Churchill?)' No. 17, April, p. 3.
'Es ist zu spät, Ihr Herren Juden! Eure Zeit ist abgelaufen! Das nationalsozialistische Deutschland ist gerüstet, mit dem Teufelsvolk der Juden endgültig fertigzuwerden.'
'Judentum ist Verbrechertum. Kurznachrichten aus dem Reich.
Jud Hirsch besaß die Frechheit, überall mit "Heil Hitler" zu grüßen. Die Düsseldorfer Strafkammer verurteilte ihn zu 4 Jahren Zuchthaus. Außerdem wurde Sicherungsverwahrung angeordnet.
Sie sind Nichtjuden. In dem von uns in der Nr. 6 unter dem Titel "Die Rebekka von Joachimsthal und ihr Rebeckchen" veröffentlichten Bild teilt

uns der Vertreter der dargestellten Personen mit, daß diese Vollarier sind.'
No. 18, May, pp. 4, 9.
'Die Judenfrage ist keine Religionsfrage. Die Juden sind eine internationale
Rasse von Verbrechern.' No. 27, July, p. 9.
'Getaufte Juden in Dänemark.

Neuerdings machen sie (Juden) ausgiebigen Gebrauch von dem Recht der
Namensänderung, das in Dänemark wegen der vielfach gleichlautenden
Familiennamen amtlich gefördert wird. So erlebt man jetzt in Kopenhagen
und anderswo, daß man irgend einem schmierigen Juden begegnet, der sich
einen schönklingenden, altnordischen Namen beigelegt hat.

Jud Levi nennt sich heut Larsen oder Lavand, aus Abraham wurde Asmild,
und Nathansohn heißt heute vielleicht Nielsen oder ähnlich. Aber auch die
altnordischen Namen vermögen aus einem geborenen Kaftanjuden ebenso
wenig einen Nichtjuden zu machen, wie man es durch die Taufe zu tun
vermag.'

'Lieber Soldat! Du hast die Juden in Polen gesehen. Daß es solche Geschöpfe
überhaupt gibt, dreckig, verschmutzt, verlaust, stinkend und einem Teufel
ähnlicher als einem Menschen, habe ich wirklich nicht gewußt! . . . Der Jude
in Frankreich verstand es nämlich wesentlich besser, sich dem gastgebenden
Volke anzupassen als dies in Holland oder gar in Polen der Fall war. Er
trägt die neuste Pariser Herrenmode. Die Hosen sind so raffiniert gefertigt,
daß man die krummen Beine kaum bemerkt. . . . Der Jude von Paris markiert
den Franzosen vom Scheitel bis zur Sohle.

'Du, Lieber Soldat, läßt Dich nicht täuschen. Du kennst die Rassenmerkmale
der Juden. Du kennst die Judenaugen, die Judenohren, den Judenmund. Du
kennst den Gang des Juden und seine typischen Bewegungen. Und wenn Du
selbst kein Wort Französisch verständest, aus der Sprache dieser "Franzosen"
hörst Du sofort den Juden heraus. E. H.' No. 28, July, pp. 10-11.

'Was viele nicht wissen.

Jede Menschenrasse hat einen nur ihr eigenen Geruch. Der Rassengeruch der
Juden ist süßlich, wie der des Negers. Senkfüße entwickeln sich schon früh-
zeitig bei Menschen, die viel stehen müssen. Plattfüße aber sind angeboren.
Man findet sie fast nur bei Negern und Juden. Für die jüdische Rasse sind
die kurzen herabhängenden Schultern typisch. Sie können auch durch in die
Kleider eingelegte Watte nicht beseitigt werden.' No. 36, September, p. 11.

'Puritanismus und Judentum. Religiöse Verwandtschaft zwischen Engländern
und Juden.' No. 37, September, 1940.

'Von Juden begangene Ritualmorde sind durch geschichtliche Zeugnisse nach-
gewiesen. Sie werden auch heute noch begangen.' No. 39, September, p. 11.

'Das tschechische Unterrichtsministerium in Prag hat einen Erlaß herausgegeben, demzufolge mit Beginn des Schuljahres 1940/41 jüdische Schüler in
tschechische Schulen nicht mehr aufgenommen werden dürfen. Jüdische
Schüler, die solche Schulen derzeit noch besuchen, werden mit Beginn des
kommenden Schuljahres von der Teilnahme am Unterricht ausgeschlossen.

'Was den Juden nicht gefällt: Daß der Polizeipräsident von Prag verfügt hat,

daß Juden auf der Straßenbahn nur den letzten Beiwagen benutzen dürfen.
Daß im Generalgouvernement die Juden nun auch zum Steinhauen ausrücken
müssen.' No. 46, November, pp. 7, 10.
'Marsch ins Konzentrationslager. Die Juden in Italien.
In Italien sind die Juden wie in Deutschland aus dem Volksleben ausgeschaltet.
. . . Wenn der Jude keine militärische Uniform tragen darf, dann kann er
dafür die Uniform eines Konzentrationslagers anziehen!
Ihr Juden alle miteinander, bereitet Euch darauf vor, den Galgen zu be-
steigen.' No. 48, November, p. 4.
'Otto Petschek der Rothschild von Prag.'
'Der Jude im Sprichwort.' No. 50, December, pp. 1-2, 4.
'Die Juden heißen es Zwangsarbeit. Jüdisches Drohnenleben nimmt ein Ende.'
'Rassenschande in Frankreich. . . . wenn weiße Frauen sich mit Negern paaren.'
No. 51, December, pp. 5, 8.
*Vol. XIX, 1941*:
'Der Segen von Dachau – ein Jude "hat in Dachau das Arbeiten gelernt".'
No. 17, April, p. 6.
'Ghettoisierung der Juden.' No. 18, May, p. 7.
'Zwangsarbeit der Juden.'
'Vor kurzem wurde der Jude Jossek Pakin wegen Verlassen des Wohngebietes
der Juden in Litzmannstadt zu 8 Monaten Gefängnis verurteilt. Es gelang
ihm zu entkommen, er wurde doch wieder gefaßt. Nun erhielt er eine Zusatz-
strafe von 8 Monaten.' No. 21, May, pp. 2, 6.
'Negerjuden in New York. Rabbi Matthews, ein Rabbiner der Neger-Juden in
New York.' No. 24, June, p. 2.
'Soldat geht durch das Ghetto.
Juden unter sich. Was Jud Peine dem Stürmer schreibt. (Egon Israel Peine,
Hamburg 13, Beneckestraße 6)
. . . "Der religiöse Jude zettelt die Kriege an . . . Würde der arische Leser alle
Gemeinheiten kennen, die die Religionsjuden und besonders die Beamten des
Hamburger Religionsverbandes begehen, so würde er dies nicht glauben, weil
sein Fassungsvermögen für solche Niederträchtigkeiten nicht ausreichend ist.
. . . "Ich hoffe, daß meine Ausführungen dazu beitragen, vielen Ariern die
Augen zu öffnen über die Verworfenheit der religiösen Juden. . . .".' No. 35,
August, p. 6.
"Beim Ostrauer Kreisgericht häufen sich jetzt Klagen, die sich mit der Fest-
stellung der Abstammung zu beschäftigen haben. Juden wollen nicht mehr
Juden sein. Sie streben ein Urteil an, worin festgestellt werden soll, daß ein
Elternteil arisch sei und daß sie demnach nicht Juden, sondern Halbjuden
wären.' No. 38, September, p. 9.
'Judenstern.
. . . So könnte dem Judentum das verbrecherische Handwerk noch schwerer
gemacht werden als bisher. Ich bin überzeugt, daß das Volk eine derartige
Verfügung mit großer Dankbarkeit begrüßen würde.' No. 43, October, p. 6.
'Denkt daran!

Wer hat noch Mitleid mit dem Juden?
Wo deutsche Männer für uns bluten
Um gutzumachen, was Epochen
An unserem deutschen Volk verbrochen,
Durch Judenliebedienerei.
Mitleid? Niemals!! Das ist vorbei!'
No. 44, October, p. 1.
'Für den Wissenden ist die Maßnahme, die zur Wiedererneuerung des Juden-
sternes geführt hat, der äußere Ausdruck der in den europäischen Völkern
gewordenen Erkenntnis, daß eine Ordnung in Europa und darüber hinaus in
der ganzen Welt nur möglich ist, wenn die Judenfrage einer endlichen Lösung
zugeführt wird.' No. 45, November, p. 4.
*Vol. XX, 1942:*
'Zum Ordnungsdienst angetreten!
Die Juden in den Ghettos haben auch ihre eigenen Ordnungsmänner. Man
beachte die typischen Plattfüße dieser Hebräer. Der Jude rechts mit dem
Gummiknüppel ist der "Oberordnungsmann". Wenn er schlecht aufgelegt ist,
haben seine Rassengenossen nichts zu lachen.'
'Frauen ohne Kennzeichnung.
Wie notwendig die Kennzeichnung der Hebräer durch den Judenstern war,
beweisen die obigen Bilder. Wer sieht diesen Weibern aus dem Generalgouver-
nement auf den ersten Blick an, daß sie Jüdinnen sind?'
'Leserbrief von SS-Sturmmann Karl Bauer "Ich bin ä armer Jud!" ...' No. 5,
January, pp. 4, 6.
'Auch Ungarn hat die Juden satt. Interniert oder abgeschoben – Genugtuung
in der Bevölkerung.' No. 11, March, p. 4.
'SS-Unterscharführer Hans Schick ... "Die Ghettos im Osten zeigen, daß diese
jüdische Weltpest mit Stumpf und Stiel ausgerottet gehört, genauso wie man
Ungeziefer in der Tierwelt vernichtet...."' No. 15, April, p. 6.
'Wiener Juden vor der Ausreise.' No. 17, April, p. 5.
'Erbärmliche Judenschwindeleien im Protektorat. Juden suchen arische Väter
– "Meine Manne hat Ehebruch getrieben." ' No. 29, July, p. 4.
'Sie wissen es. Lösen wir die Judenfrage, dann erlösen wir die Menschheit vom
Unglück der Jahrtausende ... Ob die Jüdin in der Maske des alten abgehärm-
ten Weibes Mitleid erwecken will, sie ist und bleibt die gleiche Talmudistin
wie ihr Enkelkind, das heute wegen Rassenschande und Verbrechen wider die
Kriegsgesetze vor Gericht steht. Der Jude war Verbrecher von Anfang an und
wird Verbrecher bleiben bis zu allen Zeiten. ...
Es ist völlig belanglos, ob der Jude in der Maske des hochbetagten und ver-
armten "Sternträgers" durch die Straßen wandelt, er ist und bleibt der gleiche
Gauner wie sein Sohn. ...' No. 37, September, p. 4.
*Vol. XXI, 1943:*
'Tabor ist Judenrein!
Die Stadt Tabor im Protektorat Böhmen und Mähren war seit über dreihundert
Jahren ein Lieblingsaufenthalt der Juden gewesen. Nun aber wird gemeldet, daß

auch Tabor *völlig* judenrein geworden ist. Die Bewohner der Stadt sind glücklich, die fremdrassigen Parasiten endlich losgeworden zu sein.' No. 3, January, p. 6.
'Juden und Geschlechtskrankheiten.'
'Die Pornographie im Dienste der jüdischen Weltherrschaftsbestrebungen.' No. 4, January, pp. 4-5.
'. . . wenn das Judentum sich etwa einbildet, einen internationalen Weltkrieg zur Ausrottung der europäischen Rassen herbeiführen zu können, dann wird das Ergebnis nicht die Ausrottung der europäischen Rassen, sondern die Ausrottung des Judentums in Europa sein.' (From a speech by Hitler.) No. 5, January, p. 3.
'Der Stürmer besucht Gettos des Ostens.
Man muß sich an den Kopf greifen, wie es möglich war, daß dieser Abschaum der Menschheit von den Nichtjuden jahrhundertelang als das von Gott auserwählte Volk gehalten wurde. . . . Diese Satansrasse hat wirklich keine Daseinsberechtigung.' No. 19, May, p. 4.
'Vom Wesen der jüdischen Musik.' No. 40, September, p. 2.
*Vol. XXII, 1944:*
'Die ersten Ritualmorde. Juden gestehen den Gebrauch des Christenblutes.' No. 1, January, pp. 4-6.
'Die Juden brauchen nichtjüdisches Blut für die Mazzen, das Blut dient "zum Heile der Seele".' No. 2, January, pp. 3-5.
'Teufel in Menschengestalt. (Masaryk) Umjubelt von Rabbinern. Großmeister jüdischen Verbrechertums empfingen ihren Knecht Masaryk.' No. 13, March, pp. 3-5.
'Blonde Judenkinder . . . Wie notwendig die Einführung des Judensternes auch in Ungarn war, zeigen die beiden Bilder. Wer würde diesen Kindern ansehen, daß sie Juden sind, trügen sie nicht den Judenstern bzw. Peies.' No. 23, June, p. 3.
'Durch den Talmud irrsinnig geworden.
Eine Jude, der zeit seines Lebens die Mordanweisungen des Talmud studierte, wurde schließlich geisteskrank und endete im Irrenhaus.' No. 25, June, p. 5.

---

['The Jews in Dachau did not have an easy time. They had to work in the gravel pit which, for them, was very strenuous physical labor. The guards, influenced by Eicke and by *Der Stürmer,* which was on display everywhere in their barracks and the canteens, were particularly rough with them. They were persecuted and tormented as it was as "corrupters of the German people," even by their fellow prisoners. When a display case containing *Der Stürmer* was put up in the protective custody camp, its effect on those prisoners who had hitherto not at all been anti-Semitic was immediately apparent.' Höss, *op. cit.,* p. 111.
This fact can be corroborated by this writer's experience while an inmate at Dachau in 1945.
Höss to Gilbert on April 12, 1946: 'Don't you understand, we SS men were not

supposed to think about these things; it never even occurred to us. – And besides, it was something already taken for granted that the Jews were to blame for everything. . . . we just never heard anything else. It was not just in newspapers like *Der Stürmer* but we have heard it everywhere.' Gilbert, *op. cit.*, p. 252. Cp. *ibid.*, pp. 295-296.

Höss to Gilbert on April 16, 1946: 'He [Höss] said that he read Goebbels' editorials in *Das Reich* every week for many years, as well as his books and his various speeches; furthermore Rosenberg's *The Myth of the Twentieth Century* and some of his speeches; and, of course, Hitler's *Mein Kampf*, as well as hearing and reading most of his speeches. In addition to the writings of these authors, there were the ideological pamphlets and other educational material of the SS. He read Streicher's *Stürmer* only occasionally because it was too superficial. (He noticed that those of his subordinates who had been in the habit of reading the *Stürmer* were usually men of narrow outlook.) Goebbels, Rosenberg, and Hitler gave him more food for thought. All of these writings and speeches constantly preached the idea that Jewry was Germany's enemy.' Gilbert, *op. cit.*, pp. 259-260.

The following titles and excerpts from *Der Stürmer* have been selected from editions published in the years 1940-1944.

*Vol. XVIII, 1940*:

'The former Jew, Hugo Israel Weiss, born in Vienna and most recently living in Znaim, had worn the party badge and passed himself off as a party member. He was sentenced to a thirteen-month-term in the penitentiary.'

'The stateless Eastern Jew, Alexander Israel Popper, had already been arraigned once on charges of having engaged in procuring forged baptismal certificates and other identification papers for Jewish emigrants. The amnesty he received at that time was cancelled, however, by the Provincial Supreme Court (Oberlandesgericht), and this time he received a two-month-jail sentence.' *Der Stürmer*, No. 6, February, pp. 9, 10.

'Since January 1, 1939, all Jewish persons in Germany are required to have names which reveal clearly their race. A Jew, who here-to-fore was named "Karl Franck", must now call himself "Karl Israel Franck." Or a Jewess, who bore the name "Elli Fürst", is now called "Elli Sara Fürst." '

'The Jews are responsible for the war!'

'Masaryk of Jewish descent. A Czech newspaper has published personal data concerning the founder of the former Czechoslovakian state. According to it, the first president, T. G. Masaryk, was half Jewish. His real father and progenitor was the Jew Samuel Redlich, who had an affair with Masaryk's mother, a poor servant girl. When the consequences became apparent, the Jew married the girl to his coachman, compensating him by making him a steward on one of his farms. Masaryk in turn married a full-blooded Jewess, the American citizen Charlotte Garrigue Wright.' *Der Stürmer*, No. 9, February, pp. 1-2, 7.

'Churchill, Jewish descendant (Why is Churchill lying?)' No. 17, April, p. 3.

'It is too late, you Jewish gentlemen! Your time has run out! National Socialist Germany is equipped to finish up with the Devil's folk, the Jews.'

'Jewry is outlawry. Spot news from the Reich.

'The Jew Hirsch had the gall to greet everybody with "Heil Hitler." The criminal court in Düsseldorf sentenced him to four years in the penitentiary. In addition, special security confinement was also ordered.

'They are not Jews. With respect to the picture we published in No. 6 under the title of "Rebecca of Joachimsthal and her little Rebecca," the legal representative of the persons depicted informs us that they are full Aryans.' No. 18, May, pp. 4, 9.

'The Jewish question is not a religious question. The Jews are an international race of criminals.' No. 27, July, p. 9.

'Baptized Jews in Denmark.

Recently they (the Jews) have been making extensive use of the right of changing one's name, which is officially encouraged in Denmark because so many have the same family name. Thus in Copenhagen and elsewhere one may encounter some greasy Jew who has appropriated for himself a fine-sounding old Nordic name. Jew Levi now calls himself Larsen or Lavand, Abraham has become Asmild, and Nathansohn may now be called Nielsen or something similar. But even old Nordic names are just as incapable of making a caftan Jew into a non-Jew as baptism is.'

'Dear soldier! You have seen the Jews in Poland. I really did not know that such creatures existed at all – dirty, filthy, lice-ridden, stinking, and more similar to a devil than to a human being! ...

'The fact is that the French Jew knew much better how to adapt himself to the host people than the Jews in Holland or even Poland. He wears the latest Parisian men's styles. The pants are so cleverly tailored that one hardly notices the crooked legs ... The Parisian Jew imitates the Frenchman from head to toe. You, dear soldier, do not let yourself be deceived. You know the racial characteristics of the Jews. You know the Jewish eyes, the Jewish ears, the Jewish mouth. You know the gait of the Jew and his typical movements. And even if you do not understand a word of French, you immediately recognize the Jew because of the way these "Frenchmen" speak. E.H.' No. 28, July, pp. 10-11.

'What many do not know.

'Every human race has its own smell. The Jews have a sweetish smell, as do the Negroes. Fallen arches develop early in people who have to stand a lot; but flat feet are congenital. They are found almost exclusively in Negroes and Jews. Short, downward-sloping shoulders are typical of the Jewish race. Also they cannot be concealed by cotton shoulderpads.' No. 36, September, p. 11.

'Puritanism and Judaism. The religious affinity between the English and the Jews.' No. 37, September, 1940.

'Ritual murders committed by Jews have been proven by historical documents. They are still being committed today.' No. 39, September, p. 11.

'The Czech Ministry of Education in Prague has issued a decree which provides that as of the beginning of the academic year 1940-41, Jewish pupils may no longer be admitted to Czech schools. Jewish pupils who are now attending such schools will be excluded from participation in instruction as of the beginning of the coming academic year.'

'What displeases the Jews: That the Police President of Prague has decreed that Jews may use only the last car on the street car. That in occupied Poland (Generalgouvernement) the Jews must now also work in gravel pits.' No. 46, November, pp. 7, 10.

'March to the concentration camp. The Jews in Italy.

'In Italy, as in Germany, the Jews have been excluded from community life (Volksleben) ... If the Jew may not wear a military uniform, he may, in exchange, put on the uniform of a concentration camp! All you Jews, prepare to ascend the scaffold.' No. 48, November, p. 4.

'Otto Petschek, the Rothschild of Prague.'

'The Jew in proverbs.' No. 50, December, pp. 1-2, 4.

'The Jews call it forced labor. The Jewish drone's life comes to an end.'

'Race defiling in France ... when white women mate with Negroes.' No. 51, December, pp. 5, 8.

*Vol. XIX, 1941*:

'The blessing of Dachau – a Jew "learned how to work in Dachau." ' No. 17, April, p. 6.

'Ghettoization of the Jews.' No. 18, May, p. 7.

Jewish forced labor.'

'The Jew Jossek Pakin was recently sentenced to eight months in prison for leaving the Jewish residential area in Litzmannstadt. He managed to escape, but was recaptured. Now he has received an additional sentence of eight months.' No. 21, May, pp. 2, 6.

'Negro-Jews in New York. Rabbi Matthews, a rabbi of the Negro-Jews in New York.' No. 24, June, p. 2.

'A soldier tours the ghetto.

'Jews among themselves. What the Jew Peine writes to the *Stürmer*. (Egon Israel Peine, Hamburg 13, Beneckestrasse 6)

'... The religious Jew instigates the wars ... If the Aryan reader knew all the vile tricks pulled by the religious Jews, and especially the officials of the Religious Union of Hamburg, he would not believe it because his imagination cannot conceive of such baseness.

'... I hope that my explanations will contribute to opening the eyes of many Aryans to the vileness of the religious Jews ...' No. 35, August, p. 6.

'In the Ostrau County Court (Kreisgericht) there is an accumulation of lawsuits concerned with rulings of descent. Jews no longer wish to be Jews. They aspire to a judgment declaring that one of the parents is Aryan and that, therefore, they are not Jews, but rather half-Jews.' No. 38, September, p. 9.

'Star of David.

'In this way the criminal activity of Jewry can be made still more difficult than it was before. I am convinced that the people will gratefully welcome such a decree.' No. 43, October, p. 6.

'Think about it!

'Who still has compassion for the Jew?

'At a time when German men are bleeding for us to make up for what epochs have done to our German people by kowtowing to the Jews. Compassion? Never!! That is all over!' No. 44, October, p. 1.

'For the knowledgeable person the measure which has led to the reinstatement of the Star of David is the external expression of the recognition among European peoples of the fact that order can be realized in Europe and, beyond that, the whole world only when the Jewish question has been brought to a final solution.' No. 45, November, p. 4.

*Vol. XX, 1942*:

'Entry into the Security Police!

The Jews in the ghetto also have their own security men. Notice the typical flat feet of these Hebrews. The Jew on the right, with the rubber truncheon, is the "head security man." When he is in a bad mood, his racial comrades have nothing to laugh about.'

'Women without identity badges.

The above pictures prove how necessary it was to identify the Hebrews by making them wear the Star of David. Who would recognize at first glance that these women from the Generalgouvernement are Jewesses?'

'A letter to the editor from SS-Sturmmann Karl Bauer: "I'm a poor Yid!" ...' No. 5, January, pp. 4, 6.

'Hungary, too, is fed up with the Jews. Interned or deported – population is satisfied.' No. 11, March, p. 4.

'SS-Unterscharführer Hans Schick ... "The ghettos in the East show that this universal Jewish plague should be exterminated, root and branch, just as one destroys vermin in the animal world ..." '. No. 15, April, p. 6.

'Viennese Jews before departure.' No. 17, April, p. 5.

'Contemptible Jewish swindle in the Protectorate. Jews seek Aryan fathers – "My hubby committed adultery" ("Meine Manne hat Ehebruch getrieben").' No. 29, July, p. 4.

'You know it. If we solve the Jewish question, we will redeem humanity from its millenia of misfortune ... Even if the Jewess puts on the mask of a haggard old woman to rouse sympathy, she is and remains the same Talmudist as her grandchild, who is on trial today because of race defilement and crimes against the war laws. The Jew was a criminal from the very beginning, and will remain a criminal for all time ...

'It is completely inconsequential if the Jew puts on the mask of the aged and impoverished "star-bearer" and wanders through the streets – he is and remains the same scoundrel as his son ...' No. 37, September, p. 4.

*Vol. XXI, 1943*:

'Tabor is free of Jews!

The city of Tabor in the Protectorate of Bohemia and Moravia had been a favorite place of residence for Jews for over three hundred years. However, it has now been reported that Tabor is also *completely* free of Jews. The inhabitants of the city are happy that they are finally rid of the foreign racial

parasites.' No. 3, January, p. 6.
'Jews and venereal diseases.'
'Pornography in the service of Jewish attempts to achieve world domination.'
No. 4, January, pp. 4-5.
'. . . if, indeed, Jewry imagines that it can bring about an international world war in order to exterminate the European races, the result will not be the extermination of the European races, but rather the extermination of Jewry in Europe.' (From a speech by Hitler.) No. 5, January, p. 3.
'The *Stürmer* visits ghettos in the East.
'One must hold one's head in wonder how it was possible that for centuries this scum of humanity was considered by non-Jews to be God's chosen people . . . This Satanic race really has no justification to exist.' No. 19, May, p. 4.
'On the nature of Jewish music.' No. 40, September, p. 2.
*Vol. XXII, 1944*:
'The first ritual murders. Jews admit using Christian blood.' No. 1, January, pp. 4-6.
'The Jews need non-Jewish blood for the matzoth. The blood serves the "salvation of the soul." ' No. 2, January, pp. 3-5.
'The Devil in the guise of a man. (Masaryk) cheered by rabbis. Grand masters of Jewish outlawry received their servant Masaryk.' No. 13, March, pp. 3-5.
'Blond Jewish children . . . The two pictures illustrate how necessary it was to introduce the Star of David into Hungary also. Looking at these children, who could tell that they are Jews, if they did not wear the Star of David or long curls (Peies)?' No. 23, June, p. 3.
'Crazed by the Talmud.
'A Jew who studies the Talmud's instructions for murder throughout his life finally became mentally deranged and ended up in the insane asylum.' No. 25, June, p. 5.

See also a selection of headlines and short excerpts from *Der Stürmer* in Hermann Glaser, *Das Dritte Reich: Anspruch und Wirklichkeit* (Freiburg: Herder Druck, 1963), pp. 29-40.
In contrast to *Der Stürmer* there is evidence that *Mein Kampf* – contrary to popular opinion – was less frequently read. Results of this writer's research project indicate that of a group of 229 former members of various SS formations, 114 had read *Mein Kampf* at one time or another and 115 had not; 39 had read *Mein Kampf* after 1945.
Of a comparative group of 203 veterans of the German Armed Forces, 157 had read *Mein Kampf* at one time or another and 45 had not; 31 had read *Mein Kampf* after 1945. These figures appear to indicate that the indoctrinating effect of *Mein Kampf* as a book – especially within the SS – cannot have been that decisive. One of the reasons that the book was not more frequently read should be primarily sought in the effort it takes to digest the thoughts expressed in it. Steiner and Fahrenberg, *op. cit.*, p. 557.
264. Adolf Hitler and Alfred Rosenberg (eds.), *Nationalsozialistische Monatshefte*.

*Wissenschaftliche Zeitschrift der NSDAP* (München: Franz Eher Verlag, 1931, 1932, 1933).

265. Otto Gohdes MdR., 'Unser Führer,' in *Schulungsbriefe* (Berlin: Reichsschulungsamt der NSDAP und der Deutschen Arbeitsfront, 1933), p. 30.
Alfred Rosenberg, 'Schutzfärbung,' in *ibid.*, p. 31.
Gohdes, 'Parteidisziplin,' in No. 4, *op. cit.*, pp. 46-47.
C. Wehmeyer, 'Der zweite Punkt im Programm der NSDAP,' *ibid.*, pp. 55-56.
Heinrich Härtle, 'Friedrich Nietzsche, der unerbittliche Werter des neunzehnten Jahrhunderts," in Der Reichsorganisationsleiter (ed.), *Der Schulungsbrief, Das zentrale Monatsblatt der NSDAP und Schulungsamt der DAF*. 1937, pp. 290-292, 295-299.

266. *Der Spiegel*, No. 46, November 7, 1966, p. 53. Cp. Gilbert, *op. cit.*, pp. 78, 392-395.
A similar trend of thought was expressed by Hans Frank on November 29, 1945: 'Wenn man bedenkt, daß wir wie Könige lebten und an diese Bestie glaubten! – Lassen Sie sich von niemand erzählen, daß sie nichts gewußt hätten! Jeder ahnte, daß etwas ganz und gar nicht in Ordnung war mit diesem System, auch, wenn wir nicht alle Einzelheiten wußten. Sie wollten es nicht wissen!' *Ibid.*, p. 53.

['To think that we lived like kings and believed in that beast! – Don't let anybody tell you that they had no idea! Everybody sensed that there was something horribly wrong with this system, even if we didn't know all the details. They didn't want to know!']

267. Hannah Arendt, *Eichmann in Jerusalem, op. cit.*, p. 236.
268. According to Robert Weida, intensive investigations have revealed that the refusal to obey a criminal order (such as the execution of innocent persons) had no more serious consequences than demotion or transfer to the frontlines or some other post. It is simply not true that persons who refused to obey a criminal order were summarily executed. The meaning of the continued trials of Nazi criminals is that everyone, most particularly legal, judicial, and police authorities, should realize that a criminal act remains punishable even if it is tolerated or instigated by a ruling party or in the name of the state. Cf. Robert Weida, 'NS-Gewaltverbrechen in polizeilicher Sicht' (Nazi Crimes from the Police Point of View), *Kriminalistik* (Cologne, Germany), No. 20, Vol. VII, 1966, pp. 329-335.
Cp. Richard Egenter *et al.*, 'Die NS-Prozesse. Tatsachen und Betrachtungen,' in Willehad Eckert *et al.* (ed.), *Freiburger Rundbrief* (Freiburg i. Br.), No. 57/60, January 1964, pp. 42-43.
Herbert Jäger, *Verbrechen unter totalitärer Herrschaft: Studien zur nationalistischen Gewaltkriminalität* (Freiburg i. Br.: Walter Verlag, 1967), pp. 62-71, 152-158, 252-258, 290-321. Buchheim, *loc. cit.*, pp. 257-276, 346-380. See also Gilbert, *op. cit.*, pp. 233-234, 235, 237-239, 240.
A rather representative attitude of many men serving in concentration camps,

in destruction commands, and in similar capacities was expressed by Rudolf Höss, the former commandant of Auschwitz: 'Es kam mir überhaupt nicht in den Sinn, daß ich zur Verantwortung gezogen werden würde. Sehen Sie, in Deutschland galt es als selbstverständlich, daß, wenn etwas schiefging, der Mann, der den Auftrag erteilt hatte, verantwortlich war. Deshalb dachte ich nicht daran, daß ich einmal zur Verantwortung gezogen werden würde.' *Ibid.*, p. 244.

['It didn't occur to me at all that I would be held responsible. You see, in Germany it was understood that if something went wrong, then the man who gave the orders was responsible. So I didn't think that I would ever have to answer for it myself.']

269. Kersten, *op. cit.*, p. 184.
270. Cf. Heiber, *op. cit.*, p. 158.
271. Rede des Reichsführers SS auf der Ordensburg Sonthofen, May 5, 1944, GRMA, T-175, R. 155, Fr. 2 685 456.
     Cp. Hitler to Rauschning: 'Die Vorsehung hat mich zu dem größten Befreier der Menschheit vorbestimmt.' Rauschning, *op. cit.*, p. 212.
272. Kersten, *op. cit.*, pp. 189-190.
273. *Ibid.*, p. 189.
274. Cf. *ibid.*, pp. 190, 391-392.
275. Cf. *ibid.*, p. 185.
276. *Ibid.*, p. 187. Cp. Heiber, *op. cit.*, pp. 45-46, 48.
277. On February 24, 1942, Himmler wrote the following to SS-Gruppenführer Oswald Pohl: 'Ich bitte Sie, doch noch einmal nachzuprüfen, wen wir von den Leuten der biologisch-dynamischen Düngungsweise, die sehr zur Anthroposophie neigen, in unseren Reihen haben. Dr. Ley erzählte mir kürzlich, daß bei ihm ein Mann von uns gewesen sei, mit dem er sich 2¹/₂ Stunden unterhalten habe. Dieser Mann sei zu ihm gekommen, um eine Zusammenarbeit zwischen der Forschungsstelle des Reichsführers-SS für biologisch-dynamische Düngung und Dr. Ley herbeizuführen. Ich habe den Eindruck, daß wir hier vielleicht einen solchen Mann, der einen Hof nach der biologisch-dynamischen Düngung leitet, bei uns haben, und daß dieser – wie alle Anthroposophen – das Mauscheln und Agitieren nicht sein lassen kann.
     Zur biologisch-dynamischen Düngung selbst kann ich nur noch einmal sagen: Ich stehe ihr insgesamt als Landwirt sympathisch gegenüber. Ich bin aber der Überzeugung, daß wir sie heute in der jetzigen Ernährungslage niemals einführen können; denn das wäre ein ausgesprochenes Desastre. Ich bin aber dagegen, daß die Menschen aus einer verbesserten Landbauweise eine sektenartige Religion machen, die gepredigt werden muß.' Heiber, *op. cit.*, pp. 89-90.

['I would like to ask you to check once more to determine who in our ranks is among the adherents of the biological-dynamic school of manuring, and has a strong leaning towards anthroposophy. Dr. Ley told me recently that one of our men had been to see him and that he had had a conversation with him for two and a half hours. This man had come to him to bring about a cooperation between the SS-Reichsführer's Office of Research for biological-dynamic manuring and Dr. Ley. I have the impression that we may perhaps have such a man managing a farm according to biological-dynamic manuring, and that he, like all anthroposophists, cannot refrain from agitating and mouthing like a Jew. As to biological-dynamic manuring itself, I can only repeat: As a farmer I am sympathetic to it on the whole. However, I am convinced that during the present food supply situation we could never introduce it since it would be a complete disaster. I am, however, opposed to the idea that people should convert an agricultural improvement into a secretarian-like religion that must be preached.']

278. Kersten, *op. cit.*, pp. 185, 196, 197.
279. Cf. Steiner, *op. cit.*, pp. 59-61.
280. Rauschning, *op. cit.*, p. 232. See also pp. 233-236.
281. Cf. *ibid.*, p. 236.
282. *Ibid.*, pp. 233-234.
283. Cf. *ibid.*, p. 233.
284. Cf. *ibid.*, p. 235.
285. Cf. *ibid.*, p. 237.
286. Cf. *ibid.*
287. *Ibid.*
288. *Ibid.* Cp. also Louis Pauwels, Jacques Bergier, *Aufbruch ins dritte Jahrtausend. Von der Zukunft der phantastischen Vernunft* (Bern: Scherz Verlag, 1962), pp. 383-384.
289. Rauschning, *op. cit.*, p. 238. See also Pauwels, Bergier, *op. cit.*, pp. 337-338, and Erhard Klöss (ed.), *Reden des Führers* (München: Deutscher Taschenbuch Verlag, 1967), pp. 316-318, 323.
290. Cf. Trevor-Roper, *op. cit.*, p. 138. Cp. Bronder, *op. cit.*, p. 252.
291. Cf. *ibid.*; cp. Pauwels, Bergier, *op cit.*, pp. 385-393. See also W. Schellenberg, *Memoiren* (Köln: Verlag für Politik und Wirtschaft, 1959), p. 124.
292. Cf. *ibid.*, pp. 39-40. Cp. also Bronder, *op. cit.*, p. 252. One of the leading members of this consistory was the former Obergruppenführer and General of the Waffen-SS, Karl Wolff.
Cf. also Heiber, *op. cit.*, pp. 64-65.
293. Cf. Rauschning, *op. cit.*, pp. 50, 53, 57.
294. Cf. *ibid.*, p. 50
295. Cf. *ibid.*, p. 51.
296. Cf. *ibid.*, p. 53. Cp. Hitler, *Mein Kampf*, Vol. II, *op. cit.*, pp. 71-72, 99. Cp. Gilbert, *op. cit.*, pp. 71-78, 278.
297. Cf. *ibid.*, pp. 130, 133-134, 194, 262. See especially Rauschning, *op. cit.*, p. 57. Cp. Pauwels, Bergier, *op. cit.*, p. 391.
So, for example, the former chief of Himmler's personal staff, Karl Wolff, is still wearing around his neck a silver hammer (Mjöllnir) of the God Thor,

later renamed Donar. This fact was revealed during an interview with Wolff at Stadelheim prison, in Munich, on December 7, 1964.

298. Rauschning, *op. cit.*, p. 212. Cf. T. Ravenscroft, *The Spear of Destiny*. New York: Bantam Books, 1974, *passim*.

299. *Ibid.*, p. 228. Cf. also pp. 224, 227. Cp. T. Ravenscroft, *op. cit.*, pp. 243-251. Hitler explicates the basis for his religious concept even further by declaring to Rauschning: 'Die beiden Spielarten werden sich sehr schnell von einander fort in entgegengesetzter Richtung entwickeln. Die eine wird unter den Menschen heruntersinken, die andere wird weiter über den heutigen Menschen hinaussteigen. Gottmensch und Massentier möchte ich die beiden Spielarten nennen ...
'Ja, der Mensch ist etwas, das überwunden werden muß, Nietzsche hat davon auf seine Weise allerdings bereits etwas gewußt. Er hat den Übermenschen sogar schon als eine biologische neue Spielart gesehen. Obwohl das bei ihm noch schwankt. Der Mensch wird Gott, das ist der einfache Sinn. Der Mensch ist der werdende Gott.' Rauschning, *op. cit.*, pp. 231-232.

---

['Both varieties will develop very rapidly in opposite directions. The one will sink below the human level, and the other will rise far above the human beings of today. I should like to call the two varieties God-man (Gottmensch) and mass-animal (Massentier) ...
'Yes, man is something which must be overcome. Nietzsche, in his own way, already realized something of this. He even saw the superman as a new biological variety, although he still vacillates about this. Man becomes God – that is the simple sense of it. Man is God in the process of becoming.']

300. Adolf Hitler, *Mein Kampf*, Vol. I, *op. cit.*, p. 301. See also *ibid.*, pp. 300, 155, 338, 121, 123, 264.
The religious anti-Semitism as compared to the one based on racial doctrines was in principle more conciliatory. This was demonstrated in Johann Andrea Eisenmenger's Professors der Orientalischen Sprache bey der Universität Heydelberg Entdecktes Judenthum Oder Wahrhaffter Bericht welchgestalt Die verstockte Juden die Hochheilige Drey-Einigkeit / Gott Vater / Sohn und Heil. Geist / erschrecklicher Weise Lästern und verunehren / die Heil. Mutter Christi verschmähen / das Neue Testament / die Evangelisten und Aposteln / die Christliche Religion spöttisch durch Ziehen / und die gantze Christenheit auff das äusserste verachten und verfluchen; etc.
Mit Seiner Königl. Majestät in Preussen Allergnädigsten Special Privilegio. (in 2 Theilen) Gedruckt zu Königsberg in Preussen / im Jahre nach Christi Geburt 1711. Friedrich von Gottes Gnaden König in Preussen, etc.
The following passage can serve as an illustration: 'Objewohl sehr viel Juden hin und wieder unter den Christen wohnen / so geschieht es doch gar selten / dass sich jemand von denselben zu dem Christlichen Glauben bekehre / wie solches die Erfahrung bezeuget. Ja es seynd auch unter denjenigen wenigen / welche zu uns treten / bisweilen so übel gerathene und bosshaffte Men-

schen / wann sie eine Zeit lang sich bey unss auffgehalten haben / dass sie
wieder in ihre vorige Blindheit fallen / und den Jüdischen Irrthum und falschen Glauben wiederum annehmen / welches mit genugsamen exampeln /
wann es die Noth erforderte erwiesen werden könnte. Dass aber so gar wenige
Juden den gecreutzigten Jesum vor den wahren Messiam / Heyland Selig-
macher erkennen / und an denselben glauben wollen / dessen seynd viele
Ursachen / welche sie davon abhalten und verhindern / welche zum Theil
von den Juden / theils aber von den Christen selbst herrühren.' *Op. cit.*,
XVIII Capitel, p. 980.

---

['Although very many Jews live among the Christians from time to time, it
happens very seldom that one of them converts to the Christian faith, as experience testifies. Indeed, even among those few who convert there are sometimes such ill-disposed and evil people that after they have stayed with us for a
while, they again fall into their earlier blindness and return to the Jewish er-
rors and once more embrace the false faith. There are sufficient examples to
prove this fact if the need to do so should arise. There are many reasons – some
deriving from the Jews, and others from the Christians themselves – that prevent
all but a few Jews from recognizing the crucified Jesus as the true Messiah
and Savior and from believing in him.']

Eisenmenger clearly advocates the solution of the Jewish problem through
conversion and assimilation, even if in a tone of prophylactic scepticism. In
contrast to him and to other spokesmen of his time, Hitler and the NS racists
asserted with irreconcilable finality: 'In ihnen (jüdisch-deutschen Mischlingen)
ist das deutsche Blut mit fremdem zusammengeflossen, mit dem es sich nicht
zu klarer Mischung vereinigen kann. Innere Zerspaltenheit ist das traurige
Merkmal solcher Mischwesen, und ihr deutsches Blut ist dem deutschen Volkskörper verloren. Verbindung von deutschem mit artfremden Blute ist Rassenschande! –' Or in other terms: 'Was euch nicht angehört, müsset ihr meiden;
Was euch das Inn're stört, dürft ihr nicht leiden.' Kurt Schrey, *Du und Dein
Volk* (München: Deutscher Volksverlag GmbH., 1936), p. 24.

---

['In them (persons of mixed Jewish-German blood) German blood has become
mixed with foreign, and the two cannot unite in a pure mixture. A state of
internal disunity is the sad characteristic of such mixed beings, and their
German blood is lost to the German folk-body (Volkskörper). The blending
of German and alien blood is race defilement! – Or in other terms: "What is
not a part of you, you must avoid; what disturbs your inner existence, you
must not tolerate." ']

301. Cf. Joseph Wolf, *Martin Bormann, Hitlers Schatten* (Gütersloh: Sigbert Mohn
Verlag, 1962), p. 176a and F. Steiner, *Die Armee der Geächteten, op. cit.*,
p. 132. Cp. also Kersten, *op. cit.*, p. 186.
According to results of a sociological investigation of former members of the
SS conducted by this writer from a random sample of 228 members of the

'Waffen-SS' and other non-combat SS formations, 100 (43.86 %) declared to be Protestants, 71 (31.14 %) expressed identification with the 'gottgläubig,' and 57 (25.0 %) declared to be Catholics. Steiner and Fahrenberg, *loc. cit.*, p. 555.

302. Kersten, *op. cit.*, p. 186.
303. H. R. Trevor-Roper, *Hitler's letzte Tage* (Frankfurt/M.: Ullstein Bücher, 1965), p. 65.
304. Cf. Steiner, *op. cit.*, p. 132.
305. Kersten, *op. cit.*, p. 186. Cf. also Rede des Reichsführers SS auf der Ordensburg Sonthofen, May 5, 1944, GRMA, T-175, R. 92, Fr. 2 613 495.
306. *Ibid.*, R. 155, Fr. 2 685 455.
307. *Ibid.*, R. 92, Fr. 2 613 496. Cp. Himmler's address to the Gruppenführer in Posen on October 4, 1943, in IMT, Vol. XXIX, *op. cit.*, pp. 147-148, PS-1919.
308. Schrey states: 'Dem englischen Volke war durch seine Insellage die staatliche Einheit sehr erleichtert. Ein starker Staatswille faßte alle Kräfte zusammen und bestimmte den Gang der englischen Geschichte. Seit den Jahrhunderten der Welteroberung, als Wagemutige aus allen Ländern Europas in fremde Weltteile zogen, begleitete jeden englischen Auswanderer der Schutz und die Hilfe seines mächtigen Vaterlandes. Und wo in aller Welt der Engländer siedelte, da gründete er eine Zelle seines Mutterstaates. Der Heimat ging sein Blut nicht verloren; es begann nur in einem größeren Körper zu kreisen. So entstand das britische Weltreich, dessen Herz die britische Insel bis heute geblieben ist.' Schrey, *op. cit.*, p. 40.

――――

['Its insular position made it much easier for the English people to attain political unity. A strong will towards statehood (Staatswille) brought all forces together and determined the course of English history. Since the centuries of world conquest, when daring men from all countries of Europe ventured into unknown parts of the world, the protection and help of his powerful fatherland has accompanied every English emigrant. And wherever in the wide world an Englishman settled, there he would establish a cell of his mother state. English blood was not lost to his home country; it merely began to circulate within a larger body. Thus the British Empire was formed and the British Isles remain its heart to this very day.']

This passage remained unaltered even while Germany was at war with England.
309. Hitler's trend of thought concerning his fear and uncertainty of the role of the Jewish people we find perhaps best expressed in the following passages of *Mein Kampf:* 'Als ich so durch lange Perioden menschlicher Geschichte das Wirken des jüdischen Volkes forschend betrachtete, stieg mir plötzlich die bange Frage auf, ob nicht doch vielleicht das unerforschliche Schicksal aus Gründen, die uns armseligen Menschen unbekannt, den Endsieg dieses kleinen Volkes in ewig unabänderlichem Beschlusse wünsche.
'Sollte diesem Volke, das ewig nur dieser Erde lebt, die Erde als Belohnung zugesprochen sein? Haben wir ein objektives Recht zum Kampf für unsere

Selbsterhaltung, oder ist auch dies nur subjektiv in uns begründet?' Hitler
quickly decides which course he wants to follow: . . . 'Siegt der Jude mit Hilfe
seines marxistischen Glaubensbekenntnisses über die Völker dieser Welt, dann
wird seine Krone der Totenkranz der Menschheit sein, dann wird dieser Planet
wieder wie einst vor Jahrmillionen menschenleer durch den Äther ziehen. . . .
'So glaube ich heute im Sinne des allmächtigen Schöpfers zu handeln: *Indem
ich mich des Juden erwehre, kämpfe ich für das Werk des Herrn.*' Hitler, *Mein
Kampf*, Vol. I, *op. cit.*, p. 73.

---

['While thus examining the working of the Jewish people over long periods of
history, the anxious question suddenly occurred to me whether perhaps in-
scrutable destiny, for reasons unknown to us poor mortals, had not unalterably
decreed the final victory of this little race?
'Had this people, which always had lived only for this world, been promised the
world as a reward?
'Have we the objective right to fight for our self-preservation, or is this rooted
in us only subjectively?' Hitler quickly decides which course to follow: 'If,
with the help of the Marxian creed, the Jew conquers the nations of this world,
his crown will become the funeral wreath of humanity, and once again this
planet, empty of mankind, will move through the ether as it did thousands of
years ago. . . .
'Therefore, I believe today that I am acting in the spirit of the Almighty
Creator: *By warding off the Jews I am fighting for the Lord's work.*']

Rauschning comments upon Hitler's anti-Judaic attitude as follows: 'Für Hitler
ist der Jude das schlechthin Böse. . . . Mag man dafür Erklärungen in seinem
persönlichen Erleben suchen, mag man Hitler selbst als nach den Nürnberger
Rassengesetzen nicht arisch bezeichnen, die Nachhaltigkeit seines Antisemitismus wird erst durch die mythische Übersteigerung des Juden zu einem ewigen
Prototyp der Menschen verständlich. . . . Israel, das historische Volk des geistigen Gottes, musste zum neuen deutschen auserwählten Volk, dem Volk der
Gottnatur, des neuen Baals, des Stiers der Fruchtbarkeit in abgründiger Feind-
schaft stehen. Ein Gott schloss den anderen aus. Hinter dem Hitler'schen Antisemitismus wird wirklich ein Kampf der Götter sichtbar. . . . ging nicht das
ganze, verhasste Christentum, der Erlöserglaube, die Moral, das Gewissen, der
Begriff der Sünde auf das Judentum zurück?' Rauschning, *op. cit.*, pp. 221-222.

---

['For him the Jew is evil incarnate. . . . Explanations of this may be sought in
his personal experience, and, incidentally, it may be that under the Nuremberg
legislation Hitler himself is not entitled to be classified as "Aryan"; but the
intensity of his anti-Semitism can only be explained by his inflation of the
Jew into a mythical prototype of humanity. . . . Israel, the historic people of
the spiritual God, cannot but be the irreconcilable enemy of the new, the
German, Chosen People, the people of divine nature, of the new Baal, of the
bull of fertility. One god excluded the other. At the back of Hitler's anti-

Semitism there is revealed an actual war of the gods. ... was not the whole, hated doctrine of Christianity, with its faith in redemption, its moral code, its conscience, its conception of original sin, the outcome of Judaism?']

310. Rede des Reichsführers SS auf der Ordensburg Sonthofen, May 5, 1944, GRMA, T-175, R. 92, Fr. 2 613 469.
311. *Ibid.*, Fr. 2 613 470.
312. The honorary dagger usually bore the inscription: 'In herzlicher Kameradschaft H.H.' This information was received by this writer during an interview with a former Röhm purge participant (name withheld).
313. In one of the numerous interviews with the former Obergruppenführer and General of the Waffen-SS Karl Wolff, this writer was informed that the only possession kept by Wolff on his flight to Germany in 1945 was hidden under his coat. It was the honorary sword bestowed upon him by Himmler.
314. Rede Himmlers bei der SS-Gruppenführertagung in Posen am 4. Oktober 1943, op. cit., p. 149. Cp. also Hitler's statement: '... über allem wird es den neuen Hochadel geben, die besonders verdienten und besonders verantwortlichen Führerpersönlichkeiten. ... Und ich denke in diesem einen Punkt ganz wie Darré und Himmler. ... Wir selbst aber werden uns freimachen von allen humanen und wissenschaftlichen Vorurteilen. Und darum werde ich in den Junkerschulen, die ich gründen werde und durch die alle künftigen Angehörigen unseres Herrenstandes gehen werden, das Evangelium vom freien Menschen verkünden lassen.' Rauschning, *op. cit.*, pp. 46, 47.

['And over all of these will stand the new high aristocracy, the most deserving and the most responsible leaders (Führer-personalities). ... On this point I entirely agree with Darré and Himmler. ... We ourselves, on the other hand, shall shake off all humane and scientific prejudices. This is why, in the *Junker* schools I shall found for the future members of our *Herren*-class, I shall allow the gospel of the free man to be preached ...']

315. Worte des Reichsführers SS bei der Eheweihe des SS Sturmbannführers Deutsch, April 2, 1936, see GRMA, T-175, R. 89, Frs. 2 611 595-2 611 596.
316. Rede des Reichsführers SS anläßlich der Gruppenführerbesprechung in Dachau, November 8, 1936, see GRMA, T-175, R. 89, Fr. 2 611 728.
317. *Ibid.*, Fr. 2 611 719.
318. See SS Oberabschnitt West, Die Gestaltung der Feste im Jahres- und Lebenslauf in der SS Familie, 193/6/, p. 76.
319. See *ibid*.
320. See Herbert O. Gille in *Wiking-Ruf*, No. 3, Hameln, January, 1952, p. 15. On December 16, 1962, this writer was invited to attend what can be described as a combination of a 'Julfest' and Christmas celebration which took place in Munich at the Bürgerbräukeller. The participants were former members of the 'Waffen-SS' and their wives and children, altogether about 150 persons. The group was headed by the former Obergruppenführer and General of the

'Waffen-SS' Felix Steiner. Next to him were seated eight former senior officers and those having attained a higher social status during their civilian career after the war. Their wives and children were seated at the same table. All men present were members of the 'HIAG' and by and large occupied either leading positions in German business or industry or could be placed in the middle and lower-middle social class. As far as it could be ascertained the majority of the men had been or still were 'gottgläubig,' but were now nominally affiliated with a Christian denomination, mostly for pragmatic reasons, so that their children would belong to a recognized religious community. A Protestant minister who had also been invited was unable to attend because of 'pressing official business.'

When General Steiner arrived at the meeting place and when he departed, all present – with the exception of some women and children – stood up upon command. As this gathering demonstrated, official holidays introduced by the SS creed were still observed by those present. The religious part of the festivity began with the lighting of twelve candles. This act was performed by two former SS officers who simultaneously recited verses. So, for example, it was said: 'This candle is lit for the mothers, . . . for the widows of the community, . . . for our wives, . . . for the youth and children, . . . for those killed in action, . . . for those who died in hatred and disgrace, . . . for the imprisoned, . . . for all comrades in Europe and in the world, . . . for the German nation, . . .' Then all persons sang a song entitled 'High night of the clear stars' (Hohe Nacht der klaren Sterne), in which some elements of the creed of the 'gottgläubig' are symbolically expressed.

During this festivity a former non-commissioned SS officer commented upon the events taking place, explaining to this writer in detail the meaning of these religious rituals, but soon was discredited by General Steiner and some other leaders present as an 'old criminal talking out of his head, repeating "dummes Zeug des schlampigen Romantikers Himmler".' The informant also stated that Christmas-nights (Weihnachten) had nothing to do with the birth of Christ, but rather they were consecrated nights (Rauh- und Reifnächte) because of the solstice and therefore were regarded as holy. The presented ceremonies gave the impression of a pronounced mother cult. The succeeding portions of the evening were spent in the recital of poems, short speeches, the singing of military songs ('Burschen heraus'), and social activities of general nature.

321. The 'Jul-Leuchter' and similar ceramics were manufactured in a porcelain factory located in Allach-Munich which was purchased by the 'Persönlichen Stab Reichsführer SS' in 1936. See E. Georg, 'Die wirtschaftlichen Unternehmungen der SS,' *Vierteljahreshefte für Zeitgeschichte* (Stuttgart, 1963), No. 7, pp. 16-17.

322. Cf. Rede des Reichsführers SS anläßlich der Gruppenführerbesprechung in Dachau, November 8, 1936, *op. cit.*, Fr. 2 611 729.

323. Der Reichsführer SS/SS Hauptamt, Rassenpolitik (Berlin, 194/3), p. 78.

324. Rede Himmlers bei der SS-Gruppenführertagung in Posen am 4. Oktober

1943, *op. cit.*, p. 142.

325. Rudolf Höss gives a clear account of this conversion process to Gilbert. See Gilbert, *op. cit.*, p. 261. Yet it seems that as easily as members of the SS had converted to the creed of the 'gottgläubig,' they have also reconverted to their former belief. More well-known examples are: Gauleiter and SS-Obergruppenführer Albert Forster of Danzig, Generalgouverneur of Poland and Reichsleiter Hans Frank, SS-Obersturmbannführer Rudolf Höss, and SS-Obergruppenführer and chief of the SS Wirtschafts- und Verwaltungshauptamt (WVHA) Oswald Pohl. Cf. Bronder, *op. cit.*, p. 257.

In a letter to 'Mutz' of April, 1947, Rudolf Höss writes: 'Es war ein schweres Ringen. Doch ich habe meinen Glauben an meinen Gott wiedergefunden.'

['It was a hard struggle. Still, I have recovered my belief in my God.']

The Höss file, Institut für Zeitgeschichte, Munich, *op. cit.*, p. 5.

326. In a sworn statement of January 13, 1948; the former Obersturmbannführer der 'Waffen-SS,' Richard Schulze, stated: 'Allen katholischen Junkern war es selbstverständlich gestattet, regelmäßig in Uniform am katholischen Gottesdienst der Tölzer Kirchen teilzunehmen. Verschiedentlich waren auch evangelische Pfarrer aus dem Südosten Europas als Offiziersbewerber der Reserve nach Tölz kommandiert.' In Steiner, *op. cit.*, p. 132. Schulze served in the Junkerschule Tölz in 1944 as instructor of officer candidates.

['All Catholic junkers, of course, were permitted to participate regularly in the Catholic services of the Tölz churches while wearing their uniform. At various times Protestant ministers from southeastern Europe were also posted to Tölz as officer candidates of the reserve.']

327. Although most members of the SS had become estranged from their faith, only a relatively small percentage chose to seek their spiritual salvation in the new creed. In 1937 a total of 15,809 members had left their church, and in 1938, 26,661.

### RELIGIOUS AFFILIATION OF SS MEMBERS

| | 1937 Evangelical | % | 1938 | % | 1937 Catholic | % | 1938 | % |
|---|---|---|---|---|---|---|---|---|
| Allgem. SS | 104,364 | 62.2 | 116,192 | 54.2 | 36,043 | 21.4 | 50,984 | 23.7 |
| SS VT | 4,248 | 37.6 | 4,265 | 30.0 | 2,382 | 21.2 | 2,321 | 16.4 |
| SS TV | 1,919 | 40.1 | 2,211 | 24.1 | 385 | 8.1 | 632 | 6.9 |
| TOTAL | 110,531 | 60.0 | 122,668 | 51.4 | 38,810 | 21.1 | 53,937 | 22.6 |

| | *1937 gottgläubig* | % | *1938* | % | *1937 Others* | % | *1938* | % |
|---|---|---|---|---|---|---|---|---|
| Allgem. SS | 27,242 | 16.2 | 47,053 | 21.9 | 390 | 0.2 | 524 | 0.2 |
| SS VT | 4,656 | 41.1 | 7,648 | 53.6 | 13 | 0.1 | – | – |
| SS TV | 2,471 | 51.7 | 6,329 | 69.0 | 4 | 0.1 | – | – |
| TOTAL | 34,369 | 18.7 | 61,030 | 25.8 | 407 | 0.2 | 524 | 0.2 |

| | *1937 Total* | % | *1938 Total* | % |
|---|---|---|---|---|
| Allgem. SS | 168,039 | 100 | 214,753 | 100 |
| SS VT | 11,299 | 100 | 14,234 | 100 |
| SS TV | 4,779 | 100 | 9,172 | 100 |
| TOTAL | 184,177 | 100 | 238,159 | 100 |

Figures compiled from *Statistisches Jahrbuch der Schutzstaffel der NSDAP 1937, op. cit.*, p. 79, and *Statistisches Jahrbuch der Schutzstaffel der NSDAP 1938, op. cit.*, pp. 99-100. See Appendix XII. See also footnote 301. Cp. Steiner, *op. cit.*, p. 263. Steiner states: 'Der Anteil der Konfessionen und derjenige der "Gottgläubigen" innerhalb der Waffen-SS entsprach dem Volksdurchschnitt: Über 80 % gehörten also einer Konfession an. ... Der Generaloberst der Waffen-SS, Sepp Dietrich, ist heute noch praktizierender Christ katholischer Konfession; der Verfasser dieses Buches bekennt sich seit jeher zur evangelischen Religionsgemeinschaft.' *Ibid.*

['The proportion professing a religion and the proportion of "gottgläubig" within the Waffen-SS corresponded to that of the German people as a whole. Thus over eighty percent belonged to a religion ... The Generaloberst (Colonel-General) of the Waffen-SS, Sepp Dietrich, is still a practicing Catholic today; the author of this book has always claimed membership in the Protestant religious community.']

However, Felix Steiner fails to explain that the creed of the 'gottgläubig' differs considerably from a traditional Christian or Jewish faith and that it is an expression of a legitimized belief system based on Germanic paganism. So, for example, Eichmann refused the last rites of a Protestant minister prior to his execution in Jerusalem on May 31, 1962. He claimed to be 'gottgläubig' and not a Christian. His last words were: 'After a short while, gentlemen, we shall meet again. Such is the fate of all men ....' Arendt, *Eichmann in Jerusalem, op. cit.*, p. 230.

328. Cf. Eckart, *op. cit., passim.* Cf. also Strasser, *Mein Kampf, eine politische Autobiographie* (Frankfurt/M.: Heinrich Heine Verlag, 1969), pp. 37-82.

329. Cited in Schrey, *op. cit.*, p. 23.

330. Cp. Elizabeth Nottingham, *Religion and Society* (New York: Random House,

1954), *passim.* See also Steiner and Fahrenberg, *loc. cit.*, pp. 555-556; 559-562.
331. Cf. Thomas Luckmann, *The Invisible Religion* (New York: The Macmillan Company, 1967), p. 67.
332. Cf. Morris Janowitz, 'Soziale Schichtung und Mobilität in Westdeutschland,' *Kölner Zeitschrift für Soziologie und Sozialpsychologie,* No. 10, 1958, pp. 32-33.
333. See Appendix VI. Cf. Affidavits SS-67 and -70, IMT, Vol. XLII, *op. cit.*, pp. 563-565, pp. 573-620. See also Jäger, *op. cit.*, summary of Chpt. II: 'Auch die zentrale Stelle in Ludwigsburg ist bei ihren Ermittlungen zu dem Ergebnis gelangt, daß eine Schädigung an Leib und Leben als sichere oder doch höchstwahrscheinliche Folge der Nichtausführung eines verbrecherischen Befehls mindestens generell auszuschließen ist.'

['In the course of its research, the central office in Ludwigsburg also came to the conclusion that, at least generally, a person did not incur any certain or probable danger to life and limb as a result of failure to carry out a criminal order.']

334. Cf. Arendt, *op. cit.*, pp. 95, 198-199. See Höss, *op. cit.*, pp. 158-159.
335. Statements to this effect were made to this writer by the generals Steiner, Bittrich, Wolff, and others.
336. Cp. Arendt, *op. cit.*, pp. 13-14, 93.
337. This was done in the form of promotions, decorations, appointments, etc. Cp. also *ibid.*, pp. 18-19. See also Affidavit SS-70, *op. cit.*, pp. 573-620.
338. Affidavit by Blobel, June 18, 1947, No. - 3947, in Hilberg, *op. cit.*, p. 255. Cp. Arendt, *op. cit.*, p. 212, and Höss, *op. cit.*, pp. 161-162.
339. In his unpublished autobiographical notes Kaltenbrunner writes: 'Mein Ziel war, in Österreich eine, der Volksmeinung bei Wahlen entsprechende, demokratische Regierung, die wirtschaftlich engen Anschluß an das Reich zu suchen hätte, herbeizuführen und der österreichischen Individualität weiten Raum zu lassen. Wien sollte wieder Kristallisationspunkt altösterreichischer Nachfolgestaaten werden und zur Stabilisierung wirtschaftlicher Erfordernisse in enger Fühlung mit dem Reich stehen' (p. 8). See Appendix XVI.

['My goal in Austria was to bring about a democratic government, in accordance with the will of the people as expressed by elections, that would seek a close economic tie with the Reich, and to allow Austrian individuality ample play. Vienna was once more to become the point of crystallization for the former Austrian states and to maintain a close relationship with the Reich to stabilize economic exigencies.']

340. In a conversation with the president of the German Federal Republic, Dr. Heinrich Lübke, in Bonn on July 21, 1965, this writer was told that '... es gab ja in Deutschland nur eine Handvoll Nazis.' Cp. Arendt, *op. cit.*, p. 15.

['... there were, indeed, only a handful of Nazis in Germany.']

341. So Hitler declared in Nuremberg on September 11, 1935: 'Unsere Gegner haben 15 Jahre Zeit gehabt und vordem zusammen schon mehr als 50 Jahre, um ihre Fähigkeit zu beweisen. Sie haben Deutschland moralisch, politisch und wirtschaftlich verkommen lassen. Wir haben mit ihnen daher überhaupt nicht mehr zu sprechen. Wir besitzen die Gewalt, und wir behalten sie, und wir werden nicht dulden, daß irgend jemand versucht, gegen diese Gewalt etwas zu organisieren, sondern wir werden jede Erscheinung treffen in dem Augenblick, in dem sie sich ankündigt!' *Die Reden Hitlers am Parteitag der Freiheit 1935, op. cit.,* p. 14.

   _____
   ['Our opponents have had fifteen years – and before that, more than fifty years altogether – to prove their competence. They have let Germany decay morally, politically, and economically. Hence we have no reason whatsoever to speak to them any further. We possess the power and we will keep it, and we will not tolerate anybody attempting to organize against that power but we will counter every such endeavor in the very moment in which it becomes apparent!']

342. Attempts made by this writer to introduce innovations to this effect were frequently frustrated by responsible authorities. See Stephan Quensel and John M. Steiner, 'Neue Wege kriminologischer Zusammenarbeit,' *Monatsschrift für Kriminologie und Strafrechtsreform.* Vol. XLVIII, No. 1 (January, 1965), pp. 41-44. Also cp. Steiner *et al.,* 'Group-Counseling im Erwachsenenvollzug,' *ibid.,* Vol. XLIX, No. 4 (July, 1966), pp. 160-172.

343. Arendt, *op. cit.,* p. 231. Although there may have been 'banal individuals,' who were perpetrators of evil, it is hardly appropriate to call evil 'banal' in the face of the suffering endured by the victims of NS acts of aggression. In using, as the subtitle of her book, *A Report on the Banality of Evil,* Arendt seems to succumb to the very idea the NS Regime perpetrated: that of making destruction and cruelty so ordinary that people would become accustomed to it as an acceptable and necessary everyday occurrence.

344. Karl O. Paetel, 'The Black Order: A Survey of the Literature on the SS,' *The Wiener Library Bulletin,* XII, Nos. 3-4 (London, 1959), p. 35. See also G. Reitlinger, *The SS – Alibi of a Nation,* 1922-1945 (New York: Viking Press, 1957), *passim;* Robert M. Kempner, *SS im Kreuzverhör* (München: Rütten and Loening Verlag, 1964), *passim.*

345. Cf. Herbert Jäger, *op. cit.,* see Chpts. 2, 3, 4. Cp. Affidavit SS-70, *op. cit.,* pp. 573-620.

346. According to an affidavit by August Harbaum (Stubaf., chief of WVHA A-V-4) the total number of personnel in concentration camps to July 1, 1940, was 61,035. See *SS Statistik im Bundesarchiv R 49* (Rkf. d. Fdtv. – Stabshauptamt) No. 19. In March 1942, there were about 19,000 members of the 'Waffen-SS' in concentration camps serving as guard units and as camp staff. In April 1945, there were about 30,000-35,000 members of the 'Waffen-SS,' including camp personnel, serving in concentration camps. Thus, between

March 1942, and April 1945, about 45,000 members of the 'Waffen-SS' served in concentration camps at one time or another. Statement made on March 19, 1946, D-750. These documents were made available to this writer by the Institut für Zeitgeschichte, Munich. Cp. Hilberg, *op. cit.*, p. 576. Cf. also Document SS-35, in IMT, Vol. XLII, *op. cit.*, pp. 529-531.

347. Cf. Stein, *The Waffen-SS, op. cit.*, p. 259. Cp. Broszat, 'Nationalsozialistische Konzentrationslager 1933-1945,' in Buchheim *et al., op. cit.*, pp. 99-100; Höss, *op. cit.*, 'Reichsführer-SS (RFSS) Heinrich Himmler,' p. 6.

348. Cf. *ibid.*, 'Inspekteur der KL SS-Gruppenführer Richard Glücks', p. 2. See also Hilberg, *op. cit.*, pp. 556-559.

349. See *ibid.*, Cf. Stein, *op. cit.*, pp. 260-261; Hans Buchheim, *SS und Polizei im NS-Staat* (Duisdorf bei Bonn: Selbstverlag der Studiengesellschaft für Zeitprobleme, 1964), pp. 215-217; Hans Buchheim, *Die SS – Das Herrschaftsinstrument, op. cit.*, pp. 248-253; Broszat, 1933-1945, *op. cit.*, pp. 100-103. Cp. Höss, *op. cit.*, 'Der Chef des SS-Wirtschafts-Verwaltungs-Hauptamtes (WVHA) SS-Obengruppenführer Oswald Pohl,' pp. 2-6.

350. Cf. *Die Organisation der NSDAP, 1943, op. cit.*, p. 431. Cp. Stein, *op. cit.*, p. 261; Steiner, *Die Armee der Geächteten, op. cit.*, p. 118 (footnote); Reitlinger, *op. cit.*, pp. 262-264; Höss, *op. cit.*, 'Lagerordnung für die Konzentrationslager,' p. 129.

351. Cf. *ibid*, pp. 128-129; Stein, *op. cit.*, p. 261.

352. Cf. Höss's evaluation and description of SS leaders associated with or serving in concentration camps, in which he gives a detailed account of their background, promotion, experience, attitude, and behavior. See his unpublished autobiographical notes, *op. cit.*, pp. 1-6, 12-30, 140-181. Cp. Reitlinger, *op. cit.*, p. 266.

During the last war years this writer had the opportunity (in the KL Blechhammer at Ehrenforst, Upper-Silesia) to witness the replacement of younger camp guard personnel by men of older generations. Especially during the period between December 1944, and February 1945, an increased employ of Ukrainian, Serbian, Norwegian, and other Volksdeutsche, who had been recruited into the SS, could be noticed. Some of them hardly mastered the German language. During the final stage of concentration camps, specifically during death marches, in some cases German inmates were clad in SS uniforms and ordered to serve as guards.

353. Cf. Stein, *op. cit.*, p. 262. Höss describes such a case in point: 'In 1938 SS-Obersturmbannführer Friedrich Hartjenstein was transferred from the Wehrmacht to the Death's Head Units and became the commander of a company in the concentration camp Sachsenhausen. From 1941 to 1942 he served in Eicke's Death's Head Division, but was relieved of his duty in the same year because of incompetence, and transferred to Auschwitz II, where he first served as commander of the guard detachment and later became commandant of Auschwitz-Birkenau. From May, 1944 to January, 1945 Hartjenstein was commandant of the concentration camp Natzweiler before the dissatisfied Oswald

Pohl released him again for duty at the front. 'See Höss's unpublished autobiographical notes, *op. cit.*, 'SS-Obersturmbannführer Friedrich Hartjenstein,' pp. 1-2. Cp. *War Crime Trials,* Vol. V: *The Natzweiler Trial* (London, 1949), pp. 128-130. Cf. Höss, *op. cit.*, p. 112. See also John M. Steiner and Jochen Fahrenberg, 'The Marks of Authoritarian Attitude in Former Members of the SS and the Armed Forces', *op. cit.*, pp. 351-362.

354. See 'Ansprache Himmlers an das Offizierskorps der Leibstandarte SS "Adolf Hitler" am 7. September 1940,' in IMT, *op. cit.*, p. 104, PS-1918.

355. Cp. Höss, *op. cit.*, pp. 162-163, 166, 172-173. See also Broszat, *op. cit.*, pp. 133-144.

The liberalization of conditions did not apply to 'Arbeits-Erziehungslager' (AEL) which had come into existence on May 28, 1944, constituting a category of camps which have received little attention in professional literature. Generally they were much more severe than other slave labor camps. The inmates had to work under direct and continued supervision of SS personnel who were usually armed with whips and similar weapons which they did not hesitate to use. During the dissolution of concentration camps in 1945, the inmates were frequently shot by their guards. Cp. *ibid.*, p. 121.

356. See editorial in *Der Freiwillige,* Vol. XIII, No. 7, July 1967, pp. 14-15. Cf. also Allan Dulles-Gero S. von Gaevernitz, *Unternehmen 'Sunrise': Die geheime Geschichte des Kriegsendes in Italien* (Düsseldorf: Econ-Verlag, 1967), *passim.*

357. The existence of a bias for the 'Waffen-SS' was already emphasized by Himmler on September 7, 1940: 'Ich kann ja nicht nur auf den – jetzt, bitte, werden Sie nicht eingebildet, auf den schönsten Teil, den ich in der SS habe, weil er der positivste ist, das Handwerk, was Sie betreiben, das positivste und männlichste ist, ich kann nicht nur nach dem, sondern ich muß immer die gesamte SS sehen. . . . Denn leben wird die Waffen-SS nur dann, wenn die Gesamt-SS lebt.'

---

['Indeed, I cannot look at just the most beautiful part I have in the SS – and please, do not become conceited – the most beautiful because it is the most positive trade, because the work you perform is the most positive and masculine. I cannot judge only according to that, but rather must always see the SS as a whole . . . For the Waffen-SS will live only if the entire SS lives.']

'Ansprache Himmlers an das Offizierskorps der Leibstandarte-SS Adolf Hitler,' in IMT, *op. cit.*, p. 107. Cp. Steiner, *Die Armee der Geächteten, op. cit.*, pp. 114-115.

## IV. TOTALITARIAN INSTITUTIONS AND GERMAN BUREAUCRACY: A PROCESS OF ESCALATION INTO DESTRUCTION

1. On the nature of European Fascism see H. R. Trevor-Roper, 'The Phenomenon of Fascism,' and A. J. Nicholls, 'Germany,' in S. J. Woolf (ed.), *European Fascism* (New York: Vintage Books, 1969), pp. 18-38, 61-87.

Cf. also Dietrich Eckart, *Der Bolschewismus von Moses bis Lenin, Zwiege-sprüch zwischen Adolf Hitler und mir* (München: Hoheneichen-Verlag, 1924), *passim;* and Julius Streicher (ed.),*Reichstagung in Nürnberg 1933* (Berlin: Vaterländischer Verlag C. A. Weller, 1933), pp. 41-247.
So, for example, concerning the solution of 'the Jewish question' already on December 6, 1922, Hermann Esser said the following: '500,000 Juden als Geiseln, die rücksichtslos erledigt werden, wenn auch nur ein Feind die deutsche Grenze überschreitet.' Fa-88, Gruppe III, Stück 99, Bl. 1-10. Archiv Institut für Zeitgeschichte, München (IfZ).

――――

['Five hundred thousand Jews as hostages who will be ruthlessly dispatched if even one enemy crosses the German border.']

See also Bernard Rosenberg *et al.* (ed.), *Mass Society in Crisis* (New York: The Macmillan Company, 1968), Part II.
2. Ludwig Voggenreiter (ed.), *Der Hitler-Prozeß* (Potsdam: Ludwig Voggenreiter, 1934), p. 66.
3. *Ibid.,* pp. 78, 79. See also *ibid.,* pp. 81-83.
4. *Ibid.,* pp. 62-63, 64.
5. *Ibid.,* pp. 69, 71. See also *ibid.,* p. 70.
6. *Ibid.,* p. 98. Cf. also *ibid.,* pp. 97-104. See also Hitler's defense before the court, *ibid.,* p. 14-25, 88-92, and the hearing of General Ludendorff, *ibid.,* pp. 39-50; the hearings of Captain Röhm, *ibid.,* pp. 50-52, and Dr. Frick, *ibid.,* pp. 55-59.
7. Joseph Goebbels, *Schriften der Deutschen Hochschule für Politik* (Berlin, 1934), p. 13.
8. Joseph Goebbels, 'Der Angriff,' in Hans Schwarz van Berk (ed.), *Aufsätze aus der Kampfzeit* (München: Zentralverlag der NSDAP, 1936), pp. 293-294. These editorials were written by Goebbels in the years 1927 to 1930 for the Berlin newspaper, *Der Angriff.* Goebbels was at that time Gauleiter of Berlin.
9. *Ibid.,* (1929), p. 187.
10. Under this kind of 'National Socialist' reasoning the following is subsumed: I. Material fallacies (factual). 1. Fallacy of accident. 2. Secundum quid. 3. Ignoratio elenchi; a) argument ad hominem; b) ad populum; c) ad baculum; d) ad verecundiam. 4. Petitio principii; a) circulus in probando. 5. Fallacy of the consequent. 6. Non sequitur. 7. Post hoc ergo propter hoc. 8. Plurium interrogationum. II. Logical or formal fallacies; these are fallacies which violate the formal rules of the syllogism, and include: 1. Fallacy of four terms, quaternio terminorum. 2. Fallacy of the undistributed middle term. 3. Fallacy of illicit process of major or minor term. 4. Fallacy of negative premises. This does not mean that the application of fallacious thinking did not adhere to a peculiar, yet internally consistent pattern. See especially Stuart Chase, *Guides to Straight Thinking* (New York: Harper and Brothers, 1956), *passim.*
11. Cf. Streicher, *op. cit.,* pp. 48, 56, 59, and 230. See also *Die Reden Hitlers am Parteitag der Freiheit 1935* (München: Zentralverlag der NSDAP, 1935), pp.

15, 19.
12. This is interpreted by Robert K. Merton as follows: 'The efficacy of social structure depends ultimately upon infusing group participants with appropiate attitudes and sentiments ... there are definite arrangements in bureaucracy for inculcating and reinforcing those sentiments.' R. K. Merton, 'Bureaucratic Structure and Personality,' in R. K. Merton *et al.*, *Reader in Bureaucracy* (Glencoe/Ill.: Free Press, 1960), p. 365.
   Cf. also Erving Goffman, *Stigma* (Englewood Cliffs, N. J.: Prentice Hall, 1963), *passim*, and Howard S. Becker, *Outsiders* (New York: The Free Press, 1968), *passim*.
13. Frederic S. Burin, 'Bureaucracy and National Socialism: A Reconstruction of Weberian Theory,' in Merton *et al.*, *op. cit.*, p. 35. See also *ibid.*, 37, 38, 41.
14. *Ibid.*, p. 35. Cf. also Hitler's address to the 'Amtswalter,' entitled 'Wir haben die Aufgabe, eine eherne Front zu bilden ...,' in Streicher, *op. cit.*, p. 248.
To understand the personnel composition and bureaucratic structure of the NS government, one needs to understand the fusion of the party elements and formal bureaucracy. The key to this understanding lies in the following characteristic passages of the Organisationsbuch der NSDAP 1943:
'Pflichten des Parteigenossen
Die Gebote des Nationalsozialisten:
Der Führer hat immer recht!
Verletze nie die Disziplin! ...
Recht ist, was der Bewegung und damit Deutschland, d.h. deinem Volke nützt!
II. Die Partei hat allein weltanschauliche Aufgaben ... Die Partei als weltanschauliches Erziehungsinstrument muß das Führerkorps des deutschen Volkes werden. Dieses Führerkorps ist für die restlose Durchdringung des deutschen Volkes im nationalsozialistischen Geiste und für die Überwindung der im Volk zum Teil noch wurzelnden Abhängigkeit von international gebundenen Kräften verantwortlich.
*Der politische Leiter*
Grundlage der Organisation der Partei ist der Führergedanke. ... Alle politischen Leiter gelten als vom Führer ernannt und sind ihm verantwortlich, sie genießen nach unten volle Autorität.
*Der Typ des politischen Leiters*
... Der politische Leiter ist kein Beamter, sondern immer der politische Beauftragte des Führers. ... Mit dem politischen Leiter bauen wir die politische Führung im Staate auf. ...
*Vereidigung des politischen Leiters*
... Die Vereidigungsformel lautet:
'Ich schwöre Adolf Hitler unverbrüchliche Treue. Ich schwöre ihm und den Führern, die er mir bestimmt, unbedingten Gehorsam.'
...
*Führerbesprechungen – Veranstaltungstermine*
...
Der Hoheitsträger trifft sich ... in seinem Amtsbereich mit zuständigen SA-,

SS-, NSKK-, HJ- sowie Reichsarbeitsdienst- und NSFK-Führern, um sich gegenseitig zu unterrichten.
. . .
*Politische Leiter und SS*
Die für das Verhältnis zur SA aufgeführten Vorschriften gelten sinngemäß auch für die SS.
Die SS wird zum Unterschied von der SA besonders eingesetzt für Führer-schutz und Aufgaben, bei denen einzelne Männer verwendet werden müssen.
. . .
*Politische Leiter und SA*
Die SA ist Ausbildungs- und Erziehungsinstrument der Partei. Ihr und den gleichgelagerten Gliederungen, SS und NSKK, obliegen die Erhaltung der körperlichen Tüchtigkeit und des soldatischen Geistes in ihren Einheiten und der evtl. Einsatz als innerpolitische Truppe.
. . .
*Hoheitsträger – Hoheitsgebiet*
Hoheitsträger sind:
Der Führer, die Gauleiter, die Kreisleiter, die Ortsgruppenleiter, die Zellen-leiter, die Blockleiter.
Hoheitsgebiete sind:
Das Reich, die Gaue, die Kreise, die Ortsgruppen, die Zellen, die Blocks.
. . .
*Der Führer*
Die Erkenntnis der sozialen Mißstände im Vorkriegsdeutschland, die das Entstehen einer echten Volksgemeinschaft verhinderten, das vom Kamerad-schaftsgeist erfüllte Fronterlebnis des Weltkrieges und die Abscheu vor dem volksverräterisch-pazifistischen Nachkriegsdeutschland ließen im Führer den Entschluß reifen, Politiker zu werden und dem deutschen Volke eine Staats-form zu geben, die auf Jahrhunderte seine berechtigten Lebensinteressen sichern soll.
. . .
*Die Reichsleitung der NSDAP*
In der Reichsleitung laufen die Fäden der Organisation des deutschen Volkes und des Staates zusammen. Durch die Ausstattung des Leiters der Partei-Kanzlei mit den Befugnissen eines Reichsministers und durch besondere Ver-waltungsanordnungen ist die Durchdringung des Staatsapparates mit dem politischen Willen der Partei gewährleistet.' 'Darstellung der Rechten und Pflichten der Parteigenossen und der Politischen Leiter,' in 'Der Prozess gegen die Hauptkriegsverbrecher vor dem Internationalen Militärgerichtshof (IMT), (Nürnberg, 1948), vol. XXIX, pp. 85-87, 89, 92. Doc. PS-1983.

---

['Duties of the party comrade
The commandments of National Socialism:
The Führer is always right!
Never violate discipline! . . .

Right is what is useful to the movement and, therefore, to Germany, that is, to your people!

II. Only the party has ideological (weltanschauliche) tasks ... The party, as an instrument of ideological education, must become the leadership corps for the German people. This leadership corps is responsible for the ceaseless indoctrination of the German people in the spirit of National Socialism and for the overcoming of the internationalist forces which still have a partial hold on the people.

*The political leader*

The foundation of the organization of the party is the concept of the Führer ... All political leaders are considered to have been named by the Führer and are responsible to him; they enjoy full authority with respect to those below them.

*The type of the political leader*

... The political leader is no civil servant, but rather always the political deputy of the Führer ... By means of the political leader we are building up the political leadership of the state ...

*Oath of the political leader*

... The words of the oath are:

"I swear inviolable faith to Adolf Hitler. I swear unconditional obedience to him and to the leaders he appoints."

...

*Conference of the leaders – Meeting times*

The officeholder (Hoheitsträger), within his jurisdiction, meets with appropriate leaders of the SA, SS, NSKK (Nationalsozialistisches Kraftfahrkorps, that is, NS motor corps: trans.), HJ (Hitler Youth), as well as of the Reich Labor Service and the NSFK (NS leadership corps), for the purpose of exchanging information.

...

*Political Leaders and the SS*

The regulations established for the relationship with the SA are generally also valid for the SS.

The SS, in contrast to the SA, is deployed particularly for the protection of leaders (Führerschutz) and for tasks which require the deployment of individual men.

*Political Leaders and the SA*

...

The SA is the training and education instrument of the party. The SA, the SS, the NSKK, and similarly structured formations, have the duty of maintaining good physical condition and military spirit in their units and, possibly, of serving as internal political troops.

...

*Officeholders – areas of territorial authority*

The holders of authority are:

The Führer, Gauleiter (province leaders), Kreisleiter (district leaders), Ortsgruppenleiter (local-branch-leaders), Zellenleiter (cell leaders), and Blockleiter (block

leaders).
Areas of territorial authority are:
The Reich, Gaue (provinces), Kreise (districts), Ortsgruppen (local branches), Zellen (cells), and Blocks (blocks).

*The Führer*

The recognition of the social ills in pre-war Germany which prevented the development of a genuine spirit of community, the world-war experience at the front which was permeated by the spirit of comradeship, and the loathing for the treasonable and pacifistic elements of post-war Germany – all this ripened in the Führer the decision to enter politics and to give the German people a form of government that would secure its justified existential interests for centuries.

...

*The Reich Leadership of the NSDAP*

...

In the leadership of the Reich the threads of the organization of the German people and of the state are joined. The vestment of the leader of the party chancellery with the authority of a Reich minister and the special administrative structure guarantee that the state apparatus will be permeated by the political will of the party.' 'Presentation of the rights and duties of the party comrades and the political leaders', in 'Der Prozess gegen die Hauptkriegsverbrecher vor dem Internationalen Militärgerichtshof (IMT),' (Nürnberg, 1948), Vol. XXIX, pp. 85-87, 89, 92. Doc. PS-1893.]

15. Cf. Burin, in Merton, *op. cit.,* p. 35.
16. Hermann Göring, *Aufbau einer Nation* (Berlin: Mittler, 1934), pp. 87-89. Cp. Erich Gritzbach, *Hermann Göring, Werk und Mensch* (München: Zentral-verlag der NSDAP, 1941), pp. 32-42.
    See also G. M. Gilbert, *Nürnberger Tagebuch* (Frankfurt: Fischer Bücherei, 1962), pp. 133, 185, 191, 194, 202-205, 386, 413.
    In his decree of November 20, 1934, Göring placed Heinrich Himmler, who had been appointed his deputy on April 20, 1934 (Stellvertretender Chef und Inspekteur der Preußischen Geheimen Staatspolizei), in charge of the Gestapo. 'Der Inspekteur der Geheimen Staatspolizei wird die Geschäfte der gesamten Preußischen Geheimen Staatspolizei unter Verantwortung mir gegenüber führen.' ['The Inspector of the Gestapo will henceforth transact the business of the entire Prussian Gestapo, being responsible to me alone.'] Hans Buchheim, 'Die SS – Das Herrschaftsinstrument,' in Hans Buchheim et al. (ed.), *Anatomie des SS-Staates* (Olten: Walter Verlag, 1965), Vol. I, p. 47, Doc. MA 433, Bl. 8736, Archiv IfZ.
    On April 22, 1934, Reinhard Heydrich became chief of the Preußisches Geheimes Staatspolizeiamt. *Ibid.,* p. 46.
    See also Robert Ley (ed.), Nationalsozialistisches Jahrbuch: 'Bericht über die SS seit dem Reichsparteitag 1938,' in IMT, Vol. XXIX, *op. cit.,* pp. 277-278.
17. *Ibid.,* p. 278.

Cf. Felix Steiner, *Die Armee der Geächteten* (Göttingen: Plesse Verlag, 1963), pp. 234-240. See also Himmler's argumentation in 'Rede Himmlers bei der SS-Gruppenführertagung in Posen am 4. Oktober 1943,' in IMT., *op. cit.,* pp. 121-123, PS-1919.

18. Cp. H. H. Gerth and C. Wright Mills (trans. and eds.), *From Max Weber: Essays in Sociology* (New York: Oxford University Press, 1946), pp. 215-216. See also Max Weber, *Wirtschaft und Gesellschaft* (Tübingen: J. C. B. Mohr, 1925), Vol. II, pp. 661-662; Franz L. Neumann, *Behemoth* (New York: Oxford University Press, 1944), pp. 77-80, and Burin, in Merton, *op. cit.,* p. 38.

19. Concerning the effectiveness, attitude, and influence of legal authority, see *ibid.*
Cf. also Max Weber, 'The Essentials of Bureaucratic Organizations: An Ideal-Type Construction,' in R. K. Merton *et al., op. cit.,* pp. 18-27.
See also Reinhard Bendix, 'Bureaucracy and the Problem of Power,' in *ibid.,* pp. 128-135.

20. Cf. Hannah Arendt, *Eichmann in Jerusalem, A Report on the Banality of Evil* (London: Faber and Faber, 1963), p. 103.
See also Gilbert, *op. cit.,* pp. 421-422, 448-450, and Raul Hilberg, 'The Destruction of the European Jews,' in Bernard Rosenberg *et al.* (ed.), *Mass Society in Crisis, op. cit.,* pp. 272-310.

21. Burin, in Merton, *op. cit.,* p. 39. See also Max Weber, 'The Routinization of Charisma,' in Merton *et al., op. cit.,* pp. 92-100. See also Max Weber, 'The Three Types of Legitimate Rule,' in Amitai Etzioni, *Complex Organizations* (New York: Holt, Rinehart and Winston, 1961), pp. 10-14.
Cf. also Gerth and Mills, *op. cit.:* 'Sociology of Charismatic Authority,' p. 248. See also *ibid.,* pp. 245-264. Trevor-Roper views the NS political and administrative system in the following terms:
'The structure of German politics and administration was in contrast to the assertion of the Nazis not pyramidal or monolithic but rather a pell-mell of private empires, private armies, and private intelligence services.' Trevor-Roper, *Hitlers letzte Tage* (Frankfurt/M.: Ullstein Verlag, 1965), p. 41. Hitler's views on German bureaucracy are expressed in the following passages of *Mein Kampf:* 'Was dabei den deutschen Beamtenkörper und Verwaltungsapparat besonders auszeichnete, war seine Unabhängigkeit von den einzelnen Regierungen, deren jeweilige politische Gesinnung auf die Stellung des deutschen Staatsbeamten keinen Einfluß auszuüben vermochte. ... Auf der Staatsform, dem Heere und dem Beamtenkörper beruhte die wundervolle Kraft und Stärke des alten Reiches. ...
Staatsautorität ... beruht ... auf dem allgemeinen Vertrauen, das der Leitung und Verwaltung eines Gemeinwesens entgegengebracht werden darf und kann. Dieses Vertrauen jedoch ist wieder nur das Ergebnis einer unerschütterlichen inneren Überzeugung von der Uneigennützigkeit und Redlichkeit der Regierung und Verwaltung eines Landes sowie die Übereinstimmung des Sinnes der Gesetze mit dem Gefühl der allgemeinen Moralanschauung.' *Mein Kampf* (München: Zentralverlag der NSDAP, 1940), Vol. I, p. 278.

['What thereby distinguished especially the German bureaucracy and the apparatus of administration was its independence of the various governments, whose political convictions were not able to exercise any influence on the position of German public servants. ... On the form of government, the army, and the bureaucrats rested the wonderful power and strength of the old Reich. ... State authority ... rests ... on the general confidence which may and can be shown in the management and the administration of a community. But this confidence is in turn only the result of an unshakable inner conviction of the unselfishness and the honesty of the government and the administration of a country as well as of a harmony between the meaning of the law and general moral views.']

A practical example of a conditioned attitude towards legal authority was given by General Jodl, former Chef der Operationsabteilung des OKW, when he asserted to Gilbert on April 7, 1946: „... der Rest der alten Offiziere stand von Anfang an dem Nazismus feindlich gegenüber. Wir machten nur mit, weil Hitler rechtmäßig zum Reichskanzler gewählt worden war.' Gilbert, *op. cit.,* p. 240. Cp. *ibid.,* pp. 258, 353, 373.

['... the rest of the old officers were opposed to Nazism from the very beginning. We collaborated only because he was legally chosen Reich Chancellor.']

In inoculating the bureaucratic apparatus with party ideology the NS leadership manipulated and misused the confidence of the people who anticipated a legal and traditionally just administration. This attitude can be illustrated by citing one of Jodl's plausible explanations given to Gilbert: 'Ich kämpfte in diesem Krieg im Glauben, daß er unumgänglich war und ich mein Vaterland verteidigte. Der Gedanke, daß Hitler ihn tatsächlich geplant und die Friedensangebote abgelehnt hatte. ... Hinterher ist es leicht reden. ... Aber es wäre ein furchtbarer Konflikt zwischen Gewissen und Pflicht gewesen.' Gilbert, *op. cit.,* p. 63.

['I fought the war in the belief that it was inevitable and I was protecting my country. – To think that Hitler actually planned it and turned down the offers of peace. – ... it's easy to talk after the fact – but it would have been a terrible conflict between conscience and duty.']

22. Burin, in Merton, *op. cit.,* p. 39.
23. Hitler was the prototype of a charismatic personality as defined by Weber. By charisma Weber understood: '... a certain quality of an individual personality by virtue of which he is set apart from ordinary men and treated as endowed with supernatural, superhuman, or at least specifically exceptional powers or qualities. These are such as are not accessible to the ordinary person, but are regarded as divine or as exemplary, and on the basis of them the individual concerned is treated as a leader.' Max Weber, *op. cit.,* p. 140. Cf. also Seymour Martin Lipset, *The First New Nation* (Garden City/N.Y..

Anchor Books, 1967), p. 19.
Charismatic authority, according to Weber, is outside the realm of everyday routine and the profane sphere. In this respect, he says, it is sharply opposed to traditional authority whether it is patriarchal, patrimonial, or any other form. In modern Western society the rational emphasis is on economic gain, administrative political machinery, and bureaucratic organization and often requires a pseudo-charisma or manufactured spurious charisma regarding leaders standing in the limelight. To effectuate an authority that is beyond the range of the rational, an array of techniques and manipulative devices are evolved which are to catapult an ordinary personage into the realms of the extraordinary.

In *Mein Kampf* Hitler defines this type of leadership as 'unbedingte Führerautorität.' Hitler writes:

'Die Bewegung vertritt im kleinsten wie im größten den Grundsatz der unbedingten Führerautorität, gepaart mit höchster Verantwortung. . . .
Immer wird der Führer von oben eingesetzt und gleichzeitig mit unbeschränkter Vollmacht bekleidet. Nur der Führer der Gesamtpartei wird aus vereinsgesetzlichen Gründen in der Generalmitgliederversammlung gewählt. Er ist aber der ausschließliche Führer der Bewegung. Sämtliche Ausschüsse unterstehen ihm und nicht er den Ausschüssen. Er bestimmt und trägt damit aber auch auf seinen Schultern die Verantwortung. . . .
Nur der Held ist dazu berufen.
Der Fortschritt und die Kultur der Menschheit sind nicht ein Produkt der Majorität, sondern beruhen ausschließlich auf der Genialität und der Tatkraft der Persönlichkeit. . . . Damit ist die Bewegung aber antiparlamentarisch. . . .'

———

['In the smallest things as well as in the greatest, the movement represents the principle of unconditional leadership authority (unbedingte Führerautorität), paired with supreme responsibility . . . The Führer is always appointed from above and simultaneously endowed with absolute power. Only the Führer of the entire party is elected, for reasons of organizational legality, in the general membership convention. But he is the exclusive leader of the movement. All committees are subordinated to him and not he to the committees. He decides, but thereby he also bears the responsibility on his shoulders . . .
'Only the hero is called to this responsibility.
'Human progress and culture are not the product of the majority, but rather are derived exclusively from the genius and energy of personality . . . With this, however, the movement is anti-parliamentarian, . . .']

*Mein Kampf*, Vol. I, *op. cit.*, pp. 337-338. See also *ibid.*, Vol. II, pp. 83, 90, 218, 227.
Hitler's charismatic image was reflected in 1933 in an address by Otto Dietrich (Reichspressechef of the NSDAP), entitled 'Der Kampf der heroischen Weltanschauung,' on September 2, at the Party Congress of Victory:
'Das Letzte an der Persönlichkeit Adolf Hitlers wird uns wohl immer ein

Mysterium bleiben. Der gottbegnadete Mensch geht seinen Weg, weil er ihn gehen muß. Hier gilt das Wort, daß der Glaube Berge versetzt. Der Glaube in Adolf Hitler ... an Adolf Hitler. Wie auch immer man das Geheimnis der Persönlichkeit Adolf Hitlers erklären will, der Glaube an ihn, seine unerhörte Popularität ist heute in Deutschland eine Macht von ungeheurer Stärke. Eine Macht, die neuartig und beispiellos ist in der nationalen Beherrschung der Völker. Über dieses ... Deutschland der Disziplin und Autorität herrscht kein Kaiser oder König, kein Despot oder Tyrann: das Dritte Reich wird beherrscht von der Macht der Persönlichkeit.' In Streicher (ed.), *op. cit.,* p. 180.

---

['The ultimate nature of the personality of Adolf Hitler will probably always remain a mystery for us. The divinely favored man pursues his course because he must pursue it. This is a valid illustration of the saying that faith moves mountains. Adolf Hitler's faith ... in Adolf Hitler. However one attempts to explain the secret of Adolf Hitler's personality, the faith in him and his unparalled popularity constitute an enormous power in the Germany of today. This power is new and unexampled among the national governments of the world. This ... Germany of discipline and authority is not ruled by an emperor or a king, a despot or a tyrant: The Third Reich is ruled by the power of personality.']

In 1929 Goebbels wrote perhaps the most descriptive portrayal of Hitler's persuasive appeal: '... Wenn Hitler spricht, dann bricht vor der magischen Wirkung seines Wortes aller Widerstand zusammen. Man kann nur sein Freund oder sein Feind sein ... Es gibt Menschen, die ihn zum erstenmal als seine glühendsten Gegner hörten und nach zehn Minuten waren sie seine leidenschaftlichsten Anhänger. Er ist der grosse Vereinfacher, der mit wenigen Worten von den zerrissenen Problemen der deutschen Gegenwart das Beiwerk abstreift und sie in ihrer ganzen herben, nackten, unerbittlichen Grausamkeit zeigt. Vor ihm kann keine Phrase bestehen. Was gilt das alles noch, internationaler Pazifismus, Weltfrieden und Völkerbund, wenn er spricht? Die Novemberkaiser von Deutschland haben schon gewusst, warum sie diesem Mann das Reden verboten. Von ihnen aus gesehen, passt auf Hitler das Wort, das einmal Robespierre über Marat sagte: "Der Mann ist gefährlich, er glaubt was er sagt.".. .' Dr. Joseph Goebbels (ed.), *Knorke* (München, Franz Eher Nachf., 1929), p. 36.

---

['... When Hitler speaks, then all resistance collapses in the face of the magical effect of his words. One can only be his friend or his enemy ... There are people who were among his most ardent opponents when they first heard him speak, and who became his most passionate adherents after ten minutes. He is the great simplifier, who in a few words strips the problem of disunity of present-day Gemany of its secondary elements and presents them in their entire harsh, naked, and inexorable horror. Before him, no phrase can prevail.

What validity do all these have – international pacifism, world peace, and League of Nations – when he speaks? The November emperors of Germany were well aware of why they forbade this man to speak. From their point of view, the description Robespierre once gave of Marat applies to Hitler: "The man is dangerous; he believes what he says." . . .']

See also Goebbels's pronouncement of an eulogy on Hitler in *Das Reich,* December 31, 1944, in Hans Dieter Müller (ed.), *Faksimile Querschnitt durch 'Das Reich'* (München: Scherz-Verlag, 1964), p. 18.
In December 1945 Ribbentrop disclosed to Gilbert: '. . . ich war einer seiner treuesten Anhänger. Das ist schwer für Sie, zu verstehen. Der Führer besaß eine ungeheuer magnetische Persönlichkeit. Man kann es nicht verstehen, es sei denn, man hat es erlebt. Wissen Sie, sogar jetzt, sieben Monate nach seinem Tode, kann ich mich seinem Einfluß noch nicht vollkommen entziehen. Jeder war von ihm fasziniert. Sogar, wenn berühmte Intellektuelle zu einer Diskussion zusammenkamen, hörten sie wahrhaftig nach einigen Minuten auf zu existieren, und die geistige Schärfe von Hitlers Persönlichkeit überstrahlte alle. Ja, sogar bei den Verhandlungen über das Münchener Abkommen waren Daladier und Chamberlain einfach überwältigt von seinem Charme.' Gilbert *op. cit.,* p. 67. Cp. *ibid.,* p. 70. In an interview with *Der Spiegel* on November 7, 1966 (No. 46, p. 48), Speer said: 'Er (Hitler) strahlte eine große Liebenswürdigkeit aus, war sehr besorgt um mich und meine Familie. Wenn man zum Skilaufen ging und eine Stunde später als geplant zurückkam, war er schon unruhig, daß etwas passiert sein könnte.'

['. . . I was one of his most faithful followers. That is something that is hard for you to understand. The Führer had a terrifically magnetic personality. You can't understand it unless you've experienced it. Do you know, even now, seven months after his death, I can't completely shake off his influence? Everybody was fascinated by him. Even if great intellects came together for a discussion, why, in a few minutes they just ceased to exist and the brillance of Hitler's personality shone over all. Why, even at the discussions on the Munich Pact, Daladier and Chamberlain were simply overwhelmed by his charm.']

In an interview with *Der Spiegel* on November 7, 1966 (No. 46, p. 48), Speer said ['He (Hitler) radiated a great kindness. He was very much concerned about me and my family. When one went skiing and returned an hour later than planned, he would already be afraid that something might have happened.']

Baldur von Schirach, 'Ich glaubte an Hitler,' in *Der Stern,* No. 30, July 1967, p. 41, wrote the following: 'Die deutsche Katastrophe wurde nicht allein durch das bewirkt, was Hitler aus uns gemacht hat, sondern durch das, was wir aus ihm gemacht haben. Hitler kam nicht von außen, er war nicht, wie viele ihn heute sehen, die dämonische Bestie, die, durch besondere Zeitumstände begünstigt, die Macht an sich riß. Er war, wenn wir ganz ehrlich sind, unser

Hitler, der Mann, den wir wollten und den wir selbst durch maßlose Verherrlichung zum Herrn unseres Schicksals gemacht haben. Denn es gibt einen
Hitler nur in einem Volk, das den Wunsch und den Willen hat, einen Hitler
zu haben. Es ist ein kollektives Verhängnis bei den Deutschen, daß sie Menschen
mit außerordentlichen Fähigkeiten – und diese wird niemand Hitler bestreiten
können – eine Verehrung zollen, die ihnen das Bewußtsein des Übermenschlichen und der Unfehlbarkeit suggeriert. ...' The effect of the 'leadership of
the personality' is perhaps best described by Höss when Himmler informed
him in the summer of 1941: 'Der Führer hat die Endlösung der jüdischen
Frage befohlen – und wir müssen diese Aufgabe ausführen. Aus verkehrs-
technischen und Isolierungsgründen habe ich Auschwitz dafür ausgesucht. Es
ist jetzt an Ihnen, diese harte Aufgabe durchzuführen.' To this, as Höss
explained to Gilbert, he could only respond, '... ich konnte nur "Jawohl"
sagen.' Gilbert, *op. cit.*, p. 243. See also *ibid.*, pp. 244-245, 250, 252-253,
278, 401.

---

[Baldur von Schirach, 'Ich glaubte an Hitler', in *Der Stern*, No. 30, July 17, 1967,
p. 41, wrote the following: 'The German catastrophe was brought about not
only by that which Hitler made of us, but also by that which we made of him.
Hitler did not come from the outside. He was not – as many consider him
today – the demonic beast who, favored by special circumstances of the times,
seized power. He was, if we are to be completely honest, our Hitler, the man
we wanted and the man we ourselves made the master of our destiny through
our boundless adulation. For the only people that has a Hitler is a people that
has the desire and the will to have a Hitler. It is the Germans' collective pre-
dicament to show such honor to persons endowed with extraordinary capabili-
ties and nobody can deny that Hitler possessed them – that they are persuaded
to believe in their superhumanness and infallibility. ...' The effect of the
'leadership of the personality' is perhaps best described by Höss when Himmler
informed him in the summer of 1941: 'The Führer has ordered the final solution
(Endlösung) of the Jewish question – and we have to carry out this task. For
reasons of transportation and isolation, I have picked Auschwitz for this. You
now have the hard job of carrying this out.' To this, as Höss explained to
Gilbert, 'he could only say: "Jawohl!" ']

24. Hitler's speech at Weimar, July 4, 1936, in *Völkischer Beobachter*, Berlin
    edition, July 5, 1936 (No. 187), quoted by Burin, in Merton, *op. cit.*, p. 41.
    Cp. Gilbert, *op. cit.*, p. 397.
25. Neumann observes: 'What National Socialism has done is to transform into autho-
    ritarian bodies the private organizations that in a democracy still give the indi-
    vidual the opportunity for spontaneous activity. Bureaucratization is the
    complete depersonalization of human relations. They become abstract and
    anonymous. On this structure of society, National Socialism imposes two ideol-
    ogies that are completely antagonistic to it: the ideology of the community and
    the leadership principle.' Neumann, *op. cit.*, p. 41.

26. Cf. Burin, in Merton, *op. cit.*, p. 41.

In this connection Hitler observed the following in his speech on September 16, 1935, during the 'Parteitag der Freiheit': 'Die nationalsozialistische Partei hat Ungeheures geschaffen. Nicht unsere Wirtschaftsführer, nicht unsere Professoren und Gelehrten, nicht Soldaten und Künstler, nicht Philosophen, Denker und Dichter haben unser Volk vom Abgrund zurückgerissen, sondern ausschließlich das *politische* Soldatentum unserer Partei. . . . Wieviele einsichtsvolle Männer anderer Völker würden glücklich sein, wenn ihre Nationen über eine ähnlich solid fundierte autoritäre Organisation verfügten, wie sie das heutige Deutschland besitzt, . . . ist es um so nötiger, die Autorität der Partei als letzte überwachende und entscheidende Instanz und als letzte Richterin anzuerkennen. . . . Sie bändigt den wilden Willen des Einzelnen, um einen unbändigen Willen aller zu erzielen! . . . um so nötiger, wird es aber dann, daß einer Vielheit von Erkenntnissen und Folgerungen vorgebeugt wird durch die starke und wenn nötig auch schroffe Führung der Partei durch die blinde Erhaltung ihrer Autorität. . . . Die Frage der Fehlbarkeit oder Unfehlbarkeit steht hier nicht zur Diskussion. So wenig es einem Armeeführer, dem Kommandeur eines Truppenkörpers oder gar am Ende dem einzelnen Soldaten gestattet werden kann, seine Vorstellung und Meinung als Maßstab anzulegen in der Anzweiflung der Richtigkeit eines ihm gegebenen Befehls, so wenig kann in der politischen Zielsetzung und Führung der Einzelgänger sein Handeln entschuldigen mit der behaupteten Richtigkeit *seiner* Auffassung oder mit dem Irrtum der von der Partei ausgegebenen Auffassungen, Anordnungen oder Befehle. . . . Es gibt keine Entbindung von dem Gehorsam gegen diesen Grundsatz.' Adolf Hitler, *Die Reden Hitlers am Parteitag der Freiheit 1935* (München: Zentralverlag der NSDAP, 1935), pp. 82-84.

------

['The National Socialist Party has accomplished an enormous amount. It is not our economic leaders, not our professors and scholars, not soldiers and artists, not philosophers, thinkers and poets who have pulled our people back from the edge of the abyss, but exclusively the *political* soldiers of our party who have done this . . . How many perceptive men of other countries would be happy if their nations possessed such a solidly based authoritarian organization as present-day Germany possesses . . . it is all the more necessary to recognize the authority of the party as the final supervisory and decision-making body and as the supreme judge . . . It subdues the wild will of the individual in order to create an intractable will of all! . . . but it then becomes all the more necessary to prevent the existence of a variety of opinions and judgments by means of the strong, and, if necessary, harsh leadership role of the party and by the blind maintenance of its authority . . . The issue of fallibility or infallibility is not under discussion here. Just as one cannot permit the leader of an army, the commander of an army corps, or at the lowest level the individual soldier to substitute his own ideas and opinions as a criterion because of his doubts as to the correctness of an order, the individual in the setting of political goals and in political leadership cannot justify his actions by asserting the correctness of *his* view or the error of concepts, ordinances, or orders of the party. .... There is no dispensation from obedience to this principle.']

Cp. also Hannah Arendt, 'Social Science Techniques and the Study of Concentration Camps,' *Jewish Social Studies*, New York, Vol. XII, No. 1 (January 1950), p. 50.

27. See Theodore Abel, *The Nazi Movement* (New York: Atherton Press, 1966), pp. 137-202; John Madge, *Scientific Sociology* (New York: The Free Press, 1967), pp. 377-423; Lipset, *op. cit.*, pp. 267-270, 316-326; Raul Hilberg, *The Destruction of the European Jews* (Chicago: Quadrangle Books, 1961), p. 134; Franz Neumann, *The Democratic and the Authoritarian State* (New York: The Free Press, 1966), *passim;* Manfred Danner, 'Repressives Strafrecht oder Praeventives Massnahmenrecht?', in *Aktuelle Kriminologie* (Hamburg: Kriminalistik Verlag, 1969), p. 208.

Cf. also biograms in Chpt. II and John M. Steiner and Jochen Fahrenberg, 'Die Ausprägung autoritärer Einstellung bei ehemaligen Angehörigen der SS und der Wehrmacht,' *Kölner Zeitschrift für Soziologie und Sozialpsychologie*, Vol. 22, No. 3 (1970), *passim.*

28 Burin, in Merton, *op. cit.*, p. 41.

See also Kurt Sontheimer, 'Antidemokratisches Denken in der Weimarer Republik,' and Karl Dietrich Bracher, 'Die Technik der Nationalsozialistischen Machtergreifung,' in Theodor Eschenburg *et al.* (ed.), *Der Weg in die Diktatur 1918-1933* (München: Piper Verlag, 1963), pp. 49-69, 153-174.

National Socialism provided an ideal breeding ground for what Adorno and his associates defined as 'authoritarian personality.' T. W. Adorno, Else Frenkel-Brunswik, Daniel J. Levinson, and R. Nevit Sanford, *The Authoritarian Personality* (New York: Harper, 1950), *passim.* Cases in point are many leaders of the SS and the military, individuals employed in the war production industry, judges and legal officers of the Ministry of Justice, faculty members and academicians, public servants such as Staatssekretär Ganzenmüller, coresponsible *with Hitler* for the transportation of millions of innocent individuals to destruction camps, men like Globke, responsible for the interpretation of anti-Jewish legislation, or those responsible for the realization of the euthanasia program. See also Ilse Staff, *Justiz im Dritten Reich* (Frankfurt: Fischer Bücherei, 1964), *passim.*

Cp. Keitel's and Ribbentrop's attitude towards Hitler's policy, Gilbert, *op. cit.,* pp. 241, 242, 314.

29. Adolf Hitler, *Die Reden Hitlers am Parteitag der Freiheit 1935, op. cit.*, p. 16. Here Hitler appears to be referring to the solution of 'internal problems' with extra-judicial means. The following may be cited as representative examples: the euthanasia action 'T 4'; the 'Final Solution' (cf. statement by former SS-Obersturmführer Kurt Gerstein on May 4, 1945, *Vierteljahreshefte für Zeitgeschichte*, Stuttgart, 1953, p. 189. See also the affidavit by Gerstein of April 25, 1945, cited in Hilberg, *op. cit.*, p. 572, PS- 1553), and the massacre of Babij Jar near Kiew of September 29-30, 1941, to mention only one of many

carried out by the Einsatzkommando 4a, a subsidiary command of Einsatz-gruppe C and led by SS-Standartenführer Paul Blobel, during which 33,771 Jewish men, women, and children were slaughtered. (Cp. affidavit by Albert Hartl, of October 9, 1947, No. 5384), cf. Hilberg, *op. cit.*, p. 255.
The 'Einsatzgruppen' were under the functional control of the RSHA. There were the following 'Einsatzgruppen': 'Einsatzgruppe A,' Stahlecker in charge; 'Einsatzgruppe B,' Nebe in charge; 'Einsatzgruppe C,' Rasch in charge, and 'Einsatzgruppe D,' Ohlendorf in charge. (Cf. Hilberg, *op. cit.*, p. 188.) Blobel was also in charge of 'Kommando 1005' which Himmler and the Gestapo Chief Müller had created in June 1942 in order to erase the traces of mass graves of executed 'Einsatzgruppen' victims (in the Eastern occupied territories) with the aid of funeral pyres, ovens, explosives, bone-crushing machines (Knochenmühlen), and finally by burning the corpses in open pits. Cf. affidavit by Blobel of June 18, 1947, No. 3947. See Hilberg, *op. cit.*, pp. 628-629. Cp. Burin, in Merton, *op. cit.*, p. 41.

30. The senseless persecution and destruction of religious, political, and ethnic minorities and individuals, who had in no way objectively constituted a threat to the Nazi Régime or German society in general, has to be considered as irrational and deviant from antecedent social values and norms. Cp. Herman Kahn and Anthony J. Wiener, *The Year 2000* (London: The Macmillan Company, 1969), pp. 266-267. The destructive interaction between the citizens and the 'Obrigkeit' and the misuse of authority by the National Socialists was perhaps best expressed in Gerhart Hauptmann's Dramenfragment *Der Dom:*

'Fasse, Bürger, in dein Gebet
die obrigkeitliche Autorität.
Recht, Gesetz, Verordnung, Mandat, Erlaß –
das obrigkeitliche Tintenfaß
hat Saft genung und Federn genung
zur Nationalbeschäftigung.
Der schwarze Saft, er färbt sich rot,
da heißt er Blut, da bringt er Tod.
Und daß es immer so bleiben mag,
betet zum Himmel jeden Tag.
Wie hurtig, alles ohne Verzug,
ist man nun erst beim Vollzug:
Die Galgen, die Räder auf allen Richtstätten
arbeiten herzhaft und unermüdlich.
Die Henker köpfen und martern friedlich.
Das Rathaus hängt voll eiserner Ketten.
Die eiserne Jungfrau steht bereit,
Halsringe, Käfige, Säcke zum Sacken,
Messer zum Bauchaufschlitzen,
Zangen zum Zwacken,
das wartet alles auf seine Zeit
und eitrige, nützliche Tätigkeit.

Nur braucht's ein stilles, freundliches Wetter,
da kommt auch der Holzstoß noch in Brand
und säubert von Hexen und Ketzern das Land.'
*Der Dom* (Berlin: Propyläen Verlag, 1963), Vol. VIII (3).

['Include, Citizen, in your prayer
the magisterial authority.
Jurisprudence, law, ordinance, mandate, decree –
the magisterial ink-well
has enough juice and enough pens
to keep the nation busy.
The black juice turns into red;
then it is called blood, then it brings death.
And that it so always may remain,
pray to Heaven every day.
Once one begins to prosecute,
how quickly everything goes, without delay:
The gallows, the racks at all places of execution
work valiently and indefatigably.
The executioners behead and torture peacefully.
The city hall is full of iron chains.
The iron maiden stands ready.
Strangling rings, cages, sacks,
knives for slitting of the bellies,
pincers for torture –
all this awaits its time,
awaits zealous and useful activity.
Calm and friendly weather is all that's needed
and the pyre also will ignite
and cleanse witches and heretics from the land.']

31. Cf. Burin, in Merton, *op. cit.*, p. 42. See also Buchheim, *op. cit.*, pp. 28-30.
32. Cf. H. H. Gerth, 'The Nazi Party: Its Leadership and Composition', in Merton *et al.*, *op. cit.*, pp. 109, 112-113. See Apendix III.
On the lowest hierarchical level of the party administration were the so-called 'Amtswalter.' See Hitler's address to the 'Amtswalter' entitled 'Wir haben die Aufgabe, eine eherne Front zu bilden,' in Streicher, *op. cit.*, pp. 247-250. At the Parteitag der Freiheit in 1935 Hitler stated: 'Die Partei hat sich in diesem Jahre außerordentlich gefestigt. Ihre innere Organisation wurde weiter ausgebaut. Zahlreiche Stellen des Staates wurden mit zuverlässigen Parteigenossen besetzt.' *Op. cit.*, p. 20. See also *ibid.*, p. 48: 'Es ist nicht möglich, 68 Millionen, Kopf an Kopf, an einem Platz zu vereinen, und trotzdem stehen jetzt vor mir nicht 150 000 oder 180 000 politische Leiter der Nationalsozialistischen Partei, sondern in *Euch steht jetzt vor mir Deutschland, das Deutsche Volk.* Denn dieses Deutsche Volk von heute, es hat nur *Euren*

Willen. Ihr seid ihm heute vorgesetzt als lebendige Führung des Volkes.'

———

['This year the party has consolidated itself to an extraordinary extent. Its internal organization was expanded. Numerous governmental offices were staffed with reliable party comrades.' *Op. cit.,* p. 20. See also *ibid.,* p. 48: 'It is not possible to bring together sixty-eight million people, side by side, in one place; yet there are not standing before me now one hundred and fifty or one hundred and eighty thousand political leaders of the National Socialist Party, but rather in *your persons, Germany, the German people, is now standing before me.* For this German people of today possesses *your* will. You are placed at its head today as the living leadership of the people.']

33. Burin, in Merton, *op. cit.,* p. 43. Cp. also Gilbert, *op. cit.,* pp. 397, 412-414, 431-443.
34. Cf. Bendix, 'Bureaucracy and the Problem of Power,' in Merton *et al., op. cit.,* pp. 127-133.
    See also Die Reden Hitlers am Parteitag der Freiheit 1935, op. cit., pp. 78-83. Hitler declared: 'Die Partei hat mithin aus ihrer Organisation für die Zukunft dem deutschen Staat die *oberste und allgemeine Führung* zu geben, und zweitens durch ihre Lehrtätigkeit dem nationalsozialistischen Staat *das ihn tragende nationalsozialistische Volk zu erziehen.*
    Daraus ergibt sich die klare Fixierung der Aufgabengebiete von Partei und Staat.
    *Staatsaufgabe* ist die Fortführung der historisch gewordenen und entwickelten Verwaltung der staatlichen Organisationen im Rahmen und mittels der Gesetze.
    *Parteiaufgabe ist:*
    1. Aufbau ihrer inneren Organisation zur Herstellung einer stabilen, sich selbst forterhaltenden ewigen Zelle der nationalsozialistischen Lehre.
    2. Die Erziehung des gesamten Volkes im Sinne der Gedanken dieser Idee.
    3. Die Abstellung der Erzogenen an den Staat zu seiner Führung und als seine Gefolgschaft. . . .
    Dieser Nationalsozialismus aber ist dann die weltanschauliche Grundlage der Existenz und damit der Organisation des Deutschen Reiches als nationalsozialistischer Staat. Sie ist als Weltanschauung – wenn sie sich nicht selbst preisgeben will – gezwungen, *intolerant* zu sein, das heißt die Richtigkeit ihrer Auffassungen und damit auch ihrer Entscheidungen *unter allen Umständen zu vertreten und durchzusetzen.' Ibid.,* pp. 80-81.

———

['Hence the party has the duty of furnishing from its organization *the supreme and general leadership* for the German state in the future, and secondly, in its educational role, the duty *of instructing the National Socialist people,* which is the bearer of the National Socialist state.
From this there results a clear division of the spheres of responsibility of party and state.
The task of the state is the continuation of the administration of the state

organizations within the framework of and by means of the laws – an administration which has come into being and developed as an historical process. The task of the party is:
1. The development of its internal organization for the creation of a stable, self-perpetuating, eternal cell of National Socialist doctrine.
2. The instruction of the whole people in the sense of the thrust of this idea.
3. The making available of people thus trained to the state for its leadership and as its adherents. . . .
But this National Socialism is then the philosophical (weltanschaulich) foundation for the existence and hence for the organization of the German Reich as a National Socialist state. As a Weltanschauung, it is forced – if it does not wish to surrender itself – to be *intolerant*, that is, to *represent and assert* the correctness of its views and thereby also its decisions *under all circumstances.*']

35. Cp. Gerth, in Merton, *op. cit.,* p. 113. See also Gilbert, *op. cit.,* pp. 101, 109, 173, 354. Joseph Wulf, *Martin Bormann, Hitlers Schatten* (Gütersloh: Sigbert Mohn Verlag, 1962), *passim.*
36. See especially 'Auszüge aus dem Tagebuch des Generalgouverneurs für die Besetzten Polnischen Gebiete,' Hans Frank, vom 25. Oktober 1939 bis 3. April 1945, in IMT, Vol. XXIX, *op. cit.,* pp. 356-723, PS-2233 (see also *ibid.,* PS-3465 and D-970). See also 'Aus Franks Handbuch "Deutsches Verwaltungsrecht 1937": Darstellung der Aufgaben der politischen Polizei,' in *ibid.,* pp. 354-355, PS-2232, and the unpublished autobiographical notes (biogram) of Hans Frank (see Appendix XVII).
In a lecture on October 11, 1936, before the Ausschuß für Polizeirecht der Akademie für Deutsches Recht, Himmler said the following: '. . . Ich habe mich dabei von vornherein auf den Standpunkt gestellt, ob ein Paragraph unserem Handeln entgegensteht, ist mir völlig gleichgültig; ich tue zur Erfüllung meiner Aufgaben grundsätzlich das, was ich nach meinem Gewissen in meiner Arbeit für Führer und Volk verantworten kann und dem gesunden Menschenverstand entspricht. Ob die anderen Leute über die "Brechung der Gesetze" jammerten, war in diesen Monaten und Jahren, in denen es um Leben oder Sterben des deutschen Volkes ging, gänzlich gleichgültig.' In Buchheim *op. cit.,* Vol. I, pp. 108-109.

['From the outset I worked on the assumption that it did not matter in the least if our actions were contrary to some paragraph in the law; in carrying out my job, working for the Führer and German people, I basically did that which my conscience and common sense told me was right. The fact that others were bemoaning "violations of the law" was completely immaterial in those months and years when the life or death of the German people was at stake.']

See also Gilbert, *op. cit.,* pp. 202-203.
37. Cf. Burin, in Merton, *op. cit.,* pp. 44-45. Cp. Bendix, in Merton, *op. cit.,* p. 115. The general direction which the course of the NS judiciary was to take was

outlined by Hitler in his speech on March 23, 1933, entitled ' "Das deutsche Volk will mit der Welt in Frieden leben" Regierungserklärung vom 23. März 1933': 'Unser Rechtswesen muß in erster Linie der Erhaltung dieser Volksgemeinschaft dienen. Der Unabsetzbarkeit der Richter auf der einen Seite muß die Elastizität der Urteilsfindung zum Zweck der Erhaltung der Gesellschaft entsprechen. Nicht das Individuum kann der Mittelpunkt der gesetzlichen Sorge sein, sondern das Volk! Landes- und Volksverrat sollen künftig mit barbarischer Rücksichtslosigkeit ausgebrannt werden!' Erhard Klöss (ed.), *Reden des Führers, Politik und Propaganda Adolf Hitlers 1922-1945* (München: Deutscher Taschenbuch Verlag, 1967), p. 100.

['Our legal system must, in the first place, further the preservation of this people's community. The irremovability of the judges, on the one hand, must correspond to the elasticity of judgment for the purpose of preserving the society. Not the individual, but only the people may be the focal point of legal concern! In the future, high treason and betrayal of the people must be eradicated with barbaric ruthlessness!']

38. As an example, Burin cites the SS and administrative career of the jurist and legal administrator Guenther Joel as that of a typical, succesful party bureaucrat. His professional career proceeded at the same pace as his career as party official. He began as member of the NSDAP and junior public prosecutor of the Ministry of Justice in 1934 and in 1943 had reached the rank of SS-Obersturmbannführer (Lt. Colonel) in the SD and Attorney General to the Supreme Provincial Court of Appeals in Hamm (Westfalia). U.S. Military Tribunal III, U.S. v. Altstaedter *et al.*, pp. 10868-70 of transcript of proceedings quoted in Burin, *op. cit.*, pp. 45-46.
See also Rauschning, *Gespräche mit Hitler* (Wien: Europa-Verlag, 1940), pp. 21, 182-183.
See also Staff, *op. cit.*, *passim;* Hilberg, *op. cit.*, Chpt. VIII on Deportations, pp. 257-554; cp. Rolf Seliger (ed.), *Braune Universität, Deutsche Hochschullehrer gestern und heute. Dokumentation* (München: im Selbstverlag Rolf Seliger, 1965), Vol. II, pp. 7-16, 28-31, 34-37, 60-67; see also *ibid.*, Vol. III, pp. 16-18, 91-94.
Especially to those German university professors, scholars, and intellectuals who claim for themselves authority and high social status for originating myth systems via thought processes without being able to do justice to their professional position and ethical responsibility, the psychologist and philosopher, Professor Kurt Huber (1893-1943), should be cited as one who lived up to his calling. He had belonged to the numerically small and politically irrelevant group of university professors and scientists who were actively opposed to Hitler and his National Socialism on principle and whose upright and courageous stand – specifically on racial issues – had been without equivocation. Cf. 'Über die Verantwortung eines Hochschullehrers (Aus dem Schlußwort von Professor Kurt Huber),' in Walter Hofer (ed.), *Der Nationalsozialismus: Doku-*

*mente 1933-1945* (Frankfurt/M.: Fischer Bücherei, 1965), pp. 332-333. For other members of the German opposition, see *ibid.*, Chpt. VIII 'Die Widerstandsbewegung,' pp. 314-358.

39. Hilberg, *op. cit.*, pp. 295-296.

Cp. p. 10763 of transcript of proceedings quoted in Burin, *op. cit.*, p. 47. See also Thierack's 'Instruction to the Judges (Richterbriefe),' for example Richterbrief No. 1 (signed Thierack) of October 1, 1942, NG-295, in Hilberg, *op. cit.*, pp. 102-103. In a report concerning his conference with Himmler on September 18, 1942, Reichsjustizminister Thierack wrote the following: 'Korrektur bei nicht genügenden Justizurteilen durch polizeiliche Sonderbehandlung. Es wurde auf Vorschlag des Reichsleiters Bormann zwischen Reichsführer-SS und mir folgende Vereinbarung getroffen: ... 2. Auslieferung asozialer Elemente aus dem Strafvollzug an den Reichsführer-SS zur Vernichtung durch Arbeit. Es werden restlos ausgeliefert die Sicherungsverwahrten, Juden, Zigeuner, Russen und Ukrainer, Polen über 3 Jahre Strafe, Tschechen oder Deutsche über 8 Jahre Strafe nach Entscheidung des Reichsjustizministers. Zunächst sollen die übelsten asozialen Elemente unter letzteren ausgeliefert werden. ...

'14. Es besteht Übereinstimmung darüber, daß in Rücksicht auf die von der Staatsführung für die Bereinigung der Ostfragen beabsichtigten Ziele in Zukunft Juden, Polen, Zigeuner, Russen und Ukrainer nicht mehr von den ordentlichen Gerichten, soweit es sich um Strafsachen handelt, abgeurteilt werden sollen, sondern durch den Reichsführer-SS erledigt werden. Das gilt nicht für bürgerlichen Rechtsstreit und auch nicht für Polen, die in die deutschen Volkslisten angemeldet oder eingetragen sind. Th., 'Bericht des Reichsjustizministers Thierack über eine Besprechung mit Himmler am 18. September 1942. Besprechung mit Reichsführer-SS Himmler am 18.9.1942 in seinem Feldquartier in Gegenwart des StS. (Staatssekretär) Dr. Rothenberger, SS-Gruppenführer Streckenbach und SS-Obersturmbannführer Bender.' In IMT, *op. cit.*, Vol. XXVI, pp. 200-201, 203, PS-654. Cp. Hilberg, *op. cit.*, pp. 295-296.

['Special police action for correction of inadequate legal verdicts. At the suggestion of Reichsleiter Bormann, the following agreement was made between the Reichsführer-SS and me: ... 2. Transfer of asocial elements from penal institutions to the custody of the Reichsführer-SS for destruction by labor. Persons in the following categories will be transferred without exceptions: Persons in preventive detention, Jews, Gypsies, Russians and Ukrainians, Poles serving sentences of over three years, and Czechs or Germans serving sentences of over eight years according to the decision of the Reich Minister of Justice. Initially, the worst asocial elements among the latter are to be transferred ...

14. It is agreed that in view of the goals of the state leadership for settlement of the Eastern questions, Jews, Poles, Gypsies, Russians, and Ukranians will no longer appear before the regular courts in the future – insofar as criminal actions are involved – but rather will be handled by the Reichsführer-SS. This procedure does not apply to civil suits or to Poles who are reported or

registered in the German people's rosters (Volkslisten). Th.' 'Report of Reich Minister of Justice Thierack on a Discussion with Reichsführer-SS Himmler on September 18, 1942, in his field headquarters in the presence of State Secretary (Staatssekretär) Dr. Rothenberger, SS-Gruppenführer Streckenbach, and SS-Obersturmbannführer Bender.']

See also Hubert Schorn, *Der Richter im Dritten Reich* (Frankfurt: Vittorio Klostermann, 1959), *passim.*

40. Cf. Arendt, *op. cit.,* p. 143.
41. Although the pathological aspects of status systems (statocentricism) have not been adequately investigated, it can be assumed that the exceedingly rigid status system prevalent in and applied by the SS to outgroups seems to have had a distorting effect upon the following topics considered by Barnard:
  I. The status system tends in time towards distorted evaluation of individuals.
  II. It unduly restricts the "circulation of the elite".
  III. It distorts he system of distributive justice.
  IV. It exaggerates administration to the detriment of leadership and morale.
  V. It exalts the symbolic function beyond the level of sustainment.
  VI. It limits the adaptability of an organization.'
  Chester I. Barnard. 'The Functions of Status Systems,' in Merton *et al., op. cit.,* p. 249. See also *ibid.,* pp. 50-54.
  The conflict between the assumed functions and the actual role played by the SS appears to be one of the major reasons why the status, prestige, and esteem they aspired to was never fully achieved except for a power status based on the persuasive force of violence. This can be illustrated by an implication clearly expressed by Himmler in 1936: 'Ich weiß, daß es manche *Leute* in Deutschland gibt, *denen es schlecht wird, wenn sie diesen schwarzen Rock sehen;* wir haben Verständnis dafür und erwarten nicht, daß wir von allzu vielen geliebt werden. ...' Heinrich Himmler, 'Die Schutzstaffel, 1936; Äußerungen über Gehorsamspflicht und über Sicherheitsdienst und Gestapo,' in IMT, *op. cit.,* Vol. XXIX, p. 14, PS-1851.

———
['I know that some *people* in Germany *are sickened when they see this black uniform.* We understand this and do not expect to be loved by too many people ...']

42. Theodore Abel, 'The Sociology of Concentration Camps,' *Social Forces* (Baltimore), 30, 1951, p. 155.
43. R. K. Merton, 'Bureaucratic Structure and Personality,' in Merton *et al., op. cit.,* p. 365.
44. *Ibid.,* p. 366.
45. This situation is illustrated by Merton as follows: '... tension is increased because of a discrepancy between ideology and fact: the governmental personnel are held to be "servants of the people," but in fact they are usually superordinate, and release of tension can seldom be afforded by turning to other

agencies for the necessary service.' *Ibid.*, p. 369.

The fact that these conflicts within the ranks of the SS existed was made clear by Himmler in his address to the Gruppenführer in Posen on October 4, 1943:

'Ich darf vielleicht auch eine Bitte hier aussprechen, dass Streit zwischen höheren Führern nicht auf meinem Rücken ausgetragen wird. In manchen Fällen muß da der Reichsführer-SS den Briefboten spielen, da die beiden Herren ja nicht miteinander verkehren können.' 'Rede Himmlers bei der SS-Gruppenführertagung in Posen am 4. Oktober 1943,' in IMT, *op. cit.*, Vol. XXIX. p. 161, PS-1919.

['Perhaps I may here express the request that quarrels between higher leaders not be played out on my back. In many cases the Reichsführer-SS must play the role of postman, as the two gentlemen are not on speaking terms.']

46. Hilberg, *op. cit.*, p. 134. See also *ibid.*, p. 135.
47. Cf. *ibid.*, p. 181.
48. *Loc. cit.*
49. Cf. Hilberg, *op. cit.*, pp. 182-185, and Hans Buchheim, 'Die Struktur der nationalsozialistischen Herrschaft,' in Hans Buchheim *et al.*, *Anatomie des SS-Staates, op. cit.*, Vol. I, pp. 76-77. II.
50. Text of draft dated March 26, 1941, enclosed in a letter by Wagner to Heydrich, April 4, 1941; copies to OKW/Abwehr (Canaris) and OKW/L (Warlimont), NOKW-256, in Hilberg, *op. cit.*, p. 187.
51. Affidavit by Schellenberg, November 26, 1945, PS-3710. Statement by Ohlendorf, April 24, 1947, No.-2890, in Hilberg, *op. cit.*, p. 187.
52. Cf. *ibid.*
53. Cf. Helmut Krausnick, 'Judenverfolgung,' in Hans Buchheim et al., *op. cit.*, Vol. II, pp. 410-415. See also report by SS-Untersturmführer Dr. Becker to Obersturmbannführer Rauff, Berlin, Prinz-Albrecht-Straße 8, of May 16, 1942, concerning gassing trucks (S Wagen) and killing activities, IMT, *op. cit.*, Vol. XXVI, PS-501.
54. Cf. Nürnberger Dokument No. 365 (photostatic copy in the Institut für Zeitgeschichte, Munich), quoted in Krausnick, in Buchheim, *op. cit.*, pp. 411-412.
55. T. Shibutani and K. Kwan observe: 'There is considerable evidence that the excesses of the Nazi regime rekindled consciousness of kind among Jews throughout the world who were well on their way to becoming assimilated into other groups.' They further state: 'After World War II a small number of Jews returned to Germany; when others expressed their astonishment, they replied simply that they did not feel at home anywhere else in the world. They had been assimilated to German life and had long forgotten their Jewish ancestors. These people were in fact Germans.' *Ethnic Stratification* (New York: The Macmillan Company, 1967), pp. 221, 511; see also ibid., pp. 21, 417.
56. Rauschning, *op. cit.*, p. 224. Hitler declared in a speech on April 12, 1922: 'Das internationale Börsenkapital wäre nicht denkbar und wäre nie gekom-

men ohne seine Begründer, den übernationalen, weil streng nationalen Juden.´

------

['International stock-market capitalism would not be conceivable, and would never have come, without its founders, the supranationalistic, yet strongly nationalistic, Jews.']

Klöss, *op. cit.*, p. 33. That is to say, Hitler was perfectly aware of the fact that the Jews could very well also be nationalists. How they could play these incompatible roles of being nationalists on the one hand and supranationalists on the other, he fails to explain. Cp. also Eckart, *op. cit.*, pp. 15, 16, 22, 43-46.

57. The realization of Hitler's extermination policy began with the events of the Reichskristallnacht. While Hitler was addressing the representatives of the German press in Munich on the eve of November 10, 1938, conveniently isolated from the events taking place outside and emphasizing the new ethos of journalism in Germany, nearly all synagogues were burnt, over 7,000 Jewish shops destroyed and looted, countless Jews brutally mishandled, 20,000 arrested, and 36 killed.
Thousands of men between 15 and 70 years of age were sent to concentration camps. The pretext for these acts was the assassination of Ernst vom Rath by the Jew Herschel Grynspan. Cf. Hilberg, *op. cit.*, pp. 23-28, 655; Hofer, *op. cit.*, pp. 272-273, 291-293; Martin Broszat, 'Nationalsozialistische Konzentrationslager,' in Buchheim *et al.*, *op. cit.*, pp. 94-95; Krausnick, in *ibid.*, pp. 333-335.
It is noteworthy that Hitler in his speech to the representatives of the German press did not once mention the minority that was the first and foremost to experience his wrath; instead, he reflected upon some of the following issues: 'Die Umstände haben mich gezwungen, *jahrzehntelang* fast nur vom Frieden zu reden. Nur unter der fortgesetzten Betonung des deutschen Friedenswillens und der Friedensabsichten war es mir möglich, dem deutschen Volk Stück für Stück die Freiheit zu erringen und ihm die Rüstung zu geben, die immer wieder für den nächsten Schritt als Voraussetzung notwendig war. ... Es war nunmehr notwendig, das deutsche Volk psychologisch allmählich umzustellen und ihm langsam klarzumachen, daß es Dinge gibt, die, wenn sie nicht mit friedlichen Mitteln durchgesetzt werden können, mit Mitteln der Gewalt durchgesetzt werden *müssen*. Dazu war es aber notwendig, nicht etwa nun die Gewalt als solche zu propagieren, sondern ... dem deutschen Volk bestimmte außenpolitische Vorgänge so zu beleuchten, daß die *innere* Stimme des Volkes selbst langsam nach der Gewalt zu schreien begann. ... Diese Arbeit hat Monate erfordert, sie wurde planmäßig begonnen, planmäßig fortgeführt, verstärkt. Viele haben sie nicht begriffen, meine Herren; viele waren der Meinung, das sei doch alles etwas übertrieben. Das sind jene überzüchteten Intellektuellen, die keine Ahnung haben, wie man ein Volk letzten Endes zu der Bereitschaft bringt, geradezustehen, auch wenn es zu blitzen und zu donnern beginnt. ...
Weiter aber war es notwendig, mit dieser Presse und sonstiger Propaganda

auf den Feind einzuwirken, der uns ja zunächst gegenüberstand, nämlich auf die Tschechoslowakei selber. Es hat vielleicht manche gegeben, die viele der Maßnahmen, die in diesen Jahren getroffen worden sind, nicht begriffen haben. Meine Herren! Nach dem 21. Mai war es ganz klar, daß dieses Problem gelöst werden mußte, so oder so! ...
Aber gewisse Intellektuelle, die ja immer sich in Deutschland als Wächter einer anderen Moral fühlen und vor allem verantwortlich fühlen für die sogenannte Gerechtigkeit usw., für das Maßhalten in allem und jedem. Viele solche Menschen haben das nicht verstanden. Glauben Sie, es war aber notwendig. Und letzten Endes, der Erfolg ist ja entscheidend. ...
Man muß sich geradezu hier auf das breite Volk stützen, um gegenüber dieser überzüchteten, intellektuellen und hysterischen Schichte (Gelächter) ein Gegengewicht zu halten. ...
Wenn ich so die intellektuellen Schichten bei uns ansehe, leider, man braucht sie ja; sonst könnte man sie eines Tages ja, ich weiß nicht, ausrotten oder so was (Bewegung). Aber man braucht sie leider. Wenn ich mir also diese intellektuellen Schichten ansehe und mir nun ihr Verhalten vorstelle und es überprüfe, mir gegenüber, unserer Arbeit gegenüber, dann wird mir fast angst. Denn seit ich nun politisch tätig bin und seit ich besonders das Reich führe, habe ich nur Erfolge. Und trotzdem schwimmt diese Masse herum in einer geradezu oft abscheulichen, ekelerregenden Weise. Was würde denn nun geschehen, wenn wir einmal einen Mißerfolg hätten? Auch das könnte sein, meine Herren. Wie würde dieses *Hühnervolk* denn *dann* sich erst aufführen? Die sind schon *jetzt*, da wir doch überhaupt nur Erfolge haben, und zwar weltgeschichtlich einmalige Erfolge, unzuverlässig. ... Es (das Volk) muß lernen, so *fanatisch* an den Endsieg zu glauben, daß, selbst wenn wir einmal Niederlagen erleiden würden, die Nation sie nur, ich möchte sagen, von dem höheren Gesichtspunkt aus wertet: Das ist vorübergehend; am Ende wird uns der Sieg sein! ...
Die breite Masse hat *einen einzigen* Wunsch: daß sie gut geführt wird, und daß sie der Führung vertrauen kann und daß die Führung selber nicht streitet, sondern daß diese Führung geschlossen vor sie hintritt.' 'Rede Hitlers vor der deutschen Presse,' (Nov. 10, 1938) *Vierteljahreshefte für Zeitgeschichte*, April, 1958, pp. 182, 183, 184, 186, 188-189.

---

['Circumstances have forced me to speak almost only of peace for *decades*. Only by a continued emphasis upon the German will for peace and peaceful intentions was it possible for me to win, step by step, freedom for the German people and to give them the armament which, again and again, proved to be the prerequisite for the next step. ... Since then it has been necessary to bring about gradual psychological changes in the German people and slowly make it clear to the people that there are things which, if incapable of realization by peaceful means, *must* be attained by violent means. However, to bring this about it was necessary, not to propagandize in favor of violence as such, but rather ... to explain certain events in foreign affairs to the German people in such a way that the *inner* voice of the people itself slowly began to cry out for violence ... This work required months; it was begun in a planned way, and continued and intensified in a planned way. Many did not understand it, gentlemen; many were of the opinion that all that was a bit exaggerated. Those are the over-bred intellectuals who have no idea as to how one finally brings a people to a state of readiness in which it can stand upright, even if it begins to thunder and lightning. ...

'Furthermore, however, it was necessary to use this press and other propaganda means to work upon the enemy that first confronted us, namely, upon Czechoslovakia itself. There may have been some who did not understand many of the measures that were taken in these years. Gentlemen! After the twenty-first of May, it was quite clear that this problem had to be solved, in one way or another! ...

'But there are certain intellectuals in Germany who always consider themselves as guardians of another morality and who feel responsible above all for so-called justice, etc., and for moderation in each and everything. Many such people have not understood that. But believe me, it was necessary. And, in the last analysis, success is indeed decisive. ...

'It is precisely here that one must rely upon the broad mass of the people, in order to create a counter-weight to this overbred, intellectual, and hysterical class (laughter) ...

'Despite my view of the intellectuel classes in our country, one unfortunately needs them; otherwise one could – well, I don't know – exterminate them one day, or something of that sort (movement in the audience). But unfortunately one needs them. Now when I look at these intellectual classes and reflect upon and re-examine their behavior with respect to me, to our work, I am almost afraid. For since I have been active politically, and especially since I have led the Reich, I have had only successes. And nevertheless, this mass swims around in a fashion that is really too often loathsome and detestable. So what would happen now if we once failed? That is also possible, gentlemen. How would these chickens (Hühnervolk) behave themselves then? They are already unreliable, at a time when we are experiencing only successes, indeed, successes unique in world history ... It (the people) must learn to believe so *fanatically* in the final victory that, even if we should once suffer some defeats, the nation would – if I may so express it – evaluate them from a higher standpoint: that is temporary; at the end victory will be ours! ...

'The broad masses have *one single* wish: that they be well led, and that they be able to trust the leadership, and that the leaders not fight among themselves, but that this leadership stand before them in unity.']

See also Hitler's conversation with Rauschning in 1933 in which Hitler expounds his future war plans. See Rauschning, *op. cit.,* pp. 9-17.

58. Cf. Hofer, *op. cit.,* pp. 270-273, 274-276; Krausnick, in Buchheim, *op. cit.,* pp. 360-448; Arendt, *op. cit.,* pp. 206-207; William L. Shirer, *The Rise and Fall of the Third Reich* (New York: Fawcett World Library, 1962), pp. 580-

587; and Hilberg, *op. cit.,* pp. 22-24.

59. Concern, as the term has been used here, describes the link between the destructive elements in drive-relationship to objects and the other positive aspects of relating. According to Winnicott, concern is presumed to belong to a period prior to the classical Oedipus complex, which is a relationship between three whole persons. The capacity for concern belongs to the two-body relationship between the infant and the mother-substitute. In the initial stages of the development, if there is no reliable mother-figure to receive the reparation-gesture, the guilt becomes intolerable, and concern cannot be felt. Failure of reparation leads to a losing of the capacity for concern and to its replacement by primitive forms of guilt, anxiety, and most probably leads to indifference, complacency, or aggression towards others. Cf. D. W. Winnicott, 'The Development of the Capacity for Concern,' *Bulletin of the Menninger Clinic,* XXVII, 4, 1963, pp. 167-176.

60. Hilberg, *op. cit.,* p. 122.

61. Cf. RGBI I. 1097, in *ibid.*

62. Cf. Hilberg, *op. cit.,* pp. 122-125, 291-297, and Arendt, *op. cit.,* pp. 102-119. Cp. also Paul Arnsberg and Wolfgang Scheffler, 'Zu Hannah Arendts "Eichmann in Jerusalem," ' *Aus Politik und Zeitgeschichte, Beilage zur Wochenzeitung Das Parlament,* B 45/64, November 4, 1964, pp. 12-17, 22-28.

63. Cf. Hilberg, *op. cit.,* pp. 122-123.

64. Cf. *ibid.,* pp. 296-297.
    Where the German deportation did not meet with success was Denmark. There the administration and population refused to cooperate with the German authorities and did not hand over the Jews to them. This united effort to save the Jews from deportation meant that less than 10 % of the Danish Jewry were apprehended and that finally only 477 out of 6,500 Jews were shipped to Theresienstadt. Furthermore, in an unprecedented nation-wide rescue action requiring a high degree of teamwork and esprit de corps, the administration and citizens in a combined effort ferried 5,919 'full' Jews, 13,310 'part' Jews, and 666 non-Jews married to Jews to Sweden. Cf. Hilberg, *op. cit.,* pp. 357-363.
    See also Kurt R. Grossmann, *Die unbesungenen Helden* (Berlin: Arany Verlag, 1961), pp. 386-406. The reason for this attitude of the Danish population should be sought in the democratic acceptance and integration of minorities and the marked absence of social distance. Similarly, in August 1941, Hitler ordered the euthanasia action 'T4' to be discontinued because of public pressure stemming predominantly from church groups. From this evidence, it can be concluded that the fate of Jews and other similarly situated 'non-Germans' did not cause equal concern to the general public. Cp. Krausnick, in Buchheim, *op. cit.,* pp. 407-408.

65. Cf. Arendt, *op. cit.,* pp. 104-111. Philip Friedman describes the function and role of the 'Judenräte' (Jewish Councils) as follows: 'The Judenrats presented a serious ethical and social problem. The Jewish masses hated them and bestowed upon them many derogatory nicknames to express their feelings.

Within the Ghetto there were heated debates concerning the relative utility of these councils. It is necessary to point out that discussions of the value of these councils are frequently marked by an oversimplified approach, whereas the problem is in fact very complicated. Persons of radically different caliber served on these councils for equally differing reasons. Some served voluntarily, others did so under German compulsion. Some of the Judenrats were composed of representatives of Jewish political parties. Others were dominated by cliques or by individual "strong men." In some instances the Germans dissolved Judenrats because they were too democratic and substituted Commissars of their own choice. Some Judenrats were passive instruments in German hands; others maneuvered and tried to rescue as many as they could. There were even some Judenrats which cooperated with the resistance movement and with the partisans. In any case, it is impossible to define the entire institution of Judenrats as all black or all white.' Friedman, 'Jewish Reaction to Nazism,' *Jewish Frontier,* Vol. XVII, September 1950, No. 9, p. 22.

De Jong writes about the 'Joodsche Raad' (Jewish Council) in Amsterdam as follows: 'The Joodse Raad and the administrative bodies functioned like small wheels in the complicated machinery – built into normal society – which week after week carried thousands of Jews to the gas chambers by the deportation train from Westerbork to Poland. There was hardly a branch of the Dutch administration which was not implicated in the tragedy in one way or another. Dutch police-agents, very few of them Nazis, fetched the Jews from their homes. The Amsterdam municipal trams carried them to the station from the Jewish Theatre where they were first assembled. At the station the train for Westerbork stood ready; it was a train of the Dutch State Railways, served by Dutch personnel. Neither among Jews nor among the non-Jews was there a systematic refusal to co-operate in the deportations. It was not realized how deadly necessary it was to organize this refusal.' Louis de Jong, 'Jews and Non-Jews in Nazi-Occupied Holland,' cited in Scheffler, *loc. cit.,* p. 28.

66. In addition, other services were performed such as the distribution of yellow Jewish star badges for which the consumers were obliged to pay, the securing of personal property of the deportees, assistance in the seizure of Jews and in seeing to it that they arrived at the designated collecting point at a specified time. Vacated apartments were sealed, registered, and reported to the SS authorities and the financing of the transportation to the camps settled.
Cf. Hilberg, *op. cit.,* pp. 122-124, 291. Cp. Arendt, *op. cit.,* pp. 104-105. See also Scheffler, *loc. cit.,* pp. 26-28.
However, there were also other organizations which performed vitally supportive functions as, for example, the Jewish 'Hilfsdienst' (emergency service) in Prague. This service was initiated and led by Freddy Hirsch, a young German Jewish Zionist and gymnastics instructor; one of the chief functions of this organization, which existed from 1940-1942, was to assist deportees in times of stress and see to it that their most essential belongings (which officially were not to exceed 50 kg) were made available to them at the assembly point

(Schleuße). Additional goals were to circumvent and sabotage German orders whenever possible. The group continued its activity in the ghetto Theresienstadt and the death camp Auschwitz-Birkenau until the beginning of 1944 when Freddy Hirsch committed suicide and most of the other members were sent to the gas chamber. This writer was a member of this group and most probably its sole survivor.

67. To improve their chances of survival, members of the Jewish Council (Judenräte) of the Council of the Elders (Ältestenräte) in ghettos, and function-holding prisoners in concentration and destruction camps (non-Jewish as well as Jewish), who were forced upon their fellow prisoners by the SS authorities, increasingly began to look and act like their German masters. Some even surpassed the SS in acts of cruelty.

Hilberg correctly observes: 'The Germans controlled the Jewish leadership, and that leadership, in turn, controlled the Jewish community. This system was foolproof. Truly, the Jewish communal organizations had become a self-destructive machine.' Hilberg, *op. cit.*, p. 125. See also *ibid.*, pp. 146, 291-292. Cp. Daniel Bell, 'Alphabet of Justice,' *Partisan Review*, Vol. XXX, 1963, pp. 422-423, and Krausnick, 'Judenverfolgung,' *op. cit.*, pp. 415-420.

See John M. Steiner, 'Social Structure and Human Behavior in Nazi Concentration Camps', unpubl. paper, pp. 12, 13, 15, 16.

Cp. Scheffler, *loc. cit.*, pp. 27-28.

68. The following examples may serve as illustrations: (1, 2, 3, 4): Rosenberg and Frank declared: '... viele von denen, die in die KZ gesteckt worden wären, *hätten es verdient*, weil sie die nationalen Symbole besudelt hätten – wie etwa dieses "Schwein Carl v. Ossietzky" (pazifistischer Publizist und Träger des Friedensnobelpreises 1935). Auch Piscator sei so einer von denen gewesen, die gegen die national gesinnten Deutschen agiert hätten; viele Juden hätten sich daran beteiligt.' Gilbert, *op. cit.*, p. 387.

(1, 4): Gilbert to Seyss-Inquart: 'Sie wollen sagen, nachdem Sie die Juden von der Gruppe, dem *Volk*, mit dem Sie sich selbst identifizierten, getrennt sahen, war Ihr Interesse für sie erloschen?' To this Seyss Inquart responded: 'Ich glaube, genau das ist's!' *Ibid.*, p. 375.

(3): Barnard has named this state 'zone of indifference' and Herbert A. Simon 'zone of acquiescence.' Herbert A. Simon, 'Decision-Making and Administrative Organization,' in Merton *et al.*, *op. cit.*, p. 190. See also *ibid.*, p. 189.

'Unnachgiebig forschte Sir David (Maxwell-Fyfe) weiter nach Papens Motiv für seine Zusammenarbeit mit einer Verbrecherbande. Ob er nicht gewußt hätte, daß Tausende von politischen Gegnern in Konzentrationslager geworfen wurden, als die Nazis an die Macht kamen? Papen machte Ausflüchte hinsichtlich der Anzahl; mit einigen sei es geschehen, vielleicht einigen Hunderten.' Gilbert, *op. cit.*, p. 387.

(3, 4): In two short replies to Reichsminister of Justice Gürtner, who repeatedly intervened in cases of arbitrariness, sudden death, and cruelties committed in concentration camps and finally petitioned to the Reichsführer-SS to permit those in preventive custody to receive legal aid, Himmler wrote the following on November 6, 1935:

a) 'Ich habe Ihr Schreiben vom 16.10. sowie die Aufstellung von Todesfällen in den Konzentrationslagern gelegentlich meines Vortrages am 1. November 1935 dem Führer selbst vorgelegt. Besondere Maßnahmen werden bei der ohnehin gewissenhaften Leitung der Konzentrationslager nicht als notwendig erachtet. gez. H. Himmler'

b) 'Ich habe in der Angelegenheit des an uns herangetragenen Wunsches betr. Erteilung der Genehmigung, bei Schutzhaftfällen Rechtsanwälte einzuschalten, dem Führer und Reichskanzler am 1.11.1935 Vortrag gehalten. Der Führer hat die Hinzuziehung von Rechtsanwälten verboten und mich beauftragt, Ihnen seine Entscheidung zur Kenntnis zu bringen. gez. H. Himmler' Pers. Stab RFSS, Institut für Zeitgeschichte, Rolle 40, Bl. 2 550 980 ff in Martin Broszat, 'Nationalsozialistische Konzentrationslager 1933-1945,' in Buchheim *et al.* (ed.), *op. cit.*, p. 46.

(4): 'Das "Reichsbürgergesetz" vom 15. September 1935 schließt Juden und jüdische Mischlinge von der Verleihung des Reichsbürgerrechtes und damit von der Anstellung als Beamte aus.

*'Die beiden Gesetze vom 15. September 1935 ("Nürnberger Gesetze") bedeuten den ersten folgerichtigen und entschlossenen Schritt, der – nach zwei Jahrtausenden – zur Lösung der Judenfrage getan worden ist.'* Kurt Schrey, *Du und Dein Volk* (München: Deutscher Volksverlag, 1936), p. 34. This booklet was edited by the Hauptamt für Erzieher (NSLB) and was distributed to primary and high school graduates.

----

['... that many of those thrown into concentration camps *deserved it* for besmirching the national symbols, like that "swine Carl von Ossietzky" (Pacifist, Nobel Peace Prize Winner, 1935). Piscator was one of the leaders of this nationalist-defamation movement on the stage, and there were a lot of Jews that participated in that movement.' Gilbert, *op. cit.*, p. 387.

(1, 4): Gilbert to Seyss-Inquart: 'Do you mean to say that after you saw the Jews separated from the group, the *people*, with which you yourself identified, your interest in them was extinguished?' To this Seyss-Inquart responded: 'I believe that is exactly right.' *Ibid.*, p. 375.

(3): Barnard has named this state 'zone of indifference' and Herbert A. Simon 'zone of acquiescence'. Herbert A. Simon, 'Decision-Making and Administrative Organization', in Merton *et al.*, *op. cit.*, p. 190. See also *ibid.*, p. 189.

'Sir David relentlessly pursued the theme of von Papen's collaboration with a gang of criminals. Didn't he know that thousands of political opponents were thrown into concentration camps as soon as the Nazis came to power? Von Papen equivocated over the number; there were some, perhaps hundreds.' Gilbert, *op. cit.*, p. 387.

(3, 4): In two short replies to Reichsminister of Justice, Gürtner, who repeatedly intervened in cases of arbitrariness, sudden death, and cruelties committed in concentration camps and finally petitioned to the Reichsführer-SS to permit those in preventive custody to receive legal aid, Himmler wrote the following on November 6, 1935:

a) 'On the occasion of my report of November 1, 1935, I submitted to the Führer personally your letter of October 16, together with the statement of deaths in the concentration camps. In view of the conscientious leadership of the camp, special measures are not considered necessary. (Signed) H. Himmler.'

b) 'On November 1, 1935, I transmitted to the Führer and Chancellor the request submitted to us that lawyers should be permitted to intervene in protective custody cases. The Führer has prohibited the consultation of lawyers and has asked me to inform you accordingly. (Signed) H. Himmler. Pers. Stab RFSS, Institut für Zeitgeschichte, Rolle 40, Bl. 2 550 980 ff in Martin Broszat, 'Nationalsozialistische Konzentrationslager 1933-1945', in Buchheim *et al.* (ed.), *op. cit.*, p. 46.

(4): 'The "Reich Citizenship Law" ("Reichsbürgergesetz") of September 15, 1935, excludes Jews and Jewish "Mischlinge" (those of mixed Jewish and non-Jewish blood: trans.) from receiving the right of citizenship, and hence from employment as civil servants. *The two laws of September 15, 1935 ('Nuremberg Laws') constitute the first logical and decisive step that – after two thousand years – has been taken for the solution of the Jewish question.'*]

69. Cf. William A. Westley, 'The Escalation of Violence through Legitimation,' in Marvin E. Wolfgang (ed.), *Patterns of Violence, American Academy of Political and Social Science* (Philadelphia, 1966), *Annals*, Vol. 364, pp. 120-126. Hilberg views the successive steps of the destruction process of the European Jewry by the NS Régime as follows:

| 'Step I: | Step II: |
|---|---|
| Definition | Mobile killing operations |
| Expropriation | Deportations |
| Concentration | Killing center operations' |

Cf. Hilberg, *op. cit.*, pp. 31, 32, 39.

During Step I, i.e., until the beginning of World War II, emigration was at least theoretically still possible. What appears to be missing in Hilberg's scheme is the killing process through slave labor, the final stage of the destruction process, and in some cases the actual preservation of the lives of deportees in slave labor camps because of the acute labor shortage during the final war years. Erving Goffman in 'The Characteristics of Total Institutions' lists 'for convenience' the total institutions of our society in five rough groupings. The 'Third, another type of total institution is organized to protect the community against what are thought to be intentional dangers to it; here the welfare of the persons thus sequestered is not the immediate issue. Examples are: Jails, penitentiaries, POW camps, and concentration camps.' Here Goffman does not seem to realize that the Nazi concentration camps were predominantly annihilation camps, and, therefore, can hardly be placed in the same category as prisons or POW camps. The former institutions are primarily concerned with the destruction of those who have been expelled from society, whereas the latter chiefly seek to resocialize or merely to isolate their charges without necessarily seeking their destruction. Erving Goffman, 'The Characteristics of Total Institutions,' in Amitai Etzioni, *op. cit.*, p. 313.

70. It should be emphasized that apart from Hitler's organizational talent his strength lay in his manipulative oratory and power of persuasion (as opposed to deliberation) rather than in the quality of his literary products. Goebbels described Hitler's appeal and power of persuasion as follows:

'Er besitzt die wunderbare Gabe, mit dem Instinkt zu wittern, was in der Luft liegt. Er hat die Fähigkeit, es so klar, logisch und einschränkungslos zum Ausdruck zu bringen, dass der Zuhörer in die Meinung versetzt wird, es sei seit je seine Ansicht gewesen, was da vorgetragen wird. Das ist das eigentliche Geheimnis der magischen Wirkung einer Hitler-Rede.' Joseph Goebbels, 'Der Führer als Redner,' in Adolf Hitler, *Bilder aus dem Leben des Führers,* hrsg. vom Cigaretten/Bilderdienst (Leipzig: F. A. Brockhaus, 1936), p. 31.

['He possesses the wonderful gift of being able to scent instinctively what is in the air. He has the ability to express it so clearly, logically, and unreservedly that the listener is persuaded that it is his own view which is being presented. That is the real secret of the magical effect of a Hitler speech.']

Hitler possessed the skill of telling the crowd what it wanted to hear, of being able to appeal to people's emotions, thus reinforcing their already existent stereotypes and prejudices. His lack of precision, his frequent generalizations, and the use of half-truths and categorizations of opponents or enemies of the German 'Volk' and National Socialism enabled his audience not only to look on them as scapegoats but also to associate them with what he wanted them to be associated with. All those who were associated with those belonging to the outgroup were evil, traitors, criminals. When Hitler referred to the 'good National Socialist' and model of a 'Volksgenosse,' superman, or hero of the nation, the tendency was to respond positively to these ego-inflating stimuli and identify with the assigned roles.

Thus, it is conceivable that because of Hitler's strong appeal to emotions, his speeches were frequently not taken literally but were used to channel out feelings of aggression, frustration, and violence. Nevertheless, the content of Hitler's oratory was internally consistent and quite clear as to his intentions and attitude, as in *Mein Kampf.*

So, for example, von Papen commented to Gilbert: 'Aber mein lieber Professor, wer nahm denn *Mein Kampf* schon ernst?' Gilbert, *op. cit.*, p. 121. Cp. also *ibid.,* pp. 260-261, 270, 272.

['But my dear professor, who ever took *Mein Kampf* seriously?']

In this connection it is interesting to note the contributions of various leaders of the Third Reich to the dynamics which brought about an escalation into destruction. There is an obvious discrepancy between the role they had actually played during the existence of the Régime and the way they perceived it in retrospect during the Nuremberg Trial; rationalization and a flexibility of attitudes and value norms become apparent. The following representative examples may serve as illustrations:

On April 16, 1946, Alfred Rosenberg, the former chief ideologist of the party, declared before the IMT that neither his anti-Semitic utterances concerning the destruction of Jews nor his propaganda were meant to be taken literally. Events had simply taken a different course than had been intended. Cf. Gilbert, *op. cit.*, p. 263. Cp. *ibid.*, pp. 262, 264-265. See also Alfred Rosenberg, *Der Mythos des 20. Jahrhunderts* (München: Hoheneichen Verlag, 1941), Chpts. IV: Das nordischdeutsche Recht (3. Rassenschutz als oberster Rechtsgrundsatz); VI: Ein neues Staatensystem (5. Lösung der gelben, schwarzen und Judenfrage; 6. Organische Scheidung der Rassen); VII: Die Einheit des Wesens (3. die Lüge als Krankheit der Germanen, als Lebenselement der Juden). Alfred Rosenberg, 'Die rassische Bedingtheit der Außenpolitik,' Rede auf dem Kongress des Reichsparteitages, in Streicher (ed.), *Reichstagung in Nürnberg 1933, op. cit.*, pp. 111-128.

Cp. Joseph Goebbels, 'Rassenfrage und Weltpropaganda,' in *ibid.*, pp. 131-142.

On April 16, 1946, Rudolf Höß, former commandant of Auschwitz, stated: '... nach Kriegsausbruch, erklärte Hitler, daß das Weltjudentum eine Auseinandersetzung mit dem Nationalsozialismus begonnen habe. Das war in einer Reichstagsrede zur Zeit des Frankreich-Feldzuges. Die Juden müßten vernichtet werden. Natürlich dachte damals niemand, daß es so wörtlich gemeint wäre ... es wurde immer betont (Goebbels), daß wenn Deutschland am Leben bleiben sollte, das Judentum ausgerottet werden müßte, und wir alle hielten das für die Wahrheit.' Gilbert, *op. cit.*, p. 260.

---

['... after the war started, Hitler explained that world Jewry had started a showdown with National Socialism – that was in a Reichstag speech at the time of the French campaign – and the Jews must be exterminated. Of course, nobody at that time thought that it was meant so literally. ... it was always stressed (Goebbels) that if Germany was to survive, then world Jewry must be exterminated and we all accepted it as truth.']

Sometime between April 19 and April 22, 1946, Wilhelm Frick, former Minister of the Interior, asserted: ['The mass murders were certainly not thought of as a consequence of the Nuremberg Laws ... It may have turned out that way, but it certainly was not thought of that way.'] Gilbert, *op. cit.*, p. 276.

On April 27 and April 28, 1946, Joachim von Ribbentrop, former Minister for Foreign Affairs, said to Gilbert that he was not an anti-Semite – some of his best friends were Jews – and that he had only belonged to an anti-Semitic government and thus, naturally, could not follow a pro-Semitic policy. *Ibid.*, p. 295.

On April 29, 1946, Julius Streicher, former Gauleiter of Franken and since

1923 editor-in-chief of the anti-Semitic weekly *Der Stürmer,* stated that – although he had advocated that the Jews should be exterminated – he had not meant this literally. *Ibid.,* p. 296; furthermore, Streicher declared on July 26, 1946, after having learned more about Jewish qualities (after 1945): 'Jeder, der kämpfen kann und Widerstand leisten kann ... und zusammenhalten und einer Sache treu bleiben kann – vor solchen Leuten habe ich den größten *Respekt!* Ja, sogar Hitler würde, wenn er noch lebte, zugeben, daß sie eine mutige Rasse sind! Ich wäre jetzt bereit, mich ihnen anzuschließen und ihnen in ihrem Kampf zu helfen! ... Ich habe sie 25 Jahre gewarnt, doch jetzt erkenne ich, daß die Juden Entschlossenheit und Mut haben. Sie werden noch die Welt beherrschen, ... ich wäre *froh,* wenn ich mithelfen könnte, sie zum Sieg zu führen weil sie stark und zäh sind. ... Ich habe sie so lange studiert, daß ich mich, glaube ich, ihren typischen Eigenschaften angepaßt habe – zumindest könnte ich eine Gruppe in Palästina leiten.' *Ibid.,* pp. 415-416.

['Anybody who can fight, and resist, ... and stick together, and be loyal to their cause – for such people I can only have the greatest *respect!* Yes, even Hitler, if he were living now, would also admit that they are a brave race. – I would be ready to join them now and help them in their fight! ... I warned them for twenty-five years, but now I see that the Jews have determination and courage. – They will dominate the world, ... I would be glad to help lead them to victory because they are strong and tenacious, ... I have studied them so long that I suppose I have adapted myself to their typical characteristics – at least I could lead a group in Palestine.']

On May 2, 1946, Hjalmar Schacht, former Reichsbankpräsident and Minister of Economy, claimed to have stood in opposition to Hitler and the party. Reichsminister Schacht actively supported Hitler's rearmament program and was recipient of the golden party badge (Goldenes Parteiabzeichen) and paid party dues amounting to RM 1,000 – annually. Schacht claimed that Hitler succeeded in deceiving him only until January 1939. After that he (Schacht) refused to accept any executive post because of moral reasons. Hitler demanded of Schacht to simply print more money in order to finance his armament program. These inflationary measures Schacht considered immoral. See *ibid.,* pp. 303-307, 309, 312, 419-420.

On May 5, 1946, Franz von Papen, former Chancellor (1932), Vice Chancellor (1933-1934), and German Ambassador to Vienna (1934-1938) and Ankara 1939-1944), also claimed to have been opposed to the Régime. The Nuremberg decrees and the pogroms of 1938 (Reichskristallnacht) did not arouse his concern.

The cross-examination on June 18, 1946, revealed that von Papen had referred to Hitler in one of his speeches as the one 'sent from Heaven to lead the German people out of their misery.' In spite of his own arrest, despite the murder of his adjutant and the removal of his two other aides to concentration camps during the Röhm Putsch, he remained in Hitler's staff. He did not hesitate to congratulate Hitler on the 'heroic suppression' of the uprising (Röhm Putsch). Besides, von Papen, too, received the golden party badge as well as other high Nazi decorations. All this – as von Papen claimed – he had done because of his patriotic sense of duty which included the role he had played in the realization of the 'Anschluß' of Austria. Yet, Papen's role in support of Hitler did not prevent his nomination by the members of the twentieth of July uprising to become Minister for Foreign Affairs (according to a sworn statement of Bismarck's grandson). *Ibid.,* pp. 312, 382, 385. Cp. also pp. 386-390.

On May 15, 1946, Hans Fritzsche, former chief of the broadcasting system and press section in Goebbel's Ministry of Propaganda, expressed the view that 'in essence racial prejudice constitutes the equivalent of a premeditation to murder. Anyone who is defending such prejudice is the spiritual father of a new wave of mass murder.' *Ibid.,* p. 324.

On May 24, 1946, Baldur von Schirach, former leader of the Hitler Youth, NSDAP Reichsleiter (1930-1940), and Gauleiter and Reichsstadthalter of Vienna (1940-1945), claimed that he and the German youth had aspired to a peaceful solution of the Jewish question. He further described his break with Hitler in 1943 as due to differences with him concerning cultural and Jewish problems. However, as prosecutor Dodd pointed out during the cross-examination, this did not prevent von Schirach from coming to an agreement with Himmler. The agreement stipulated that members of the Hitler Youth were to join SS Death's Head Units assigned for duty in concentration camps or similar commands. Furthermore, von Schirach's office received weekly reports from the RSHA concerning their destruction activities. *Ibid.,* pp. 338-341, 346-348.

On June 1 and June 2, 1946, SS-Obergruppenführer Oswald Pohl, former chief of the Wirtschafts- und Verwaltungshauptamt (WVHA) and as of March 3, 1942, in charge of concentration camps, stated in a conversation with Gilbert that conditions in concentration camps had not been so bad as depicted in the film shown to the accused and members of the IMT. Although he realized that nutrition in the camps was insufficient, there was nothing he could do but offer suggestions to Himmler. He (Pohl) wanted to abandon the concentration camps to the advancing enemy. Due to the constant evacuation of prisoners into the interior of the country more people were starving to death than before. He also did not feel responsible for the extermination of the Jews – a fact, he claimed, known to everyone in the country. This activity belonged to the scope of duties of Eichmann and Müller who, in turn, were responsible to Kaltenbrunner. He further stated that Kaltenbrunner as chief of the RSHA and Security Police was superordinate to him and after Himmler the second in charge. He, Pohl, was merely commissioned with the distribution of supplies. See Gilbert, *op. cit.,* pp. 242-245.

On June 4, 1946, Generalmajor Alfred Jodl declared before the tribunal that he had had no knowledge of the terror and destruction activities in concentration camps – except for the deportation of the Jews from Denmark. He defended the principle of loyalty to the head of the state, and along with Dönitz felt that the politicians were solely responsible for having started World

War II. Cf. *ibid.,* pp. 354, 356-357.

On April 6 and April 7, Jodl asserted: 'We only cooperated because Hitler had become the lawfully elected chancellor.' *Ibid.,* p. 240. Cp. also *ibid.,* p. 326.

On June 6, 1946, the former Reichsmarschall Hermann Göring, also former Minister of the Air Force, expressed the conviction that if the interests of a nation are at stake, moral considerations, words of honor, or agreements need not be kept. See *ibid.,* p. 361.

On June 11, 1946, Arthur Seyss-Inquart, former Reichsstatthalter of the 'Ost-mark' (1938-1939) and Reichskommissar for the occupied Netherland territories (1940-1945), admitted that the sterilization of Jews had found his approval, although he had dissuaded the SS from sterilizing Jewish women. He further admitted to having deported 250,000 Dutch workers to serve in Germany as slave laborers. Concerning the deportation of Jews to concentration camps, Seyss-Inquart insisted that he was ignorant as to their fate although he was aware of the fact that several of Hitler's opponents had perished in camps. He accepted the responsibility for having ordered the shooting of hostages, his role in the 'Anschluß' of Austria, and the fact that his actions had been in discord with the law of nations and the right of man. Cf. *ibid.,* pp. 371, 373.

To Gilbert's suggestion 'Das also ist nun die Entwicklung vom Antisemitismus, ... zunächst Reden, dann Nürnberger Recht, dann Gettos ...,' Seyss-Inquart responded 'Nein, vor den Gettos war noch die *Kristallnacht* am 9. November 1938, ... Deshalb glaubten wir damals, daß Gettos notwendig seien. Es schien der einzig vernünftige Weg, künftig solche Ausschreitungen zu vermeiden.'

---

['So that is the development of anti-Semitism ... first speeches, then Nuremberg Law, then ghettoes, ...' Seyss-Inquart responded: 'No, before the ghettoes there was the *Night of Broken Crystal* (Reichskristallnacht) of November 9, 1938 ... That is the reason why we believed at that time that ghettoes were necessary. It seemed the only reasonable way to avoid such excesses in the future.']

He also claimed to have been too preoccupied with other more urgent business to contemplate the fate of the Jews. He regarded them as alien foreigners and thought it logical that they should be removed from the war area. Cf. *ibid.,* p. 374. See also pp. 375-377.

Hitler himself appears to have felt that his action program and 'prophecies' concerning the fate of the Jews were not taken seriously. In a speech on September 30, 1942, in Berlin he said the following. 'Die Juden haben einst auch in Deutschland über meine Prophezeiung gelacht. Ich weiß nicht, ob sie auch heute noch lachen, oder ob ihnen das Lachen bereits vergangen ist. Ich kann aber auch jetzt nur versichern: Es wird ihnen das Lachen überall ver-gehen. Und ich werde auch mit diesen Prophezeiungen recht behalten.' Erhard Klöss, *op. cit.,* p. 292.

---

['Once the Jews in Germany also laughed at my prophecy. I do not know whether they are still laughing today, or whether laughter has already deserted them. But I can now assert: They will lose the ability to laugh everywhere. And I will be proved right in this prophecy as well.']

71. See the testimonies of Otto Ohlendorf, Gilbert, *op. cit.*, p. 104; of Dieter Wisliceny, *ibid.*, p. 105; of Rudolf Höß, *ibid.*, pp. 242-244, 327; of Wilhelm Keitel, *ibid.*, p. 239; cf. also *ibid.*, pp. 67, 74, 80, 162, 172-173, 224, 237, 250, 369-370, 406-407.

   In a hand-signed memo written by Himmler concerning his report to the Führer at the Obersalzberg on June 19, 1943, he recorded the following: 'Der Führer sprach auf meinen Vortrag in der Judenfrage hin aus, daß die Eva-kuierung der Juden trotz der dadurch in den nächsten 3 bis 4 Monaten noch entstehenden Unruhe radikal durchzuführen sei und durchgestanden werden müsse!'

   ---

   ['The Führer talked to me about the Jewish problem and said that the deporta-tion of the Jews must go on regardless of any unrest it might cause during the next three or four months, and that it must be carried out ruthlessly and must be seen through!']

   ---

   Hand-signed memo by Himmler of June 1943; original copy in the Bundes-archiv, Koblenz, in Helmut Krausnick, *Judenverfolgung, op. cit.*, p. 447. Cf. also *ibid.*, pp. 411-417, 419.

   As in the case of Denmark, Finland's leaders refused to yield to Hitler's and Himmler's pressure to send Finnish Jews into German destruction camps. Cf. Felix Kersten, *Totenkopf und Treue*, (Hamburg: Robert Mölich Verlag), pp. 178-181.

72. Trevor-Roper mentions the following incident during a tea-party given by Hitler in honor of Mussolini on July 20, 1944: 'Dann erwähnte irgendeiner ganz plötzlich die andere berühmte "Verschwörung" in der Geschichte des Nazismus, das Röhmkomplott vom 30. Juni 1934 und das Blutbad, das darauf folgte. In diesem Augenblick sprang Hitler in einem Tobsuchtsanfall mit Schaum vor dem Mund auf und schrie, daß er an allen Verrätern Rache nehmen werde. Die Vorsehung hätte wieder einmal gezeigt, kreischte er, daß sie ihn auserwählt hatte, Weltgeschichte zu machen. Und er drohte mit fürch-terlichen Strafen für die Frauen und Kinder – sie alle würden in Konzentra-tionslager gesteckt werden – Auge um Auge und Zahn um Zahn –, keiner sollte verschont werden, der sich der göttlichen Vorsehung entgegenstellte. Während der Führer eine halbe Stunde lang raste, war der Hof verstummt; die Besucher dachten, er müsse verrückt sein – "Ich weiß nicht", sagte einer von ihnen, "warum ich nicht auf der Stelle zu den Alliierten überging." '

   ---

   ['Then, quite suddenly, someone mentioned that other famous "plot" in Nazi history – the Röhm plot of June 30th, 1934, and the bloody purge which follow-ed it. Immediately Hitler leapt up in a fit of frenzy, with foam on his lips, and shouted that he would be revenged on all traitors. Providence had just shown him

once again, he screamed, that he had been chosen to make world history; and
he ranted wildly about terrible punishments for women and children, – all of
them would be thrown into concentration camps – an eye for an eye, and a
tooth for a tooth – none should be spared who set himself against divine Providence. The court fell silent as the Führer raged for a full half-hour; the visitors
thought he must be mad, – "I don't know," said one of them, "why I didn't go
over to the Allies there and then." ']

Trevor-Roper, *Hitlers letzte Tage, op. cit.*, p. 64. See also *ibid.*, pp. 102-111.
The social-psychological interpretation that attempts to explain the eventual,
all-embracing destruction which took place during the existence of the Third
Reich and spared no one is commented upon by Alexander as follows: 'It is
one of the laws of psychology, which is in harmony also with more general
physiological principles, that destructive urges of great magnitude and depth
and destructive concepts arising therefrom cannot remain limited or focused
but must inevitably spread and be directed against one's own group and
ultimately against the self.' Leo Alexander, 'War Crimes: Their Social-
Psychological Aspects,' *American Journal of Psychiatry*, CV, 1948, p. 172.
Cp. also Leo Alexander, 'Destructive and Self-Destructive Trends in Criminalized Society,' *Journal of Criminal Law and Criminology*, January-February,
1949, Vol. XXXIX, p. 559.
Cf. also Rauschning, *op. cit., passim.*
Otto Strasser, *Hitler und ich* (Konstanz: Johannes Asmus Verlag, 1948), *passim;*
see also Wolfgang Treher, *Hitler, Steiner, Schreber* (Emmendingen: Selbst-
auflage, 1966), Chpt. on Hitler; Wilhelm Lange-Eichbaum and Wolfram Kurth,
*Genie, Irrsinn und Ruhm* (München-Basel: Ernst Reinhardt Verlag, 1967), pp.
381-388;
J. Recktenwald, *Woran hat Adolf Hitler gelitten?* (München-Basel: Ernst
Reinhardt Verlag, 1964), *passim;* cp. Gilbert, *op. cit.*, pp. 106, 169, 209-210,
233, 236, 238, 366, 376, 381, 393-394.
73. Hitler, *Mein Kampf*, Vol. II, *op. cit.*, pp. 322, 323.
Mr. Elwyn Jones, member of the International Military Tribunal, summed
up in his indictment of January 8, 1946: 'From *Mein Kampf* the path directly
leads to the crematories of Auschwitz and the gas chambers of Maidanek.'
Gilbert, *op. cit.*, p. 117.
In this connection it may also be interesting to note that according to Hans
Frank, Hitler referred to humanity as 'Planetenbazillen.' *Ibid.*, p. 145. Cf.
also *ibid.*, p. 117. Furthermore, Hitler in his speech before the Reichstag on
January 30, 1939, stressed that 'Wenn es dem internationalen Finanzjudentum
inner- und außerhalb Europas gelingen sollte, die Völker noch einmal in einen
Weltkrieg zu stürzen, dann wird das Ergebnis nicht die Bolschewisierung der
Erde und damit der Sieg des Judentums sein, sondern die Vernichtung der
jüdischen Rasse in Europa!' Hofer *op. cit.*, p. 277.

---

['If international financial Jewry inside and outside Europe should succeed in plunging the people once more into a world war, the result will not be the bolshevization of the world and hence the victory of Jewry, but rather the destruction of the Jewish race in Europe!']

74. Erich Fromm, *Escape from Freedom* (New York: Farrar and Straus, 1941), p. 236.
75. Paul Halmos, *Towards a Measure of Man: The Frontiers of Normal Adjustment* (London: Routledge and Kegan Paul, 1957), p. 134.
    Cp. Amitai Etzioni, *A Comparative Analysis of Complex Organizations* (New York: The Free Press, 1965), pp. 201-232.
76. Cf. C. G. Jung, *Flying Saucers* (New York: Signet Books, 1969), p. 80. See also *ibid.*, pp. 71-79, 81-84, 107-113.
77. Cf. Emile Durkheim, 'On Anomie,' in C. Wright Mills, *Images of Man* (New York: George Braziller, 1967), pp. 449-458; Robert K. Merton, 'Social Structure and Anomie,' in William A. Rushing (ed.), *Deviant Behavior and Social Process* (Chicago: Rand McNally, 1969), pp. 79-86; José Ortega y Gasset, *Man and Crisis* (New York: W. W. Norton, 1962), pp. 139-142.
78. *Ibid.*, p. 139.
79. *Ibid.*, p. 156.
80. Cf. *ibid.*, p. 98.
81. Here the relativity of concepts may become more obvious when we consider their differential perception and emphasis on meanings according to a specific ranking order determined by experienced urgencies in time and space. (A propos Einstein's theory of relativity E-MC$^2$.)
    1. So, for example, the following dependent variables held in common by man in most situations may be viewed as determinants:
       a) fear of death (death instinct)
       b) urge of self-preservation (survival)
       c) physical and mental suffering (anguish)
    2. As intervening or independent variables may be considered:
       a) individual difference
       aa) ego defence mechanisms (escape, suppression, displacement, deferral, transfer, inhibition, retreat, denial)
       b) difference in vested interests, emotions, and experiences
       c) difference in the interpretation and emphasis on meaning of values and norms, models, reference groups, and awareness of and identification with historic events and past experiences.
82. Cf. Ortega y Gasset, *op. cit.*, pp. 154-155.
83. *Ibid.*, pp. 142, 146. See I. Horowitz, *Three Worlds of Development: The Theory and Practice of International Stratification* (New York: Oxford University Press, 1966), pp. 291-332.
84. Ortega y Gasset, *op. cit.*, p. 96. Cp. Rauschning, *op. cit.*, p. 78. Cf. also Robert A. Nisbet, *Social Change and History* (New York: Oxford University Press, 1969), p. 205.
85. Ortega y Gasset, *op. cit.*, pp. 155, 97, 99.

86. Ortega y Gasset, *The Revolt of the Masses* (New York: W. W. Norton 1932), pp. 80, 82, 83.
    A 'civilized' response of man to an existential crisis set off by a cultural lag is described by Y Gasset as follows: 'The man in the forest reacts to his problems by creating a culture. To that end he manages to retreat from the forest and withdraw into himself. ... the man who is too cultivated and socialized, who is living on top of a culture which has already become false, is in urgent need of another culture, that is to say a culture which is genuine. But this can only start in the sincere and naked depth of his own personal self.' *Man and Crisis, op. cit.,* p. 100. Cf. also Nisbet, *op. cit.,* p. 205.
87. Cf. Hugh Dalziel Duncan, *Communication and Social Order* (New York: Oxford University Press, 1968), Chpt. XVII: 'Rhetoric as an Instrument of Domination through Unreason: Hitler's *Mein Kampf,'* and Chpt. XVIII: 'Social Order Based on Unreason: The Perversion of Religion by the State,' pp. 225-248.
    Cf. also Ortega y Gasset, *Man and Crisis, op. cit.,* p. 114.
88. Ortega y Gasset, *The Revolt of the Masses, op. cit.,* p. 103. Here, Y Gasset refers to all those who have for some reason or another not become a part of the civilizational process and have chosen to participate in a process of retrogression, involution, and decay (vulgus, turba).
89. Ortega y Gasset, *The Revolt of the Masses, op. cit.,* p. 141.
90. Ortega y Gasset, *Man and Crisis, op. cit.,* p. 154.
91. *Ibid.,* p. 147.
92. Cf. Ortega y Gasset, *The Revolt of the Masses, op. cit.,* pp. 107-108.
93. Ortega y Gasset, *Man and Crisis, op. cit.,* p. 108.
94. Ortega y Gasset, *The Revolt of the Masses, op. cit.,* pp. 89, 97. Cf. also *ibid.,* pp. 56-57, 75-76. Terms reflecting Ortega y Gasset's connotation of the masses are for example infima plebs, multitudo, faex populi, sentina civitatis.
95. Cf. Abel, *op. cit.,* pp. 5-6; Otto Strasser, *Der Faschismus* (München: Günter Olzog Verlag, 1965), pp. 26-35; C. Wright Mills, *Power, Politics and People* (New York: Ballantine Books, 1963), pp. 59-61; Ernst Nolte, *Three Faces of Fascism* (New York: Holt, Rinehart and Winston, 1966), pp. 17, 26, 315, 434; S. J. Woolf (ed.), *European Fascism* (New York: Vintage Books, 1969), pp. 4-5; Ortega y Gasset, *The Revolt of the Masses, op. cit.,* p. 199.
96. Ortega y Gasset, *Man and Crisis, op. cit.,* p. 139.
    Rauschning records the following claims made by Hitler in 1932: The creative genius stands always outside the circle of experts. I have the gift of reducing all problems to their simplest foundation ... the theories of Feder and Lawaczek do not bother me. I have a gift for tracing back all theories to their roots in reality ... I have nothing to do with fantasies. ... I have the gift of simplification and then everything works itself out. Difficulties exist only in the imagination!' Rauschning, *op. cit.,* pp. 12, 26.
    This revolt against realism is astutely described by Hannah Arendt: 'The masses' escape from reality is a verdict against the world in which they are forced to live and in which they cannot exist, since coincidence has become

Its supreme master and human beings need the constant transformation of chaotic and accidental conditions into a man-made pattern of relative consistency. The revolt of the masses against "realism," common sense, and all "the plausibilities of the world" (Burke) was the result of their atomization, of their loss of social status along with which they lost the whole sector of communal relationships in whose framework common sense makes sense. ... Totalitarian propaganda can outrageously insult common sense only where common sense has lost its validity.' Arendt, *The Origins of Totalitarianism* (New York: Meridian Books, 1952), p. 352.

97. For a definition of the meaning and function of intellectualism, see Ortega y Gasset, *Man and Crisis, op. cit.*, pp. 111-114.

Cf. Adolf Hitler, *Mein Kampf*, Vol. I, *op. cit.*, pp. 222-223, 260, 334-336; Vol. II, *op. cit.*, pp. 71-72; Strasser, *Hitler und Ich, op. cit.*, pp. 69, 79; Rauschning, *op. cit.*, pp. 173, 198, 212, 237.

In these passages Hitler's anti-intellectual attitude is clearly expressed. From these and other data it can be assumed that the average type of follower of the Hitler movement had anti-intellectual inclinations.

98. Ortega y Gasset, *The Revolt of the Masses, op. cit.*, p. 97. In this context Parsons' reflection on charismatic movements seems appropriate: 'Charismatic movements of various sorts seem to function in the situation as mechanisms of "reintegration" which gives large numbers of disorganized insecure people a definite orientation, gives meaning to their lives.' Talcott Parsons, 'Max Weber and the Contemporary Political Crisis,' *Review of Politics,* 1942, No. 4, pp. 75-76.

99. Ortega y Gasset, *Man and Crisis, op. cit.*, pp. 148-149.

100. Cf. Elton B. MacNeil, 'Violence and Human Development,' in Marvin E. Wolfgang (ed.), *op. cit.*, pp. 149-157.

So, for example, James C. Hackler's findings show that statistical associations between pairs of variables permit the formulation of a plausible sequence. Low esteem by society leads to prediction by others that ego will achieve little in life and therefore will be led to commit deviant acts. Perceiving that others anticipate deviance, ego has little to lose by actual participation in deviant behavior; after acting in this manner, ego begins to think of himself as a deviant and finally comes to endorse deviant norms. Although such an individual may appear tough and courageous superficially, basically he is frightened of society and its demands. See J. C. Hackler, *A Sequential Mode of Deviant Behavior,* doctoral dissertation, University of Washington, 1945. Ann Arbor, University Microfilms, 1965, *passim.*

101. See especially Leo Alexander, 'War Crimes: Their Social-Psychological Aspects,' *American Journal of Psychiatry,* No. 105, 1948, pp. 170-177; E. Federn, 'Some Clinical Remarks on the Psychopathology of Genocide,' *Psychiatric Quarterly,* Vol. XXXIV, No. 3, 1960, pp. 538-549; F. Cavero Javega, 'War Crimes' (Crimenes de Guerra), *Policia Espanola,* Vol. II, No. 15, 1963, p. 12; O. Wormser-Migot *et al., 'La Prophylaxie du Génocide,' Etudes Internationales de Psycho-Sociologie Criminelle,* Nos. 11-12-13, Paris, 1967, pp. 3-59.

102. Arendt, *Eichmann in Jerusalem, op. cit.,* p. 247.
     Cf. also Arthur Everett *et al., Calley* (New York: Dell Publ., 1971), *passim.*
103. Gilbert, *op. cit.,* p. 76. Similarly Fritzsche attempted to explain that the propaganda only endeavored to isolate the Jews. *Ibid.,* p. 174.
     Göring stated the following to Gilbert on March 22, 1946, in connection with anti-Semitic measures: 'Nein, um Gottes Willen! Nach dem, was ich jetzt weiß? Um Gottes Willen, glauben Sie, ich hätte sie je befürwortet, wenn ich nur die leiseste Idee gehabt hätte, daß sie zum Massenmord führt? Ich versichere Ihnen, wir hatten so etwas nie im Sinn. Ich dachte nur, wir würden die Juden aus ihren Stellungen in der Wirtschaft und Regierung entfernen, und dabei würde es bleiben. Aber vergessen Sie nicht, sie haben auch eine schreckliche Kampagne gegen uns in der ganzen Welt geführt.' *Ibid.,* p. 205.

['*Nein, um Gotteswillen!* – After what I know now? – For heaven's sake, do you think I would ever have supported it if I had had the slightest idea that it would lead to mass murder. I assure you we never for a moment had such things in mind. I only thought we would eliminate Jews from positions in big business and government, and that would have been that. – But don't forget they carried on a terrific campaign against us too, all over the world.']

For statements by Höss and Rosenberg, see footnote 70. For similar comments by Ribbentrop and Frank, see Gilbert, *op. cit.,* pp. 224, 229-230, 272. See Appendices XVII, XVIII.
The SS judge Dr. Konrad Morgen stated in an affidavit on July 19, 1946, '...Der Reichsarzt-SS, SS-Gruppenführer Dr. Grawitz erklärte mir, Hitler selbst habe den Befehl zur Judenvernichtung gegeben.'

['... Dr. Grawitz, Reichsarzt-SS and SS-Gruppenführer, explained to me that Hitler himself had given the order for the destruction of the Jews.']

Dr. Konrad Morgen, Richter d. Reserve und Untersuchungsführer des Reichs-kriminalhauptamtes (RKPA). Affidavit SS-67, Dr. K. Morgen, July 19, 1946, in IMT, Vol. XLII, *op. cit.,* pp. 563, 565.
Morgen further testified: '... er (Himmler) persönlich sei an der Judenfrage gar nicht interessiert. Von ihm aus könnten die Juden machen, was sie wollten. Er sei aber Soldat ... und habe daher widerspruchslos die Befehle des obersten militärischen Vorgesetzten auszuführen, so schwer ihm das auch werde. ...' *Ibid.*

['... he (Himmler) was personally not at all interested in the Jewish question. As far as he was concerned the Jews could do as they wished. But he was a soldier ... and hence he had to carry out the orders of the supreme military commander without contradicting them, however difficult that might be for him ...']

104. Cf. Lipset, *op. cit.*, pp. 266-274, 313-365.
105. Cf. Oron James Hale (ed.), 'Gottfried Feder calls Hitler to Order: An Unpublished Letter on Nazi Party Affairs,' *The Journal of Modern History*, December, 1958, Vol. XXX, No. 4, p. 362.
106. Christian Fürchtegott Gellert, *Sämtliche Fabeln und Erzählungen* (Leipzig. in der Hahn'schen Verlags-Buchhandlung, 1836), p. 152.
107. Ortega y Gasset, *The Revolt of the Masses*, *op. cit.*, p. 133.
108. *Ibid.*, p. 134.
109. *Ibid.*
110. During his election campaign in Hamburg Hitler said the following in 1932: 'The streets of our country are in turmoil. The universities are filled with students rebelling and rioting. Communists are seeking to destroy our country. Russia is threatening us with her might, and the Republic is in danger. Yes, danger from within and from without. We need law and order. Yes, without law and order, our Nation cannot survive. Elect us and we shall restore law and order.' Paul Omelich in an editorial entitled 'Ominous Changes in Police Tactics,' in the *San Francisco Chronicle*, May 28, 1969, No. 147, p. 46. Cf. also Ortega y Gasset, *The Revolt of the Masses*, *op. cit.*, p. 135.
111. Cf. *ibid.*, pp. 148, 195, 201.

## V. SOCIOLOGICAL IMPLICATIONS OF DEVIANCE AND ACCOUNTABILITY IN NS POLITICAL AND BUREAUCRATIC INSTITUTIONS

1. Erich Fromm sees in Rank's Weltanschauung '... a close kinship with the essentials of Fascist philosophy.' Erich Fromm, 'The Social Philosophy of "Will Therapy",' *Psychiatry*, II, No. 2, May, 1939, pp. 234-235.
2. Otto Rank, *Will Therapy and Truth and Reality* (New York: Alfred A. Knopf, 1950), p. 200.
In contrast to the above quotation it might be of interest to cite in this context Thomas S. Szasz's stand on the definition of mental illness. He posits that '... contemporary psychotherapists deal with problems in living, rather than with mental illnesses and their cures, [which] stands in opposition to a currently prevalent claim, according to which mental illness is just as "real" and "objective" as bodily illness. ... instead of calling attention to conflicting human needs, aspirations, and values, the notion of mental illness provides an amoral and impersonal "thing" (an "illness") as an explanation for *problems in living* (Szasz, 1959). ... The belief in mental illness, as something other than man's trouble in getting along with his fellow man, is the proper heir to the belief in demonology and witchcraft. Mental illness exists or is "real" in exactly the same sense in which witches existed or were "real". ... My argument was limited to the proposition that mental illness is a myth, whose function it is to disguise and thus render more palatable the bitter pill of moral conflicts in human relations.' Thomas S. Szasz, 'The Myth of Mental Illness,' in Thomas J. Scheff (ed.), *Mental Illness and Social Processes* (New

York: Harper and Row, 1967), pp. 249, 251, 254.
However, the fact that violators of human ethics by their conduct can do grave harm to their fellow men as well as to themselves cannot be easily discarded as outdated. Ausubel observes: '... some individuals, either because of the magnitude of the stress involved, or because of genically or environmentally induced susceptibility to ordinary degrees of stress, respond to the problems of living with behavior that is either seriously distorted or sufficiently unadaptive to prevent normal interpersonal relations and vocational functioning. The latter outcome – gross deviation from a designated range of desirable behavioral variability – conforms to the generally understood meaning of mental illness. . . .

'Modern students of personality disorder do not regard mental illness as a cause of human disharmony, but as a co-manifestation with it of inherent difficulties in personal adjustment and interpersonal relations; ... psychopathologists do not conceive of mental illness as a cause of particular behavior symptoms but as a generic term under which these symptoms can be subsumed. ... one can plausibly accept the proposition that psychiatrists and clinical psychologists have erred in trying to divorce behavioral evaluation from ethical considerations, in conducting psychotherapy in an amoral setting, and in confusing the psychological explanation of unethical behavior with absolution from accountability for same, *without* necessarily endorsing the view that personality disorders are basically a reflection of sin, and that victims of these disorders are less ill than responsible for their symptoms. . . .

'In the first place, it is possible in most instances (although admittedly difficult in some) to distinguish quite unambiguously between mental illness and ordinary cases of immorality. The vast majority of persons who are guilty of moral lapses knowingly violate their own ethical precepts for expediential reasons – despite being volitionally capable at the time, both of choosing the more moral alternative and of exercising the necessary inhibitory control. ... Such persons, also, usually do not exhibit any signs of behavior disorder. At crucial choice points in facing the problem of living they simply choose the opportunistic instead of the moral alternative. They are not mentally ill, but they are clearly accountable for their misconduct. Hence, since personality disorder and immorality are neither co-extensive nor mutually exclusive conditions, the concept of mental illness need not necessarily obscure the issue of moral accountability.' David P. Ausubel, 'Personality Disorder is Disease,' in Thomas J. Scheff (ed.), *op. cit.*, pp. 261, 262, 263.

Cf. also Erik H. Erikson, *Insight and Responsibility* (New York: W. W. Norton, 1964), pp. 54-56, and Erich Fromm, *May Man Prevail?* (Garden City/N.Y.: Doubleday, 1964), pp. 7-13, 17-30.

3. Walther Rathenau, *Zur Kritik der Zeit* (Berlin: S. Fischer Verlag, 1912), p. 27. Otto Strasser views Rathenau's influence on his time as follows: 'Rathenau nun war es, der mit der Autorität des Wirschaftlers und des Staatsmannes Inhalt und Form jener neuen, besseren Ordnung in klarster Weise darstellte – in einer Weise, die ihn zu einem Wegbereiter des Faschismus machte.' Otto

Strasser, *Der Faschismus, Geschichte und Gefahr* (München: G. Olzog Verlag, 1965), p. 37. See also *ibid.*, pp. 38-41.

['Now it was Rathenau who, with the authority of an economist and a states-man, gave the clearest pictures of the content and form of that new, better order, in such a manner as to make him a trail-blazer for fascism.']

Cp. also J. W. von Goethe, *Wilhelm Meisters Wanderjahre* (Stuttgart: Cot-ta'sche Buchhandlung, 1821), pp. 155-198, 543-550. Here Goethe gives an account of his concept of authority and the three types of reverence rendered to persons in supervisory (Aufseher) capacity and social leadership positions.
4. Cf. Rathenau, *op. cit.*, p. 70.
Gottfried Feder, one of the co-founders of the NSDAP, wrote in an admonitory letter to Hitler on August 10, 1923, the following: 'Wir wollen alle im Geiste Friedrich des Großen *Diener* des Staates sein, wir räumen Ihnen gerne die erste Stelle ein, aber für tyrannische Neigungen haben wir kein Verständnis.' Oron James Hale (ed.), 'Gottfried Feder calls Hitler to Order: An Unpublished Letter on Nazi Affairs,' *The Journal of Modern History*, Vol. XXX, No. 4, December 1958, pp. 358-362.

['We all want to be *servants* of the state in the spirit of Federick the Great; we gladly grant you the first place, but we have no sympathy for tyrannical in-clinations.']

Cp. Karel Čapek, *Hovory s T. G. Masarykem (Conversations with T. G. Masaryk)*, (Praha: Fr. Borovy, 1947), p. 280. Masaryk traces the traditional attitude of the masses towards spiritual and political authority to the model of the total and exclusive leadership of the ecclesia which was subsequently adopted and substituted by the political aristocracy. He suggests that the present state of the authority-subject relationship is in a state of transition. The claim to and practice of authority still exercised by many a political, religious, and social leader is now being challenged by the mass-educated members of society whose dependency relationship is in a state of flux and whose autonomy is in progression. This also applies to the increasingly negative attitude towards rigid traditional, hierarchically organized institutions among segments of Central European and Western peoples in general.
For a further discussion of Masaryk's social theory, which today could be defined as humanistic sociology and an interactionist approach, see especially *ibid.*, pp. 290-291.
Cp. Otto Strasser's review of Masaryk's social and political thought, Strasser, *op. cit.*, pp. 71-73.
Cf. also Harry Elmer Barnes and Howard Becker, *Social Thought from Lore to Science* (Washington D.C.: Harren Press, 1952), Vol. II, pp. 1060-1067.
5. Rathenau, *op. cit.*, pp. 90-91.
Some consequences of 'transitory states' brought about by technological (and

other) innovations have been astutely described by Erikson: 'Where historical and technological developments severely encroach upon deeply rooted or strongly emerging identities (i.e., agrarian, feudal, patrician) on a large scale, youth feels endangered, individually and collectively, whereupon it becomes ready to support doctrines offering a total immersion in a synthetic identity (extreme nationalism, racism, or class consciousness) and a collective condemnation of a totally stereotyped enemy of the new identity. The fear of loss of identity which fosters such indoctrination contributes significantly to that mixture of righteousness and criminality which, under totalitarian conditions, becomes available for organized terror and for the establishment of major industries of extermination. Since conditions undermining a sense of identity also fixate older individuals on adolescent alternatives, a great number of adults fall in line or are paralyzed in their resistance.' Erikson, *op. cit.*, p. 93. See also *ibid.*, p. 93.

6. Rathenau, *op. cit.*, pp. 98-99.
7. *Ibid.* pp. 104-105.
8. *Ibid.*, pp. 109-111.
9. *Ibid.*, pp. 111-112, 114. Cp. also Čapek, *op. cit.*, pp. 232-241. See also *ibid.*, pp. 219-280.
10. Rathenau, *op. cit.*, p. 125.
11. *Ibid.*, pp. 135-137, 139, 141, 143, 145-146, 148, 157. See also John M. Steiner, 'Goethe's Concept of Art, the Artist, the Public, and his Evaluation of Mass Media,' unpublished manuscript, pp. 36-38.
12. Ernst Benda, Minister of the Interior of the Federal Republic of Germany, cited in 'Radical Fringe "Inevitable" in Any Democracy' in *The Bulletin (A Weekly Survey of German Affairs)*, Bonn, 1968, Vol. XVI, No. 43, p. 328.
13. Cf. Oswald Spengler, *Jahre der Entscheidung*, Part I: *Deutschland und die weltgeschichtliche Entwicklung* (München: Beck'sche Verlagsbuchhandlung, 1933), *passim*. Otto Strasser writes: 'Die naturalistische Philosophie, die dem Naturalismus in der Dichtung seine geistige Überzeugung und Ausrichtung gab, lief auf ein mechanistisches Weltbild hinaus, in dem der Mensch als ein – durch biologische, gesellschaftliche oder sonstige kausal bedingte Naturkräfte – passives Wesen determiniert wurde. Die naturwissenschaftlichen Erkenntnisse wurden auf alles und alle, so auch auf den Menschen, angewandt; in ihrer gesetzlichen Enge hatte er zu leben.

Immer stärker wurde der Einfluß der Milieutheorie des Historikers Hippolyte Taine und der 'Kampf ums Dasein' – Theorie Darwins auf die Dichter der achtziger Jahre. Nach Taine (1828-1893) wurde der Mensch ausschließlich durch die Verhältnisse und Zeitumstände beeinflußt, ja geformt. Bei ihm war der Mensch das Produkt seines Milieus – ohne eigenen, gestaltenden Willen, dem geschichtlichen Prozeß in kausaler Abhängigkeit ausgeliefert. Man kann dies ohne Übertreibung als geistige Vorbereitung auf die unbedingte Abhängigkeit des Menschen (beim Faschismus vom Staat und beim Bolschewismus von den ökonomischen Verhältnissen) von der 'politischen Großmacht' ansehen –
. . .

'Eine packende Zusammenfassung dieser geistigen Struktur der Jahrhundertwende und ihrer Folgen gibt Werner Mahrholz in seiner "Deutschen Literatur der Gegenwart" mit den Worten: "Die ganze Generation befindet sich in dieser seltsam zwiespältigen Stellung zu ihrer Umwelt: sie fühlt die große Qual der Unterdrückung des einzelnen und seiner Seele durch die gesellschaftliche Mechanerie aufs bitterste und klagt deshalb diese Gesellschaft leidenschaftlich an; zugleich aber ist sie besessen von der Dämonie des Zeitalters, der Expansion auf wirtschaftlichem, technischem, politischem, wissenschaftlichem Gebiet. An diesem Zwiespalt der Empfindungen und an dem Mangel an Entscheidungskraft ihm gegenüber leidet die junge Generation, welche die Welt, in der sie zu leben gezwungen ist, zugleich in einem Atem haßt und liebt, bewundert und verachtet, anklagt und lobpreist." Und Fritz Martini in seiner 'Deutschen Literaturgeschichte' sekundiert ihm, wenn er schreibt:
'Das Gefühl einer unentrinnbaren Kulturzersetzung löste den Glauben an eine sinngebende Einheit des Daseins ab. Im radikalen Protest gegen die bestehenden Zustände suchte die junge Generation eine neue Daseinsordnung zu finden. ....' Man wird die Brüchigkeit unserer Zeit und ihre Anfälligkeit gegenüber Faschismus und Kommunismus nicht verstehen, wenn man diese seelische Haltung des modernen Menschen nicht kennt – und ihr Rechnung trägt.'

---

['The naturalistic philosophy, which furnished naturalism in poetry with its spiritual conviction and technique, resulted in a mechanistic picture of the world in which the human being is a passive being whose fate is determined by biological, social, or other causally conditioned natural forces. The knowledge of physical science was applied to everything and everybody, including human beings, who had to live within the narrow confines of its laws.
The influence of the milieu theory of the historian Hippolyte Taine and of the "struggle-for-existence" theory of Darwin on the poets of the 1880s became ever stronger. According to Taine (1828-1893), human beings are influenced, and even formed, exclusively by their relationships and the circumstances of the times. To him man was the product of his milieu – existing without his own formative will and left to the mercy of the historical process in a causal dependence upon it. Without exaggerating, one can regard this as a spiritual preparation for the unconditional dependence of man (on the state, in the case of Fascism, and on economic relationships in the case of Bolshevism) on the "political great power" –
. . .
'Werner Mahrholz, in his "Deutsche Literatur der Gegenwart" (Present-day German Literature), gives an arresting summary of this spiritual structure of the turn of the century and of its consequences in these words: "The whole generation finds itself in a position vis-à-vis its environment that is characterized by an odd dichotomy: it feels very bitterly the great torment of the repression of the individual and of his soul by the social mechanism, and therefore passionately accuses this society; but at the same time it is possessed by the demon of the age, expansion in the economic, technical, political, and scientific spheres.

The young generation suffers from this dichotomy in its sentiments and from its lack of decisiveness with respect to it. In one breath (it) both hates the world in which it is forced to live and loves it, admires it and despises it, accuses it and praises it." And Fritz Martini, in his "Deutsche Literaturgeschichte" (History of German Literature), seconds him when he writes:
"The feeling of an ineluctable cultural decay dissolves the faith in a meaningful unity of existence. In a radical protest against the existing circumstances, the young generation is trying to find a new order of existence . . ." One will not understand the fragility of our time and its susceptibility to Fascism and Communism if one is not acquainted with this spiritual attitude of modern man – and if one does not take it into account.']

Strasser, *op. cit.*, pp. 29, 34-35. Cf. also *ibid.*, pp. 46-47, 48-95. See also Heinrich von Kleist, 'Über das Marionettentheater,' as well as some of his other major writings in Heinrich von Kleist, *Sämtliche Werke* (Darmstadt: Verlag der Heimbücherei, 1951), pp. 825-831.

14. Cf. Thomas G. Bergin (ed.), *Niccolò Machiavelli, The Prince* (New York: Appleton-Century-Crofts, 1947), VIII: 'On Those Who Have Become Princes by Crime,' pp. 23-26.

15. Fromm, *loc. cit.*, p. 229.

16. Cf. Martin Trow, 'Small Businessmen, Political Tolerance, and Support for McCarthy,' mimeographed manuscript, p. 13. On the social character and political orientations of the lower middle class in Germany as shaped by their insecure and continually deteriorating social and economic positions before the rise of Hitler, see Hans H. Gerth, 'The Nazi Party: Its Leadership and Composition,' in Robert K. Merton *et al.* (ed.), *Reader in Bureaucracy* (New York: The Free Press, 1967), pp. 104-107; Erich Fromm, *Escape from Freedom* (New York: Farrar and Strauss, 1941), pp. 211-216; Emil Lederer, *The State of the Masses* (New York: W. W. Norton, 1940), pp. 51-53; Karl Mannheim, *Man and Society in an Age of Reconstruction* (New York: Harcourt, Brace, 1940), p. 102; C. Wright Mills, *Power, Politics, and People* (New York: Ballantine Books, 1963), pp. 59-61; Sigmund Neumann, *Permanent Revolution* (New York: Harper and Bros., 1942), p. 28.
Cf. Theodore Abel, *The Nazi Movement* (New York: Atherton Press, 1966), pp. 4-5, 81, 183-186, 13-53.
Cf. also the occupational distribution of members of the SS in 1938, Appendices IV a – d.

17. Cf. Trow, *op. cit.*, p. 13. Cf. also Adolf Hitler, *Mein Kampf*, Vol. I., *op. cit.*, pp. 154-156, 208-223, 232-234, 310-312, and facsimile of NS bill-posters (Plakatanhang) announcing the themes of Hitler's speeches and other party activities. See Appendix XXI.
Sea also Strasser, *Hitler und ich* (Buenos Aires: Editorial Trenkelbach, 1940), pp. 66-88, 107.

18. *Ibid.*, p. 112.
Cf. Gottfried Feder's reproving letter to Hitler of August 10, 1923, in which

he attempts to save Hitler's 'workingman's soul' from too great an involvement with Munich's high society, artist circles, and the company of beautiful women. Hitler was criticized by founding members of the party for his social activity which gave rise to the expression 'Arbeitsführer bei Sekt und schönen Frauen.' See Hale, *op. cit.*, pp. 359-360. See also Hermann Rauschning, *Gespräche mit Hitler* (Wien: Europa-Verlag, 1940), pp. 176-181; Mills, *op. cit.*, pp. 170-178; Ernst Nolte, *Three Faces of Fascism* (New York: Holt, Rinehart and Winston, 1966). pp. 335-340.

19. Thomas S. Szasz, *Law, Liberty, and Psychiatry* (New York: Collier Books, 1968), pp. 12, 15, 16-17.
20. Patrick Mullahy, *Oedipus: Myth and Complex: A Review of Psychiatric Theory* (New York: Hermitage Press, 1948), p. 320.
21. Sigmund Freud, *Civilization and Its Discontents* (London: Hogarth Press, 1930), p. 102.
22. *Ibid.*, pp. 102-103.
23. Karen Horney, *Neurosis and Human Growth: The Struggle toward Self-Realization* (New York: W. W. Norton 1950), p. 377.
24. Read Bain, 'Sociology and Psychoanalysis,' *American Sociological Review*, Vol. I, No. 2, April 1936, p. 206.
25. Cf. Frederic Wertham, 'Freud Now,' *Scientific American*, Vol. CLXXXI, No. 4, October, 1949, p. 53.
26. *Ibid.*, p. 54.
27. The following communication written by Himmler to SS-Obergruppenführer Ernst Sachs seems to reflect the official attitude towards Freud and his theory:
    '25.6.44; A:RF; E:SS-Ogruf. Ernst Sachs, Chef Fernmeldewesen.
    Lieber Sachs!
    Bei Übernahme des Dienstschreibtisches des Kommandeurs Oberehnheim durch SS-Obersturmbannführer Prechter wurde ein Buch "Freude – Sexualtheorie"* gefunden. Ich ersuche Sie, den SS-Standartenführer Dilcher sofort zu sich zu bestellen und ihn zu befragen:
    1. Wie kommt dieses Buch in den Dienstschreibtisch?
    2. Ist Dilcher der Besitzer dieses Buches?
    Bitte um baldigste schriftliche Antwort. Das Buch befindet sich bei mir. SS-Staf. Dilcher hat Berlin nicht zu verlassen, bis ich es wieder genehmige.
    *Heil Hitler!*
    Ihr gez. H. Himmler·

['25.6.44; A:RF; E:SS-Ogruf. Ernst Sachs, Chef Fernmeldewesen.
Dear Sachs:
When SS-Obersturmbannführer Prechter took over the desk of Commanding Officer Oberehnheim, a book, "Freude (sic) – Sexual Theory"*, was found. I request you to summon SS-Standartenführer Dilcher immediately and to ask him the following:

* Here Himmler is referring to Freud's book but misspelled his name in the letter.

1. How did this book get into the desk?
2. Is Dilcher the owner of this book?
I request a written answer as soon as possible. The book is in my possession.
SS-Staf. Dilcher is not to leave Berlin without my authorization.

*Heil Hitler!*

Yours,
(Signed) H. Himmler']

Schriftgutverwaltung des persönlichen Stabes Reichsführer-SS, T-175, Rolle 62, p. 7859 (Guides to German Records Microfilmed at Alexandria/Va.) in Helmut Heiber (ed.), *Reichsführer!* ... *Briefe an und von Himmler* (Stuttgart: Deutsche Verlags-Anstalt, 1968), p. 269, No. 325.

On November 10, 1940, Kersten cites Himmler as follows: 'Sie wollen mir doch nicht etwa beibringen, daß die Psychotherapeuten, dieser Verein der Seelenzerschneider mit ihrem jüdischen Ehrenpräsidenten Freud an der Spitze, den sie jetzt allerdings schamhaft verleugnen oder sich von ihm aus Zweckmäßigkeitsgründen distanzieren, die Homosexualität heilen könnten!' Felix Kersten, *Totenkopf und Treue* (Hamburg: Robert Mölich Verlag, 1952), p. 70.

———

['Surely you don't mean to tell me that the psychotherapists – this association of soul-dissectors headed by their Jewish honorary president Freud, whom they now shamefully deny or from whom they now distance themselves for reasons of expediency – could cure homosexuality!']

The human anguish and destruction of lives brought down upon mankind by turning the concrete into a stigmatizing, abstract label is incalculable.

28. Cf. *ibid.*, pp. 186-190.
See also Dietrich Eckart, *Der Bolschewismus von Moses bis Lenin: Zwiegespräch zwischen Adolf Hitler und mir* (München: Hoheneichen-Verlag, 1924), pp. 45-49.

29. Eckart writes: 'Die Zeiten sind vorbei, wo uns die jüdische Religion schnuppe war. Wir kümmern uns jetzt sogar sehr um sie. Auf Schritt und Tritt gehen wir ihr nach und haben schon bei der ersten Bekanntschaft herausgefunden, daß das, was die Juden ihre Religion nennen, haargenau mit ihrem Charakter übereinstimmt. ...
Eine Religion das? Dieses Wühlen im Schmutz, dieser Haß, diese Bosheit, dieser Hochmut, diese Scheinheiligkeit, diese Rabulistik, diese Aneiferung zu Betrug und Mord – eine Religion? Dann hat es noch nie etwas Religiöseres gegeben als den Teufel. Die jüdische *Wesenheit* ist es, der jüdische *Charakter*, und damit Punktum! Man probiere es doch einmal und lehre einem anständigen Menschen solches Zeug, was der dazu sagen wird? Nein, wer so etwas wie lauter Leckerbissen hinunterfrißt, ist ein Scheusal von Haus aus.' *Ibid.*, pp. 45-46.

———

['The times are past when the Jewish religion was a matter of indifference to

us. Now we are very much concerned about it. We are investigating it, step by step, and on first acquaintance we learned that that which the Jews call their religion is in exact agreement with their character ...
'That, a religion? This grubbing in the dirt, this hate, this evil, this arrogance, this hypocrisy, this pettifogging, this stimulus to deception and murder – is this a religion? If so, there has never been anything more religious than the Devil. It is the Jewish *nature*, the Jewish *character*, and that is all! If one once tried to teach a decent person such stuff, what would he say? No, anybody who could gulp something like that as if it were a dainty titbit is a monster by nature.']

30. Cf. Himmler's communications of July 19, 1942, to SS-Obergruppenführer Friedrich-Wilhelm Krüger, HSSPF Ost, Krakau; of July 27, 1942, to SS-Obergruppenführer Arthur Greiser, Gauleiter und Reichsstatthalter im Wartheland; of July 28, 1942, to SS-Gruppenführer Gottlob Berger, Chef SSHA und Verbindungsführer zum Reichsminister für die besetzten Ostgebiete; of October 2, 1942, to SS-Obergruppenführer Oswald Pohl, WVHA et al.; of October 27, 1942, to SS-Obergruppenführer Hans Prützmann, HSSPF Ukraine; of November 20, 1942, to SS-Gruppenführer Heinrich Müller, Chef Amt IV/RSHA; of June 21, 1943, to HSSPF Ostland (Riga) und Chef WVHA; and finally of July 31, 1944, to Martin Mutschmann, Gauleiter und Reichsstatthalter in Sachsen. See Heiber, *op. cit.*, pp. 131, 133-134, 151-152, 165, 169, 214-215, 275-276.
Cp. Kersten, *op. cit.*, pp. 131, 201, 151.

31. On September 13, 1942, Himmler said the following to Kersten: 'Wir gehen lediglich soweit, zu erklären, daß reinrassiges, germanisches Blut die Voraussetzung für höchste geistige und seelische Eigenschaften seien ... Reinrassiges Blut ist aber auch die Voraussetzung dafür, daß sich lichte Kräfte und Wesenheiten, die uns artverwandt sind, in unserm germanischen Menschen verkörpern. Hier liegt die religiöse Seite des Problems ... Mit der rassischen Substanz ändert sich nicht nur die leibliche, sondern auch die geistige und die seelische Struktur eines Volkes. ...' *Ibid.*, pp. 193-194.

['We go only so far as to declare that racially pure, Teutonic blood is the prerequisite for the highest mental and spiritual qualities ... But racially pure blood is also the prerequisite for divine forces and characteristics which are very similar to our own, to be incarnated in our Teutonic people. This is the religious aspect of the problem ... With a change in the racial substance, not only the physical, but also the mental and the spiritual structure of a people changes ...']

32. On December 1, 1943, SS-Obergruppenführer Richard Hildebrandt, Chef RuSHA, wrote to Himmler concerning the SS-Rottenführer Julius and Rolf Sütterlin, the common ancestor of whom was the Jew Abraham Reinau, born in 1663: 'Ich bin der Meinung, daß das Ausmendeln des jüdischen Blutes

wahrscheinlich ist, wenn sich durch die rassischen und charakterlichen Beurteilungen keine jüdischen Züge mehr nachweisen lassen.' To this Himmler replied on December 17, 1943: 'Das Gutachten des Prof. Dr. B. K. Schultz kann ich in keiner Weise anerkennen. Es ist wissenschaftlich in meinen Augen überhaupt nicht haltbar. Denn mit derselben Berechtigung, mit der er erzählt, daß in der dritten Generation von dem Vorhandensein auch nur eines vom Juden stammenden Chromosoms nicht mehr gerechnet werden kann, könnte man behaupten, daß die Chromosome aller anderen Vorfahren ebenfalls verschwinden. Dann muß ich die Frage stellen: woher bekommt der Mensch überhaupt das Erbgut, wenn nach der dritten Generation von den Chromosomen seiner Vorfahren nichts mehr vorhanden ist?' T-175, R. 83, p. 9238-9 and p. 9236-7 (Guides to German Records Microfilmed at Alexandria/Va.), in Heiber *op. cit.*, pp. 245-246, 247, No. 288a-b.

On January 18-19, 1941, Kersten writes: 'Er (Himmler) verfocht dabei die These, daß man auf dem Gebiete der Menschenzucht dieselben Zuchterfolge zu erreichen vermöge, wie im Bereiche der Tierzucht und ein wirkliches Vollmenschentum mit höchster körperlicher, seelischer und geistiger Leistungsfähigkeit herangebildet werden könnte. . . .

Nietzsches Übermensch war für ihn auf züchterischem Wege zu erreichen. Er war der festen Überzeugung, daß bestimmte geistige und seelische Eigenschaften in der gleichen Weise zu vererben seien wie körperliche und betrachtete jeden, der dies leugnete, im Grunde als einen Feind der germanischen Rasse und seinen persönlichen Gegner dazu, den er am liebsten eingesperrt hätte, um einen solchen Irrlehrer von weiterem schädlichen Wirken abzuhalten. Wenn er blonde Kinder, Jungen wie Mädchen sah, konnte er vor Rührung weich werden.' Kersten, *op. cit.*, pp. 99-100.

——

[On December 1, 1943, SS-Obergruppenführer Richard Hildebrandt, Chef RuSHA, wrote to Himmler concerning the SS-Rottenführer Julius and Rolf Sütterlin, the common ancestor of whom was the Jew Abraham Reinau, born in 1663: 'I am of the opinion that it is probable that the Jewish blood has died out (ausgemendelt) when the racial and character examinations give no indications of Jewish traits.' To this Himmler replied on December 17, 1943: 'I can in no way accept the opinion of Professor B. K. Schultz. In my view it is completely untenable scientifically. For just as he claims that in the third generation one cannot expect the presence of even one chromosome coming from Jewish ancestors, one could assert that the chromosomes of all other ancestors likewise disappear. Then I must ask the question: Where does a human being acquire his heredity in the first place if no chromosomes of his ancestors are present after the third generation??' T-175, R. 83, p. 9238-9 and p. 9236-7 (Guides to German Records Microfilmed at Alexandria/Va.), in Heiber, *op. cit.*, pp. 245-246, 247, No. 288 a-b.

On January 18-19, 1941, Kersten writes: 'He (Himmler) always maintained the theory that men could be bred just as successfully as animals and that a race of men could be created possessing the highest spiritual, intellectual, and physical qualities . . . Through breeding he meant to produce Nietzsche's Superman. He was firmly convinced that definite intellectual and spiritual traits were inherited no less than physical ones; and he regarded anyone who denied this as an enemy of the Germanic race, and a personal enemy to boot, whom he would have liked to throw into jail before such fallacies could do further damage.

'Wenn he saw blond children, boys or girls, he could become tender with emotion.' Kersten, *op. cit.*, pp. 99-100.]

33. Cf. Himmler's letter to SS-Standartenführer Viktor Brack, Stabsleiter des Chefs der Kanzlei des Führers der NSDAP, of December 19, 1940:
'Lieber Brack!
Wie ich höre, ist auf der Alb wegen der Anstalt Grafeneck eine große Erregung. Die Bevölkerung kennt das graue Auto der SS und glaubt zu wissen, was sich in dem dauernd rauchenden Krematorium abspielt. Was dort geschieht, ist ein Geheimnis und ist es doch nicht mehr.
Somit ist dort die schlimmste Stimmung ausgebrochen, und es bleibt meines Erachtens nur übrig, an dieser Stelle die Verwendung der Anstalt einzustellen und allenfalls in einer klugen und vernünftigen Weise aufklärend zu wirken, indem man gerade in der dortigen Gegend Filme über Erb- und Geisteskranke laufen läßt.
Ich darf Sie um eine Mitteilung bitten, wie dieses schwierige Problem gelöst wurde.

Heil Hitler<br>Ihr HH'

_____

['Dear Brack:
As I hear, people in the Alb region are very upset because of the Grafeneck institution. The population knows the grey SS automobile and thinks it knows what is happening in the crematorium, which is continuously smoking. What is happening there is a secret, yet isn't secret any longer.
This has created the worst possible mood, and in my opinion, the only thing to do is to stop the operation of the institution at this time and, at best, explain things in an intelligent and reasonable way by showing films, especially in that region, about people who are hereditarily and mentally sick.
May I ask you to inform me how this difficult problem is going to be solved?

Heil Hitler!<br>Your HH']

ND-018, Nürnberger Dokumentenreihe in Heiber, *op. cit.*, p. 83, No. 72.
Cp. Eckardt's and Hitler's preoccupation with radical extermination, Eckart, *op. cit.*, pp. 47-50.
See also Kersten, *op. cit.*, pp. 200-201.
34. *Ibid.*, pp. 149-150.
35. Carl G. Jung, *Essays on Contemporary Events* (London: Routledge and Kegan

Paul, 1947), p. 44.

36. Cf. Rudolf Steiner, *Die Philosophie der Freiheit, Grundzüge einer modernen Weltanschauung* (Berlin: Philosophisch-Anthroposophischer Verlag, 1918), *passim*.

37. M. Brachyhu, 'A Contribution towards the Psychology of the Parties,' *Psychoanalytical Review*, XXXVI, 1949, p. 431.

38. Helen Merrell Lynd, 'Must Psychology Aid Reaction?,' *The Nation*, CLXVIII, No. 3, January 1949, p. 76.

39. Clyde Kluckholm and Henry A. Murray (eds.), *Personality in Nature, Society and Culture* (New York: Alfred A. Knopf, 1950), pp. XI-XII.

40. Cf Erikson, *op. cit.*, p. 204.
See also Fromm, *May Man Prevail?*, *op. cit.*, pp. 3-30, 167-174.

41. Erikson, *op. cit.*, p. 80.

42. Cf. R. D. Laing, *The Politics of Experience* (New York: Ballantine Books, 1970), pp. 17-56.

43. Glaser, Barney and Strauss, Anselm H., *Status Passage* (London: Routledge and Kegan Paul, 1971), p. 79.

44. By egocide we understand an intentional extinction of the self as an individually creative entity acting upon preferences which are distinctly personal and unique. Egocide can also be viewed as murder of the mind for the purpose of eliminating undesirable expression of an individually reflected choice by subtle persuasive (e.g., 'technology of behavior'; Skinner) or coercive totalitarian means for personal, economic, or political gain. Egocide can also be self-induced to obliterate the ego by means of subliminal persuasion, 'psychotechnology' (Kenneth Clark), or other techniques and practices used against oneself to escape from stress and anxiety situations experienced as intolerable.
A brilliant and powerful scenario characterizing the effect of egocide is drawn by Anthony Burgess in *A Clockwork Orange* (New York: Ballantine Books, 1972). Referring to the 'Ludovico Technique,' Burgess describes how Alex, the novel's fifteen-year-old main character, is 'reconditioned' into a model citizen, deprived by science of choice, turned into a mindless pawn in the hands of England's cynical socialist authorities at some future time. Alex is indeed transformed into a 'clockwork orange', something mechanical that appears organic. However, in his former activities Alex was already approaching such a state by acting in an almost robot-like fashion, far below the level of choice, a machine for mechanical violence, in a society which itself had become a giant clockwork orange.

# Appendices

# EXPLANATORY NOTE FOR APPENDICES IVa-XII

Appendices IVa to XII are photostatic copies of original SS statistical documents for the years 1937 and 1938, published by the Reichsführer-SS, *Statistisches Jahrbuch der Schutzstaffel der NSDAP.*

1. Appendices IVa to IVe reflect the occupational background and statistical distribution of members of the entire SS in all formations and units for the years 1937 and 1938.

2. Appendices V to VId give a statistical analysis of dismissals, exclusions, and expulsions from the SS, including the figures on those SS-men who had died, for the years 1937 and 1938.

3. Appendices VII to XI give the numerical development of the entire SS for the years 1935, 1936, 1937, and 1938.

4. Appendix XII shows the religious affiliation of all members of the SS for the year 1938.

## SS AND ARMY RANKS

| SS | German Armed Forces | U.S. Army | British Army |
|---|---|---|---|
| **GENERAL OFFICERS (GENERALSTABSOFFIZIERE)** | | | |
| Reichsführer-SS | Generalfeldmarschall | General of the Army | Field Marshal |
| SS-Oberstgruppenführer (from 1942 only) | Generaloberst | no equivalent | (Lit. Colonel-General) |
| SS-Obergruppenführer | General | General | General |
| SS-Gruppenführer | Generalleutnant | Lieutenant-General | Lieutenant-General |
| SS-Brigadeführer | Generalmajor | Major-General | Major-General |
| **STAFF OR SENIOR OFFICERS (STABSOFFIZIERE)** | | | |
| SS-Oberführer | no equivalent | Brigadier-General | Brigadier |
| SS-Standartenführer | Oberst | Colonel | Colonel |
| SS-Obersturmbannführer | Oberstleutnant | Lieutenant-Colonel | Lieutenant-Colonel |
| SS-Sturmbannführer | Major | Major | Major |
| **JUNIOR OFFICERS (HAUPTMÄNNER UND LEUTNANTE)** | | | |
| SS-Hauptsturmführer | Hauptmann | Captain | Captain |
| SS-Obersturmführer | Oberleutnant | 1st Lieutenant | 1st Lieutenant |
| SS-Untersturmführer | Leutnant | 2nd Lieutenant | 2nd Lieutenant |

## STAFF SERGEANTS AND NON-COMMISSIONED OFFICERS
### (STABSFELDWEBEL, UNTEROFFIZIERE MIT PORTEPEE)

| SS-Sturmscharführer | Stabsoberfeldwebel | Sergeant-Major | Regimental Sergeant-Major |
|---|---|---|---|
| SS-Hauptscharführer | Oberfeldwebel | Master-Sergeant | Sergeant-Major |
| SS-Oberscharführer | Feldwebel | Technical Sergeant | Quartermaster-Sergeant |

## SERGEANTS (FELDWEBEL, UNTEROFFIZIERE OHNE PORTEPEE)

| SS-Scharführer | Unterfeldwebel | Staff Sergeant | Staff Sergeant |
|---|---|---|---|
| SS-Unterscharführer | Unteroffizier | Sergeant | Sergeant |

## ENLISTED MEN (MANNSCHAFTEN)

| SS-Rottenführer | Gefreiter | Corporal | Corporal |
|---|---|---|---|
| SS-Sturmmann | Obersoldat | Private 1st Class | Senior Private |
| SS-Mann | Soldat | Private | Private |
| SS-Anwärter | no equivalent | no equivalent | no equivalent |
| (SS-Candidate) | | | |

# ORGANIZATIONAL CHART OF THE SS (1943)

```
                    REICHSFÜHRER—SS
                    UND CHEF DER
                    DEUTSCHEN POLIZEI
```

ARMY FIELD COMMAND

RASSE UND SIEDLUNGS- HAUPTAMT

HAUPTAMT ORDNUNGS- POLIZEI

DIENSTSTELLE SS—O-GRUF. HEISSMEYER

HAUPTAMT VOLKSDEUTSCHE MITTELSTELLE

STABSHAUPTAMT DES REICHSKOM— MISSARS FÜR DIE FESTIGUNG DEUT— SCHEN VOLKSTUMS

PERSÖNLICHER STAB RF—SS

SS— HAUPTAMT

SS—FÜHRUNGS— HAUPTAMT

SS—PERSONAL— HAUPTAMT

HAUPTAMT SS—GERICHT

REICHS— SICHERHEITS— HAUPTAMT

HAUPTAMT VERWALTUNG U. WIRTSCHAFT

CONCENTRATION, EXTERMINATION, & SLAVE LABOR CAMPS; GHETTOS (AEL)◆

ALLGEMEINE—SS

HÖHERE SS UND POLIZEIFÜHRER

WAFFEN SS

FIELD UNITS

RESERVE AND TRAINING UNITS

SECURITY AND ANTIPARTISAN OPERATIONS

ADMINISTRATION & MILITARY TRAINING

RECRUITING—IDEOLOGICAL TRAINING

TACTICAL COMMAND

◆(AEL) = ARBEITSERZIEHUNGSLAGER [WORK TRAINING CAMP]

# POWER STRUCTURE OF THE THIRD REICH

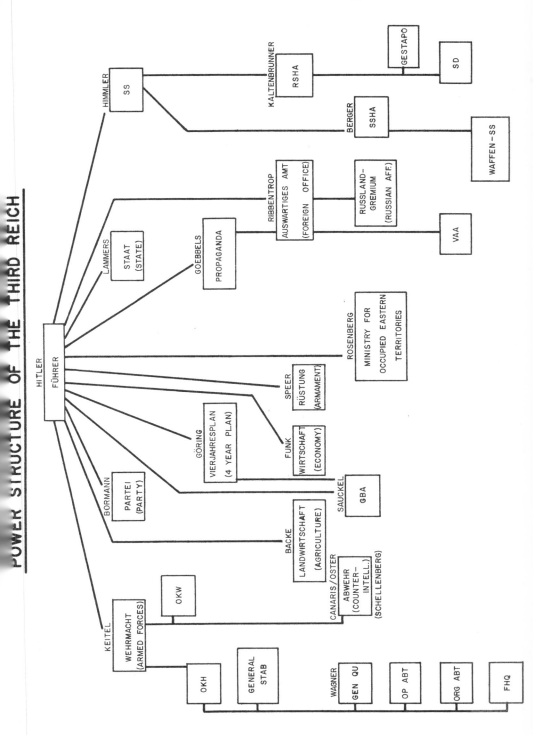

# Die Berufe in der ⚡⚡

| Berufe | Stärke am 31.12.37 | | Zugang 1938 | | | Abgang 1938 | Stärke am 31.12.38 |
|---|---|---|---|---|---|---|---|
| | ohne Bewerber, SD, VT, TV | mit Bewerber, SD, VT, TV | Altreich | Ober-abschnitt Donau | Gesamt | | |
| **I** | | | | | | | |
| Landwirtschaft, Gärtnerei, Tierzucht u. ä. ......... | **15 807** | **17 479** | **2 085** | **919** | **3 004** | **556** | **19 927** |
| Bauern .............. | 11 476 | 12 661 | 1 642 | 243 | 1 885 | 396 | 14 150 |
| Landwirtschaftliche Inspektoren .............. | 671 | 742 | 56 | 34 | 90 | 16 | 816 |
| Knechte und landwirtschaftliche Arbeiter ........ | 1 493 | 1 651 | 158 | 365 | 523 | 82 | 2 092 |
| Gärtner .............. | 1 376 | 1 521 | 165 | 62 | 227 | 52 | 1 696 |
| Jäger und Förster ....... | 635 | 719 | 51 | 148 | 199 | 7 | 911 |
| Fischer .............. | 74 | 88 | 6 | 8 | 14 | 1 | 101 |
| Winzer .............. | 82 | 97 | 7 | 59 | 66 | 2 | 161 |
| Bergbau ................ | **1 052** | **1 162** | **41** | **132** | **173** | **45** | **1 290** |
| Steiger .............. | 73 | 84 | 2 | 13 | 15 | 4 | 95 |
| Bergleute und Hauer ..... | 979 | 1 078 | 39 | 119 | 158 | 41 | 1 195 |
| Gewinnung und Verarbeitung von Stein und Erde ..... | **763** | **834** | **89** | **48** | **137** | **29** | **942** |
| Töpfer .............. | 232 | 254 | 18 | 19 | 37 | 5 | 286 |
| Glasbläser .............. | 205 | 224 | 34 | 17 | 51 | 10 | 265 |
| Steinmetzen ........... | 197 | 215 | 25 | 3 | 28 | 7 | 236 |
| Sonstige Berufe der Steinverarbeitung ........ | 129 | 141 | 12 | 9 | 21 | 7 | 155 |
| Metallgewinnung und Metallverarbeitung ........... | **25 356** | **28 012** | **1 926** | **1 982** | **3 908** | **1 272** | **30 648** |
| Metallarbeiter .......... | 1 439 | 1 582 | 112 | 149 | 261 | 79 | 1 764 |
| Schmiede .............. | 1 381 | 1 522 | 115 | 124 | 239 | 67 | 1 694 |
| Goldschmied ........... | 114 | 126 | 2 | 3 | 5 | 4 | 127 |
| Schlosser, Mechaniker, Monteure | 12 170 | 13 447 | 1 231 | 995 | 2 226 | 781 | 14 892 |
| Optiker .............. | 114 | 125 | 3 | 5 | 8 | 3 | 130 |
| Uhrmacher .............. | 250 | 277 | 27 | 43 | 70 | 12 | 335 |
| Schweißer .............. | 225 | 249 | 12 | 25 | 37 | 4 | 282 |
| Klempner .............. | 4 321 | 4 779 | 103 | 144 | 247 | 84 | 4 942 |
| Ingenieure und Techniker .. | 5 253 | 5 807 | 291 | 465 | 756 | 228 | 6 335 |
| Sonstige .............. | 89 | 98 | 30 | 29 | 59 | 10 | 147 |
| Chemische Industrie ....... | **458** | **506** | **21** | **47** | **68** | **19** | **555** |
| Chemiker .............. | 214 | 236 | 12 | 39 | 51 | 11 | 276 |
| Chemotechniker und Laboranten .............. | 244 | 270 | 9 | 8 | 17 | 8 | 279 |
| Textilherstellung .......... | **727** | **803** | **62** | **95** | **157** | **33** | **927** |
| Weber .............. | 416 | 458 | 34 | 32 | 66 | 16 | 508 |
| Sonstige .............. | 311 | 345 | 28 | 63 | 91 | 17 | 419 |
| Papierverarbeitung und Vervielfältigung ........... | **1 528** | **1 688** | **203** | **124** | **327** | **68** | **1 947** |
| Buchdrucker ........... | 560 | 618 | 66 | 49 | 115 | 30 | 703 |
| Schriftsetzer ........... | 655 | 724 | 107 | 34 | 141 | 29 | 836 |
| Buchbinder ........... | 152 | 168 | 20 | 15 | 35 | 7 | 196 |
| Sonstige .............. | 161 | 178 | 10 | 26 | 36 | 2 | 212 |

II

| Berufe | Stärke am 31.12.37 | | Zugang 1938 | | | Abgang 1938 | Stärke am 31.12.38 |
|---|---|---|---|---|---|---|---|
| | ohne Bewerber, SD, VT, TV | mit Bewerber, SD, VT, TV | Altreich | Ober- abschnitt Donau | Gesamt | | |
| Lederherstellung und Verarbeitung | 534 | 592 | 32 | 46 | 78 | 28 | 642 |
| Gerber | 433 | 478 | 8 | 19 | 27 | 3 | 502 |
| Sonstige | 101 | 114 | 24 | 27 | 51 | 25 | 140 |
| Berufe der Holzverarbeitung | 4 560 | 5 041 | 402 | 422 | 824 | 212 | 5 653 |
| Tischler | 3 484 | 3 851 | 319 | 303 | 622 | 165 | 4 308 |
| Stellmacher | 441 | 487 | 22 | 22 | 44 | 17 | 514 |
| Sonstige | 635 | 703 | 61 | 97 | 158 | 30 | 831 |
| Nahrungs- und Genußmittelherstellung | 6 121 | 6 767 | 601 | 792 | 1 393 | 278 | 7 882 |
| Müller | 389 | 431 | 30 | 71 | 101 | 19 | 513 |
| Bäcker | 2 345 | 2 593 | 274 | 295 | 569 | 107 | 3 055 |
| Konditoren | 391 | 433 | 47 | 39 | 86 | 23 | 496 |
| Fleischer | 2 277 | 2 514 | 181 | 329 | 510 | 103 | 2 921 |
| Brenner | 335 | 371 | 30 | 23 | 53 | 12 | 412 |
| Meier | 359 | 397 | 34 | 35 | 69 | 12 | 454 |
| Sonstige | 25 | 28 | 5 | — | 5 | 2 | 31 |
| Berufe der Herstellung von Bekleidungsgegenständen | 1 921 | 2 121 | 175 | 232 | 407 | 84 | 2 444 |
| Schneider | 1 064 | 1 174 | 80 | 105 | 185 | 51 | 1 308 |
| Schuhmacher | 755 | 834 | 79 | 100 | 179 | 23 | 990 |
| Sonstige | 102 | 113 | 16 | 27 | 43 | 10 | 146 |
| Berufe des Baugewerbes und Baunebengewerbes | 8 488 | 9 387 | 668 | 639 | 1 307 | 371 | 10 323 |
| Architekten und Baumeister | 656 | 726 | 45 | 60 | 105 | 20 | 811 |
| Landmesser | 261 | 289 | 34 | 14 | 48 | 13 | 324 |
| Maurer | 2 230 | 2 467 | 184 | 183 | 367 | 109 | 2 725 |
| Zimmerer | 1 320 | 1 460 | 62 | 122 | 184 | 64 | 1 580 |
| Dachdecker | 303 | 335 | 17 | 9 | 26 | 12 | 349 |
| Maler | 2 330 | 2 577 | 232 | 136 | 368 | 104 | 2 841 |
| Tapezierer | 555 | 610 | 38 | 29 | 67 | 28 | 649 |
| Steinsetzer | 207 | 230 | 9 | 7 | 16 | 2 | 244 |
| Schornsteinfeger | 250 | 277 | 33 | 60 | 93 | 5 | 365 |
| Sonstige | 376 | 416 | 14 | 19 | 33 | 14 | 435 |
| Berufe des Handels | 31 686 | 35 209 | 2 730 | 2 426 | 5 156 | 1 571 | 38 794 |
| Prokuristen | 338 | 376 | 21 | 13 | 34 | 11 | 399 |
| Reisende | 792 | 880 | 18 | 64 | 82 | 44 | 918 |
| Kaufleute u. Händler | 5 066 | 5 635 | 130 | 387 | 517 | 154 | 5 998 |
| Verkäufer | 516 | 574 | 32 | 67 | 99 | 28 | 645 |
| Kaufmännische Angestellte | 22 966 | 25 511 | 2 381 | 1 768 | 4 149 | 1 248 | 28 412 |
| Lageristen | 408 | 454 | 21 | 11 | 32 | 25 | 461 |
| Drogisten | 726 | 807 | 72 | 56 | 128 | 32 | 903 |
| Boten | 518 | 576 | 30 | 35 | 65 | 22 | 619 |
| Sonstige | 356 | 396 | 25 | 25 | 50 | 7 | 439 |
| Berufe des Verkehrswesens | 6 906 | 7 539 | 269 | 495 | 764 | 279 | 8 024 |
| Schaffner | 285 | 311 | 1 | 1 | 2 | 18 | 295 |
| Posthelfer | 562 | 613 | 27 | 34 | 61 | 18 | 656 |
| Telephon- und Telegraphenarbeiter | 525 | 573 | 37 | 7 | 44 | 21 | 596 |
| Kraftwagenführer | 4 696 | 5 128 | 166 | 426 | 592 | 180 | 5 540 |
| Kutscher | 443 | 483 | 6 | 8 | 14 | 12 | 485 |
| Sonstige | 395 | 431 | 32 | 19 | 51 | 30 | 452 |

| Berufe | Stärke am 31.12.37 ohne Bewerber, SD, VT, TV | Stärke am 31.12.37 mit Bewerber, SD, VT, TV | Zugang 1938 Altreich | Zugang 1938 Oberabschnitt Donau | Zugang 1938 Gesamt | Abgang 1938 | Stärke am 31.12.38 |
|---|---|---|---|---|---|---|---|
| **III** | | | | | | | |
| Berufe des Gast- und Schankstättengewerbes ........ | 378 | 418 | 27 | 68 | 95 | 24 | 489 |
| Kellner .............. | 207 | 230 | 13 | 52 | 65 | 11 | 284 |
| Sonstige .............. | 171 | 188 | 14 | 16 | 30 | 13 | 205 |
| Schulen, Verwaltung, Justiz | 9 629 | 10 646 | 680 | 898 | 1 578 | 251 | 11 973 |
| Richter und Staatsanwälte . | 139 | 154 | 7 | 12 | 19 | — | 173 |
| Sonstige Juristen ........ | 2 475 | 2 737 | 167 | 123 | 290 | 75 | 2 952 |
| Angestellte bei Behörden .. | 4 920 | 5 439 | 313 | 460 | 773 | 97 | 6 115 |
| Lehrer an Volksschulen ... | 1 336 | 1 478 | 111 | 221 | 332 | 52 | 1 758 |
| Lehrkräfte an höheren Schulen ............. | 525 | 580 | 6 | 47 | 53 | 1 | 632 |
| Hochschullehrer .......... | 234 | 258 | 76 | 35 | 111 | 26 | 343 |
| Freie und künstlerische Berufe | 1 859 | 2 056 | 183 | 138 | 321 | 151 | 2 226 |
| Redakteure ............. | 226 | 250 | 27 | 5 | 32 | 6 | 276 |
| Musiker ............... | 878 | 971 | 73 | 29 | 102 | 103 | 970 |
| Sonstige .............. | 755 | 835 | 83 | 104 | 187 | 42 | 980 |
| Gesundheitswesen und sonstige hygienische Berufe.. | 5 604 | 6 203 | 449 | 640 | 1 089 | 177 | 7 115 |
| Ärzte ................. | 2 166 | 2 399 | 171 | 325 | 496 | 57 | 2 838 |
| Zahnärzte ............. | 1 207 | 1 339 | 110 | 115 | 225 | 47 | 1 517 |
| Apotheker ............. | 444 | 491 | 20 | 27 | 47 | 13 | 525 |
| Friseure .............. | 845 | 934 | 97 | 102 | 199 | 34 | 1 099 |
| Krankenpfleger ......... | 347 | 383 | 17 | 19 | 36 | 14 | 405 |
| Feuerwehrleute ......... | 292 | 322 | 10 | 20 | 30 | 5 | 347 |
| Sonstige .............. | 303 | 335 | 24 | 32 | 56 | 7 | 384 |
| Angestellte der Polizei, Partei und 〓 ................. | 4 881 | 9 381 | 1 318 | 1 631 | 2 949 | 83 | 12 247 |
| Polizei ............... | 768 | 1 268 | 828 | 1 150 | 1 978 | 6 | 3 240 |
| Angestellte der Partei, DAF, NSV u. ä. ........... | 1 138 | 1 338 | 142 | 348 | 490 | 48 | 1 780 |
| Angestellte in der 〓 ..... (ohne VT und TV) | 2 975 | 6 775 | 348 | 133 | 481 | 29 | 7 227 |
| Ungelernte und angelernte Arbeiter ............... | 12 885 | 14 242 | 661 | 1 344 | 2 005 | 568 | 15 679 |
| Werkmeister ............ | 2 522 | 2 787 | 42 | 105 | 147 | 8 | 2 926 |
| Schüler und Studenten .... | 7 156 | 10 583 | 1 333 | 1 429 | 2 762 | 398 | 12 947 |
| Wachmänner ............ | 4 866 | 5 280 | 381 | 784 | 1 165 | 115 | 6 330 |
| Zollangestellte und Iliga ... | 2 245 | 2 382 | 62 | 38 | 100 | 21 | 2 461 |
| Beamte ................ | 5 149 | 5 393 | 455 | 498 | 953 | 140 | 6 206 |
| Beamte der Reichspost ... | 746 | 781 | 66 | 73 | 139 | 25 | 895 |
| Beamte der Reichsbahn ... | 961 | 1 007 | 84 | 93 | 177 | 23 | 1 161 |
| Beamte der Kommunalbehörden ............. | 1 231 | 1 288 | 109 | 116 | 225 | 37 | 1 476 |
| Beamte der anderen Behörden ............. | 2 184 | 2 289 | 189 | 209 | 398 | 51 | 2 636 |
| Ehemalige Offiziere ....... | 27 | 28 | 7 | 7 | 14 | 4 | 38 |
| Sonstige ............... | 3 825 | 4 465 | 704 | 239 | 943 | 1 252 | 4 156 |
| Verfügungstruppe ......... | — | 12 069 | — | — | — | — | 14 234 |
| Totenkopfverbände ........ | — | 5 319 | — | — | — | — | 9 172 |

# Prozentualer Anteil
## der Berufsgruppen in der ## im Vergleich zum Reich

### Deutsches Reich

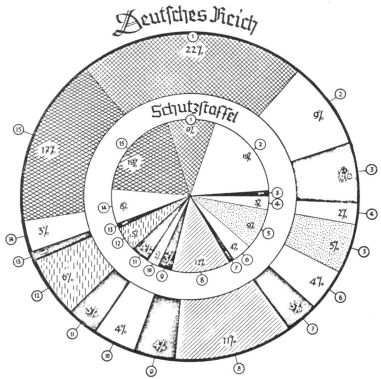

### Facharbeiter u. Handwerker

① Landwirtschaft
② Handel
③ freie Berufe
④ Gesundheitspflege u. Hygiene
⑤ Beamte u. Behördenangestellte
⑥ Verkehr

⑦ Bergbau-Stein u. Erde
⑧ Metall
⑨ Holz
⑩ Textil u. Bekleidung
⑪ Nahrung u. Genuß
⑫ Bau
⑬ Papier u. Druck

⑭ ungelernte u. angelernte Arbeiter
⑮ Sonstige

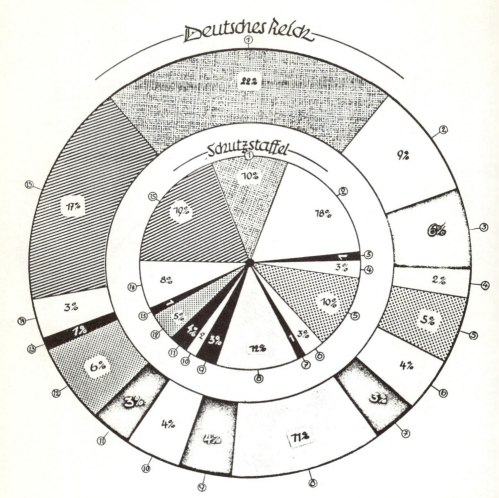

**Facharbeiter u. Handwerker**

① Landwirtschaft
② Handel
③ Freie Berufe
④ Gesundheitspflege u. Hygiene
⑤ Beamte u. Behördenangestellte
⑥ Verkehr

⑦ Bergbau-Stein u. Erde
⑧ Metall
⑨ Holz
⑩ Textil und Bekleidung
⑪ Nahrung u. Genuß
⑫ Bau
⑬ Papier u. Druck
⑭ ungelernte u. angelernte Arb.
⑮ Sonstige

# Geheim

## Gründe der Ausschlüsse und Ausstoßungen

| Grund | Ausschluß | Ausstoßung |
|---|---|---|
| Disziplinlosigkeit . . . . . . . . . . . . . . . . . . . . . . . | 1 290 | 44 |
| Heirat ohne Genehmigung . . . . . . . . . . . . . . . . . | 307 | 1 |
| Verstoß gegen die Kameradschaft . . . . . . . . . . . . | 13 | 1 |
| Fahnenflucht . . . . . . . . . . . . . . . . . . . . . . . . . . | 8 | 11 |
| Landesverrat . . . . . . . . . . . . . . . . . . . . . . . . . . | 6 | 1 |
| Parteiausschluß . . . . . . . . . . . . . . . . . . . . . . . . | 7 | — |
| Verkehr mit Juden . . . . . . . . . . . . . . . . . . . . . . | 50 | 4 |
| Ehrenwortbruch, Meineid . . . . . . . . . . . . . . . . . | 37 | 6 |
| Trunkenheit . . . . . . . . . . . . . . . . . . . . . . . . . . | 74 | 13 |
| Roheit, Schlägerei, Totschlag . . . . . . . . . . . . . . | 42 | 2 |
| Amtsmißbrauch . . . . . . . . . . . . . . . . . . . . . . . . | 3 | 1 |
| § 175 . . . . . . . . . . . . . . . . . . . . . . . . . . . . . . . | 23 | 29 |
| Abtreibung . . . . . . . . . . . . . . . . . . . . . . . . . . . | 15 | 13 |
| Notzuchtverbrechen . . . . . . . . . . . . . . . . . . . . . | 9 | 4 |
| Ehebruch . . . . . . . . . . . . . . . . . . . . . . . . . . . . | 20 | 2 |
| Rassenschande . . . . . . . . . . . . . . . . . . . . . . . . . | 3 | 2 |
| Sonstige Sittlichkeitsverbrechen . . . . . . . . . . . . . | 34 | 13 |
| Unterschlagung . . . . . . . . . . . . . . . . . . . . . . . . | 214 | 47 |
| Urkundenfälschung . . . . . . . . . . . . . . . . . . . . . | 20 | 9 |
| Betrug . . . . . . . . . . . . . . . . . . . . . . . . . . . . . . | 72 | 13 |
| Diebstahl (Kameradendiebstahl) . . . . . . . . . . . . . | 129 | 60 |
| Schulden . . . . . . . . . . . . . . . . . . . . . . . . . . . . . | 22 | 3 |
| Zechprellerei . . . . . . . . . . . . . . . . . . . . . . . . . . | 3 | — |
| Sonstige Gründe . . . . . . . . . . . . . . . . . . . . . . . . | 88 | 7 |
| **Gesamt** | **2 489** | **286** |

# Ausscheidungen 1937

## unterteilt nach Entlassung, Ausschluß, Ausstoßung und Tod

### Nach Monaten

| | Entlassung | Ausschluß | Ausstoßung | Tod | Gesamt |
|---|---|---|---|---|---|
| Januar | 624 | 133 | 21 | 45 | 823 |
| Februar | 937 | 267 | 29 | 37 | 1 270 |
| März | 798 | 215 | 20 | 32 | 1 065 |
| April | 844 | 217 | 20 | 56 | 1 137 |
| Mai | 703 | 221 | 25 | 49 | 998 |
| Juni | 759 | 294 | 37 | 49 | 1 139 |
| Juli[2]) | 9 | 4 | 5 | 37 | 55 |
| August | 875 | 305 | 28 | 47 | 1 255 |
| September | 474 | 158 | 21 | 38 | 691 |
| Oktober | 526 | 218 | 26 | 50 | 820 |
| November | 781 | 254 | 30 | 45 | 1 110 |
| Dezember | 630 | 203 | 24 | 33 | 890 |
| Gesamt | 7 960 | 2 489 | 286 | 518 | 11 253 |
| Gesamt in Prozenten | 70% | 22% | 3% | 5% | 100% |

¹) Juli war Urlaubsmonat der Allgemeinen ꜰꜰ.

### Nach Oberabschnitten, VT. und TV.

| | Entlassung | Ausschluß | Ausstoßung | Tod | Gesamt |
|---|---|---|---|---|---|
| Süd | 284 | 79 | 14 | 21 | 398 |
| Südwest | 702 | 125 | 16 | 51 | 894 |
| Rhein | 573 | 150 | 11 | 37 | 771 |
| West | 1 037 | 269 | 14 | 51 | 1 371 |
| Nordwest | 652 | 233 | 20 | 40 | 945 |
| Nord | 414 | 251 | 7 | 29 | 701 |
| Nordost | 704 | 258 | 14 | 32 | 1 008 |
| Ost | 734 | 229 | 32 | 38 | 1 033 |
| Südost | 485 | 201 | 8 | 35 | 729 |
| Elbe | 521 | 127 | 10 | 33 | 691 |
| Main | 347 | 87 | 6 | 15 | 455 |
| Fulda-Werra | 539 | 115 | 6 | 39 | 699 |
| Mitte | 654 | 266 | 21 | 34 | 975 |
| Sonder-Einheiten | 84 | 35 | 13 | 20 | 152 |
| Allgemeine ꜰꜰ | 7 730 | 2 425 | 192 | 475 | 10 822 |
| Verfügungstruppe | 84 | 40 | 56 | 27 | 207 |
| Totenkopfverbände | 146 | 24 | 38 | 16 | 224 |
| Gesamt ꜰꜰ | 7 960 | 2 489 | 286 | 518 | 11 253 |

# Gründe der Entlassungen

| | 1 Eigener Antrag | 2 Dienstlich ungeeignet | 3 Gesundheitlich untauglich | 4 Weltanschaulich ungeeignet | 5 Charakterlich ungeeignet | Gesamt |
|---|---|---|---|---|---|---|
| Süd | 247 | 32 | — | — | 5 | 284 |
| Südwest | 665 | 30 | 4 | 1 | 2 | 702 |
| Rhein | 500 | 51 | 10 | — | 12 | 573 |
| West | 876 | 107 | 24 | 14 | 16 | 1 037 |
| Nordwest | 557 | 48 | 24 | 1 | 22 | 652 |
| Nord | 379 | 22 | 7 | — | 6 | 414 |
| Nordost | 510 | 156 | 27 | 1 | 10 | 704 |
| Ost | 635 | 55 | 28 | 4 | 12 | 734 |
| Südost | 391 | 63 | 12 | 5 | 14 | 485 |
| Elbe | 459 | 42 | 9 | 2 | 9 | 521 |
| Main | 302 | 31 | 3 | — | 11 | 347 |
| Fulda-Werra | 500 | 24 | 12 | 1 | 2 | 539 |
| Mitte | 556 | 53 | 12 | 2 | 31 | 654 |
| Sondereinheiten | 40 | 33 | 5 | — | 6 | 84 |
| Verfügungstruppe | 23 | 24 | 15 | 1 | 21 | 84 |
| Totenkopfverbände | 81 | 23 | 19 | 4 | 19 | 146 |
| Gesamt | 6 721 | 794 | 211 | 36 | 198 | 7 960 |
| in Prozenten | 84,4 % | 10,0 % | 2,6 % | 0,5 % | 2,5 % | 100 % |

## Nähere Erläuterung der Gründe zu Spalte 1 und 2

| | Übertritt zum Heer oder RAD. | Übertritt zu einer anderen Gliederung | Auslandsaufenthalt | Gesundheit | Beruf | Interesselos | Verlobungsbefehl | Weltanschauung | Sonstige Gründe | Gesamt |
|---|---|---|---|---|---|---|---|---|---|---|
| Süd | 28 | 46 | 4 | 25 | 137 | 16 | 2 | 2 | 19 | 279 |
| Südwest | 47 | 56 | 11 | 111 | 385 | 27 | 30 | 3 | 25 | 695 |
| Rhein | 60 | 55 | 5 | 94 | 235 | 30 | 19 | 17 | 36 | 551 |
| West | 77 | 82 | 5 | 126 | 472 | 101 | 29 | 55 | 36 | 983 |
| Nordwest | 91 | 54 | 18 | 123 | 248 | 20 | 18 | 4 | 29 | 605 |
| Nord | 44 | 25 | 2 | 78 | 182 | 18 | 8 | 20 | 24 | 401 |
| Nordost | 82 | 37 | 2 | 101 | 247 | 132 | 23 | 3 | 39 | 666 |
| Ost | 130 | 35 | 16 | 154 | 260 | 32 | 22 | 3 | 38 | 680 |
| Südost | 94 | 38 | 2 | 85 | 113 | 51 | 26 | 7 | 38 | 454 |
| Elbe | 81 | 45 | 1 | 74 | 196 | 31 | 39 | 4 | 30 | 501 |
| Main | 42 | 31 | 1 | 42 | 151 | 21 | 14 | 3 | 28 | 333 |
| Fulda-Werra | 43 | 50 | 5 | 80 | 231 | 19 | 64 | 10 | 22 | 524 |
| Mitte | 43 | 33 | 3 | 108 | 296 | 53 | 20 | 17 | 36 | 609 |
| Sondereinheiten | 8 | 4 | 1 | 9 | 9 | 3 | — | 6 | 33 | 73 |
| Verfügungstruppe | 5 | 4 | — | 5 | 3 | 1 | 6 | 1 | 22 | 47 |
| Totenkopfverbände | 13 | — | — | 14 | 40 | — | — | 5 | 32 | 104 |
| Gesamt | 888 | 595 | 76 | 1 229 | 3 205 | 555 | 320 | 160 | 487 | 7 515 |

# Gründe der Entlassungen

| Oberabschnitt | a<br>eigener<br>Antrag[1]) | b<br>dienstliche<br>Unge-<br>eignetheit[1]) | Welt-<br>anschauliche<br>Unge-<br>eignetheit | Charak-<br>terliche<br>Unge-<br>eignetheit | Gesund-<br>heitliche<br>Untauglich-<br>keit | Gesamt |
|---|---|---|---|---|---|---|
| Donau ............ | 5 | 1 | — | 1 | 1 | 8 |
| Süd ............. | 212 | 9 | 3 | 5 | 5 | 234 |
| Südwest ......... | 402 | 31 | 4 | 2 | 3 | 442 |
| Rhein ........... | 380 | 23 | 5 | 12 | 6 | 426 |
| West ............ | 578 | 38 | 2 | 5 | 13 | 636 |
| Nordwest ........ | 518 | 46 | 3 | 5 | 19 | 591 |
| Nord ............ | 228 | 5 | — | 2 | 2 | 237 |
| Nordost ......... | 394 | 35 | — | 6 | 9 | 444 |
| Ost ............. | 560 | 39 | 4 | 3 | 6 | 612 |
| Südost .......... | 316 | 21 | 4 | 4 | 6 | 351 |
| Elbe ............ | 403 | 26 | 8 | — | 2 | 439 |
| Main ............ | 162 | 31 | — | 3 | 2 | 198 |
| Fulda-Werra ...... | 514 | 30 | — | 2 | 8 | 554 |
| Mitte ............ | 392 | 15 | — | 3 | 3 | 413 |
| Sondereinheiten ... | 40 | 7 | 1 | 3 | 2 | 53 |
| **Insgesamt** ....... | **5 104** | **357** | **34** | **56** | **87** | **5 638** |
| In Prozenten .... | *90,6* | *6,3* | *0,6* | *1,0* | *1,5* | *100* |

[1]) Erläuterung zu a und b siehe S. 69.

## Erläuterung der Entlassungsgründe
### zu Spalte a »eigener Antrag«

| Oberabschnitt | Übertritt zur WM | Übertritt zum RAD | Übertritt zu einer anderen Gliederung | Krankheit | Beruf | Auslandsaufenthalt | Verlobungsbefehl | Sonstige Gründe | Gesamt |
|---|---|---|---|---|---|---|---|---|---|
| Donau ........ | 1 | — | — | 1 | — | — | — | 3 | 5 |
| Süd .......... | 22 | 4 | 37 | 36 | 91 | 3 | 6 | 13 | 212 |
| Südwest ...... | 41 | 12 | 47 | 80 | 188 | 5 | 4 | 25 | 402 |
| Rhein ........ | 34 | 8 | 41 | 79 | 181 | 3 | 6 | 28 | 380 |
| West ......... | 58 | 15 | 65 | 88 | 289 | 5 | 12 | 46 | 578 |
| Nordwest ..... | 70 | 16 | 50 | 94 | 237 | 7 | 13 | 31 | 518 |
| Nord ......... | 29 | 4 | 22 | 62 | 85 | — | 1 | 25 | 228 |
| Nordost ...... | 98 | 6 | 39 | 68 | 122 | 2 | 3 | 56 | 394 |
| Ost .......... | 100 | 12 | 42 | 143 | 211 | 11 | 8 | 33 | 560 |
| Südost ....... | 121 | 18 | 22 | 45 | 78 | — | 5 | 27 | 316 |
| Elbe ......... | 56 | 2 | 47 | 64 | 179 | 1 | 12 | 42 | 403 |
| Main ......... | 15 | — | 18 | 22 | 88 | 2 | — | 17 | 162 |
| Fulda-Werra .. | 257 | 30 | 33 | 52 | 102 | 5 | 5 | 30 | 514 |
| Mitte ........ | 29 | 2 | 32 | 66 | 223 | 1 | 4 | 35 | 392 |
| Sondereinheiten | 5 | 1 | 4 | 5 | — | — | 4 | 21 | 40 |
| **Insgesamt ..** | **936** | **130** | **499** | **905** | **2 074** | **45** | **83** | **432** | **5 104** |

## Erläuterung der Entlassungsgründe
### zu Spalte b »dienstliche Ungeeignetheit«

| Oberabschnitt | Interesselos | Befehlsverweigerung | Verlobungsbefehl | Parteiangelegenheiten | Sonstige Gründe | Gesamt |
|---|---|---|---|---|---|---|
| Donau ........ | 1 | — | — | — | — | 1 |
| Süd .......... | 2 | — | 1 | 1 | 5 | 9 |
| Südwest ...... | 11 | 4 | 3 | 3 | 10 | 31 |
| Rhein ........ | 14 | 1 | 2 | 3 | 3 | 23 |
| West ......... | 23 | — | 1 | 3 | 11 | 38 |
| Nordwest ..... | 19 | 1 | 2 | 15 | 9 | 46 |
| Nord ......... | 3 | 1 | — | — | 1 | 5 |
| Nordost ...... | 18 | 1 | 1 | 10 | 5 | 35 |
| Ost .......... | 13 | 2 | 3 | 12 | 8 | 39 |
| Südost ....... | 4 | — | 1 | 15 | 1 | 21 |
| Elbe ......... | 13 | 1 | 3 | 2 | 7 | 26 |
| Main ......... | 20 | 1 | 4 | — | 6 | 31 |
| Fulda-Werra .. | 21 | 1 | 3 | 1 | 4 | 30 |
| Mitte ........ | 10 | 1 | — | — | 4 | 15 |
| Sondereinheiten | — | — | — | 3 | 4 | 7 |
| **Insgesamt...** | **173** | **14** | **24** | **68** | **78** | **357** |

## Zahlenmäßige Entwicklung der gesamten ⚡⚡ in den Jahren 1935, 1936, 1937

| Jahr | Monat | Allgemeine ⚡⚡ | ⚡⚡ Verfügungstruppe | ⚡⚡ Totenkopfverbände | Gesamt |
|---|---|---|---|---|---|
| 1935 | Januar | 189 628 | 4 984 | 1 987 | **196 599** |
| | Februar | 186 947 | 6 098 | 1 977 | **195 022** |
| | März | 181 036 | 6 383 | 1 998 | **189 417** |
| | April[1]) | 197 266 | 7 610 | 2 093 | **206 969** |
| | Mai | 196 875 | 8 459 | 2 241 | **207 575** |
| | Juni | 191 561 | 8 620 | 2 220 | **202 401** |
| | Juli | 190 974 | 8 779 | 2 252 | **202 005** |
| | August | 189 510 | 8 912 | 2 273 | **200 695** |
| | September | 188 658 | 8 943 | 2 338 | **199 939** |
| | Oktober | 188 159 | 9 185 | 2 411 | **199 755** |
| | November | 188 675 | 9 206 | 2 550 | **200 431** |
| | Dezember | 188 108 | 9 261 | 2 546 | **199 915** |
| 1936 | Januar | 188 974 | 9 212 | 2 855 | **201 041** |
| | Februar | 188 595 | 9 163 | 2 818 | **200 576** |
| | März | 187 512 | 9 073 | 2 733 | **199 318** |
| | April | 186 210 | 9 188 | 2 876 | **198 274** |
| | Mai | 185 431 | 9 277 | 3 222 | **197 930** |
| | Juni | 185 409 | 9 223 | 3 359 | **197 991** |
| | Juli | 185 409 | 9 136 | 3 502 | **198 047** |
| | August | 184 793 | 9 162 | 3 506 | **197 461** |
| | September | 184 798 | 9 159 | 3 548 | **197 505** |
| | Oktober | 184 350 | 10 464 | 3 667 | **198 481** |
| | November | 186 061 | 10 647 | 3 804 | **200 512** |
| | Dezember | 185 656 | 10 643 | 3 830 | **200 129** |
| 1937 | Januar | 185 607 | 10 641 | 3 892 | **200 140** |
| | Februar | 185 364 | 10 691 | 3 947 | **200 002** |
| | März | 185 294 | 10 703 | 3 924 | **199 921** |
| | April | 184 769 | 11 394 | 3 976 | **200 139** |
| | Mai | 184 971 | 11 168 | 4 053 | **200 192** |
| | Juni | 185 435 | 11 300 | 4 300 | **201 035** |
| | Juli | 185 435 | 11 329 | 4 746 | **201 510** |
| | August | 185 868 | 11 299 | 4 779 | **201 946** |
| | September | 186 510 | 11 223 | 4 840 | **202 573** |
| | Oktober | 189 027 | 11 274 | 5 200 | **205 501** |
| | November | 190 430 | 12 097 | 5 301 | **207 828** |
| | Dezember | 190 976 | 12 069 | 5 319 | **208 364** |

[1]) Erstmals einschließlich ⚡⚡-Bewerber und ⚡⚡-Zugehörige.

# Entwicklung der SS-Totenkopfverbände¹)
## 1935—1937

### 1935—1936

| Monat | KL Dachau | KL Esterwegen | KL Lichtenburg | KL Sachsenburg | KL Columbia | KL Brandenburg | San.-Abt. SS-TV. | Stab J.KL u. SS-TV. | Gesamt¹) |
|---|---|---|---|---|---|---|---|---|---|
| **1935** | | | | | | | | | |
| Januar | 838 | 368 | 335 | 380 | 61 | — | — | 5 | 1 987 |
| Februar | 837 | 371 | 328 | 372 | 63 | — | — | 6 | 1 977 |
| März | 844 | 366 | 313 | 411 | 59 | — | — | 5 | 1 998 |
| April | 778 | 355 | 347 | 388 | 26 | 194 | — | 5 | 2 093 |
| Mai | 774 | 359 | 348 | 389 | 29 | 337 | — | 5 | 2 241 |
| Juni | 764 | 356 | 341 | 390 | 27 | 336 | — | 5 | 2 220 |
| Juli | 772 | 359 | 352 | 403 | 23 | 336 | — | 6 | 2 252 |
| August | 812 | 364 | 358 | 404 | 24 | 304 | — | 7 | 2 273 |
| September | 855 | 356 | 355 | 405 | 26 | 334 | — | 7 | 2 338 |
| Oktober | 856 | 352 | 358 | 469 | 28 | 338 | — | 7 | 2 411 |
| November | 974 | 362 | 358 | 474 | 29 | 342 | — | 10 | 2 550 |
| Dezember | 971 | 360 | 359 | 473 | 27 | 345 | — | 11 | 2 546 |
| **1936** | | | | | | | | | |
| Januar | 1 034 | 359 | 381 | 623 | 27 | 420 | — | 11 | 2 855 |
| Februar | 1 033 | 358 | 402 | 548 | 27 | 439 | — | 11 | 2 818 |
| März | 996 | 358 | 405 | 531 | 22 | 373 | 37 | 11 | 2 733 |

### Neugliederung ab 1. April 1936

| Monat | I SS-TV. Oberbayern | II SS-TV. Elbe | III SS-TV. Sachsen | IV SS-TV. Ostfriesland | V SS-TV. Brandenburg | Unterführerschule | KL Esterwegen | KL Sachsenburg | KL Lichtenburg | KL Dachau | KL Columbia | KL Sachsenhausen | KL Julia | San.-Abt. SS-TV. | Stab J.KL u. SS-TV. | Gesamt¹) |
|---|---|---|---|---|---|---|---|---|---|---|---|---|---|---|---|---|
| April | 871 | 355 | 487 | 391 | 475 | — | 46 | 36 | 35 | 83 | 22 | — | 4 | 47 | 24 | 2 876 |
| Mai | 847 | 539 | 536 | 482 | 497 | — | 46 | 36 | 35 | 83 | 23 | — | 4 | 69 | 25 | 3 222 |
| Juni | 881 | 571 | 534 | 538 | 508 | — | 45 | 36 | 35 | 83 | 26 | — | 5 | 74 | 23 | 3 359 |
| Juli | 1 008 | 597 | 531 | 533 | 498 | — | 44 | 36 | 35 | 82 | 33 | — | 7 | 73 | 25 | 3 502 |
| August | 1 009 | 607 | 527 | 531 | 493 | — | 44 | 36 | 35 | 81 | 33 | — | 7 | 75 | 28 | 3 506 |
| September | 1 021 | 624 | 521 | 530 | 512 | — | — | 35 | 35 | 81 | 31 | 44 | 8 | 76 | 30 | 3 548 |
| Oktober²) | 947 | 618 | 496 | 488 | 531 | — | — | 34 | 35 | 85 | 30 | 40 | 9 | 74 | 28 | 3 415 |
| November | 1 038 | 628 | 491 | 513 | 530 | — | — | 37 | 34 | 86 | — | 70 | 9 | 76 | 29 | 3 541 |
| Dezember | 1 041 | 640 | 492 | 521 | 521 | — | — | 37 | 34 | 88 | — | 70 | 10 | 79 | 32 | 3 565 |
| **1937** | | | | | | | | | | | | | | | | |
| Januar | 1 044 | 636 | 525 | 542 | 536 | — | — | 37 | 34 | 87 | — | 67 | 10 | 78 | 30 | 3 626 |
| Februar | 1 019 | 620 | 510 | 541 | 570 | 77 | — | 35 | 35 | 88 | — | 68 | 10 | 78 | 31 | 3 682 |
| März | 996 | 618 | 512 | 537 | 566 | 77 | — | 35 | 34 | 89 | — | 68 | 10 | 76 | 31 | 3 649 |
| April | 1 021 | 616 | 496 | 551 | 571 | 77 | — | 36 | 34 | 88 | — | 68 | 10 | 77 | 31 | 3 676 |
| Mai | 1 061 | 656 | 498 | 550 | 552 | 79 | — | 37 | 36 | 89 | — | 72 | 10 | 78 | 35 | 3 753 |
| Juni | 1 229 | 672 | 486 | 563 | 610 | 78 | — | 41 | 37 | 89 | — | 70 | 9 | 81 | 35 | 4 000 |

### Neugliederung ab 1. Juli 1937

| Monat | 1. SS-TV. Oberbayern | 2. SS-TV. Brandenburg | 3. SS-TV. Thüringen | | | | | | | San.-Abt. SS-TV. | Stab | Gesamt¹) |
|---|---|---|---|---|---|---|---|---|---|---|---|---|
| Juli | 1 473 | 1 375 | 1 180 | — | 40 | 37 | 87 | — | 68 | 9 | 144 | 36 | 4 449 |

### Neugliederung ab 1. August 1937

| Monat | 1. SS-TV. Oberbayern | 2. SS-TV. Brandenburg | 3. SS-TV. Thüringen | KL Buchenwald | KL Dachau | KL Sachsenhausen | San.-Abt. SS-TV. | Stab | Gesamt¹) |
|---|---|---|---|---|---|---|---|---|---|
| August | 1 428 | 1 391 | 1 116 | 120 | 121 | 111 | 152 | 43 | 4 482 |
| September | 1 492 | 1 394 | 1 107 | 119 | 122 | 115 | 153 | 43 | 4 545 |
| Oktober | 1 630 | 1 547 | 1 169 | 118 | 123 | 114 | 154 | 52 | 4 907 |
| November | 1 630 | 1 560 | 1 080 | 109 | 117 | 115 | 151 | 52 | 4 814 |
| Dezember | 1 621 | 1 617 | 1 066 | 112 | 116 | 109 | 143 | 49 | 4 833 |

¹) Männer und Anwärter. Ohne SS-Zugehörige. ²) Seit Oktober 1936 werden in den Totenkopfverbänden auch SS-Zugehörige geführt.

## Entwicklung der SS-Verfügungstruppe
### 1935—1937

| Monat | Leibstandarte SS Adolf Hitler | SS Deutschland | SS Germania | SS-Nachrichtensturmbann | SS-Pioniersturmbann | SS Nürnberg | SS Junkerschulen | Inspektion SS-Verfügungstruppe | Sanitätsabteilung SS-VT. | Gesamt |
|---|---|---|---|---|---|---|---|---|---|---|
| **1935** | | | | | | | | | | |
| Januar.... | 2 531 | 1 722 | 526 | — | — | — | 205 | — | — | 4 984 |
| Februar ... | 2 627 | 2 617 | 590 | — | 59 | — | 205 | — | — | 6 098 |
| März...... | 2 544 | 2 589 | 698 | — | 139 | — | 413 | — | — | 6 383 |
| April...... | 2 633 | 2 511 | 1 091 | 365 | 257 | — | 753 | — | — | 7 610 |
| Mai....... | 2 660 | 2 556 | 1 855 | 375 | 254 | — | 759 | — | — | 8 459 |
| Juni...... | 2 648 | 2 596 | 1 895 | 357 | 387 | — | 737 | — | — | 8 620 |
| Juli...... | 2 654 | 2 592 | 2 043 | 360 | 414 | — | 716 | — | — | 8 779 |
| August .... | 2 634 | 2 563 | 2 184 | 350 | 467 | — | 714 | — | — | 8 912 |
| September . | 2 601 | 2 558 | 2 275 | 356 | 462 | — | 691 | — | — | 8 943 |
| Oktober.... | 2 576 | 2 622 | 2 488 | 352 | 455 | — | 692 | — | — | 9 185 |
| November.. | 2 665 | 2 618 | 2 458 | 356 | 461 | — | 648 | — | — | 9 206 |
| Dezember .. | 2 660 | 2 611 | 2 518 | 364 | 458 | — | 650 | — | — | 9 261 |
| **1936** | | | | | | | | | | |
| Januar.... | 2 650 | 2 580 | 2 514 | 366 | 460 | — | 642 | — | — | 9 212 |
| Februar ... | 2 636 | 2 557 | 2 516 | 361 | 458 | — | 635 | — | — | 9 163 |
| März...... | 2 597 | 2 499 | 2 509 | 368 | 454 | — | 646 | — | — | 9 073 |
| April...... | 2 671 | 2 516 | 2 493 | 370 | 454 | — | 684 | — | — | 9 188 |
| Mai....... | 2 786 | 2 495 | 2 493 | 373 | 456 | — | 674 | — | — | 9 277 |
| Juni...... | 2 756 | 2 486 | 2 486 | 370 | 458 | — | 667 | — | — | 9 223 |
| Juli...... | 2 722 | 2 468 | 2 461 | 372 | 444 | — | 669 | — | — | 9 136 |
| August .... | 2 651 | 2 329 | 2 421 | 364 | 433 | 135 | 646 | 18 | 165 | 9 162 |
| September . | 2 630 | 2 336 | 2 418 | 363 | 430 | 153 | 645 | 17 | 167 | 9 159 |
| Oktober.... | 3 228 | 2 911 | 2 508 | 359 | 427 | 264 | 565 | 18 | 184 | 10 464 |
| November.. | 3 216 | 2 936 | 2 522 | 365 | 500 | 351 | 537 | 17 | 203 | 10 647 |
| Dezember .. | 3 201 | 2 932 | 2 523 | 364 | 497 | 355 | 539 | 17 | 215 | 10 643 |
| **1937** | | | | | | | | | | |
| Januar.... | 3 177 | 2 951 | 2 509 | 361 | 509 | 350 | 531 | 18 | 235 | 10 641 |
| Februar ... | 3 205 | 2 970 | 2 506 | 358 | 508 | 348 | 543 | 17 | 236 | 10 691 |
| März...... | 3 192 | 3 004 | 2 500 | 356 | 505 | 347 | 542 | 17 | 240 | 10 703 |
| April...... | 3 662 | 3 026 | 2 538 | 389 | 542 | 423 | 557 | 16 | 241 | 11 394 |
| Mai....... | 3 688 | 3 021 | 2 485 | 409 | 545 | 423 | 342 | 16 | 239 | 11 168 |
| Juni...... | 3 678 | 3 004 | 2 522 | 423 | 538 | 472 | 355 | 31 | 277 | 11 300 |
| Juli...... | 3 661 | 2 985 | 2 550 | 415 | 545 | 494 | 374 | 31 | 274 | 11 329 |
| August .... | 3 664 | 2 948 | 2 554 | 408 | 542 | 502 | 375 | 32 | 274 | 11 299 |
| September . | 3 610 | 2 933 | 2 543 | 406 | 540 | 507 | 383 | 35 | 266 | 11 223 |
| Oktober.... | 3 614 | 2 857 | 2 485 | 391 | 517 | 522 | 588 | 38 | 262 | 11 274 |
| November.. | 3 653 | 3 178 | 2 610 | 409 | 575 | 615 | 742 | 39 | 276 | 12 097 |
| Dezember .. | 3 622 | 3 161 | 2 621 | 414 | 580 | 617 | 738 | 41 | 275 | 12 069 |

## Zusammensetzung und zahlenmäßige Entwicklung der Allgemeinen ᛋᛋ in den Jahren 1936 und 1937

| Monat | Bewerber | Anwärter | Männer | Anwärter und Männer | Zugehörige | Gesamt |
|---|---|---|---|---|---|---|
| **1936** | | | | | | |
| Januar .............. | 12 515 | 4 785 | 154 360 | **159 145** | 17 314 | **188 974** |
| Februar .............. | 12 535 | 5 161 | 153 568 | **158 729** | 17 331 | **188 595** |
| März ............... | 12 397 | 5 400 | 151 895 | **157 295** | 17 820 | **187 512** |
| April ............... | 10 976 | 6 408 | 149 596 | **156 004** | 19 230 | **186 210** |
| Mai ............... | 11 124 | 6 289 | 148 386 | **154 675** | 19 632 | **185 431** |
| Juni................ | 11 397 | 6 361 | 147 887 | **154 248** | 19 764 | **185 409** |
| Juli¹)............... | 11 397 | 6 361 | 147 887 | **154 248** | 19 764 | **185 409** |
| August.............. | 11 491 | 6 547 | 147 107 | **153 654** | 19 648 | **184 793** |
| September............ | 11 448 | 6 734 | 146 602 | **153 336** | 20 014 | **184 798** |
| Oktober ............. | 11 735 | 6 519 | 144 842 | **151 361** | 21 254 | **184 350** |
| November ............ | 14 073 | 6 420 | 144 490 | **150 910** | 21 078 | **186 061** |
| Dezember............ | 13 864 | o 695 | 144 422 | **151 117** | 20 675 | **185 656** |
| **1937** | | | | | | |
| Januar .............. | 13 409 | 7 393 | 144 341 | **151 734** | 20 464 | **185 607** |
| Februar .............. | 13 031 | 8 126 | 143 941 | **152 067** | 20 266 | **185 364** |
| März ............... | 12 476 | 8 415 | 143 672 | **152 087** | 20 731 | **185 294** |
| April ............... | 11 900 | 8 345 | 142 720 | **151 065** | 21 804 | **184 769** |
| Mai ............... | 12 210 | 8 540 | 142 472 | **151 012** | 21 749 | **184 971** |
| Juni................ | 12 682 | 8 520 | 142 600 | **151 120** | 21 633 | **185 435** |
| Juli¹)............... | 12 682 | 8 520 | 142 600 | **151 120** | 21 633 | **185 435** |
| August.............. | 13 637 | 7 768 | 143 010 | **150 778** | 21 453 | **185 868** |
| September............ | 13 941 | 5 835 | 145 383 | **151 218** | 21 351 | **186 510** |
| Oktober ............. | 16 683 | 4 821 | 146 452 | **151 273** | 21 071 | **189 027** |
| November ............ | 18 654 | 4 419 | 145 598 | **150 017** | 21 759 | **190 430** |
| Dezember ............ | 19 155 | 4 437 | 146 100 | **150 537** | 21 284 | **190 976** |

¹) Urlaubsmonat der Allgemeinen ᛋᛋ.

# Gesamtüberblick
## über die Zusammensetzung und
### die monatlichen Stärken der ⚡-Totenkopfverbände

| Monat | 1/T.St. Ober-bay-ern | 2/T.St. Bran-den-burg | 3/T.St. Thü-rin-gen | 4/T.St. Ost-mark | KL Bu-chen-wald | KL Dach-au | KL Flos-sen-bürg | KL Lich-ten-burg | KL Maut-hau-sen | KL Sach-sen-hau-sen | San.-Abt. ⚡-T.St. | Stab F.KL u. ⚡- T.St. | Trup-pen-ver-wal-tungs-amt | Stab-nach-richten-zug ⚡-TV. | Ge-samt |
|---|---|---|---|---|---|---|---|---|---|---|---|---|---|---|---|
| **Anwärter** | | | | | | | | | | | | | | | |
| Januar .... | 1 050 | 1 062 | 444 | — | 10 | 4 | — | — | — | 11 | 35 | 10 | — | — | 2 626 |
| Februar ... | 1 030 | 1 129 | 435 | — | 10 | 4 | — | — | — | 10 | 40 | 9 | — | — | 2 667 |
| März...... | 1 017 | 925 | 633 | — | 7 | 4 | — | — | — | 9 | 41 | 7 | — | — | 2 643 |
| April...... | 2 550 | 1 840 | 605 | — | 5 | 4 | — | — | — | 10 | 41 | 7 | — | — | 5 062 |
| Mai....... | 2 418 | 2 353 | 565 | — | 5 | 4 | — | — | — | 14 | 36 | 7 | — | — | 5 402 |
| Juni ...... | 2 252 | 1 765 | 1 387 | — | 4 | 3 | — | — | — | 14 | 32 | 6 | — | — | 5 463 |
| Juli....... | 2 252 | 1 765 | 1 387 | — | 4 | 3 | — | — | — | 14 | 32 | 6 | — | — | 5 463 |
| August .... | 1 773 | 1 693 | 1 288 | 479 | 4 | 5 | 2 | — | 1 | 8 | 37 | 1 | — | — | 5 291 |
| September . | 1 773 | 1 693 | 1 288 | 479 | 4 | 5 | 2 | — | 1 | 8 | 37 | 1 | — | — | 5 291 |
| Oktober ... | 1 773 | 1 693 | 1 288 | 479 | 4 | 5 | 2 | — | 1 | 8 | 37 | 1 | — | — | 5 291 |
| November . | 1 693 | 1 903 | 1 329 | 700 | 5 | 5 | 6 | — | 8 | 16 | 50 | 6 | — | 12 | 5 733 |
| Dezember.. | 1 693 | 1 903 | 1 329 | 700 | 5 | 5 | 6 | — | 8 | 16 | 50 | 6 | — | 12 | 5 733 |
| **Männer** | | | | | | | | | | | | | | | |
| Januar .... | 603 | 562 | 634 | — | 100 | 112 | — | 9 | — | 95 | 107 | 40 | — | — | 2 262 |
| Februar ... | 596 | 565 | 596 | — | 99 | 111 | — | 12 | — | 96 | 114 | 39 | — | — | 2 228 |
| März...... | 610 | 495 | 668 | — | 94 | 113 | — | 15 | — | 98 | 123 | 40 | — | — | 2 256 |
| April...... | 563 | 467 | 602 | — | 107 | 116 | — | 15 | — | 99 | 119 | 41 | — | — | 2 129 |
| Mai....... | 637 | 461 | 611 | — | 118 | 124 | — | 17 | — | 119 | 125 | 41 | — | — | 2 253 |
| Juni ...... | 719 | 470 | 605 | — | 127 | 126 | — | 17 | — | 114 | 127 | 41 | — | — | 2 346 |
| Juli....... | 719 | 470 | 605 | — | 127 | 126 | — | 17 | — | 114 | 127 | 41 | — | — | 2 346 |
| August .... | 574 | 495 | 600 | 149 | 120 | 129 | 29 | 17 | 6 | 116 | 139 | 43 | — | — | 2 417 |
| September . | 574 | 495 | 600 | 149 | 120 | 129 | 29 | 17 | 6 | 116 | 139 | 43 | — | — | 2 417 |
| Oktober ... | 574 | 495 | 600 | 149 | 120 | 129 | 29 | 17 | 6 | 116 | 139 | 43 | — | — | 2 417 |
| November . | 632 | 593 | 612 | 154 | 129 | 122 | 38 | 19 | 57 | 144 | 155 | 38 | 35 | 23 | 2 751 |
| Dezember.. | 632 | 593 | 612 | 154 | 129 | 122 | 38 | 19 | 57 | 144 | 155 | 38 | 35 | 23 | 2 751 |
| **Zugehörige** | | | | | | | | | | | | | | | |
| Januar .... | 145 | 126 | 184 | — | 5 | 7 | — | — | — | 5 | 10 | 1 | — | — | 483 |
| Februar ... | 145 | 126 | 182 | — | 5 | 7 | — | — | — | 5 | 10 | 1 | — | — | 481 |
| März...... | 145 | 121 | 177 | — | 5 | 7 | — | — | — | 5 | 10 | 1 | — | — | 471 |
| April...... | 222 | 175 | 228 | — | 7 | 7 | — | — | — | 5 | 11 | 1 | — | — | 656 |
| Mai....... | 220 | 175 | 228 | — | 7 | 7 | — | — | — | 5 | 11 | 1 | — | — | 654 |
| Juni ...... | 219 | 175 | 228 | — | 7 | 7 | — | — | — | 5 | 11 | 1 | — | — | 653 |
| Juli....... | 219 | 175 | 228 | — | 7 | 7 | — | — | — | 5 | 11 | 1 | — | — | 653 |
| August ... | 217 | 174 | 227 | — | 7 | 7 | — | — | — | 5 | 11 | 1 | — | — | 649 |
| September. | 217 | 174 | 227 | — | 7 | 7 | — | — | — | 5 | 11 | 1 | — | — | 649 |
| Oktober ... | 217 | 174 | 227 | — | 7 | 7 | — | — | — | 5 | 11 | 1 | — | — | 649 |
| November . | 197 | 199 | 235 | 13 | 8 | 6 | 1 | — | 1 | 12 | 13 | 1 | — | 2 | 688 |
| Dezember.. | 197 | 199 | 235 | 13 | 8 | 6 | 1 | — | 1 | 12 | 13 | 1 | — | 2 | 688 |
| **Insgesamt** | | | | | | | | | | | | | | | |
| Januar... | 1 798 | 1 750 | 1 262 | — | 115 | 123 | — | 9 | — | 111 | 152 | 51 | — | — | 5 371 |
| Februar .. | 1 771 | 1 820 | 1 213 | — | 114 | 122 | — | 12 | — | 111 | 164 | 49 | — | — | 5 376 |
| März..... | 1 772 | 1 541 | 1 478 | — | 106 | 124 | — | 15 | — | 112 | 174 | 48 | — | — | 5 370 |
| April .... | 3 335 | 2 482 | 1 435 | — | 119 | 127 | — | 15 | — | 114 | 171 | 49 | — | — | 7 847 |
| Mai ..... | 3 275 | 2 989 | 1 404 | — | 130 | 135 | — | 17 | — | 138 | 172 | 49 | — | — | 8 309 |
| Juni ..... | 3 190 | 2 410 | 2 220 | — | 138 | 136 | — | 17 | — | 133 | 170 | 48 | — | — | 8 462 |
| Juli ..... | 3 190 | 2 410 | 2 220 | — | 138 | 136 | — | 17 | — | 133 | 170 | 48 | — | — | 8 462 |
| August .. | 2 564 | 2 362 | 2 115 | 628 | 131 | 141 | 31 | 17 | 7 | 129 | 187 | 45 | — | — | 8 357 |
| September | 2 564 | 2 362 | 2 115 | 628 | 131 | 141 | 31 | 17 | 7 | 129 | 187 | 45 | — | — | 8 357 |
| Oktober.. | 2 564 | 2 362 | 2 115 | 628 | 131 | 141 | 31 | 17 | 7 | 129 | 187 | 45 | — | — | 8 357 |
| November | 2 522 | 2 695 | 2 176 | 867 | 142 | 133 | 45 | 19 | 66 | 172 | 218 | 45 | 35 | 37 | 9 172 |
| Dezember | 2 522 | 2 695 | 2 176 | 867 | 142 | 133 | 45 | 19 | 66 | 172 | 218 | 45 | 35 | 37 | 9 172 |

# Konfession der ᛋᛋ-Angehörigen
# 31. 12. 1938

| Oberabschnitte, Sondereinheiten, ᛋᛋ-Verfügungstruppe und ᛋᛋ-Totenkopfverbände | Gesamtstärke | Konfession | | | | Konfession ausgedrückt in % | | | |
|---|---|---|---|---|---|---|---|---|---|
| | | evgl. | kath. | gottgl. | sonstige | evgl. | kath. | gottgl. | sonst. |
| Donau ........ | 17 435 | 1 715 | 11 852 | 3 850 | 18 | 9,8 | 68,0 | 22,1 | 0,1 |
| Süd .......... | 10 122 | 2 237 | 6 771 | 1 098 | 16 | 22,1 | 66,9 | 10,9 | 0,1 |
| Südwest ....... | 13 289 | 7 328 | 4 172 | 1 759 | 30 | 55,3 | 31,4 | 13,2 | 0,1 |
| Rhein ........ | 15 124 | 7 535 | 5 096 | 2 467 | 26 | 49,8 | 33,7 | 16,3 | 0,2 |
| West ......... | 21 346 | 6 139 | 5 940 | 9 251 | 16 | 28,8 | 27,8 | 43,3 | 0,1 |
| Nordwest ...... | 16 899 | 12 166 | 910 | 3 802 | 21 | 72,0 | 5,4 | 22,5 | 0,1 |
| Nord ......... | 13 323 | 10 828 | 756 | 1 718 | 21 | 81,2 | 5,7 | 12,9 | 0,2 |
| Nordost ....... | 12 902 | 9 133 | 1 570 | 1 994 | 205 | 70,7 | 12,2 | 15,5 | 1,6 |
| Ost .......... | 19 393 | 14 826 | 1 537 | 2 969 | 61 | 76,5 | 7,9 | 15,3 | 0,3 |
| Südost ........ | 13 263 | 6 621 | 5 079 | 1 554 | 9 | 49,9 | 38,3 | 11,7 | 0,1 |
| Elbe .......... | 13 321 | 10 308 | 558 | 2 421 | 34 | 77,3 | 4,2 | 18,2 | 0,3 |
| Main .......... | 8 808 | 4 424 | 3 236 | 1 144 | 4 | 50,2 | 36,7 | 13,0 | 0,1 |
| Fulda-Werra ... | 16 195 | 11 606 | 1 759 | 2 808 | 22 | 71,7 | 10,9 | 17,3 | 0,1 |
| Mitte ......... | 12 218 | 7 926 | 728 | 3 540 | 24 | 64,9 | 5,9 | 29,0 | 0,2 |
| Sondereinheiten | 11 115 | 3 400 | 1 020 | 6 678 | 17 | 30,6 | 9,2 | 60,1 | 0,1 |
| Allgemeine ᛋᛋ | 214 753 | 116 192 | 50 984 | 47 053 | 524 | 54,2 | 23,7 | 21,9 | 0,2 |
| ᛋᛋ-Verfügungstruppe | 14 234 | 4 265 | 2 321 | 7 648 | — | 30,0 | 16,4 | 53,6 | — |
| ᛋᛋ-Totenkopfverbände .. | 9 172 | 2 211 | 632 | 6 329 | — | 24,1 | 6,9 | 69,0 | — |
| Insgesamt ... | 238 159 | 122 668 | 53 937 | 61 030 | 524 | 51,4 | 22,6 | 25,8 | 0,2 |

Biogram by Hermann Göring, written for Major Douglas M. Kelley
at Nuremberg prison during the latter part of 1945.

Hermann Göring.
Für Major M. Kelley

*Lebenslauf*

Ich bin am 12.I.1893 in Rosenheim in Bayern geboren. Mein Vater war
zweimal verheiratet. Aus seiner ersten Ehe (Frau gestorben) stammen
drei Halbbrüder von mir, von denen zwei noch am Leben sind, und
eine bereits verstorbene Halbschwester. Aus seiner zweiten Ehe ist mein
ältester Bruder an seinen schweren Verletzungen aus dem ersten Weltkrieg gestorben. Zwei Schwestern, die beide älter sind als ich sind verheiratet, ausserdem habe ich noch einen jüngeren Bruder, der sich zur Zeit
auch hier im Nürnberger Zellengefängnis befindet. Mein Vater war
erster Gouvernör unserer Kolonie Südwestafrika, später Ministerresident.
Meine Jugend verlebte ich auf unseren Besitzungen Veldenstein bei
Nürnberg und Schloss Mauterndorf in den oesterreichischen Alpen.
Dadurch bin ich sehr früh Hochtourist geworden und habe im Laufe der Jahre, vor allem bis 1923 sehr viele und schwere Bergbestei-
gungen durchgeführt. Da ich den aktiven Offizierberuf erwählte, kam
ich nach der Erziehung im elterlichen Hause in das Kadettencorps.
Ich wurde dann Leutnant in einem Infanterieregiment und ging mit
diesem Regiment in den ersten Weltkrieg. Bis Oktober 1914 machte
ich die grossen Schlachten in Lothringen mit. Dann kam ich zur Flie-
gerei, für die ich mich schon immer sehr interessierte. Zuerst als Beobachter, wurde ich 1915 selbst Pilot und führte ein Bombenflugzeug.
1916 wurde ich Jagdflieger. Als solcher wurde ich am 2. November
1916 schwer im Luftkampf verwundet und schied drei Monate (Lazarett) aus. Dann flog ich wieder. Ich schoß damals 28 feindliche Flug-
zeuge ab und erhielt die höchste Kriegsauszeichnung des kaiserlichen
Deutschlands, den Orden 'Pour le mérite'. Als der Krieg zu Ende war,
schied ich als Hauptmann aus der Armee und ging bald darauf als
Flieger nach Dänemark, später nach Schweden. Dort lernte ich meine
erste Frau kennen und heiratete. Ich ging dann nach Deutschland
zurück und wohnte in der Nähe von München. Ich besuchte ein Jahr

Appendix XIII   383

die Universität München, um Geschichte und Staatswissenschaften zu
hören. Ende 1922 lernte ich Adolf Hitler kennen und trat seiner Bewegung bei. Ich erhielt von ihm den Auftrag, die S.A. zu organisieren.
November 1923 kam es zu dem Münchner Putsch, bei welchem ich
schwer verwundet wurde. Ich mußte damals sofort ins Ausland trans-
portiert werden. 1924 ging ich nach Italien, wo ich bis März 1925
(Rom-Venedig) blieb. Von dort reiste ich mit meiner Frau nach Schweden. Bis 1927 blieb ich dort, unterbrochen von Reisen nach der Türkei.
Ab 1927 lebte ich teils in Deutschland, teils in Schweden. (Reisen
nach England etc.) Mai 1928 wurde ich in den Reichstag als Abge-
ordneter gewählt und nahm meine politische Tätigkeit wieder auf. 1931
(Oktober) starb meine Frau an einem Herzleiden. Ich lebte nun
dauernd in Berlin. 1932 wurde ich Präsident des Reichstages und Hitlers
politischer Beauftragter. 1933 kam unsere Regierungsbildung und ich
wurde zunächst Reichsluftfahrtminister und Preußischer Innenminister.
April 1933 wurde ich Preußischer Ministerpräsident. 1934 dazu Reichs-
forstmeister (Forstminister) und Reichsjägermeister, da ich mich stets
für Natur und auch die Jagd interessierte. 1935 Oberbefehlshaber der
Luftwaffe und Generaloberst. Gleichzeitig erklärte mich der Führer in
seinem Staatstestament zu seinem Nachfolger. 1936 Beauftragter für
den 4 Jahresplan und damit oberster Leiter der gesamten deutschen
Wirtschaft und Ernährung. 1938 wurde ich Generalfeldmarschall.
Während dieser Zeit machte ich viele offizielle und inoffizielle Reisen
ins Ausland (Europa) und lernte fast alle bedeutenden leitenden Männer kennen. 1935 habe ich mich wieder verheiratet und 1938 (Juni)
wurde meine Tochter Edda geboren. Neben den militärischen, wirtschaftlichen und Staatsaufgaben, galt mein grosses Interesse der Kunst.
Ich leitete persönlich die preussischen Staatstheater (Staatsoper, Schau-
spielhaus) und stand mit den Künstlern in engem Kontakt. Ich gründete die 'Hermann Göring Meisterschule für Malerei', der noch eine
Gobelinweberei angeschlossen wurde. Desgleichen legte ich den Grund-
stock für eine neue Galerie (Malerei, Statuen, Kunstgewerbe). Ich
unterstützte alle Zweige der Kunst und Wissenschaft. Ich war deshalb
auch Präsident des Reichsforschungsrates, wo alle Forschungen zu-
sammenliefen. Sportlich betätigte ich mich auf der Jagd und im Reiten.
1939 kam der Krieg, der meine Arbeitskraft bis an die Grenze der
äussersten Möglichkeiten in Anspruch nahm und an die Nerven die
höchsten Anforderungen stellte. 1940 wurde ich der Reichsmarschall

des Deutschen Reiches. – Gesundheitlich ist folgendes zu berichten. Ausser Gelenkrheumatismus (infolge von Scharlach) und häufigen Anginas, war ich immer gesund. Der Rheumatismus ging nach der Verwundung 1923 weg, ebenso die Angina. Ab 1939 tritt paroschinale Tachicarty (parochiale Tachycardie), seit 1945 immer häufiger auf. Ebenfalls leide ich manchmal an schwerer Gesichtsneuralgie.

Mai 1945 kam ich in amerikanische Gefangenschaft.

Hermann Göring

----

Biogram by Hermann Göring, written for Major Douglas M. Kelley at Nuremberg prison during the latter part of 1945.

Hermann Göring.
For Major Kelley

*Curriculum vitae*

I was born in Rosenheim, in Bavaria, on January 12, 1893. My father was married twice. Children from his marriage with his first wife (who died) were my three stepbrothers (two of whom are still alive) and my stepsister (now dead). Of the children of his second marriage, my oldest brother died of the severe wounds he received in World War I. Two sisters, both older than I, are married; and I still have a younger brother, who is now also here in the Nuremberg prison. My father was the first governor of our colony 'Southwest Africa,' and later Resident Minister. I spent my youth at our homes Veldenstein, near Nuremberg, and Mauterndorf Castle, in the Austrian Alps. This made me an accomplished mountain-climber at an early age, and in the course of the years, especially up to 1923, I went on many and difficult mountain-climbing expeditions. Since I had decided to become a military officer, I joined the Corps of Cadets after my education in my parents' house. I then became 2nd Lieutenant in an infantry regiment and accompanied this regiment to the front in World War I. Until October 1914, I participated in the great battles in Lorraine. Then I got into flying, which had always interested me very much. Initially an observer, I became a pilot myself in 1915 and flew a bomber. In 1916 I became a fighter pilot, and as such I was severely wounded in a dogfight on November 2, 1916, and was hospitalized for three months. Then I resumed flying. I shot down twenty-eight enemy planes and received the highest military decoration of Imperial Germany, the order 'Pour le mérite.' When the war was over, I was discharged from the army as a captain, and soon thereafter I went first to Denmark and later to Sweden as a pilot. There I met and married my first wife. I then returned to Germany and lived near Munich. For one year I attended Munich University to study history and political science. At the end of 1922 I became acquainted with Adolf Hitler and joined his movement. I was assigned the task of organizing the SA (Sturmabteilung). In November 1923 came the Munich putsch, in which I was seriously wounded. I had to be taken abroad immediately. In 1924 I went to Italy where I remained (in Rome and Venice) until March 1925. From there my wife and I traveled to Sweden. Except for visits to Turkey, I remained there until 1927. From 1927 on I lived partly in Germany and partly in Sweden (some trips to England, etc.). In May 1928 I was elected to the Reichstag as a deputy and resumed my political activity. In 1931 (October) my wife died of a heart condition. From then on I lived in Berlin permanently. In 1932 I became President of the Reichstag and Hitler's political deputy. In 1933 we formed a government and I initially became Reich Minister of the German Air Force and Prussian Minister of the Interior. In April 1933 I became Governor of Prussia. In 1934 I also became Reich Minister of Forestry (Forstminister) and Chief Ranger of the Reich, as I had always been interested in nature and hunting. In 1935 I became Commander in Chief of the Air Force and Colonel General. At the same time the Führer named me his successor in his political testament. In 1936 I was put in charge of the Four-Year-Plan and thus became chief director of the over-all German economy and food-supply system. In 1938 I became Field Marshal. During this period I made many official and unofficial trips abroad (Europe) and became acquainted with almost all the important political leaders. I had remarried in 1935, and in 1938 (June) my daughter Edda was born. Along with my military, economic, and governmental duties, my special interest was in the arts. I personally supervised the Prussian State Theaters (State Opera and Drama Theater) and was in close contact with the artists. I founded the 'Hermann Göring Master School for Painting', to which a Gobelin weaving establishment was added.

Likewise, I donated a collection as the nucleus for a new gallery (painting, sculpture, decorative arts). I supported all branches of the arts and sciences. Consequently, I was also president of the Reich Research Council, which coordinated all research activities. With regards to sports, I was an active hunter and rider. In 1939 came the war, which challenged my energies to their extreme limits and placed the greatest possible demands on my nerves. In 1940 I became Reich Marshal (Reichsmarschall) of the German Reich.

As to my health, I can report the following. With the exception of rheumatoid arthritis (a consequence of scarlet fever) and frequent attacks of angina, I have always been healthy. After my injuries in 1923, the rheumatism disappeared, and so did the angina. Beginning in 1939, parochial tachycardia appeared, becoming ever more frequent since 1945. I also suffer sometimes from severe facial neuralgia.

In May 1945 I was captured by the Americans.

Hermann Göring

Autobiographical Note by Hitler of November 29, 1921.
FA 88 St. 17 a, Bl. 1-3.
Institut für Zeitgeschichte, Munich.

*Abschrift*

München, den 29. November 1921

Lieber Herr Doktor!

Wie mir Herr *Eckart* mitteilt, haben Sie wieder einmal Interesse über meine Entwicklung zum Parteiführer gezeigt.

Ich erlaube mir deshalb, Ihnen einen kurzen Aufriss über meine Person zu geben:

Ich bin am 20. April 1889 zu Braunau a. Inn als Sohn des dortigen Postoffizials Alois *Hitler* geboren. Meine gesamte Schulbildung umfaßt 5 Klassen Volksschule und 4 Klassen Unterrealschule. Ziel meiner Jugend war, Baumeister zu werden und ich glaube auch nicht, daß, wenn mich die Politik nicht gefaßt hätte, ich mich einem anderen Beruf jemals zugewandt haben würde. Da ich, wie Sie wahrscheinlich wissen, bereits mit 17 Jahren väterlicher- und mütterlicherseits verwaist war, im übrigen ohne jedes Vermögen dastand, mein gesamter Barbetrag bei meiner Reise nach Wien betrug rund 80 Kronen, war ich gezwungen, sofort als gewöhnlicher Arbeiter mir mein Brot zu verdienen. – Ich ging als noch nicht 18 jähriger als Hilfsarbeiter auf einen Bau und habe nun im Verlaufe von 2 Jahren so ziemlich alle Arten von Beschäftigungen des gewöhnlichen Taglöhners durchgemacht. Nebenbei studierte ich, soweit meine Mittel es zuliessen, Kunstgeschichte, Kulturgeschichte, Baugeschichte und beschäftigte mich nebenbei mit politischen Problemen. Aus einer mehr weltbürgerlich empfindenden Familie stammend, war ich unter der Schule der härtesten Wirklichkeit in kaum einem Jahr Antisemit geworden. Schon damals jedoch konnte ich mich keiner der bereits bestehenden Parteien anschliessen.

Unter unendlicher Mühe gelang es mir, mich nebenbei als Maler soweit auszubilden, daß ich durch diese Beschäftigung von meinem 20. Lebensjahr ab ein, wenn auch zunächst kärgliches, Auskommen fand.

Ich wurde Architektur-Zeichner und Architektur-Maler und war praktisch mit meinem 21. Lebensjahr vollkommen selbständig. 1912 ging ich in dieser Eigenschaft dauernd nach München. Im Verlauf der 4 Jahre, vom 20. bis 24. hatte ich mich mehr und mehr mit politischen Dingen beschäftigt, weniger durch Besuch von Versammlungen als vielmehr durch gründliches Studium volkswirtschaftlicher Lehren, sowie der damals zur Verfügung stehenden gesamten antisemitischen Literatur.

Seit meinem 22. Jahr warf ich mich mit besonderem Feuereifer über militärpolitische Schriften und unterliess die ganzen Jahre niemals, mich in sehr eindringlicher Weise mit der allgemeinen Weltgeschichte zu beschäftigen.

Aktiv betätigt habe ich mich in der Politik auch in diesen Jahren nicht. Ich vermied es, irgendwo als Redner aufzutreten schon aus dem Grunde, weil keine der damals bestehenden Parteien mir innerlich irgendwie sympathisch gewesen wäre.

Auch in dieser Zeit war das letzte Ziel unverrückbar, Baumeister zu werden.

Am 5. August 1914 meldete ich mich auf Grund eines genehmigten Majestätsgesuches beim 1. Bayr. Inf. Regiment zum Eintritt in die deutsche Armee. Nach einigen Tagen zurückgestellt wurde ich dem 2. Inf. Regiment überwiesen und trat am 16. August in die damals in Aufstellung begriffenen Formationen des Bayr. Res. Inf. Regt.s Nr. 16 ein. Das Regiment marschierte unter dem Namen: Regiment 'List' als erstes Bayrisches Freiwilligen-Regiment ins Feld und empfing Ende Oktober 1914 in der 'Schlacht an der Yser' die Feuertaufe.

Es war eines jener Freiwilligen-Regimenter, die damals im Verlauf von wenigen Tagen oft nahezu vollständig aufgerieben wurden.

Am 2. Dez. 1914 erhielt ich das Eiserne Kreuz 2. Klasse. Ich blieb dauernd beim Regiment und wurde in der Schlacht an der Somme am 7. Okt. 1916 zum erstenmal verwundet (durch Granatsplitter am linken Oberschenkel) und kam am 10. Okt. 1916, am Jahrestage meines Ausmarsches, als Verwundeter zum ersten Male wieder in die Heimat.

Nach 2 monatlicher Behandlung im Lazarett Beelitz bei Berlin wurde ich im Dez. 1916 dem Ersatzbatl. 2. Inf. Reg. München überwiesen und meldete mich wieder freiwillig ins Feld. Am 1. März 1917 war ich wieder bei meinem Stammregiment und erhielt am 17.9.1917 das Militärverdienstkreuz 3. Kl. mit Schwertern, am 9. Mai 1918 das Regiments-

diplom, am 4.8.1918 das Eiserne Kreuz 1. Kl., am 18.5.1918 das Verwundetenabzeichen in schwarz und am 25.8.1918 die Dienstauszeichnung 3. Klasse.

In der Schlacht vom 13./14. Oktober 1918 erhielt ich eine schwere
Gelbkreuzvergiftung, im Verlaufe deren ich zunächst vollständig er-
blindete. Ich wurde von Werwick in Flandern abtransportiert und dem
Vereinslazarett Pasewalk bei Stettin überwiesen. Da meine Erblindung
in verhältnismäßig kurzer Zeit wieder wich, und das Augenlicht allmählich wieder zurückkehrte, außerdem ja am 9. November die Revolution ausgebrochen war, ersuchte ich um möglichst schnelle Überführung nach München und war seit Dez. 18 wieder beim Ers. Batl. 2. Inf.
Reg. Während der Räteperiode auf der Konskriptionsliste stehend, wurde ich nach Niederschlagung der roten Herrschaft in die Untersuch.
Kommiss. des 2. Inf. Reg. kommandiert und von dort als Bildungsoffizier dem Schützenregiment 41 überwiesen. Ich hielt in diesem Regiment
sowie in anderen Formationen nun zahlreiche Aufklärungsvorträge über
den Wahnsinn der roten Blutdiktatur und konnte mit Freude erleben,
daß aus den infolge der allgemeinen Reichswehrverminderung aus dieser ausscheidenden Heeresangehörige die 1. Truppe meiner späteren
Anhänger entstand.

Im Juni 1919 schloß ich mich der damals 7 Mitglieder zählenden
Deutschen Arbeiterpartei an, in der ich nun endlich auf politischem
Gebiete die Bewegung gefunden zu haben glaubte, die meinem Ideal
entsprach. – Heute ist die Zahl ihrer Anhänger in München allein auf
über 4$^1$/$_2$ Tausend gewachsen, und ich darf mit Stolz wohl einen grossen
Teil an dieser Arbeit mir zuschreiben.

Gestatten Sie mir, daß ich nun schliesse und verbleibe ich

mit vorzüglicher Hochachtung
Ihr (gez.) *A. Hitler.*


F. d. R. der Abschrift:

*Richter*

Seal: Nationalsoz. Deutsche Arbeiterpartei Hauptarchiv

**26. Aug. 1941**

Autobiographical Note by Hitler of November 29, 1921.
FA 88 St. 17 a, Bl. 1-3.
Institut für Zeitgeschichte, Munich.

*Copy*

Munich, November 29, 1921

Dear Doctor:

As Mr. *Eckart* informs me, you have again displayed interest in the course of my development to party leader.

I, therefore, take the liberty to give you a short outline of my personal life.

I was born on April 20, 1889, at Braunau on the Inn River, the son of Alois *Hitler*, a postal official there. My total schooling consisted of five years of grade school (Volksschule) and four years of junior high school (Unterrealschule). As a youth, it was my ambition to become an architetct (Baumeister); and I do not believe that, if politics had not got hold of me, I would ever have turned to another occupation. As you probably know, I became an orphan at the early age of seventeen and, in addition to this, did not have any funds at all. On my trip to Vienna, I had a total of approximately eighty crowns in my possession. Therefore, I was forced to begin working immediately as an ordinary worker in order to earn a living. Before I even turned eighteen, I started out as an unskilled worker on a construction site. In the course of the following two years, I went through just about every possible job available to the ordinary day-laborer. In my spare time, insofar as my means permitted, I also studied art history, the history of culture, the history of building, and got involved in political problems. Coming from a family which had a rather cosmopolitan outlook on life, and confronted with harsh reality, I had become an anti-Semite in hardly a year. Even at that time I was unable to join any of the then-existing parties.

Going through endless hardships, I simultaneously succeeded in acquiring sufficient training as a painter, so that this occupation provided me with an income – although initially minimal – from my twentieth year on. I became an architectural draftsman and architectural painter, and, at the age of twenty-one, had practically become completely independent. In 1912 I used this independence to move to Munich. During the preceding four years, from age twenty to twenty-four, I had concerned myself more and more with political issues, not so much by attending meetings, but rather by the thorough study of economic doctrines as well as of the entire anti-Semitic literature available at that time.

Beginning at age twenty-two, I immersed myself with special enthusiasm in military-political writings, and for all these years I have never ceased to occupy myself deeply with general world history.

Also during those years I did not participate actively in politics. I avoided appearing as a speaker anywhere, simply because I could not feel sympathetic toward any of the then existing political parties.

During this time as well, my ultimate goal of becoming an architect remained irrevocable.

After having successfully appealed to the German emporer [Hitler, at that time, was Austrian: trans.], I reported, on August 5, 1914, to the First Bavarian Infantry Regiment for entry into the German army. After a few days' deferment, I was transferred to the Second Infantery Regiment, and on August 16, I joined the Bavarian Reserve Infantry Regiment No. 16, which was then in the process of formation. This regiment, marching under the name of 'List Regiment,' was the first Bavarian volunteer regiment to go to the front, and at the end of October 1914, it came under fire for the first time in the 'Battle on the Yser.'

It was one of those volunteer regiments which, at that time, was often virtually wiped out in the course of only a few days.

On December 2, 1914, I received the Iron Cross Second Class (Eisernes Kreuz Zweiter Klasse, EK II), I stayed with this regiment, and in the Battle on the Somme, on October 7, 1916, I was wounded for the first time (by grenade fragments), on the left thigh. On October 10, 1916, the anniversary of my departure, I returned to my home, as a veteran, for the first time.

After two months of treatment in the Beelitz Military Hospital near Berlin, I was transferred to the Replacement Battalion, Second Infantry Regiment Munich, and again volunteered for the front. On March 1, 1917, I was once more with my old regiment. On September 17, 1917, I received the Military Service Cross Third Class with

Swords (Militärverdienstkreuz Dritter Klasse mit Schwertern); on May 9, 1918, the Regimental Diploma (Regimentsdiplom); on August 4, 1918, the Iron Cross First Class (Eisernes Kreuz Erster Klasse); on May 18, 1918, the Wounded Decoration in Black (Verwundetenabzeichen in Schwarz); and on August 25, 1918, the Service Decoration Third Class (Dienstauszeichnung Dritter Klasse).

In the battle of October 13-14, 1918, I was seriously poisoned by mustard gas and was initially completely blinded. I was evacuated from Werwick, Flanders, and transferred to the Union Military Hospital in Pasewalk, near Stettin. As my blindness yielded to treatment in a relatively short time, and my sight gradually returned, and, moreover, revolution had broken out on November 9, I asked for my transfer to Munich as soon as possible. As of December 18, I was again with the First Battalion of the Second Infantry Regiment. Being on the conscription list during the Red Guard period (Räterepublik), I was ordered to the Investigating Committee (Untersuchungskommission) of the Second Infantry Regiment, after the defeat of the Red rule, and from there I was transferred to the Schützenregiment No. 41 as indoctrination officer (Bildungsoffizier). Both in that regiment and in other units I gave numerous lectures to enlighten them regarding the insanity of the bloody Red dictatorship; and I saw with joy that the first group of my later adherents was composed of these soldiers, who were being discharged as the result of the general reduction in the Armed Forces of the Reich.

In June of 1919, I joined the Deutsche Arbeiterpartei (German Workers' Party), which then had seven members. I believed that in this party I had finally found, in the political sphere, the movement that corresponded to my ideal. Today the number of its adherents in Munich alone has grown to over 4,500, and I may certainly proudly claim a large share in this work.

Allow me to conclude now. I remain,

Respectfully Yours,
(signed) *A. Hitler.*

Accuracy of Copy verified by:
Richter

Seal: NSDAP Main Archives

August 26, 1941

Letter to Major Douglas M. Kelley, written by Alfred Rosenberg at Nuremberg prison on December 26, 1945.

Nürnberg 26.12.45

An Herrn Oberstabsarzt Major Kelly.

Sehr geehrter Major Kelly!

Ihr Fortgehen aus Nürnberg bedauere ich, sicher auch die mit mir gefangenen Kameraden. Ich danke Ihnen für ihr menschliches Verhalten und das Bemühen, auch *unsere* Beweggründe zu verstehen.

Ich spreche dabei meine Überzeugung aus, dass viele Konflikte nie eine solche Schärfe in der Welt angenommen hätten, wenn man auch in der Politik die Gesetze der Natur beachtet hätte. Die Natur zeigt uns *Gestalt*, in der Pflanzen-, Tier- und Menschenwelt. Die Achtung der von der Natur in bestimmten Räumen geschaffenen Gestalten (Europa, Afrika, Ostasien) ist nicht Rassenhass, sondern Rassenachtung. Das Zusammenleben verwandter Rassen (z.B. der europäischen) bedeutet nicht Vermischung mit an sich achtenswerten afrikanischen oder syrisch-orientalischen. Ich glaube, dass nur wenige Jahrzehnte vergehen werden und man wird uns dann verstehen lernen. Man hat meiner Überzeugung gegen Weisse *und* Schwarze gesündigt, dass man diese aus ihrem dörflichen Raum in die grosstädtische Zivilisation hereinzog. Der soziale Kampf wird somit auch ein rassischer werden, weil im *gleichen Raum* eine Auseinandersetzung stattfindet. Eine weise Politik hätte die Neger auf dem *Lande* gelassen und ihnen alle *eigenen* Möglichkeiten ihrer Sitten und dörflichen Verwaltung ausbauen müssen. Wenn das nicht – mit schrittweiser Rücksiedlung nach Afrika – nachgeholt wird, wird es in 50 Jahren vielleicht 20 Millionen zerstreute Schwarze und Millionen Mulatten geben. Nach 150 Jahren dann aber kein Amerika mehr, sondern ein unschöpferisches Gemisch. Da die weissen Kräfte aber immerhin bis dahin noch sich aufraffen dürften, könnte es eine nie dagewesene blutige Revolution geben.

Das gleiche gilt für das Judentum. Ein Volk, das eine eigene Kultur ausbauen will, kann in seiner wirtschaftlichen Hauptstadt nicht $2^1/_2$ Millionen Juden haben. Sie kontrollieren in New-York schon das ganze Erziehungswesen. Die *gesamte* grosse Flugproduktion – das grosse

Geschäft – ist heute in jüdischen Händen. Die politischen Parteien von heute sind unfähig, sich von jüdischem Einfluss zu befreien.

Ihre Ideologie (welche Gleichberechtigung zwischen Europäern mit Forderungen von Orientalen verwechselt) hindert sie ebenso daran, wie das Wahlgeld und die Stimmenzahl. Es ist also im *gleichen Raum* der Kampf um die *Führung* da. Siegt der jüdische Anspruch, dann haben die Pioniere von einst umsonst gekämpft. Angesichts der Ereignisse in Europa wird vorerst niemand wagen, das Problem zu berühren. Aber das Leben wird Amerika einst *zwingen*, sich zu entscheiden. Ich hoffe, dass das angelsächsich-skandinavisch-deutsche Blut in USA dann so stark sein wird, um das schöne, von den Vätern eroberte Land nicht kampflos in die Hände orientalischer Händler übergehen zu lassen. Auch dieser Kampf dann wird harte Formen annehmen, weil die Juden – heute 150 % 'amerikanisch' – sicher die Schwarzen mobilisieren werden!

Ich glaube zu wissen, dass manche, ihr Land liebende Amerikaner ähnliche Befürchtungen haben. Ihre *Pflicht* ist es dann, eine *rein amerikanische* Bewegung zum Schutz ihres Landes, seiner inneren Freiheit und des sozialen Ausgleiches zu schaffen.

Was *mich* in 25 Jahren Kampf bewegt hat, waren Gedanken, die wohl dem *deutschen* Volke dienen wollten, die aber stets ganz Europa, das ganze weisse Menschentum im Auge hatten.

Ich wünsche Ihnen Glück für Ihr späteres Leben.

Mit herzlichem Gruss und nochmaligem Dank

Alfred Rosenberg

Letter to Major Douglas M. Kelley, written by Alfred Rosenberg at Nuremberg prison on December 26, 1945.

To Chief Staff Physician Major Kelley

Nuremberg, December 26, 1945

Dear Major Kelley:

I regret the fact that you are leaving Nuremberg, and the comrades imprisoned with me certainly also regret it. I thank you for your human attitude and for your endeavors to understand *our* motives as well.

In saying this I wish to express my conviction that many of the conflicts of the world would never have become so severe if people had observed the laws of nature in politics as well. Nature shows us *Gestalt*, in the plant, animal, and human worlds. Respect for the different categories (Gestalten), which nature created in certain regions (Europe, Africa, East Asia), is not hatred of races, but rather respect for races. The fact that related races (the European, for example) live together does not mean that they should mix with African or Syrian-Oriental races, though these are worthy of respect in themselves. I believe that only a few decades will pass before we are understood. I am convinced that it was a sin against both Whites and Blacks to have pulled the latter away from their villages into the civilization of the big cities. The social struggle will thereby also become a racial one, since a confrontation takes place in *the same space*. It would have been a wise policy to leave the Negroes on the *land* and help them to develop their *own* customs and village administration. If this mistake is not remedied by gradual resettlement of Blacks in Africa, in fifty years there will be, perhaps, twenty million Blacks and millions of Mulattoes scattered all over the world. Then, after one hundred and fifty years, there will be no more America, but only an uncreative mixture. But since the white forces may well pull themselves together before that time, there could be a bloody revolution such as has never been seen before.

The same goes for the Jews. A people that wants to develop its own culture cannot have two and one half million Jews in its economic capital. In New York they already control the entire educational system. Today the *entire* large-scale production of airplanes – all big business – is in Jewish hands. Today's political parties are incapable of freeing themselves of Jewish influence.

Their ideology (which confuses equal rights among Europeans with demands from Orientals) prevents them from doing so, as do campaign contributions and the voter totals. Thus there are two competitors struggling for *leadership* in the *same space*. If the Jewish pretentions win, the pioneers of yesteryear have fought in vain. In view of the events in Europe, nobody will dare to approach this problem for the time being. But life will one day *force* Americans to make a decision. I hope that the Anglo-Saxon-Scandinavian-German blood in the United States will then be strong enough to prevent the beautiful land, conquered by their forefathers, from passing into the hands of Oriental traders without resistance. This struggle, too, will be severe, since the Jews – today 150% 'American' – will certainly mobilize the Blacks!

I think I know that many Americans who love their country have similar fears. It will be their *duty* to create a *purely American* movement for the protection of their country, its internal freedom, and its social equilibrium.

What has moved *me* during twenty-five years of struggle was to serve the *German* people, without losing sight of all Europe, indeed, of all of white mankind.

I wish you good luck for the future.

Best regards and thanks again.

Alfred Rosenberg

Biogram by Ernst Kaltenbrunner, written for Major Douglas M. Kelley at Nuremberg prison during the latter part of 1945.

*Kaltenbrunner*

Meine Vorfahren väterlicherseits lebten durch viele Generationen in Micheldorf-Kremstal (Oberösterreich). Sie gehörten dem Stande der 'Hammerherren' an, denn sie betrieben Sensenhammer, verbunden mit einer mittleren Landwirtschaft. Die Sensen und Sicheln dieser Handwerker wurden nach Russland geliefert, was nicht nur einen gewissen Wohlstand herbeiführte, sondern auch bürgerliches Ansehen und eigene Standesgesetze.

Mein Urgrossvater, der sich infolge zahlreicher älterer Geschwister einem anderen Berufe zuwenden musste, war kaiserlicher Beamter der Hof-Rechnungskanzlei. Er war auch ein bekannter Dichter der oberösterreichischen Mundart (Dialekt) und man setzte ihm in Ems O.Ö. ein Denkmal. Er heisst Karl Adam Kaltenbrunner.

Mein Grossvater war der Rechtsanwalt Dr. Karl Kaltenbrunner in Grieskirchen, bekannt durch seine Gründung der ersten grossen, bürgerlich-bäuerlichen Sparkasse in dieser Landstadt Oberösterreichs. Er übersiedelte im Jahre 1868 nach Eferding, einer Kreisstadt, 20 km westlich von Linz. Er lebte dort bis 1910 und war mehr als 20 Jahre Bürgermeister dieser Stadt. Er hatte vier Kinder, 2 Söhne 2 Töchter. Der älteste war mein Vater, Hugo K., der 1875 zur Welt kam und als Rechtsanwalt im Jahre 1938 in Linz starb. Sein Bruder Oskar war Psychiater und Leiter der Landes-Heilanstalt in Ybbs in Nieder-Österr. Er starb ca. 1929 dortselbst. Die Schwester Paula meines Vaters wurde die Frau des Direktors des steiermärkischen Landes-Archives in Graz, des bekannten Historikers Hofrat Dr. Doblinger. Die andere Schwester starb an Dyphterie im jugendl. Alter.

Mein Vater heiratete 1902 meine Mutter Therese K., geborene Udvardy. Sie starb 1943 in Linz.

Ich kam im Jahre 1903 in Ried, Oberösterreich zur Welt. Mein Vater eröffnete 1905 in Raab, O.Ö. seine Rechtsanwaltkanzlei, die er 1918 nach Linz verlegte. Meine Jugendzeit verlebte ich also in Raab, einem ländlichen Marktflecken, mit rein bäuerlicher Umgebung. Diese erste Jugendzeit war nicht nur wegen des harmonischen Elternhauses schön für mich, sondern blieb für meine ganze innere und persönliche Entwicklung von Einfluss, weil sie mich mit grosser Liebe zur Natur, Interesse für Landwirtschaft und Freude an einfachem Leben erfüllte. Auch als meine Eltern 1918 nach Linz übersiedelten, verbrachte ich meine Ferienzeit stets auf dem Lande in Raab und arbeitete dort bei Bauern zur Erntezeit.

Vom Jahre 1909-1913 besuchte ich in Raab die Volksschule und kam 1913 nach Linz zum Besuch des Real-Gymnasiums. Im Jahre 1921 legte ich dort in Linz die Matura-Prüfung ab.

In früher Kindheit hatte ich Scharlach und die sonst normalen Kinderkrankheiten.

In den Jahren des Weltkrieges 1914-1918 und noch hernach hatten wir als Allgemeinerscheinung unter Lebensmittelmangel zu leiden. Dauernde Gesundheitsschäden verblieben nicht.

Von 1913-1918 wohnte ich mit sieben anderen Studenten bei der Rechtsanwaltswitwe Berta Katzer in Linz, Walterstrasse 2.

In den drei letzten Jahren meiner Mittelschulzeit lebte ich wieder im Haushalte meiner Eltern in Linz.

Im Herbst 1921 ging ich nach Graz zum Besuch der chemisch-techn. Fakultät der dortigen Technischen Hochschule. Mein erstes Ziel war, Chemiker zu werden um angesichts der aussichtslosen Arbeitslage in der Heimat in die niederländischen Kolonien gehen zu können.

Da sich inzwischen die Vermögenslage meines Vaters immer mehr verschlechterte, war ich genötigt, mir mein Brot selbst zu verdienen. Dies gelang mir, indem ich als Kohlentrimmer am Grazer Bahnhof in der Nachtschicht arbeitete. Nach damaligen Verhältnissen konnte ich mit diesem Lohn meine Auslagen für Wohnung, Essen und übrigen, nötigsten Lebensbedarf decken. Als infolge der herantretenden Teilprüfungen das Studium mehr Zeit erforderte, übernahm ich die Erteilung von Nachhilfestunden an Gymnasiasten und gab die Schwerarbeit auf.

Da mein Vater im Frühjahr 1923 ernstlich erkrankte, bat mich meine Mutter, anstelle des Chemiefachs, das Jurastudium aufzunehmen, um notfalls in die Praxis meines Vaters eintreten zu können. Ich erfüllte diesen Wunsch meiner Eltern und ergriff das Studium an der Universität von Graz. Dort legte ich alle drei Staatsprüfungen, sowie die drei Rigorosen ab und wurde im Sommer 1926 zum Doktor juris utriusque promoviert.

Ich habe neben meinem Studium und Erwerb auch noch Zeit gefunden, mich mit geographischen und wirtschaftlichen Problemen, besonders des Balkans zu beschäftigen, habe viel darüber gelesen und vor allem auch einige persönliche Freunde unter den Studenten dieser Länder gehabt. Im Kreise der bulgarischen Studenten lernte ich den späteren Träger des Nobel-Preises, Professor Dr. Pregl kennen, mit dem mich bis zu seinem Tode eine enge Freundschaft verband.

Ich habe aber auch die fröhlichen Seiten des Studentenlebens kennen gelernt und auch einige Mensuren gefochten, wie dies in Graz auch ausserhalb der Korporationen üblich war.

Im Herbst 1926 begann ich am Landesgericht in Linz meine, für den Rechtsanwaltsberuf in Österreich erforderliche Praxis. Sie bestand aus einem Gerichtsjahr und 6 Jahren in einem Anwaltsbüro.

Im Jahre 1927 ging ich zu Rechtsanwalt Dr. Vilas nach Salzburg, wo ich 1 Jahr Praxis ablegte, hernach wieder nach Linz in das Büro meines Vaters.

Im Jahre 1930 lernte ich meine Frau kennen, die ich im Januar 1934 heiratete. Sie stammt aus einer Kaufmannsfamilie aus Linz und schenkte mir drei Kinder. Wir wohnten im Hause ihrer Eltern, sodass wir auch die Zeit meiner Arbeitslosigkeit von 1935-1938 mit meinem Erwerb aus dem An- und Verkauf von Briefmarken überdauern konnten.

Seit dem Jahre 1934 leide ich mit grösseren Unterbrechungen an einer Entzündung des Gallenganges, sonst sind mir keine Krankheiten bekannt.

1938 wurde ich nach Wien berufen und daraufhin Staatssekretär der österreichischen Landesregierung.

Meine politische Entwicklung gehört wahrscheinlich in diesen ärztlichgeforderten Lebenslauf nicht hinein. Ich will sie daher neben den bereits mündlich gegebenen Aufklärungen wie folgt kurz zusammenfassen:

Elternhaus deutschnationale Volkspartei, demokratisch. Hochschulzeit keiner Partei angehörig gewesen. 1929-32 österr. Heimatschutz – Starhemberg. 1932 NSDAP-1933. Dann Parteiverbot in Österreich. 1934 mit ca. 1500 anderen Parteimitgliedern von Regierung in Praeventivhaft genommen. Herbst 1934 Angehöriger des sogenannten Befriedungs-Kommittées. Am Juliputsch 1934 nicht beteiligt gewesen, was schon aus der Zugehörigkeit zu diesem Kommitée hervorgeht, das von der Regierung gebilligt war. Bis 1938 mit Wissen und Billigung der Regierung Verbindung zu SS-Kreisen gehalten und gegen jeden Bolschewis-

mus Stellung genommen. Mein Ziel war, in Österreich eine, der Volksmeinung bei Wahlen entsprechende demokratische Regierung, die wirtschaftlich engen Anschluss an das Reich zu suchen hätte, herbeizuführen und der österreichischen Individualität weiten Raum zu lassen.
Wien sollte wieder Kristallisationspunkt altösterreichischer Nachfolgestaaten werden und zur Stabilisierung wirtschaftlicher Erfordernisse in
enger Fühlung mit dem Reich stehen.

Kaltenbrunner

———

Biogram by Ernst Kaltenbrunner, written for Major Douglas M. Kelley
at Nuremberg prison during the latter part of 1945.

*Kaltenbrunner*

For many generations my ancestors on my father's side lived in Micheldorf-Kremstal, in Upper Austria. They belonged to the class of the
'forge-masters' ('Hammerherren'), for they operated scythe-forges in
conjunction with a medium-sized farm. The scythes and sickles of these
artisans were shipped to Russia, a fact which brought them not only a
certain prosperity, but also middle-class esteem and their own code of
ethics as a class (Standesgesetze).

My great-grandfather, who had to turn to another occupation because of numerous older brothers and sisters, was an imperial civil
servant in the court's audit chancellery. He was also a well-known
poet, writing in the dialect of Upper Austria, and a monument was
erected in Ems, Upper Austria. His name was Karl Adam Kaltenbrunner.

My grandfather was the lawyer Dr. Karl Kaltenbrunner of Grieskirchen, known as the founder of the first large savings and loan
association for the middle class and the farmers in this rural town in
Upper Austria. In 1868 he moved to Eferding, a county seat, twenty
kilometers west of Linz. He lived there until 1910 and was mayor of
that city for over twenty years. He had four children, two sons and two
daughters. The oldest was my father, Hugo Kaltenbrunner, who was
born in 1875 and died as an attorney in Linz, in the year 1938. His
brother Oskar was a psychiatrist and director of the provincial sana-

torium at Ybbs, in Lower Austria. He died there in about 1929. My father's sister Paula became the wife of the director of the provincial archives of Styria in Graz, the noted historian (and Privy Councillor) Dr. Doblinger. The other sister died of diphteria at an early age.

In 1902 my father married my mother, Therese Kaltenbrunner, née Udvardy. She died in Linz in 1943.

I was born in 1903 in Ried, Upper Austria. In 1905 my father opened his law office in Raab, Upper Austria, transferring it to Linz in 1918. Thus I spent my youth in Raab, a country market town, in a strictly peasant environment. My early youth was not only a beautiful time for me because of the harmony of my parents' home, but remained an influence on my entire inner and personal development because it filled me with a great love for nature, interest in agriculture, and joy in the simple life. Even when my parents moved to Linz in 1918, I always spent my vacations in the country at Raab and worked for farmers there at harvest time.

I attended grade school (Volksschule) in Raab from 1909 to 1913, and in 1913 entered the Real-Gymnasium in Linz. In 1921 I passed the Matura examination [corresponding to Junior College graduation in the United States: trans.] in Linz.

In early childhood I had scarlet fever, and otherwise the usual childhood illnesses.

During World War I, 1914-1918, and afterward, we suffered from a lack of food, which was a general occurrence. Permanent damages to my health were not incurred.

From 1913 to 1918 seven other pupils and I lived with Berta Katzer, widow of an attorney, at Walterstraße No. 2, in Linz.

For the last three years of my secondary education I again lived in my parents' home in Linz.

In the fall of 1921 I went to Graz to attend the chemical-technical department of the Institute of Technology. My first goal was to become a chemist in order to be able to work in the Dutch colonies, given the hopeless employment situation at home.

Since the financial position of my father had become increasingly worse in the meantime, I was forced to earn my living myself. I succeeded in this by working at the Graz railroad station as a coal-loader on the night shift. Under the conditions which prevailed then, the wages covered my lodging, meals, and the other most urgent necessities of life. When my studies began to take up more time due to forthcoming preliminary examinations, I began to tutor gymnasium-level (high school) students and gave up the hard labor.

As my father became seriously ill in the spring of 1923, my mother requested me to take up the study of law, rather than chemistry, in order to be able to enter my father's law practice if necessary. I fulfilled this wish of my parents and began studies at the University of Graz. There I passed all three state examinations as well as the three oral examinations (Rigorosen) and received the degree of doctor juris utriusque in the summer of 1926.

In addition to the time taken up by my study and employment I also found time to study geographical and economic problems, especially those of the Balkan countries. I read a lot about them and, above all, I had several personal friends among the students from those countries. Among the circle of Bulgarian students I became acquainted with the future Nobel Prize winner, Professor Dr. Pregl, with whom I maintained a close friendship until his death.

However, I also became acquainted with the more cheerful aspects of student life and also fought several duels, as was customary in Graz, even for those outside the student dueling fraternities.

In the fall of 1926 I started practical training, a requirement for entering the legal profession in Austria, at the assize court in Linz. The practical training consisted of one year in a court and six years in a law firm.

In 1927 I joined the lawyer Dr. Vilas in Salzburg, where I put in one year of practical training, after which I again moved to Linz to work in my father's office.

In 1930 I became acquainted with my wife, whom I married in 1934. She is the daughter of a Linz family of merchants and presented me with three children. We lived in the home of her parents, so that we were able to get through the period of my unemployment from 1935 to 1938 with my earnings from buying and selling stamps.

Since 1934 I have suffered at fairly long intervals from an inflammation of the bile duct; I know of no other illnesses.

In 1938 I was called to Vienna and subsequently became a high-ranking official (Staatssekretär) of the Austrian state government (Landesregierung).

My political development probably does not belong in this biographical sketch written at the doctor's request. Hence, in addition to the oral statements I have already made, I will briefly summarize my political development as follows:

My parents' political stance: German-national Volkspartei, democratic. As a student, I did not belong to any party. From 1929-1932 I belonged to the Austrian Home Guard (Heimatschutz) – Starhemberg. 1932-1933 NSDAP (Nazi Party). After that the party was outlawed. In 1934 I was placed in preventive custody, along with about fifteen hundred other party members. In the fall of 1934 I was a member of the so-called Appeasement Committee (Befriedungs-Komitées). I was not involved in the July putsch of 1934, as is already shown by my membership in that committee, which was approved by the government. I maintained a relationship with SS circles and opposed every form of Bolshevism. My goal in Austria was to bring about a democratic government, in accordance with the will of the people as expressed by elections, that would seek a close economic tie with the Reich, and to allow Austrian individuality ample play. Vienna was once more to become the point of crystallization for the former Austrian states and to maintain a close relationship with the Reich to stabilize economic exigencies.

Kaltenbrunner

Biogram by Hans Frank, written for Major Douglas M. Kelley at Nuremberg prison during the latter part of 1945.

*Lebenslauf*

Ich Dr. jur *Hans* Michael *Frank* wurde am 23. Mai 1900 in Karlsruhe (in Baden) als Sohn des Rechtsanwalts Karl Frank und dessen Ehefrau Magdalena geborene Buchmeier geboren.

Mein Vater stammt aus einer alten rheinpfälzischen Familie und hatte am 22. April 1869 das Licht der Welt in Edenkoben (Rheinpfalz-Bayern) erblickt. Sein Vater war Oelmüller und Bürgermeister der Stadt.

Meine Mutter ist ein Kind oberbayrischer Eltern und wurde am 16. Juni 1874 in München geboren. Ihr Vater war Ratsbürger der Stadt München und Großkaufmann.

Mein Vater starb am 15 Januar 1945 in Gernlinden bei München; ob meine Mutter noch lebt, ist mir ungewiß, da ich seit über ³/₄ Jahren (Januar 1945) ohne Nachricht über ihr Schicksal bin.

Mein Vater war protestantisch, meine Mutter ist altkatholisch. Aus ihrer Ehe entstammen drei Kinder:

1. Mein Bruder Karl geboren am 17. September 1892 – im Weltkrieg (1914-1918) an einer Gasvergiftung gestorben am 29. Juni 1916. Er war Zahnarzt und in kinderloser Ehe jung verheiratet.
2. Ich.
3. Meine Schwester Elisabeth geb. 27. September 1903 (in Rotthalmünster); seit 29. September 1942 mit dem Regierungsrat Dr. Schultze am Reichspatentamt (in Berlin) verheiratet.

Entsprechend der in Deutschland geltenden Übung wurden wir Kinder altkatholisch getauft (nach der Mutter) –

Unsere Familie wohnte von 1901 ab in *München*: – (Mit einer Unterbrechung von etwa 5 Jahren – 190*3*/190*8* – innerhalb deren wir in Rotthalmünster in Niederbayern wohnten)   –

Ich kann also wohl mich als 'echten' Münchener bezeichnen. Ich besuchte nach Erledigung von vier Jahren Volksschule von 1910 bis 1919 das Maximilians-Gymnasium in München und studierte von 1919 bis 1923 an den Universitäten München und Kiel (Winter Semester

1921-22 und Sommersemester 1922) Rechtswissenschaft, Nationalöko-
nomie und Philosophie, bestand im Sommer 1923 das Referendar-
examen, im Sommer 1924 die Prüfung zum Dr. der Rechtswissenschaft
(in Kiel) und im Herbst 1926 das große juristische Staatsexamen
(Assessorprüfung). – Sportlich liegt mir Bergsport und Schwimmen am
meisten.

Im Sommer 1927 wurde ich zum Mitglied des Lehrkörpers der Technischen Hochschule München (juristische Abteilung) berufen mit dem
Ziele meiner Habilitation als Professor der Rechtswissenschaft. Gleichzeitig habe ich mich in München als Rechtsanwalt niedergelassen.

Am 2. April 1925 heiratete ich Frl. Brigitte *Herbst*, die in Eitorf (an
der Sieg-Westfalen) als Tochter des Textilfabrikdirektors Heinrich
Herbst und dessen Ehefrau Maria geborene Lemger am 29. Dezember
1895 geboren wurde – die heute noch meine Frau ist.

Aus unserer Ehe sind folgende Kinder geboren:
1. *Sigrid* Leonore geboren in München 17. März 1927;
2. *Norman* Karl geboren in München 3. Juni 1928;
3. *Brigitte* Maria geboren in München 13. Januar 1935;
4. *Michael* Hans geboren in München 15. Februar 1937;
5. *Nicklas* geboren in München 9. März 1939 –
Nennenswerte Krankheiten weder bei mir noch in der Familie. Sie
gehören sämtlich – meine Frau ist römisch-katholisch – der römisch-
katholischen Kirche an.

Seit 1928 gehöre ich der Nationalsozialistischen Partei als Mitglied an
und vertrat die Rechtsidee. 1931 wurde ich in meiner Eigenschaft als
Leiter der Rechtsabteilung *Reichsleiter*. 1933 wurde ich zum Bayrischen
Staatsminister der Justiz ernannt. Nach Abberufung von diesem Amte
wurde ich am 19. Dezember 1934 mit Titel und Rang eines *Reichsministers* (ohne Portefeuille) begabt. Ich war seit 1933 *Führer* des
Nationalsozialistischen Juristenbundes und *Präsident* der Akademie für
Deutsches Recht. Am 26. Oktober 1939 wurde ich zum *Generalgouverneur* in Krakau ernannt.

Meine sämtlichen politischen Ämter als Reichsleiter der Partei, als
Reichsführer des Juristenbundes und als Präsident der Rechtsakademie
wurden mir im August 1942 von Adolf Hitler strafweise entzogen, da
ich in aller Öffentlichkeit – insbesondere durch vier Universitätsreden

in Berlin, Wien, München und Heidelberg, die ungeheures Aufsehen erregt hatten – in dauernder schwerster Opposition gegen das Gewaltregime der Konzentrationslager usw. *Opposition* machte. Seit dieser Degradierung bin ich nur noch einfaches Parteimitglied gewesen. Meine übrigen Ämter waren mir damals ('aus außenpolitischen Gründen' – wie mir Reichsminister Lammers auf Befehl Adolf Hitlers mitteilte) belassen worden: Meine diesbezüglichen dauernden Rücktrittsgesuche nicht angenommen. –

Am 17. Januar 1945 verließ ich einen Tag vor dem Einmarsch der Bolschewisten Krakau. Am 3. Mai 1945 wurde ich in Neuhaus am Schliersee von den Amerikanern, denen ich mich gestellt hatte, verhaftet. –

Was diese äußere Lebensgestaltung an Arbeit und Sorgen, an Last und Unruhe auf mich gebürdet hat, ist vorstellbar.

Als Gewinn blieb mir eine reiche Kenntnis des Daseins, eine liebe Familie und der tiefe demütige Glaube an Gott, der ins Herz sieht.

———

Biogram by Hans Frank, written for Major Douglas M. Kelley at Nuremberg prison during the latter part of 1945.

*Curriculum vitae*

I, Doctor of Law *Hans* Michael *Frank*, was born on May 23, 1900, in Karlsruhe (Baden), the son of the lawyer Karl Frank and his wife Magdalena, née Buchmeier.

My father comes from an old family of the Rhineland-Palatinate and was born on April 22, 1869, in Edenkoben (Rhineland-Palatinate-Bavaria). His father had been an oil miller and mayor of the city.

My mother is the daughter of a family of Upper Bavaria and was born on June 16, 1874, in Munich. Her father was a councilman of the city of Munich and a wholesale merchant.

My father died on January 15, 1945, at Gernlinden, near Munich. I am unsure whether my mother is still alive, as I have not had news of her for over nine months (January 1945).

My father was Protestant; my mother is Old-Catholic. Three children were born of their marriage:

1. My brother Karl, born September 17, 1892. He died from poison gas on June 29, 1916, during World War I (1914-1918). He was a dentist and married young; he had no children.
2. Myself.
3. My sister Elisabeth, born September 27, 1903 (in Rotthalmünster). Since September 29, 1942, she has been married to Regierungsrat Dr. Schultze of the Reich Patent Office in Berlin. In accordance with the custom in Germany, we children were baptized Old-Catholic (following the faith of the mother). –

From 1901 on, our family lived in Munich (with an interruption of about five years, 1903-1908, during which we lived in Rotthalmünster in Lower Bavaria). Thus, I can certainly call myself a 'genuine' citizen of Munich (Münchner).

After having finished four years of grade school (Volksschule), I attended the Maximilians-Gymnasium in Munich from 1910 to 1919. From 1919 to 1923 I attended the Universities of Munich and Kiel (winter semester 1921-22 and summer semester 1922), studying jurisprudence, economics, and philosophy. In the summer of 1924 I took the examination to become doctor of jurisprudence (in Kiel) and in the fall of 1926 the comprehensive legal state examination (Assessorprüfung). – In sports I am most interested in mountain climbing and swimming.

In the summer of 1927 I was invited to become a member of the faculty of the Institute of Technology of Munich (Law Department) for the purpose of qualifying as a professor of jurisprudence (Habilitation). At the same time I established my own law firm in Munich.

On April 2, 1925, I had married Miss Brigitte *Herbst*, who was born in Eitorf (on the Sieg River in Westphalia), on December 29, 1895, the daughter of Heinrich Herbst, manager of a textile factory, and his wife Maria, née Lemger. She is still my wife.

The following children were born to us:
1. *Sigrid* Leonore, born in Munich, on March 17, 1927;
2. *Norman* Karl, born in Munich, on June 3, 1928;
3. *Brigitte* Maria, born in Munich, on January 13, 1935;
4. *Michael* Hans, born in Munich, on February 15, 1937;
5. *Nicklas*, born in Munich, on March 9, 1939.

Neither I nor any members of my family have had any serious illnesses. Since my wife is Roman Catholic, all of the children belong to the Roman Catholic Church.

Since 1928 I have been a member of the National Socialist party, and I advocated the idea of legal justice. In 1931 I became *Reich Leader* [Reichsleiter, that is, the highest ranking Nazi party official: trans.] in my capacity as leader of the Law Department. In 1933 I was named Bavarian Attorney General. After leaving this post, I was given the title and rank of a Reich Minister (without portfolio) on December 19, 1934. From 1933 on I was *Führer* of the National Socialist League of Jurists and *President* of the Academy of German Law. On October 26, 1939, I was named Governor General in Cracow.

In August 1942, as a punitive action, Adolf Hitler stripped me of all my political offices as Reichsleiter of the party, as Reichsführer of the League of Jurists, and as President of the Academy of Law. The reason for this action was that – particularly in four speeches at the Universities of Berlin, Vienna, Munich, and Heidelberg, which had attracted enormous attention – I had quite publicly evinced continuous and very strong *opposition* to the rule of violence exemplified by the concentration camps, etc. Since this degradation I have been only an ordinary party member. At that time I retained my other offices ('on grounds of foreign policy', as Reich Minister Lammers informed me, at Adolf Hitler's order). My repeated requests to be allowed to resign these offices were not accepted. –

On January 17, 1945, I left Cracow one day before the Bolsheviks marched in. On May 3, 1945, I was arrested in Neuhaus on the Schliersee by the Americans, to whom I had given myself up. –

One can imagine the amount of work and worry, what burden and anxiety this kind of life brought upon me.

What I am left with is a deep awareness of human existence, a devoted family, and a profound and humble belief in God who sees into the heart.

Biogram by Alfred Rosenberg, written for Major Douglas M. Kelley at Nuremberg prison during the latter part of 1945.

*Alfred Rosenberg*, geb. 12.1.93. Reval.

Großvater väterlicherseits Martin R. Handwerksmeister (Aeltermann seiner Gilde in Reval). Er und meine Großmutter starben in recht hohem Alter. Sie hatten vier Söhne und zwei Töchter. Der älteste Dr. med. Alexander R. starb etwa 55-jährig an einer akuten Krankheit. Der zweite, mein Vater, Waldemar Wilhelm R. erkrankte durch Ansteckung mit meiner Mutter an Tuberkulose, starb mit 44 Jahren. Der dritte Sohn starb jung an einer Kehlkopfkrankheit, der jüngste lebte noch 73-jährig in voller Rüstigkeit, sein jetziges Schicksal ist mir unbekannt. Meine beiden Tanten sind heute 87-jährig und 83-jährig; waren in voller Rüstigkeit. – Meine Großeltern mütterlicherseits waren wohl 75 Jahre als sie kurz nacheinander starben; von ihren sechs Kindern sind drei alt geworden, ein Sohn an Lungenentzündung gestorben; ebenfalls eine Tochter; und meine Mutter an Schwindsucht. Ich hatte nur einen Bruder. Dieser war kerngesund, kämpfte gegen den Bolschewismus, war in Sowjetgefängnissen, wo er die Schwindsucht bekam. In Deutschland konnte er sich nur schlecht erholen und starb mit 44 Jahren in Schörnberg.

Ich habe in meinem Leben keine innere schwere Krankheit gehabt; bin in der Jugend nur blutarm gewesen und leide an Schwindelanfällen. Seit über 10 Jahren stellen sich Gelenkerkrankungen ein: Blutergüsse und Entzündungen im großen Zehgelenk. Ablagerungen am Rückgrat drücken Nerven und Muskeln, so daß ein längeres Stehen beschwerlich wird, ein Aufrichten von jedem Bücken macht Mühe. Kuren in Schlamm und Moorbädern. – In letzten Jahren Empfindlichkeit der Augen, leicht entzündbar.

In der Jugend Sport getrieben: Tennis, Schlittschuh, Fechten.

Ab 1910 Studium der Architektur an der Technischen Hochschule zu Riga. Daneben Fortführen der Studien von Geschichte, Philosophie. Dauernde Fortbildung im Malen.

Bei Annäherung der Front 1915 Verlegung der Rigaer Technischen Hochschule nach Moskau. Dort weiteres Studium, im Februar 1918 Staatsexamen mit Diplom 1. Grades als Ingenieur-Architekt. Rückkehr in die Heimatstadt Reval. Herbst 1918 Reise nach Deutschland. In München Bekanntschaft mit Hitler und Mitarbeit in der national-sozialistischen Bewegung. Bücher und Aufsätze über die Ziele der Partei, Marxismus und Judenfrage. Hauptschriftleiter des 'Völkischen Beobachters'. 1930 Mitglied des Reichstags. Nach 1933 vom Führer mit der Überwachung der geistigen Erziehung der Partei beauftragt. Im Juli 1941 zum Reichsminister für die besetzten Ostgebiete ernannt.

Verheiratet zwei Mal. Meine erste Frau stammte aus dem Baltikum, auch sie zog sich im damaligen Petrograd (Leningrad) eine Lungenentzündung zu, die sie in der Schweiz zu kurieren suchte. 1923 Scheidung.

Seit 1925 zum zweiten Mal verheiratet mit Hedwig Kramer (aus Niedersachsen). Meine Frau bis auf nervöse Herzerkrankung und eine geheilte Frauenkrankheit bis zuletzt gesund gewesen. Ein Sohn starb nach der Geburt. 1930 wurde meine Tochter Irene geboren. Beide habe ich im Mai 1945 in Flensburg zurückgelassen. Über ihr Schicksal habe ich nichts erfahren. Ebenfalls nichts über das Schicksal meiner nach Bayern gereisten 83- und 87-jährigen Tanten. Meine jetzt 15-jährige Tochter ist bisher nie ernstlich krank gewesen. Hoch aufgeschossen, etwas mager, ist sie doch widerstandsfähig geblieben.

Überblicke ich somit meine Familie, so sind alle 4 Großeltern kerngesund gewesen und im hohen Alter gestorben. Unter den 12 Kindern der beiden Familien mehrere Fälle an Schwindsucht, daneben aber ebenso gesunde wie die Eltern. Meine Tanten und Onkel väter- und mütterlicherseits haben etwa 26 Kinder gehabt; auch die meistens gesund.

Meine Rückenerkrankung ist seit 1935 von Prof *Gebhardt* (hier im Gefängnis) genau untersucht und behandelt worden. Ebenso die Entzündungen und Blutergüsse in den Gelenken (etwa 10 an der Zahl, vielleicht auch mehr). Sie sind wohl auf gichtischer Grundlage entstanden, bei stärkerer Beanspruchung des Gelenkes beim Gehen. Meine Rückenerkrankung hatte sich in Mondorf stark bemerkbar gemacht.

12.10.45 A. Rosenberg

---

Biogram by Alfred Rosenberg, written for Major Douglas M. Kelley at Nuremberg prison during the latter part of 1945.

*Alfred Rosenberg*, born January 12, 1893, in Reval.

Paternal grandfather, Martin Rosenberg. Master artisan (elder of his guild in Reval). He and my grandmother died at quite an advanced age. They had four sons and two daughters. The eldest, Alexander Rosenberg (a medical doctor), died of an acute illness at the age of about fifty-five. The second, Waldemar Wilhelm Rosenberg (my father), contracted tuberculosis from my mother and died at the age of forty-four. The third son died young, of a disease of the larynx. The youngest still had his full vigor at the age of seventy-three; I do not know his present situation. My two aunts, now eighty-seven and eighty-three years old respectively, had their full vigor. – My maternal grandparents were probably seventy-five years old when they died, one shortly after the other. Of their six children, three lived into old age –, one son and one daughter died of infection of the lungs, and my mother died of consumption. I had only one brother. He was sound as a bell, fought against Bolshevism, and was in Soviet prisons, where he came down with consumption. He made a poor recovery in Germany and died in Schörnberg at the age of 44.

During my life I have had no serious illnesses; my only complaint in youth was anaemia, and I suffer from dizzy spells. For over ten years I have been the victim of arthritis; I have also had ecchymoses and inflammations in the joint of the big toe. Deposits on the spinal column press against nerves and muscles, so that it becomes difficult to stand for a long time; resuming an upright position after bending over is a chore. I have taken mud-bath cures. – In the last few years my eyes have been sentitive and are easily inflamed.

When I was young I enjoyed tennis, skating, and fencing.

From 1910 on I studied architecture at the Institute of Technology in Riga. On the side I continued the study of history and philosophy and took continuous instruction in painting.

As the front moved closer in 1915, the Riga Institute of Technology was transferred to Moscow. There I continued my studies; in February 1918, I passed my state examination with a first-degree diploma and became an engineer-architect. Return to my hometown, Reval (Estonia). Fall of 1918, trip to Germany. In Munich I became acquainted with Hitler and worked for the National Socialist movement. I wrote books and essays on the goals of the party, Marxism, and the Jewish question.

Chief editor of the *Völkischer Beobachter*. In 1930 I became a member of the Reichstag. After 1933 I was entrusted by the Führer with the supervision of the intellectual training of the party. In July 1941 I was named Reich Minister for the occupied Eastern territories.

I have been married twice. My first wife came from the Baltic region. She also contracted an inflammation of the lungs in Leningrad (then Petrograd), which she attempted to cure in Switzerland. Divorce in 1923.

Since 1925 I have been married to Hedwig Kramer (from Lower Saxony). Except for a heart ailment of nervous origin and a female complaint of which she was cured, my wife was healthy until recently. One son died after birth. In 1930 my daughter Irene was born. I left both [wife and daughter: trans.] in Flensburg in May 1945. I have heard nothing about their fate. Nor have I heard about the fate of my eighty-three- and eighty-seven-year-old aunts, who went to Bavaria. My daughter, who is now fifteen years old, has never been seriously ill. Quite tall and somewhat skinny, she has nevertheless remained hardy.

Surveying my family, all four of my grandparents were sound as a bell and died at an advanced age. Among the twelve children of both families, there were several cases of consumption, but otherwise they were healthy as the parents. My paternal and maternal aunts and uncles have had about twenty-six children, most of them also healthy.

My back ailment has been carefully examined and treated by Professor *Gebhardt* (in this prison) since 1935. Likewise the inflammations and ecchymoses in the joints (numbering about ten, or perhaps more). They are probably of arthritic origin, arising from great demands placed on the joint in the process of walking. In Mondorf my back condition had become quite noticeable.

October 12, 1945. A. Rosenberg

Order by Himmler of January 31, 1945, to punish expelled members of the SS for their dereliction of duty and cowardice in the face of the enemy.
Fa 91/5 Bl. 1251
Institut für Zeitgeschichte, Munich.


*Der Höhere SS- und Polizeiführer Main*
in den Gauen Bayreuth, Franken und Mainfranken
und im Wehrkreis XIII.

Nr. 1376/45                          Nürnberg, den 31. Jan. 1945

*Befehl*

Der Reichsführer-SS hat befohlen, dass sein nachstehender an den höheren SS- und Polizeiführer Danzig gerichteter Befehl unverzüglich allen Polizeiverwaltern und allen Kommandeuren bekanntzugeben ist:
1.  Der frühere SS-Standartenführer und Polizeipräsident von Bromberg, von *Salisch*, wird von mir wegen Feigheit und Pflichtvergessenheit degradiert und ist unverzüglich zu erschiessen!
2.  Der frühere Regierungspräsident *Kühn*, Bromberg, der frühere Bürgermeister *Ernst*, Bromberg, werden wegen Feigheit und Pflichtvergessenheit ihren Würden und Ämter entkleidet und degradiert. Sie kommen als Bewährungssoldaten in das Bewährungsbatl., *nachdem sie vorher der Exekution des v. Salisch beigewohnt haben.* Die beiden letzteren sind im Bewährungsbatl. für *besonders* schwierige und gefährliche Aufgaben vorzusehen.
3.  Der durch den Leiter der Parteikanzlei degradierte und aus der Partei ausgestossene Kreisleiter von Bromberg, *Rampf*, kommt ebenfalls in das Bewährungsbatl. und ist wie Kühn und Ernst einzusetzen.

gez. H. Himmler

Ich bitte um weitestgehende Bekanntgabe des Befehls an alle unterstellten Einheiten, Führer, Unterführer und Männer.

(Signature illegible)
SS-Obergruppenführer
General der Waffen-SS und Polizei

*grosser Verteiler!*

Order by Himmler of January 31, 1945, to punish expelled members of the SS for their dereliction of duty and cowardice in the face of the enemy.
Fa 91/5Bl. 1251
Institut für Zeitgeschichte, Munich.

*The Higher SS and Police Leader Main*
in den Gauen Bayreuth, Franken und Mainfranken
und im Wehrkreis XIII.

No. 1376/45                                      Nuremberg, January 31, 1945

*Order*

The Reichsführer-SS had ordered that the following order, directed to the Higher SS and Police Leader in Danzig be made known at once to all police administrators and commanders:

1.  The former SS-Standartenführer and Police President of Bromberg, von *Salisch*, is degraded by me because of cowardice and dereliction of duty and is to be shot immediately!

2.  The former Regierungspräsident [a senior government official of a sub-division of a province or district: trans.] of Bromberg, *Kühn*, the former mayor of Bromberg, *Ernst*, are stripped of their offices and degraded because of cowardice and dereliction of duty. They will be sent as soldiers to the probationary battalion, *after they have first attended the execution of von Salisch*. Especially difficult and dangerous tasks in the probationary battalion are to be assigned to the latter.

3.  The Kreisleiter [official of the Nazi Party in charge of a district or county: trans] of Bromberg, *Rampf*, degraded and expelled from the Party by the Leader of the Party Chancellery, is likewise to be sent to the probationary battalion, and assigned as Kühn and Ernst.

signed H. Himmler

I request widest possible dissemination of this order to all subordinated units, leaders, sub-leaders, and men.

(Signature illegible)
SS-Obergruppenführer
General der Waffen-SS und Polizei

*Wide Distribution!*

Complaint of an SS officer and member of the news staff of *Das Schwarze Korps* against cruelties committed against Jewish deportees at the 'Clou' in Berlin, dated March 4, 1943.
MA-322, pp. 2143-44.
Institut für Zeitgeschichte, Munich.

### *Das Schwarze Korps*

Zeitung der Schutzstaffeln der NSDAP, Organ der Reichsführung SS

Zentralverlag der NSDAP Rü/J.
Franz Eher Nachf. GmbH.

Zweigniederlassung
Berlin SW 68
Zimmerstrasse 88
Ferngespräche
Sammelnummer:  11 00 71
Ortsgespräche:   11 00 22

SS-Obersturmbannführer *Dr. Brandt*
Pers. Stab RFSS

*Berlin SW 11*
Prinz Albrecht-Str. 8

4. März 1943

*Persönlich gegen Quittung!*

Abl bei mir R.

Lieber Kamerad Dr. Brandt!

Ich möchte Ihnen heute einen Vorfall schildern, dem m.E. grundsätzliche Bedeutung zukommt.
Seit einigen Tagen sitzen hier bei uns in der Zimmerstrasse im 'Clou' – ehemals eine bürgerliche Unterhaltungsstätte – scharenweise die Juden, die auf ihren Weitertransport warten. Der 'Clou' hat nun einen Notausgang, der zwischen den Gebäuden des Eher-Verlages mündet und zwar auf einen Hof hinaus. Dieser Ausgang wurde für An- und Abtransport benutzt. Während die Heranbringung durch Lastwagen ordnungsgemäss vor sich ging, wurde ich am gestrigen Mittwoch von meinen schreckensbleichen Sekretärinnen gebeten, doch einmal schnell ins Zimmer unseres Registrators zu kommen (von wo aus man den Abtransport genau beobachten kann). Die Juden würden ohne ersichtlichen Grund sinnlos von einem Mann mit Hundepeitsche verprügelt.

Ich stellte durch Augenschein folgendes fest: ein Lastwagen war gerade heraus. Es kam ein neuer. Die augenscheinlich abgezählten Juden stürmten beim Ankommen des Wagens im Eilschritt aus dem 'Clou' und versuchten, so schnell wie möglich über besondere Hocker, die jüdische Ordner aufgestellt hatten, auf den Wagen zu kommen. Als ungefähr die Hälfte der Juden auf dem Wagen war (schneller ging es wirklich nicht), kam ein Zivilist, mit der Zigarette im Mund, eine Hundepeitsche schwingend, ebenfalls aus dem 'Clou' gelaufen und schlug wie ein Wildgewordener auf die zum Einsteigen drängenden Juden ein. Ich muß bemerken, dass sich unter diesen Jüdinnen mit kleinen Kindern auf dem Arm befanden. – Der Anblick war entwürdigend und beschämend zugleich.

Ich darf dazu bemerken, dass währenddessen an allen Fenstern und Türen der hohen umliegenden Gebäude des Eher-Verlages Arbeiter und Angestellte standen, die diese Vorgänge beobachteten. Direkt am Rand des Hofes ist die Druckerei des Eher-Verlages und überhaupt der technische Betrieb, in dem zahllose Ausländer aller Schattierungen und vor allem auch Frauen beschäftigt werden.

Als die Aufladung unter den eben geschilderten Formen erledigt war, spielte sich zum zweiten Mal genau der gleiche Vorgang ab. – Es kann also keine Rede davon sein, dass es sich vielleicht um einen Wutanfall aus besonderem Anlass gehandelt haben könnte. Der Mann mit der Hundepeitsche war offensichtlich der Leiter des gesamten Unternehmens 'Clou', augenscheinlich ein Assessor der Geheimen Staatspolizei. – Als ich aus dem Zimmer ging, um wegen dieser unmöglichen und politisch geradezu irrsinnigen Handlungsweise mit Sturmbannführer Dr. Fitzner zu sprechen, berichteten mir meine Sekretärinnen, dass der Mann beim nächsten Transport wiederum und vor allem auf Frauen eingeschlagen hätte und zwar so, dass es ein grosses Geschrei gab, worauf der Mann zu den umliegenden Häusern heraufbrüllte, die Fenster seien zu schliessen.

Sturmbannführer Dr. Fitzner verwies mich gleich an den Hauptsturmführer Fälschlein (?), mit dem ich auch gesprochen habe, der sofort die Unmöglichkeit dieses Vorgangs einsah und auch umgehend für Abhilfe sorgte. Zwischendurch konnte ich dann allerdings feststellen, dass diese Methode um sich gegriffen hatte: ein Mann der Waffen-SS hatte anscheinend einem Juden einen dicken Spazierstock weggenommen und schlug nun seinerseits genau so blödsinnig auf Juden ein, die sogar an der Wagenseite standen, also überhaupt nicht aufsteigen konnten. Das Gleiche tat ein Polizeibeamter mit einem kleineren Stock.

Sturmbannführer Dr. Fitzner kam nachher noch zu mir rüber, um sich die Sache anzusehen. Da ging jedoch bereits alles vorschriftsmässig und ruhig vonstatten. – Nachher erhielt ich noch einen Anruf von der Stapo, in dem man mir mitteilte, es sei auch von dort direkt jemand dagewesen, um die Angelegenheit zu kontrollieren, man habe jedoch nichts gesehen, sondern nur festgestellt, dass auf einem Tisch eine Hundepeitsche lag. Nach der Herkunft befragt, habe man erklärt, die sei nur dahingelegt worden, um den Juden Angst zu machen! Die jüdischen Ordner selbst befragt, ob alles ruhig vonstatten ginge, hätten das bejaht. – Man sagte mir jedoch zu, dass der Fall noch eingehend untersucht und der Verantwortliche zur Rechenschaft gezogen werden sollte.

Wenn ich Ihnen diesen Vorgang trotzdem so ausführlich schilderte, lieber Kamerad Dr. Brandt, so deshalb, weil ich glaube, dass es vielleicht einmal gut wäre, intern alle zuständigen Stellen darauf aufmerksam zu machen, dass das mit Humanität oder Gefühlsduselei aber auch nicht das Geringste zu tun hat, wenn verlangt wird, dass jede Amtshandlung, ganz gleich, was geschieht, unter strengster Wahrung der Form zu geschehen hat, gerade in solchen Fällen. Denn ich glaube, auch Sie sind der Auffassung, lieber Kamerad Dr. Brandt, dass etwas anderes sich mit germanischer Haltung nicht vereinbaren läßt. Schließlich wollen wir ja nicht den Anschein blindwütiger Sadisten erwecken, die vielleicht noch persönliche Befriedigung bei solchen Szenen empfinden und die beste Verhütung derartiger Auswüchse ist m.E. neben einer entsprechenden charakterlichen Auslese die unbedingte Wahrung der Form, was selbstverständlich nicht ausschliesst, dass man, wenn es am Platz ist, bei aller Form auch mal einen Juden in den Hintern treten kann, aber selbst dazu gehört m.E. Anstand. – Auf die politische Seite – nämlich die Nahrungsquelle für übelste Greuelberichte – brauche ich wohl nicht einzugehen.

Mit herzlichem Gruss,  
Ihr  
Heil Hitler!  
Rudolf aus den Rüschen  
SS Hauptsturmführer  

*Durchschrift Panzerschrank!*

Complaint of an SS officer and member of the news staff of *Das Schwarze Korps* against cruelties committed against Jewish deportees at the 'Clou' in Berlin, dated March 4, 1943.

MA-322, pp. 2143-44.
Institut für Zeitgeschichte, Munich.


### *Das Schwarze Korps*

Newspaper of the Protection Detachment [SS: trans.] of the NSDAP,
Organ of the Reich leadership SS

Zentralverlag der NSDAP Rü/J.
Franz Eher Nachf. GmbH.

Branch Office
Berlin SW 68
Zimmerstrasse 88
Telephone
Collective Number:   11 00 71
Local Calls:          11 00 22

SS-Obersturmbannführer Dr. Brandt
Personal Staff RFSS

*Berlin SW11*
Prinz Albrecht-Str. 8                                      March 4, 1943

*Personal receipt required!*

Copy to my File R.

Dear Comrade Dr. Brandt:

Today I would like to describe an incident to you which, in my opinion, is of fundamental significance.

With us here in Zimmerstrasse, in the 'Clou,' formerly a middle class place of entertainment, loads of Jews have been sitting for several

days, waiting for their deportation. Now, there is an emergency exit
from the 'Clou' which is between two buildings of the Eher Publishing
Firm and which leads out onto a courtyard. This exit was used for arrivals as well as departures [of Jewish transports: trans.]. While bringing the Jews here on trucks usually proceeds in an orderly fashion,
yesterday, a Wednesday, my secretaries, pale with fright, asked me to
please quickly come to our registrar's office (from which the departure
can be closely observed) claiming that the Jews were being soundly
beaten, for no apparent reason, by a man with a dog whip.

Through personal observation I ascertained the following: one truck
had just left; another came. On its arrival, the Jews, who apparently
had been counted off, rushed out of the 'Clou,' nearly running, and,
with the help of special stools which had been placed there by Jewish
orderlies, tried to climb onto the truck as quickly as possible. When
about half of the Jews were on the truck (there was no way it could
have been done faster), a civilian with a cigarette in his mouth and
swinging a dog whip also came running out of the 'Clou,' beating like
a madman on the Jews who were pushing to get onto the truck.

I have to mention that among the Jews there were Jewesses with small
children on their arms. This sight was both degrading and shameful.

I would like to point out that while all this was going on, workers
and employees of the Eher Publishing Firm were observing these incidents from all the windows and doors of the surrounding high buildings. Directly at the edge of the courtyard the printing press of the
Eher Publishing Firm is located and all the workshops in which countless foreigners of all types and, above all, women are employed.

As soon as the boarding of the truck was completed in the above-
mentioned manner, the whole procedure started all over again in
exactly the same way. Thus it is quite out of the question to assume
that this perhaps could have been a fit of rage caused by a specific
occurrence. Apparently the man with the dog whip was the leader of
the entire operation 'Clou,' evidently an Assessor [a relatively minor
rank: trans.] of the State Secret Police. – As I left the room to talk to
Sturmbannführer Dr. Fitzner regarding this impossible and, politically
speaking, a downright insane way of handling the situation, my secretaries
told me that during the following transport this man had again beaten
people, especially women, indeed in such a way that it caused loud
screaming, whereupon this man yelled up at the surrounding buildings

that the windows were to be closed.

Subsequently, Sturmbannführer Dr. Fitzner referred me at once to Hauptsturmführer Fälschlein (?) with whom I also talked. He immediately realized the impossibility of this incident and arranged for immediate relief. Meanwhile, however, I was able to ascertain that this method had spread: evidently a man belonging to the Waffen-SS had taken a thick walking stick away from a Jew, and in his turn, just as insanely now proceeded to beat the Jews, who already stood by the side of the truck and thus were really unable to climb in. The same was done by a police officer with a smaller stick.

Sturmbannführer Dr. Fitzner came over to me later on to take a look at the situation. By then, however, everything was going smoothly, according to regulations. – In addition I later received a phone call from the State Police in which I was informed that the Stapo had also sent someone there to immediately check out the matter. Nothing had been seen, however, but it was merely ascertained that a dog whip was lying on the table. When questioned about it, it was claimed that the dog whip had only been placed there to frighten the Jews! When the Jewish orderlies themselves were asked whether everything had gone along smoothly, they answered in the affirmative. – Nevertheless, I was promised that the case would be thoroughly investigated and the responsible individual called to account.

Dear comrade Dr. Brandt, if I am nevertheless giving you such a detailed description of this incident, it is only because I believe that it perhaps would be desirable to internally draw the attention of all appropriate authorities to the fact that it has nothing to do whatsoever with humanitarianism or sentimentality if it is insisted that every official act – regardless what is happening – take place under the strictest adherence to form, especially in such cases. For I do believe, dear comrade Dr. Brandt, that you, too, share my view that anything else cannot be reconciled with Germanic deportment. After all, we do not want to create the impression of blindly raging sadists who maybe even experience personal satisfaction during such scenes. The best way, in my opinion, to prevent such excesses, is, besides an appropriate selection on the basis of character, the unconditional adherence to form. This does not exclude that, when the time comes, with all due form, one can occasionally give a Jew a kick in the rear, but even then it should be done with decency. – I hardly need to go into the political aspect – that is, the fact that such incidents breed the most evil rumors about atrocities.

Cordially Yours,
Heil Hitler!
Rudolf aus den Rüschen
SS-Hauptsturmführer

*Copy to vault!*

# Nationalsozialistische Deutsche Arbeiter-Partei

Schlagwörter über Schlagwörter praffeln auf unfer Volk hernieder.

## !Internationale Solidarität!

Zwischen Engländern und Hottentotten, Chinefen und Zulukaffern, Franzofen und Japanern Ruffen und Deutfchen ufw. foll ein Zuftand idealer, inniger Verbrüderung eintreten! Sie find Menfchen und damit alle gleich!

Wenn auch die Farben verfchieden find, Gehirnmenge und Körperbau nicht ftimmt, Denkart und Leiftungen fich nicht gleichen, der Jude aber behauptet: Sie find gleich, und damit find fie es auch. Eine Folge diefer Gleichheit ift dann auch die „internationale Solidarität".

Aber während die Völker von ihr träumen, zertrümmert der gleiche Jude die einzige natur- gemäße und verftändlichfte Solidarität, die es geben follte, die jedes einzelnen Volkes felber. Unermeßliches Elend hat fich heute auf Deutfchland gefenkt. In dauerndem Gemetzel finken Tau- fende von Volksgenoffen in Oberfchlefien ins Grab.

Die fchwarze Schande wütet am Rhein, Weiber, Mädchen und Kinder büßen die Luft ver- tierter Reger mit ihrem Tode. Ein ununterbrochener Strom von Gift und Krankheit fließt in das Blut unferes Volkes. Marokkanifche Syphilis treibt Taufende von Opfern einem graufamen Tode entgegen. — Zehntaufende junger Deutfcher werden teils im Traume, teils im Raufche in die Fremdenlegion gefchleift.

Hunderttaufende unferer Kinder fiechen an langfamer Unterernährung dahin. Und nun fragen wir: Wo bleibt fie, die internationale Solidarität der Hilfe?

## Blutiger Hohn!

Während uns die Entente über eine Million Rinder raubt, gibt fie uns als Zeichen der Weltver- brüderung ein Gefchenk von 6000 gnädig zurück. Und während man noch in Paris die ftrikte Er- füllung der Friedensverträge fordert, verfichert man uns des Mitleids des franzöfifchen Proletariats.

## Rein, fo wird Deutfchland nicht frei!

### Auf internationale Hilfe trauen, heißt bauen auf Rebel und Dunft.

Das follte jeder Deutfche heute fchon begriffen haben, daß international und folidarifch nur eines ift, das

## Lumpen-, Gauner- und Schiebertum

International endlich nur die Weltbörfe, ihre Träger und Trabantengarde, die

## Jüdifche Raffe.

Wir deutfche Nationalfozialiften haben erkannt, daß nicht die internationale Solidarität die Völker befreit aus den Banden des internationalen Kapitals, fondern die

## organifierte nationale Kraft.

Die Vorausfetzung jeder über das eigene Zoll hinausreichenden Solidarität der Nationen fetzt erft voraus die Solidarität der eigenen. Diefe aber heißt Zufammenfchluß der fchaffenden Kräfte, gleich ob es Geiftes- oder Handarbeiter, zur Partei der fchaffenden Arbeit gegenüber den zehrenden Drohnen. **Deutfche Volksgenoffen!**

Die Nationalfozialiftifche Deutfche Arbeiter-Partei fordert Euch auf:

### kommt alle Donnerstag, den 25. August, 1921, in den

## Zirkus Krone zur Riefenkundgebung

gegen die dauernde Befchwindelung unferes Volkes durch die jüdifchen Agenten des inter- nationalen Weltbörfenkapitals!

Es werden fprechen: Herr **Dr. A. Schilling**, Schriftfteller, Führer der Nationalfoz. Partei, Mährifch-Oftrau, und Herr **A. Hitler**, München, über die

# Internationale Solidarität, ein jüdifcher Weltbetrug

Beginn der Verfammlung 8 Uhr abends, Ende 10½ Uhr.       Juden haben keinen Zutritt. Eintritt zur Deckung der Saal- und Plakatunkoften M. 1.—, Kriegsbefchädigte frei. Einberufer: Für die Parteileitung A. Drexler.

**Das Kampfblatt** der nationalfozialiftifchen Bewegung Großdeutfchlands ift der „Völkifche Beobachter", München, Thierfchftraße 15. In der heutigen Nummer: Unfere Gegenrechnung. — Was wir wollen, wenn wir wollen.

Die Verfammlung war von über 6000 Perfonen befucht.

# Bibliography

NOTATION OF SOURCES

1. *Documentary and Manuscript Material*

a) International Military Tribunal, *Trial of the Major War Criminals (Nuremberg, 1947-1949)*, 42 Vols. (in German), referred to as IMT.
b) War Crime Trials (London, 1949), Vol. V: *The Natzweiler Trial*.
c) Captured German Records, mostly included in the collection of the World War II Record Division of the National Archives at Alexandria, Virginia, Adjutant General's Office, Departmental Records Branch, U.S. Army. Most of these volumes have been published in various series of volumes, collected, microfilmed, and deposited in libraries.
A portion of these documents is now available at the Institut für Zeitgeschichte, Munich, referred to as MA – ... and FA ... Most of these documents were microfilmed by the American Historical Association's Committee for the Study of War Documents in cooperation with the National Archives and the Department of the Army. They are designated as U.S. National Archives Microcopy and deposited in the National Archives, Washington, D.C.
In this study were used:
1) Records of the Reich Leader of the SS and Chief of the German Police (Reichsführer SS und Chef der Deutschen Polizei), Washington: U.S. National Archives, Microcopy T-175. (Cited as GRMA, T-175).
2) Captured German Records Microfilmed at the Berlin Document Center, made available by the American Historical Association and the University of Nebraska, here referred to as BDC, T-580 and T-611.
Other abbreviations used: R. – Roll, F. – File, Fr. – Frame.
d) Interviews, First-Hand Accounts, and Biograms by former members of the SS were utilized. The names of some correspondents had to be withheld.

1a. *Autobiographies, Biograms, Memoirs, and Diaries by Former National Socialist Officials*

Bach-Zelewski, Erich von dem. 'Leben eines SS-Generals'. *Aufbau*/Reconstruction. New York, 1946.
Bormann, Martin. *The Bormann Letters*. Edited by H. R. Trevor-Roper, London: Weidenfeld & Nicolson, 1954.
Frank, Hans. Unpublished letter written to Major Douglas M. Kelly at Nuremberg prison during the latter part of 1945.
Gisevius, Hans. *To the Bitter End*. Boston: Houghton Mifflin Co., 1947.
Göring, Hermann. Unpublished biogram written for Major Douglas M. Kelley at Nuremberg prison during the latter part of 1945.
Hagen, Louis (ed. and trans.). *Hitler's Secret Service: Memoirs of Walter Schellenberg*. New York: Pyramid Books, 1958.

Hagen, Walter. *Die geheime Front*. Linz & Wien: Nibelungen-Verlag, 1950.

Hitler, Adolf. *Autobiographical Note by Adolf Hitler of November 29, 1921*. Institut für Zeitgeschichte, Munich: FA 88 St. 17a, Bl. 1-3.

Höss, Rudolf. *Kommandant in Auschwitz, autobiographische Aufzeichnungen*. Edited by Martin Broszat, München: Deutscher Taschenbuch-Verlag, 1964.

— Unpublished Autobiographical Note. Institut für Zeitgeschichte, Munich: Höss folder.

Kaltenbrunner, Ernst. Unpublished biogram written for Major Douglas M. Kelley at Nuremberg prison during the latter part of 1945.

Kersten, Felix, *Totenkopf und Treue*. Hamburg: Robert Mölich Verlag, 1952.

Rauschning, Hermann. *Gespräche mit Hitler*. Wien: Europa-Verlag, 1940.

Röhm, Ernst. *Geschichte eines Hochverräters*. München: Franz Eher, Nachfolger, 1930.

Rosenberg, Alfred. Unpublished biogram written for Major Douglas M. Kelley at Nuremberg prison on October 12, 1945.

— Unpublished letter written to Major Douglas M. Kelley at Nuremberg prison on December 26, 1945.

Schellenberg Walter. *Memoiren*. Köln: Verlag für Politik und Wirtschaft, 1959.

Schlabrendorff, Fabian von. *Offiziere gegen Hitler*. Zürich: Europa Verlag, 1946.

Speer, Albert, *Erinnerungen*. Berlin: Propyläen Verlag, 1969.

Steiner, Felix. *Die Freiwilligen: Idee und Opfergang*. Göttingen: Plesse Verlag, 1958.

— *Die Armee der Geächteten*. Göttingen: Plesse Verlag, 1963.

Strasser, Otto. *Hitler und ich*. Buenos Aires: Editorial Trenkelbach, 1940.

— *Hitler und ich*. Konstanz: Johannes Asmus Verlag, 1948.

— *Mein Kampf. Eine politische Autobiographie*. Frankfurt/M.: Heinrich Heine Verlag, 1969.

1.b  *Other Autobiographies, Biograms, Memoirs, and Diaries*

Andrus, Burton C. *I was the Nuremberg Jailer*. New York: Tower Publications, 1970.

Behrend-Rosenfeld, Else. *Ich stand nicht allein*. Hamburg: Europäische Verlagsanstalt, 1949.

Buber-Neumann, Margarete. *Als Gefangene bei Stalin und Hitler*. München: Deutscher Taschenbuch Verlag, 1962.

Diels, Rudolf. *Lucifer ante portas ... es spricht der erste Chef der Gestapo ...* Stuttgart: Deutsche Verlags-Anstalt, 1950.

Granzow, Klaus. *Tagebuch eines Hitlerjungen*. Bremen: Carl Schünemann Verlag, 1965.

Herbermann, Nanda. *Der gesegnete Abgrund: Schutzhäftling Nr. 6582 im Frauen K. Z. Ravensbrück*. Nürnberg: Glock & Lutz. Second edition, 1948.

Joos, Joseph. *Leben auf Widerruf*. Trier: Paulinsdruckerei (second edition), 1948.

Kardorff, Ursula v. *Berliner Aufzeichnungen*. München: Biederstein Verlag, 1962.

Kautsky, Benedikt. *Teufel und Verdammte*. Zürich: Büchergilde Gutenberg, 1946.

Kraus, Ota, und Kulka, Erich. *Die Todesfabrik*. Berlin: Kongress-Verlag, 1958.

Lengyel, O. *Five Chimneys: The Story of Auschwitz*. Chicago: University of Chicago Press, 1947.

Levi, Primo. *Survival in Auschwitz*. New York: Collier Books, 1961.

Lingens-Reiner, Ella. *Prisoners of Fear*. London: Victor Gollancz, 1948.

Marcuse, Bruno. *Erlebnisse im KZ Theresienstadt*. Ulm: Ebner, 1946.

Maschmann, Melita. *Fazit*. Stuttgart: Deutsche Verlags-Anstalt, 1963.

Maurel, Micheline. *The Slave*. New York: Belmont Books, 1958.

Nyiszli, Miklos. *Auschwitz: A Doctor's Eyewitness Account*. With a foreword by Bruno Bettelheim. New York: Frederick Fell Inc. Publishers, 1960.

Poller, Walter. *Arztschreiber in Buchenwald*. Offenbach: Verlag Das Segel. 1960.

Rassinier, Paul. *Die Lüge des Odysseus*. Wiesbaden: Verlag Karl Heinz Priester, 1959.

— *Was nun, Odysseus? Zur Bewältigung der Vergangenheit*. Wiesbaden: Verlag Karl Heinz Priester, 1960.

Roeder, Bernhard. *Das Katorgan: Traktat über die moderne Sklaverei*. Berlin: Kiepenheuer & Witsch, 1956.

Schoenberner, Gerhard (ed.). *Wir haben es gesehen*. Hamburg: Rütten & Loening Verlag, 1962.

Seger, Gerhart. *Oranienburg*. With a foreword by Heinrich Mann. Karlsbad: Verlagsanstalt 'Graphia', 1934.

Vermehren, Isa. *Reise durch den letzten Akt*. Hamburg: Christian Wegner Verlag, 1947.

Vrba, Rudolf and Bestic, Alan. *I Cannot Forgive*. New York: Bantam Books, 1964.

Wechsberg, Joseph (ed.). *The Murderers Among Us: The Simon Wiesenthal Memoirs*. New York: Bantam Books, 1968.

## 2. *National Socialist Literature*

### a) *Books, Official Publications, and Pamphlets*

Bayer, Ernst. *Geschichte, Arbeit, Zweck und Organisation der S.A. Aus den Schriften der Hochschule für Politik*. Berlin: Junker und Dünnhaupt Verlag, 1938.

Best, Werner. *Die Deutsche Polizei*. Darmstadt: Wittich Verlag, 1940.

D'Alquen, Günter. *Die SS, Geschichte, Aufgabe und Organisation der Schutzstaffel der NSDAP. Aus den Schriften der Hochschule für Politik*. Berlin: Junker und Dünnhaupt Verlag, 1939.

Darré, Walter. *Das Bauerntum als Lebensquell der Nordischen Rasse*. München: Lehmann, 1933.

Eckart, Dietrich. *Der Bolschewismus von Moses bis Lenin: Zwiegespräch zwischen Adolf Hitler und mir*. München: Hoheneichen-Verlag, 1924.

Goebbels, Joseph (ed.). *Knorke, ein neues Buch Isidor für Zeitgenossen.* München: Franz Eher, Nachfolger, 1929.

— *Michael. Ein deutsches Schicksal in Tagebuchblättern.* München: Franz Eher, Nachfolger, 1935.

Göring, Hermann. *Aufbau einer Nation.* Berlin: Mittler, 1934.

Gritzbach, Erich. *Hermann Göring, Werk und Mensch.* München: Franz Eher, Nachfolger, 1941.

Hitler, Adolf. *Mein Kampf,* 2 Vols. München: Franz Eher, Nachfolger, 1940.

— *Die Reden Hitlers am Parteitag der Freiheit 1935.* München: Franz Eher, Nachfolger, 1935.

— *Bilder aus dem Leben des Führers.* Edited by Cigaretten/Bilderdienst. Leipzig: F. A. Brockhaus, 1936.

Koch, W. H. Karl. *Das Ehrenbuch der SA.* Düsseldorf: Friedrich Floeder Verlag, 1934.

Reich, Albert. *Dietrich Eckart.* München: Franz Eher, Nachfolger, 1933.

Der Reichsführer SS. *Dienstaltersliste der Schutzstaffel der NSDAP. Stand vom 1. Juli 1935, bearbeitet von der Personalkanzlei des Reichsführers-SS, Berlin,* 1935.

— *Statistisches Jahrbuch der Schutzstaffel der NSDAP 1937.* Berlin 1938.

— *Statistisches Jahrbuch der Schutzstaffel der NSDAP 1938.* Berlin 1939.

— *Dich ruft die SS.* Berlin: SS-Hauptamt, 1942.

— *Aufbruch. Briefe von germanischen Freiwilligen der SS-Division Wiking.* Berlin-Leipzig: Nibelungen-Verlag, 1943.

— *Rassenpolitik.* Berlin: SS-Hauptamt, 1943.

— *Dienstaltersliste der Schutzstaffel der NSDAP. Stand vom 9. November 1944, herausgegeben vom SS-Personalamt, Berlin,* 1944.

Der Reichsorganisationsleiter. *Die Organisation der NSDAP.* München: Franz Eher, Nachfolger, 1943.

Rosenberg, Alfred. *Wesen, Grundsätze und Ziele der NSDAP.* München: Deutscher Volksverlag, 1932.

— *Der Mythos des 20. Jahrhunderts.* München: Hoheneichen-Verlag, 1941.

Schrey, Kurt. *Du und Dein Volk. Herausgegeben von der Reichsleitung der NSDAP, Hauptamt für Erzieher (NSLB).* München: Deutscher Volksverlag, 1936.

Schwarz van Berk, Hans (ed.). *Aufsätze aus der Kampfzeit.* München: Franz Eher, Nachfolger, 1936.

SS Oberabschnitt West. *Die Gestaltung der Feste im Jahres- und Lebenslauf in der SS Familie.* 1936.

Streicher, Julius (ed.). *Reichstagung in Nürnberg 1933.* Berlin: Vaterländischer Verlag C. A. Weller, 1933.

Stuckart, Wilhelm, and Globke, Hans. *Kommentare zur deutschen Rassengesetzgebung.* Berlin: Beck'sche Verlagsbuchhandlung, 1936.

Voggenreiter, Ludwig (ed.). *Der Hitler-Prozess.* Potsdam: Ludwig Voggenreiter, 1934.

b) *Journals, Periodicals, and Articles*

Berchtold, Joseph. 'S.A.-Geist hat gesiegt,' *Völkischer Beobachter* (Juli, 1934), p. 1.

Eckart, Dietrich (ed.). 'Auf gut Deutsch,' *Wochenschrift für Ordnung und Recht* (München, 1920).

'Der Führer erhebt die SS zur selbständigen Organisation' (Editorial), *Völkischer Beobachter*, Ausgabe A/Süddeutsche Ausgabe (July, 1934), p. 1.

Gohdes, Otto. 'Unser Führer!,' *Schulungsbriefe des Reichsschulungsamtes der NSDAP und der Deutschen Arbeitsfront*, Vol. I, No. 3 (August, 1933), p. 30.

Gohdes, Otto. 'Parteidisziplin,' *Schulungsbriefe des Reichsschulungsamtes der NSDAP und der Deutschen Arbeitsfront*, Vol. I, No. 4 (September, 1933), pp. 46-47.

Hartle, Heinrich, 'Friedrich Nietzsche, der unerbittliche Werter des neunzehnten Jahrhunderts,' *Schulungsbriefe des Reichsschulungsamtes der NSDAP und der Deutschen Arbeitsfront*, Vol. IV, No. 8 (August, 1937), pp. 290-292, 295-299.

Hitler, Adolf, and Rosenberg, Alfred (eds.). *Nationalsozialistische Monatshefte. Wissenschaftliche Zeitschrift der NSDAP*. München: Franz Eher, Nachfolger, 1931, 1932, 1933.

Der Reichsführer SS (ed.). *SS-Leithefte*, Vol. VII, No. 1b (Berlin), pp. 10-11.

Rosenberg, Alfred. 'Schutzfärbung,' *Schulungsbriefe des Reichsschulungsamtes der NSDAP und der Deutschen Arbeitsfront*, Vol. I, No. 3 (August, 1933), pp. 31-32.

'Staat und evangelische Kirche im neunzehnten Jahrhundert' (Editiorial, author's name omitted), *Schulungsbriefe des Reischsschulungsamtes der NSDAP und der Deutschen Arbeitsfront*, Vol. IV, No. 8 (August, 1937), p. 317.

Strasser, Otto (auth. & ed.). 'Die Gefahr der Aufteilung Deutschlands,' *Die Deutsche Revolution (Organ der Schwarzen Front)*, Vol. XII, No. 1 (Prague, 1937), pp. 1-2.

Streicher, Julius (ed.). *Der Stürmer*. Excerpts 1940-1944.

Wehmeyer, C. 'Der zweite Punkt im Programm der NSDAP,' *Schulungsbriefe des Reichsschulungsamtes der NSDAP und der Deutschen Arbeitsfront*, Vol. I, No. 4 (September, 1933), pp. 55-56.

3. *Books in the Social Sciences*

Abel, Theodore, *The Nazi Movement*. New York: Atherton Press, 1965.

Adorno, Theodor *et al. The Authoritarian Personality*. New York: Harper, 1950.

Allport, Gordon W. *The Nature of Prejudice*. Garden City, N.Y.: Doubleday & Co., 1958.

Arendt, Hannah. *The Origins of Totalitarianism*. New York: Meridian Books, 1952.

— *Eichmann in Jerusalem.* London: Faber & Faber, 1963.

— *On Violence.* New York: Harcourt, Brace & World, Inc., 1970.

Barnes, Harry Elmer, and Becker, Howard. *Social Thought from Lore to Science.* Washington, D.C.: Harren Press, 1952.

Becker, Howard. *Outsiders.* New York: The Free Press, 1968, Vol. 2.

Bettelheim, Bruno. *The Informed Heart.* Glencoe, Ill.: The Free Press (fourth printing), 1963.

Bracher, Karl D. *et al. Die nationalsozialistische Machtergreifung.* Köln: Westdeutscher Verlag (second edition), 1967.

Bronder, Dietrich. *Bevor Hitler kam.* Hannover: Pfeiffer Verlag, 1964.

Buchheim, Hans. *Totalitäre Herrschaft, Wesen und Merkmale.* München: Kosel-Verlag, 1962.

— *SS und Polizei im NS-Staat.* Duisdorf bei Bonn: Selbstverlag der Studiengesellschaft für Zeitprobleme, 1964.

— *et al. Anatomie des SS-Staates.* Freiburg: Walter-Verlag, 1965, 2 Vols.

Cattell, Raymond. *The Scientific Analysis of Personality.* Harmondsworth/Middlesex: Penguin Books, 1965.

Christie, Richard, and Jahoda, Marie (eds.). *Studies in the Scope and Method of 'The Authoritarian Personality'.* Glencoe, Ill.: The Free Press, 1954.

Cohen, E. *Human Behavior in the Concentration Camp.* New York: Grosset & Dunlap, 1953.

Coser, Lewis A. *The Functions of Social Conflict.* Glencoe, Ill.: The Free Press, 1965.

— (ed.). *Political Sociology.* New York: Harper Torchbooks, 1966.

Crankshaw, Edward. *Die Gestapo.* Berlin: Colloquium Verlag. 1959.

Djilas, Milovan. *The New Class.* New York: Praeger (fifteenth printing), 1961.

Döring, Hans Joachim. *Die Zigeuner im NS-Staat.* Hamburg: Kriminalistik Verlag, 1964.

Duncan, Hugh Dalziel. *Communication and Social Order.* New York: Oxford University Press, 1968.

Durkheim, Emile. *Les Règles de la méthode sociologique.* Paris: Librairie Félix Alcan, 1927.

Erikson, Erik H. *Childhood and Society.* New York: W. W. Norton & Co., Inc. (second edition), 1963.

— *Insight and Responsibility.* New York: W. W. Norton & Co., 1964.

Eschenburg, Theodor *et al. Der Weg in die Diktatur 1918-1933.* München: Piper Verlag, 1963.

Etzioni, Amitai (ed.). *Complex Organizations.* New York: Holt, Rinehart and Winston, 1961.

— *A Comparative Analysis of Complex Organizations.* New York: The Free Press, 1965.

Falk, Richard A., Kolko, Gabriel, and Lifton, Robert Jay (eds.). *Crimes of War.* New York: Vintage Books, 1971.

Frankl, Viktor E. *Ein Psychologe erlebt das KZ.* Wien: Verlag für Jugend und Volk (second edition), 1947.

Freud, Anna. *The Ego and the Mechanisms of Defense.* New York: International Universities Press, 1946.

Freud, Sigmund. *Civilization and Its Discontents.* London: Hogarth Press, 1930.

— and Bullitt, William. *Thomas Woodrow Wilson: Twenty-Eighth President of the United States: A Psychological Study.* Boston: Houghton Mifflin Co., 1967.

Frischauer, Willi. *Himmler: The Evil Genius of the Third Reich.* Boston: The Beacon Press, 1953.

Fromm, Erich. *Escape from Freedom.* New York: Farrar & Strauss, 1941.

— *May Man Prevail?* Garden City, N.Y.: Doubleday & Co., 1964.

George, Alexander L. and Juliette L. *Woodrow Wilson and Colonel House.* New York: Dover Publications, 1956.

Gerth, Hans H., and Mills, C. Wright (trans. and eds.). *From Max Weber: Essays in Sociology.* New York: Oxford University Press, 1946.

— *Character and Social Structure.* London: Routledge & Kegan Paul, 1961.

Gilbert, G. M. *Nürnberger Tagebuch.* Frankfurt/M: Fischer Bücherei, 1962.

Glaser, Barney, and Strauss, Anselm H. *Status Passage.* London: Routledge and Kegan Paul, 1971.

Glaser, Hermann. *Das Dritte Reich: Anspruch und Wirklichkeit.* Freiburg/Br.: Herder Druck, 1963.

Goffman, Erving. *The Presentation of Self in Everyday Life.* New York: Doubleday Anchor, Inc., 1959.

— *Asylums.* New York: Doubleday & Co., Inc., 1961.

— *Behavior in Public Places.* New York: The Free Press of Glencoe, Inc., 1963.

— *Stigma.* Englewood Cliffs, N.J.: Prentice-Hall, 1963.

— *Interaction Ritual.* New York: Doubleday & Co., Inc., 1967.

Halmos, Paul. *Towards a Measure of Man. The Frontiers of Normal Adjustment.* London: Routledge & Kegan Paul, 1957.

Heiber, Helmut. *Joseph Goebbels.* München: Deutscher Taschenbuch Verlag, 1965.

— (ed.). *Reichsführer! . . . Briefe an und von Himmler.* Stuttgart: Deutsche Verlags-Anstalt, 1968.

Hilberg, Raul. *The Destruction of the European Jews.* Chicago: Quadrangle Books, 1961.

Hofer, Walter (ed.). *Der Nationalsozialismus: Dokumente 1933-1945.* Frankfurt/M.: Fischer Bücherei, 1965.

Horney, Karen. *Neurosis and Human Growth: The Struggle toward Self-Realization.* New York: W. W. Norton & Co., 1950.

Horowitz, Irving Louis. *The War Game.* New York: Ballantine Books, 1963.

— *Three Worlds of Development: The Theory and Practice of International Stratification.* New York: Oxford University Press, 1966.

Hottinger, A. et al. *Hungerkrankheit, Hungerödem, Hungertuberkulose.* Basel: B. Schwabe, 1948.

Jäger, Herbert. *Verbrechen unter totalitärer Herrschaft. Studien zur national-sozialistischen Gewaltkriminalität.* Freiburg/Br.: Walter Verlag, 1967.

Jung, Carl G. *Essays on Contemporary Events.* London: Routledge & Kegan Paul, 1947.

— *Flying Saucers.* New York: Signet Books, 1969.

Kahn, Hermann, and Wiener, Anthony S. *The Year 2000.* London: The Macmillan Company, 1969.

Kelley, Douglas M. *22 Männer um Hitler.* Bern: Delphin Verlag, 1947.

Kluckhohn Clyde, and Murray, Henry A. (eds.). *Personality in Nature, Society and Culture.* New York: Alfred A. Knopf, 1950.

Kogon, Eugen. *Der SS-Staat.* München: K. Alber, 1946.

Krausnick, Helmut. *Zur Zahl der jüdischen Opfer des Nationalsozialismus.* Edited by Bundeszentrale für Heimatdienst. Bonn, 1956, No. 9.

Kriminalistik (ed.). *Aktuelle Kriminologie.* Hamburg: Kriminalistik Verlag, 1969.

Laing, Er. D. *The Politics of Experience.* New York: Ballantine Books (fifth printing), 1970.

Lange-Eichbaum, Wilhelm, and Kurth, Wolfram. *Genie, Irrsinn und Ruhm.* München: Ernst Reinhardt, 1967.

Lederer, Emil. *The State of the Masses.* New York: W. W. Norton & Co., 1940.

Lewin, Kurt. *Resolving Social Conflict.* New York: Harper and Row, 1948.

Liddel Hart, B. H. *Strategy.* New York: Frederick A. Praeger (tenth printing), 1964.

Lipset, Seymour Martin. *The First New Nation.* Garden City, N.Y.: Anchor Books, 1967.

Lofland, John. *Deviance and Identity.* Englewood Cliffs, N.J.: Prentice-Hall, 1969.

Luckmann, Thomas. *The Invisible Religion.* New York: The Macmillan Company, 1967.

Lynd, Robert S. *Knowledge for what? The Place of Social Science in American Culture.* Princeton: Princeton University Press, 1939.

Machiavelli, Niccolo. *The Prince.* Edited by Bergin, Thomas G. New York: Appleton-Century-Crofts, 1947.

Madge, John. *The Tools of Social Science.* London: Longmans, Green, 1953.

— *The Origins of Scientific Sociology.* Glencoe, Ill.: The Free Press, 1964.

— *Scientific Sociology.* New York: The Free Press, 1967.

Malinowski, Bronislow. *A Scientific Theory of Culture and Other Essays.* New York: Oxford University Press (fourth printing), 1966.

Mannheim, Karl. *Man and Society in an Age of Reconstruction.* New York: Harcourt, Brace, 1940.

Matson, Floyd W. *The Broken Image: Man, Science and Society.* New York: George Braziller, 1964.

Mead, Heorge H. *Mind, Self, and Society.* Chicago: University of Chicago Press, 1934.

Meisel, James H. (ed.). *Pareto & Mosca.* Englewood Cliffs, N.J.: Prentice Hall, 1965.

Merton, Robert K. *et al. Reader in Bureaucracy.* Glencoe, Ill.: The Free Press, 1960.
— *Social Theory and Social Structure* (enlarged edition). New York: The Free Press, 1968.
Mills, C. Wright. *Power, Politics and People.* New York: Ballantine Books, 1963.
— (ed.). *Klassik der Soziologie: eine polemische Auslese.* Frankfurt/M.: S. Fischer Verlag, 1966.
— *Images of Man.* New York: George Braziller, 1967.
—*The Sociological Imagination.* New York: Oxford University Press, 1968.
— *The Power Elite.* New York: Oxford University Press, 1969.
Mitzman, Arthur. *The Iron Cage: An Historical Interpretation of Max Weber.* New York: Alfred Knopf, 1970.
Mullahy, Patrick. *Oedipus: Myth and Complex: A Review of Psychiatric Theory.* New York: Hermitage Press, 1948.
Myrdal, Gunnar *et al. An American Dilemma.* New York: Harper, 1944.
Neumann, Franz. *Behemoth.* New York: Oxford University Press, 1944.
— *The Democratic and the Authoritarian State.* New York: The Free Press, 1966.
Neumann, Sigmund. *Permanent Revolution.* New York: Harper and Bros., 1942.
Neusüss-Hunkel, Ermenhild. *Die SS.* Hannover: Norddeutsche Verlagsanstalt, 1956.
Nisbet, Robert A. *Social Change and History.* New York: Oxford University Press, 1969.
Nolte, Ernst. *Three Faces of Fascism.* New York: Holt, Rinehart and Winston. 1966.
Nottingham, Elizabeth. *Religion and Society.* New York: Random House, 1954.
Orleans, Peter (ed.). *Social Structure and Social Process.* Boston, Mass.: Allyn and Bacon, Inc., 1969.
Ortega y Gasset, José. *The Revolt of the Masses.* New York: W. W. Norton & Co., 1932.
— *Man and Crisis.* New York: W. W. Norton & Co., 1962.
Perls, F. S. *Ego, Hunger and Aggression.* New York: Vintage Books, 1969.
Poliakov, Leon. *Harvest of Hate: The Nazi Program for the Destruction of Jews in Europe.* Syracuse: Syracuse University Press, 1954.
— and Wulf, J. *Das Dritte Reich und die Juden.* Berlin: Arany Verlag, 1955.
Pulzer, Peter G. *Die Entstehung des politischen Antisemitismus in Deutschland und Österreich 1867-1914.* Gütersloh: Sigbert Mohn Verlag, 1966.
Rank, Otto. *Will Therapy and Truth and Reality.* New York: Alfred A. Knopf, 1950.
Rathenau, Walther. *Zur Kritik der Zeit.* Berlin : S. Fischer Verlag, 1912.
Recktenwald, J. *Woran hat Adolf Hitler gelitten?* München: Ernst Reinhardt Verlag, 1964.
Reitlinger, Gerald. *The SS: Alibi of a Nation, 1922-1945.* New York: Viking Press, 1957.
Rosenberg, Bernard *et al.* (ed.). *Mass Society in Crisis.* New York: The Macmil-

lan Company, 1968.

Rothfels, Hans. *Die deutsche Opposition gegen Hitler*. Frankfurt/M.: Fischer Bücherei, 1958.

Rubington, Earl, and Weinberg, Martin S. (eds.). *Deviance: The Interactionist Perspective*. New York: The Macmillan Company, 1968.

Rushing, William A. (ed.). *Deviant Behavior and Social Process*. Chicago: Rand McNally Co., 1969.

Scheff, Thomas J. *Mental Illness and Social Process*. New York: Harper and Row, 1967.

Schoenbaum, David. *Hitler's Social Revolution: Class and Status in Nazi Germany 1933-1939*. Garden City, New York: Anchor Books Doubleday & Company, Inc., 1967.

Shibutani, T., and Kwan, K. *Ethnic Stratification*. New York: The Macmillan Company, 1967.

Simmel, Georg. *Conflict and the Web of Group Affiliations*. Trans. by Kurt Wolff and Reinhard Bendix. Glenco, Ill.: The Free Press, 1955.

Spengler, Oswald. *Jahre der Entscheidung*, Part I: *Deutschland und die weltgeschichtliche Entwicklung*. München: Beck'sche Verlagsbuchhandlung, 1933.

Spitzer, Stephan P. (ed.). *The Sociology of Personality*. New York: Van Nostrand Reinhold Co., 1969.

Staff, Ilse. *Justiz im Dritten Reich*. Frankfurt/M.: Fischer Bücherei, 1964.

Stein, George H. *The Waffen SS: Hitler's Elite Guard at War 1939-1945*. Ithaca, N.Y.: Cornell University Press, 1966.

Szasz, Thomas S. *The Myth of Mental Illness*. New York: Dell Publishing Company, 1961.

— *Law, Liberty and Psychiatry*, New York: Collier Books, 1968.

Toennies, Ferdinand. *Community and Society*. Trans. by Charles P. Loomis. New York: Harper & Row, 1957.

Treher, W. *Hitler, Steiner, Schreber. Ein Beitrag zur Phänomenologie des kranken Geistes*. Emmendingen/Br.: im Selbstverlag, 1966.

Trevor-Roper, H. R. (ed.). *Hitler's Secret Conversations 1941-1944*. New York: Ferrar & Strauss, 1953.

— *Hitler's letzte Tage*. Frankfurt/M.: Ullstein Bücher, 1965.

Utitz, Emil. *Psychologie des Lebens im Konzentrationslager Theresienstadt*. Wien: Continental, 1948.

Walace, Walter L. (ed.). *Sociological Theory*. Chicago: Aldine Publication Company, 1969.

Walter, Eugene. *Terror and Resistance*. New York: Oxford University Press, 1969.

Weber, Max. *Gemeinschaft und Gesellschaft*. Tübingen: J. C. B. Mohr, 1922.

— *Wirtschaft und Gesellschaft*, Tübingen: J. C. B. Mohr, 1925.

Wheaton, Eliot Barculo. *The Nazi Revolution. 1933-1935: Prelude to Calamity*. Garden City, New York: Anchor Books. Doubleday & Company, Inc., 1969.

Wolfenstein, M. *Disaster: A Psychological Essay. Glencoe*, Ill.: The Free Press, 1957.

Wolff, Kurt H. (trans. & ed.). *The Sociology of Georg Simmel*. Glencoe, Ill.: The Free Press, 1950.

Woolf, S. J. (ed.). *European Fascism*. New York: Vintage Books, 1969.

Wulf, Joseph. *Martin Bormann, Hitlers Schatten*. Gütersloh: Sigbert Mohn Verlag, 1962.

— Aus dem Lexikon der Mörder. 'Sonderbehandlung' und verwandte Worte in nationalsozialistischen Dokumenten. Gütersloh: Sigbert Mohn Verlag, 1963.


### 4. *Professional Periodicals*

Abel, Theodore, 'The Sociology of Concentration Camps,' *Social Forces*, XXX (Baltimore, 1951).

Alexander, Leo. 'War Crimes: Their Social-Psychological Aspects,' *American Journal of Psychiatry*, Vol. CV, No. 4 (September, 1948), pp. 170-177.

— 'Destructive and Self-Destructive Trends in Criminalized Society,' *Journal of Criminal Law and Criminology*, XXXIX (January- February, 1949), p. 559.

Angress, Werner T., and Smith, Bradley F. 'Diaries of Heinrich Himmler's Early Years,' *The Journal of Modern History*, Vol. XXXI, No. 3 (September, 1959), pp. 206-224.

Arendt, Hannah. 'Social Science Techniques and the Study of Concentration Camps,' *Jewish Social Studies*, Vol. XII, No. 1 (January, 1950), p. 50.

Bain, Read. 'Sociology and Psychoanalysis,' *American Sociological Review*, Vol. I, No. 2 (April, 1936), p. 206.

Bell, Daniel. 'The Alphabet of Justice,' *Partisan Review*, XXX (1963), pp. 422-423.

Bluhm, Hilde O. 'How did they survive? Mechanisms of Defense in Nazi Concentration Camps,' *American Journal of Psycho-Therapy*, II (1948), pp. 3-32.

Bondy, C. 'Problems in Internment Camps,' *Journal of Abnormal and Social Psychology*, Vol. XXXVIII, No. 4 (October, 1943), pp. 453-475.

Brachyahu, M. 'A Contribution toward the Psychology of the Parties,' *Psychoanalytic Review*, XXXVI (1949), p. 431.

Cameron, Norman. 'The Paranoial Pseudo-Community Revisited,' *American Journal of Sociology*, LXV (July, 1959), p. 58.

Clifford, W. 'The Role of Frustration in Anti-Social Behavior,' *Justice of the Peace and Local Government Review (U.K.)*, Vol. CXXVI, No. 47 (1962), pp. 735-736.

Cohen, A. K. 'The Sociology of the Deviant Act: Anomie Theory and Beyond,' *American Sociological Review*, Vol. XXX, No. 1 (1965), pp. 5-14.

Coser, Lewis A. 'Some Social Functions of Violence,' in *American Academy of Political and Social Science. Patterns of Violence*. Edited by Marvin E. Wolfgang. *Annals*, CCCLXIV (Philadelphia, 1966), pp. 8-18.

Dubin, Robert. 'Power, Function, and Organization,' *Pacific Sociological Review*, VI (Spring, 1963), pp. 16-22.

Egenter, Richard *et al.* 'Die NS-Prozesse. Tatsachen und Betrachtungen,' *Freiburger Rundbrief*, Vol. XV, Nos. 57/60 (January, 1964), pp. 32-52.

Emerson, Richard H. 'Power-Dependence Relations,' *American Sociological Review*, XXVII (February, 1962), pp. 31-37, 39-41.

Farris, Charles D. 'Authoritarianism as a Political Behavior Variable,' *Journal of Politics*, XVIII (1956), pp. 61-82.

Federn, E. 'Some Clinical Remarks on the Psychopathology of Genocide,' *Psychiatric Quarterly*, Vol. XXXIV, No. 3 (1960), pp. 538-549.

Frenkel-Brunswik, Else. 'Interaction of Psychological and Sociological Factors in Political Behavior,' *The American Political Science Review*, Vol. XLVI, No. 1 (March, 1952), pp. 44-65.

Friedman, Philip. 'Jewish Reaction to Nazism,' *Jewish Frontier*, Vol. XVII, No. 9 (September, 1950), p. 22.

Fromm, Erich. 'The Social Philosophy of "Will Therapy",' *Psychiatry*, Vol. II, No. 2 (May, 1939), pp. 234-235.

Georg, Enno. 'Die wirtschaftlichen Unternehmungen der SS.' *Vierteljahrshefte für Zeitgeschichte*, Vol. XI, No. 7 (Stuttgart, 1963), pp. 16-17.

Gerstein, Kurt, 'Niederschrift vom 4. Mai 1945 über Massenvergasung am 18. August 1942,' *Vierteljahrshefte für Zeitgeschichte*, Vol. I, No. 2 (April, 1953), pp. 189-191.

Hale, Oron James (ed.). 'Gottfried Feder calls Hitler to Order: An Unpublished Letter on Nazi Affairs,' *The Journal of Modern History*, Vol. XXX, No. 4 (December, 1958), pp. 358-362.

Janowitz, Morris. 'Soziale Schichtung und Mobilität in Westdeutschland,' *Kölner Zeitschrift für Soziologie and Sozialpsychologie*, X (1958), pp. 32-33.

Javega, Cavero F. 'War Crimes' (Crimines de Guerra), *Politica española*, Vol. II, No. 15 (1963), p. 12.

Lewin, Kurt, and Lippitt, R. 'An Experimental Study of the Effect of Democratic and Authoritarian Group Atmospheres,' *University of Iowa Studies in Child Welfare*, Vol. XVI, No. 3 (1940), pp. 45-198.

Lynd, Helen M. 'Must Psychology Aid Reaction?,' *The Nation*, Vol CLXVIII, No. 3 (January, 1949), p. 76.

McClosky, H., and Schaar, J. 'Psychological Dimensions of Anomy,' *American Sociological Review*, Vol. XXX, No. 1 (Washington, D.C., 1965), pp. 14-40.

MacNeil, Elton B. 'Violence and Human Development,' in *American Academy of Political and Social Science, Patterns of Violence.* Edited by Marvin E. Wolfgang. Annals, CCCLXIV (Philadelphia, 1966), pp. 149-157.

Paetel, Karl O. 'The Black Order: A Survey of the Literature on the SS,' *The Wiener Library Bulletin*, Vol. XII, Nos. 3-4 (London, 1959), pp. 33-35.

Parsons, Talcott. 'Max Weber and the Contemporary Political Crisis,' *Review of Politics*, No. 4 (1942), pp. 75, 76.

Peterson, E. N. 'Die Bürokratie und die NSDAP,' *Der Staat, Zeitschrift für öffentliches Recht und Verfassungsgeschichte*, Vol. VI, No. 2 (1967), pp. 151-173.

Scheffler, Wolfgang. 'Hannah Arendt und der Mensch im totalitären Staat,'

*Aus Politik und Zeitgeschichte, Beilage zur Wochenzeitung Das Parlament,* B 45/64 (November, 1964), pp. 19-38.

Schreier, Fritz. 'German Aggressiveness – Its Reasons and Types,' *The Journal of Abnormal and Social Psychology,* XXXVIII (1943), pp. 211-224.

Steiner, John, M., and Quensel, Stephan. 'Neue Wege kriminologischer Zusammenarbeit.' *Monatsschrift für Kriminologie und Strafrechtsreform.* Vol. XLVIII, No. 1 (January, 1965), pp. 41-44.

— *et al.* 'Group-Counseling im Erwachsenenvollzug,' *Monatschrift für Kriminologie und Srafrechtsreform,* Vol. XLIX, No. 4 (July, 1966), pp. 160-172.

— and Fahrenberg, Jochen. 'The Marks of Authoritarian Attitude in Former Members of the SS and the Armed Forces,' *Abstracts on Criminology and Penology,* Vol. X, No. 4 (July/August, 1970), pp. 351 362.

— and Fahrenberg, Jochen. 'Die Ausprägung autoritärer Einstellung bei ehemaligen Angehörigen der SS und der Wehrmacht,' *Kölner Zeitschrift für Soziologie und Sozialpsychologie,* Vol. XXII, No. 3 (1970), pp. 551-566.

Toby, Jackson. 'Violence and the Masculine Ideal: Some Qualitative Data,' in *American Academy of Political and Social Science. Patterns of Violence.* Edited by Marvin E. Wolfgang. *Annals,* CCCLXIV (Philadelphia, 1966), pp. 19-27.

Treue, Wilhelm (ed.). 'Rede Himmlers vor der deutschen Presse,' *Vierteljahrshefte für Zeitgeschichte,* Vol VI, No. 2 (April, 1958), pp. 175-191.

Trevor-Roper, H. R. 'The Strange Case of Himmler's Doctor: Felix Kersten and Count Bernadotte,' *Commentary* (April, 1957), pp. 356-364.

Trow, Martin. 'Small Businessmen, Political Tolerance, and Support for McCarthy,' *American Journal of Sociology,* Vol. LXIV, No. 3 (1958), pp. 270-281

Weida, Robert. 'NS-Gewaltverbrechen in polizeilicher Sicht,' *Kriminalistik.* Vol. VII, No. 20 (Köln, 1966), pp. 329-335.

Wertham, Frederic, 'Freud Now,' *Scientific American,* Vol. CLXXXI, No. 4 (October, 1949), p. 53.

West, L. J. 'The Psychobiology of Racial Violence,' *Mental Health Digest.* National Institute of Mental Health, Chevy Chase, Maryland. (December, 1966), p. 24.

Westley, William A. 'The Escalation of Violence through Legitimation,' in *American Academy of Political and Social Science. Patterns of Violence.* Edited by Marvin E. Wolfgang. *Annals,* CCCLXIV (Philadelphia, 1966), pp. 120-126.

Winnicott, D. W. 'The Development of the Capacity for Concern,' *Bulletin of the Menninger Clinic,* Vol XXVII, No. 4 (Topeka, Kansas, 1963), pp. 167-176.

Wormser-Migot, O. *et al.* 'La prophylaxie du génocide,' *Etudes Internationales de Psycho-Sociologie Criminelle, Nos. 11-13 (Juillet, 1967), pp. 3-59.*

5. *Unpublished Sources*

Aronson, Shlomo. Heydrich und die Anfänge der Gestapo und des SD. Doctoral dissertation (Berlin, 1966).

Bommersheim, Elli. Unpublished letter to the editor of *Der Spiegel*, Heinz Höhne, of January 3, 1967.

Hackler, J. C. A Sequential Mode of Deviant Behavior. Doctoral dissertation (University of Washington, 1965).

Haytin, Daniel L. The Methodological Validity of the Case Study in the Social Sciences. Doctoral dissertation (University of California, Berkeley, 1969).

Rattner, Leo. The SS: A Study of Nazi Terrorism. Doctoral dissertation (New School for Social Research, New York, 1962).

Steiner, John M. Social Structure and Human Behavior in Nazi Concentration Camps. Unpublished paper.

— Goethe's Concept of Art, the Artist, the Public, and his Evaluation of Mass Media. Unpublished manuscript.

Wiesenthal, Simon. Die Beteiligung von Österreichern an Nazi-Verbrechen und deren strafrechtliche Verfolgung. Unpublished mimeographed memorandum (Vienna, 1966).


6. *General Works*

Adler, H. G. *Die verheimlichte Wahrheit*. Tübingen: J. C. B. Mohr, 1958.

— *Theresienstadt 1941-1945*. Tübingen: J. C. B. Mohr (second edition), 1960.

— *et al. Auschwitz. Zeugnisse und Berichte*. Frankfurt: Europäische Verlagsanstalt, 1962.

Aretin, Erwein von. *Krone und Ketten*. Edited by Buchheim, Karl, and Aretin, Karl Otmar von. München: Süddeutscher Verlag, 1955.

*Ausnahme-Gesetze gegen Juden in den von Nazi-Deutschland besetzten Gebieten Europas*. London: Wiener Library, 1956.

Baum, Bruno. *Widerstand in Auschwitz*. Berlin: Kongress-Verlag, 1957.

Bayern, Prinz von, Konstantin. *Der Papst*. Berlin: Ullstein Bücher, 1958.

Beradt, Charlotte. *Das Dritte Reich des Traums*. München: Nymphenburger Verlagshandlung, 1966.

Berning, Cornelia. *Vom 'Abstammungsnachweis' zum 'Zuchtwart', Vokabular des Nationalsozialismus*. Berlin: Walter de Gruyter, 1964.

Burgess, Anthony. *A Clockwork Orange*. New York: Balantine Books, 1972.

Busch, Wilhelm. *Humoristischer Hausschatz*. München: Verlag Friedrich Bassermann, Jubiläumsausgabe, 1924.

Čapek, Karel, *Hovory s T. G. Masarykem (Conversations with T. G. Masaryk)*. Praha: Fr. Borovíj, 1947.

Chase, Stuart. *Guides to Straight Thinking*. New York: Harper and Bros., 1956.

Crossman, Richard (ed.). *The God that Failed*. New York: Bantam Books, 1959.

Deutsch, H. *Verschwörung gegen den Krieg*. München: C. H. Beck, 1969.

Dulles, Allan, and Gaevernitz, Gero S. von. *Unternehmen 'Sunrise'. Die geheime Geschichte des Kriegsendes in Italien.* Düsseldorf: Econ-Verlag, 1967.

Eisenmenger, Johann Andrea. *Entdecktes Judentum* . . . Königsberg in Preussen, 1711.

Everett, Arthur *et al. Calley.* New York: Dell Publications, 1971.

Fuchs, Eduard. *Die Juden in der Karikatur.* München: A. Langen, 1921.

Gellert, Christian Fürchtegott. *Sämtliche Fabeln und Erzählungen.* Leipzig: in der Hahn'schen Verlags-Buchhandlung, 1836.

Goethe, Johann Wolfgang von. *Wilhelm Meisters Wanderjahre.* Stuttgart: Cotta'sche Buchhandlung, 1821.

Graml, Hermann. *Der 9. November 1938 'Reichskristallnacht.'* Edited by Bundeszentrale für Heimatdienst. Bonn, 1957, No. 2.

Grossmann, Kurt. *Die unbesungenen Helden.* Berlin: Arany Verlag, 1961.

Grygier, Tadeusz. *Oppression.* London: Routledge & Kegan Paul, 1954.

Guibert, Graf von. *Lobschrift auf Friedrich den Zweiten.* Trans. and ed. by Zöllner, Johann Friedrich. Berlin: by Lagarde & Friedrich, 1788.

Hauptmann, Gerhart. *Der Dom. Dramenfragment.* Berlin: Propyläen Verlag, 1963.

Heidecker, Joe J., and Johannes Leeb. *Der Nürnberger Prozess. Bilanz der 1000 Jahre.* Berlin: Kiepenheuer & Witsch, 1958.

Henkys, Reinhard. *Die nationalsozialistischen Gewaltverbrechen.* Ed. by Dietrich Goldschmidt, Stuttgart: Kreuz Verlag, 1964.

Hersh, Seymour M. *My Lai 4: Report of the Massacre and its Aftermath.* New York: Random House, 1970.

Hirsch, Kurt. *SS gestern, heute und* . . . Frankfurt/M.: Verlag Schaffende Jugend, 1957.

Hunter, Edward. *Brainwashing.* New York: Pyramid Books Edition (second printing), 1961.

Joffroy, Pierre. *A Spy for God: The Ordeal of Kurt Gerstein.* New York: Harcourt Brace Jovanovich, 1971.

Kafka, Franz. *The Trial.* Harmondsworth, Middlesex: Penguin Books, 1953.

— *The Castle.* New York: The Modern Library, 1969.

Kempner, M. W. *SS im Kreuzverhör.* München: Rütten & Loening Verlag, 1964.

Kleist, Heinrich von. *Sämtliche Werke.* Darmstadt: Verlag der Heimbücherei, 1951.

Kloss, Erhard (ed.). *Reden des Führers, Politik und Propaganda Adolf Hitlers 1922-1945.* München: Deutscher Taschenbuch Verlag, 1967.

Konzentrationslager. *Ein Appell an das Gewissen der Welt.* Ed. and publ. by Verlagsanstalt 'Graphia,' Karlsbad, 1934.

Littell, Robert (ed.). *The Czech Black Book.* New York: Praeger, 1969.

Lübke, Heinrich. *Aufgabe und Verpflichtung.* Bonn: Athenäum Verlag, 1965.

McCarthy, Joe. *McCarthyism: The Fight for America.* New York: The Devin-Adair Co.: Publishers, 1952.

Manvell, Roger, and Fraenkel, Heinrich. *Himmler.* New York: Paperback Library, 1968.

March, Hans. *Verfolgung und Angst*. Stuttgart: Ernst Klett Verlag, 1960.

Mitscherlich, Alexander, and Mielke, Fred (eds.). *Medizin ohne Menschlichkeit*. Frankfurt/M.: Fischer Bücherei, 1960.

Mňačko, Ladislav. *Taste of Power*, New York: Frederick A. Praeger, 1967.

Müller, Hans Dieter (ed.). *Faksimile Querschnitt durch 'Das Reich.'* München: Scherz-Verlag, 1964.

Nolting-Hauff, W. JMI's (Jüdische Mischlinge 1. Grades). *Chronik einer Verbannung*. Bremen: Trüjen, 1946.

Orwell, George. *Nineteen Eighty-Four*. New York: Harcourt, Brace, 1949.

Pauwels, Louis, and Bergier, Jacques. *Aufbruch ins dritte Jahrtausend*. Bern: Scherz-Verlag, 1962.

Ravenscroft, Trevor. *The Spear of Destiny*. New York: Bantam Books, 1974.

Reichmann, Eva. *Die Flucht in den Hass*. Frankfurt/M.: Europäische Verlagsanstalt, 1956.

Riemann, Hugo. *Musik-Lexikon*, Leipzig: Max Hesse Verlag, 1916.

Rost, Nico. *Goethe in Dachau. Literatur und Wirklichkeit*. Trans. by Edith Rost-Blumberg. Berlin: Verlag Volk & Welt. 1948.

Schlabrendorff, Fabian von. *Offiziere gegen Hitler*. Frankfurt/M.: Fischer, Bücherei, 1959.

Schnabel, Reimund. *Macht ohne Moral*. Frankfurt/M.: Röderbergverlag (second edition), 1958.

Schorn, Hubert. *Der Richter im Dritten Reich*. Frankfurt/M.: Klostermann, 1959.

Schwarz, Hans. *SS-Sonderformation 'Dirlewanger' und das KZ Neuengamme*. Hamburg: Sekretariat der Arbeitsgemeinschaft Neuengamme, 1961.

Seliger, Rolf (ed.). *Braune Universität, Deutsche Hochschullehrer gestern und heute*. München: im Selbstverlag Rolf Seliger, 1965.

Shirer, William L. *The Rise and Fall of the Third Reich*. Greenwich/Conn.: Fawcett Publications, 1962.

Steiner, Rudolf. *Die Philosophie der Freiheit, Grundzüge einer modernen Weltanschauung*. Berlin: Philosophisch-Anthroposophischer Verlag, 1918.

Strasser, Otto. *Die Deutsche Bartholomäusnacht*. Prag-Zürich, Brüssel: Verlag Die dritte Front (seventh edition), 1938.

— *Der Faschismus, Geschichte und Gefahr*. München: Günter Olzog Verlag, 1965.

Stuckart, Wilhelm, and Globke, Hans. *Kommentar zur deutschen Rassengesetzgebung*. Berlin: Beck'sche Verlagsbuchhandlung, 1936.

Taylor, T. *Die Nürnberger Prozesse*. Zürich: Europa Verlag, 1951.

Tenenbaum, Joseph. *Race and Reich*. New York: Twayne Publishers, 1956.

Thadden, Adolf von. *Richter und Antisemiten*. Hannover: Reichsruf-Verlag, 1959.

Thieme, Karl (ed.). *Judenfeindschaft*. Frankfurt/M.: Fischer Bücherei, 1963.

Trott zu Solz, Werner von. *Der Untergang des Vaterlandes*. Freiburg/Br.: Walter Verlag, 1965.

*Das Urteil im I.G.-Farben-Prozess*. Offenbach: Bollwerk-Verlag, 1948.

Van Dam, H.G. *et al. KZ-Verbrechen vor Deutschen Gerichten. Dokumente aus den Prozessen gegen Sommer (KZ Buchenwald), Sorge, Schubert (KZ Sach-*

*senhausen), Unkelbach (Ghetto in Czenstochau).* Frankfurt/M.: Europäische Verlagsanstalt, 1962.

Weber, Carl Julius. *Das Ritterwesen.* Stuttgart: Hallberger'sche Verlagshandlung, 1836.

Wiesel, E. *Die Nacht zu begraben Elischa.* Esslingen: Bechtle Verlag, 1961.

Wighton, V. *Heydrich, Hitler's Most Evil Henchman.* Philadelphia: Chilton Company, 1962.


7. *Periodicals*


Benda, Ernst. 'Radical Fringe "Inevitable" in any Democracy.' *The Bulletin (A Weekly Survey of German Affairs).* Vol. XVI, No. 43 (Bonn, 1968), p. 328.

Bloch, Eduard. 'My Patient Hitler.' *Collier's* (New York, March, 1941).

*Der Freiwillige/Wiking-Ruf:* Kameradschaftsblatt der HIAG. The minor title was changed to: *Für Einigkeit und Recht und Freiheit.* Osnabrück: Verlag Der Freiwillige, later Munin-Verlag. Vols. 1958-1967.

Omelich, Paul. 'Ominous Changes in Police Tactics' (Editorial), *San Francisco Chronicle,* No. 147 (May 28, 1969), p. 46.

Schirach, Baldur von. 'Ich glaubte an Hitler.' *Der Spiegel,* No. 30 (Hamburg, July 17, 1967), p. 41.

Speer, Albert, 'Interview mit Speer.' *Der Spiegel,* No. 46 (Hamburg, November 7, 1969), p. 48.

Strasser, Otto. Letter to the editor. *Der Spiegel.* No. 47 (Hamburg, November 14, 1966), pp. 14-15.

*Wiking-Ruf.* Mitteilungsblatt der ehemaligen europäischen Soldaten der Waffen-SS für Vermissten-, Such- und Hilfsdienst, Hameln und Hannover. Subsequently this monthly periodical was published by the Wiking-Ruf Verlag in Hannover and then at Stemmen über Hannover. 1951-1958.

# Name Index

Abel, Theodore, 144, 194
Adenauer, Konrad, 123
Alexander, Leo, 342
Andus, Burton C., 204
Angerer, (Major), 60
Arco auf Valley, Anton Graf von, 58
Arendt, Hannah, 4, 122, 257, 304, 344-345
Aronson, Shlomo, 257
Attila, 82
Ausubel, David P., 348
Baarová, Lida, 260
Bach-Zelewski, Erich von dem, 83, 98
Baeck, Leo, 151
Bain, Read, 189
Barnard, Chester I., 326
Bauer, Fritz, 123
Baumgarten, Eduard, 95n
Bender, Horst Gerhard, 268
Berchtold, Joseph, 47, 48, 50, 51
Berger, Gottlob, 68, 69
Bernadotte, Folke Graf von, 127
Bernstorff, Ingrid von, 256
Best, Werner, 64
Bierwirth, Karl, 219, 220
Bittrich, Wilhelm, 63
Blobel, Paul, 122, 320
Bloch, Eduard, 274
Blumer, Herbert, 194
Bommersheim, Ellie, 264
Bormann, Martin, 17, 41, 113, 143, 198, 256, 325
Brachyahu, M., 194
Brack, Viktor, 357
Brandt, Rudolf, 261, 266, 418
Breder, Reinhard, 218, 219
Breithaupt, Franz, 270
Breysig, Kurt, 160
Brezhnev, Leonid, 25
Bronder, Dietrich, 234, 257

Brüning, Heinrich, 224
Brunner, Alois, 247
Brunner, Anton, 247
Bülow, Harry von, 63
Büth, Hans, 219
Burger, Anton, 247
Burgess, Anthony, 358
Burin, Frederic S., 39, 138, 324
Busch, Wilhelm, 73, 250
Caligula, XVIII
Calley, William L. Jr., 5, 11
Cameron, Norman, 10
Carter, Herbert, 5
Chamberlain, Arthur Neville, 316
Coser, Lewis, A., 42
Daladier, Edouard, 316
Daluege, Kurt, 50, 53-54
Darré, Richard Walther, 38, 72, 78, 85, 113
Dewey, John, 194
Diels, Rudolf, 140
Dietrich, Josef, 60, 127
Dietrich, Otto, 68, 314-315
Dörffler-Schuband, Werner, 63
Dollard, John, 123
Dulles, Allan, 126
Durkheim, Emile, 204-205
Eckart, Dietrich, 74, 354-355
Eichmann, Adolf, VII, 17, 123, 147, 214, 247, 268, 269, 273, 280, 339
Eicke, Theodor, 71, 124, 125, 265, 286
Eisenmenger, Johann Andrea, 295, 296
Ellsberg, Daniel, 5, 6
Engler-Füßlin, Friedrich, 85
Erikson, Erik, 194-195
Esser, Hermann, 307
Fahrenberg, Jochen, 291, 296-97
Feder, Gottfried, 349, 352-353
Feitenhansl, Karl, 261
Fischböck, Hans, 248

Forster, Albert, 68, 274, 301
Frank, Hans, 265, 292, 301, 333, 342, 406-408
Frank, Karl Hermann, 268
Frederick the Great, 130, 171
Freisler, Roland, 143
Frenkel-Brunswik, Else, 42, 123
Freud, Sigmund, XVI 189, 190, 353, 354
Frick, Wilhelm, 143, 151, 337
Friedman, Philip, 331-332
Fritzsche, Hans, 339, 346
Fromm, Erich, XVI, 123, 154-155, 185, 194, 347
Ganzenmüller, Theodor, 222, 319
Gellert, Christian Fürchtegott, 163-164
Gerstein, Kurt, 319
Gerth, Hans H., 194, 223, 226
Ghengis-Khan, XVIII, 83
Gilbert, G. M., 265, 334
Gille, Herbert, 63, 127, 276
Glaser, Barney, 197
Globke, Hans, 319
Globocnik, Odilo, 247
Goebbels, Joseph, 17, 44, 73, 136, 137, 138, 143, 150, 198, 260, 287, 315, 336
Göring, Hermann, 17, 48, 64, 139, 140, 142, 229, 311, 340, 346, 384-386
Goeth, Amon, 248
Goethe, Johann Wolfgang von, 168, 349
Goffman, Erving, 186, 194, 335
Grabner, Maximilian, 268
Grawitz, Ernst-Robert, 269, 346
Grimm, Wilhelm, 68
Grosse, Ernst, 217, 218
Grynspan, Herschel, 150, 328
Günther, Hans F. K., 119
Gürtner, Franz, 143, 334
Guibert de, Comte, XIX
Hackler, James C., 345
Härtel, Siegfried, 268
Hagen, Walter, 257
Halmos, Paul, 155
Hammeran, Erna, 218
Harbaum, August, 304
Hartjenstein, Friedrich, 305
Hasselbach, Hans Karl von, 95n
Hauptmann, Gerhart, 320
Haußer, Paul, 63, 261, 276

Haytin, Daniel L., XVI
Heidegger, Martin, 190
Heiden, Erhard, 49, 51, 55
Henry the Lion, 106
Hentschel, Willibald, 71
Heraclitus, 2
Hess, Rudolf, 17, 73, 143
Heydrich, Bruno, 257, 265
Heydrich, Heinz, 264, 265
Heydrich, Reinhard, 17, 53, 81, 86, 140, 145-146, 213, 257, 258, 259, 264, 265
Hilberg, Raul, 145, 257, 331, 333, 335
Hildebrandt, Friedrich, 68
Hildebrandt, Richard, 270, 356
Himmler, Ernst, 54
Himmler, Gebhard, 54
Himmler, Gebhard Jr., 54
Himmler, Heinrich, see Appendix
Hinkler, Paul, 140
Hirsch, Freddy, 332
Hitler, Adolf, see Appendix
Höfle, Hermann, 247
Höhne, Heinz, 264
Höss, Rudolf, 17, 97, 265-266, 268, 271, 272, 273, 279-280, 286-287, 293, 301, 305, 337
Horace, 168
Horney, Karen, 189, 194
Huber, Kurt, 324
Hugenberg, Alfred, 32
Hummel, Friedrich, 219, 220
Jäger, Herbert, 124
Jaspers, Karl, 2
Jodl, Alfred, 339-340
Joel, Guenther, 324
Jones, Elwyn, 342
Jong, Louis de, 332
Jüttner, Hans, 124
Kahr, Gustav Ritter von, 131
Kaltenbrunner, Ernst, 17, 123, 140, 213, 247, 303, 339, 400-403
Katzenstein, SS-Rottenführer, 86
Kaufmann, Karl, 68
Keitel, Wilhelm, 17
Kempner, Robert, 264
Kennedy, John F., 4
Keppler, Georg, 63, 127
Kerrl, Hans, 151
Kersten, Felix, 26, 226, 356-357

Klaus, Josef, 70
Klintzsch, Johann Ulrich, 47
Kloppel, Karl, 219
Kluckhohn, Clyde, 195
Koch, Karl-Otto, 211, 213
Koch, Karl W.H., 49, 228
Köhler, Adolf, 219
Krüger, Walter, 262-263
Kube, Wilhelm, 68
Küchlin, Walter, 86
Kumm, Otto, 276
Kunz, Johann, 247
Kwan, K., 327
Lechler, Fritz, 235, 274
Lenin, Vladimir Ilyich, 83
Lettow, Bruno, 63
Lewin, Kurt, 232
Ley, Robert, 109, 293-294, 294
Liddell Hart, Basil H., XX
Liebhenschel, Arthur, 272
Loeper, Wilhelm, 68
Lösener, Bernard, 151
Loritz, Hans, 268
Lossow, Otto von, 133
Ludendorff, Erich von, 48
Lübke, Heinrich, 123, 303
Lutze, Viktor, 61
Lynd, Helen Merrell, 194
Machiavelli, Niccolo, 3, 34, 185, 188
Mack, Hans, 217
Madge, John, XV
Mahrholz, Werner, 351-352
Malinowski, Bronislaw Kasper, XVI
Mansson, H., X
Mao Tse-tung, 159, 164
Marat, Jean Paul, 316
Martini, Fritz, 352
Masaryk, Thomas G., 287, 291, 349
Mauersberg, SS-Hauptsturmführer, 260
Maurer, Helmut, 264
Maurice, Emil, 47, 61, 257
Maxwell-Fyfe, Sir David, 334
Mayr-Miesbach, SS-Obersturmführer, 261
Mead, George Herbert, 194
Medina, Ernest L., 5
Menthon, François de, 103
Merton, Robert K., 308, 326
Meyer, Kurt, 127, 279
Milgram, Stanley, X

Mills, C. Wright, 194, 196, 203
Milton, John, VII, X
Mñačko, Ladislav, 203
Montigny, Baron von, 63
Morgen, Konrad, 266, 268-270, 346
Müller, Heinrich, 213, 269, 320, 339
Murer, Franz, 247
Murr, Wilhelm, 68
Murray, Henry A., 195
Mussolini, Benito, 159, 164
Nebe, Arthur, 219, 320
Nellen, Fritz, 218
Nero, XVIII
Neumann, Franz, 203, 317
Nietzsche, Friedrich, 72, 169, 295
Nottingham, Elizabeth, 119
Novak, Franz, 247
Novotný, Antonin, 25
Ohlendorf, Otto, 120, 213, 225, 266, 275, 280, 320
Opton, N., X
Ortega y Gasset, José, 3, 161, 164, 344
Orwell, George, X
Ossietzky, Carl von, 334
Paetel, Karl O., 124
Papen, Franz von, 334, 336, 338
Pareto, Vilfredo, 9, 165
Parsons, Talcott, 345
Paulmann, Werner, 268
Pavlov, Ivan Petrovich, XVIII
Peterson, Edward N., 20, 222, 223
Petschek, Otto, 289
Pfeffer, Franz von, 50, 55, 56, 233
Piscator, Erwin, 334
Poche, Oswald, 218
Podgorny, Nicolai V., 25
Pohl, Oswald, 124, 268, 301, 305, 339
Popitz, Johannes, 64
Rajakowitsch, Erich, 247
Rank, Otto, 169
Rasch, Otto, 320
Rath, Ernst vom, 150, **328**
Rathenau, Walther, 58, 130, 160, 170-171, 172-173, 174-176, 177-178, 179, 180, 182-184, 193, 348
Rauschning, Hermann, 26, 68, 231, 232, 257, 265, 298
Rauter, Hanns, 248, 268
Reinau, Abraham, 85, 356
Reitlinger, Gerald, 264

Ribbentrop, Joachim von, 316, 337
Robespierre, Maximilien de, 316
Röhm, Ernst, 48, 49, 56, 57, 60, 233
Roschmann, Eduard, 247
Rosenberg, Alfred, 72-73, 74, 101, 113, 143, 162, 287, 333, 337, 395-396, 410-412
Rüschen, Rudolf aus den, 418-421
Rust, Bernard, 151
Sachs, Ernst, 353
Samuel, Lazarus 261
Sauckel, Fritz, 68
Schacht, Hjalmar, 338
Schädig, Richard, 274
Scheff, Thomas J., 194
Schele, Werner Freiherr von, 63
Schellenberg, Walter, 120, 127, 266
Schick, Hans, 290
Schirach, Baldur von, 317, 339
Schlegelberger, Franz, 143
Schmidt-Klevenow, Kurt, 269
Schmitt, Walter, 260
Schreck, Julius, 49, 50
Schulenburg, Friedrich Werner Graf von der, 281
Schultz, B. K., 75
Schwarz, Franz Xaver, 68
Seidl, Siegfried, 247
Seisser, Hans Ritter von, 134
Seyss-Inquart, Artur, 248, 334, 340
Shelest, Pëtr Yefimovich, 25
Shibutani, Tamotsu, 194, 327
Simmel, Georg, XVI, 42
Speer, Albert, 17, 102-103, 316
Spengler, Oswald, 185
Stahl, Heinrich, 151
Stahlecker, Franz, 320
Stalin, Joseph, XVIII, 25, 83, 159, 164
Stangel, Franz, 247
Stein, George, H., 125
Stein, Lorenz von, 223
Steiner, Felix, 63, 92, 103, 127, 235-236, 265, 266, 274-275, 276, 279, 280, 281, 300
Steiner, John M., 279, 291, 296-97, 299-300
Steiner, Rudolf, 194

Stenglein, Ludwig, 131
Stennes, Walter, 232, 233
Strasser, Gregor, 55, 232, 234
Strasser, Otto, 26, 232, 233, 234, 257, 348, 350-351
Strauss, Anselm H., 197
Strauss, Georg, 219
Streicher, Julius, 337-338
Sütterlin, Julius, 86, 356
Sütterlin, Rolf, 86, 356
Sullivan, Harry S., 195
Szasz, Thomas, 194, 347
Taine, Hippolyte, 351
Tamerlane, 83
Tanzmann, Bruno, 71
Thierack, Otto Georg, 143, 325
Thormeyer, Walter, 273
Thorn, Rudi, 219, 220
Toennies, Ferdinand, 10, 205
Treher, Wolfgang, 95
Trevor-Roper, Hugh Redwald, 226, 312
Ulbricht, Walter, 25
Vogt, Josef, 269
Voss, Bernhard, 63
Wächter, Gustav Otto, 247
Wagner, Eduard, 146
Wahl, Karl, 68
Waldeck und Pyrmont, Josias Erbprinz zu, 268
Weber, Carl Julius, 7
Weber, Christian, 61
Weber, Max, XV, XVI, 7, 15, 17, 18, 20, 21, 22, 25, 26, 28, 39, 41, 155, 199, 222-223, 313, 314
Weida, Robert, 292
Wertham, Frederic, 189-190
Wetzel, Ernst, 146
Weymar, Karl Ludwig, 219
Wiesel, Eli, VII
Wiesenthal, Simon, 70, 247, 274
Wilson, Woodrow, 203
Winnicott, D. W., 331
Wittelsbach, Heinrich Prinz von, 58
Wolff, Karl, 126, 222, 233, 235, 255, 256, 266, 280, 294, 299
Zimbardo, Philip G., VII-X

# Appendix to Name Index

**Heinrich Himmler:**
Anthroposophist, 293-294
appearance, 92, 274
attitude towards SS, 326
bigamy, 256
biological-dynamic manuring, 293-294
bureaucracy, 26, 43, 224
   party bureaucracy, 34, 120, 124, 125
Catholic Church, 106-107
concentration and destruction camps, 222, 280, 335
control over political police, 64-65, 140
criteria for selection into SS, 67-68, 75-77
dereliction of duty in the SS, 414
destruction (Final Solution) of Jews, 98-99, 190, 192-193, 275
euthanasia action T 4, 357
foremost task of Schutzstaffel, 95-96
Freud, Sigmund, 353-354
Gestapo, 311
ideological opponents, 118
illegitimate children, 255
indoctrination, 100, 104, 105, 120, 281
Jewish and non-German descent of SS members, 81-82, 85-86, 258-259, 261-262, 263, 264, 356
Kommando 1005, 320
law and legality, 225, 323, 335
leadership, 41, 95
Lebensborn, 80-81
marriage order, 78, 79
mystical belief, 72, 104-106, 234
mystical romanticism, 108
obedience, 271, 317, 414
personal and professional development, 54-60, 233
political ideology, 95
probationary units, 273
racial ideology, 38, 71, 72-74, 75, 82,
   84, 88-89, 99, 115, 142, 143, 144, 355, 356-357
Reichsführer-SS, 51-53
relations with Jews, 84, 92
romantic whims, 97, 235, 300
Slavs, 82-83
speech to the Gruppenführer in Posen, 88-89, 249, 271, 279, 327
SS as monastic order, 116
SS as religious movement, 116-118
suicide, on, 91
Weltanschauung, 99

**Adolf Hitler:**
anti-Semitism, 298
autobiographical note, 390-392
British, 115
bureaucracy, 26, 141, 142, 154, 165, 188, 312, 319-320, 322
controversy with Röhm, 48, 341-342
charisma, 52, 160, 188, 313, 315-316, 317
Christianity, 110, 299
creation of SS, 47
demands on SS, 50
destruction of opponents, 153, 319-320, 328, 330
dilettante, 25
duelling, 91
education, 36, 109, 221
euthanasia action T 4, 319, 331
expectations, 5
experts, 224
fear of Chosen People, 115, 298-299
file on influential and abnormal individuals, 32
Final Solution, 190, 213, 271, 280, 291, 317, 319, 340-341
future SS, 93
gassing of Jews, 154, 275

God, 113-114, 295, 298-299
homosexuality, 91
idée fixe, 159
indoctrination, 221, 281, 287, 329-330
intellectuals, 330, 345
Jewish family physician, 274
Jewish people, 298, 328
Jewish religion, 112-113
leadership, 17, 41, 95, 141, 188, 314, 317
legal system, 324
madness, VIII
mass murder, 275, 337, 340-341, 342
middle class, prejudice of, 80
National Socialism, more than a religion, 108
New German cult, 111
non-German nationals in SS formations, 69
NS revolution, 142
oath of loyalty, 90
obedience, unconditional, 188
policies, 8

political legacy, 250
power politics, 32-34, 50, 165, 188, 304, 329-330
propaganda, 135, 160, 211, 221, 281
racist and political ideology, 16, 72-74, 82, 160, 163, 190, 296
rhetorical gift, 133, 135
Reichskristallnacht, 328
rejection of, XVIII
religious concept, 295
schizophrenia, 95
sense of reality, 134, 344-345
sickness report, 95, 276
social order, 37-38, 322
SS as religious order, 113
SS-Verfügungstruppen, 77
support from Jews, 149
supreme law lord, 39
terror system, 94
trial, 131-135
turn against SS, 42
war machine, 20
Weltanschauung, 94-95, 295

# Subject Index

Accident, situational, 7, 121
Ältestenrat, see Jewish Council of Elders
Aggression, 91, 186, 331
  acts of, 28, 212
  frustration-aggression pattern, 123
  indoctrination of, 100, 279
  motivation for, 120
  policy of, 74
  tendency to, 11, 189
  victims of NS-, 44
Alcohol, consumption of, 68
Alienation, 9, 183
  between the ruled and the ruling élite, 5
Allgemeine SS, 61, 62, 63, 65, 71
Allies, 204
  victorious, 10
Alternatives, see Choice
Amalgamation, 40-41
  of the civil service and the party, 145
  of party elements and formal bureaucracy, 308, 313, 322
  of positions, 142-143
  of SS and police, 145-146
Americans, 217
Annexation
  of the Memel territory, 68
  of Sudetenland, 68
Anomie, 155
Anschluß, of Austria, 68, 339, 340
Anthroposophists, 106, 293-294
Anti-intellectualism, 161, 164, 345
Anti-Judaism, 148, 299
Anti-Semitism, 174, 211
  discussion on, 151, 173
  exposure to, 265
  Hitler's, 298
  measures of, 346
  racial, 72, 73, 74, 295

religious, 73, 295
Appearance, of Himmler, 274
Arbeits-Erziehungslager (AEL), 306
Aristocracy, 37
  Nazi, 95
  new, 299
  political, 349
Artaman League, 71-72
Aryan, 289, 290
  Hitler as an, 298
  paragraph, 74
  persecutors, 74
  as superman, 190
  super-religion, 109-110
Ascension Commandos, (Himmelfahrtkommandos), see SS-Probationary Units
Asocial elements, 325
Assassination, 198
  of Heydrich, 221
  of Hitler, 281
Assimilation, 296, 327
Atheists, 114-115
Atrocities
  judged posthumously, 122
  opposition to, 280
Attitude, 308, 349
  ambivalent, 98, 100
  towards animals, 89
  of inmates, 333
  of the SS, 100, 114, 115, 119, 125
Auschwitz, IX, XIX, 44, 218, 219, 266, 269, 272, 280, 317, 333, 342
Austria, Kaltenbrunner's goal in, 303
  Austrians, 70, 247
Authoritarianism, 15, 141, 170, 317
  authoritarian character, 155
  authoritarian personality structure, 123, 319
  functions of, 188

régime of the Third Reich, 278
Authoritativeness, 21, 170, 188, 197
Authority, 5, 198
  acceptance of, 170
  admiration for, 163
  appearance of, 197
  bureaucratization of, 19
  charismatic, 314
  charismatic legitimation of, 141
  dissipation of, 132
  forces of public, 3, 164
  functions of, 188
  Goethe's concept of, 349
  independent, 188
  misuse of, 320
  persuasive, 21
  over prisoners, 214
  respect for, 226
  role, 188
  of the state, 132
  -subject relationship, 349
  submission to, 141, 170
  superior, 86
  traditional, 314
  true, 15, 173
Autobiographical note, by Hitler, 390-
  392
Autobiographical accounts by former
  members of the SS, 206-222
Autonomy, 197, 349
Auxiliary police, 217
Banality of evil, 124, 304
Barbarism, 158
  barbarians, 157
  barbaric ruthlessness, 324
Befehlsnotstand, 103-104, 212, 213, 214,
  292, 303
Behavior
  blueprint of, 3
  conformistic, 11
  deviant political, 10, 11
  deviant social, 9
Belgium, 69
Belief
  in Hitler, 292
  Indo-German, 105-106
  sincere, 3
Berchtesgaden, 251
Berlin Jewish Community, 151
Bigamy, 256

by Frank, 406-408
Biogram
  by Göring, 384-386
  by Kaltenbrunner, 400-403
  by Rosenberg, 410-412
Blechhammer-Ehrenforst, 44, 99, 305
Blutfahne, 49
Bolshevism, 3, 34, 100
Bourgeoisie, 37, 38, 56, 94, 137, 160,
  176, 177
Brack's facilities, 147
Brainwashing, 205
Breeding policy, 83
British Empire, 297
Buchenwald, 211, 214
Bürgerbräukeller, 135
Bureaucracy, 15, 24, 41, 225, 312, 313
  cooperation of, 44
  deficient, 142
  Hitler's views on German, 313
  ideological, 141, 144
  ministerial, 140
Bureaucrat, 20, 21, 154, 223
  characteristic features of a, 43
  Himmler on, 224
  Hitler's use of, 26
Bureaucratization, 22, 308, 313, 317,
  322
  of authority, 19
  of life, 164
  bureaucratic structure of NS govern-
    ment, 308
Byzantine Monarchy, 134
Calling, XV
Capitalism, 149, 174
  private, 25
Card index of influential persons, 32
Cartoons, 73
  caricatures, 73
Categories of SS affiliation, see SS
  Affiliation
Catholic Church
  conversion to, 73
  Himmler's characterization of, 106-
    107
  Himmler's conflict with, 54, 58, 73,
    107
  marriage as achievement of, 256
  as model, 110
Change

social, 119
socio-cultural, 186
socio-political, 3
Charisma
  appeal, 52, 121, 231
  charismatic personage, 160
  defined, 313
  pseudo, 314
  spurious, 314
Charlie Company, 5, 6
Chauvinism, 16
Checks and balances, 7, 16, 141, 188, 198
Choice
  alternatives, 99, 103, 123, 160
  freedom of, 36
  moral, XVII
Christianity, 110, 179, 188, 299
  conversion to, 296
  reconversion to, 301
Civil service, 15, 43, 141, 222, 227, 318
Class
  intellectual, 330
  ruling, 144
  slave, 38
  working class, 134
Class subculture, 11
Clockwork orange, 358
Collaboration
  of the Dutch administration, 332
  of Jews, 151-152, 269-270, 333
  lack of, in Denmark, 331
  of SS members, 270
Collegiate body, 27
Columbia Haus, 60
Command, chain of, 4, 6, 214
Commandments of National Socialism, 309-310
Communism, 69, 352
Compassion, 100, 110, 177-178, 211, 214, 290
Compensation, for insecurity, 52
Competence, 123, 198
Complacency, 25, 197, 331
Complaint, of an SS officer, 418-421
Compliance, 17, 142, 271, 275, 346
Concentration and destruction camps,
  Auschwitz, XIX, 44, 218, 219, 266, 269, 272, 280, 317, 333, 342
  Blechhammer, 44, 99, 305

Buchenwald, 211, 214
  Dachau, 60, 273, 286, 289
  Maidanek, 342
  Matzkau, 273
  Natzweiler, 305
  Sachsenhausen, 305
  Theresienstadt, 220, 333
  Treblinka, 222
Concentration camps, 6, 40, 44, 91, 136, 280-281, 342
  antagonism towards Jews in, 150
  conditions in, 335, 339
  under control of Gestapo, 238
  under control of SS Main Economic and Administrative Office, 145
  death march, 305
  establishment of, 64, 139
  guard personnel in, 6, 125, 126, 304-305
  inspectorate of, 124
  service in, 63, 69, 70, 103, 212, 304
  transferral to, 325
Concern
  capacity for, 10, 102, 163
  defined, 331
  lack of, 17, 25, 104, 150, 163, 187, 204, 214, 338
Condottieri types, 265
Conflict
  with one's conscience, 122
  with other groups, 42
  with the law, 121
  nonrealistic, 6
  resolution of, 6
  social, 9, 194, 195, 196, 197
  with secular institutions, 119
  unrealistic, 5
  unresolved, 161
Conformism, 11
Confusion
  mental, 160
  moral, 156-157, 160
  of the persecuted, 136
Con men, 197
Conscience, 111, 122, 203, 234, 323
Consent, passive, 44
Consumer habits, 176
Contract, social, 8
Control, VIII
  over bureaucracy, 39

ideological, 8
social, 8, 186, 188
total, 144
Conviction, ideological, 23
Correction of legal verdicts, 325
Corruption, 232
Cosmopolitanism, 180
Coup d'état, 132
Cowardice in the face of the enemy, 122
Creed of the SS, 52, 119
Crime
economic, 9
against honor of the people, 137
against humanity, 40, 162
against human status, 9, 103, 122, 162
political, 9, 25, 162
in retrospect, 122
tried in SS courts, 91-92
Criminal
actions, 325
justice, NS concept of, 143-144
Nazi war, 6
white collar, 9
Cross, 110
Cruelty
acts of, 123, 333
complaint against, 418-421
in concentration camps, 334
mindless, XVII
revealing of, 40
sanction of, XVIII
Cultural lag, 344
Culture, 157, 161, 189, 232, 314, 344
ancient, 73
and personality, 189, 195
Czechoslovakia
Czechs, 88
founder of, 287
occupation of, 3, 26, 330
Dachau, 60, 273, 286, 289
Darwinism, 71
selection, 115
social, 186
Death
march, 305
penalty, 137
Decision-making, democratic process of, XX, 10

Demagogue, 16, 18, 198
Democracy, Hellenic, 18
Democrat
bourgeois, 33
democratic means, 136
Democratization, passive, 15
Demos, 15, 25
Denmark, 69
Jews in, 288, 331
opposition in, 331
population of, 331
Dependency relations, XVII, XX, 4, 7, 9, 10, 11, 23, 165, 186-187, 188, 349, 351
Deportation
apparatus of, 152
from Denmark, 331
from Holland, 332
of Jewish and Gypsy minorities, 44, 220, 222, 340
selection for, 67
Deprivation, 226
Der Freiwillige, 126-127, 277, 278
Desk perpetrators, 160
Destruction
camps, 145, 269-270, 339
destructive urge, 342
by labor, 325-326
machinery of, 270
participation of Austrians in, 247
process of, 148, 153, 335
program of, 151-152, 279-280
Determinism, 190, 351
Deviant, 11, 17, 122
acts of deviance, 345
socially constructive, XV
Dialogue, 52, 123
suppression of, 138
Dichotomy, of value-norms, 97-98
Dictatorship, Hitler's, 134
Dilettante, 27
Hitler as a, 25
political master as, 223
Discrimination
against enemies, 152
measures of, 92, 102, 346
participation of Austrians in, 70
Disparities, 16
Dissenters, 17, 139-140
Distress, psychological, 212

Division of labor, 173
Divorce, 256
Doctrine
  ideological, 279
  of love, 179
Domination, 4, 17, 19, 27, 33, 203
Dominion, see Domination
Drift, 16
Duty, dereliction of, 414
Ecocide, 197
Ecstatic joy, 4
Education, 109
  educational ideal, 19
Egocide, 197
  defined, 358
Ego-survival, XVIII
Ego-threat, 95, 99
Ehrenforst, see Blechhammer
Eicke's Death's Head regiments, 103, 124
Einsatzgruppe, 121, 122, 280, 320
Einsatzkommandos, 213, 280
  Austrians in the, 70
    on the front line, 146
  massacres of, 320
  personality-profile of, 100
Elation, 4, 156
Elite, XIX
  circulation of, 9, 165, 326
  counter-, 9, 23, 138
  criteria for, 76-77
  power, 8, 9
  ruling, 5, 8
  SS as, 52, 115
Enemies
  adversary, 137
  internal, 136, 142
  stereotype, 350
Ermächtigungsgesetz, 149-150
Escalation
  into brutality, 154
  into economic and political crime, 9
  into extermination, 121
  into mass destruction, 44, 131, 162, 336-337
  process of, 131, 144
  into totalitarianism, 198
  of violence, 122, 152, 165
Escape reaction, XVIII
Esprit de corps, 42, 120

  lack of, 44
  of the SS, 87, 127
Europe, 17, 95, 96
  European volunteer formations, 69
  'SS Standarte Nordland', 69
  'SS Standarte Westland', 69
Euthanasia program, 44, 121, 319, 331, 357
Evil, VII, VIII XVII, 124, 304
Exclusiveness, 11, 21, 204
Executions, 67, 212-213
  firing squad, 99, 214
Exhaustion in war, XX
Existential necessity, 5
Expansionism, aggressive, 17
Expectations of the voter, 198
Experience, 196, 197
Expert, 7, 25, 27, 188, 344
  bureaucratic, 223
  Fachmenschentypus, 18
  Hitler's aversion to, 224
  on Jewish affairs, 219
Extermination
  of Christianity, 110-111
  of the clergy, 107
  of Gypsies, 121, 143
  Hitler's policy of, 328
  industries, 350
  of the intellectual classes, 330
  of Jews, 70, 121, 143, 193, 218, 291, 337, 338
  mass, 20, 63, 98, 213
  of Russians, 143
  of Slavs, 121
Fascism, 3, 157, 160, 349, 352
Fear, 94, 205
Fermentation theory, 174-175
Final Solution, X, 92, 97, 150, 153, 190, 271, 290, 317, 319
  definite solution of Jewish question, 317, 335, 339, 341
Finland, opposition in, 341
Förderndes Mitglied of the SS, 51, 230
Follower, 60, 204
  status, XX
France, 73
  Jews in, 288
Frankfurt/Main 217, 219
Fraternity, 54, 58
Fratricide, 197

Frontbann, 48, 49
Führer, 8, 105, 226, 228, 258, 310
    charismatic, 52
    decree, 141, 149
    development of, 311
    escape on July 20th, 114
    on Final Solution, 341
    illness of, 276
    personality of, 38, 299, 342
    role of, 314
Gassing, 154, 270
    gas chamber, 219, 332
    of Jews, 218, 219
    machinery, 146
    vans, 275
Gauleiter, 142
    von Pfeffer, 50
Gemeinschaftsrelations, 10, 205
Genealogical record, 76, 81
Geneva Conventions, 274
Genocide, 9, 121, 197, 213
    in East Pakistan, 3
    yield to, 25
German Armed Forces, 23, 145, 277, 291
German Cross in Gold, 256
German people, 5, 10, 29, 37, 74, 89, 278, 323
German Reich, 132
Gesellschafts-relationships, 10, 205
Gesetz über die Errichtung eines Geheimen Staatspolizeiamts (Gestapo), 64
Gesetz zur Wiederherstellung des Berufsbeamtentums, 20
Gestapo, 39, 40, 60, 64, 212, 214, 217-220, 311
    Austrians in, 70
    defined, 238
    fear of, 145
    origin of, 64, 139
    special police action of, 325
Ghetto, 332, 333, 340
    Warsaw, 44, 221
Goal
    aspiration, 4
    displacement of, 144
    orientation, 50
God, 184, 295
    Altvater, 104

der Uralte, 104
    war of the Gods, 299
    of nature, 110
    of the National Socialists, 115
    Thor, 110, 294
    Wodan, 110
Gottgläubig, 104, 113, 118, 119, 300, 301
Großdeutsches Reich, 17
Group-dynamics, 123
Guilt
    feeling of, 122, 123, 331
    rationalization, 123
Gypsies, 44, 143, 325
    status of, 29
    origin, 82
Handlanger, see Henchman
Hauptamt SS, see Main Office SS
Henchman, 11, 28, 160
Hero worship, 231
    heroism, 256
    hero as leader, 314
Herrenbewußtsein, of the SS, 52
Herrenmenschen, 73, 76
Herrschaftsbeziehungen, 22
HIAG (Hilfsgemeinschaft auf Gegenseitigkeit), 96, 126, 276-279, 300
Hierarchy, of party members, 38
High Command of the Army, 146
Higher SS and Police Court, 92, 222
Higher SS and Police leaders, 65
Hiroshima, 184
Hitler Youth, 50, 339
Holland, 69
Homosexuality, 91, 272, 354
Honorary dagger, 299
    leader, 68, 116
    sword, 299
Honorific symbols, 115-117, 299
Hostility, collective, 17
Human
    being, insignificance of, 111
    ethics, 348
    rights, 19
    status, 204
Humanistic sociology, 349
Humanity
    referred to by Hitler as 'Planetenbazillen', 342
    servant of, 171

Ideals
  ethic, 177-178
  religious, 179
  political, 180
Identification
  with aggressors, 169-170
  with assigned roles, 100, 336
  with NS ideology, 92
Identity, VIII, 4, 9, 164, 195
  distortion of, 197
  ethnic, 17
  of Jews, 122, 170
  national, 17
  need for, 155
  reaffirmation of, 42
  in search of, 86
  synthetic, 350
Ideographic approach, XVI
Ideology, 3, 144, 326
  ideological doctrines, 279
  ideological opponents, 118
  ideological penetration, 89
  ideological prejudice, 131
  NS, 190
  party, 141
  persuasive, 28
  political, 9, 25
  of the SS and Christian faith, 114
  supernatural, 155
Ignorance, 19
Imperialism, 180
Imperial Presidency, 198
Individualism, in the SS, 87
Indoctrination, 100, 102, 221, 281
  ideological, 77, 125, 287
  integration of NS values, 99
  of the people, 138, 310, 330
  psychological, 211, 212
  of racial materialism in the SS, 92,
    125
  Sprachregelung, 98
  strategies of, 104
Inequality, 37
Influence, 5
  of the Catholic Church, 107-108
  cross-cultural, 120
  elimination of Jewish, 346
  of Hitler's personality, 315-316
  of Jews, 107
  SS sphere of, 69

Ingroup
  esprit de corps of, 42
  persecution of members of, 122
Injustice, 11
Inmates
  asocial elements, 212
  confusion of, 136
  German, 305
  habitual criminals, 212
  Jewish, 152, 219, 269, 333
  political, 212
Innocence, XIX
Institutional function, IX
Institutions, 203, 204
  National Socialist, 5, 136
  total, defined, 335-336
Intellectuals, 330
  intellectual subculture, 52
  anti-intellectuals, 345
Intelligentsia, 62
Interaction, XX, 7, 116, 195, 196, 320
Interdependencies, VIII, XX, 196
  excessive, 7
  functional, 23
  patterns of, 4
  socio-cultural, 123
Interrelations, 131, 196
  insight into, 52, 198
  interrelated facts, 192
Inventors, 177
Italy, Jews in, 289
Jewish administration, 151-152, 269, 333
Jewish ancestry, of members of the SS,
  81, 85-86, 257, 258-259, 263, 264-265,
  274, 356-357
Jewish auxiliary police, 152
Jewish communal organization, 151
  -152, 333
Jewish Council of Elders, 151, 152,
  269, 333
Jewish family physician, of Hitler, 274
Jewish Hilfsdienst, in Prague, 332-333
Jewish order squad, 270
Jewish, blood, 112, 263, 296, 356
  descent, 287, 335
  people, 98, 298
  question, 44, 288, 290, 344
  religion, 355
  smell, 288
  support for Hitler, 149

traits, **356**
Jews, 58, 95, 143, 148, 149, 163, 165, 169, 174-175, 192-193, 211, 328
  abolition of privileges of citizenship for, 149-150
  admiration for, 99-100, 338
  as alien foreigners, 340
  as man's antagonist, 111
  appearance of, 74
  association with, 261, 272, 273
  in camp, 221
  as Chosen People, III, 115, 291, 298
  consciousness of kind among, 327
  as converts, 296
  as counterpart of the German, 111
  decent, 99, 337
  deportation of, 222, 325, 328, 332, 341
  destruction of, 218, 247, 343, 346
  elimination of, 147
  exclusion from schools, 288-289
  extermination of, 70
  gassing of, 218
  Hitler's fear of, 297
  as hostages, 307
  identification of, 169-170
  influence of, 107, 269
  introduction of names revealing Jewish race, 287
  loss of citizenship, 44
  trying to destroy the Nordic man, 73
  participation in destruction process, 151, 152, 269-270
  portrayals of Jews in Der Stürmer, 287-291
  racial characteristics of, 250-251, 356
  resettlement of, 269
  and revolutions, 192
  as scapegoats, 287
  sterilization of, 340
  as Untermenschen, 73, 92
Joodsche Raad, see Judenrat
Judenrat, 151, 331-332, 333
Judeo-Christian heritage, 113
Jud Süß, 212
Jüdischer Ordnungsdienst, see Jewish auxiliary police
Jul-Fest, 117, 299-300
Jul-Leuchter, 117, 300
Junkerschulen, 109

Kampfbund, 134, 135
Kapo, VII
Karma, 105, 106
Killing centers, deportation to, 222
Knight's Cross, 256
Knowledge, 36
Know-how, 156
Know-why, 156
Kommando 1005, 320
Kreisleiter, 142
Kulturmenschentum, 18
Kultusgemeinden, see Jewish communal organizations
Law and order, XX, 3, 140, 164
  facade of, 143
  need of, 25
  in the SS, 87
Law(s)
  Asiatic, 88
  basic, 262
  of the forest, 84
  Germanic, 88
  of life, 84
  respect for, 132
  of reason, 115
  commissar's rules, 88
Lawyers, 225
Leader
  charismatic, XX, 17, 155, 193, 226
  exclusive, 314
  incompetent, 16
  political, 16, 310, 322
  quarrels among SS leaders, 327
  responsible, 299
  supreme, 161
Leadership
  charismatic, 26, 29, 155
  corps, 165
  people's confidence in, 330
  of the personality, 141, 317
  political, 349
  power position of, 25
  qualities, 68
  Reich leadership of the NSDAP, 311
  role, 5, 7
  SA-, 53
  SS-, 142
  totalitarian, 25, 26
  types of, 17
  unconditional, defined, 314

Lebensborn, 80-81, 255
Legal aid in cases of preventive custody, 334-335
Legality, 135, 323, 324, 325
Legislature, 20, 152
Leibstandarte SS 'Adolf Hitler', 60, 65, 78, 239-240
Letter(s)
  admonitory, to Hitler, 349, 353
  by Rosenberg, 395-396
  by members of the Waffen-SS, 92
Level, psychogenic, 10
  sociogenic, 7, 10, 204
Leveling of the governed, 15, 16
Lex talionis, 119, 204
Liberal, 15
  learning, 199
Liberalism, 36, 73
Life style, aspired, 4
Lime light, 4
Liquidation, see Extermination
Logical or formal fallacies, 307
Machtergreifung, see Power
Machtpolitik, see Power politics
Maidanek, 342
Main Office(s) SS, 69, 145
  Development, structure and range of activity of, 243-245
  Economic and Administrative Department, 124, 126, 140, 145, 153, 304, 339
  Ordnungspolizei (Police), 54
  Race and Settlement, 78-79, 270
  Reich Security, 140, 145-146, 153, 213, 219, 268, 320, 339
  of the SS, 124
  SS-Gericht (SS-Tribunal and Legal Department), 91-92, 222, 266, 270, 346
Malevolence, XVII
Man
  abnormal, Hitler's use of, 32
  cultivated, 18, 19, 157
  of the future, 108
  as procreation-assistant, 80
Maoism, 3
Marginality, 86, 122
Marriage
  approval, 78, 262
  laws, 256, 261

order, 78, 90, 271
permission, 255, 263
vows, 116
Marxism, 3, 37, 73, 139
Mas(es)
  broad, 330
  destruction, 145, 146
  its escape from reality, 344-345
  formation, 50
  man, 161, 164
  media, 17, 197
  murder, 266, 275, 337, 346
  new mentality of the, 157-158
  shooting, 275
  traditional attitude of, 349
Massacre, see My Lai
Materialism, 182, 183, 190
Matzkau, 273
Mechanistic thinking, 184
Mechanization, XVIII, 172, 173, 175, 177, 178, 182, 183, 184
Mein Kampf, 77, 153-154, 211, 287, 291, 298, 312, 314, 336, 342
Memoirs, by Höss, 281, 286
Mental illness, 347, 348, 356
Method
  classic, of the founding of power, 34
  overt revolutionary, 131
Middle class, 80, 226
Militia, 48
Ministry of the Interior, 40
Minority, 17, 44, 187, 331
Mischling, Heydrich as, 86, 257, 258-259, 264-265
Mobilization, perpetual, 17
Modernism, 174
Modus operandi, 158
Monogamy, 256
Moral
  choice, XVII
  code of the SS, 89
  ideals, objection to, 81
  response, 196
  revolution, 320
Morality
  Christian, 110
  considerations of, 340
  of the intellectuals, 330
  mundane, 3
  new, XVIII

NS, 136, 323
Movement
  anti-parliamentarian, 314
  charismatic, 345
  National Socialist, 15, 29, 134, 135, 314
  revolutionary, 135
  salvationary, 226
Munich
  Pact, 316
  party center in, 49
  SA leadership in, 50
Mutual Aid Society, see HIAG
My Lai, X, 5, 6
Myth system, 3, 9, 104, 163
Nagasaki, 184
Nationaldemokratische Partei Deutschlands (NPD), 29
Nationalism, 16, 180
  bounds of, 38
  false, 278
  national destiny, 154
National Socialism, 3, 227, 303, 317, 323
  Hitler's view of, 108
  ideology of, 155, 190
  opposition to, 324
  political schooling of, 221
  Weltanschauung of, 94, 323
Nationalsozialistische Führungsoffiziere (NSFO), see Political officers
Natzweiler, 305
Needs
  personal, 3
  psychogenic, 7
  unfulfilled, 155
Nivellierung der Beherrschten, see Leveling of the governed
Nomothetic approach, XVI
Norms, social, 8
Nietzsche's Superman, 357
Norway, 69
NS poster, facsimile of, 423
NS Press, address to German representatives of the, 328
  Nationalsozialistische Monatshefte, 101
  Das Reich, 101, 287
  Das Schwarze Korps, 101
  Schulungsbriefe des Reichsschulungs-

amtes der NSDAP und der Deutschen Arbeitsfront, 101
Der Stürmer, 73, 101, 281, 286, 287-291, 338
Der Völkische Beobachter, 47, 49, 101
NS revolution, 89, 122, 135, 136, 140
Nuremberg Laws, 44, 113, 121, 150, 335, 337, 338
Nuremberg Trial, 6, 337-340
Oath of personal allegiance to Hitler, 40, 78, 90
Obedience, 163, 170, 232
  compliance, 142
  loyalty in the SS, 90, 116
  loyalty to head of the state, 339-340
  military, 63, 213, 271, 280, 346
  Obrigkeitshörigkeit, 131, 155
  strict, 103
  unconditional, 53, 76, 97, 121, 188
  uncritical, 124, 162, 256, 317, 318-319
Befehl (Order), 6, 211
  compliance with, 142, 152, 212, 214, 231, 271, 280
  to punish expelled members of the SS, 414
  for mass murder, 275, 292
  refusal to obey, 292
  sabotage of, 333
Oberkommando des Heeres, see High Command of the Army
Obrigkeitshörigkeit, 131
Occult exercises, 110
Occupation, 25
  of Belgium, 69
  of Czechoslovakia, 3, 26, 330
  of Denmark, 69
  of Holland, 69
  of Norway, 69
Officeholders, 310-311
Opposition, see Resistance
Orden, 34
  of good blood, 82
  Ordensburgen, 109
  Thule-Orden, 234
Order, see Befehl
Order
  new social, 37, 38
  new world, 89

socio-political, 52
Ordnertruppe, 47, 228
Organization, 23, 40, 55, 99, 159, 186, 318
Orwellian thesis, X, 193
Outgroup, 20, 42, 122, 336
Parallelism, 39
Parkinson's disease, 95
Participant-observer, IX
Participation, reflective, 10
Party
  accomplishments of, 318-319
  and bureaucracy, 38-39
  bureaucracy, 17, 26, 27
  center in Munich, 49
  consolidation of, 322
  ideology, 141
  as leadership corps, 310, 318
  organization of, 309-311
  political will of, 311
  slogans, 188
  tasks of, 322-323
Patriotism, 33
Pentagon study, 5-6
People's court, 142, 143
Peoples of perpetual dawn, 160
Perception, of their role as leading Nazis, 336-337
Perpetrators, 11
  desk-chair, 6, 9, 28, 160
Perpetuation, of power, 4
Personality
  characteristics, 7, 100, 190
  charismatic, 313
  cultivated, 19
  and culture, 189, 195
  ethnocentric, 42
  of former members of the SS, 8
  of Hitler, 154-155, 315, 316
  human, 195, 278
  structure, 4, 8, 10, 11, 123, 203, 204
  surrender of, 52
  unintegrated, 17
Persuasion
  coercive, 23
  Hitler's gift of simplification, 344
  Hitler's persuasive appeal, 315-316
  Hitler's power of, 336
Philo-Semitism, 338
Pilot, XVIII

Pluralism, destruction of, 17
Poland, 332
  Jews in, 288
Poles, 143, 325
Political aristocracy, 349
Political authority, 349
Political crime, 9, 25, 162
Political master, 223, 317
Political officers (NSFO), 77
Political police, 23, 217
  construction of, 64-65
  reorganization of, 139
Posen, Himmler's speech in, 87-90, 98-99, 118, 249, 271, 279, 327
Power, VIII, 204, 226
  conflict, 65
  craving for, 155
  defined, 4
  dictatorial, 226
  élite, XVII, XVIII, XIX, 6, 8, 9, 156
  expertise in harnessing of, 7
  imbalance of, 165
  instrument of, 47
  monopolization of, 198, 304
  of personality, 315
  political, 50
  politics, 32, 188, 304
  position, 4, 25
  relation, 22, 134
  relationship, defined, 11
  role, 4, 5, 7, 8
  search for, 203
  seizure of, 47-48, 62, 67, 120, 136, 138
  structure, 365
  struggle, IX, X, 37, 50, 145
  trimmings of, 120
Precipitating conditions, 10
Prejudice, 80, 131, 338, 339
Preventive detention, see Protective custody
Priesthood, 117, 118, 231
Privileged, 9
Prisoners, see Inmates
Problems
  of living, 156, 160
  in living, 187, 196,
  defined, 347
Program, eugenic, 84

Propaganda, 17, 135, 197, 280
   anti-Jewish, 281
   propagandists, 278
   rallies, 49, 230
   of Rosenberg, 337
   totalitarian, 345
Protective custody, 218
   camp, 286
   legal and in cases of, 334-335
   preventive detention of minorities,
   315
Protectorate of Bohemia and Moravia,
   290
Providence, 95, 113, 115, 118, 155-156,
   160, 342
Prussia
   civil servants in, 43
   military tradition of, 63
   tradition of, 163
Psychoanalysis, 189, 353
Psychopath, affectothyme, 27
Psychotherapists, 354
Public, 197, 331
Punishment camps, of the SS, 273
Purification, 278
Putsch
   Bierhallen, 54
   Hitler, 48
   Röhm, XX, 53, 60, 61, 121, 338-339,
   341
   Stennes, 53, 232
Race, 190
   alien, 38
   breeding of men, 356-357
   defiler, 92, 220, 296
   defined, 119
   hatred, 211
   Himmler's and Hitler's agreement
   on, 72
   Himmler's doctrine of, 71-72
   Nordic, 74, 80
   racism, 274-275
   Rosenberg's concept of, 73
Racial
   appearance, 76, 274
   characteristics of Jews, 73, 113, 250,
   356-357
   prejudice, 339
   propagation, 79, 80
   purity of SS, 61, 75, 355

racist revolution, 122
Radicalism, 194, 352
Rationality, 138, 141, 226
Reality, 4, 5, 6, 196
   escape from, 344-345
   Hitler's sense of, 134
   social, IX, 8
   withdrawal from, 156
Rebirth, see Reincarnation
Reflections, autobiographical, 210-222
Régime
   authoritarian, 278
   totalitarian, 27
Reich, existence of, 84, 132
Reich Association of Jews in Germany,
   151
Reich Citizenship Law, 335
Reich Security Main office, 40, 70
Reichsführer, 50, 55, 61, 105, 262, 294
   criminal jurisdiction of, 143-144
   Himmler appointed, 53
   as postman, 327
Reichskriegsflagge, 54
Reichskristallnacht, 44, 121, 150, 328,
   338, 340
Reichsprotektor, Daluege as, 54
Reichssicherheits-Hauptamt, see Reich
   Security Main Office
Reichsvereinigung    der    Juden    in
   Deutschland, see Reich Association
   of Jews in Germany.
Reichsvertretung der Juden in Deutsch-
   land, see Reich Association of Jews
   in Germany
Reincarnation, 105-106
Relativity, 343
Religion
   Aryan, 109-111
   Hitler's Menschheitsreligion, 108,
   295
   Indian, 107
   Jewish, 111-112, 354-355
   Nazi, 110
   SS religious affiliation, 301-302
Renaissance, 73
Repression, 351
Resistance, 141
   from foreign countries, 269
   opposition to Hitler, 121-122, 324,
   388

paralyzed, 350
of persecuted individuals, 44
of SS personnel, 99-100, 212, 279, 418-421
Respectability, of Himmler's orders, 225
Responsibility, 10, 123, 213
    delegation of, 165
    of the Führer, 314
    individual, XX, 160, 214, 271
    lack of, 187
    for mass killings, 266, 293, 339, 346
Retrogression into direct action, 164
Reward, 4, 172
Rhetoric, 8
    Hitler's, 132, 135, 232, 336, 344
Ritual murder, 288, 291
Rivalry between SA and SS, 56-57
Robots, 144, 358
Role
    identification, 100
    incompatibility of, 145, 328
Role assignment, 11
Rorschach method, XVI
Ruling process, participation in, 16
Ruling stratum, membership in, 19
Russians, 88, 143, 325
Sachsenhausen, 305
Safety, 23, 25, 164
Salvation, 226
Sanction, XVIII, 8, 11, 115
Scapegoating, 42, 123, 287
Schizophrenia, 95
Schutzstaffel (SS) (Protection Squad)
    as anti-intellectual organization, 186
    as anti-Bolshevistic combat organization, 95-96
    apologists of, 96, 124
    assumed functions and actual control of, 145, 326
    Austrians in, 70
    average age in, 246
    as biological élite, 95
    breeding policy, 83
    chasm in, 126
    clan book of, 79
    code of honor, 90
    combative spirit of, 65
    criminal code of, 91
    criteria for selection into, 70, 76-77,
        254
    discharge from, 271
    dismissal from, 67-68, 90, 261, 271
    dismissal, exclusion, and expulsion from, in the years 1937 and 1938, 371-375
    distinctions within, 121
    as ecclesia militans, 116, 119
    eclecticism within, 99
    as the elect, 105
    exclusion from, 246, 271
    expulsion from, 75, 246, 271, 274
    goal orientation of, 50
    identification with NS ideology, 97
    independence within NSDAP of, 60-61, 236
    influx into, 67
    intellectual aptitude of, 76
    Jewish ancestry of members of, 81, 85-86, 257, 258-259, 263, 264-265, 274, 356-357
    legal proceedings against members of, 266, 268-270
    marginal position of, 50
    models of, 127
    as monolithic organization, 65
    as multi-purpose organization, 87
    membership in, 81-83
    members of, married to Jewish women, 82, 84, 85
    non-Germans in, 305
    numerical development of entire SS, 1935, 1936, 1937, 1938, 376-380
    numerical strength of, 246
    occupational background of, 61-62
    occupations in, for 1937 and 1938, 366-370
    offenses in, 91-92
    personal accounts of former members of, 206-222
    as police force, 56
    procreation assistants of, 80
    racist indoctrination of, 125
    reconversion of, 301
    release from, 271
    religious affiliation of, 296-297, 301-302, 381
    as religious movement, 116-119
    as scapegoat, 123
    selective breeding, 75, 356-357

socio-economic background of, 125
staff members of, 6
transformation into an élite, 61
Secret state Police Bureau, 139, 198
Security Police, 67
Self-
concept, 59, 86
destructive, 151
esteem, 59, 203, 345
image, 4, 204
interest, 25
Sentimentality, 84
Servant, of the state, 349
Shock Troops, 47, 49, 93, 233
Sicherheitsdienst (SD), 65, 67, 68, 120, 221, 222
Significant other, 5
Slaves, 88
human animals, 89
slave labor, 126, 326, 335, 340
slave labor camps, 306
Slavs, 82-83, 88-89, 98, 121
Social
change, 119
conflict, 9, 194, 196, 197
control, 188
distance, 9, 331
engineer, XV
fact, 204
identity, 9
imagination, 163, 196, 198
norms, 8
order, 4, 38
perspective, 4
reality, IX, 8
sanction, 8, 11
status, 120
stratification, 9, 34
structure, VIII, 29, 123, 308
system, 136, 193
theory, 194, 349
Social Democrats, 139, 140
Socialization, process of, 195
Social psychiatry, findings of, 19
Society
classless, 37
totalitarian, 205
Sonderkommandos, 60, 146
Sonderkommando '1005', 122
Soviet Union, 3

Special police action, 325
Specialist, 18, 19
Specialization, functional, 24
SS Academy, 77
SS Affiliation, categories of, 252-253
SS and comparable army Ranks, 362
SS-Applicants, 252-253
SS-Candidates, 77-78, 116, 120-121, 253
SS Chart, 364
SS Cloisters, 109-110
SS family, 79
SS-Hauptämter, see Main Office
SS-Men, 253
SS Orders to the Last Sons, 81
SS Organization, 364
SS Physicians, 269
SS Probationary Units, 273
Ascension Commandos, 273
SS-Totenkopfverbände (TV) (Death's Head Units), 62, 63, 66, 70, 71, 78, 125
defined, 248
SS Trainees, 251
SS-Verfügungstruppe (VT), 60, 62, 63, 70, 78
defined, 248
SS Volunteers, 69
SS-Wirtschafts-Verwaltungs-Hauptamt, see Main Office SS
Waffen-SS (Combat SS), 62, 65, 67, 70, 71, 96, 125, 145, 221, 299
as most beautiful part of SS, 306
bias for, 306
conflict with leadership of German Armed Forces, 63-64
letters by members of, 92
false nationalism in, 278
origin and function of, 239-240, 304-305
racism in, 274-275
status of, 277, 279
Stabswache, 47, 51, 60
Staffel, 229
Stanford Prison Experiment, X
Star of David, 44, 289, 290, 291, 332
Statocentricism, 326
Stimmvieh, 16
Stormtroopers, 47, 49, 53, 211, 228, 231, 232
Stoßtrupp, see Shock Troops

Stoßtrupp Hitler, 48, 50, 51
Struggle, time of, 136
Sturmabteilung (SA), see Stormtroopers
Subculture, 16, 52, 163, 193
Subhuman, 73, 83, 92, 115
Submission, 164, 170, 185, 205
Suicide, 91, 212, 214, 272
Supreme law lord, 111, 212, 314, 346
Survival, 11, 115, 173, 214, 280
Swastika, 110
Symbols, religious, 117-118
Syndicalism, 157
System(s)
  belief, 51, 52, 155
  bureaucratic, 21
  legal, 324
  myth, 3, 9, 104, 163
  NS, 163
  social, 193
  status, 326
  terror, 93
  totalitarian, 141
Tactics, 225, 226
Talmud, 112, 291
Target orientation, 63
Team, symbiotic, 28
Technocrat, amorality of, 102
Technological Warfare, XVIII
Terror, 33-34, 93, 137, 138, 140, 142,
  350
Theory
  evil seed, VIII
  fermentation, 174-175
  Marxist, 3
  milieu, 351
  sexual, 353-354
  social, 349
Theosophists, 106
Theresienstadt, 220, 333
Third Reich, power structure of, 365
Thule-Order, 234
Tolerance of ambiguity, 196
Total institutions, defined, 335-336
Totalitarianism, XVIII, IX, 140
Transcendentalism, 174-175
Transition, 120
Transitory state, 349-350
Transport escort squads, 269
Transportation, 229
Treason, 122, 127, 324

Treblinka, 222
Trial
  of Eichmann, 123
  of Hitler, 131-132
Tribal community, 34
Twentieth of July Movement, 121-122,
  281, 339, 341-342
Ukrainians, 325
Unconditional surrender, 278
Understanding (Verstehen), IX, XV,
  XVI, 164, 184, 198, 278
United States of America, 197
University, 223, 324
University of Hawaii, study of, X
Untermensch, see Subhuman
Unterrasse, see Subhuman
Utopia, 25
Values, 99, 136, 187, 320
Variables, 343
Verstehen, see Understanding
Vertical invaders, 160
Victims, 44, 122, 169, 170
Vietnam, X, 3, 5, 6, 204
Violence
  acts of, XVII, 11, 161
  forms of, 152, 330
  impulses of, 19, 206
  indoctrination of, 100
  legitimate means of, 23
  mechanical, 358
  to the mind, 138
  necessity of, 329-330
  persuasive force of, 326
  as prima ratio, 158
  prophets of, 3
  subculture of, 163, 193
  use of, 19
  violent means, 132
Vorsehung, see Providence
Warsaw ghetto, 221
Watergate, 198
Weimar Republic, 10, 40, 52, 132
Weltanschauung, XVII, 10, 52, 67, 94,
  99, 116, 120, 153, 193, 222, 323, 347
Wertfreiheit, XV
Wewelsburg, see SS Cloisters
White collar criminal, see Perpetrators
Wiking-Ruf, 278
World War I, 51, 64
World War II, 64

Zeitgeist, 165, 185
Zone, of acquiescence, 334
  of indifference, 334